THE REINVE[
MAGNA CART,

This new account of the influence of Magna Carta on the development of English public law is based largely on unpublished manuscripts. The story was discontinuous. Between the fourteenth century and the sixteenth the charter was practically a spent force. Late-medieval law lectures gave no hint of its later importance, and even in the 1550s a commentary on Magna Carta by William Fleetwood was still cast in the late-medieval mould. Constitutional issues rarely surfaced in the courts. But a new impetus was given to chapter 29 in 1581 by the 'Puritan' barrister Robert Snagge, and by the speeches and tracts of his colleagues, and by 1587 it was being exploited by lawyers in a variety of contexts. Edward Coke seized on the new learning at once. He made extensive claims for chapter 29 while at the bar, linking it with *habeas corpus*, and then as a judge (1606–16) he deployed it with effect in challenging encroachments on the common law. The book ends in 1616 with the lectures of Francis Ashley, summarising the new learning, and (a few weeks later) Coke's dismissal for defending too vigorously the liberty of the subject under the common law.

SIR JOHN BAKER taught at the University of Cambridge from 1971 to 2011, latterly as Downing Professor of the Laws of England. He also served for thirty years as Literary Director of the Selden Society and was knighted for services to legal history in 2003. He is the author of *Collected Papers on English Legal History* (2013) and *Introduction to English Legal History* (4th edn, 2002).

CAMBRIDGE STUDIES IN ENGLISH LEGAL HISTORY

Edited by
Sir John Baker
Fellow of St Catharine's College, Cambridge

Recent series titles include

The Reinvention of Magna Carta 1216–1616
John Baker

Insurance in Elizabethan England: The London Code
Guido Rossi

The Law of Contract 1670–1870
Warren Swain

A History of English Tort Law 1900–1950
Paul Mitchell

Sir Edward Coke and the Reformation of the Laws Religion, Politics and Jurisprudence, 1578–1616
David Chan Smith

Medieval English Conveyances
John M. Kaye

Marriage Law and Practices in the Long Eighteenth Century: A Reassessment
Rebecca Probert

The Rise and Fall of the English Ecclesiastical Courts, 1500–1860
R. B. Outhwaite

Law Courts and Lawyers in the City of London, 1300–1550
Penny Tucker

Legal Foundations of Tribunals in Nineteenth-century England
Chantal Stebbings

Pettyfoggers and Vipers of the Commonwealth The 'Lower Branch' of the Legal Profession in Early Modern England
C. W. Brooks

Roman Canon Law in Reformation England
R. H. Helmholz

Sir Henry Maine: A Study in Victorian Jurisprudence
R. C. J. Cocks

Sir William Scott, Lord Stowell Judge of the High Court of Admiralty, 1798–1828
Henry J. Bourguignon

The Early History of the Law of Bills and Notes: A Study of the Origins of Anglo-American Commercial Law
James Steven Rogers

The Law of Treason in England in the Later Middle Ages
J. G. Bellamy

William Sheppard, Cromwell's Law Reformer
Nancy L. Matthews

THE REINVENTION OF
MAGNA CARTA 1216–1616

SIR JOHN BAKER

CAMBRIDGE
UNIVERSITY PRESS

CAMBRIDGE
UNIVERSITY PRESS

University Printing House, Cambridge CB2 8BS, United Kingdom

One Liberty Plaza, 20th Floor, New York, NY 10006, USA

477 Williamstown Road, Port Melbourne, VIC 3207, Australia

314-321, 3rd Floor, Plot 3, Splendor Forum, Jasola District Centre, New Delhi - 110025, India

79 Anson Road, #06-04/06, Singapore 079906

Cambridge University Press is part of the University of Cambridge.

It furthers the University's mission by disseminating knowledge in the pursuit of education, learning and research at the highest international levels of excellence.

www.cambridge.org
Information on this title: www.cambridge.org/9781316637579
10.1017/9781316940990

© John Baker 2017

First published 2017
First paperback edition 2018

A catalogue record for this publication is available from the British Library

Library of Congress Cataloging in Publication data
Names: Baker, John H. (John Hamilton), author.
Title: The reinvention of Magna Carta 1216-1616 / Sir John Baker.
Description: Cambridge, United Kingdom ; New York, NY, USA : Cambridge University Press, 2017. | Includes bibliographical references and index.
Identifiers: LCCN 2016034384 | ISBN 9781107187054 (hardback : alk. paper)
Subjects: LCSH: Magna Carta–Influence. | Constitutional history–England–To 1500. | Constitutional history–England–16th century. | Constitutional history–England–17th century.
Classification: LCC KD3946 .B35 2017 | DDC 342.4202/9–dc23 LC record available at https://lccn.loc.gov/2016034384

ISBN 978-1-107-18705-4 Hardback
ISBN 978-1-316-63757-9 Paperback

CONTENTS

PREFACE

The year 2015 witnessed one of the most remarkable historical anniversaries ever celebrated, stretching across continents and civilisations. Every scholar with an interest in Magna Carta was expected to say or write something about it, and much was learned about the events in and around 1215. It was right, of course, to concentrate on 1215, since that was the occasion for the anniversary and it was the beginning of all that followed. But the Charter of Runnymede itself had a short life. The timelessness and ubiquity of what it came to represent can only be explained over the longer term. Its enduring spiritual force was nowhere more clearly demonstrated last year than by the decision of the Chinese authorities to ban the general public display of the 1217 charter sent on loan from Hereford Cathedral. There are few people with the ability to read such a charter, even in England, and yet its physical presence alone was enough to alarm an authoritarian regime on the other side of the world. Magna Carta has evidently acquired a symbolic power which transcends language and culture and even history. Such a remarkable phenomenon cannot be accounted for merely by the turbulent events of 1215. Indeed, were it not for its reinvention in the early-modern period, the charter would be known today only to a few medieval specialists. This obvious fact may be widely acknowledged, and yet the details of the later story have become lost in a shimmering haze, with flashes of sunlight in 1628 and 1787. Even the meticulous book by Faith Thompson, published in 1948 after decades of research, a work which opened up many of the topics pursued in the present book, did not fully bring out the legal context of the reinvention, or its chronology.

The reason why the story has not been fully unravelled before is that it is primarily a legal story. Political and constitutional historians have not generally cared to consult legal sources other than statutes, while most English legal historians in the century after Maitland have ignored public law completely. There has in consequence been a considerable lack of clarity about the story of the charter in the three centuries between

Edward III and the Petition of Right. Some have assumed that its incandescence remained undimmed through the centuries, others that it sank into obscurity until it was rediscovered by Sir Edward Coke in the 1620s. Neither view is correct, but much of the story has been hidden away in legal manuscripts which no one reads.

The manuscripts are not written in English, and their substantive content is often embedded in procedural contexts which to the uninitiated can seem unfathomable. Leaving aside, however, the abbreviated hieroglyphs in which it was written, law French is not a particularly difficult language, compared with Latin, and in fact the law reports when deciphered make more sense and contain far more information than the garbled and often unintelligible English reports of what the same lawyers were saying in the House of Commons. The barrier in scholarship is professional rather than linguistic. Lawyer historians who grapple with the thoughts and arguments of lawyers in the past are liable to be dismissed by their non-legal colleagues as 'internalists' who accord too much weight to the doctrinal mysteries and arcane procedures of the legal world. There is no doubt that contingent remainders and *indebitatus assumpsit* will never compete on equal terms with kings and queens, parliaments and battles. But the history of the common law belongs on a different plane from the history of events because it is, at least in part, an intellectual history, and it is impossible to understand legal thinking, or indeed its practical effects in the real world, without understanding the procedures and technical concepts which set the terms of reference and often evolved over long periods of time.

This book is necessarily internalist, in that it is based heavily on sources which few people outside the law school have ever thought worth reading. Yet the story of Magna Carta cannot be reconstructed without them. Surprisingly little reference was made to the charter in popular literature or drama, or in philosophical writing. The core of the story – before, that is, the historians took it over in the seventeenth century – is the way lawyers thought about it and deployed it for forensic purposes in the courts, for political purposes in the House of Commons, and for educational purposes in the inns of court. The law which they found in the charter was far from static. In reality, the Magna Carta of 1616 was completely different from that of 1216, despite the fact that the words which still mattered were identical. This has sometimes led to misunderstanding. Heavy criticism has been heaped upon the lawyers who cultivated new perceptions of Magna Carta, represented first and foremost by Coke, for being bad historians. But that is to miss the point.

Although the common lawyer's relationship with history is central to the present account, it was not the same as that of the historian. Lawyers were, in fact, more interested in history than almost anyone else was, and they were duly critical in evaluating historical evidence. But when they used old books for forensic purposes, they were looking for useful law rather than indulging in antiquarian curiosity for its own sake. Moreover, the thinking of lawyers has its own history, especially when it involves the development of traditional learning to meet the exigencies of the moment. It turns out that, when the legal sources are brought into play, more significant changes of thought can be discerned over time than the statute-book alone might lead the casual observer to suppose.

The book is based on a number of lectures given in 2014–15, as enumerated in the acknowledgements. Something of the tone of the lectures has been preserved, but the details have been augmented from further research in the huge corpus of early-modern legal manuscripts. Underlying both the lectures and the book were the four new discoveries revealed in the Selden Society volume for 2015, *Readings and Commentaries on Magna Carta 1400–1604*. The first, a negative discovery but a surprising one, was the absence of any coherent constitutional learning in the many lectures on Magna Carta which survive from the late-medieval and early-Tudor inns of court. The second was the legal and historical treatise on Magna Carta by William Fleetwood, which, though written as late as the 1550s, was still closer to the medieval learning than to the mentality of Coke. The third was the almost complete absence of Magna Carta from constitutional discussions in reported cases before the 1580s, when all of a sudden chapter 29 became common currency in forensic argument. This chronology suggested a possible link with the first known reading in an inn of court devoted entirely to chapter 29, that given by Robert Snagge in 1581. And the fourth discovery was the treatise on chapter 29 written by Sir Edward Coke, not when he was leading the opposition in the House of Commons in the 1620s, but when he was the king's principal law officer in 1604. These discoveries, especially in conjunction, pointed to a very different history of Magna Carta from that which has prevailed before now.

Instead of printing the original papers as a collection of separate essays, their content has been reworked into a chronological arrangement, ending with the dismissal of Coke from the office of lord chief justice in 1616. The story is preceded by a more general chapter straddling the centuries, the purpose of which is to examine different views about the legal character of Magna Carta and its special place in the common-law tradition. After further chapters exploring the legal profession's awareness and understanding of the great charter from the late-medieval period up to the sixteenth century, the central chapters show how most of the constitutional issues which came eventually to be linked with Magna Carta were initially addressed without drawing upon its assistance at all. The process of reinvention is then recounted, with some attempt at an explanation, in the later chapters. Religion played a crucial part in that story, because of the struggle for freedom of thought and the campaign by 'Puritan' members of Parliament against the ecclesiastical High Commission. Another preliminary chapter therefore surveys briefly the treatment of heresy in England, an unsavoury story of religious intolerance which continued to inform debates about the High Commission and due process. There were concurrent concerns also about secular liberty and the rule of law, concerns which within a single generation united conservative and progressive lawyers in a newfound devotion to the great charter. Magna Carta rapidly became a symbol of national glory and stability in the later years of Queen Elizabeth, and in the next reign a bulwark against the disturbing constitutional ideas which the new king brought with him from Scotland.

The main purpose of the book is to investigate how, when and why English lawyers began to think about connections between personal liberty, constitutional monarchy, the rule of law and Magna Carta, and the story is related from their point of view. The process of reinvention largely concerned a single provision, the world-famous chapter 29, the rest of the statute (with a few exceptions) having lost its practical relevance before Tudor times. The fine words had always been known to lawyers, but they were of little or no forensic consequence until they were resurrected for practical purposes in the 1580s and rapidly turned into holy scripture. Their apotheosis came in Francis Ashley's reading in the Middle Temple, delivered a few weeks before Coke's dismissal in 1616. Within this short period of under forty years, the exegesis of chapter 29 had stretched its reach almost to the limits. The present account therefore ends in 1616, rather than in 1628. There remained one high hurdle to overcome, the availability of *habeas corpus* to challenge an imprisonment by the king's immediate command. That would require a change of mind by Coke, and a great deal of debate. In other respects, however, the new implications of chapter 29 had all been settled before the end of Coke's chief justiceship. Coke played such a prominent role in the story that it has been related at some length, though it will be shown that he was responsible neither for the initial revival of Magna Carta nor for the myths which posterity has attributed to him.

Many of the sources used here have never been printed, and are not written in English, and so translations of a small selection of them are provided in the appendices. Quotations from English texts have throughout the book been rendered into modern orthography, with adjusted punctuation, even when taken from printed editions, since the language is that still in use. There is no merit in preserving exactly the immaterial features of transcripts of lost autograph texts, and no obvious merit even in the case of autograph material. Latin spelling has also been standardised, and one consequence of this is that Charta is rendered throughout as Carta. Quotations which have been translated from French or Latin are marked 'tr.'.

John Baker
April 2016

ACKNOWLEDGEMENTS

The chapters in this book enlarge upon the following lectures and essays by the author:

1 'The Legal Force and Effect of Magna Carta' in *Magna Carta: Muse & Mentor*, ed. R. J. Holland ([Washington, DC], 2014), pp. 65–84, (notes) 258–61.

2 'Chapter 29 of Magna Carta in the Fourteenth Century' in *Texts and Contexts in Legal History: Essays in Honor of Charles Donahue*, ed. J. Witte, S. McDougall and A. de Robilant (Berkeley, 2016), ch. 15, pp. 223–44.

3–4 *Selected Readings and Commentaries on Magna Carta 1400–1604* (132 SS, 2015), introduction, pp. xxxix–lxxxv.

5 'Magna Carta and Personal Liberty' in *Magna Carta, Religion and the Rule of Law*, ed. R. Griffith-Jones and M. Hill (Cambridge, 2015), pp. 81–108; *Reports from the Lost Notebooks of Sir James Dyer*, vol. i (109 SS, 1994), introduction, pp. lxii–lxxvi.

6 *Reports from the Lost Notebooks of Sir James Dyer*, vol. i (109 SS, 1994), introduction, pp. li–liv, lxxvi–lxxxv; 'Personal Liberty under the Common Law 1200–1600' (1991), reprinted in *Collected Papers on English Legal History* (Cambridge, 2013), ii. 871–900.

7–8 'Magna Carta: The Emergence of the Myth', lecture at the British Legal History Conference (on a boat starting from Runnymede), 8 July 2015, and in a revised form at a meeting of the American Inns of Court Foundation, Washington, DC, 23 October 2015; 'Magna Carta and the Templars 1215–1628', lecture in the Inner Temple, 23 November 2015.

9–10 *Selected Readings and Commentaries on Magna Carta 1400–1604* (132 SS, 2015), introduction, pp. lxxxviii–xci; 'Sir Edward Coke and Magna Carta', lecture delivered to the Stoke Poges Historical Society, 14 July 2015; 'The Common Lawyers and the Chancery: 1616' (1969) reprinted in *Collected Papers on English Legal History* (Cambridge, 2013), i. 481–512.

TABLE OF STATUTES AND GENERAL CHARTERS

TABLE OF CASES

Year-book Cases

Cases Cited by Name

LIST OF ABBREVIATIONS

All the printed law reports are cited by the standard abbreviations used by lawyers, to avoid tediously lengthy bibliographical references. There is a guide in P. G. Osborn, *A Concise Law Dictionary for Students and Practitioners* (new edn, 2013). All the cases in the printed reports between the YB and 1865 were reprinted (from the latest editions, some of which were English translations) in the *English Reports* (1900–32), 178 vols., with the original pagination preserved in brackets. Translations here are the author's, using the original French editions.

APC	*Acts of the Privy Council* (new series) (1895–1925), 34 volumes. The coverage is incomplete because some of the original registers (including all the years 1602–13) were destroyed in a fire. The volumes themselves do not bear numbers, but are cited here according to the numbers by which they are usually cited, and which are given in the digitised version published in British History Online.
Ashley's reading	Reading by Francis Ashley (d. 1635) in the Middle Temple, Autumn 1616, on Magna Carta, c. 29. The text cited here, unless otherwise stated, is BL MS. Harley 4841, which was probably the reader's own manuscript (though not in his hand). Cases from the reading are in CUL MS. Ee.6.3, fos. 100–21.
Att.-Gen.	attorney-general
B.	Baron of the Exchequer
Baker, *Collected Papers*	J.[H.] Baker, *Collected Papers on English Legal History* (Cambridge, 2013), three volumes.
Baker, 'Legal Force and Effect of Magna Carta'	J. [H.] Baker, 'The Legal Force and Effect of Magna Carta' in *Magna Carta: Muse & Mentor*, ed. R. J. Holland (Library of Congress [Washington, DC], 2014), pp. 65–84, (notes) 258–61.

Birch, *Court and Times* [T. Birch], *The Court and Times of James I Illustrated by Confidential and Authentic Letters*, ed. R. F. Williams (1848), two volumes. Birch (d. 1766) collected in this work, inter alia, the letters between John Chamberlain and Dudley Carleton from the Stowe MSS. in the British Library.

BL British Library, London.

Bodl. Lib. Bodleian Library, Oxford.

Bowyer, *Parliamentary Diary* *The Parliamentary Diary of Robert Bowyer 1606–1607*, ed. D. H. Wilson (Minneapolis, 1931).

Boyer, *Coke and the Elizabethan Age* A. D. Boyer, *Sir Edward Coke and the Elizabethan Age* (Stanford, CA, 2003).

Bracton *Bracton on the Laws and Customs of England*, ed. G. E. Woodbine and S. E. Thorne (1968–77), four volumes.

Bro. Abr. R. Brooke, *La Graunde Abridgement* (1573), two volumes. Cited by alphabetical title.

Brooks, *Law, Politics and Society* C. W. Brooks, *Law, Politics and Society in Early Modern England* (Cambridge, 2008).

c. chapter

c. *circa*

Caesar's minutes Autograph minutes by Sir Julius Caesar LLD, chancellor of the Exchequer, of proceedings in the Privy Council concerning prohibitions (1608–11) BL MS. Lansdowne 160, fos. 405–431v (bound up from folded papers). This is a period for which the Privy Council registers are missing. Caesar was directly interested in the subject as master of the Court of Requests, judge of the Admiralty and ecclesiastical commissioner.

Calth. MS. Autograph reports of Henry Calthorpe (d. 1637) of the Middle Temple (called to the bar 1614), from Michaelmas 1611 to Trinity 1619, in BL MSS. Hargrave 385 (with full subject index) and 386 (with a similar index in MS. 387). These notebooks, uniformly written in a tiny crabbed hand, contain a very minute account of the business of the King's Bench during Coke's chief justiceship. Calthorpe was knighted as solicitor-general to Queen Henrietta Maria in 1635 and was briefly recorder of London (1635–6) and Attorney-General of the Wards (1636–7). His reports of cases relating to the city of London (commonly cited as Calth.) were printed in 1655.

CB	Chief baron of the Exchequer. (*see* CJ)
CCR	*Calendar of Close Rolls.*
CELMC	J. H. Baker, *Catalogue of English Legal Manuscripts in Cambridge University Library* (Woodbridge, 1996).
CJ	Chief justice. Postnominal judicial titles have been used sparingly, e.g. where they are useful as indicating a speaker's legal position at the time of speaking.
CJCP	Chief Justice of the Common Pleas
CJKB	Chief Justice of the King's Bench
cl.	clause
Co. Inst.	Sir Edward Coke, *Institutes of the Laws of England* (1628–44), four volumes. The first volume (the commentary on Littleton's *Tenures*, 1st edn, 1628), is cited as Co. Litt.
Co. Litt.	*See* Co. Inst.
Co. Rep.	*The Reports of Sir Edward Coke*, first published in French in thirteen parts, under various titles, between 1600 and 1615, with two further parts (in English translation only) published posthumously in 1658–9. The last edition to include Coke's prefaces was that by J. H. Thomas and J. F. Fraser (1826), six volumes, with the whole text in translation only. The translation was reprinted in the *English Reports*, as to which see the remarks at the beginning of this section. Citations are always to the original folio numbering, which is preserved in all editions in addition to the varying pagination.
Coke, 'Dangerous and Absurd Opinions'	Sir Edward Coke, 'Dangerous et absurd opinions affirme devant le Roy' [by Lord Ellesmere] (1608–16), in Coke's autograph notebook, CUL MS. Ii.5.21, fos. 47v–48, continued in the margins on both pages. This was begun in 1608, using a space left blank in Pas. 1607, and continued over the next eight years. There are several manuscript copies.
Collinson, *Bancroft*	P. Collinson, *Richard Bancroft and Elizabethan Anti-Puritanism* (Cambridge, 2013).
CP 40	Plea rolls of the Court of Common Pleas (PRO).
CPR	Calendar of Patent Rolls.
Crompton, *Courts*	R. Crompton, *L'Authoritie et Jurisdiction des Courts* (1594).
CSPD	Calendar of State Papers (Domestic).
CUL	Cambridge University Library.

Dawson, 'Privy Council'   J. P. Dawson, 'The Privy Council and Private Law in the Tudor and Stuart Period' (1950) 48 *Michigan Law Review* 393–428, 627–56.

DCL   doctor of the civil law

Discourse upon Statutes   [W. Fleetwood], *A Discourse upon the Exposicion & Understandinge of Statutes With Sir Thomas Egerton's Additions: Edited from Manuscripts in the Huntington Library*, ed. S. E. Thorne (San Marino, CA, 1942). This is another version of Fleetwood, *Statutes*. For the authorship see below, pp. 232–7.

Dyer   J. Dyer, *Ascuns Novel Cases* (1585/6).

Dyer's Notebooks   *Reports from the Lost Notebooks of Sir James Dyer*, ed. J. H. Baker (109–10 SS, 1994–5), two volumes.

EHR   *English Historical Review*

Ellesmere, 'Observations upon Coke's Reports'   T. Egerton, Lord Ellesmere, 'Observations upon the Lord Coke's Reports' [1616], in *Law and Politics in Jacobean England: The Tracts of Lord Chancellor Ellesmere*, ed. L. A. Knafla (Cambridge, 1977), pp. 297–318.

ELMUSA   J. H. Baker, *English Legal Manuscripts in the United States of America*, (Selden Society, 1985).

FBL   The Francis Bacon Library, founded by Walter and Louise Arensberg in Clarement, California, and donated to the Huntington Library in 1995.

Fitz. Abr.   A. Fitzherbert, *La Graunde Abridgement* [1514–16] (3rd edn, 1577). Cited by alphabetical title.

Fleetwood, *Of Forests*   W. Fleetwood, *Of Forests* (1571), with a historical 'proheme' (fos. 3–6) and an appendix (fos. 49–59) explaining Anglo-Saxon words ('De expositione antiquorum verborum'), BL MS. Harley 5194. The dedication to Sir Nicholas Bacon LK is dated 8 June 1571. HLS MS. 15 is a copy in Fleetwood's hand dated 21 March 1581; here he says he wrote it about thirteen years earlier, i.e. around 1568, and that the vocabulary was prepared in connection with his reading (1565). There are other versions in BL MS. Add. 26047; LMA, CLC/270, MS. 86, fos. 60–86.

Fleetwood, *Itinerarium ad Windsor*   *The Name of a Queen: William Fleetwood's Itinerarium ad Windsor*, ed. D. Moore and C. Beem (New York, 2013).

Fleetwood, *Justice*   W. Fleetwood, *The Office of a Justice of Peace* ('1658', *recte* 1657). The Harvard Law School copy has an

	ownership inscription dated 27 July 1657, and the Thomason copy in the British Library is also annotated with a correction of the date.
Fleetwood, *Liber Fleetwood*	See *Liber Fleetwood*.
Fleetwood, *Magna Carta*	Fleetwood's commentary on Magna Carta (*c.* 1558) CUL MS. Gg.5.18, fos. 3–41v, partly printed (with translation) in *Selected Readings on Magna Carta*, pp. 366–92.
Fleetwood, 'Miscellanea'	A collection of miscellaneous drafts by Fleetwood, some of them incomplete, LMA, CLC/270, MS. 86. For the history of this manuscript see below, p. 234.
Fleetwood, 'Notes for Arguments'	BL MS. Hargrave 4, fos. 289v–342, identifed below (pp. 238–40) as notes made by Serjeant Fleetwood for use in arguing cases at the bar. Other similar notes in BL MS. Harley 4717, here attributed to Fleetwood, are cited by that reference.
Fleetwood, *Statutes*	W. Fleetwood, 'Instructions how and in what Manner Statutes are to be Expounded' printed as the second part of *The Office of a Justice of Peace, together with Instructions how and in what Manner Statutes shall be Expounded. Written by W. Fleetwood, Esq; sometime Recorder of London* ('1658', *recte* 1657), at pp. 97–164. This is another version of *Discourse upon Statutes*. The first edition of Wing wrongly attributed it to the contemporary Colonel Fleetwood.
FNB	A. Fitzherbert, *La Novel Natura Brevium* (1538).
Forrest, *Detection of Heresy*	I. Forrest, *The Detection of Heresy in Late Medieval England* (Oxford, 2005).
Fuller, *Argument*	*The Argument of Master Nicholas Fuller in the Case of Thomas Lad and Richard Maunsell* (1607).
gl.	gloss, glossing
Glanvill	*The Treatise on the Laws and Customs of the Realm of England commonly called Glanvill*, ed. G. D. G. Hall (1965).
Gray, 'Self-Incrimination'	C. M. Gray, 'Self-Incrimination in Interjurisdictional Law' in *The Privilege against Self-Incrimination*, ed. R. H. Helmholz and others (Chicago, 1997), pp. 47–81.
Gray, *Writ of Prohibition*	C. M. Gray, *The Writ of Prohibition: Jurisdiction in Early Modern English Law* (New York, 1994), two volumes.

Hake, *Epieikeia*
E. Hake, *Epieikeia: A Dialogue on Equity in Three Parts*, ed. D. E. C. Yale (New Haven, 1953). The treatise was largely written in the 1590s and finished *c.* 1603.

Halliday, *Habeas Corpus*
P. Halliday, *Habeas Corpus: From England to Empire* (Cambridge, MA, 2010).

Hatfield House MSS.
Calendar of the Manuscripts of the Most Honourable the Marquis of Salisbury preserved at Hatfield House (1883–1976), twenty-four volumes. These are sometimes known as the Cecil Papers.

Hawarde
J. Hawarde, *Les Reportes del Cases in Camera Stellata 1593–1609*, ed. W. P. Baildon (privately printed, 1894).

Henderson, *Foundations*
E. G. Henderson, *Foundations of English Administrative Law* (Cambridge, MA, 1963).

HLS MS.
Manuscript in Harvard Law School Library, Cambridge, Massachusetts. The manuscripts are cited here by the numbers which were in use in the Library in 1990 and cited in J. H. Baker, *English Legal Manuscripts in the United States of America*, vol. ii (1990). Some of them have since been altered.

Holkham MS.
Manuscript belonging to the earl of Leicester, Holkham Hall, Norfolk.

HPHC 1509–58
The History of Parliament: The House of Commons 1509–1558, ed. S. T. Bindoff (1982), three volumes.

HPHC 1558–1603
The History of Parliament: The House of Commons 1558–1603, ed. P. W. Hasler (1981), three volumes.

HPHC 1604–29
The History of Parliament: The House of Commons 1604–1629, ed. A. Thrush and J. Ferris (2010), six volumes.

IT MS.
Manuscript in the library of the Inner Temple, London.

J.
Justice (*see* CJ.)

JCP
Justice of the Common Pleas

JHC
Journal of the House of Commons, vol. i (1547–1629) (1802).

Jones, *Elizabethan Chancery*
W. J. Jones, *The Elizabethan Court of Chancery* (Oxford, 1967).

JP
Justice of the Peace

KB 27
Plea rolls of the Court of King's Bench (PRO).

KB 29
Controlment rolls of the clerk of the crown in the King's Bench (PRO).

Lambarde, *Archeion*
W. Lambarde, *Archeion: or, A Discourse on upon the High Courts of Justice in England*, ed. C. H. McIlwain

	and L. Ward (Cambridge, MA, 1957). This was written *c.* 1591 and first printed in 1635.
LC	Lord Chancellor
Letters and Life of Bacon	*The Letters and the Life of Francis Bacon*, the subsidiary title given to volumes 8–14 of The *Works of Francis Bacon* (q.v.), which were also numbered separately as 1–7 (1861–74).
LI MS.	Manuscript in Lincoln's Inn library, London.
Lib. Ass.	*Liber Assisarum*, now printed as part of the year-book series. The most recent edition is that of 1679.
Liber Fleetwood	W. Fleetwood, collection of London records and documents entitled 'Liber Fleetwood', LMA, COL/CS/ 01/11 (formerly Corporation of London Record Office, Cust. 11); microfilm, X112/018. The preface is dated 31 July 1576. A copy, which also apparently belonged to Fleetwood, is in the Folger Shakespeare Library, Washington, MS. V.b.9.
Litt.	T. Littleton, *Tenures* [1st edn, *c.* 1482] (reprinted in Co. Litt.), cited by section.
LK	Lord Keeper of the Great Seal
LMA	London Metropolitan Archives. This repository now houses the holdings of the former Corporation of London Record Office and the Guildhall Library manuscript collection.
LQR	*Law Quarterly Review*
m.	membrane
Magna Carta Commemoration Essays	*Magna Carta Commemoration Essays*, ed. H. E. Malden (1917).
Men of Court (The)	J. [H.] Baker, *The Men of Court 1440–1550: A Prosopography of the Inns of Court and Chancery and the Courts of Law* (18 SS Suppl. Series, 2012), two volumes.
More, *Debellation of Salem and Bizance*	*The Debellation of Salem and Bizance*, ed. J. Guy (10 *Complete Works of St Thomas More*, New Haven, CT, 1987).
Morice's reading	Reading by James Morice (d. 1597) in the Middle Temple, Autumn 1578, on Westminster I, c. 50, concerning the rights of the crown. Unless otherwise stated, references are to BL MS. Egerton 3376, a redaction prepared at the instance of Lord Burghley. What seems to be the first part of the reader's original

	autograph version is BL MS. Add. 36081, fos. 229–74. Arguments on the reader's cases on some of the divisions are reported in BL MS. Add. 16169, fos. 39–57.
MP	Member of Parliament
MTR	*Middle Temple Records: Minutes of Parliament of the Middle Temple*, vol. i (1501–1603), ed. C. A. Hopwood (1904).
ODNB	*Oxford Dictionary of National Biography*, ed. H. C. G. Matthew and B. Harrison (Oxford, 2004), sixty-one volumes.
OHLE, vi.	J. [H.] Baker, vol. vi (1483–1558) of the *Oxford History of the Laws of England* (Oxford, 2003).
Ordinary Gloss on Magna Carta	The widely circulated reading (or collection of readings) on the whole of Magna Carta, dating from the early fifteenth century, which exists in several manuscripts and is partly printed in *Selected Readings on Magna Carta*: see below, pp. 71–4. Although the term is used here for convenience, it was an academical expression not in fact used in the inns of court.
Owen, *Common Law*	Sir Roger Owen (d. 1617), treatise on the antiquity and excellency of the common law (*c.* 1615), which survives (without title) in disordered fragments: BL MS. Harley 6604–6 (corrupt copy of chapters 1–2, 4–6, 15–20); MS. Lansdowne 646 (chapters 7, 16–18); MS. Harley 1572; MS. Harley 3627 (chapters 1–6); LI MS. Misc. 207 (chapters 1–7, 13, 15–20); it is possible that chapters 8–12 and 14 were never written. Owen was a non-practising but resident barrister of Lincoln's Inn, an MP, and a voracious student of historical manuscripts and foreign books. He referred to William Lambarde as 'a late ornament of our university of Lincoln's Inn' (MS. Harley 6604, fo. 251v).
PCC	Prerogative Court of Canterbury will registers (PROB 11 in the PRO).
pl.	placitum: see YB.
Plowd.	*Les Comentaries ou Reports de Edmund Plowden* (1571, 1579), two parts with continuous folio numbering.
Pocock, *Ancient Constitution*	J. G. A. Pocock, *The Ancient Constitution and the Feudal Law* (reissue of the 1957 edn, with a retrospective essay, Cambridge, 1987).

PRO	Public Record Office, Kew, the statutory English record repository overseen by the National Archives.
Proc. Parl. 1558–81	*Proceedings in the Parliaments of Elizabeth I*, vol. i: 1558–1581, ed. T. E. Hartley (Leicester, 1981).
Proc. Parl. 1584–9	*Proceedings in the Parliaments of Elizabeth I*, vol. ii: 1584–1589, ed. T. E. Hartley (Leicester, 1995).
Proc. Parl. 1593–1601	*Proceedings in the Parliaments of Elizabeth I*, vol. iii: 1593–1601, ed. T. E. Hartley (Leicester, 1995).
Proc. Parl. 1610	*Proceedings in Parliament 1610*, ed. E. R. Foster (New Haven, CT, 1966), two volumes.
Proc. Parl. 1614	*Proceedings in Parliament 1614 (House of Commons)*, ed. M. Jansson (Philadelphia, 1988).
Readers and Readings	J. H. Baker, *Readers and Readings in the Inns of Court and Chancery* (13 SS Suppl. Series, 2000).
Rights and Liberties	*The Rights and Liberties of the English Church: Readings from the Pre-Reformation Inns of Court*, ed. M. McGlynn (129 SS, 2015).
Rot. Parl.	*Rotuli Parliamentorum ut et Petitiones et Placita in Parliamento* [1767–7].
RS	Rolls Series
S.	Section
SC 8	PRO, Special Collections.
Selected Readings on Magna Carta	*Selected Readings and Commentaries on Magna Carta 1400–1604*, ed. J. [H.] Baker (132 SS, 2015).
sig.	signature
sjt	serjeant at law
Smith, *Sir Edward Coke*	D. C. Smith, *Sir Edward Coke and the Reformation of the Laws: Religion, Politics and Jurisprudence 1579–1616* (Cambridge, 2014).
Snagge, *Antiquity of the Chancery*	[R.] Snagge, *The Antiquity and Original of the High Court of Chancery and Authority of the Lord Chancellor of England*, ed. T. L. (1654). A revised extract from Snagge's reading in the Middle Temple (1581), with a dedication addressed to Sir Christopher Hatton in 1587.
Sol.-Gen.	solicitor-general
SP	PRO, State Papers.
SS	Publications of the Selden Society.
Spelman's Reports	*The Reports of Sir John Spelman*, ed. J. H. Baker (93–4 SS, 1977–78), two volumes, the second containing the introduction (paginated in italic arabics) and records.

St. Tr.	*Cobbett's Complete Collection of State Trials*, vol. i (1163–1600), vol. ii (1603–27) and vol. iii (1627-40) [ed. T. B. Howell] (1809).
Sta. P.C.	W. Staundforde (Staunford), *Les Plees del Coron* (1557).
Statham	The abridgement of cases compiled c. 1460 and printed anonymously, without title, in Rouen (*c.* 1490). It has always been attributed to Nicholas Statham of Lincoln's Inn.
Statutes of the Realm	*Statutes of the Realm* (Record Commission, 1810–28), twelve volumes.
sub nom.	*sub nomine*, i.e. (reported) under the (variant) name (of).
Suppl.	Supplementary
Thompson, *Magna Carta*	F. Thompson, *Magna Carta: Its Role in the Making of the English Constitution 1300-1629* (Minneapolis, 1948).
Tourneur	Reports of cases, mostly in the King's Bench 1615–17, by Timothy Tourneur (d. 1677), BL MS. Add. 35957 (autograph). Earlier and later reports by him are cited in some of the marginalia, but they have not been found. Tourneur was a barrister of Gray's Inn (called 1611, bencher 1632), and in 1670 at the age of 86 was knighted as one of the king's serjeants.
tr.	Here translated into English; translated as follows.
Usher, *High Commission*	R. G. Usher, *The Rise and Fall of the High Commission* (Oxford, 1913).
Usher, *Reconstruction*	R. G. Usher, *The Reconstruction of the English Church* (1910; reprinted in facsimile, Farnborough, 1969), two volumes.
Wilbraham, *Journal*	*The Journal of Sir Roger Wilbraham ... 1593-1616*, ed. H. S. Scott (10 Camden Miscellany, 1902).
Works of Francis Bacon	*The Works of Francis Bacon*, ed. J. Spedding, R. L. Ellis and D. D. Heath (1857–74), fourteen volumes. The last seven volumes were given the subsidiary title *The Letters and The Life of Francis Bacon* and are cited here as *Letters and Life of Bacon.*
YB	year book, cited by term, regnal year, folio and 'placitum' (or case-number) from the vulgate edition of 1679–80.

Yelverton's abridegment	Abridgement of cases compiled by Sir Henry Yelverton, BL MS Add. 48486.
YLS	Yale Law School Library, New Haven, CT.
Youngs	F. A. Youngs, *Proclamations of the Tudor Queens* (Cambridge, 1976).

The Legal Character of Magna Carta

Magna Carta is universally considered to be one of the world's great documents, 'worthy to be written in letters of gold',[1] treasured syllable by syllable,[2] quoted on the walls of law schools and courts, perhaps even on official notepaper,[3] taught to all schoolchildren and so forth. There is no doubt that it has had an immense influence on hearts and minds around the world. Yet it is not always understood that this influence has been achieved more by reputation than by the operation of positive law. The charter was not a constitutional document.[4] It did not address the law-making process at all, because it did not contemplate future legislative change. It did not specify in general terms what kinds of authority the king's government could exercise; nor did it provide any remedies by way of an action at law against the crown if the government acted despotically.[5] Its purpose was more immediate: to restore, declare and preserve the previous common law. In many respects this was achieved rapidly and without the need for sanctions, in that Henry III did much of what was promised and stopped doing things which had been the source of complaint.[6] Whether it had a future was a very different matter. It was

---

[1] So said Coke in the *Case of Purveyance* (c. 1605), cited in Ashley's reading, fo. 24v ('cel statute fuit digne d'estre escript en lettres de or'). It was actually the first English book to be printed in gold: Blackstone's edition of 1759 was reprinted in gold on vellum, with hand-painted decoration, in 1816.

[2] Co. Inst. ii. 57: 'As the gold-finer will not out of the dust, threads or shreds of gold, let pass the least crumb, in respect of the excellency of the metal: so ought not the learned reader to let pass any syllable of this law, in respect of the excellency of its matter.'

[3] Lord Bingham suggested that the wording of c. 29 should be inscribed on the stationery of the Ministry of Justice and Home Office: *The Rule of Law* (2010), p. 10.

[4] Cf. W. H. Dunham, 'Magna Carta & British Constitutionalism' in *The Great Charter: Four Essays on Magna Carta and the History of our Liberty* (New York, 1965), pp. 26–50.

[5] No action at law could be brought against the crown until 1947. The elaborate enforcement system in clause 61 of the 1215 charter had no parallel in the statutory version.

[6] For a measured assessment of the thirteenth-century effects see D. Carpenter, *Magna Carta* (2015), ch. 14.

certainly not a document to be forgotten. But some of the wording was unclear, and within a century open reference was being made in high places to its doubts and obscurities.[7] This was not merely a tactful way of complaining that the king was ignoring it. Doubts about the true meaning of the most fundamentally important chapter led to its being adjusted in 1331 and completely reworded in 1354,[8] though the original text remained on the statute-book alongside the recensions, and the texts had to be read together.[9] In 1377 the Commons asked for the whole charter to be expounded, point by point, with the help of the judges and serjeants at law,[10] though this attempt to turn Parliament into a law school was quietly ignored. By that time much of it was obsolete anyway, and the phrase-by-phrase commentaries provided in the inns of court lectures were probably well on their way to becoming highly technical and destructively critical. Generations of lawyers and students sharpened their wits exploring its intricacies, and in so doing identified many more doubts and obscurities.[11] It is truly remarkable, in view of all this, that Magna Carta achieved such lasting and widespread fame in later periods. The stages by which this became possible will be explored in this book, in chronological order. But first it may be helpful to make some general observations about the legal character of the charter as seen across the centuries.

Magna Carta as a Statute

The charter of 1215 might have been seen fleetingly as a statute, in the sense of a declaration or enactment intended to lay down rules for the future.[12] Yet it was clearly never a statute in the sense which has prevailed among English lawyers since the fourteenth century, namely an

---

[7] E.g. the New Ordinances (1311) Rot. Parl. i. 281 (doubtful points to be clarified by the lords ordainers), 286 (doubtful points to be clarified in the next parliament by the barons, justices 'et autres sages gentz de la lei'); *Statutes of the Realm*, i. 158, no. 6; and i. 167, no. 38. In 1327 the Commons petitioned that those points of 'la chartre du franchises' which were in need of clarification should be clarified in Parliament: Rot. Parl. ii. 7, no. 3. This probably referred to the *Earl of Lancaster's Case*, discussed below, p. 54.

[8] Below, p. 33. For the obscurity of its wording see below, pp. 32–40.

[9] The late-medieval inns of court largely ignored the 1354 version, no doubt because it gave less scope for destructive analysis: below, p. 92.

[10] Rot. Parl. iii. 15, nos. 44–5.   [11] See Chapter 3, below.

[12] For the early forms of English legislation and their various descriptions see T. F. T. Plucknett, *Statutes and their Interpretation in the First Half of the Fourteenth Century* (Cambridge, 1922), pp. 1, 8–12.

enactment made by the king with the advice of the peers and commons in Parliament assembled.[13] Not only was there nothing resembling Parliament at the time,[14] but only a few weeks after it was agreed the charter was repudiated by King John, with the blessing of Pope Innocent III. The beleaguered king had an arguable case for treating it as void for duress, and for the avoidance of doubt he procured a bull from the pope forbidding him, on pain of eternal anathema, from keeping his solemn promises.[15] The charter was a dead letter, and it failed even as a means of securing a peace. The importance of the 1215 document was not that it ever had any legal effect itself, but that it inspired modified versions extracted from King Henry III. For centuries Magna Carta was almost universally understood to be the charter which Henry III granted in 1225,[16] and which Edward I and subsequent kings confirmed, rather than the Charter of Runnymede, which was a passing historical event.[17] It is surprising how many reputable historians have been careless about this, referring to the clauses of the 1215 charter – clause 39, in particular[18] – as if they operated as law in later periods.

[13] T. F. T. Plucknett, *The Legislation of Edward I* (Oxford, 1949), pp. 10–15; J. H. Baker, *Introduction to English Legal History* (4th edn, 2002), pp. 203–6.

[14] There was an assembly of bishops and barons at Runnymede, but they were there to negotiate terms rather than deliberate, and no mention is made of participation by commoners.

[15] The pope, who was an advocate of absolutism (below, p. 120), also regarded it as shameful and demeaning for a king to make such concessions to his people. Both grounds were expressed in the bull (*Etsi karissimus*, 24 August 1215), which survives in the British Library and is printed in C. Bémont, *Chartes des Libertés Anglaises* (Paris, 1892), pp. 41–4.

[16] Two sixteenth-century readers, however, thought it was John's charter which was later turned into a statute: *Rights and Liberties*, pp. 87 (made a statute by Edward I), and 140 (made a statute at Marlborough). They were in error, since it was not the 1215 charter which was confirmed in 1267 and 1297. They had probably not seen the 1215 text. Only one reader is known to have lectured on a clause of the 1215 charter, presumably relying on an old manuscript: *Selected Readings on Magna Carta*, p. 210 (Baldwin Malet, 1512, on cl. 27, *Si quis liber homo intestatus decesseri*).

[17] See this distinction drawn by William Fleetwood, below, p. 243. Cf. J. Cowell, *The Interpreter* (1607), sig. Ss4v: 'Magna Carta ... is a charter containing a number of laws ordained the ninth year of Henry the third ... I read in Holinshed that King John to appease his barons yielded to laws or articles of government much like to this great charter.'

[18] The original charters were not written with distinct paragraphs, let alone divided into numbered chapters. In medieval texts and citations the numbering varies, but it became fixed in the printed editions. There were fewer clauses in the later versions, and clauses 39–40 of the 1215 charter became c. 29 of the 1225 statute.

The 1225 version was the text usually found in statute-books, both manuscript and printed,[19] and was the basis of Coke's commentary four centuries later.[20] Although the 1215 charter was occasionally copied out for reference purposes, or in the hope that it might somehow be of use,[21] it was usually distinguished from the great charter by a special title.[22] There was no proper edition of it before Blackstone.[23] It was little more than a footnote to history. The despicable King John could hardly be given credit for something which had turned out so well, particularly since he was against the very idea of it. When Shakespeare wrote a play in the 1590s about King John, first published in 1623, he did not see fit to mention the episode at Runnymede at all.[24] Obviously Shakespeare knew about Magna Carta – even Justice Shallow would have heard of it, as a student in Clement's Inn – but it was not associated with King John.[25]

---

[19] In fourteenth-century manuscripts the text was often copied from the 1297 confirmation of the 1225 charter, but only because it was the most authentic evidence of what had been enacted in 1225: see below, pp. 8–10. In a few manuscripts the text is a conflation of the 1217 and 1225 texts.

[20] Co. Inst. ii. 1–78.

[21] The 'magna carta Johannis Regis de Ronemede' (cl. 56) was pleaded in *Mortimer v. Tony* (1290) in an unsuccessful attempt to prevent the justices at Hereford from entertaining a suit relating to land in the marches of Wales: KB 27/129, m. 61 (formerly m. 58); abridged in *Placitorum Abbreviatio* (1811), p. 58. Some other examples are given in F. Thompson, *The First Century of Magna Carta* (Minneapolis, 1925), p. 65; J. C. Holt, *Magna Carta* (3rd edn), pp. 47, 328–30. See also Carpenter, *Magna Carta*, pp. 432–4.

[22] E.g. CUL MS. Ee.6.1, fos. 154–156v ('Carta Johannis Regis que vocatur Runnemede'); MS. Ee.2.19, fos. 1–5 ('Carta Johannis'); MS. Gg.1.12, fos. 21–25v ('Provisio de Ronnemde'). Richard Hesketh referred to the 'charter of Runnymede' in his Gray's Inn reading (c. 1506): *Selected Readings on Magna Carta*, p. 362. But cf. Co. Inst. ii, proeme: 'King John in the 17. yeare of his raigne had granted the like, which was also called Magna Carta, as appeareth by a record before this Great Charter made by King H. 3' (citing Matthew Paris); below, p. 532.

[23] W. Blackstone, *The Great Charter* (Oxford, 1759). Before then it was generally known only from Matthew Paris (printed in 1571), or Roger of Wendover, whose account of it (as Blackstone revealed) was badly garbled. A facsimile of one of the Cottonian charters, with hand-painted coats of arms, was engraved by John Pine, Bluemantle Pursuivant, and published in 1733; a copy was sold at Bonham's on 12 November 2013, lot 227, for £32,500.

[24] Cf., however, William Fleetwood's remark in the 1550s that the story of King John and Magna Carta was well known even to those who knew nothing of history: *Rights and Liberties*, p. 133.

[25] It is true that the readers in the inns of court usually noted that the charter was originally granted by John, but they immediately explained that it was not a statute until Henry III: *Rights and Liberties*, pp. 71, 83, 87, 97, 139. They probably knew about the 1215 charter only from chronicles, not from direct access to a copy, and were unaware of textual differences.

This cannot be dismissed as a playwright's inattention to historical detail, for no less a historical scholar than John Selden wrote in 1610, without a hint of irony, that little of relevance to legal history occurred in John's reign.[26] As will be shown later, Magna Carta was already, by the time of Shakespeare and Selden, a topic of great and growing interest; but it was Henry III's charter, not John's, which went by the epithet 'Magna'.[27] Coke once went so far as to suggest that John's charter was of no more significance than that of Henry I (1100), though he may not at that time have been closely familiar with either of them.[28]

The resurrection of Magna Carta began on 12 November 1216, a month after King John's death, with the so-called 'reissue' under the seals of the king's regent William Marshal and the papal legate Guala. It is misleading to call it a reissue, since it was a substantially pared down and carefully redrafted revision.[29] If the original document was in essence a peace treaty,[30] this was now a charter freely agreed by the government and sanctioned from the outset by papal authority,[31] even if (as seems certain) the new pope himself knew nothing about it.[32] This, then, was

[26] J. Selden, *Janus Anglorum* (1610), preface, sig. A6v.

[27] Coke said that this reflected its importance: *La Huictieme Part des Reports* (1611), sig. §§5 ('not in respect of the quantity but of the weight'); cf. Co. Litt. 81 ('it is called the great charter in respect of the great weightiness and weighty greatness of the matter contained in it in few words ... it is *multum in parvo*'); Co. Inst. ii, proeme. As a matter of history, however, it seems that the adjective 'Magna' at first merely distinguished the charter from its little sister, the *Carta de Foresta*: Cowell, *The Interpreter*, sig. Ss4v; A. B. White, 'The Name Magna Carta' (1915) 30 EHR 472–5; Carpenter, *Magna Carta*, pp. 4–8.

[28] *Bulthorpe v. Ladbrook* (1607) CUL MS. Gg.5.6, fo. 52; translated below, p. 532. Four years later he went still further and said that the laws of William I, confirming those of Edward the Confessor, were 'a Magna Carta, the groundwork of all those that after followed': *La Huictieme Part des Report* (1611), preface, sig. §§4v. Cf. Co. Litt. 81, citing Fitz. Abr., *Mordauncester*, pl. 53, dated Pas. 5 Hen. III (1221), which refers to the 'statute of Magna Carta'; Coke thought this must have been John's charter, but the entry is more probably misdated and belongs to the last decade of Henry III's reign.

[29] The first serious discussion of this charter, and of the changes which it made, was in Blackstone, *The Great Charter*, pp. xxvii–xxxi. Only one sealed version survives, in Durham cathedral.

[30] This is a controverted point: see, e.g., Holt, *Magna Carta*, pp. 224, 228. But the charter itself said (cl. 61) that it was (tr.) 'for the better settling of the discord which has arisen between us and our barons'. Cf. F. Pollock and F. W. Maitland, *The History of English Law before the Time of Edward I* (2nd edn, Cambridge, 1898), i. 171 ('In form a donation ... in reality a treaty').

[31] N. Vincent, *Magna Carta: A Very Short Introduction* (Oxford, 2012), p. 82; Carpenter, *Magna Carta*, pp. 406–11; Holt, *Magna Carta*, pp. 316–17.

[32] Innocent III, who had damned the 1215 charter, died in July 1216 and was succeeded by Honorius III.

the first revival, without which nothing else would have followed. With further revisions made in 1217, it was the basis of the great charter issued under the seal of the seventeen-year-old King Henry III at a major assembly of prelates, barons and knights on 11 February 1225.

The 1225 charter was free from the coercion which vitiated the charter of John. It said so itself.[33] But was it a statute? The king was a minor at the time, but this did not invalidate the charter in the eyes of succeeding generations. Many things were done in the name of infant kings. If explanation were needed, the later solution was to say that the king had two bodies, and in his 'royal and politique capacity' (as Coke was to put it) he was deemed always to be of full age.[34] For this reason, Coke considered the later confirmations of the 1225 charter to have been politically understandable but legally unnecessary.[35] A more difficult question for the later observer was its form. It was not cast in the form of a parliamentary statute. In its operative words, at the beginning and end, it was phrased like a conveyance. It was a grant and gift of liberties from the king to the people, to be 'held' within his realm for ever.[36] The only known reading on the *Articuli super Cartas* (1300) taught that the *Articuli* were not statutory, because they took the form of a grant and confirmation by the king, prelates and peers, without mention of the commons.[37] Coke took a similar view of the *Carta de Foresta*.[38] The great charter of 1225, however, seemed on its face to have been more than

---

[33] This was noted by a fifteenth-century reader: HLS MS. 13, p. 7; *Rights and Liberties*, p. 82. Likewise Co. Inst. ii. 2, gl. *spontanea et bona voluntate nostra*.

[34] Co. Inst. ii, proeme; explained more fully in *Calvin's Case* (1608) 7 Co. Rep. 1 at fos. 10–12. This had been settled in *Earl of March* v. *Earl of Salisbury* (1352) 26 Edw. III, Lib. Ass., pl. 54. Cf. *Anon.* (1332) YB Mich. 6 Edw. III, fo. 50, pl. 49, *per* Shardelow J. ('Our lord the king is always under age when it suits him (*a son avauntage*), and always of full age when it suits him'); *Case of the Duchy of Lancaster* (1562) Pl. Com. 212v; Dyer 209; *Dyer's Notebooks*, i. 30; KB 27/1181, m. 156 (identifiable as *Bunye* v. *Stubley*); *Le Case pur Prender de Apprentices* (c. 1585/90) BL MS. Harley 1693, fo. 95v, *per* Fleetwood sjt (something granted 'during the king's pleasure' does not expire on the king's death, because he is a body politic); Fleetwood, *Itinerarium ad Windsor*, p. 37.

[35] *Bulthorpe* v. *Ladbrook* (1607) CUL MS. Gg.5.6, fo. 52; translated below, p. 532. See also Co. Litt. 43.

[36] The word *tenendas* does not necessarily denote feudal tenure, as in grants of real property, but might be better translated here as 'kept' or 'retained'. The 1215 charter was defective in having no operative words of grant (except in cl. 1) until cls. 60–1.

[37] *Selected Readings on Magna Carta*, p. 350. But Snede (in 1511) thought the *Articuli* were statutory: *Rights and Liberties*, p. 97. So did Coke: 10 Co. Rep. 74; Co. Inst. ii. 600.

[38] He argued that the *Carta de Foresta* was only an ordinance and not a statute: *Anon.* (1596) BL MS. Add. 25201, fo. 121v (anonymous case).

simply a unilateral gift from the king, or a pact between the king and the barons. The expressed consideration for it was a fifteenth granted to the king by the bishops, abbots, priors, barons, knights, freeholders and 'everyone of our realm', comprehensive words which seemed to imply a major assembly in which everyone in the realm was somehow represented.[39] This was, surely, a parliament of some sort.[40] Some have dismissed this as 'bad history',[41] and yet it is difficult to see why the assemblies at Merton (1236) or Marlborough (1267) were parliaments if this was not.[42] It is a matter of definition.[43] At any rate, the charter was close enough to the concept of parliamentary legislation for it to be received, as a matter of law, as the first statute in the notional 'statute-book'. Even if not a parliamentary statute *ab initio*, it was confirmed many times by undoubted parliaments, beginning with that held at Marlborough in 1267,[44] and that would have given it statutory

---

[39] Selden made a similar point in 3 St. Tr. at col. 169 (1628): 'some have published that Magna Carta is but a charter and no law. But it is an Act of Parliament; and let men speak what they will, that was the fashion of statutes till printing came in ... Also the body of Magna Carta is, that it is consented to by all the earls etc. and for the assent there was a fifteenth granted, and clearly that cannot be without an Act of Parliament.'

[40] R. Holinshed, *Chronicles of England, Irelande and Scotlande* (1577), p. 626; Lambarde, *Archeion* [c. 1591], pp. 136–7; Owen, *Common Law* (c. 1615) BL MS. Harley 6604, fo. 313v ('The great charter of England established by Act of Parliament in the 9th year of Henry the third'); Ashley's reading, fos. 2v–3; Co. Litt. 81; Co. Inst. ii, proeme, and p. 77.

[41] Dunham in *The Great Charter*, p. 36.

[42] It was widely held that Merton was not. An anonymous reader of Gray's Inn c. 1515 held that Marlborough was the first statute: *Rights and Liberties*, p. 131. Serjeant Fleetwood said in 1582 that Merton was never a statute, but was now taken to be one: below, Appendix 5, p. 478. William Hakewill said in his speech on impositions (1610) that Merton was no other than an ordinance, lacking the consent of the Commons, but 'yet hath it by continuance of time gotten not only the strength but the name of a statute': *The Libertie of the Subject against the pretended Power of Impositions* (1641), p. 61. Camden, likewise, held that the assembly at Merton was not a parliament because the commonalty were not mentioned: F. S. Fussner, ed., 'William Camden's "Discourse concerning the Prerogative of the King" [c. 1615]' (1957) 101 *Proceedings of the American Philosophical Society* 204–15, at p. 215. Cf. Co. Inst. ii. 99 (that the dissent of the bishops from c. 9 did not prevent it being an Act of Parliament).

[43] Cf. James Morice in his Middle Temple reading (1578) BL MS. Add. 36081, fo. 269, criticising the dictum of Saunders CB in 1560 (Pl. Com. 209) that the Statute of Rhuddlan was not a statute but a constitution made by the king without Parliament: 'yet can I see no cause at all why the same ... should not have the force and authority of a law, in such sort as the liberties of England contained in the Great Charter before the same were confirmed by Act of Parliament'.

[44] Statute of Marlborough, c. 5. The statute was repealed in 1881; but, by virtue of the Interpretation Act (below, p. 11 n. 60), this repeal should not itself have any effect on what the statute confirmed.

force anyway. That was the view taken by earlier Tudor lawyers.[45] The 1225 charter contained the final text, but it became a permanent statute at the latest by confirmation in 1267.[46]

Some took the later confirmation by Edward I, in 1297, to be the ultimate statutory form, though this was a matter of evidence rather than of substantive law. It was certainly an authentic text, being enrolled in Chancery, albeit the roll was not an official statute roll as later understood.[47] Yet it was only a confirmation of the earlier statute, not a new one.[48] There was no doubt that the statute of Magna Carta dated from 1225, not from the reign of Edward I. When Edward I confirmed Magna Carta again, in 1301, without setting out the text, it was his father's charter which he mentioned in the patent of confirmation, not his own.[49] This had never been a matter of contention, and it was finally settled for legal purposes in 1607, when the Court of Common Pleas held that the 1225 charter was itself an Act of Parliament. An action had been brought on chapter 29, reciting the charter of Henry III rather than its confirmation, and an objection on the ground that it was not a statute

---

[45] Cf. the 'Ordinary Gloss' of *c.* 1400/25 (below, p. 71), which says that until Henry III the charter was only a treaty or treatise ('trete') made at Runnymede, implying that it became a statute in 1225: *Rights and Liberties*, p. 71. George Willoughby, in his Inner Temple reading (1549), held that before the 1267 confirmation Magna Carta was no more than a treatise on the common law: BL MS. Harley 1691, fo. 197; cited in M. McGlynn, *The Royal Prerogative and the Learning of the Inns of Court* (Cambridge, 2003), p. 76.

[46] So said the elusive Hervy of the Inner Temple, in the last quarter of the fifteenth century: HLS MS. 88, fo. 1; BL MS. Hargrave 87, fo. 195; *Rights and Liberties*, p. 87. It became the orthodoxy in the early sixteenth century, though some readers began the story with John: see *Rights and Liberties*, pp. 97, 131, 139; reading on Marlborough, c. 5, in Gray's Inn MS. 25, fo. 92 (tr. 'before this statute Magna Carta was only a charter and no statute').

[47] It is the version often found in manuscript statute-books, indicated by the first word *Edwardus* rather than *Henricus*. One fifteenth-century reader attributed the statutory character to both confirmations: HLS MS. 13, p. 7; *Rights and Liberties*, p. 83 (cf. ibid. 78, where the reader used the Edwardian version as his text). For a valuable study of the 1297 charter see [N. Vincent], *The Magna Carta* (Sotheby's catalogue 8461, New York, 2007), especially at pp. 21–48.

[48] It contained one discrepancy, the correction of an error in c. 2 as to the amount of a relief due from a barony (£100 corrected to 100 marks). It has been said that this was 'either a deliberate falsification or a mistake': S. Reynolds, 'Magna Carta 1297 and the Uses of Literacy' (1989) 62 *Historical Research* 233–44, at p. 233. It is true that a mere confirmation could not change the text confirmed, but this could perhaps be understood as a concession by the king (*non obstante* the confirmation) that he would not take advantage of the error and claim the unintended larger sum.

[49] *Statutes of the Realm*, i. 44 (14 February 1301). Cf. the confirmation of the 1225 charter on 28 March 1300: ibid. 38.

was overruled.[50] Coke CJ said the fact that it had been confirmed – by thirty-two parliaments at least[51] – was no argument to prove that it was not an Act of Parliament prior to confirmation.

Although it is the royal confirmation of 1297 which is now treated as an Act of Parliament, and as the only official version of the few parts that remain, the instrument itself made no mention of any kind of legislative assembly. It began in the usual form of an *inspeximus* charter,[52] setting out a transcript of the 1225 text, and concluded with words of grant, confirmation and renewal, 'willing and granting for our self and our heirs that the aforesaid charter shall be firmly and inviolably observed in all its articles for ever'. The king himself was at Ghent, in Flanders, when the charter was sealed on the authority of his regency council, and witnessed by his thirteen-year-old son Prince Edward.[53] Although the regency council had summoned a parliament to discuss the reissue of the charter, there is no indication in the 1297 charter itself or in any other record that it was an Act of Parliament.[54] The king was personally against it, and in 1305 he emulated King John by obtaining a papal dispensation from his oath to observe it, with a purported annulment of his confirmation. Pope Clement V no more approved of constitutional monarchy than did Innocent III (another notable canonist), declaring that the presumed concessions by Edward were 'a loss of his honour and to the detriment of his royal supremacy'.[55] But it was too late this time to undo a document of such force, and no king would ever again presume to do so. The pope was simply ignored.

---

[50] *Bulthorpe v. Ladbrook* (1607) CUL MS. Mm.1.21, fo. 92; printed in translation below, Appendix 10, pp. 531–3. Sixteenth-century actions on c. 29 had all been framed on the charter of 9 Hen. III as 'a statute lately made in Parliament': see Appendix 1, below.

[51] Cf. below, pp. 264, 352, 396.

[52] I.e. a charter or patent exemplifying an earlier charter, setting out the original text in full, preceded by the phrase *Inspeximus ... in haec verba* ('We have inspected ... in these words'). The prime purpose of an exemplification was to serve as an authentic transcript of a royal document, certified under the great seal.

[53] Richard Snede pointed out in his reading that the king had been overseas at the time of the grant: *Rights and Liberties*, p. 96. The patent was tested at Westminster, but the king was in Flanders.

[54] The further confirmation of 28 March 1300 was granted in Parliament, but this too was not cast in the form of an Act of Parliament: *Statutes of the Realm*, i, Charters of Liberties, p. 38.

[55] By the bull *Regalis devotionis integritas*, dated 29 December 1305: Bémont, *Chartes des Libertés Anglaises*, p. 110, at p. 111 ('in tui honoris dispendium et regalis excellentie detrimentum').

Although the supposed primacy of the 1297 text resulted from its being the first version of Magna Carta to be enrolled in Chancery, which made it more reliable than the variable versions found in private statute-books, whether it was evidentially more reliable than the sealed charters was another matter. Blackstone took the view that the 1297 text was necessarily inferior to those found in the contemporary charters.[56] But the latter had probably not been available to the editors of the old *Statutes at Large*, and they may have been unfamiliar even to historical scholars such as Selden.[57] When they became available, their legal superiority was not universally acknowledged, since it was apparently considered that for legal purposes a Chancery enrolment took precedence over a sealed engrossment.

The editors of the *Statutes of the Realm* (1810) departed from the earlier tradition of the *Statutes at Large* by putting the Provisions of Merton 1236 first in the main text and relegating the various charters of liberties to a preliminary section, separately paginated. The reason given, in respect of Magna Carta, was that there was no text of the Henry III charter on the statute roll, and that previous printed editions – while placing Magna Carta first, as a statute of 1225 – had been based on the enrolled Edwardian text.[58] They therefore printed the 1297 text, in its chronological position, as the best version. This was sensible enough as an archival or evidential reason, since they were setting out the texts they had used in the order of their creation as records, though it was not a legal decision about the nature of the 1297 charter. The sub-commissioners did include in the main body of statutes – in their appropriate chronological place – the Provisions of Merton and the other statutes made between 1225 and 1278, even though they were not enrolled. But they had not been confirmed in the same way as Magna Carta, and so it was necessary to have recourse for the texts to 'inferior

---

[56] Blackstone, *The Great Charter*, p. i.
[57] Ibid., p. xlv. Selden was aware that the 1215 charter was different from the Magna Carta of 1225 but confused the texts (by relying on the Matthew Paris version) in his earlier works. He was indeed to be faulted by Sir Robert Heath, Att.-Gen., for relying on Matthew Paris, though Heath had not seen the original either: *The Five Knights' Case* (1627) 3 St. Tr. 1 at 38; CUL MS. Mm.6.63, fo. 190v. By 1631 he had seen an original from 1215, possibly one of Camden's: *Titles of Honor* (1631), p. 671 ('I have used an original of it that had been sealed by King John'). At some stage he acquired a full transcript of the text: LI MS. Hale 12, fo. 184. (Professor D. Carpenter, who drew attention to the Hale manuscript, thinks it may have been taken from a damaged version no longer extant.)
[58] *Statutes of the Realm*, i, introduction, pp. xxix, xxxiii.

sources'. Again, this was a perfectly sensible editorial decision. When, however, sixty years later the Statute Law Committee produced a semi-official chronological table of statutes, showing which statutes were still in force and which repealed, they were seemingly misled by the arrangement of the 1810 edition into listing Merton as the first Act of Parliament and omitting the 1225 charter from the table.[59] In so doing, they silently abandoned six centuries of previous legal tradition. Perhaps the committee were also influenced by current thinking about the origins of Parliament. But the assembly at Merton in 1236 was just as remote from the Parliament of 1870 as that which negotiated the granting of Magna Carta in return for a fifteenth in 1225. To treat these ancient meetings as being organically connected to the Parliament which still continues to possess legislative sovereignty in the United Kingdom is, on any view, a brazen legal fiction. But it is the fiction upon which sovereignty of Parliament now rests. The Statute of Treasons 1351, written in French, still governs the most serious of criminal offences, and is no less a statute because the parliaments of Edward III were almost unrecognisably different from those of Elizabeth II. The difficulty only arises when law is confused with history. A lawyer in 2016 has no difficulty treating the parliament of 1351 as Parliament, for current legal purposes, whereas for historical purposes such a proposition is factually meaningless.

The piecemeal repeal by Parliament of most of the content of the 1297 *inspeximus* has seemingly left three chapters in force (1, 9 and 29). Even the opening words of grant used in 1297 have been repealed, though the words of confirmation and renewal at the end have been retained as a new 'chapter' 37. The 1225 charter, on the other hand, has escaped explicit repeal. This has left the law in a muddle. Even on the assumption that the 1297 charter of confirmation was an Act of Parliament, which it seems not to have been, it remains doubtful whether the repeal of a confirming statute or instrument could have the effect of abrogating what was confirmed.[60] It may be, therefore, that all the repeals of provisions in Magna Carta from 1863 onwards have been nugatory.[61] But the puzzle is of little consequence, since the chapters which have purportedly been

---

[59] *Chronological Table and Index of the Statutes* (1870). The history of this work is traced in C. Ilbert, *Legislative Methods and Forms* (Oxford, 1901), pp. 63–5.

[60] The Interpretation Act 1978 (c. 30), s. 16, provides that 'where an Act repeals an enactment, the repeal does not, unless the contrary intention appears, ... affect the previous operation of the enactment repealed'.

[61] The first series was contained in the Statute Law Revision Act 1863, 26 & 27 Vict., c. 125, which purported to repeal cc. 5, 13, 19–21, 24, 27, 31, 33 and 36. When c. 26 (concerning

repealed – over 90 per cent of the text – had already been rendered obsolete by implied repeal, and implied repeals must by their nature extend to each and every statutory version. The charter lives on so vigorously in the imagination that no one is really interested in the question of whether or not, or to what extent, it is still legally in force.

Magna Carta as a Grant

The 1225 charter was expressed as a grant to the archbishops, bishops, abbots, priors, earls, barons 'and everyone of our realm of England', in perpetuity. At the end were the words, 'We have also granted to the same, on behalf of our self and our heirs, that neither we nor our heirs will seek to do anything whereby the liberties contained in this charter would be infringed or weakened, and if anything of the kind is attempted it shall be taken as null and void.' The language was similar to that used in granting franchises to corporations or individuals.[62] But, leaving aside the question of whether the charter had statutory force, could any grant of liberties enure, as a matter of property law, to all of the people? The strict answer under the developed common law would have to be, no. A grant could not be made to a fluctuating body unless it was first incorporated.[63] In the thirteenth century the law of corporations was in its infancy and this problem would not have been perceived. But in the two succeeding centuries it became clear that if the king granted liberties to the inhabitants of a place, they would be impliedly incorporated for the purpose of taking the grant. Magna Carta was seen in 1215 as a grant by the king to his kingdom.[64] No one, however, suggested that all the people of England were a corporation capable of suing for their liberties and being sued. A grant of liberties to all the people of England was therefore an exercise in rhetoric rather than a meaningful piece of

---

the writ *de odio et atia*) was repealed by the Offences against the Person Act 1828, 9 Geo. IV, c. 31, s. 1, both the 'Great Charter' of 1225 and the 'Statute' of 1297 were mentioned.

[62] Some readers in the inns of court therefore thought it appropriate to devote several of their lectures on Magna Carta to the topic of royal grants and the words of grant used in conveyancing: *Rights and Liberties*, pp. 97–106 (Richard Snede, Inner Temple, Lent 1511), 141–8 (anonymous, *c.* 1546/50).

[63] No mention was made of 'heirs', as was necessary for a perpetual grant to individuals. A perpetual grant to a corporate body used the word 'successors'.

[64] The Articles of the Barons (1215), c. 48, referred to the liberties granted by the king to the realm ('libertates quas rex concessit regno'): Holt, *Magna Carta*, p. 368. In the charter itself (cl. 60) the reference was altered to the liberties to be kept within the realm.

conveyancing. Moreover, many of the provisions of the charter were not liberties, or even analogous to liberties, as understood in the law of property. Some even took away previous rights. For such reasons, the learned men of the inns of court treated the charter not as a constitutional document or grant but as a statute like any other, confirming or clarifying numerous particular rules of law.

Magna Carta, even so, was not like any other statute. The attempt to bind posterity showed that. Moreover, despite the language of perpetuity, intended to ensure that 'this great parliamentary charter might live and take effect in all successions of ages for ever',[65] it was for generations seen as representing also a compact imposing a moral obligation on the king as an individual,[66] a process to be replicated under every king (sometimes repeatedly) until Edward III.[67] It has been suggested that this repeated confirmation was only necessary because the charter had failed to do its work;[68] but this is surely to underestimate its political and emotional force. It was repeatedly confirmed precisely because it lived on vigorously in the minds of the king's greater subjects, who deemed it expedient that kings also should be regularly reminded of its existence and sworn to its observance. There were a number of respects in which its character was out of the ordinary.

Magna Carta as Common Law

The *Confirmatio Cartarum* of 1297 declared that Magna Carta should be 'allowed' by the king's judges and ministers as common law ('le facent alower ... come ley commune').[69] In one sense this is not difficult to understand. It was widely held over the centuries that it was merely declaratory of the common law, or a restoration of the earlier common law,[70] and that had indeed been its original purpose. The barons'

---

[65] Co. Inst. ii. 2, gl. *Pro nobis et haeredibus nostris imperpetuum*. The word *imperpetuum* was omitted from the Durham cathedral copy printed in *Statutes of the Realm*, but it occurs in other copies and printed versions.

[66] It was thought to be included, at least by implication, in the coronation oath: below, p. 253.

[67] In 1416, Henry V in Parliament confirmed Magna Carta 'and all other statutes and ordinances ... not repealed': 4 Hen. V, c. 1. It is ambiguous whether 'repealed' here extended to repeals of Magna Carta.

[68] E. Jenks, 'The Myth of Magna Carta' (1905) 4 *Independent Review* 260–73, at p. 271 ('Why was it necessary to insist on the repeated confirmation of the charter? Obviously, because it failed to do its work.'). But it may be that Jenks's thought-provoking *jeu d'esprit* was deliberately exaggerated: see further below, p. **.

[69] *Statutes of the Realm*, i. 123.   [70] Below, pp. 15–16, 90 n. 101, 532.

demand, at a critical meeting in the Temple, had been to confirm Henry I's coronation charter of 1100,[71] which in turn confirmed the old law of Edward the Confessor's time, and those laws were doubtless seen (however incorrectly) as having been formulations of the common law of the land.[72] But 'allowed as common law' does present difficulties to the legal mind, since statute has come to be regarded as a superior form of law to unwritten law, and Magna Carta has sometimes been revered as superior to any other statute. Common law certainly denoted unwritten law by 1297, and was already sometimes contrasted with statute law.[73] But it cannot bear that sense in the *Confirmatio* of 1297. Coke noticed this difficulty, and explained the words as meaning that Magna Carta was to be 'law common to all'.[74] His explanation may betray bewilderment and yet be nearer the mark than any other.

The meaning was investigated in 1915 by McIlwain, who concluded that Coke was right but for a reason other than the one he had in mind.[75] According to McIlwain, the common law was 'in a very real sense, a fundamental law'.[76] Even Acts of Parliament were not conceived of as altering this common law, but rather as affirming it by removing abuses and clarifying its operation. They might, in so doing, have brought about substantive changes in the law, but change was not their prime purpose. Abrogating the common law itself was unthinkable, whereas statutes might well be repealed solely on the grounds that they conflicted with the law of the land. In affirming the common law, statutes partook of its nature, namely its permanence, its generality of application, and its supremacy. The original Magna Carta, McIlwain argued, was granted primarily to the king's tenants in chief and their men, and was a predominantly feudal document; but it was perceived by the end of the thirteenth century as a

---

[71] *Wendover's Chronicle* (RS), ii. 83, whence M. Paris, *Chronica Majora* (RS), ii. 584; Holt, *Magna Carta*, pp. 199–200; Carpenter, *Magna Carta*, pp. 310–13.

[72] This was what Samuel Johnson meant when he said that Magna Carta was born with a grey beard: [S. Johnson], *A History and Defence of Magna Carta* (1769), pp. 4–5. For the cult of Edward the Confessor and his laws see J. Greenberg, *The Radical Face of the Ancient Constitution: St Edward's 'Laws' in Early Modern Political Thought* (Cambridge, 2001).

[73] See, e.g., *Anon.* (1292) YB 20 & 21 Edw. I (RS), pp. 355–7, *per* Lisle sjt: (tr.) 'The usage which he alleges was common law before the Statute of Merton . . . which common law is undone by Merton . . . and by Westminster II.'

[74] Co. Inst. ii. 526.

[75] C. H. McIlwain, 'Magna Carta and Common Law' in *Magna Carta Commemoration Essays*, ed. H. E. Malden (1917), pp. 122–79.

[76] Ibid. 131.

grant of liberties to all free persons in general, and as law which was common to all. It was therefore 'an enactment in affirmance of fundamental common law, to be confirmed and observed as a part of that law'.[77]

McIlwain's general thesis about the relationship between common law and statute, which he had been developing since before 1910,[78] provoked strong criticism from Plucknett,[79] who argued that there was no good evidence for regarding the medieval common law as 'fundamental'. The fourteenth-century year books frequently referred to statutes as 'special ley' or 'novel ley', and made it plain that legislation could defeat or undo the common law. This difference of opinion is more apparent than real, since it turns largely on what is meant by fundamental. If McIlwain meant that statute could not override common law, this could be true only of the most fundamental principles of the common law, and correct only as a political rather than a legal proposition. Legislation was certainly criticised in Parliament on the grounds that it was inconsistent with the law of the land, but it was no argument in the world outside. And the distinction between unalterable common law – such as the basic principles of feudal tenure – and particular rules of common law which were found unsatisfactory and in need of reform, was a distinction which could only be drawn in Parliament or in the law school.[80] Part of the historical problem is that what McIlwain seems to have meant by 'fundamental' is not the only sense of the word. It might be better to say that the common law was foundational, and that much medieval legislation was calculated to make it clearer or more effective, reinforcing its basic principles rather than supplanting them. That was presumably what Coke meant when he wrote that Magna Carta was 'for the most part declaratory of the principal grounds of the fundamental laws of England, and for the residue it is additional to supply some defects of the common law'.[81] Indeed, he once claimed that all but one or two of its provisions were law in Edward the Confessor's time. He said he had seen this in an

---

[77] Ibid. 178.
[78] C. H. McIlwain, *The High Court of Parliament and its Supremacy* (New Haven, 1910), pp. 46–51, 249–300.
[79] Plucknett, *Statutes and their Interpretation in the First Half of the Fourteenth Century*, pp. 26–31. For Plucknett's more nuanced view of thirteenth-century legislation see his *Legislation of Edward I*, pp. 6–14. See also W. S. Holdsworth, *History of English Law*, vol. ii (4th edn, 1936), pp. 441–2; J. W. Tubbs, *The Common Law Mind: Medieval and Early Modern Perceptions* (Baltimore, 2000), pp. 29–35.
[80] See the Gray's Inn moot cited below, pp. 90–1.
[81] Co. Inst. ii, proeme. Cf. Co. Litt. 81.

old book of great authority, though Walmsley J., sitting beside him, reacted with characteristic (and justified) scepticism.[82]

A further complication is that the 'law of the land', protected by chapter 29 of Magna Carta,[83] was not immutable. It was not discussed in earlier times whether this *lex terrae* was the same as *jus regni*,[84] or whether it had any specific meaning at all.[85] It was certainly never asserted that it was set in stone, so that conflicts between judicial opinions had to be resolved in favour of the earliest, or that *Glanvill* (being pre-1215) must be preferred to *Bracton* or Littleton. On the contrary, common lawyers always followed the developing currents of professional understanding and recognised that these could change.[86] No particular rules of law were entrenched in 1225. The 'law of the land' could only mean the law in operation for the time being. Chapter 29 was therefore an expression of what is now called the rule of law. Governments were not to act arbitrarily, disregarding or changing the law as they pleased, but had to operate within the law as it stood. The same principle was extended by William Fleetwood in the 1550s to the whole of Magna Carta. In so far as it was a confirmation of the common law, it partook of the organic nature of the common law and could evolve over time.[87] And it was, or soon became, orthodox legal learning that the whole charter was 'declarative of the ancient common law of England'.[88] This point was of more than antiquarian interest. If it were once allowed

---

[82] *Bulthorpe* v. *Ladbrook* (1607) CUL MS. Mm.1.21, fo. 92; printed in translation below, p. 532. Roger Owen argued (*c.* 1615) that the contents of Magna Carta must have been the same as the laws of Edward the Confessor, with a few 'new articles' added: BL MS. Harley 6605, fos. 56v–60.

[83] For c. 29 see below, p. 32.

[84] Cf. M. Radin, 'Glanvill on the Common Law: *Lex Terrae* and *Ius Regni*' (1933) 82 *University of Pennsylvania Law Review* 26–36.

[85] Selden once thought that *lex terrae* meant wager of law, a meaning which is found in *Glanvill*: Thompson, *Magna Carta*, p. 242. But in Magna Carta 1215, cl. 55, which Selden may not then have seen, *lex terrae* clearly did not mean wager of law. He later changed his mind: see below, p. 38 n. 215.

[86] Tubbs, *The Common Law Mind*, pp. 30–2.

[87] Fleetwood, *Magna Carta*, fos. 7v–8; below, pp. 244–5. Note also Frowyk's argument (1495) that, since Magna Carta was common law, it was possible for it to be clarified by *Prerogativa Regis*, even though that was not a statute: McGlynn, *The Royal Prerogative and the Learning of the Inns of Court*, p. 88. As to the possibility of prescribing against Magna Carta, on the footing that it was common law, see below, pp. 25–6.

[88] *Hall* v. *Stanley: Case of the Marshalsea* (1612) 10 Co. Rep. 68 at fo. 74v (tr.). Further down the page, Coke CJ explained that the *Articuli super Cartas* were (tr.) 'the explanations of the charter, i.e. of the common law'. See also Co. Litt. 81 ('a confirmation or restitution of the common law'); Co. Inst. ii. 8. Cf. *Case of Purveyance of Timber* (1604) BL MS.

that the liberties of the subject derived from a royal grant, they might be taken away again. It was therefore important that they should be anterior to Magna Carta, as old as the fields and villages of England, even if out of those old fields might spring and grow new corn.[89]

Magna Carta as Fundamental Law

The question remains whether McIlwain's thesis might be uniquely true of Magna Carta, which is the context in which he first advanced it.[90] Whether or not the common law was fundamental, perhaps Magna Carta was fundamental, in the sense that it enshrined principles which could not be subverted. And yet, despite occasional later assertions that the liberties granted by Magna Carta could not legally be taken away,[91] even this proposition could not easily be squared with legal thinking. It is difficult to propound a constitutional theory whereby a sovereign ruler could bind himself and future sovereigns never to change the law. This was doubtless the difficulty which prompted the series of general excommunications pronounced by the Church against all those who should go about to break the provisions of the charter. If legal entrenchment was impossible, perhaps spiritual forces might be effective.[92] The idea may well have been Stephen Langton's. He had issued the first such sentence at the time of the 1225 charter, following the precedent of the general excommunications laid down in 1222 (in the provincial council

---

Add. 35955, fo. 29 (Star Chamber), *per* Lord Ellesmere LC, Popham and Fleming CJJ (tr. 'the statute of Magna Carta is but an affirmation of the common law'). Thomas Hedley MP said in the Commons in 1610, 'I do not take Magna Carta to be a new grant or statute, but a restoring or confirming of the ancient laws and liberties of the kingdom, which by the Conquest before had been much impeded or obscured': *Proc. Parl. 1610*, ii. 190. Heneage Finch MP said it was 'nothing else but the common law put into a charter': ibid. 227. There were antecedents of such views in the fifteenth century: below, p. 89.

[89] Coke's metaphor, borrowed from Chaucer, was used in the preface to 1 Co. Rep.

[90] J. W. Gough, *Fundamental Law in English Constitutional History* (Oxford, 1955), pp. 15–17, rejected McIlwain's thesis, apparently on the ground that it was inconsistent with the repeated confirmations of Magna Carta. The discussion there is not easy to follow.

[91] E.g. in 1423 Parliament referred to the liberties of the people which had not been repealed *nor were by the common law repealable* ('ne par la commune leie repellables'): Rot. Parl. iv. 169B; 2 Hen. VI, c. 1.

[92] See M. McGlynn, 'From Charter to Common Law: The Rights and Liberties of the Pre-Reformation Church' in *Magna Carta, Religion and the Rule of Law*, ed. R. Griffith-Jones and M. Hill (Cambridge, 2015), at pp. 54–6.

at Oxford) to reinforce the decisions of the Lateran Council of 1215.[93] Another followed in 1237.[94] The better known *Sentencia Lata in Transgressores Cartarum* of 1253 was solemnly pronounced in Westminster Hall, with burning candles, by Archbishop Boniface and a dozen other bishops, the king being personally present, and was confirmed by Pope Innocent IV in 1254.[95] It anathematised not only occasional transgressors but also those who passed statutes or introduced new customs which infringed the charter, or who observed or presumed to adjudicate in accordance with such innovations.[96] It even cursed, for good measure, those who presumed to disturb the peace of the king and the realm. This was the boldest attempt ever made in England to entrench legislation, by calling down terrifying spiritual sanctions. But could such ecclesiastical fire and thunder keep Magna Carta inviolate?

The strident fulminations were by no means ignored. They were copied into statute-books,[97] repeated at the time of the 1297 confirmation[98] and proclaimed from time to time by bishops.[99] How far they made any real difference, however, is questionable. Sentences of general excommunication were not an ideal legal mechanism, because pronouncing judgment before trial was the very opposite of the due process of law and made no practical sense. There had to be some judicial procedure for determining who had fallen within them, and for lifting the excommunication when it had achieved its purpose. Langton's Oxford provisions of 1222 were enforced through an inquisitorial procedure to determine who should be punished under them, most notably in relation to defamation, and to give the accused an opportunity to be heard.[100] But as yet no historian has uncovered any such proceedings to punish specific

---

[93] *Councils & Synods and other Documents relating to the English Church*, ed. F. M. Powicke and C. R. Cheney, vol. ii (Oxford, 1964), 100–25, 138 n. 1. An earlier precedent was the canon *Si quis suadente* of the Lateran Council 1139, which excommunicated all those who laid violent hands on a clergyman or monk.

[94] *Councils & Synods*, ed. Powicke and Cheney, ii. 205–7.

[95] There is a copy of the bull in the Lincoln statute-book, CUL MS. Dd.10.28, fo. 72v.

[96] *Councils & Synods*, ed. Powicke and Cheney, ii. 477–9; *Statutes of the Realm*, i. 6; Blackstone, *The Great Charter*, pp. liv, 70–2.

[97] There are fifteen texts in CUL manuscripts of the *Statuta Vetera*: CELMC, p. 680.

[98] *Councils & Synods*, ed. Powicke and Cheney, ii. 1177 n. 2, 1193–4; *Statutes of the Realm*, i. 126. This is also found in some medieval statute-books: e.g. CUL MSS Dd.10.28, fo. 11; Ee.1.5, fo. 12v; Ee.6.33, fo. 11; Gg.5.7, fo. 16v.

[99] Thompson, *Magna Carta*, pp. 125–8.

[100] R. H. Helmholz, *Select Cases on Defamation to 1600* (101 SS, 1985), pp. xiv–xvi R. H. Helmholz, *The Oxford History of the Laws of England*, vol. i; *The Canon Law and Ecclesiastical Jurisdiction from 597 to the 1640s* (Oxford, 2004), pp. 574–5.

infringements of Magna Carta. This is not surprising, because if such a procedure had developed it would have led before long to a serious jurisdictional impasse.[101] The exposition of statutes restoring or defining rights under the common law could hardly be left in the care of bishops and canon lawyers.[102] Nor could the bishops assume a jurisdiction over common-law crimes under the 'king's peace' clause, since Magna Carta itself had strictly limited that sphere of jurisdiction, and the judges guarded it jealously with writs of prohibition. Even less could the Church be allowed to exercise a veto over the legislative activities of the king in Parliament. It can hardly be supposed that the ecclesiastical establishment would have wanted such a responsibility anyway. The only real interest of the Church was in the enforcement of chapter 1, the preservation of its own liberties, and it would have been an extraordinary and dangerous measure to invoke judicial measures against the king himself. At best, the sentence of anathema may have helped to promote a general public awareness of Magna Carta as an important document. It is said to have been read out in churches four times a year,[103] which meant that copies were supposedly available at parochial level, and parish clergy were encouraged to teach their flocks that infringements incurred automatic excommunication.[104] As late as the reign of Henry VIII, churchgoers were told of the great curse visited upon 'all those who break any point of the king's great charter, or the charter of the forest, in which charters be written the freedoms of the land that divers kings

---

[101] Cf. the impasse over the punishment of defamation, under the Provisions of Oxford, in cases where the defamatory words charged a common-law crime: see *OHLE*, i. 593–6; vi. 242, 782–3.

[102] This very difficulty occurred to Henry III and his magnates in 1253, when they dissented from that part of the *Sentencia* which appeared to give unfettered jurisdiction (*arbitrium*) to the bishops, and replaced it with 'the judgment of the king's court': *Councils & Synods*, ed. Powicke and Cheney, ii. 479; D. Carpenter, 'More Light on Henry III's Confirmation of Magna Carta in 1253' (2013) 86 *Historical Research* 191–5; Carpenter, *Magna Carta*, p. 447.

[103] It had been so ordered by the *Articuli super Cartas* (1300), c. 1, a measure which Ferdinando Pulton praised in 1578, without indicating whether it was still observed: *An Abstract of all the Penall Statutes* (1578), preface, sig. Aij^v; reprinted in *A Kalender, or Table, comprehending the Effect of all the Statutes* (2nd edn, 1608), preface, sig. Aiiij.

[104] For this reason, Magna Carta was included in William de Pagula's fourteenth-century pastoral manuals *Oculus Sacerdotis* and *Pupilla Oculum*. For discussion of this see F. C. Hill, 'Magna Carta, Canon Law and Pastoral Care: Excommunication and the Church's Publication of the Charter' (2016) 89 *Historical Research* (forthcoming). It does not seem, however, that Magna Carta was known to clergy in detail in the later fourteenth century: see Wycliffe's remark, below, p. 66.

have granted to every man, both to the learned and to the lewd'.[105] But such vague threats to sequester those in authority from Holy Church, whatever impression they made on the lewd, were not in practice a viable method of legal entrenchment.

Another solution to the problem of entrenchment might have been to treat the grant of liberties as a personal guarantee by each king in succession. An Act of Parliament has always required the royal assent, and so a solemn promise by a king to keep the provisions of Magna Carta inviolate might on the face of it prevent him from assenting to any new statute which threatened to contravene them. But it was difficult to suppose that the solemn concessions in the charter, reinforced by the coronation oath to govern according to law, could realistically be taken to impose on a king the duty to refrain from making laws contrary to the charter, or to stop such laws from being made. Legal consequences from the oath were sometimes hinted at,[106] and a controversial civilian lawyer in the time of James I went so far as to argue that but for his oath the king could make any law he liked,[107] though the notion was never pressed very far. A constitutional monarch could hardly encroach on the judicial sphere by taking it upon himself to decide what Magna Carta meant. Edward I's confirmation of Magna Carta in 1301 promised that if any statutes had been made contrary to the 1225 charter they would be amended or even annulled, but was careful to add that this would be

---

[105] 'Articuli Generales Majoris Excommunicationis', printed in *Ceremonies and Processions of the Cathedral Church of Salisbury*, ed. C. Holdsworth (Cambridge, 1901), pp. 252–3. 'Lewd' here means uneducated.

[106] It was declared in 1322 that the pardon granted in Parliament to the pursuers of the Despensers was contrary to the king's coronation oath: *Statutes of the Realm*, i. 186. The accusation that King Richard II had broken his coronation oath referred in part to legislative wrongs: see below, Chapter 2, at p. 63. Henry IV on his accession declared his intention of keeping the old laws and statutes 'according to his oath': Rot. Parl. iii. 434, no. 108. Sir Thomas More at his trial in 1535 suggested that the statute of Henry VIII declaring the king's supremacy was contrary to his coronation oath: J. D. M. Derrett, 'The Trial of Sir Thomas More' (1964) 79 EHR 449–77, at p. 472. Nicholas Fuller referred to it in *Darcy* v. *Allen* (1602) Noy 174. Edward Hake said that Magna Carta was confirmed by every king in his coronation oath: *Epieikeia* (1603), p. 73. See also *Anon.* (c. 1607) BL MS. Harley 4814, fo. 172; below, p. 381, per Walmsley J. Coke said that Magna Carta was declaratory of the ancient common laws of England, 'to the observation and keeping whereof the king was bound and sworn': Co. Inst. ii, proeme.

[107] Cowell, *The Interpreter*, sig. Qq1: 'though for the better and equal course in making laws he do admit the three estates, that is the Lords spiritual, Lord temporal, and the Commons unto counsel, yet this (in divers men's opinions) is not of constraint but of his own benignity, or by reason of his promise made upon oath at the time of his coronation'.

done 'in due manner by the common council of our realm'.[108] In any case, there never was any specific mention of Magna Carta in the coronation oath.[109] The law mentioned in the oath must have meant the law for the time being, rather than the law at the time when the oath was taken, for the oath could hardly bind the monarch to stop all change. The contrary position, if taken to its logical conclusion, would have prevented the king from assenting to any change in any law whatsoever. That caused enough trouble for the Medes and Persians.[110]

There was a provision in the charter itself, repeated in the *Confirmatio Cartarum* of 1297, that anything done contrary to the charter should be void. In a parliamentary world, that could only be read as applying to governmental acts by the king and his ministers, not to legislative acts by the king in Parliament. But in 1368 Parliament went further and declared that all statutes contrary to Magna Carta were void.[111] Did this not entrench the charter as a form of higher law? That may have been the intention, but it was never held by any court to have done so.[112] It presumably applied only to changes detrimental to the liberties granted by the charter, for improvements in the wording, or the addition of new remedies, could not be said to contradict it.[113] Even the retrospective effect of the provision was uncertain. On the one hand, Coke held that the 1368 Act had the effect of repealing some pre-1368 legislation which was inconsistent with the charter,[114] so that, for example, the statute had revived the writ *de odio et atia*, which had been confirmed by chapter 26 of Magna Carta but abolished in 1354 (if not earlier).[115] This example

---

[108] *Statutes of the Realm*, i. 44.

[109] The fourteenth-century oath did, however, refer to the laws of Edward the Confessor: below, p. 253 n. 23.

[110] *Daniel*, vi. 12–13.

[111] 42 Edw. III, c. 1. This was in response to a Commons' petition: Rot. Parl. ii. 295, no. 10. For other assertions that Magna Carta might defeat other legislation see McIlwain, 'Magna Carta and Common Law', at pp. 173–6.

[112] It was sometimes cited in later times as reinforcing Magna Carta, without explaining its exact effect: e.g. Fleetwood's treatise, below, p. 244; Hake, *Epieikeia*, p. 72; *Bagg's Case* (1615) below, p. 396, *per* Coke CJ.

[113] *Bracton*, ii. 21 ('Non destruitur quod in melius commutatur'). Elsewhere the author distinguished between alterations *contra jus* and those merely *praeter jus*: *Bracton*, ii. 289.

[114] See Co. Inst. ii, proeme. Cf. Co. Inst. iv. 52 ('it is to be remembered, that by the statute of 42 Edw. III, c. 1, all statutes are repealed that are against Magna Carta').

[115] Co. Inst. ii, proeme, and pp. 43 ('and so in like cases upon all the branches of Magna Carta'), 55; argument at the parliamentary conference on the liberty of the subject (1628) 3 St. Tr. at col. 129. Coke attributed the repeal to 28 Edw. III, c. 9. Cf. the next note.

was questionable, however, since it had been common learning in the inns of court that the writ was gone.[116] On the other hand, Coke did not attempt to reconcile his thesis with the fact that many other pre-1368 statutes had unquestionably modified the law as stated in Magna Carta. For instance, the 1368 statute had not taken away the power of justices of nisi prius to give judgment in darrein presentment and *quare impedit*, a power given them by statute in 1285, contrary to chapter 13 of Magna Carta.[117] Moreover, Coke positively praised the statute *Quia Emptores* as containing 'many excellent things' in alteration of Magna Carta.[118] Those were, however, improvements rather than flat contradictions. When it suited him, as when speaking in the House of Commons in the 1620s, Coke would make very broad claims for the statute of 1368; but it has been persuasively argued that these claims were rhetorical rather than legal. He was not maintaining that Parliament was legally unable to repeal provisions in Magna Carta, only that it could not be done without great danger.[119] It was axiomatic that Parliament could not be bound by earlier statutes, since such a restraint would not only limit the sovereign power of the king but also the liberty of the subject, who was represented in Parliament.[120] In the dispute over prohibitions to the High Commission in the time of James I, the attorney-general (Sir Henry Hobart) argued that any reliance on chapter 29 was 'out of season', because it had been modified by subsequent statutes, 'and the statutes are infinite that have given imprisonment in sundry cases since that statute of Magna Carta'.[121] Coke himself tacitly accepted this, and made no mention of chapter 29 in his defence of the prohibitions.[122]

---

[116] *Selected Readings on Magna Carta*, p. 232 ('Therefore this statute of Magna Carta is void', attributing the repeal to the *Articuli super Cartas* in 1300). This was also Fleetwood's view in the mid-sixteenth century: ibid. 382 (attributing the repeal to Gloucester, c. 9, in 1278). Cf. the fifteenth-century reading on Westminster I, c. 11, in CUL MS. Ee.5.22, fo. 128v. If the writ survived at all, it was long obsolete when it was finally abolished by the Offences against the Person Act 1828, 9 Geo. IV, c. 31, s. 1.

[117] Co. Inst. ii. 17.   [118] Co. Inst. ii. 66.

[119] M. Lobban, *A History of the Philosophy of Law in the Common Law World, 1600–1900* (Dordrecht, 2007), p. 46.

[120] Co. Inst. iv. 42–3. Coke here cited a maxim that later laws abrogate earlier ones to the contrary (*leges posteriores leges priores contrarias abrogant*), a 'ground' which he had quoted as attorney-general in *Grene* v. *Buskyn* (1596) BL MS. Harley 1697, fo. 101 (tr.); sub nom. *Gregory* v. *Blashfield* (1596) BL MS. Hargrave 356, fo. 115v.

[121] BL Cotton MS. Cleopatra F. I, fo. 131; BL MS. Add. 58218, fo. 4v.

[122] BL MS. Add. 58218, fo. 10–25v (Coke's own draft); copy in BL Cotton MS. Cleopatra F. I, fos. 135–48. See further below, p. 370.

If there had ever been a notion that statutes interfering with due process could be reviewed judicially by reference to some fundamental law enshrined in Magna Carta, it received its final death sentence under the Cromwellian regime.[123] Colonel Euseby Andrewes, in peace-time a barrister of Lincoln's Inn, was arraigned for his life before the so-called High Court of Justice, a tribunal established by the Rump Parliament in 1650, without being indicted by a grand jury and without any right to trial by petty jury. Relying on the statute of 1368, he submitted on his application for *habeas corpus* that the statute erecting the court was invalid because it was contrary to Magna Carta, and that he was entitled to be tried by his peers before a regular court of law. He was beheaded.[124] Three years later Colonel Streater, who in later life became a law pub-lisher, sought release from imprisonment by order of Parliament on the ground that it was contrary to Magna Carta. His counsel, Edward Freeman of Gray's Inn, is said to have argued that all 'laws' against the law of the land were void. Either he or the reporter evidently saw no inherent contradiction in this proposition, but probably the reporter garbled what was said. It was certainly part of his submission that a mere order of Parliament, as opposed to an Act of Parliament, was not the law of the land. The court responded that 'an inferior court cannot control what the Parliament does. If Parliament should do one thing and we the contrary here, things would run around. We must submit to the legisla-tive power.' The following year Streater was released, because the parlia-ment had been dissolved and so the order had lapsed.[125] Ten years later the Acts of the Rump Parliament would all be treated as void, for want of the royal assent. But the principle of parliamentary supremacy has not been seriously questioned since. It is connected with parliamentary privilege, the separation of powers, and the doctrine of estoppel by record. The record of a court can only be questioned in a superior court, and there is no court superior to Parliament. The doings of the High Court of Parliament, whether of a judicial or legislative character, cannot therefore be questioned in any other court.[126] But the ordinary courts retain the power of interpretation. And there is good authority for saying

---

[123] Oliver Cromwell's own view of 'Magna F–a' is too coarse to be repeated.

[124] *Euseby Andrewes's Case* (1650) 5 St. Tr. 1. These proceedings were regarded after 1660 as those of an illegal regime; but the principle remained in place with respect to legitimate Acts of Parliament.

[125] *Streater's Case* (1653) ibid. 365 at col. 372, 386.

[126] Parliament could itself dispense with this inveterate rule by making particular parlia-mentary proceedings justiciable, and it has come close to doing so (inadvertently) on

that, even at the present day, a general statute will not be understood as having impliedly repealed a provision of Magna Carta.[127]

Magna Carta as the Paramount Statute

Any legal priority accorded to Magna Carta was therefore perhaps only a canon of interpretation. According to Coke, 'A general law shall not take away any part of Magna Carta'.[128] It would need explicit language. This was sometimes offered as an explanation for the proposition that cities and towns could prescribe against generally worded statutes, such as the Statute of Mortmain 1279, because their prescriptive liberties had been confirmed by Magna Carta.[129] Another explanation of the mortmain custom, in London, was that the city charter was itself confirmed by Parliament subsequently to the statute.[130] This analysis, however,

---

recent occasions. An early exception (the absence of peers without permission) was noted by Coke: below, Appendix 8, at pp. 503–4.

[127] *Thoburn v. Sunderland City Council* [2003] QB 151 at pp. 186–7, *per* Laws LJ; *R. (Buckinghamshire County Council) v. Secretary of State for Transport* [2014] 1 WLR 324.

[128] *R. v. Allen and Tooley* (1614) 2 Bulst. 186 at p. 191, *per* Coke CJ. Cf. Calth. MS. i. 267: (tr.) 'the general words of a statute shall never repeal any part of the statute of Magna Carta'. Fuller, *Argument*, p. 29, made a related point: 'if the statute of [42] Edw. III did so highly regard [Magna Carta] as to make void acts of Parliament contrary to the same, it would a fortiori make void all construction of statutes contrary to Magna Carta which have no express words'.

[129] For the proposition see *Case of the Abbot of Winchcombe* (1493) YB Trin. 8 Hen. VII, fo. 1, pl. 1 (called the *Abbot of Tewkesbury's Case:* but see *Reports of Cases by John Caryll*, ed. J. H. Baker, vol. i (115 SS, 1999) p. 151, at fo. 4, *per* Bryan CJ; *Snellinge v. Norton* (1595) BL MS. Add. 25200, fo. 62, *per* Danyell; *R. v. Bagshaw* (1634) Cro. Car. 347. Cf. *Case of the Prior of St Mary Overy* (1371) YB Trin. 45 Edw. III, fo. 26, pl. 39 (apparently assumed); *Dale v. Broune* (1496), *The Notebook of Sir John Port*, ed. J. H. Baker (102 SS, 1986), p. 19, *per* Fairfax J. (common knowledge). Some sources attribute the survival of mortmain customs to royal charters, perhaps treating them (like individual licences to alienate in mortmain) as dispensations from the statute of 1279: e.g. *Case of St John's Hospital* (1354) 28 Edw. III, Lib. Ass., pl. 24 (grant of 1 Edw. III); *Re Sir Otes Grandison* (1364) 38 Edw. III, Lib. Ass., pl. 18 (charter of 11 Edw. II).

[130] *Anon.* (1428) YB Mich. 7 Hen. VI, Statham, pl. [3] (tr. 'if someone wishes to say that there is a custom in London that they may devise in mortmain without licence, he must show confirmation of their customs since the statute *De Religiosis* ... and yet it is said that a general statute does not defeat a custom except by express words'); *Case of the Abbot of Winchcombe* (1493), previous note, at fo. 4 (tr. 'this is by the statute of Magna Carta, c. 9, which has been confirmed'); *Waggoner v. Fish* (1609) 2 Br. & G. 285; BL MS. Add. 25211, fo. 191v, *per* Daniel and Foster JJ (London charter granting power to make bye-laws confirmed by statute of 7 Ric. II); *R. v. Allen and Tooley* (1614) 2 Bulst. 186 at pp. 187, *per* Coke CJ ('their customs were confirmed after the said statute made to the

depended on the dubious assumption that a generally worded confirmation of customs could somehow revive those which had already been abolished, and it would also have caused a difficulty with respect to statutes passed since the latest confirmation, a difficulty which was sometimes ignored.[131] The point was debated inconclusively in the Common Pleas in the 1580s, when Serjeant Fleetwood argued that the confirmation of London customs in chapter 9 of Magna Carta rendered them proof against a statute of 1401, citing the example of mortmain. Against this, it was argued by Serjeant Peryam that the custom as to mortmain depended for its validity on the confirmation of Magna Carta in 1340, which was after the Statute of Mortmain 1279, whereas there was no confirmation after 1401.[132] The case was adjourned for further consideration of a different point, whence it seems that Fleetwood lost the argument.[133]

On either view, the arguments about confirmation of customs did not rest on any fundamental quality of Magna Carta. If they had, it would have been impossible ever to change any municipal customs, since (being notionally immemorial)[134] they were all by definition in being in 1225 and therefore confirmed by chapter 9.[135] But that was never asserted to be the law. It was simply a matter of statutory interpretation. Likewise, it was possible in some cases to prescribe against Magna Carta, for instance by asserting a custom to hold local courts at times and places other than those specified in chapter 35.[136] The best explanation for this

---

contrary, and this confirmation had relation to their former usage by custom', citing the case in Statham), and 189; differently reported in Calth. MS. i. 266v.

[131] E.g. *Chibborne's Case* (1564) Dyer 229 (where the judges, without giving reasons, held that cities were exempt from the Statute of Enrolments 1536); *City of London* v. *Bernardiston* (1661) 1 Lev. 14 at p. 15 ('The customs of London are of such force that they shall stand against negative acts of Parliament').

[132] Peryam must have overlooked the confirmation of 1416: 4 Hen. V, c. 1.

[133] *Le Case pur Prender de Apprentices* (c. 1585/90) BL MS. Harley 1693, fo. 95v. The statute was 7 Hen. IV, c. 17, concerning the qualifications for apprentices, which had been repealed by 8 Hen. VI, c. 11, and partially revived by 5 Eliz. I, c. 4.

[134] To be valid, a local custom must have been in existence, at least in contemplation of law, since 1189.

[135] 'The city of London shall have all its ancient liberties and free customs. We further will and grant that all other cities and boroughs, and towns, and the barons of the Cinque Ports, and all ports, shall have all their liberties and free customs.' The word 'ancient' may have implied immemorial antiquity, but it was only used in relation to London. The meaning of 'free' here is obscure: cf. the liberties and 'free customs' of free men in c. 29.

[136] Thomas Harlakenden's reading (Gray's Inn, 1525) in *Selected Readings on Magna Carta*, at pp. 283–4; *Att.-Gen.* v. *Partriche* (1589) BL MS. Harley 1633, fo. 36; Lansdowne 1087,

was that where a statute merely confirmed the common law it did not abolish contrary customs, since immemorial customs were allowed by the law of the land as exceptions to the general law.[137] Again it was a matter of interpretation, applying the principle that *Generalia specialibus non derogant*. On the other hand, it was not possible to set up a custom to imprison without due process, since that would contravene chapter 29,[138] which was declaratory of a fundamental principle of the common law.[139] That reasoning did not rest on the special character of Magna Carta either, for such a custom would fail to meet the common-law requirement of reasonableness, regardless of the charter. In 1614 it seems even to have been argued, by the prerogative-minded Serjeant Montagu, that the king could in some cases dispense with provisions of Magna Carta by letters patent, instancing the grant of trading privileges to English merchants which seemed to infringe the liberty of foreign merchants under chapter 30.[140] Once again, however, this would be better seen as a matter of statutory interpretation rather than of constitutional law.

In 1600 the matter was debated again in the Common Pleas, in a notable case which is known principally from manuscripts.[141] In an action for damages for a false imprisonment in Sandwich, the defendant pleaded a custom of the Cinque Ports that if a citizen of London was

---

fo. 72 (accepting Coke's argument, in a *quo warranto*). This may have been because of the saving of liberties in the *ita scilicet* clause of c. 35. In *Partriche v. Platte* (1589) BL MS. Lansdowne 1087, fo. 72, it was argued by Popham Att.-Gen. that a man could not prescribe to hold a leet at a time and place contrary to c. 35; but the court accepted Coke's argument that he could, provided he pleaded the custom, (tr.) 'for we cannot presume it, contrary to the statute of Magna Carta'.

[137] Coke CJ stated this explicitly in relation to the *Carta de Foresta* in *Webb's Case* (1616) 3 Bulst. 213.

[138] For the wording of c. 29 see below, p. 32.

[139] *Mayor of Lincoln's Case* (1401) YB Pas. 2 Hen. IV, fo. 19, pl. 16, as explained in Jenk. Cent. 79; *Paramour v. Verrall and others*, n. 141 below. See also the Elizabethan cases discussed below.

[140] *Proc. Parl. 1614*, p. 111, citing a charter granted to Exeter merchants. The report is so garbled that it is impossible to make complete sense of it. For the dispensing power see below, pp. 187–90.

[141] *Paramour v. Verrall and others* (1597–1600) BL MS. Harley 4814, fos. 78–87v; MS. Lansdowne 1065, fos. 58–63; CUL MS. Add. 8080, fos. 96v–97v; 2 And. 151; extracts translated below, Appendix 5, pp. 489–94; less fully reported in BL MS. Harley 1575, fo. 29; BL MS. Harley 1693, fos. 194v–196; BL MS. Hargrave 51, fos. 128–129v; CUL MS. Add. 8080, 96v–97; Moo. 603; cited anonymously by Coke CJ in *Davenant v. Hurdys* (1600) below, p. 317; in *Sir William Wade's Case* (1611) YLS MS. G.R29.16, fo. 468 (where a similar custom was alleged by the lieutenant of the Tower); and in *Case of the Cinque Ports* (1612) 2 Br. & G. 191 (below, p. 494 n. 102).

indebted to one of the barons (freemen) of the Cinque Ports, a letter was sent to the mayor of London to cause the party to put in a sufficient plea or else send his body; if he failed after two further letters missive, judgment was given against the mayor and corporation of London and could be levied against the body and goods of any citizen of London who happened thereafter to come into the Cinque Ports. Serjeant Glanville, for the plaintiff, argued that such a custom was unreasonable and void. It was against the law of God, the law of nature, the common law of the land, chapter 29 of Magna Carta, and all the Edwardian statutes of due process. It was a maxim that no one should be punished for another person's wrong (*nemo pro alieno delicto est puniendus*). Moreover, the sending of letters missive between mayors was not due process. It was answered by the defendant, inter alia, that the liberties of the barons of the Cinque Ports had been expressly confirmed by chapter 9 of Magna Carta,[142] and by the *Articuli super Cartas* 1300, and that they had survived for the same reason as the London custom of mortmain. The custom in question was also part of the *jus gentium*, being a common usage on the Continent, for instance in Normandy (Rouen and Dieppe) and the Low Countries (Dunkirk, Middelburg, Nieeuwpoort and Sluys). In reply, the plaintiff argued that chapter 9 was 'answered' by chapter 29, presumably meaning that it was overridden. The court unanimously preferred that argument.[143] According to Anderson CJ, the custom of imprisoning strangers was bad. It reminded him of the story of Henry VIII's fool, Will Somer, who was accustomed, when angry with someone out of reach, to hit the person nearest him instead.[144] It was contrary to Magna Carta and the statutes of due process, and when a custom was abrogated by statute it was gone for ever, unless the statute contained an express exception preserving it, or it was revived by a subsequent statute. The London custom of mortmain had on this footing been abolished by the general statute of 1290 but then revived by the

---

[142] It had been assumed by the readers in the inns of court that 'free customs' in c. 9 meant all local customs operating within a city or town, and this seems also to be the assumption of early-modern and modern commentators. The meaning of 'free' was not explained.

[143] Walmsley J. disagreed with respect to the seizure of goods, because the privileges of the Cinque Ports were justified by their special position as 'the gates of the realm' and the need to guard against invasion: below, Appendix 5, at p. 493. But he held the imprisonment to be actionable.

[144] BL MS. Lansdowne 1065, at fo. 63. Somer was fool to Henry VIII, Edward VI and Mary, and many stories circulated about him in Elizabethan times.

statute of 1340.[145] The supposed custom in the present case, however, was bad in origin and therefore no custom at all. The confirmation of a void custom, even by Magna Carta, could not make it good. As to the prevalence of the custom in foreign countries, that was irrelevant: it was to be explained either by the law of war (*jure belli*), or because the places were under several governments, so that the ordinary course of justice could not be so easily obtained, whereas London and Sandwich and the other Cinque Ports 'have one prince, one law and one government, and therefore it is unfitting for such a commonwealth to allow such martial proceedings'.[146] Judgment was given for the plaintiff.[147] Since both sides relied on Magna Carta, the decision involved a choice between two potentially inconsistent enactments of the same date and had no bearing on the question of entrenchment. The decision might perhaps be taken as judicial authority for the overriding importance coming to be attached to chapter 29,[148] because it reversed the usual rule that a general provision did not derogate from the specific.[149] On the other hand, the courts had taken the view since at least the fifteenth century that the charter only confirmed lawful liberties,[150] and therefore an alleged liberty or custom was not rendered immune to challenge by chapter 9; if it was unreasonable, it could not in law exist and its confirmation could therefore have no effect.[151] It is difficult to fault this logic, and yet it rendered chapter 9 completely meaningless.[152]

---

[145] BL MS. Harley 4814, fo. 87v.   [146] CUL MS. Add. 8080, fo. 97 (tr.).

[147] The like conclusion had been reached by the chief justices a few years earlier in respect of a similar claim for the liberty of the Tower of London: *Anon.* (1582/92) cited in *Dr Palmer's Case* (1613) 33 APC 133 ('altogether against the laws of the realm'); but in *Paramour v. Verrall* (1600) BL MS. Harley 4814, fo. 81, Serjeant Williams asserted that the custom had been 'allowed'. Cf. *Sir William Wade's Case* (1611) above, p. 26 n. 141.

[148] See Chapter 7, below.

[149] Cf. the opinion of Coke CJ that London could prescribe for a court of equity, even though it was against the statutes of due process: see opposite at n. 155.

[150] *Anon.* (1465) YB Pas. 5 Edw. IV, *Long Quinto*, fos. 30–32, at fo. 32, *per* Danby CJ, rejecting Serjeant Littleton's argument that a custom of London had been confirmed by royal charters and by Parliament. This was relied upon by Serjeant Daniel in *Paramour v. Verrall*, above.

[151] This was also argued in *The Chamberlain of London's Case* (1628) Palm. 539, citing Magna Carta, c. 29, but without a clear conclusion.

[152] See the readings on Magna Carta, c. 9, in *John Spelman's Reading on Quo Warranto*, ed. J. H. Baker (113 SS, 1997), pp. 1–14. One anonymous reader (ibid. 2) actually said the chapter was void. Cf. *Paramour v. Verrall* (1597) BL MS. Lansdowne 1065, fo. 60v, *per* Kingsmill J. (tr. 'although their customs are confirmed by Parliament, nevertheless this extends only to those which are just and reasonable usages'); *Deane's Case* (1599) BL MS.

The logic was not readily acknowledged by the city of London. Serjeant Fleetwood, supported by Coke, persuaded the King's Bench in 1590 that the city had the customary power to make bye-laws, enforceable by fines, relying on the argument that its customs had been confirmed by chapter 9 of Magna Carta, and that Magna Carta had been confirmed by the Statute of Marlborough and numerous later statutes.[153] Many years later, when he was chief justice, Coke held that London was able to hold a customary court of equity, even though prescribing for such a court was against Magna Carta and the statutes of due process,[154] on the ground that its customs had been confirmed by statute.[155] Well might erstwhile recorders of London make such arguments,[156] but their reasoning is difficult to follow. It seems contrary to the decision in the Cinque Ports case, since it subordinated chapter 29 to chapter 9.[157] Unreasonable local customs were not validated by Magna Carta, whereas reasonable customs and privileges were perfectly good in law without royal or statutory confirmation and could only be abrogated by Act of Parliament. This was as true of the customs of, say, the manor of Piddletrenthide as of those of the City of London. It is ironic that, while chapter 9 has been repeatedly saved from repeal, out of deference to the City, it can have no legal effect whatever. The same might even be said of chapter 29, since Coke himself was forced to admit that it gave no better redress than that available under the common law.[158]

The only other provision considered to be still in force, chapter 1, has likewise been of questionable scope. Chapter 1 granted that the English

---

Add. 25223, fo. 68, per Anderson CJ (the customs of London are not confirmed unless they stand with law and reason; the lord mayor may not by custom commit someone for a private offence).

[153] *Chamberlain of London's Case* (1590) Fleetwood, 'Notes for Arguments', fos. 335–6; 3 Leo. 264; BL MS. Harley 1633, fo. 181; BL MS. Add. 25200, fo. 20v. Coke's report (5 Co. Rep. 62) says 'confirmed by divers Acts of Parliament', not naming Magna Carta.

[154] Coke CJ recalled: (tr.) 'it was held by all the justices in the time of Queen Elizabeth, when Gilbert Gerrard was attorney-general [1559/81], that since the making of those statutes a chancery court may not be erected by letters patent, nor may anyone prescribe since those statutes to have a court of chancery with equity ... against those statutes'. Cf. *Perrot v. Mathew* (1588) below, p. 265.

[155] *Anon.* (c. 1610) Warburton's reports, CUL MS. Ii.5.25, fo. 100. This was perhaps a dictum rather than a decision (it begins, tr., 'Note, by the report of Coke CJ').

[156] Fleetwood was recorder of London from 1571 to 1591, Coke from 1591 to 1592 (when he became solicitor-general).

[157] Cf. *Anon.* (1612) 2 Br. & G. 191, where Coke CJ cited the Cinque Ports case, apparently with approval.

[158] *Bulthorpe v. Ladbrook* (1607) CUL MS. Gg.5.6, fo. 52; translated below, pp. 531–3.

Church should be free and should have all its rights and liberties inviolate. The readers in the late-medieval and early-Tudor inns of court
developed an agreed interpretation of this.[159] The word 'free' meant
freedom from taxation (by laymen), and also that priests should not be
villeins; 'rights' meant the jurisdiction of the Church over spiritual
causes; and 'liberties' meant temporal franchises.[160] Attempts to stretch
the meaning further generally failed. As early as 1297, the prelates
complained that the Statute of Mortmain 1279 was in breach of this
chapter, since it violated the privilege of religious institutions to amass
landed wealth without hindrance; but they were given short shrift by the
king's advisers, who said it 'proceeded from old law', presumably chapter
36 of Magna Carta.[161] In the sixteenth century the stately guarantee even
failed to prevent the statutory curtailment of benefit of clergy, one of the
rights and liberties which medieval lawyers thought the framers had
foremost in mind.[162] Whether the break with the papacy in 1534 was
also a breach of chapter 1 depended on one's point of view. On one view
it was an interference with the Church by Parliament,[163] denying the
papal supremacy which was embodied in canon law.[164] On the other, it
was a perfection of the freedom granted to the *Ecclesia Anglicana*,
liberating it from foreign power and restoring its primitive autonomy.[165]
The latter may not have been close to the original intent, but it did make
sense of the words *Ecclesia Anglicana*, which seemed to later eyes calculated to distinguish the English Church as a separate entity from the
Ecclesia Romana. Sir Thomas More, at his trial in 1535, advocated the

---

[159] *Rights and Liberties*, part II. It was held in the mid-sixteenth century that c. 1 extended to
the Church in Wales, which was part of England in the earlier thirteenth century, but not
to Ireland: ibid. 148.

[160] The provision included the 'privileges' of benefit of clergy and sanctuary, but there was
no unanimity as to whether these were rights or liberties.

[161] *Councils & Synods*, ed. Powicke and Cheney, ii. 1217.

[162] *OHLE*, vi. 531–40. The Becket affair and the Compromise of Avranches (1172) were still
relatively recent history in 1215. The readers in the inns of court consistently treated c. 1
as guaranteeing the benefit of clergy, though by the fifteenth century it was becoming a
lay privilege.

[163] Robert Aske complained in the 1530s that while, until recently, it had been customary at
the beginning of each parliament to confirm c. 1, this had been stopped: Thompson,
Magna Carta, p. 141.

[164] For the canon law as to papal supremacy see F. W. Maitland, 'William of Drogheda and
the Universal Ordinary', reprinted in *Roman Canon Law in the Church of England*
(Cambridge, 1898), pp. 100–31; R. H. Helmholz, *The Spirit of Classical Canon Law*
(Athens, GA, 1996), pp. 311–38.

[165] This interpretation was not an invention of the sixteenth century: below, pp. 65–6.

former interpretation. He submitted that the statute of 1534 under which he was convicted of treason, in denying the king's supremacy,[166] was contrary to chapter 1, apparently on the basis that the Church had thereby been exempted in perpetuity from any parliamentary interference with the 'general law' of the Church.[167] The fragmentary reports of his trial afford no clue as to how the argument was presented, in terms either of the entrenchment of Magna Carta or of the relevance to his own case, as an individual, of a grant of freedom and liberties to the English Church. All we know for certain is that the submission was rejected.[168] As late as the 1580s Serjeant Fleetwood glossed the chapter in the medieval manner as confirming the jurisdictional immunities of the Church, benefit of clergy and sanctuary,[169] though he would have accepted that by his time the former had been validly altered by statute and the latter abolished. Doctors of law were still relying on chapter 1 at the end of the sixteenth century as guaranteeing the independence of ecclesiastical jurisdiction,[170] but the common-law judges never accepted their interpretation. Someone had to decide what liberties were protected by chapter 1, and, whatever canon lawyers might think, the practical authority to make and enforce such decisions rested with the royal judges. As with the liberties of London, therefore, so with the Church, the charter gave no more than the law of the land allowed.

Although Magna Carta could not be legally entrenched, it remained a powerful argument in the fourteenth century that Parliament ought not to infringe it, and that it should itself reverse any infringements found to have occurred in its past Acts. That was the only sense in which it was, or approached to being, fundamental or paramount law. It was accepted that Parliament, of all courts, should observe the rule of law. It should not, for instance, condemn people to death without being heard,[171]

---

[166] 26 Hen. VIII, c. 13.

[167] Parliament had, however, done this on several previous occasions: see R. H. Helmholz in *Thomas More's Trial by Jury* (next note), at pp. 67–8. A Lincoln's Inn reader around the turn of the century had maintained that 'all her rights' in c. 1 did not include the whole of the canon law, but only matters of faith and spiritual causes, and that the rights had to be reasonable: *Rights and Liberties*, p. 85.

[168] Derrett, 'The Trial of Sir Thomas More' p. 472. The only relevant source on this point is William Roper's biography. No further light could be thrown on the matter by the very thorough recent study, *Thomas More's Trial by Jury*, ed. H. A. Kelly, L. W. Karlin and G. B. Wegemer (Woodbridge, 2011), as to which see the review by I. S. Williams in 33 *Journal of Legal History* 123–6.

[169] *Specott v. Bishop of Exeter* (1588) in Fleetwood, 'Notes for Arguments', fo. 329.

[170] Below, p. 274.   [171] See Chapter 2, below, pp. 53–7.

or modify rules of law to suit favoured individuals.[172] But there was no doubt that it could do so, as Coke himself accepted. Coke related, on the authority of Sir Thomas Gawdy, that Henry VIII once consulted the judges as to whether a man could be attainted of treason by Parliament without being first called to answer a charge. Their response had been that it ought never to happen, but that, if it did, no inferior court could question it. Coke thought they should have referred to chapter 29, to bolster their warning, but he admitted that it would not have affected the conclusion.[173] The unnamed person against whom the procedure was proposed was not in the event attainted, though the king acted on the advice when Thomas Cromwell was condemned in 1540.[174] Coke expressed confidence that it would never happen again.

The Exegesis of Chapter 29

The most important of all the provisions of Magna Carta, from the fourteenth century onwards, was chapter 29:[175]

> No free person (*Nullus liber homo*) shall be taken or imprisoned, or disseised of any free tenement or of his liberties or free customs,[176] or outlawed, or exiled, or in any way destroyed, nor shall we go against him or send against him, except by the lawful judgment of his peers (*per legale judicium parium suorum*) or by the law of the land (*vel per legem terrae*); to no one shall we sell, to no one deny or delay, right or justice.

Never mind that this was for some reason hidden away in the middle of the charter.[177] Anyone who reads the resounding words, which have never been repealed, instinctively understands what they are about and

---

[172] E.g. *Statutes of the Realm*, i. 186 (where the statutory pardon granted to the pursuers of the Despensers was revoked in 1322 as being against Magna Carta and the coronation oath, apparently because it barred appeals and thereby denied justice); Rot. Parl. iii. 321, no. 44 (where the Commons prayed in 1378 that the common law should not be changed for the benefit of particular parties).

[173] Co. Inst. iv. 37–8.

[174] Ibid. 38. There were also several instances in the same parliament of attainders without trial for adhering to the bishop of Rome, and according to Hall some of those so attainted were burned for heresy: *OHLE*, vi. 244 n. 110.

[175] Translated. For the numbering see above, p. 3 n. 18.

[176] This phrase echoes the wording of c. 9 (above, p. 25). In the settled common law, however, it was impossible for an individual to claim a customary right peculiar to himself.

[177] This is a puzzle, since its much shorter precursor in the 'Unknown Charter' (c. 1215) was given pride of place as cl. 1: Holt, *Magna Carta*, p. 352. In the 1215 charter of

why they matter. According to a fifteenth-century verse summary of Magna Carta, they mean simply that a free person should only be treated in accordance with law.[178] And yet the exact legal interpretation of the words has caused much perplexity to lawyers since at least the fourteenth century. This was perhaps the most obscure provision in the whole charter.

Against whom was the chapter directed? It begins as a general prohibition in the passive voice – 'No free person shall be taken' – which would apply as well to a private imprisonment as to action by the king. But then it turns active and adopts the royal we – 'Nor shall *we* go or send'. Was it therefore intended to make distinctions between private and governmental action? Such a conclusion might seem to be ruled out by a provision at the very end of the charter that all the provisions to be observed by the king were to be observed by everyone in the realm, including the clergy, with respect to their own men (*erga suos*). This was not, however, a comprehensive answer to the question. The word *suos* presupposed a feudal relationship, the usual context for imprisoning and oppressing people. They meant, for instance, that the clergy were bound by the provisions as feudal lords, but they did not require the Church as an institution to observe due process in exercising its canon-law jurisdiction.[179]

The scope of chapter 29 was widened in 1354 by avoiding the royal first person and making the whole provision passive: 'no man . . . shall be put out from land or tenement or arrested, imprisoned or disinherited or put to death without being brought to answer by due process of law'.[180] This brought all inferior forms of authority under the same regime, whether or not the authority had been conferred directly by the king, and whether or not it was derived from lordship over men. Since the grant was to the people of the realm, it was arguably limited to England, though it might be extended by grant or analogy to the men of Ireland and the other dominions of the crown.[181] By the seventeenth

---

Runnymede, however, it was placed much later, as cl. 39–40 of sixty-three clauses in total.

[178] CUL MS. Ee.5.22, fo. 15 ('Et non tratectur homo liber nisi per [*reads* per nisi] legem'). The manuscript dates from *c.* 1485: *CELMC*, p. 219.

[179] It did not always do so, e.g. in cases of heresy: below, pp. 119.

[180] 28 Edw. III, c. 3 (tr.).

[181] In 1297 the people of Ireland petitioned to have Magna Carta granted to them, with due process by writ rather than by bill: SC 8/53/2463. But by 1342 it was assumed to extend to Ireland, which had been made subject to English law: see the Petition of the Prelates,

century no inconsistency would be seen in attributing *habeas corpus* to Magna Carta and also allowing its availability outside the realm.[182] And whatever limitations as to persons might be read into the obscure language of chapter 29, the wording of the statutes of due process was wide enough to include aliens. Chapter 30 also showed that alien merchants had rights, and it was cited in 1611 to persuade the King's Bench that an alien merchant could bring an action for defamation in England.[183]

The charter as a whole was addressed to *omnes*, all the people of the realm. But was not chapter 29 limited by its opening words? It was always clear that *homo* included women,[184] as it did in classical Latin,[185] and indeed children. The opening word *Nullus* is a masculine adjective, but that is because *homo* is a masculine noun, at any rate when used inclusively.[186] Conversely, a man may be *persona grata*, since *persona* is a feminine noun. But the statute said 'No *free* person'. Did this not exclude the unfree men and women, the villeins? There must have been a doubt about this, because the statute of 1354 changed the wording to read 'no person, of whatever estate or condition'. The alteration may have reflected changed social conditions after the Black Death. But later medieval lawyers considered the alteration to have been otiose, except in the case of the king's villeins, because villeinage was relative. A man might be unfree against his own lord, but he was free against everyone

---

Earls, Barons and Commons of Ireland (1342) printed, from the Close Roll, in W. Prynne, *Brief Animadversions on the Fourth Part of the Institutes* (1669), pp. 278–85, at p. 281 (referring to c. 29). Coke held that Magna Carta extended to Ireland only as a consequence of Poynings' Law (1495), which incorporated English statutes into Irish law: Co. Inst. ii. 2. Cf. the reading of *c.* 1500, below, Appendix 1, p. 454, where it was held that the laws in Ireland were *lex terrae*, and the early sixteenth-century reading in BL MS. Harley 4990, fo. 161v, where it is held that the Irish were not *legales homines* for the purpose of Magna Carta because it applied only to England.

[182] See below, p. 301.

[183] *Tirlot v. Morris* (1611) 1 Bulst. 134; sub nom. *Truelock v. Morrison*, CUL MS. Ee.3.54, fo. 30v. Williams J. said it was the first case of its kind.

[184] The doubt mentioned in the statute 20 Hen. VI, c. 9, concerning the wives of peers and c. 29, was related to the concept of peerage rather than to the meaning of *homo*: see *Selected Readings on Magna Carta*, pp. 170, 253, 264. Fleetwood may have confused the two questions: ibid. 384.

[185] *Selected Readings on Magna Carta*, p. lxxi. *Glanvill*, ix. 3, referred to 'libero homini tam masculo quam femine' (free human being, whether male or female). In an action founded on c. 29 of Magna Carta in 1502, Juliana Draper pleaded that she had the liberties of a *liber homo*: *Draper v. Claver* (1502) KB 27/965, m. 25.

[186] A female defendant, alleging that a deed had been misread to her, might plead that she was *homo laica*: CP 40/1026, m. 556 (1519); CP 40/1102, m. 448 (1539).

else, including the king.[187] Locking up other people's villeins was an infringement of chapter 29, a false imprisonment actionable by the villein as well as the lord. On the other hand, lords could continue to imprison their own villeins, because that was allowed by the law of the land.[188] The great charter of liberties did not extend liberty to anyone who was born unfree, and certainly did not authorise the king to do so. Indeed, in 1381 the Lords and Commons agreed with one voice to confirm the annulment of all charters of enfranchisement granted by the crown to appease villeins during the Peasants' Revolt. Granting freedom to villeins was a disinheritance of their lords and therefore unlawful, without their agreement, which agreement (they said) they would never give to their dying day.[189] This might seem to have been England's *Dred Scott* moment,[190] but it was not. The objection was to taking away property by executive action, in a time of crisis, rather than by Act of Parliament. As it turned out, the eventual ending of villeinage in England was not the work of Parliament either.[191] Slavery was different. It was not recognised by the common law,[192] and it was held in the time of Elizabeth I that if a slave was brought to England from abroad he or she would immediately become free.[193] *Liber homo*, therefore, whatever it may have meant in 1225, came in due course to include everyone.[194]

---

[187] *Selected Readings on Magna Carta*, p. lxxiii. The law was so stated also in Co. Inst. ii. 4.

[188] Cf. R. B. Pugh, *Imprisonment in Medieval England* (Cambridge, 1968), p. 53, where the effect of c. 29 is misunderstood.

[189] Rot. Parl. iii. 100, no. 13.

[190] *Dred Scott v. Sandford*, 60 US 393 (1857), in which the Supreme Court of the United States held that the 'due process' clause in the Constitution (derived from Magna Carta) protected the property rights of slave-owners and therefore legislation freeing slaves was unconstitutional. It was not the finest hour of American jurisprudence, though 'due process' is still considered to be a ground on which legislation may be struck down by the American Supreme Court.

[191] See *OHLE*, vi. 602–7; Baker, *Collected Papers*, ii. 881–7.

[192] See the remark in Parliament in 1378, below, pp. 60–1.

[193] The position was so stated by the Revd William Harrison in his 'Description of England' (*c.* 1577): Baker, *Collected Papers*, ii. 886. The observation may have been prompted by the case of one Cartwright, who was said to have been condemned in 1569 for whipping someone he claimed was a slave brought from Russia. When this case was cited by counsel in the House of Lords in 1640, counsel said 'it was resolved that England was too pure an air for slaves to breathe in': J. Rushworth, *Historical Collections* (1721), ii. 468; cf. 2 St. Tr. 1354, where the speaker is identified as John Cook. Counsel went on to mention the Star Chamber, but he did not state (as is often supposed) that *Cartwright's Case* was heard there.

[194] For some supposed exceptions, not generally recognised, see Francis Ashley's reading (1616) below, p. 431.

The only interference with property mentioned in chapter 29 was the disseisin of a free tenement,[195] a sensible enough provision in a document much concerned with feudal relationships. The primary sense of disseisin was the removal of a tenant by his own lord, and this clause of chapter 29 was meant to protect tenants, especially the king's tenants, from eviction. Concerns in the fourteenth century about attainders for treason without due process led to an enlargement of the scope of this provision in 1331 to include the seizure of goods and chattels into the king's hands.[196] This emendation is missing from the later fourteenth-century statutes of due process, which seem to be more focused on preventing the Council and Chancery from meddling with life, limb or freehold property. But it remained on the statute-book and would prove very helpful in the seventeenth century in supporting the argument that the king could not impose taxation without Parliament.

There was much puzzlement over the centuries about the meaning of 'going' and 'sending' upon (or against) people, and most of the readers of the inns of court simply passed over the words when glossing chapter 29, or took them to apply only to peers. The original sense of going upon people was to attack them with force,[197] though in the later printed editions *super eum ibimus* was watered down as 'pass upon him'.[198] Francis Ashley in 1616 held it to mean primarily an arraignment on a criminal charge, but he also suggested – taking an audacious advantage of its obscurity – that it included making people incriminate themselves.[199] The original sense of sending or putting upon people may have been sending someone with the king's authority against them, which Fleetwood took to mean sending process.[200] But this was far from obvious. St German said that the words confirmed an old custom of the realm that no one should be put to answer or suffer judgment except in accordance with the law of the land.[201] Coke said of the clause only that 'it extends to his life', meaning a prosecution for felony.[202] Selden confessed that the

---

[195] Disseisin of 'liberties' would also have referred to franchises granted as free tenements.

[196] 5 Edw. III, c. 9.

[197] See the Articles of the Barons, c. 29, in Holt, *Magna Carta*, at p. 364 ('nec rex eat vel mittat super eum vi'); letters patent of 10 May 1215, ibid. 414 ('super eos per vim vel per arma ibimus'); F. Stenton, *The First Century of English Feudalism* (2nd edn, 1961), p. 251 n. 3.

[198] Thompson, *Magna Carta*, p. 151, citing George Ferrers's translation of 1534.

[199] CUL MS. Ee.6.3, fos. 119, 120.　　[200] Below, p. 464.

[201] *St German's Doctor and Student*, ed. T. F. T. Plucknett and J. L. Barton (91 SS, 1974 49).

[202] Memorandum on c. 29 (1604) below, p. 500. Cf. Co. Inst. ii. 48–9, where he passes over the words, save to observe that they confine the trial of peers to prosecutions by the king.

words had no obvious meaning – 'a man cannot find any fit sense for them' – but, relying on Matthew Paris, suggested that the words 'to prison' must have been omitted after 'send'. This would have resulted in a pointless repetition of 'imprisoned' in the first clause, as Sir Robert Heath was quick to point out in setting him right.[203]

Even more difficulty arose from the phrase *judicium parium suorum* ('judgment of his peers'). In the seventeenth and eighteenth centuries this was usually taken to mean trial by jury, a benign error which may have influenced the framers of the United States Constitution. But there was no trial by jury in 1215, in criminal cases,[204] and in any case a verdict was not a *judicium*.[205] Until the seventeenth century the word 'peers' here was usually taken to mean temporal lords of Parliament rather than jurors.[206] Thomas Williams, when he gave a course of lectures in 1558 on trial by jury, did not think to mention Magna Carta at all.[207] An early attempt to argue that commoners were entitled to a jury of their equals, so that knights should be tried by knights, might be evidence that judgment of peers was associated even in the late thirteenth century with jury trial,[208] and it was certainly easy to mix up the peers with the due process;[209] but the idea that a jury should consist of social peers did not take root.[210] The connection of the phrase with peers of the realm was

---

[203] *The Five Knights' Case* (1627) 3 St. Tr. 1, at col. 18, 79 (and see Noy's argument at col. 14). Heath's refutation is at col. 38. Selden had earlier suggested that *super eum ibimus* also included entering upon someone's possession: Thompson, *Magna Carta*, p. 242.

[204] The recognitors in an assize were sworn, and were therefore a kind of jury charged to answer a specific question.

[205] The original intent was focused more on the *judicium* than the *pares*. In the draft 'Unknown Charter' (*c.* 1215), the king was not to arrest anyone without judgment, but there is no mention of peers: Holt, *Magna Carta*, p. 352. In the king's summary of the provision on 10 May 1215, the emphasis was on a judgment in the king's court: ibid. 414 ('per judicium parium suorum *in curia nostra*').

[206] In a trial by peers the triers were not jurors because they were not sworn.

[207] Below, p. 247 n. 206.

[208] Such a claim seems to have been accepted in R. v. *Sir Hugh FitzHenry* (1293/4) YB 30 & 31 Edw. I (RS), pp. 529–32 (misdated). Although Magna Carta was not mentioned, the defendant's objection 'non debeo judicari nisi per meos pares' (tr. 'I ought not to be judged except by my peers') seems to allude to c. 29. See also the unorthodox reading of c. 1455/60, below, Appendix 1, p. 452.

[209] See the petition of the earl of Arundel (1330) Rot. Parl. ii. 55, no. 13 (tr. 'the great charter wills that no earl, baron *or anyone else* of the realm, should be judged except by process of his peers').

[210] No precedents could be found in 1554, when the notion was firmly rejected as to an esquire: R. v. *Thomas* (1554) Dyer 99. The doubt there had arisen from the phrase 'gentz de lour condition' in the Statute of Treasons 1351.

still espoused by Coke,[211] though he implied that it could also refer to the common jury.[212] Lambarde had already suggested that it referred to trial by jury,[213] and this was accepted by Crompton[214] and later by Selden.[215] Since the general assumption at the time was that the jury existed before the Norman conquest,[216] no one was thereby implying that jury trial was introduced by Magna Carta; it was seen rather as being guaranteed and protected by it,[217] through the provision that no one could be imprisoned without such a trial.[218] Chapter 29 therefore, by reinterpretation, came to be more about trial than judgment.[219]

Then there is the problem of the word *vel*. The restriction of the 'peers' clause to lords of Parliament would have led to an impossible difficulty if *vel* was construed conjunctively, as some modern historians have forcefully contended.[220] It could hardly be supposed that the whole chapter applied only to peers of the realm, in view of the opening words 'No free person', and so the phrase 'by the lawful judgment of his peers or by the law of the land' would have to be confined to going and sending against people. But that would mean that no free person could be imprisoned or outlawed at all, even by the law of the land, which would be equally absurd. A plausible way out of the difficulty for the conjunctivists, unless they are prepared to become subdisjunctivists,[221] might be to read the words as meaning that judgments should always be given by subjects, not

---

[211] Co. Inst. ii. 55.   [212] Ibid. 46.

[213] W. Lambarde, *Eirenarcha* (1581), p. 436; *Archeion*, p. 62.

[214] Crompton, *Courts* (1594), fo. 97v: (tr.) 'lawful judgment of his peers (that is, his equals)'.

[215] See G. J. Toomer, *John Selden: A Life in Scholarship* (Oxford, 2009), i. 81, 185. Selden's original opinion was that *lex terrae* meant wager of law (as it did in *Glanvill*), and was thus a natural complement to the jury trial of *judicium parium*, though he later changed his mind and held that it meant English as opposed to Roman law.

[216] As early as 1579 Coke told the students of Lyons Inn that trial by jury must have existed before the Norman conquest, because tenants in ancient demesne in Edward the Confessor's time were exempt from jury service: Reading on the Statute *De Finibus*, prefaced to Co. Litt. (1738 edn), p. 3 (wrongly dated 1592). See also *La Huictieme Part des Reports* (1611), sig. §§6.

[217] *Sedgwick v. Archbishop of York and Ingram* (1612) Godb. 201; below, p. 385.

[218] *Maunsell's Case* (1607) below, Appendix 9, at p. 517, *per* Nicholas Fuller.

[219] See Pulton, *A Kalender, or Table, comprehending the Effect of all the Statutes*, fo. 1v, where the effect is rendered as 'No man shall be condemned but by lawful trial'.

[220] See W. Ullmann, *The Individual and Society* (1966), p. 71 n. 21, where he suggested that Holt in reading it disjunctively was 'obviously unfamiliar with the basic jurisprudential problems'. Ullmann's interpretation is effectively refuted in Holt, *Magna Carta*, pp. 276–7 n. 154.

[221] Pollock and Maitland, *The History of English Law before the Time of Edward I*, i. 173 n. 3, pointed out that *vel* sometimes meant and/or.

by the king in person, and that those giving judgment should apply the law of the land. As it happens, there was a provision in the 1215 charter (clause 45), not included in the later versions, that justices should know the law of land. And there is some near-contemporary evidence that judgment of peers could indeed be understood as judgment by justices rather than by the king.[222] But this interpretation never occurred to lawyers trying to make sense of chapter 29 in later generations. It never occurred to Sir Edward Coke, who famously told King James I that he could not sit judicially in his own courts because he did not know enough law, to found his unwelcome advice on the *judicium parium* clause.[223]

For these reasons, the disjunctive interpretation is the only one capable of making legal sense. An arrest by a humble constable involved no judgment of peers, and yet it was a taking allowed by the law of the land.[224] The procedure of outlawry never (in civil cases)[225] required a judgment of peers, though no one suggested that outlawries were thereby invalidated. It is true that the disjunctive interpretation of *vel* might seem prima facie to carry the implication that judgment by peers was somehow an alternative to the law of the land. But it had to be *legale judicium*, a lawful judgment, not an arbitrary proceeding outside the law. Trial and judgment by peers of the realm was accordingly, down the centuries, controlled by the common law.[226] It was limited by the law to indictments for treason, murder and felony, and was conducted in accordance with the law of the land. In other criminal cases, including appeals of felony, peers were subject to the same procedural law as commoners, save that in civil cases they were entitled to a

---

[222] Matthew Paris reported Peter des Roches as saying in 1233, 'There are no peers in England, as in France, and so the king is allowed through the agency of justices *(per justiciarios)* to condemn by judgment anyone of the realm': *Chronica Majora*, ed. H. R. Luard (RS, 1872–83), iii. 252 (tr.).

[223] *Prohibitions del Roy* (1608) 12 Co. Rep. 63; below, pp. 366–7.

[224] See the reading of *c.* 1455/60, below, Appendix 1, p. 453. This was to be Sir Edward Littleton's argument in 1628: CUL MS. Mm.6.63, fo. 190; 3 St. Tr. at p. 152. The coercive powers of constables were much debated in the 1580s and 1590s, though without reference to Magna Carta: *Beale* v. *Clarke* (1589) 1 Leo. 327; Owen 98; BL MS. Harley 4814, fo. 98; *Smith* v. *Browne* (*c.* 1590) BL MS. Add. 35948, fos. 98v–99; BL MS. Harley 4814, fo. 114v; *Skarett* v. *Hanmer* (1595) CUL MS. Ii.5.24, fos. 41v–43v; BL MS. Add. 25223, fo. 32; sub nom. *Sharrock* v. *Hannemer*, Cro. Eliz. 375; sub nom. *Scarret* v. *Tanner* (1593) Owen 105.

[225] As to criminal cases, cf. *Gilbert Basset's Case* (1234) in *Bracton's Note Book*, ed. F. W. Maitland (Cambridge, 1887), ii. 664–7; discussed by F. M. Powicke in *Magna Carta Commemoration Essays* (1917), pp. 105–7.

[226] It was, indeed, sometimes said to be provided by the common law: e.g. *Lord Latimer* v. *Gascoigne* (1565) BL MS. Hargrave 4, fo. 224v, at fo. 225, *per* Browne J.

jury containing at least some knights.[227] The phrase therefore added nothing of substance to *lex terrae*. Whatever *legale judicium* had meant to the draftsmen of 1215, by the fourteenth century it had come to represent nothing other than a vague and indirect confirmation of the common-law privilege of trial by peers,[228] or perhaps – disregarding *parium suorum* altogether – as a general requirement of lawful judgment.[229]

The prohibition on selling justice did not prevent the king from charging fees for access to justice, through the issuing of writs,[230] and the prohibition on delays did not prevent procedures such as protections and *non procedendo rege inconsulto*, since they were delays which the common law permitted.[231] The only remaining sense which could be given to this clause bordered on the bizarre.[232] Here again, therefore, chapter 29 had no very specific meaning in relation to the king, other than that the king was bound to observe the rule of law. In relation to the king's ministers, judges and officials, assuming them to be included in the royal first person, the *nulli vendemus* clause could no doubt be interpreted as forbidding bribery, and that was Fleetwood's conclusion;[233] but, as with original writs, it was necessary to distinguish bribery from the charging of acceptable routine fees.[234]

Due Process

In the fourteenth century, chapter 29 was already coming to be seen as the most important of the provisions in Magna Carta,[235] and in

---

[227] *OHLE*, vi. 354; *Lord Latimer v. Gascoigne* (1565) BL MS. Hargrave 4, fo. 224v; *Earl of Pembroke's Case* (1567) ibid. fo. 273 (holding that the privilege could be waived). This rule does not seem to have been related to c. 29, but to medieval requirements of substantial juries in important cases: see *Anon.* (1323) Mich. 17 Edw. II, Fitz. Abr., *Attaint*, pl. 69; *Helygan v. Bishop of Exeter* (1340) YB Trin. 13 Edw. III (RS), 283, pl. 1, at p. 291; Fitz. Abr., *Challenge*, pl. 115; CP 40/319, m. 303.

[228] If such it was. Peers might sometimes have preferred a common jury. But in *R. v. Lord Dacre of the North* (1534) *Spelman's Reports* i. 54, it was held that in a treason case a lord of Parliament could not refuse trial by peers and be tried by jury, because of c. 29.

[229] *Pokelyngton v. Exebrigge* (1397) C 1/68/7, where c. 29 is abridged in French as forbidding imprisonment, (tr.) 'except by lawful judgment or by law of the land'.

[230] Below, pp. 47–8.   [231] Below, pp. 107, 174–9, 181–3.   [232] Below, pp. 48, 93.

[233] Below, Appendix 3, p. 465. It would be cited in proceedings against two lord chancellors accused of bribery, Bacon (1621) and Macclesfield (1725).

[234] See the discussion in Sir Roger Owen's treatise on the common law (*c.* 1615) BL MS. Harley 6605, fos. 255 *et seq*. More difficult to distinguish were spontaneous 'presents': *OHLE*, vi. 413–14.

[235] See Chapter 2.

1354 some of the obscurity of its original language was dispelled by replacing it with the reference to due process.[236] The restatement was not intended as a change in the law, but as a clarification of what it had always been. Much has been made of the phrase 'due process' in the United States, but it was not in the fourteenth century a technical concept. It obviously did not mean that the legal procedures used in 1225 could never be altered.[237] It was a compendious reformulation of the principle that people must not be treated arbitrarily, but only in accordance with the regular legal procedures of the day; and it had been used in that sense well before 1354.[238] It was not particularly novel or peculiarly English.[239] What qualified as due process varied with the context. The sheriff or village constable did not require written pleadings and submissions by counsel before arresting someone for felony, or to quell a breach of the peace, and he could use force if resisted.[240] Even in litigation, regular due process would have to give way to special procedures on occasion, to prevent a denial of justice.[241] And due process could be overridden by parliamentary legislation. For example, if Parliament erected a new court with a power to adjudicate according to its discretion, this was effective because the statutory provision became the law of the land.[242] The reason why 'due process' has acquired such significance in the United States is that the words were incorporated into the written Constitution and were later seized upon as

---

[236] Above, p. 33.

[237] Serjeant Fleetwood argued that the effect of the Edwardian confirmations was that 'Magna Carta shall be guided according to the course of the common laws': *Earl of Pembroke v. Earl of Hertford* (1591) in Fleetwood's 'Notes for Arguments', fo. 337 (tr.).

[238] See below, pp. 51–2.

[239] There is a parallel, contemporaneous with Magna Carta, in the Golden Bull of King Alexander II of Hungary (1222), which enacted in cl. 2 that serjeanty tenants should not be arrested or destroyed without being first summoned to appear (*primo citati*) and subsequently convicted by due judicial process (*ordine judiciario*): E. Hantos, *The Magna Carta of the English and of the Hungarian Constitution* (1904), p. 187.

[240] Lord Ellesmere LC said in the Star Chamber in 1606 that 'whoever comes to arrest someone comes with the king's sceptre and sword, which sceptre is that he ought to arrest him peaceably, but if the party who is arrested makes resistance the sword ought to help the sceptre': BL MS. Add. 35955, fo. 28v. It was decided in that case that a sheriff could not issue arrest warrants in blank.

[241] E.g. where an action was brought against the mayor and corporation of York, which was a county in itself, the writ and process would have to go the sheriff of Yorkshire (a different county), contrary to the normal rules about venue, (tr.) 'for the queen does not wish that right should fail her subjects': *Anon.* (1565) BL MS. Hargrave 4, fo. 211v.

[242] Robert Snagge's reading in the Middle Temple (1581), *Selected Readings on Magna Carta*, p. 259. For this important reading see below, pp. 251–5.

imposing restrictions on the capacity of the legislature, restraints which could be policed by the Supreme Court. That did not happen in England, where Acts of the High Court of Parliament could not be questioned by lower courts on the grounds that they seemed to infringe Magna Carta. The statutory duty to observe due process was laid upon the government, not upon the representatives of the people.

Remedies

The strict enforcement provisions in clause 61 of the 1215 charter were not carried into the charter of 1216 or the statute of 1225, and this omission led to some uncertainty over the centuries about the enforceability of Magna Carta. In the thirteenth century it was approached in political and military rather than judicial terms: according to the author of *Bracton*, it was still implicit that the earls and barons, as the king's associates, could rein him in if he broke the law.[243] In the less turbulent fourteenth century it became more a matter of pressing kings in Parliament to grant repeated confirmations, lest they should forget what had been conceded by their forebears. But these were not legal remedies, providing redress to individual subjects in specific cases. The *Mirror of Justices*, written in about 1290, listed numerous 'abuses' in (or contrary to) Magna Carta, and one of them was that the charter itself provided no remedy if the Church or free persons were deprived of their liberties.[244] The absence of remedies would be a constant refrain in the readings in the inns of court. For example, the provision in chapter 6 that 'Lords should marry off their wards without disparagement' did not indicate how this should be enforced; indeed, it was not even framed as a prohibition. The remedy came in 1236, when the Provisions of Merton provided an action for damages. Likewise the provision for a widow's quarantine in chapter 7 was seemingly unenforceable before Merton provided the writ *de quarantina habenda*.[245] But the most serious lacuna seemed to be in the nobly worded chapter 29. As the readers pointed out, no indication was given in the charter as to whether or how freedom from arbitrary imprisonment, or from the other less explicit forms of official oppression, could be protected by

---

[243] *Bracton*, ii. 110; iii. 43.
[244] *The Mirror of Justices*, ed. W. J. Whitaker (7 SS, 1893), pp. 175–82.
[245] See below, p. 89.

legal means.[246] The king could not be sued in his own courts. For this reason, there was no possibility of an action for damages against a government department until the Crown Proceedings Act 1947. Did this mean that chapter 29 was merely a statement of the king's best intentions, rather than a statute binding kings for ever? Worse than that, was it a mere figment of the political imagination to suppose that the king, as *Bracton* taught,[247] was under the law at all?

Mere textual analysis might suggest defeatist answers to these questions. But this is where the common lawyers revealed their ingenuity, and the common law its innate strength. When the medieval benchers of the inns of court explored the limitations of Magna Carta as a document, they were very properly inculcating in their students a precise critical approach to words and statutory interpretation.[248] Whatever the law schools taught, however, their graduates were equal to the challenge of finding practical solutions. It did not matter that no remedies were set out, if the charter was seen as merely declaratory of the common law, because the common law could provide the remedies. And so it did. In due course the solutions would become retrospectively linked to Magna Carta so as to create a powerful illusion of cause and effect. Trial by jury was one of them. By the fourteenth century the common-law position was that no one could lawfully be sentenced to death without a specific accusation followed by a trial before twelve sworn members of the public.[249] Another was the petition of right. If a subject's property or money came wrongfully into the hands of the crown, he could not sue the king but he could sue *to* the king for restitution, and the suit would be heard by judges applying rules of law. The king could only make out a title to property by matter of record, and therefore when facts occurred which gave him a right it was necessary to summon a jury to establish and record the facts, such as an inquisition *post mortem* after the death of

---

[246] They seem to have overlooked the proivisions of the Statute of Marlborough, c. 5, which sanctioned the issue of writs to enforce Magna Carta. The Ordinary Gloss on Marlborough made little of it: CUL MSS. Hh.2.6, fo. 42; Ee.5.19, fo. 202v; Ii.5.43, fo. 55 (tr. 'this statute is only affirmative of Magna Carta, and provides that it shall be kept as well against the king as against the party'). Some readers just ignored it: MSS. Hh.2.6, fo. 66v; Hh.2.8, fo. 17v.

[247] *Bracton*, ii. 33 (tr. 'the king ought not to be under man, but under God and the law, because it is the law which makes a king'). On this passage see further below, p. 344.

[248] See Chapter 3, below, at pp. 82–3, 109.

[249] This did not prevent an attainder by Parliament, which was a legislative act, though the exception was controversial: above, p. 32.

a tenant in chief or an inquisition after an attainder for treason. It was possible for interested parties to 'traverse' such an inquisition, in the Chancery, alleging that the facts had not been truly found, or to admit the facts as found but show further facts establishing their own right (the 'monstrans de droit').[250] The Chancery would routinely call on the judges for advice in such cases, and it became the practice to send the cases to the King's Bench for trial of any disputed facts by jury.[251] The many cases of this kind in the law reports show that royal property rights were frequently the subject of legal dispute, and that the judges were free to decide against the king.[252] The rights of the king could also be questioned defensively, by pleading against the king in actions at common law.[253]

Besides the assertion of rights there was the annulment of wrongs. Although the king was not subject to any 'mandatory law', he was subject to law in a negative way.[254] The year books are full of judicial statements about things the king could not do – for instance, the king could not grant a franchise which would defeat justice,[255] or which would harm his people,[256] or which would change the law,[257] and the same was true of quasi-judicial commissions.[258] In such cases the remedy was simply to

---

[250] 36 Edw. III, stat. 1, c. 13. In 1378 the Commons prayed that lands should not be granted out by patent without an inquest or evidence given in a court of record, so that a subject should not be deprived of them without answer, contrary to Magna Carta: Rot. Parl. iii. 46, no. 66. The petition was granted. In *Anon.* (1587) BL MS. Hargrave 15, fo. 110, Fleetwood argued in Chancery that the 'monstrans de droit' was available at common law, but Popham Att.-Gen. held clearly that it was not.

[251] E.g. *Gervaise Clifton's Case* (1348) YB Pas. 22 Edw. III, fo. 5, pl. 12. See also the fifteenth-century reading in Appendix 1, below, at p. 453.

[252] For examples see below, pp. 61–2.

[253] An early example is *Beauchamp v. Trayly* (c. 1275/8) in *Casus Placitorum*, ed. W. H. Dunham (69 SS, 1952), p. 105, pl. 7. It is perhaps the only case in the year-book period where c. 29 was successfully cited against the crown.

[254] In *Warren v. Smith* (1615) Calth. MS. i. fo. 363v, Coke CJ said that (tr.) 'although the king is under the direction of the laws, he is not under the penalty of laws, and so no mandatory law will bind the king, for he is not subject to the command of any but God'.

[255] *Eyre of London 1321* (86 SS), p. 296.

[256] E.g. *Jurdan's Case* (1375) YB 49 Edw. III, Lib. Ass., pl. 8; *Chancellor of Oxford's Case* (1430) YB Hil. 8 Hen. VI, fo. 19, pl. 6; *Prior of St Bartholomew's Case* (1435/6) YB 14 Hen. VI, fo. 11, pl. 43; *Anon.* (1458) YB Mich. 37 Hen. VI, fo. 26, pl. 3; *Anon.* (1491) YB Trin. 6 Hen. VII, fo. 4, pl. 4. These cases were all cited by William Fleetwood in his opinion on the Bridewell commission: *The Oxford Francis Bacon*, vol. i: *Early Writings 1584–96*, ed. A. Stewart, pp. 51–3 (where they are not all identified); below, p. 241.

[257] *Abbot of Glastonbury's Case* (1411) YB Hil. 12 Hen. IV, fo. 12, pl. 3, at fo. 13, *per* Hankford J.

[258] Below, pp. 58–61.

treat the grant or commission as invalid. From this developed, in the fifteenth century, the fundamentally important principle that the king can do no wrong. Few principles of law have been more misunderstood,[259] and yet it was a major reinforcement of the rule of law. It had nothing to do with the monarch's personal or political behaviour. Kings as human beings could obviously do wrong, and kings were better placed to do wrong than most people.[260] Nor was it about the immunity of the king from suit in his own courts, an immunity shared by every manorial lord. It meant rather that the king in his royal capacity could only, as a matter of law, do right. He could not lawfully do or command something legally wrong, and so wrongs could not be done on his behalf. If, therefore, a minister, official or servant of the crown, high or low, claimed to be acting under the king's authority, any defence on that footing fell away if the command was one which the king could not lawfully have given. And it worked in other ways. The rule that the king could not be a wrongdoer meant that if the king's officers seized another person's land without title, and it was then granted to someone else by patent, the person entitled could lawfully enter upon the patentee or bring an assize against him to recover possession.[261] Similarly, according to all the judges of England advising the Chancery in 1483, if someone disseised a man to the king's use, the king would not acquire an equitable interest because he could not be a disseisor.[262] None of this was explicitly attributed to Magna Carta, but it is easy to see how it could become linked to the words 'No free person shall be disseised'.[263]

It was held in 1438 that the king could not lawfully send anyone to prison by his own discretion, because the king could not command

---

[259] Even, perhaps, by Selden: *Table Talk of John Selden*, ed. F. Pollock (1927), p. 63.

[260] Christopher Yelverton said in the 1560s that a murder by a great prince was as much a crime as a murder by a private soldier: Brooks, *Law, Politics and Society*, p. 89. For a well-meaning murder committed by King James I see below, p. 340.

[261] *Knotting's Case* (1407) YB Mich. 9 Hen. IV, fo. 4, pl. 17; *Select Cases in the Exchequer Chamber*, ed. M. Hemmant (51 SS, 1933), p. 5, *per* Gascoine CJ, but denied by Hankford J.; cf. Mich. 4 Edw. IV, fo. 25, pl. 3; Mich. 7 Edw. IV, fo. 16, pl. 11. Cf. *Bishop of Winchester* v. *Prior of the Carmelite Friary, Winchester* (1343) YB Mich. 17 Edw. III (RS), p. 263, pl. 58 (patent granting land repealed in Chancery because it wronged the plaintiff).

[262] YB Trin. 1 Edw. V, fo. 8, pl. 13, where there is the first explicit statement that the king can do no wrong. Coke derived it from Bracton: below, p. 323. In *Warren* v. *Smith* (1615) Calth. MS. i. 365v, 1 Rolle Rep. 166, the principle is attributed to Fortescue, though the Latin quotation has not been found in *De Laudibus*.

[263] The year-book cases were discussed by Hake in the context of c. 29: *Epieikeia* (1603), p. 83. The point had also occurred to a reader of Lincoln's Inn in the mid-fifteenth century: below, Appendix 1, at p. 453.

anything without matter of record.[264] The remedy in such a case was an action of trespass against the person who carried out the command, including the gaoler, since he would have had no lawful authority to arrest or detain his prisoner. This might have placed the gaoler in an awkward quandary; but a gaoler's lot was not a happy one. A century later the remedy would be the writ of *habeas corpus*, which went to the gaoler but did not make him personally liable. In either case the courts of law were enabled to consider whether the imprisonment was lawful, and in the latter could also decide whether to bail or discharge the prisoner. During the sixteenth century *habeas corpus* was increasingly used to challenge imprisonment by statesmen and by various royal courts.[265]

Sir Edward Coke was prominent in tying all these strands together. He dismissed the late-medieval doctrine that there was no way of enforcing the provisions of chapter 29. True it might be that no express remedies were mentioned, but every statute made against an injury, mischief or grievance implied a remedy, and Magna Carta was clearly such a statute.[266] The statute was, moreover, for the most part a declaration of the common law, and so the common law could provide supportive remedies without reference to statutory authority.[267] Coke listed them in 1604 as *habeas corpus*, actions of false imprisonment, actions on the statute, indictments on the statute, and writs *de homine replegiando*, to which he soon afterwards added the prerogative writs of prohibition and *mandamus*.[268] By the time he was dismissed from office in 1616, chapter 29 was seen as guaranteeing effectively all the liberties to which the subject was inheritable under the law.[269] How this came about is the question to be addressed in this book.

---

[264] *Anon.* (1438) Trin. 16 Hen. VI, Fitz. Abr., *Monstrans de faits*, pl. 182. Cf. *Tresham's Case* (temp. Edw. IV), remembered in YB Mich. 1 Hen. VII, fo. 4, pl. 5, *per* Hussey CJ (tr. 'the king cannot arrest a man on suspicion of treason or felony, as his other lieges may, because if he does wrong the party cannot have an action'). Cf. *Serjeant Browne's Case* (1532), below, p. 100.

[265] See Chapter 5, below, pp. 155–70.

[266] Memorandum on Magna Carta, c. 29, printed for the first time in *Selected Readings on Magna Carta*, pp. 394–402; below, pp. 500–10; Co. Inst. ii. 55.

[267] On this see also *Bulthorpe v. Ladbrook* (1607) below, p. 531.   [268] Below, p. 503.

[269] See Francis Ashley's reading, below, pp. 427–35.

2

Chapter 29 in the Fourteenth Century

For many centuries the noble words of chapter 29 of Magna Carta have been hailed as a clear declaration of the core principles of constitutional monarchy and the rule of law. But it is far from clear that chapter 29 had as much clout in the medieval period. There are remarkably few references to it in the year books. In one of the earliest of them, in 1311, objection was taken to a new type of generally worded writ of protection on the grounds that the king had promised not to deny or delay right or justice.[1] Bereford CJ responded that 'The king, in whose place we are, has commanded us that the defendant should be quit of all pleas ... how, then, can we hold pleas against his command?'[2] And so the great Bereford, with impeccable logic, laid the *nulli differemus* provision to rest for nearly two hundred years.[3] As to *nulli vendemus*, selling justice most obviously meant making people pay for access to royal justice.[4] In 1351 the Commons understood it in that way when they complained that writs were 'the first part of [the king's] law, which law is [the] supreme right of his realm and his crown (*quele leie est soverein droit de son roialme et de sa corone*)', and that to charge fees for them was against chapter 29. The king's response, however, was that he was entitled to charge for writs of grace, albeit the chancellor could show grace in ease of the people.[5] A similar complaint was given even shorter shrift when it

---

[1] A protection placed a defendant temporarily beyond the reach of legal process while he was engaged, or about to be engaged, in the king's service outside the realm. Only two years earlier, the commonalty of the realm had complained of protections delaying proceedings in the benches: SC 8/294/14698. See further below, pp. 107, 174–9.

[2] *Abbot of Croyland's Case* (1311) YB Mich. 5 Edw. II (63 SS, 1994), p. 6, pl. 4 (slightly paraphrased). The protection in question did not disclose the cause.

[3] It might still apply to other forms of deferment: see *R. v. Gisors* (1321) *Eyre of London* (85 SS), p. 67, where an alleged custom to bail prisoners for felony until the next eyre was held bad because, eyres having become rare, it would delay justice; it was just as well, since there never was another eyre of London. Cf. also *Devykke v. Halman* (1495) below, p. 175.

[4] It could hardly mean allowing people to pay for exemption from justice.

[5] Rot. Parl. ii. 241, no. 30. Cf. a similar petition and response in 1377: ibid. 370, no. 51.

was raised in Parliament in 1381. King Richard II responded that he was not willing to abandon a source of revenue which had been enjoyed by all his forebears, both before and after the charter.[6]

Lecturers in the late-medieval inns of court, attempting to reconcile the reality with the wording of chapter 29, concluded that 'right' could only mean writs of right, and that 'justice' could only mean writs of *justicies*, an interpretation which led to the miserable consequence that this noble guarantee of justice was limited to certain proceedings in inferior courts.[7] Although the author of *Bracton* had proclaimed, around or not long after 1225, that the king was under the law, because it was the law which made him king,[8] the inns of court in the next century seem not to have been aware of this doctrine. Shocking though it may seem, the Ordinary Gloss (as it may be termed) – which probably brought together the common learning of the fourteenth century – actually declared, in the form of a Latin maxim, that the king was above or beyond the law (*Rex est supra legem*).[9]

Whether this negative approach to chapter 29 reflected the virtual absence of reported case-law on the matter, or vice versa, can only be a matter for conjecture. What is clear is that Magna Carta had not yet acquired its mystical symbolic power, which has depended on not reading the words too closely, and therefore it is hardly surprising that chapter 29 was not yet considered to contain law which was forensically useful for ordinary purposes. Its objects would be attained in other ways, and then retrospectively attributed to Magna Carta. That story lay in the centuries ahead and will be pursued in later chapters. Nevertheless, chapter 29 was not wholly dormant in the fourteenth century, and there were a few applications in that earlier part of its story which deserve attention.

Parliament and Council

The king could not be sued in his own courts, not so much because he was king as because he had no peer in his own land.[10] It was an immunity shared with every inferior lord. In the case of the king, however, there was no superior court in which he could be sued. The most obvious way of obtaining a remedy against the crown, without suing the king, was to

---

[6] Rot. Parl. iii. 116, no. 88. See further Thompson, *Magna Carta*, pp. 98–9.
[7] See below, p. 93.   [8] Above, p. 43; below, p. 344.   [9] See below, p. 86.
[10] *Hadelow's Case* (1348) YB Hil. 22 Edw. III, fo. 3, pl. 25, *per* Thorp CJ (in Parliament).

sue *to* the king. The formal way of doing this was the petition of right, or (where appropriate) the monstrans de droit.[11] It was also possible, besides this formal procedure for recovering property, to seek administrative justice in Council, or legislative justice in Parliament, by invoking chapter 29. Magna Carta was mentioned in a number of petitions to Parliament and the Council in the first half of the fourteenth century,[12] usually quoting or alluding to chapter 29, and broad claims were sometimes made as to its scope. Perhaps the broadest was made in 1319. An attorney of the Sheriffs' Court in the city of London complained that one of the sheriffs' clerks had despicably and unlawfully refused to allow him to act as an attorney, against the law of the land ('vileynment, a tort e encountere ley de terre'), and had thereby taken away his living, 'in breach of the lord king's great charter of the liberties of the land' ('en blemisement de la graunt chartre nostre seygnur le roy de fraunchises de la terre'). He claimed damages of £100.[13] The complaint was addressed to the king and his 'enquerours', but no outcome is recorded. It is an interesting document for four reasons. First, because the plaintiff relied on Magna Carta as a statute of the current king, Edward II, thereby showing that the king was thought to be especially bound by his own confirmation.[14] Second, chapter 29 was treated as applying not only to wrongs done by the king and feudal lords, but also to wrongs by minor civic officials such as a sheriff's clerk. Third, the provision was treated as applying not only to freehold land and franchises but also to a professional person's means of earning a living.[15] Finally, the plaintiff assumed that a remedy could be given in damages. In all these respects the humble London attorney had seen far into the future; but his ideas were not yet to be, either in his own century or the next. Although seemingly sanctioned by the Statute of Marlborough 1267, actions for damages founded on chapter 29 are not found until 1501 and never became numerous.[16]

---

[11] See above, p. 44.

[12] See also A. Musson, 'Magna Carta in the Later Middle Ages' in *Magna Carta: The Foundation of Freedom*, ed. N. Vincent [2015], at pp. 92–3.

[13] *Moumby* v. *Hardyngham* (1319) SC 8/320/E455. Attorneys were lesser practitioners attached to the court and regulated by the court. The attorneys of the city courts were doubtless, as in slightly later times, professionally separate from those of the royal courts, who in turn were inferior to learned counsel.

[14] Edward II did not reissue the charter, or issue an exemplification, but merely granted a parliamentary confirmation of the old one in general terms.

[15] This notion was not reinvented until the later sixteenth century: below, pp. 190, 257.

[16] See below, p. 97.

Chapter 29 was not commonly mentioned in Chancery petitions, but there was an instance in 1397. The defendants were alleged to have arrested, on their own authority, several chaplains while robed and attending divine service, showing contempt of a Chancery subpoena by casting it down, and violently disturbing a consistory court when it subsequently investigated the arrests. This was alleged to be contrary to the statute 'that no free man should be taken or imprisoned unless by lawful judgment or by the law of the land', subtly dropping the reference to peers.[17] The background is unclear, but the case was probably rooted in local politics or even in popular religion. The plaintiff was a Chancery clerk suing on the king's behalf, and this seems to be a downward use of Magna Carta by the king against his subjects, in dealing with troublesome townsmen, rather than an upwards complaint about governmental power. The paucity of appeals to chapter 29 in later conciliar petitions might have a number of explanations. For one thing, it was only a confirmation of the common law, and once the legal system was more settled there was less point in referring to it. Moreover, the teaching of the inns of court, as outlined in the next chapter, had found it upon analysis to have little or no specific meaning. In any case, for the Chancery or Council to award damages would itself have been contrary to law. The jurisdiction of the Council was restricted in the fourteenth century precisely because it threatened to infringe Magna Carta.[18]

It was a different story in the world of Parliament, at any rate in the fourteenth century. Here the king could be personally challenged to honour his obligations as a constitutional monarch. Magna Carta was frequently confirmed by kings in Parliament. Edward III confirmed it no fewer than fifteen times, and in 1331 – perhaps prompted by the earl of

---

[17] *Pokelyngton* v. *Exebrigge and others* (1397) C 1/68/7 (tr.). This was brought to light by N. Le Poidevin QC. The proceedings in the consistory are mentioned in F. C. Hingeston-Randolph, *Register of Edmund Stafford (AD 1395–1419): An Index and Abstract of its Contents* (1886), p. 134. The matter is further complicated by the fact that Bishop Stafford was also lord chancellor.

[18] 25 Edw. III, stat. 5, c. 4 (no one to be arrested upon a petition or suggestion to the king or Council except by indictment or presentment, or by process made by writ original at the common law). Cf. also 37 Edw. III, c. 18 (concerning false suggestions to the king, contrary to c. 29); 42 Edw. III, c. 3 (to eschew the mischiefs arising from false accusations before the King's Council, and otherwise, no one to be put to answer without presentment, or matter of record, or due process and writ original according to the old law of the land). Some ingenuity would later be required to square the coercive powers of the Chancery and Star Chamber with these statutes.

Arundel's case in 1330[19] – chapter 29 was paraphrased or explained in the following words: 'no man from henceforth shall be attached by any accusation, or forejudged of life or limb, nor his lands, tenements, goods or chattels seized into the king's hands, against the form of the great charter and the law of the land.'[20] The word 'accusation' here is obviously to be contrasted with a proper indictment and arraignment, and it either referred to proceedings before the King's Council – a concern addressed later in the reign – or to impeachments initiated by the king. Chapter 29 was further expounded in 1354: 'no person, of whatever estate or condition he be, shall be put out from land or tenement or arrested, imprisoned or disinherited or put to death without being brought to answer by due process of law'.[21] The words 'no man' (or person) brought villeins more clearly within its compass, and this was reinforced by 'whatever estate or condition'. Villeins could hardly be excluded from the great charter, especially after the social upheaval of the Black Death,[22] though they could still be imprisoned by their own lords, since that was the law of the land.[23] The right to be heard, and 'due process of law', were easier to understand than the obscure language of 1215 and 1225, though they only codified the previous understanding. Also helpful was the transition from the royal first person. By using passive language, Parliament clarified the general application of the legislation.

These statutes were to prove important in the seventeenth century. Remarkably, however, they were not made the subject of any known lectures in the inns of court, where the curriculum seemed – until the Tudor period – immovably rooted in the *Statuta Vetera*, the legislation prior to Edward III. There are therefore no learned commentaries on 'due process', though it is apparent from conciliar petitions that it was merely an encapsulation of the received sense of chapter 29 as protecting what is now known as the rule of law. For example, in 1328 the countess of Pembroke petitioned the king in Council that no writ should issue to oust her from a castle without her being summoned by due process according to the law of the realm.[24] This was presumably an allusion to

---

[19] Below, p. 57.

[20] 5 Edw. III, c. 9. This did not replace c. 29, which remained in force as part of the 1225 charter.

[21] 28 Edw. III, c. 3.

[22] In *Russell* v. *Hirde* (1388) a bondman of the king complained in Chancery that he had been put out of his unfree tenement in Tintagel by bailiffs, acting without due process of law, and the matter was referred to the sheriff and escheator of Cornwall to investigate: CPR 1385–9, p. 474.

[23] See above, p. 35.   [24] *Countess of Pembroke* v. *Robert de Holand* (1328) SC 8/11/510.

Magna Carta, which in the same year was reinforced by the parliamentary enactment that the judges should not desist from doing justice by reason of any command under the great or petty seal.[25] And in about 1330 the archbishop of York complained to the king in Council that the king's bailiff had seized the franchises of the port of Hull without judgment or due process, contrary to Magna Carta, again presumably referring to chapter 29.[26] Due process was not an arcane constitutional mystery, but the ordinary procedure of the common law as opposed to the arbitrary whim of those in power. It was well understood that people should not be dispossessed of their property without regular legal proceedings to establish the true title, and should not be condemned to death or prison without an opportunity to be heard before a court of law following the procedure of the common law.

Repeated confirmation might be seen as a sign of the precarious impermanence of Magna Carta in the fourteenth century rather than of its firm effectiveness. In the records of Parliament, however, may be found a number of successful invocations of chapter 29 in real cases. In 1311 a customs duty imposed by the *Carta Mercatoria* was struck down as being against Magna Carta, because it was not approved by the Lords as well as the Commons, an indication that the bicameral Parliament was itself being somehow incorporated into the general understanding of the charter.[27] In 1322 the exile and disinheritance of Hugh le Despenser, the elder, was reversed in Parliament, on a writ of error, upon complaint (*inter alia*) that it was against the provision in Magna Carta that no man should be exiled[28] or ruined or in any way destroyed except by judgment

---

[25] 2 Edw. III, c. 8. This was repeated in 14 Edw. III, stat. 1, c. 14, and inserted in the judges' oath in 1344 (18 Edw. III, stat. 4; recited in 20 Edw. III, c. 1): (tr.) 'You shall deny to no man common right by the king's letters ... and in case any letters come to you contrary to law, you shall do nothing by such letters, but shall certify the king thereof and go on to do the law notwithstanding the said letters.' The precise bearing of this prohibition requires further investigation. It looks like an attempted check on the nascent equitable jurisdictions of the Council and Chancery, but might refer to the writ of *non procedendo rege inconsulto*.

[26] SC 8/11/515. The allusion to c. 29 rather than c. 9, which guaranteed the liberties of towns and ports, is shown by the reference to judgment and due process.

[27] New Ordinances 1311, *Statutes of the Realm*, i. 159, no. 11.

[28] The text says 'forjugge', which the editors of the new edition of *The Parliament Rolls of Medieval England 1275–1504* (Leicester, 2005) have rendered as 'judged', but in view of the prefix 'for-' (from the Latin *foris*) it more naturally means exiled or outlawed, following the wording of c. 29. The judgment in the same record actually uses the word 'exile' in paraphrasing c. 29, and unlawful exile was part of the complaint. References here to Rot. Parl. are to the printed edition

of his peers or by the law of the land. The former decision had been made without summoning[29] Hugh to any court to answer, and in the absence of the bishops, who were peers of the realm, and no record was made of the prosecution.[30] The reversal was promptly annulled after Edward III's accession in 1326, but confirmed in 1397. The legal interest, however, lies more in the wording of the parliamentary record than its practical effect. It demonstrates again that, well before the statute of 1354, chapter 29 was understood to guarantee a right to be heard and to due process of law. It was also understood to guarantee that peers of the realm should be tried by their peers.

Similar use was made of chapter 29 in 1327, by the opposite political faction, in order to reverse the attainders for treason of Thomas, earl of Lancaster, Bartholomew, Lord Badlesmere, and Roger Mortimer, earl of March.[31] Lord Badlesmere had been sentenced to death on 14 April 1322 before Lord Cobham, Edmund de Passeley (king's serjeant at law) and other justices at Canterbury on the basis of common knowledge and 'the king's record'. The king's record in this instance was a privy seal instrument, in French, setting out Badlesmere's offences and directing the judges to pronounce judgment. There was no trial. It was, in effect, an improper exercise of martial law in peace-time.[32] In the first term of Edward III's reign, the judgment was reversed in Parliament on three grounds.[33] The first was that judgment had been pronounced without the accused being arraigned for any felony, or given an opportunity to be heard, contrary to the law and custom of the realm. The second was that the king could not make a record of such crimes except in respect of his enemies in time of war, when the king rode out with banners

---

[29] The text says 'appeletz en court', which the editors of the new edition have rendered in one place as 'appealed in court' and in another as 'summoned to court'. The latter interpretation seems preferable, especially since the judgment uses the phrase 'sauntz appeler ... en respouns'.

[30] *Hugh Le Despenser's Case* (1322), record in French recited in the 1397 proceedings in Rot. Parl. iii. 361–7; *CCR 1318–23*, pp. 542–6; L. W. V. Harcourt, *His Grace the Steward and Trial of Peers* (1907), pp. 324–6 (French text from the close roll). The Despensers had been granted a safe-conduct on 8 December 1321 to pursue their petition: *CPR 1321–24*, p. 45.

[31] The records of all three cases are printed, in their original languages, in Harcourt, *His Grace the Steward*, pp. 327–34.

[32] Hale so characterised it: *Sir Matthew Hale's Prerogatives of the King*, ed. D. E. C. Yale (92 SS, 1976), pp. 121–2. On these cases See also M. Hale, *Historia Placitorum Coronae*, ed. S. Emlyn (1736), i. 344–8, 499–500.

[33] Ibid. 332–4; *CPR 1338–40*, pp. 208–10 (record exemplified in 1339).

displayed, and not in time of peace, whereas at the time of the judgment the chancellor and the justices of both benches were sitting to administer justice.[34] And the third was that Badlesmere was not tried by his peers as required by Magna Carta. It will be noted that chapter 29 was cited only in respect of trial by peers. The right to be heard, before judgment of death could be pronounced, was on this occasion treated as common law.[35]

In the same term, Parliament heard the case of Thomas, late earl of Lancaster.[36] On 22 March 1322 the earl had been charged with treason and murder before the king, seven earls, and others of the Council, at Pontefract, and because the treason and murder were open and notorious (*manifesta, notoria et nota*) to the earls, barons, magnates and people of the realm, and were recorded by the king, judgment of death was given. The earl's son, Henry of Lancaster, now in 1327 presented a petition in French, seeking the removal of the record into Parliament because his father had been adjudged to death unrighteously (*nounresonablement*). When it was removed he assigned two specific errors. The first was that every subject arrested for treason, homicide, robbery, arson and other felonies in time of peace should by the law and custom of the realm be arraigned, put to answer, and convicted according to law, before he could be adjudged to death; and although Thomas was a subject of the king's father and arrested in time of peace, and brought before the king himself, the king had recorded that he was guilty of treasons and felonies without his being arraigned or put to answer as was customary according to the law and custom of the realm, and so the judgment of death was erroneous,[37] especially since the Chancery and other courts were open all the time and doing justice, and the king was not riding with banners displayed. The second was that, whereas Thomas was one of the peers and great men of the realm, and it is provided in *Magna Carta de Libertatibus Angliae* that no free man should be destroyed except by lawful judgment of his peers or by the law of the land, Thomas had been

---

[34] For this understanding of peace-time see also *Countess of Kent* v. *Abbot of Ramsey* (1340) YB Pas. 14 Edw. III (RS), p. 127, pl. 54; cited on this point, from the manuscript, in Co. Inst. iii. 52.

[35] In the statute of 1354, mentioned above, it was also treated as implicit in c. 29.

[36] This is the case cited in Co. Inst. iii. 52 as 'Anno 14 E. 4'.

[37] This was cited in *Mareschal* v. *Bamburgh* (1340) YB Hil. 13 Edw. III (RS), p. 97, pl. 12, where the plaintiff argued that the king could only record matters by due process; Willoughby CJ said the king could only record conclusively what had occurred within his own sight.

erroneously adjudged to death as aforesaid without arraignment, or answer, or lawful judgment of his peers, against the tenor of Magna Carta. Judgment was given in Parliament by the king, peers, magnates, and the whole community of the realm, that the judgment should be reversed as erroneous.[38] The reasons were the same as in Badlesmere's case, though reduced to two in such a way that the right to be properly charged and heard was now attributed to chapter 29 as well as to the common law. The third case heard by Parliament in Hilary term 1327 was that of Roger Mortimer.[39] He had been sentenced to death without trial at Westminster on 3 August 1322, by a commission including two justices of the Common Bench (William de Herle and John de Stonore), following a similar direction from the king, though he had escaped to France. The judgment was reversed on the same grounds. A Latin document in very similar words, conjecturally assigned to 1327,[40] concerned Lancaster's associate John, Lord Mowbray, who had likewise been executed in 1322 following the battle of Boroughbridge. The Mowbray heirs were told to sue for their inheritance by due process, as was customary (*processu debito inde faciendo, prout moris est*).

However coloured they may have been by the politics of the moment, these were principled declarations of some importance. Trial by common notoriety was no longer thought consistent with the rule of law.[41] A person accused of a capital offence was entitled to a summons, and an opportunity to be heard, before judgment was given. Moreover, the king could not record a person's guilt without trial, except by martial law on the field of battle, and it was unlawful for his judges to obey his command to give judgment upon such a record.[42] It was around the

---

[38] Harcourt, *Trial of Peers*, pp. 327–9 (printed in Latin from the exemplification on the patent and close rolls); Rot. Parl. ii. 55–6, no. 13; *CCR 1327–30*, pp. 105–6; KB 27/418, m. 49, cited in Co. Inst. ii. 48 (certification of the same record in Easter term 1365).

[39] *CPR 1327–30*, 141–3; Latin text in Harcourt, *Trial of Peers*, pp. 329–32. He had been convicted by the peers on the ground that his offences were notorious: Rot. Parl. ii. 52, no. 1.

[40] SC 8/196/9788.

[41] Plucknett considered that it had previously been common, and that it might have been the origin of impeachment, though Thompson questioned this: T. F. T. Plucknett, 'The Origin of Impeachment' (1942) 24 *Transactions of the Royal Historical Society* (4th series) 47–71; 'The Impeachments of 1376' (1951) 1 *Transactions of the Royal Historical Society* (5th series) 153–64, reprinted in *Studies in English Legal History* (1983), ch. viii; Thompson, *Magna Carta*, pp. 75–6.

[42] Conviction by the king's record alone was used after the battle of Blackheath in 1497 and was considered to be good law by Edward Hales in 1512: reading in the Inner Temple on Magna Carta, c. 11, printed in *Selected Readings on Magna Carta*, at p. 148. See also the

same period that the law turned against the old notion that offenders caught redhanded (or in possession of stolen goods soon after the event) could be executed, or at least brought to trial, summarily.[43]

These important decisions of 1327 were temporarily forgotten or laid aside in 1330 when Roger Mortimer, earl of March, was again condemned to death on account of the notoriety of his guilt, 'without any accusation, and without being brought to judgment after hearing his response (*sanz estre mesne en juggement ou en respons*)'; this time he was executed. But justice of a sort prevailed in 1354, when the judgment of 1330 was reversed on account of this defect.[44] Also in 1330, John Mautravers (or Maltravers), first Baron Maltravers (d. 1364), was condemned to death by Parliament for complicity in the death of the earl of Kent, and fled abroad. His exile is briefly alluded to in the year books.[45] His disgrace was of a modified nature, since he acted on behalf of Edward III while in exile in Flanders, and in 1339 and 1345 he petitioned to be allowed to return. The reason given in his first petition was that by the law and custom of the realm, and the ordinance lately made therein in Parliament, no one ought to be condemned unheard, that he had been condemned without any appeal or indictment, and that he was willing to come back and be tried by his peers.[46] The petitions were not immediately successful, and Maltravers tried again in 1348, alleging that he had been sentenced to death in his absence, 'not being indicted, [arraigned] or summoned to make answer, contrary to the laws and approved usages of the realm'.[47] There is no recorded response to this petition either, but he was finally pardoned in 1352 and returned

---

reading of *c.* 1529, below, p. 107. Dr Cowell was probably ignorant of all this when he asserted that 'the king's only testimony of anything done in his presence is of as high nature and credit as any record': J. Cowell, *The Interpreter* (1607), sg. Qq1.

[43] Baker, *Collected Papers*, ii. 973–4; cf. *Collett v. Webbe* (1587) below, pp. 478–9, *per* Fleetwood sjt. For a supposed customary survival, in the form of the 'Halifax gibbet law', see below, p. 263.

[44] Rot. Parl. ii. 255–6, nos. 8–12 (tr.).

[45] Rot. Parl. ii. 53, no. 3 (record of the judgment only, omitting to mention any process against him); YB Mich. 10 Edw. III, fo. 53, pl. 37 (referring to her husband's exile 'for a certain cause'); cited in Co. Inst. ii. 47, in the margin. See also *ODNB*, sub nom. Maltravers, John.

[46] *Rotuli Parliamentorum hactenus Inediti*, ed. H. G. Richardson and G. O. Sayles (1935), pp. 285–6 (1339 petition); *CPR 1343–5*, p. 535 (and see p. 541). As the 1339 petition made clear, the ordinance referred to was the clarification of Magna Carta in 1327 in the context of the earl of Lancaster's case: *Rotuli Parliamentorum hactenus Inediti*, p. 117 ('qe desormais soit nul mys a la mort par record le roy saunz responz iugez').

[47] Rot. Parl. ii. 173, no. 65 (tr.). The word *atteintz* seems to be an error for *arreine*.

to England.[48] What is particularly notable about the case is that the claim was made, and seemingly accepted, that even Parliament could not override the requirement of natural justice. The same conclusion was reached in the earl of Arundel's case in 1330, when a judgment confirmed by Parliament in 1327 was held to be erroneous and void in that it had been given without due process of law.[49] This may have prompted the legislation of 1331 concerning due process.[50] For jurisdictional reasons, however, it was for Parliament alone to set aside its own erroneous judgments. Since there was no higher court, only the king in Parliament could redress an error or injustice committed by an earlier parliament.

A seemingly aberrant case occurred in 1340, when Richard Willoughby, chief justice of the King's Bench, was arraigned before commissioners for misconduct in office. He was said to have perverted and sold the laws as if they were cattle, though the precise background to his prosecution remains unclear. He challenged the proceedings because the king had not been informed of the accusation by indictment or by suit of a party, with pledges, but Parving CJ (Willoughby's successor) responded that the king had been informed by the clamour of the people, as if that was sufficient.[51] Willoughby was clearly appealing to the requirement of due process, though it is not obvious that it had been denied in a substantive sense. The accusations were indeed made without pledges or good suit, and therefore fell short of an action of trespass. Clamour of the people, however, was arguably equivalent to an indictment by grand jury, especially since the accusations had been put into written bills. The defendant was given an opportunity to be heard, and was even allowed counsel, since no felony was alleged. How he would be tried did not become a question, because in the end he said he would not plead with the king and threw himself upon the king's mercy. After a heavy fine, Willoughby was pardoned, and the king reappointed him to

---

[48] Rot. Parl. ii. 243, nos. 54–6. See also *Earl of Hertford* v. *Earl of Oxford* (1355) YB Pas. 29 Edw. III, fo. 24.

[49] Rot. Parl. ii. 55–6, no. 13; ibid. 256–7, nos. 13–15; *CCR 1330–3*, pp. 291–3. Cf. the case of John Montagu, earl of Salisbury, who was murdered by a mob in 1400 and attainted. His son's petition of 1409 to reverse the attainder, relying on c. 29, was adjourned: Rot. Parl. iv. 18, no. 12. The son was nevertheless summoned to Parliament as earl of Salisbury in 1409.

[50] 5 Edw. III, c. 9; above, p. 51.

[51] R. v. *Willoughby* (1340) YB Mich. 14 Edw. III (RS), pp. 258–63, pl. 109; G. O. Sayles, *Select Cases in the Court of King's Bench*, ed. G. O. Sayles, vol. vi, (82 SS, 1965), p. xvii.

the bench in 1343. The case was therefore not such an aberration as might at first sight appear.

Reported Cases in the 1360s

Later in the reign of Edward III two notable cases were reported in the year books, and they appear to be the only reported cases in the fourteenth century (or the next) in which chapter 29 was given effect, albeit indirectly and not in ordinary legal proceedings.[52] The first is known only from the *Liber Assisarum*, an atypical year book which reported cases occurring before royal justices away from Westminster.[53] A commission of oyer and terminer was opened in June 1368 at Chelmsford in Essex before the two chief justices, John Knyvet and Robert Thorp,[54] together with Thomas Lodelow, chief baron of the Exchequer, and it was presented before them that one John Clerk of Ewell and Sir John atte Lee[55] had arrested Thomas 'Scuryngge' of 'Toll',[56] with certain goods and chattels, taken him to Colchester castle,[57] and imprisoned him there for four weeks until he had made fine to them in

---

[52] Cf. an obscure case of 24 Edw. III (1350), abridged in Bro. Abr., *Commissions*, pl. 3 (tr. 'Note that commissions [were issued] to certain persons to arrest everyone notoriously slandered of felony and trespass, even though not indicted; this is against law'). This is the case cited by Fleetwood in his discourse on the Bridewell commission: *The Oxford Francis Bacon*, vol. i: *Early Writings 1584–96*, ed. A. Stewart (Oxford, 2012), p. 60 (untraced there). He also cited it in the *Case of the Tallow Chandlers* (1583) Fleetwood, 'Notes for Arguments', fo. 292; and in *Collett v. Webbe* (1587) below, p. 479.

[53] *Sir John atte Lee's Case* (1368) 42 Edw. III, Lib. Ass., pl. 5; corrected from CUL MS. Mm.2.16, fo. 96 (which supplies the missing names) and BL MS. Harley 6691, fo. 66. The report is missing from most other manuscript texts of the *Liber Assisarum*, which contain only an abridged version of the year 42 Edw. III. The record of the commissioners' session in Hertfordshire, which included other proceedings against Lee, are preserved in PRO JUST 1/339; the Essex rolls seem not to have survived.

[54] Knyvet was CJKB, and Thorp was CJCP. They were acting under a special commission of oyer and terminer issued on 3 June, which extended to five counties (Norfolk, Suffolk, Cambridgeshire, Essex and Hertfordshire): *CPR 1367–70*, pp. 189–90. Only the previous year Lee himself had served on a similar commission with the same judges: *CPR 1364–67*, p. 438.

[55] This name might be modernised as Attlee, but that form, though made famous by a prime minister, was an uncommon survival. Just as atte Style became Style, so atte Lee usually became Lee.

[56] These names are only in the Cambridge manuscript. The Harleian manuscript says 'S. de T.', while the vulgate has 'T. S. de S.'. 'Toll' might be Tolleshunt, Essex, or even Colchester.

[57] The printed *Liber Assisarum* says Gloucester, but this is obviously a mistake for 'Colcestre' (as it is spelt in the manuscripts). Colchester is in Essex.

£40, half of which was paid for his deliverance. Lee produced in court a commission from the Chancery, issued to him and others, to arrest Thomas and his goods and chattels and take him to Colchester castle, which is what he did, and said that he handed Thomas over to John Oliver, the sheriff,[58] by indenture, 'without this, that he took any fine'. Thereupon the justices, evidently with a note of outrage, exclaimed that 'this commission was against the law, to take a man and his goods without indictment or suit of a party, or other due process', and said they would take the commission away with them and show it to the King's Council. Magna Carta was not expressly mentioned, but the principle relied on was evidently that enshrined in chapter 29 and the due-process statute of 1354. It was, however, no ordinary case. Sir John Lee (d. 1370) was steward the household and had been imprisoned in the Tower of London a month earlier after various complaints, presented to the king by Thorp CJ, of his high-handedness and extortion.[59] A little earlier in the same Parliament a petition had been presented 'that no man shall be put to answer without presentment before justices, or matter of record, or by due process and original writ according to the ancient law of the land, and if anything henceforth shall be done to the contrary it shall be void in law and treated as being in error'. The king assented to this on the grounds that it was one of the articles of Magna Carta.[60] It seems, therefore, that the justices of oyer and terminer at Chelmsford were simply implementing the recent confirmation of Magna Carta in the context of investigations prompted by Parliament itself. But the case had a greater significance. It was not so much that it uncovered another instance of Lee's manifold offences against the rule of law, which was merely a historical event, but rather that the judges were prepared to

---

[58] John Oliver was sheriff of Essex 1366–8, and according to the *Liber Assisarum* was himself indicted for extortion.

[59] Rot. Parl. ii. 297–8, nos. 20–28; *ODNB*, sub nom. Lee, Sir John (d. 1370); and see now W. M. Ormrod 'Parliamentary Scrutiny of Royal Ministers and Courtiers in Fourteenth-Century England: The Disgrace of Sir John Atte Lee (1368)' in *Law, Governance and Justice: New Views on Medieval Constitutionalism*, ed. R. W. Kaeuper (Leiden, 2013), pp. 161–88, and the sources cited there (which do not include the proceedings at Chelmsford).

[60] Rot. Parl. ii. 295, no. 12. This followed a petition to confirm Magna Carta generally. The resulting statute was 42 Edw. III, c. 3. The Commons had complained in 1341 and 1369 that people were often imprisoned without due process, contrary to Magna Carta: Rot. Parl. ii. 129, no. 21; 130, no. 28; 15 Edw. III, stat. 2, c. 3; Rot. Parl. ii. 270, no. 12; cf. 37 Edw. III, c. 18. It was again a grievance in the 1390s and 1400s: ibid. iii. 319, no. 37; iv. 470, no. 60.

overturn a commission issued by the Chancery. The mere fact that persons acted under the authority of the great seal of England, and therefore at least notionally with the authority of the king's chancellor (in this case William of Wykeham), did not prove that they had followed due process.[61]

The decision was not in conflict with a seemingly contrary precedent two years earlier.[62] In 1366 the Common Pleas had accepted the validity of a charter granted to the chancellor of Oxford University whereby 'clerks' or scholars were given the privilege of taking up lodgings in preference to laymen, and the chancellor of the university was given the power to determine disputes about such lettings. The printed year book contains a comment that 'the king as chief guardian of the common weal has power and authority by his prerogative to grant many privileges by the pretence of a public good, even if prima facie they appear wholly against common right'. This was much cited in the early seventeenth century, but it was a Tudor interpolation. The charter did not authorise the chancellor to proceed without due process, and the privileges of scholars may have been considered universal and immemorial;[63] the principal objection made at the time was that the king could not confer a jurisdiction over freehold property. This objection was easily answered. The chancellor had not been empowered to try title to freehold, but only the allocation of lodgings which their owners had chosen to make available for letting.

Commissions which bypassed due process were nevertheless frequent enough to remain a grievance. In 1378 the Commons complained that the commissions authorised by a statute passed in the last Parliament, which empowered commissioners to arrest troublemakers without indictment or other process of law, were 'tres-horrible et perillouse', and threatened

---

[61] In another case the same year, Knyvet CJ by the advice of all the justices quashed a writ from the Chancery giving an ad hoc criminal jurisdiction to justices of labourers, on the grounds that it was not warranted without a commission: 42 Edw. III, Lib. Ass., pl. 12. Serjeant Fleetwood, citing this together with *Lee's Case*, said it was 'most notable to behold the grave judgments given in Edward III's days and how deeply did those honourable judges conceive of such matters as this': *Case of the Tallow Chandlers* (1583) in 'Notes for Arguments', fo. 293.

[62] *Case of Oxford University* (1366) YB Hil. 40 Edw. III, fo. 17, pl. 8.

[63] Before the chancellor of Oxford was driven to produce the charter, his counsel had been minded to claim the privileges as an immemorial custom. Similar privileges were claimed by apprentices of the law following the king's courts, and in their case there was no charter: Baker, *Collected Papers*, i. 147 n. 48; *The Eyre of Northamptonshire, 1329–30*, vol. i, ed. D. W. Sutherland (97 SS, 1981), p. 33.

every free man with slavery (*servage*), contrary to Magna Carta and the statutes of due process. The statute was thereupon repealed.[64] A less successful petition was presented in 1415 by the men of Sandwich, who complained of a commission to charge them with a supposed debt to a Flemish widow, without giving them an opportunity to answer, contrary to chapter 29. The response this time was that the lord chancellor should proceed in accordance with the terms of the treaty with Flanders.[65]

The second case in the *Liber Assisarum* occurred the year after Lee's case, but in an entirely different context.[66] Mary de Valence (*née* de St Pol), dowager countess of Pembroke, was in 1345 granted the advowson of Tilney, Norfolk, with an acre of land, by John Bardolf (d. 1363), Lord Bardolf, and the grant was confirmed by a final concord levied in Hilary term 1346. In 1347 the countess founded Valence Mary Hall in Cambridge, now Pembroke College,[67] and among many other endowments gave them the advowson, with the sanction of a mortmain licence, in 1358. After Lord Bardolf's death in 1363, the king seized his heir as a ward and later (on 14 October 1369) presented to the benefice, which had fallen vacant during the wardship, on the footing that the advowson had descended to the heir;[68] the king's clerk, William Humberston, was then admitted by the archbishop of Canterbury *sede vacante*. The college immediately presented a petition of right. According to the report in the *Liber Assisarum*, the college's complaint was that they had been ousted of their presentment without an opportunity to object ('sans responder'), which was absolutely contrary to the great charter and other statutes to the same effect (*purement contre la grande chartre et auters divers statutes de ceo faits*). Counsel for the crown argued that the parol should demur[69] until the

---

[64] 2 Ric. II, stat. 1, c. 6; Rot. Parl. iii. 65, no. 46; 2 Ric. II, stat. 2, c. 2.

[65] *Kalewartes v. Town of Sandwich* (1415) Rot. Parl. iv. 67; SC 8/303/15127 (petition); SC 8/23/1145 (answer); *CPR 1413–16*, 110 (commission).

[66] *Valence Mary Hall, Cambridge v. Regem* (1369) CP 40/440, m. 590 (petition of right, in French, and its outcome, pleaded in the replication in a *quare impedit* against Bardolf and the presentee, Humberston); 43 Edw. III, Lib. Ass., pl. 21 (the petition of right in the Chancery); YB Mich. 44 Edw. III, fos. 35–6, pl. 24; C 44/5/20 (petition of right); Pembroke College Archives, B.1–20 (located with the help of Dr Jayne Ringrose, the college archivist).

[67] In the *quare impedit*, Serjeant Kirton pleaded misnomer in that the plaintiffs' true name was Pembroke Hall. This was disputed, and the point seems to have been abandoned.

[68] The presentation was enrolled in Chancery: *CPR 1367–70*, p. 310.

[69] I.e. that the proceedings should stand over during the minority, which was the usual course in real actions brought against infants.

boy came of age, but it was decided that the case should proceed, since the petition was in the nature of a *quare impedit* – the usual form of action for recovering an advowson against a disturber, which could not be delayed for infancy. It was then suggested that John Bardolf had been a tenant in tail, and therefore had no power to bar his issue by the final concord of 1346. A hearing was held in Chancery on 19 November 1369, in the presence of the two chief justices, Knyvet and Thorp, and other judges. The king's serjeants on this occasion could not prove that John was a tenant in tail, and so judgment was given against the king. The king thereupon revoked the presentation, and the college proceeded to recover the advowson by an ordinary writ of *quare impedit*. The college records show that a writ was sent to the bishop to give effect to the judgment;[70] the king regranted the advowson to the college, and Humberston was granted a pension and a room in college in return for his loss. The reference in the petition to Magna Carta must have been to the disseisin clause of chapter 29, and the 'sans responder' looks very like the principle of natural justice encountered in the cases of the 1320s. Coke so cited it, adding: '*nota bene*, the usurpation to an advowson is within this Act'.[71] Thus, although no action could be brought against the crown, and no execution of judgment could be awarded against the king, a remedy could be obtained by due process against the usurper on the principle that the king could do no wrong.[72] It was by no means a unique or even a new case,[73] but its inclusion in the year books gave it greater prominence than any other of its kind.

---

[70] Pembroke College Archives, B.16–17. The presentation by the king was revoked by patent (*CPR 1367–70*, p. 332), and whether this patent was effective was one of the matters discussed in the Common Bench: YB Mich. 44 Edw. III, fo. 36, pl. 24.

[71] Co. Inst. ii. 46, margin.   [72] For this principle see the previous chapter, at pp. 45–6.

[73] See, e.g., *Earl of Surrey's Case* (1346), in which John de Warenne complained that the escheator of Norfolk had seized his manor of Thetford without warning or summoning him first, contrary to Magna Carta: *CCR 1346–9*, p. 29; C 54/179, m. 7 (quoted in Thompson, *Magna Carta*, p. 77 n. 29). Two other Chancery cases mention due process, perhaps alluding to Magna Carta. In *Robert de Barton's Case* (1348) a collation to a prebend in York cathedral, made by the king *sede vacante*, was revoked when the chancellor decided that the king's right could not be proved, and Barton was told to pursue his right by due process of law: *CPR 1348–50*, pp. 102–3. And in *John de Lisle's Case* (1355) a grant of the custody of a priory was revoked upon the prior's complaint that, since he had been inducted into the freehold, he could not be deprived without being brought to answer by due process of law: *CPR 1354–8*, p. 266.

The Deposition of King Richard II

In 1399 the great charter played its part in the weightiest case of the century, the deposition, or forced abdication, of a king.[74] It was not on the face of it a prominent part, since the case against Richard II was framed chiefly in terms of the king's obligation, arising from his coronation oath, to uphold the laws of the realm in general. The case was set out in a series of charges (*objectus contra regem*) which formed part of the formal record of the deposition.[75] The king, it was alleged, had been unwilling to preserve and protect the just laws and customs of the realm, in accordance with his oath, but had claimed that the laws lay in his own mouth, or in his breast, and that he alone could change and make laws.[76] He had said that the life, lands and goods of his subjects were at his will, which was contrary to the laws always used in former times with respect to free men.[77] He had forced the judges to give an opinion as to the law of treason against their better judgment,[78] and by colour of that had proceeded to the destruction of the duke of Gloucester, the earls of Arundel and Warwick, and Lord Cobham, without due process, 'contrary to justice and the laws of his realm, and his oath'.[79] Furthermore, Archbishop Arundel had been sentenced to exile, in his absence, without any process of law.[80] How far these allegations were meritorious it is difficult to say. There is no clear evidence that the judges had approved of convictions without trial. According to the record, the earl of Warwick had pleaded guilty, while the earl of Arundel and Lord Cobham had been arraigned in Parliament and asked what they had to say.[81] But the opportunity to speak seems in their case to have been in the manner of an *allocutus*, that is, the calling upon a defendant after conviction to say why judgment should not be given according to law.

---

[74] Edward II's deposition in 1327 was less formal and did not use judicial forms: *Taswell-Langmead's English Constitutional History*, ed. T. F. T. Plucknett (1960), pp. 487–9. The 'six articles' against him, drawn up by John de Stratford, bishop of Winchester, did not mention Magna Carta.

[75] Rot. Parl. iii. 418–21. There is a translation in 1 St. Tr. 140–51.

[76] Rot. Parl. iii. 419, no. 33.   [77] Rot. Parl. iii. 420, no. 43.

[78] As to this see S. B. Chrimes, 'Richard II's Questions to the Judges' (1956) 72 LQR 365–90; N. Saul, *Richard II* (1997), pp. 173–5.

[79] Rot. Parl. iii. 418, nos. 19, 21 (tr.). Cobham's sentence was commuted to exile, since what he had done had been with the king's express authority.

[80] Rot. Parl. iii. 421, nos. 47, 50. Tresilian CJ had also been sentenced *in absentia*: ibid. 238.

[81] 1 St. Tr. 125–36, at cols. 129, 174. The duke of Gloucester, having already been murdered, was attainted posthumously.

That would explain why Arundel relied on nothing other than a pardon, which the king rejected as void for misrepresentation. The real gravamen must have been that they were not tried by their peers, upon a specified charge, and with evidence given openly. Impeachment had been veering in the wrong direction, under royal pressure.[82]

All these accusations against the king contained echoes of chapter 29, but the statute was not expressly cited until the forty-fourth charge, which was that men had been accused before the earl marshal's court (*in curia militari*), and only allowed to defend themselves by battle, even when they were old and their accusers young and fit, contrary to chapter 29 (which was recited in full) and to the king's oath.[83] One other explicit breach of the statute, in this case chapter 1, was that the king had sent prohibitions to church courts under his signet seal, contrary to the ecclesiastical liberties approved in the great charter.[84] This complaint was not about prohibitions in general, but about irregular writs of prohibition without involving any court; indeed, the charge was that the king had sent them after the chancellor had refused to grant a regular prohibition. Some of these grievances undoubtedly had substance, while others may have been exaggerated or distorted. That is not the point. The great point of principle was that the rule of law, which had found expression in the broadest provisions of the great charter, did not spare kings. But it was not Magna Carta itself which justified deposal, since the 1225 version provided no such remedy. The true justification had to be that kings took a solemn oath, before they were crowned, to uphold the laws, and it followed that arbitrary government outside the law amounted both to perjury and to a breach of the conditions on which kings were crowned.[85] Nevertheless, the constitutional principle that kings were under the law, a law which protected life, liberty and property,

---

[82] For the development of more regular procedure earlier in the reign see Plucknett, 'The Impeachments of 1376' (above, n. 41). For the later proceedings see his *Studies in English Legal History* (1983), chs. ix–x.

[83] Rot. Parl. iii. 420, no. 44. See A. Tuck, *Richard II and the English Nobility* (1973), pp. 197–8.

[84] Rot. Parl. iii. 421, no. 46.

[85] For the constitutional significance of the coronation oath see C. Carpenter, 'Resisting and Deposing Kings in England in the 13th, 14th and 15th Centuries' in *Murder and Monarchy: Regicide in European History 1300–1500*, ed. R. von Friedeburg (Basingstoke, 2004), pp. 99–121; A. Spencer, 'The Coronation Oath in English Politics 1272–1399' in *Political Society in Late Medieval England: A Festschrift for Christine Carpenter*, ed. B. Thompson and J. Watts (Woodbridge, 2015), pp. 38–54.

had also come to be associated indelibly with Magna Carta. It would in future be taken for granted, without the need for repeated confirmation.

General Awareness of Magna Carta

Most of the cases considered in this chapter were high matters of state. How far Magna Carta had entered the popular consciousness in the fourteenth century is difficult to gauge. There are some apparent allusions to its basic principles in political verse of the early fourteenth century.[86] One verse in particular, from the time of Edward II, refers to the king' charter – presumably the confirmation of Magna Carta – which had (metaphorically) been held too near the fire so that the wax had melted; the sorry consequence was that 'Might is right, the land is lawless'.[87] A petition from the first quarter of the century, by a group of 'poor tenants' to their manorial lord, complaining of abuses by the steward, seems to indicate reliance on chapter 14 by the lowest orders of society and their lowly lawyers. They did not have the exact wording in their heads, because they supposed it granted them a right to be amerced by their 'peers', though they were doubtless right to treat the 'honest and lawful men of the neighbourhood' as meaning the same thing.[88] Such texts are rare, and yet it is perfectly possible that a general and vague knowledge of the charter percolated society at every level, especially perhaps at the level where it had least practical effect.[89] It is true that the peasants who revolted in 1381 were not Magna Chartists,[90] and yet the charter did have a potentially subversive quality. John Wycliffe regarded the liberties of the *Ecclesia Anglicana* guaranteed by chapter 1

---

[86] D. Matthews, *Writing to the King: Nation, Kingship and Literature in England 1250–1350* (Cambridge, 2010), pp. i, 8, 39, 118.

[87] 'On the King breaking his Confirmation of Magna Carta' in *The Political Songs of England from the Reign of John to that of Edward III*, ed. T. Wright (Camden Soc., 1839), pp. 253–8. The title in Wright's edition is not in the manuscripts. For the date, and a second manuscript, see Matthews (previous note), p. 118

[88] J. F. Nichols, 'An Early Fourteenth-Century Petition from the Tenants of Bocking to their Manorial Lord' (1930) 2 *Economic History Review* 300–7, at p. 306, art. 3. Amercement by peers was, according to the words of c. 14, limited to earls and barons.

[89] For the possibility that this was brought about by reading the charter aloud in parish churches see above, p. 19.

[90] As to whether they had any legal ideals or were essentially anarchic see A. Musson, *Medieval Law in Context: The Growth of Legal Consciousness from Magna Carta to the Peasants' Revolt* (Manchester, 2001), pp. 241–55. Wat Tyler had demanded, rather puzzlingly, that there should be no law other than 'the law of Winchester'.

as including a measure of freedom from interference by the Roman Curia,[91] a notion perhaps reflected in the twenty-seventh charge against Richard II,[92] but hardly the orthodoxy of the day. He wrote scathingly in the 1370s that

> much treasure, and much time of many hundred clerks in universities, is foul wasted about books of the emperor's law and study about them ... It seemeth the curates should rather learn and teach the king's statutes, and namely the great charter, than the emperor's law or much part of the pope's; for men in our realm are bound to obey the king and his rightful laws and not so the emperor's, and they might wondrous well be saved though many laws of the pope had never been spoken ...[93]

The universities did not, however, condescend to teach Magna Carta, and it is doubtful whether their doctors would have been more constructive in their exegesis of its clauses than the learned laymen in the inns of court, or what parts of it could possibly have helped the cause of religious freedom. It helped the Wycliffites and Lollards no more than it did the aggrieved peasants. For most purposes, Magna Carta was still the property of the upper levels of society and their lawyers. In the fifteenth century, chapter 29 would disappear completely from the law reports, except in relation to the trial of peers of the realm. And it disappeared from petitions as well. One of the last to mention it was presented to the King's Council in the 1420s by Nicholas Stanshawe, a member of Lincoln's Inn, who complained of being sued in Council by bill in a matter determinable at common law, and of being adjourned there from term to term, to his great harm, annoyance and expense, and potential final destruction, contrary to Magna Carta.[94] But he was confronting a newer legal world. The bill jurisdiction of the Star Chamber and Chancery was

---

[91] See E. Tatnall, 'John Wyclif and *Ecclesia Anglicana*' (1969) 20 *Journal of Ecclesiastical History* 19–43.

[92] Rot. Parl. iii. 419, no. 27. The grievance was stated to be that, whereas the realm (*regnum*) had always been so free that neither the pope nor anyone else outside the realm could meddle with it (*se intromittere debeat*), Richard had petitioned the pope to confirm certain Acts of Parliament, contrary to his royal crown and dignity and against the statutes and liberties of the realm. The *regnum* was doubtless not thought to comprehend the *ecclesia*.

[93] Quoted in F. W. Maitland, *English Law and the Renaissance* (Cambridge, 1901), p. 53 (here modernised).

[94] *Stanshawe v. Wydecombe* (?1427) SC 8/341/16080 (almost illegible). There is no visible endorsement, but the case went to arbitration (AC/D/3/10-12). For Stanshawe, an apprentice of the law (what would later be called a barrister), see *The Men of Court*, ii. 1451–2. Slightly earlier conciliar petitions relying on c. 29 are those of the Englishmen of

in its infancy, though over the next century it would grow until it seemed to challenge the common law itself. The procedure by subpoena, English bill and depositions was not the due process contemplated in Edward III's reign, but it would soon be accommodated as part of the law of the land.[95] Even so, these courts were not supposed to meddle with the common law contrary to Magna Carta, and Stanshawe's grievances would be resurrected a century later.[96]

As for the inns of court, their teaching in the fifteenth century – doubtless derived from that of the fourteenth – would minimise the practical effectiveness of chapter 29.[97] Nevertheless, it is evident from the great cases discussed above that the underlying notions of due process and the rule of law had been kept alive in appropriate cases during the fourteenth century. The inns of court were a professional law school, and their mode of teaching – borrowed from the universities – was to gloss texts, word by word, as a way of inculcating a critical approach to written law and its interpretation. They did not provide lectures on constitutional law or human rights, or try to read into statutes more than was there. Participants in their exercises of learning were introduced to the problems and opportunities raised by looseness of language, and it was left to the real world to circumvent the problems or seize the opportunities. A glimpse of that real world is provided by the parliamentary and conciliar records, though in the high-level cases of 1322, 1327 and 1330 it was the king himself who took advantage of chapter 29 to benefit political supporters. In clarifying and endorsing the concept of due process, the cases might seem to be, and no doubt to some extent were, significant steps in the development of the rule of law. And yet, even in relation to attainders, they were disingenuous and of little enduring consequence. Striking down attainders by reference to Magna Carta threatened the very idea of a parliamentary attainder, which no king was willing to abandon. During the fifteenth-century conflict between Lancaster and York, there were numerous attainders by Parliament, and reversals and restitutions, ending with a display of juristic legerdemain in which Henry Tudor was allowed as king de facto to summon a parliament and give the royal assent to a statute effectively annulling the attainder which had rendered him incapable of inheriting the

---

Pembrokeshire (1402) SC 8/22/1092 (with the royal assent in Rot. Parl. iii. 518, no. 16) and of John Barber (*c.* 1422) *SC* 8/199/9926.
[95] See below, p. 103.   [96] See below, p. 97.   [97] See Chapter 3.

crown.[98] Magna Carta was no longer mentioned in such proceedings. Parliament had supreme legal authority, and could condemn or absolve as it saw fit.[99]

The fourteenth-century law reports were less ostentatious than the parliamentary records but more enduring in their legacy. They did not yet show the judiciary, independently of Parliament, daring to challenge the agents of a ruling government, as Coke was to do in the time of James I. The judges were nevertheless confident enough, in suitable cases, to invoke the principle of due process against royal officials on behalf of private subjects and institutions. And the year books gave lawyers a long collective memory. The 1368 report was destined to bear a heavy load in the sixteenth and seventeenth centuries, when its original context was forgotten, and it was assumed to be a direct application of chapter 29.[100] It came to be revered as an ancient proof that the king could not commission judges or officials to interfere with the persons or property of his subjects except by due process of law. The king could not authorise others to do what he could not do himself; and the king could not change the law of the land.

---

[98] YB Mich. 1 Hen. VII, fo. 4, pl. 5; *OHLE*, vi. 58. Since the attainder of high treason in 1484 (Rot. Parl. vi. 244–9) had rendered him and his followers incapable of enjoying any dignity or inheritance, the conundrum was whether he had the capacity to summon a parliament in order to remove the incapacity. In the event, his title to the throne was confirmed without express reference to the attainder, which was reversed with respect to all his followers: Rot. Parl. vi. 270, 273–5.

[99] For renewed doubts in the sixteenth century about the legitimacy of attainders without trial see above, p. 32.

[100] Popham cited it in *Att. -Gen.* v. *Joiners' Company* (1582) below, p. 470. Fleetwood cited it in the *Case of the Tallow Chandlers* (1583): Fleetwood, 'Notes for Arguments', fo. 292v. It was mentioned in *Parsons* v. *Locke* (1595), an action founded on Magna Carta: below, p. 278. And it was cited by Edward Hake in discussing c. 29: *Epieikeia* (1603), p. 73. It was cited in Coke's memorandum on c. 29 (1604): below, p. 501; cf. Co. Inst. ii. 48. Several later examples are given below.

3

Magna Carta in The Inns of Court 1340–1540

Although Wycliffe thought the university schools would do well to teach Magna Carta,[1] the university law faculties by the fourteenth century had long since waived any potential interest in English law. Their concern was universal jurisprudence, and so the law of any one country was beneath their notice.[2] The common lawyers therefore set up their own law schools, perhaps at first in Westminster Hall, where students learned law partly by watching the king's courts in action, and partly through their own versions of academical exercise. In the thirteenth century the exercises were focused on procedure, on the writs which provided access to royal justice, and on the artificial pleadings whereby questions were framed for decision: law was not taught in the abstract. The need for accommodation combined with technical instruction was met by the establishment of a collegiate system in the first half of the fourteenth century, probably at the moment when the courts returned to Westminster from their long exile in York in early 1339.[3] At the very same time, colleges were being formed within the universities at Paris, Oxford and Cambridge, both to house the increasing numbers of non-monastic students and to hold them more firmly to the discipline of lectures and disputations. In the legal quarter of London, between the busy city and the royal courts in Westminster Hall, the equivalent colleges were called the *hospicia hominum curiae*, the hostels or inns of the men of court, and they were to monopolise education in English law

---

[1] Above, p. 66.

[2] Some very elementary English law was included in the conveyancing lectures given at Oxford, but these did not lead to a degree and the teachers were not lawyers: see Baker, *Collected Papers*, i. 257–69. It is very unlikely that those who took these courses were destined for attorneyship, let alone the Bar.

[3] William Lambarde planned in 1579 to write about them but could not find 'any certain monument' of their beginning: *Archeion*, fo. 25. It became a topic of discussion in the Elizabethan society of antiquaries, but they could find no certain evidence either. For the likely origins see Baker, *Collected Papers*, i. 145–57, 273–7.

until the eighteenth century. The inns of court were, and still are, unique institutions. They had no founders, no endowments, and no charters of incorporation, but unwritten constitutions which evolved continuously over time.

The system of education in the lawyers' inns was adapted from that of the universities, which was the only system known, and it seems to be for this reason that lectures on statutes were introduced.[4] Since a *lectura* was understood to be the reading out and glossing of a written text, the inns of court decided early on that the lectures (called 'readings') must be on the statutes of the realm rather than the unwritten common law.[5] The consequence of this deference to academical convention was to insulate law-teaching from coherent legal analysis. The readers went through the statutes phrase by phrase, word by word, explaining the Latin text in commentaries which may have been delivered in English but were written down in law French. There was no order in the syllabus save for that of the statute book. One day the subject might be feudal wardship, the next day the rights of widows, followed by the customs of London, or whatever. These commentaries were illustrated with 'cases', factual examples which illustrated how the reader supposed his statute to apply in practice. Any of these cases could be taken up by the assembled company and disputed. Each course of lectures would last for about a month, in one of the vacations, and then in the next learning-vacation another lecturer would take over. In addition to this newer regime there continued, throughout the law terms, to be exercises in the formulation of writs and pleadings; these were called 'moots'. As in the universities, there was – at least by the middle of the fifteenth century – a graduation system. The 'utter barrister' graduated by performing an exercise at the bar: that is, standing outside the bar in the hall of his inn, to argue a moot. After ten years or so he was called upon to deliver a course of lectures, after which he was one of those who sat on the bench at moots, the 'benchers' or masters of the bench. A bencher was expected in due course to deliver a second reading; these 'double readings' attracted special notice, and were sometimes attended by judges.

---

[4] Coke conjectured, anachronistically and without any evidence, that it was the teaching of Magna Carta as early as the reign of Henry III which led to the ban on law schools in the city of London in 1234: Co. Inst. ii, proeme; Baker, *Collected Papers*, i. 271–3.

[5] In a later period, Thomas Hedley of Gray's Inn asserted that they were given on statutes because they raised more difficult questions of interpretation than the common law: *Proc. Parl. 1610*, ii. 180.

It was suggested by Professor Thorne that, under the original lecture system, the reader did not have a choice of subject but simply began where his predecessor left off. That would have corresponded with the system in the university law schools of the time, where the lectures proceeded in order through the Digest or the Decretals. The direct evidence for this supposition is sketchy, and there are signs that it was not the normal system by the end of the fifteenth century;[6] yet it is an attractive hypothesis which would explain the nature of the earliest manuscripts. However arranged, the syllabus was certainly confined at first to the legislation of the thirteenth century, beginning with Magna Carta. There are some remains of statute-based exercises, called *Quaestiones compilatae de Statutis*, dating from around the first decade of the inns' existence in the 1340s, and they begin with a few elementary discussions of points arising from Magna Carta.[7] These *Quaestiones*, with their brief determinations, were probably direct ancestors of the readings which began to circulate in the early fifteenth century, distilled from the disputations over which the readers presided. The same *quaestio ... dicitur* formula occurs in some of the fifteenth-century manuscripts, including the much circulated text which is referred to below as the Ordinary Gloss.[8] One of the very cases arising in a mid-fifteenth-century reading on chapter 7 concerned a widow's right to remain in a castle, and the *quaestio* (as well as its solution) seems identical with one found in the fourteenth-century *Quaestiones*.[9] There is, however, a hiatus in the surviving texts between the 1340s and the early 1400s.

Readings in the Fifteenth Century

The earlier fifteenth-century texts survive in some quantity, but they are generally of poor quality in terms of grammar and sense, and in places difficult to translate into comprehensible English. In fact, they seem to be several degrees lower in textual quality than the manuscript year

---

[6] See *Readings and Moots at the Inns of Court in the Fifteenth Century*, vol. i, *Readings* ed. S. E. Thorne (71 SS, 1952), pp. xv–xviii; Baker, *Readers and Readings*, p. 3. The present writer was less wavering in *Collected Papers*, i. 277, 323–4, 342, 406. But Thorne himself admitted that the evidence was 'meagre and late'.

[7] CUL MSS Hh.2.8, fos. 115–120v; Ll.4.17, fos. 219–222v; Thorne, *Readings*, pp. xxi-xxv; Baker, *Collected Papers*, i. 322–3. A selection of the cases, including all those on Magna Carta, is printed in Thorne, *Readings*, pp. cxlii–cli.

[8] *Selected Readings on Magna Carta*, pp. 22, 32, 159–60, 197, 266, 275.

[9] *Ibid.* 21, no. 5, and p. 32; Thorne, *Readings*, p. cxlv, no. 5; below, p. 89.

books of cases, and were seemingly copied either by young students who had not proceeded very far in their studies or by scribes who knew little or nothing of law or its peculiar French dialect. Despite their shortcomings, most of the texts exist in several versions and must have been in wide circulation. The commonest of them cover the whole of Magna Carta, and they are paralleled by others covering Merton, Marlborough, Gloucester and the two first Statutes of Westminster. These may be regarded as the Ordinary Gloss, to appropriate a convenient academical term which was not used in the inns of court. There are many questions as yet unanswered about these anonymous series. None of the texts is exactly the same; some are abridged, some augmented; most have haplographies and other errors which can only be corrected by collation.[10] Some versions have occasional whole chapters or shorter interpolations which are uncollatably different from the rest. A manuscript dating from the 1450s at Northwestern University begins with unique readings on Magna Carta, but by chapter 20 converges with the vulgate text.[11] Another of similar date, at Cambridge, contains interpolations attributed to William Catesby (d. 1485) of the Inner Temple, and also some whole chapters which differ from the vulgate.[12] These wide textual divergences between versions of the basic text demonstrate that the surviving corpus is only a small proportion of what must once have been a large number of manuscripts which circulated over many decades.

The former existence of so many copies suggests that the world of legal learning, for much of the fifteenth century, was largely satisfied with this standard text as an exposition of Magna Carta, with occasional tweaking. And the likely explanation for this is that substantially the same lectures were repeated over the decades by successive readers, perhaps following the conjectured cycle from chapter 1 of Magna Carta to *Quia Emptores* 1290. It has been shown that repetition of that kind happened a century later with the lectures on *Quo Warranto*,[13] and perhaps with the first

---

[10] For similar observations see *Rights and Liberties*, pp. xiv–xv, xxviii.

[11] *Selected Readings on Magna Carta*, pp. xi–xii, xli. The same volume contains a reading by John Sulyard (d. 1488), which must have been given in Lincoln's Inn in the 1450s or 1460s.

[12] CUL MS. Ee.5.22, fos. 18–51. One of the divergent chapters is c. 26, printed in *Selected Readings on Magna Carta*, p. 233.

[13] See *John Spelman's Reading on Quo Warranto*, ed. J. H. Baker (113 SS, 1997), pp. xvi–xxi. To the readings derived ultimately from Edmund Dudley's (*c.* 1490), listed ibid. xvi, should probably be added that of Francis Browne (Gray's Inn, 1528) BL MS. Add. 35959, fos. 201–2.

chapter of Westminster I, *De Pace Regni*.[14] A tradition of repetition would explain the prevalent anonymity. We cannot put a name to any individual reading before the 1430s, and names are uncommon before the 1460s. The only indications of the reader's personal presence are the occasional remark or question in the first person.[15] Yet there would have been no interest in names if the lectures were not seen as individual performances, if they were passing on the 'inherited core' of which Thorne wrote.[16] An alternative hypothesis is that these are compilations of scattered readings given by different individuals over a longer period and assembled retrospectively in chapter order. The fourteenth-century *Quaestiones compilatae* appear themselves to be such a composition – a *compilatio* – and the Chaloner manuscript from early sixteenth-century Gray's Inn seems to have at least two different series of readings on Magna Carta combined in that way.[17]

The Ordinary Gloss is for these reasons difficult to date, if indeed it has a single date. In so far as cases are cited, which is not often, they are predominantly from Edward III's reign, with nothing from the year books after 1410,[18] although under chapter 29 of Magna Carta there is mention of *Lord Cobham's Case* (1413) without a citation.[19] A statute of 1357 is cited as 'one of the new statutes';[20] an interpolation in one version corrects the text in the light of a statute of 1430;[21] and some of the content of the old gloss was being denied by the 1450s.[22] It seems most

---

[14] Thomas Marow (1503) drew on Thomas Kebell (*c.* 1475): see B. H. Putnam, *Early Treatises on Justices of the Peace in the Fifteenth and Sixteenth Centuries* (Oxford, 1924), pp. 154–5; *Rights and Liberties*, pp. xviii–xix. Kebell's reading is printed in *Rights and Liberties*, pp. 21–31. Marow was used in turn by Thomas Harlakenden (1525): *Selected Readings on Magna Carta*, pp. liii, lxiv.

[15] E.g. in the Ordinary Gloss 'jeo crey' (*Selected Readings on Magna Carta*, p. 159, *bis*) and 'jeo pose' (ibid. 274). It is possible that 'jeo pose' represents an impersonal 'suppose': see the passages in the Library of Congress text (*c.* 1455/60) as translated ibid. at pp. 37, 164, 199, 200, 235, 241, 250.

[16] Thorne, *Readings*, pp. lxiv, lxvii ('in the early fifteenth century a lawyer called upon for a reading seems not to have been expected to do more than repeat the work of his predecessors ... Since the reading remained substantially the same, it made little difference who the particular reader was'); cf. *Spelman's Reading on Quo Warranto*, pp. xvii–xx.

[17] Gray's Inn Library, MS. 25, fos. 20–59; *Selected Readings on Magna Carta*, pp. xlvii–xlviii. Cf. *Rights and Liberties*, pp. xxii, xxxviii–xl, where it is likewise suggested that these manuscripts are composite texts which grew organically over multiple generations.

[18] A case of 1410 is cited under c. 14 (*Selected Readings on Magna Carta*, p. 160). The case of 1409 cited under c. 34 is in an interpolation (ibid. 267).

[19] *Selected Readings on Magna Carta*, pp. 247–8.   [20] Ibid. 274.   [21] Ibid. 266.

[22] See, e.g., Ibid. 250.

likely, therefore, to belong to the first quarter of the century. Thorne dated the parallel glosses on the other *Statuta Vetera* to the same period.[23] But the difficulty in assigning a date to the collection may be connected with the variety of its contents. Attention has already been drawn to the enduring presence of a *quaestio* from the mid-fourteenth century. If the corpus of readings was an accumulation over time, the text which circulated may well have contained a substantial quantity of material originating in the fourteenth century, bridging the chasm between the *Quaestiones* of the 1340s and the named readings of the 1450s and 1460s.

By the end of the fifteenth century we find several distinctly different readings on Magna Carta, some by named individuals, and it seems that the older 'core' was no longer sacrosanct.[24] The readers of the Yorkist and early Tudor periods made use of the old material but revised and developed it in their own way, sometimes inserting chunks of learning made familiar by readings on other statutes,[25] or sometimes simply lecturing on the common law or the legal system with only minimal reference to the legislative purpose or subsequent effects of Magna Carta itself.[26] The earliest identifiable compiler is one 'Eltoñ', whose manuscript includes Nicholas Statham's reading in Lincoln's Inn on the Statute of Marlborough, datable to around 1460, and an anonymous reading on Magna Carta.[27] He is probably John Eltonhead (d. 1479/80), who was admitted to Lincoln's Inn in 1445 and went out of residence in 1464, and

---

[23] See also *Rights and Liberties*, p. xvi, where the readings on Westminster I are dated 'shortly before 1430'.

[24] This was the view also of Thorne, *Readings*, p. lxviii.

[25] E.g. the overlap between *Quo Warranto*, the *Carta de Foresta* and Magna Carta, c. 9 (Baker, *Spelman's Reading on Quo Warranto*, pp. xviii–xix); or between Westminster I, c. 1 (justices of the peace) and Magna Carta, c. 35, according to Harlakenden (*Selected Readings on Magna Carta*, pp. liii–liv). Much of the learning on liberties and grants in the readings on *Quo Warranto* was also incorporated into readings on the liberties of the Church (Magna Carta, c. 1, and Westminster I, c. 1), and it may also be found elsewhere (e.g. in John Hales's reading on Westminster II, c. 39, in Gray's Inn MS. 25, fos. 296–7). Discussions of wreck, which overlap considerably in content, are found not only in readings on Westminster I, c. 4, and *Prerogativa Regis*, c. 13 (Baker, *Spelman's Reading on Quo Warranto* p. xix), but even in a case argued at Harlakenden's reading on Magna Carta, c. 35 (below, p. 79).

[26] The prime example is Kidwelly's reading on c. 11: opposite. Another is Robert Brooke's on c. 17 (partly printed in *Selected Readings on Magna Carta*, pp. 186–95), which concentrates on the words *placita coronae* rather than the jurisdictional point of the enactment.

[27] Library of Congress, MS. 139; *Selected Readings on Magna Carta*, pp. x–xi.

is known to have owned a number of legal manuscripts. The Magna Carta text is long winded and tediously repetitive, often saying the same thing twice in succession in almost the same words. Whether this reflects the style of the readers or of the note-taker is a matter for conjecture.

A slightly later reading on the first eight chapters of Magna Carta is attributed to one Hervy, an otherwise unknown reader of the Inner Temple, probably the Humphrey Hervy of that inn who was active in the 1480s and died around the time its records begin in 1505.[28] The reading cites cases as late as 1482 and refers to 'Magister Litilton' (Thomas Littleton), meaning the *Tenures* which were published in the same year, though a reference to 'the time of Edward IV' indicates that it was given in the time of Richard III or Henry VII.[29] Hervy's commentary is far superior to the old gloss, both in its detail and in the clarity of its exposition, though it belongs to the same tradition.

Morgan Kidwelly's Reading

We seem to be in a very different world when we encounter Morgan Kidwelly's reading of 1483, although it must have been nearly contemporaneous with Hervy's and was delivered in the same inn. Kidwelly was one of a quartet of Yorkist Inner Templars who were in the ascendant that year.[30] Only two months after the reading he was appointed attorney-general to the infant King Edward V, and he continued in office under Richard III. Thomas Lyneham, the new solicitor-general, was from the same inn, as also was William Catesby, a bencher, who became chancellor of the Exchequer. The accession of the Tudors two years later dashed all their hopes of further advancement. Catesby was beheaded soon after the battle of Bosworth; Lyneham lived on for another thirty-five years out of the public eye. Kidwelly, though knighted in 1501, when he was still serving as counsel to the queen dowager, Elizabeth of York, and continuing as a governor of the Inner Temple until his death, lost his life appointment as attorney-general and

---

[28] HLS MS. 88; BL MS. Hargrave 87, fos. 195–218 (with variations). For his identity see *The Men of Court*, i. 94, 828, sub nom. Harvey.

[29] Lecture on c. 1, printed in *Rights and Liberties*, pp. 89, 91, 94. There is another reference to Littleton in the lecture on c. 7: *Selected Readings on Magna Carta*, p. 53. These references rule out Nicholas Hervy (d. 1471), recorder of Bristol 1468–71, who was possibly Humphrey's father.

[30] The fourth was John Vavasour, the only king's serjeant appointed by Richard III, who became a judge under Henry VII.

held no further major office. But the chance survival of the reading is cause enough to remember him.

The sole text of Kidwelly's reading is an extraordinary text of an extraordinary series of lectures.[31] His exposition of chapter 11 of Magna Carta, concerning common pleas, was written for delivery over four weeks during the Lent vacation 1483, which proved to be the last month of the reign of King Edward IV. The surviving copy was made in the 1510s by Walter Atwell of Gray's Inn. Next to nothing is known of Atwell, who described himself as a bachelor of arts, though it appears from his memoranda that he had some connection with Anthony Fitzherbert. He was presumably related to Kidwelly's chaplain of the same surname, and it would seem that he had come into possession of Kidwelly's own notes. Atwell added somewhat of his own, for instance references to Fitzherbert's abridgement (published in 1514–16), to a year book of Henry VII belonging to Fitzherbert, and to later readings in Gray's Inn, including Fitzherbert's. But there are numerous passages written in the first person of the composer, and references to what must have been Kidwelly's own books, such as would not occur in normal lecture notes. A few passages are out of order, there is some repetition, and there are some unfinished portions, all features which show that this was a draft found on loose sheets rather than a report of the lectures as actually given.

The timetable set out at the beginning is unique for the period. And the introductory lecture, giving an account of the origin of the common law, is highly unusual. It is not easy to understand, but the thesis seems to be that William the Conqueror in the fourth year of his reign decided to allow the old law of England to remain in force, with some additions from the Danelaw and a few innovations, after apparently rejecting Roman law as a possible alternative. No single source has been identified for Kidwelly's legal history. There is a marginal reference to the 'book of decrees of William the Conqueror', but the principal source may have been the twelfth-century treatise usually known as the *Leges Edwardi Confessoris*, possibly augmented from chronicles. Kidwelly went on to indicate that there had been some legal changes under Henry II, before proceeding to Magna Carta. It is notable that a lecturer in the Temple in 1483 should have made the attempt to place English law and the legal system in a historical context. Only a few years earlier, in the same reign,

---

[31] CUL MS. Ee.5.18, fos. 26–41; *Selected Readings on Magna Carta*, pp. xliii–xlvi, 97–142.

some common lawyers had proclaimed their law to be literally immemorial.[32]

Kidwelly's presentation of the legal material is also unique for the period. Instead of providing a string of unattributed cases and queries, most of his illustrative cases (following the explanatory linking passages) are real cases, for which citations are given. His year-book reports would have been manuscripts, in some cases taken from abridgements rather than books of terms, and there are occasional references to Littleton's *Tenures*, printed the previous year. The method is not unlike that of an abridgement,[33] and Kidwelly referred in passing to his own abridgement; but he arranged the cases more systematically than in any general abridgement, inserted some queries arising from them, and offered his own thoughts where appropriate.

This is perhaps the closest insight we can gain into the process of composition of an innovatory fifteenth-century reading. It admittedly has all the deficiencies of rough notes. The text is imperfect, particularly with regard to the conjugation of verbs and grammatical constructions, and lacks legal coherence. Sometimes the connection between the cases assembled by the reader and the subject in hand is elusive. And yet, making due allowance for the fact that these were merely private notes, mangled by a copyist, the document represents a significant new departure in legal education. Indeed, it is the first known reading in a newer and more idiosyncratic style, soon to be followed by Thomas Kebell (1486),[34] Gregory Adgore (1489/90) and Thomas Frowyk (1495) in the same inn, and by Edmund Dudley in Gray's Inn (around 1490). The new method was to lecture in depth on a specific branch of the common law which was touched upon in a statute. Although formally an exposition of chapter 11 of Magna Carta, that 'common pleas shall not follow our court', Kidwelly's reading was really an essay on the entire system of courts as it was in 1483, with excursions into miscellaneous topics not found in other readings, such as the workings of Parliament and the law

---

[32] Below, pp. 85–6.

[33] Abridgements of cases began to be compiled in the middle of the fifteenth century: see Baker, *Collected Papers*, ii. 619–20.

[34] The evidence for his supposed reading on Magna Carta is flimsy: *Readings*, p. 68. In addition to the reference there, see Owen, *Common Law* (c. 1615) BL MS. Lansdowne 646, fo. 4, who quotes 'Keeble, the reader', on c. 11, referring to him as 'our nimble and ingenious common lawyer of H. 7 time in his reading upon the statute of Magna Carta'. But the words quoted by Owen (in translation) are very close to those of the Ordinary Gloss (*Selected Readings on Magna Carta*, p. 91), which was of earlier origin.

relating to aliens. As a minutely detailed exposition of the words 'our court' (*curia nostra*) in chapter 11, it was very strained, not to say legally absurd, since it included the Common Bench as one of the species and thereby destroyed the original meaning. But Kidwelly was obviously untroubled by such difficulties. He was not a history professor, but was introducing his young audience to the complexities of the English legal system, choosing two words in the statute as a formal pretext for expounding the common law. The wonder is that so few other examples of his technique survive. Students in general had to manage without a written introduction to the legal system – or, indeed, the substantive common law – until the next century.[35] The only student treatise worthy of the name in the fifteenth century was that already mentioned, the lucid elementary exposition of the land law by Sir Thomas Littleton, justice of the Common Pleas and formerly a bencher of the Inner Temple. It was immediately recognised as authoritative, and was the earliest English law book to be printed. Kidwelly himself, and Hervy soon afterwards, both of whom would have known the author, cited 'Master Littleton' without title.[36] Chief Justice Montagu asserted in 1550 that it was 'the true and most sure register of the foundations and principles of our law', and a writer in 1600 went so far as to say that 'Littleton is not now the name of a lawyer, but of the law itself'. Elizabethan students bought interleaved and extra-marginated copies to stuff with masses of annotation. Sir Roger Owen even suggested that Littleton should have his own holy day.[37] The true bible of the common-law student after 1482 was not Magna Carta, but Littleton's *Tenures*.

Thomas Harlakenden's Reading

Thomas Harlakenden's reading on chapter 35 of Magna Carta, given in Gray's Inn in 1525, was another extensive essay on the legal system, more or less unrelated to the original intent.[38] Since texts survive both of the lectures and of some of the disputations, it illustrates clearly the

---

[35] The first comparable work in print was Crompton, *Courts* (1594), though a shorter work, *Le Diversité des Courtes*, appeared in 1526.
[36] *Selected Readings on Magna Carta*, pp. xliii, 109, 123, 132; *Rights and Liberties*, p. 89.
[37] J. H. Baker, 'Sir Thomas Littleton', in *ODNB*; Owen, *Common Law*, LI MS. Misc. 207, at fo. 1v of ch. 3.
[38] *Selected Readings on Magna Carta*, pp. 280–331 (on c. 35). They are a considerable jumble, perhaps a result of wide circulation, though there seems to have been more than one reporter: ibid. lii–liv.

established system of exercise, which has been described elsewhere.[39] The text of the statute was read out and then the reader expounded it, clause by clause, illustrating each of his propositions with a string of real or imaginary cases. Some of those cases were then picked out for discussion, with arguments made for and against by the students, barristers, benchers – and, on occasion, judges – who were present. There were three named speakers at Harlakenden's reading, besides himself, two of whom were judges: Richard Broke, justice of the Common Pleas, and John Hales, baron of the Exchequer. The cases were very wide ranging, but those which remain came only from that part of the reading which dealt with leets and liberties. Sometimes they bore no relation at all to Magna Carta, as where the learned assembly debated the vexed puzzle whether the lord of a villein could lay claim to the villein's goods when they had been shipwrecked.[40] This was really a question arising from the interpretation of chapter 4 of Westminster I, but it had arisen because of the mention of liberties in chapter 35, and wreck was one of the liberties explored in detail in the reading. It can hardly have been uppermost in the thoughts of the framers of Magna Carta, but such flights from the text were, or were to become, normal.[41]

The superior quality of the report of Harlakenden's reading gives the impression of a more sophisticated treatment than is found in the less polished fifteenth-century texts. The reader began by referring to what *Glanvill* and *Bracton* had to say about counties, sheriffs and coroners, in order to place chapter 35 in its historical context. And here he had a subtle point to make about the relationship between the charter and the common law. The requirement that counties be held monthly was common law, but it was introduced into the charter because the common law was not being observed; the result was that, whereas at common law proceedings held at the wrong intervals were erroneous rather than void, the direct prohibition in Magna Carta had the legal consequence of making the proceedings invalid rather than merely erroneous. Harlakenden's gloss on chapter 35 thereafter followed a systematic progression: an account of sheriffs and coroners, how they were appointed, and what they could and could not do in the county court; an account of the sheriff's tourn and view of frankpledge; then, because of the saving of

---

[39] *Readings and Moots*, vol. ii, *Moots and Readers' Cases*, ed. J. H. Baker, and S. E. Thorne (105 SS, 1989), pp. xlv–lxxiii; *Collected Papers*, i. 329–32, 405–8.
[40] Ibid. 285, 318–20.
[41] See, e.g., *Spelman's Reports*, ii. 135 n. 2; Thorne, *Readings*, pp. ii, xv.

liberties, an account of liberties and *quo warranto*, which seems to owe most of its content to Spelman's reading of 1519 on *Quo Warranto*, including the excursus on wreck; next, tithings and leets; and finally (upon the *pax nostra* clause) the appointment of justices and conservators of the peace, and the taking of sureties to keep the peace. Much, if not all, of this last section was taken verbatim from Thomas Marow's 1503 reading in the Inner Temple on chapter 1 of Westminster I.[42] Even such abstruse details as the existence of conservators of the spiritual peace before the Conquest, citing the laws of Cnut, was taken from Marow. Also Marow's was the distinction between a 'breach' of the peace and something which was merely against the peace, an esoteric distinction which would continue to mystify future generations. In true scholastic manner, he explained how a breach of the peace could sometimes be committed by the person who was beaten rather than the person who beat him. Much legal virtuosity was displayed in connection with battery by a servant in defence of his master: what if two masters retained the same servant, and one master was assaulting the other? Or what if a servant himself had a servant, who was proposing to defend his master's master? Again, however, all of this was derived from Marow, and it was very typical of the inns of court pedagogic mentality.

Whereas with poorer texts we find merely piles of disjointed cases, in Harlakenden's reading – as in Marow's – we can see more clearly how the cases were used to illustrate a coherent exposition of the matters addressed. It is a good question whether Harlakenden's reading was untypical in this regard. The existence of several versions may be evidence that it was. Yet he was not eminent in the profession and this may simply be a chance survival. Unless the difference in quality from one reading to the next was vast, the likely explanation is that we just have very inferior notes of the others. The sheer length and detail of Harlakenden's lectures, when compared with most of what we have, strongly suggest that the bulk of our surviving texts are mere summaries of far more substantial performances; and this would readily

---

[42] Printed without translation in B. H. Putnam, *Early Treatises on Justices of the Peace in the Fifteenth and Sixteenth Centuries* (Oxford, 1924), pp. 289–413. Chapter 1 had probably been the subject of a Middle Temple reading by Thomas Wode (subsequently CJCP) at the end of Edward IV's reign: *Readers and Readings*, p. 146. But Marow's reading was widely circulated in manuscript and was probably known outside the Inner Temple. Much of it was reproduced in W. Fleetwood, *The Office of a Justice of Peace* (1658) [written in 1563], as to which see below, p. 236.

explain the lapses in sense and general lack of coherence. There were other surviving readings of similar quality, such as those by Marow (1503) and Spelman (1519), which were partly adopted by Harlakenden, and the earlier readings on *Quo Warranto* which were reused by Spelman.

The Obsolescence of Magna Carta

Most of the learning derived from the great charter, whether found in the statute itself or in the glosses, was obsolescent even by the beginning of the fifteenth century. It may have been kept alive purely for educational purposes, perhaps in order to preserve the cycle of statutory texts, if indeed there was one. It is therefore no great surprise to find that lectures on Magna Carta peter out almost completely in the sixteenth century. Raphael Holinshed's remark that 'a great part of the law now in use' depended on Magna Carta,[43] while it must have reflected some kind of popular perception, only betrayed his lack of a legal education. Most of the serious interest in the inns of court had always lain in the first few chapters alone. The grant of ecclesiastical liberties in chapter 1 was a pretext for discussing such miscellaneous topics as sanctuary and benefit of clergy.[44] Difficult questions about spiritual jurisdiction were avoided before the sixteenth century, and even then the principal expositions of the jurisdictional divide were to be found in readings on other statutes.[45] Wardship, treated in chapters 2 to 6, and 27, was still of practical importance, even though it was increasingly avoided by means of feoffments to uses, whereas dower (chapter 7), on which considerable time was spent, had in practice largely given way to jointure. Readings on jointure would be given with some regularity once the Statute of Uses 1536 provided a suitable text for exposition, but the subject was not worked into the commentaries on Magna Carta; nor were uses. Some of the later provisions in the charter, even if still in force, had become riddled with exceptions. For example, that as to common pleas

---

[43] *Chronicles of England, Irelande and Scotlande* (1577), p. 626. This was cited by J. Cowell, *The Interpreter* (1607), sig. Ss4v, to support his even broader assertion that 'all the law we have is thought in some sort to depend of it'.

[44] These lectures have all now been published in *Rights and Liberties*, part II.

[45] The first detailed account was in the preface to Richard Gynes's reading in the Inner Temple (Lent 1568) on 2 & 3 Edw. VI, c. 13, concerning tithes: below, p. 220. There were earlier readings on specific topics lying on the boundary, such as Baldwin Malet's reading of 1512 on the administration of estates: *Selected Readings on Magna Carta*, pp. 210–15.

(chapter 11) had been historically significant as the origin of the Common Bench, but all the legal interest for the readers lay in the various cases where (despite Magna Carta) common pleas did not have to be held 'in a certain place'.

As Kidwelly's lectures show, it became acceptable for a reader to choose a single phrase in a statute as a pretext for lecturing on some broad area of common law. The content of such lectures owed nothing to the provisions of the charter itself. William Fleetwood would call them 'vain and wandering excursions'.[46] But adverse criticisms such as this rested on the assumption that readers were supposed to concentrate on the original purpose of their statute, or at least indicate what had become of it over time. In reality, however, the words of the text were becoming mere verbal pegs on which to hang whatever the reader chose to address. It would have been a sensible and helpful reform if more readers had made such wandering excursions, and brought more of the common law within the taught curriculum. Their failure to do so would doom the whole system to extinction in the seventeenth century.

The obsolescence of Magna Carta did not matter too much to the inns of court if the purpose of readings was not so much to impart useful information as to provide students with an introduction to legal method and reasoning, and to familiarise them with the 'common learning'[47] and grounds[48] of the law. Some of this learning was as artificial as law teachers could make it. Emulating the academic tradition of the university law schools, the readers in court seem to have delighted in legalistic but perfectly logical conclusions which might cause surprise or challenge the mind.[49] This approach is evident from the treatment of the very first words of Magna Carta, chapter 1, *Concessimus Deo*. They prompted the lawyerly point, taken in nearly all the manuscripts, that a grant could not be made to God, since he was not a corporate body known to the law.[50]

---

[46] Below, p. 237.

[47] For 'comen erudition' see J. Dawson, *Oracles of the Law* (Ann Arbor, 1968), p. 64 n. 55; *Spelman's Reports* ii. 161; Thorne and Baker, *Moots and Readers' Cases*, p. lxii; J. H. Baker, *The Law's Two Bodies* (Oxford, 2001), pp. 67–70; *OHLE*, vi. 467–472. The phrase occurs in the readings: e.g. B. & M. 64; *Moots and Readers' Cases*, pp. 155, 272, 273, 298; Baker, *Spelman's Reading on one Warranto*, p. xxi n. 73; *Rights and Liberties*, p. 130.

[48] For 'grounds', or basic principles, see *Spelman's Reports*, ii. 161; *OHLE*, vi. 468 n. 174; Thorne and Baker, *Moots and Readers' Cases*, pp. 67, 94, 119, 124, 144, 322, 323.

[49] For a canon law parallel see J. H. Baker, *Monuments of Endlesse Labours: English Canonists and their Work 1300–1900* (1998), pp. 39–40.

[50] *Rights and Liberties*, pp. 70, 71, 73, 78, 82, 87, 96.

The words were, perhaps, simply a personal vow.[51] Nor, for that matter, was the *Ecclesia Anglicana* mentioned in the chapter a corporate body capable of taking by grant.[52] Some readers also held that a grant could not be made to an individual church, since a church was merely a mass of bricks and stones. They usually went on to acknowledge that the words were really metonymic shorthand, and that grants should be construed according to the usage of the times when they were made.[53] But some readers nevertheless pursued the pernickety earlier logic to the perverse conclusion that if the grant of freedom to the Church could not refer to the institution or to buildings it must refer to the clergy, since they were capable legal persons,[54] and that therefore it must be taken to mean either that unfree men should not be ordained[55] or, conversely (and more intelligibly), that if villeins were ordained they became in some sense free.[56] A more tortuous example of the same kind of thing is afforded by the proposition, arising in relation to chapter 6, that offering a male ward a marriage with a widow was a disparagement because, if he married her, he would become a *bigamus* in the canon law and therefore disqualified from claiming clergy if he were ever unfortunate enough to be convicted of felony.[57] There was no converse objection to a woman marrying a widower, since she could never claim clergy. Other examples may be found throughout the readings. What if the king married a woman who

---

[51] William Fleetwood, arguing as a serjeant in *The Bishop of Exeter's Case* (1587) BL MS. Lansdowne 1087, fo. 234, said of c. 1, (tr.) 'this is a vow by the king to God, and not a grant, but although he thereby vowed that the rights of the Holy Church should not be altered or violated he did not thereby vow that the spiritual judges should have the jurisdiction to try spiritual matters ... which previously belonged to the common law'.

[52] It was discussed in Gray's Inn whether it was impliedly incorporated by this provision: *Rights and Liberties*, p. 128.

[53] See, e.g., *Rights and Liberties*, pp. 73 (the Ordinary Gloss), 87, 97, 135, 141–5. This point was also made by Fleetwood, who wryly observed that in old charters one word made more legal sense than twenty in his day: ibid. 135. It had some judicial support: see *Prior of Huntingdon v. Stanley* (1520) YB Mich. 12 Hen. VIII, 119 SS 33 at p. 37, *per* Brudenell CJ. Cf. Co. Inst. ii. 2, gl. *Concessimus Deo*.

[54] *Rights and Liberties*, pp. 84, 148, 167. It could also refer to religious corporations, whose members (being dead in law) were not capable individual grantees.

[55] Ibid. 71, 79.

[56] This became the orthodox learning, with qualifications: *Selected Readings on Magna Carta*, pp. lvii, 84, 128; *OHLE*, vi. 601–2. Fleetwood referred to both opinions, but opted for this one: *Rights and Liberties*, p. 136.

[57] *Selected Readings on Magna Carta*, pp. 2, 11 (from readings on c. 6). Bigamy in the modern sense was no bar to ordination, even if the second wife was a widow, since the second marriage was void: below, p. 111. The conclusion was logical enough, even if the theological premises were bizarre.

happened to be a hereditary sheriff: was the shrievalty in suspense?[58] Or a female hereditary sheriff married a justice of the peace?[59] (It mattered not a whit that there were no female hereditary sheriffs at the time.) What if a hereditary office of gaoler descended to one of the prisoners: was it an escape if he walked out? If it was, could he license himself to go out? Then again, what if such an office descended to a woman, she married one of the prisoners, and he walked out: could he be guilty of an escape from the custody of his own wife?[60] What if a testator appointed the diocesan bishop and the metropolitan as his executors: who then should grant probate?[61] None of this was practically useful learning in itself, since the factual situations were deliberately far fetched. It was playful teasing with abstract principles for educational purposes.

Sometimes antiquated learning was kept alive for its own sake. The readers discussed at length the necessity for the king's widow – that is, the widow of a tenant in chief – to obtain the king's licence to marry, though one of them let slip that the king was no longer allowed to refuse it, or to charge for it.[62] Matters such as castle-ward were still expounded, and in far more detail than their current relevance warranted. Although one of the readers admitted that the service was never performed, since there were no longer any wars within the realm, he contrived to make it relevant on the ground that there might still be a payment of money in lieu.[63] Yet even the law of castles, however useless, was replete with pedagogic potential. What if the castle fell down? What if it was then rebuilt? What if a man was obliged by different tenures to guard two castles? What if there were two castles in the same vill, and one of the constables bought goods by way of purveyance but left them in the possession of the seller: could the other constable seize them by way of purveyance?[64] But the most pervasive method of exposition in the readings was the drawing out of analogies and 'diversities'. Legal principles are more readily understood, and their limits tested, through

---

[58] See ibid. 282 (from Harlakenden's reading on c. 35). The answer was, yes.
[59] See ibid. 294 (from Harlakenden's reading on c. 35). A justice could not be a sheriff.
[60] These examples are from Kebell's reading on Westminster I, printed in *Rights and Liberties*, at pp. 129–30. Kebell was perhaps thinking of the wardenship of the Fleet, which had descended to a woman (Elizabeth Venour) in his own time.
[61] Baldwin Malet's reading (1512) in *Selected Readings on Magna Carta*, p. 211. The answer was, the prior of Christ Church, Canterbury. But what if there was no prior? Probate would then have to await the election of a new prior.
[62] *Selected Readings on Magna Carta*, p. 41.   [63] Ibid. 226.
[64] Ibid. lviii, 220, 222, 229.

the identification of similarities and distinctions.[65] That is how the legal mind was, and is, formed.

The Role of History in Legal Education

Since the readers on Magna Carta were glossing a text produced two or three hundred years before their own time, and since it was normal to begin a reading by explaining the 'mischief' which gave rise to the legislation, some attempt at explaining the historical context was expected. This history mostly took the form of assertions about the state of the law before 1225 – 'le comen ley devant le feasance de cest estatute' – which was usually deduced from the terms of the charter itself. When the mischief was thus gathered by deduction from the text alone, it was often wrong.[66] For instance, all the readers said that a woman could bring any kind of appeal of death before the restriction in chapter 34, but it is evident from *Glanvill* that this was not so. Occasional acquaintance with *Glanvill* and *Bracton* is nevertheless in evidence, even in the fifteenth century, and Harlakenden – borrowing from Marow – cited both.[67] There are a few examples of more specific reliance on histories, notably in Kidwelly's fanciful account of William I's settling of English law after the conquest.[68] Kidwelly also discovered, presumably from a chronicle, that the *murdrum* fine was not Norman but had been introduced by King Cnut with respect to Danes and then adopted by William I.[69] Richard Hesketh relied on the 'laws and decrees' of William the Conqueror, and on the laws of Athelstan, for information about villeinage and frank-pledge.[70] But the general sense conveyed by the readings is that, although lawyers were well aware of legal change, and were trained to believe that legislation must be understood from its historical context, their law school was only marginally more advanced in historical scholarship than other contemporary academies. Many lawyers believed the common law to be immemorial in the literal sense, more ancient even than

---

[65] For a 'common distinction held by those who moot in court and chancery' see Plowd. 62v (1550).

[66] See William Fleetwood's complaint about this, below, p. 222.

[67] *Selected Readings on Magna Carta*, pp. 27, 280; Baker, *Spelman's Reading on Quo Warranto*, pp. 19, 20. For a possible citation of *Britton* see *Selected Readings*, p. 346.

[68] Above, p. 76.   [69] *Selected Readings on Magna Carta*, pp. xlv, 98, 105.

[70] Reading on the *Carta de Foresta* (Gray's Inn, *c.* 1506), BL MS. Lansdowne 1145, fos. 71v, 72. The laws of William I are seemingly taken from the *Carta Regis Willelmi*, found in the Red Book of the Exchequer.

Roman law,[71] and evidence of a legal culture among the ancient Britons was found in the tales of the legendary King Brut and King Lucius.[72] Immemorial antiquity would in due course be reconciled to the lawyers' appreciation of change by supposing that it was only the details which changed with the times.[73] The essential principles of the common law were 'pure and tried reason' and must therefore have existed in some form for as long as men had been capable of rational thought.[74]

The Dearth of Constitutional Learning

The most striking feature of all but the latest readings on Magna Carta is the almost complete absence of any significant constitutional content. There is no indication in the fifteenth-century texts that Magna Carta was anything other than an ordinary statute. It was, to be sure, the 'great charter of the liberties of England';[75] but no one thought of it as a bill of rights, in the seventeenth-century sense, let alone as a constitution for England or a charter of human rights. The Ordinary Gloss even proclaimed that the king was above or beyond the law – *Rex est supra legem* – and therefore not bound by chapter 11 with respect to his own pleas.[76] Later generations would achieve the same result by interpretation: the king was not bound by any statute without express mention,[77] and in any case the king's pleas were not 'common' pleas[78] or were not within the

---

[71] J. Fortescue, *De Laudibus Legum Anglie*, ed. S. B. Chrimes (Cambridge, 1942), ch. 17; YB Pas. 10 Edw. IV, fo. 4, pl. 9, *per* Catesby sjt (tr. 'Common law has always been, since the creation of the world'). Cf. the anonymous reading of *c.* 1546/50 (*Rights and Liberties*, p. 139) which attributed the amalgam of English laws to legislation by successive ancient monarchs: the British King Lucius, the Danish King Cnut, the Anglo-Saxon King Edward, and the Norman King William.

[72] *OHLE*, vi. 18–22. See further below, pp. 223–4.   [73] Below, p. 349.

[74] Francis Rodes said in his Gray's Inn reading (1576), 'The common law is defined to be nothing else but pure and tried reason . . . As Tully was bold to convey the pedigree of his law from the great god Jupiter, even so am I bold [to say] in the person of our common law, "When reason came into England, then came I'" etc.': Fleetwood, 'Miscellananea', fo. 104v.

[75] For the meaning of 'magna' see above, p. 5.

[76] *Selected Readings on Magna Carta*, p. 92. Cf. YB Hil. 8 Edw. II (41 SS), 73, pl. 33, *per* Bereford CJ ('le roy . . . est sur la ley'); Mich. 8 Hen. IV, fo. 9, pl. 12, *per* Stourton (*Potestas principis non est inclusa sub legibus*); *Grymmesby* v. *Eyre* (1456) YB [Mich.] 35 Hen. VI, 51 SS 118 at p. 120, *per* Hindeston sjt ('le roy est desuis la ley').

[77] So said Broke J., in another context, at Harlakenden's reading (1525): *Selected Readings on Magna Carta*, p. 317.

[78] So said Morgan Kidwelly in 1483: ibid. 111.

intended purview.[79] Nevertheless, the fact that a standard text of the early fifteenth century could offer the explanation in the form of such a general maxim, without seeking to qualify it,[80] provides a noteworthy counterbalance to *Bracton*. The theme of constitutional governance which by the seventeenth century was inseparably attached to the great charter was not yet embedded in every legal mind. In fact, the charter was seen primarily as a source of what would now be called private law.[81]

No one lectured on the fourteenth-century confirmations of Magna Carta, and there was no discussion of the enactment in 1368 that all statutes contrary to Magna Carta were void.[82] It would have been a difficult position to maintain, for the reasons discussed earlier.[83] Some readers simply assumed, without seeing any point worth arguing, that parts of Magna Carta had been repealed by pre-1368 legislation.[84] Far from asserting its inviolability, readers in the inns of court regularly took the position that provisions of the charter had been repealed, even impliedly repealed, by later statutes. Nowadays we attribute this to the notion that Parliament is sovereign and that therefore any statute, including that of 1368, can be repealed provided there is a clear intention to do so. Some such idea is implicit in the readings, but the approach seems more pragmatic. If in fact there were provisions of Magna Carta which were no longer seen to be in operation, that was prima facie evidence that they were no longer law, and that had to be attributed either to repeal or to initial invalidity. Parliament itself was part of the *lex terrae*, and its enactments were *lex terrae*. This raised no questions; but it was presumably squared with chapter 29 either because Parliament was deemed to have existed in 1225 or because the charter of

---

[79] Morice's reading (1578), fo. 14v, explained it as an application of the principle that the king was not usually bound by a statute unless he was explicitly or impliedly named. Although there were qualifications to this principle, in the cases where it applied the prerogative was said to 'surmount the force and authority of the law' and to have a 'preeminency above the law': ibid. 16v, 17. Fleming CJ, in *Calvin's Case* (1608) Hawarde 363, said the king was 'above the laws, but not to abrogate them, which he can not do'.

[80] It was perhaps taken for granted that *lex* should be understood as written legislation, in which case there was no implication that the king was above the common law. The king was not always bound by statute, whereas he could not dispense with the common law. On the other hand, 'legem' is singular, and most naturally translates as 'the law'.

[81] Cf. Thompson, *Magna Carta*, p. 139.   [82] 42 Edw. III, c. 1.   [83] See above, pp. 21–2.

[84] E.g. Gray's Inn MS. 25, fo. 47 (*c.* 1520), where a reader held that c. 25 (as to standard measures of wine), had been overtaken by statutes of 1340 and 1351. A little later in the same manuscript (fo. 54) it is pointed out that c. 32 (restricting subinfeudations) had been repealed by *Quia Emptores*.

1225 had acquired its statutory authority by virtue of later parliamentary confirmation. There is an extensive treatment of Parliament and its procedures in Kidwelly's reading (1483), but it was included only because the reader deemed the High Court of Parliament to occupy the uppermost place in the system of courts, as the first and foremost example of *curia nostra*. The constitutional supremacy of Parliament was assumed, but not taught. It was not, in any case, derived from Magna Carta.

Not only is there no indication in the readings that Magna Carta was regarded as a form of higher law, but several of its provisions were even held by the readers to be 'void'.[85] They might be void because they did not reflect the law as currently understood, as with the provision in chapter 7 that widows should not marry without the lord's consent,[86] or those in chapter 18 as to registering the king's debts and attaching them 'in lay fee',[87] or even that about selling justice in chapter 29, which did not prevent fines being charged for writs.[88] They might alternatively be void because they could not be reconciled with other provisions in the charter: for instance the provision in chapter 14 that villeins should be amerced 'saving their wainage' was held by some to be inconsistent with the overriding principle, embodied in the same chapter, that everyone should be amerced according to the gravity of their offence.[89] The phrase 'saving their contenement' in the first clause of the same chapter was held by one reader to be void on a similar policy ground, because it would enable the impecunious to commit offences with impunity.[90] And some parts of the charter were held void because they were simply nugatory. The provision in chapter 7 about the king's widow giving surety not to marry without the king's consent was held void on this ground, because she could be fined for marrying without the king's consent whether or

---

[85] Below, note 102. Cf. *Reports of Cases from the Time of Henry VIII*, ed. J. H. Baker, vol. ii (121 SS, 2004), p. 468, *per* Saunders sjt (1544): 'Sometimes the words of a statute are void: for instance, the statute of Magna Carta, c. 3, "no one shall have the wardship of any heir before he has taken his homage" ...'. Fleetwood was less sure about c. 3: see *Magna Carta*, fo. 7v (tr. 'the law was altered and the words of the statute seem to be void ... and yet various constructions have been made to make the statute good').

[86] The Ordinary Gloss in *Selected Readings on Magna Carta*, p. 22 ('for the contrary is frequently seen'); cf. ibid. 26, 29.

[87] Ibid. 198.   [88] Ibid. 250.

[89] Ibid. 161. A similar argument was made about ecclesiastical persons being amerced in respect of their lay fee and not their spiritual fee: ibid. 159.

[90] Ibid. 166. Cf. the Ordinary Gloss, ibid. 159, which says an amercement should be according to the seriousness of the offence even if the offender cannot bear it.

not she had given surety.[91] Others held the provisions in chapter 14 about the amercement of villeins to be void on the grounds that villeins had no goods of their own with which to pay amercements.[92] A provision might also be void on the ground that it was too loosely drafted to make sense.[93] Some provisions were ambiguous, such as 'unless the house is a castle' in chapter 7, which was usually taken as a direct prohibition on claiming dower in a castle but was sometimes interpreted in favour of widows, contrary to the strict wording.[94] This was one of the oldest moot-points on Magna Carta,[95] not finally settled (in the widow's favour) until 1581.[96] Others pointed out where remedies provided by Magna Carta were ineffective and had been overtaken or impliedly repealed by subsequent legislation. For instance, the widow's quarantine introduced by chapter 7 was seemingly unenforceable before the Provisions of Merton gave a remedy in 1236. And the failure of chapter 6 to prohibit disparagement of wards, or furnish a remedy for disparagement, was held by one reader to render it void.[97] The standard learning on chapter 26, which provided that writs of inquisition of life and member should be granted freely and not denied, was that it did not prevent the Chancery clerks from charging fees for writing and sealing such writs, and that (if this should be doubted) the chapter had been impliedly repealed in 1300.[98] Other provisions were held to do no more than confirm the common law, and were for that reason 'void'.[99] This came close to dismissing the legal effect of the entire charter. One reader regarded all its provisions as confirmations of the common law,[100] and that was later to be Coke's

---

[91] Ibid. 40. Hervy held it invalid as to lords other than the king, because no oath could be given to anyone other than the king's widow: ibid. 58.

[92] Ibid. 161, 166. There is a flaw in this argument, in that villeins could own goods and money until they were seized by the lord, and could give good title to others before seizure.

[93] E.g. c. 7 ('all the lands which were his'): ibid. 36.

[94] Ibid. 21, 31, 76, 84; cf., to the contrary, ibid. 32, 34, 44, 45, 49, 63, 66.

[95] The solution in the *Quaestiones de Statutis* was ambiguous: ibid. 21.

[96] *Ilderton's Case* (1581) *Dyer's Notebooks*, ii. 392 ('notwithstanding Magna Carta'); BL MS. Lansdowne 1078, fo. 59 (tr. 'it appears from Magna Carta, c. 7, that a woman shall not have dower of a castle, but the justices held the contrary').

[97] *Selected Readings on Magna Carta*, pp. lxv, 6.

[98] Ibid. 232, 233, 234. It was this repeal which Coke held had been undone by the statute of 1368.

[99] E.g. the provision in c. 7 that a widow should have her inheritance: ibid. 21 (the Ordinary Gloss) and 68.

[100] Library of Congress MS. 139, p. 3; *Selected Readings on Magna Carta*, p. 330.

position as well,[101] though any suggestion that the whole of Magna Carta was in consequence 'void' would have struck him as most inconvenient.

The notion that any Act of Parliament could be treated as void might seem to conflict with the concept of parliamentary supremacy, even if the word 'void' is taken to import ineffectiveness rather than defectiveness. Coke's contention in 1610 that the courts could declare a statute void[102] was lambasted by Lord Ellesmere[103] and has been rejected by some as an unnecessary obiter dictum.[104] At least it seemed to later English lawyers notably eccentric. But Coke was not claiming a power of judicial review in the modern American sense. His assertion that legislation contrary to reason was ineffective was simply the application of a common-sense presumption that Parliament could not have intended something manifestly irrational, unjust or absurd, or perhaps an acknowledgement of the factual impossibility that legislation could make something just which was unjust.[105] This was not an aberration by the wayward Coke, but derived from the older learning of the inns of court. It was common well before Coke's time to reject the efficacy of statutes which made no legal sense, and the benchers of Gray's Inn discussed this very proposition in the 1520s.[106] What if Parliament granted land on condition that it should

---

[101] See, e.g., *Case of the Marshalsea* (1612) 10 Co. Rep. 68 at p. 74, *per* Coke CJ: 'This statute of *Articuli super Cartas* is not introductory of new law, but an explanation of the great charter, which was declaratory of the ancient common law of England.' See also above, p. 16; below, p. 501.

[102] *Dr Bonham's Case* (1610) 8 Co. Rep. 114; 2 Bro. & Golds. 255 at p. 265. For recent comment see I. Williams, 'Dr Bonham's Case and "Void" Statutes' (2006) 27 *Journal of Legal History* 111–28; R. H. Helmholz, 'Bonham's Case, Judicial Review, and the Law of Nature' (2009) 1 *Journal of Legal Analysis* 324–53; Smith, *Sir Edward Coke*, pp. 168–73.

[103] Ellesmere, 'Observations upon Coke's Reports', pp. 306–7; speech on the installation of Montagu CJ, below, p. 439.

[104] See, e.g., C. M. Gray, 'Bonham's Case Revisited' (1972) 116 *Proceedings of the American Philosophical Society* 35–58. Substantial parallel manuscript reports of *Bonham's Case* (e.g. BL MS. Add. 9844, fos. 89v–93v) make no mention of Coke's doctrine. But cf. *Darcy v. Allen* (1602) Noy 173 at p. 180, *per* Fuller ('an Act of Parliament against the law of God directly is void', e.g. a statute prohibiting a man from living by his own labour); *Doylie's Case* (1605) BL MS. Hargrave 19, fo. 179v, *per* Tanfield (repugnancy in an act of Parliament makes it void); anonymous note on *Bate's Case* (1606) BL MS. Hargrave 34, fo. 54 ('The judges may, to avoid an inconvenience in law, control an Act of Parliament'); *Day v. Savadge* (1615) Hob. 85 at p. 87.

[105] Baker, *Collected Papers*, i. 209; ii. 940–1; below, p. 477. Coke CJ himself said the point he made in *Bonham's Case* was about repugnancy: *Rowles v. Mason* (1612) 2 Bro. & Gold. 192 at p. 198.

[106] BL MS. Add. 35939, fo. 269 (*c.* 1526/9); printed in translation in Baker, *Collected Papers*, ii. 942–4; see also below, pp. 103–4.

not escheat to the lord from whom it was held, or that it should not descend to heirs? These were such incomprehensible conditions, in the thinking of the time,[107] that several of the benchers thought they would be invalid; no sensible effect could be given to them. 'Parliament,' said Robert Wroth,[108] 'may not do something which is against law and reason.' Even the solicitor-general, Christopher Hales, who had served in the parliament of 1523–5, maintained that Parliament could not make a law which was absurd, such as removing a piece of land from human ownership. The benchers who argued on the other side asked how a statute could ever be invalid, since everyone in the realm had consented to it through their representatives in Parliament.[109] But Hales hinted that it was all a matter of interpretation. An Act of Parliament was to be construed according to common law and reason, and if it was so obscure that it could not be understood by law or reason it could hardly be given any effect.[110] The courts might on the same principle correct obvious verbal errors in Acts of Parliament.[111] In the days before official printing guaranteed an authentic text, the result could be achieved by presuming that the received text was corrupt, or even that the clerk of the parliaments must have misunderstood what Parliament had agreed.[112] What is more surprising about the readings discussed above is the general assumption that parts of Magna Carta could be treated as 'void' without any sign of an explicit intention to abrogate them, a position which has been rejected in the present age.[113]

---

[107] Parliament did abolish descent to heirs in 1925, but not escheat.

[108] Wroth (d. 1535) became a MP in 1529 and attorney-general of the duchy of Lancaster in 1531.

[109] For this doctrine see *Merton College, Oxford* v. *Woodlark* (1463) YB Trin. 3 Edw. IV, fo. 1, pl. 1, at fo. 2. The defendant, Robert Woodlark, was sued as provost of King's College, Cambridge: see the record, CP 40/809, m. 122.

[110] John Kitchin said in 1564 that if Parliament granted the manor of Dale in Middlesex, and there was no such manor, nothing would pass: reading in Gray's Inn, BL MS. Lansdowne 1134, fo. 47. But he said that Parliament could grant land to a married woman, alien or monk, presumably because they could be given legal capacity by legislation.

[111] E.g. where Parliament introduced a new criminal offence and enacted that those who did *not* commit the offence should be punished: *Lord Cromwell's Case* (c. 1581/2) 4 Co. Rep. 12; autograph version in BL MS. Harley 6687, fo. 313v (noted in 1582).

[112] HLS MS. 13, fo. 253 (from a late fifteenth-century moot); *Spelman's Reports*, p. 44.

[113] *Thoburn* v. *Sunderland City Council* [2003] QB 151 at pp. 186–7, *per* Laws LJ; above, p. 24. These current references to Magna Carta, however, must be taken to refer solely to c. 29.

There is no trace, then, of an elevated constitutional theme to be found in the workaday common learning passed on through the readings. Far from glittering in gold letters, Magna Carta seems still to be written in ever-fading sepia ink. Even the lectures on chapter 29 showed no hint of its later fame. It was stock learning (glossing the word *capiatur*) that its main consequence was to prevent the issue of a judicial writ of *capias* to arrest a party where there was no original writ, and that was merely a reinforcement of the common law. The words 'judgment of his peers' were particularly problematic.[114] They were held to protect – if not introduce[115] – trial by peers for the peerage, the lords of Parliament. But, if that was so, it seemed to follow that the entire provision about going and sending against people – whatever that meant – was confined to the peerage, and in consequence that 'unless by the law of the land' was similarly confined. That was perhaps one understanding in the fifteenth century,[116] and it explained why trial by peers was not available in an appeal of felony brought against a peer by a subject, but it made grammatical nonsense of the earlier words. The word-by-word analysing of the text, to which lawyers were accustomed, threatened to deprive chapter 29 of most of its meaning.

Although some of the problems with chapter 29 were removed in 1354,[117] the readers generally ignored the statutory revisions and explanations of Magna Carta. The Ordinary Gloss mentioned the 1354 statute in passing, but it was not given close attention.[118] Due process was not seen as a particularly telling phrase, and little time was spent on it.[119] It was not a 'concept' at all, since it meant no more than the ordinary procedure of the law, a procedure which could always be altered by statute. Moreover, as another reader pointed out, a man could in some cases be lawfully imprisoned without any due process, as where he was arrested on suspicion of felony.[120]

The meaning of 'peers' was not explored with any rigour, for the provision in chapter 14 that earls and barons were to be amerced by

---

[114] See above, pp. 37–8.

[115] See *Lord Grey of Codnor's Case*, identifiable as *Preston* v. *Lord Grey of Codnor* (1442) KB 27/725, m. 94, cited in YB Pas. 10 Edw. IV (47 SS), p. 63, pl. 17, *per* Littleton sjt.

[116] *Selected Readings on Magna Carta*, pp. 247, 253, 254. It is also found as late as 1544: ibid. 256.

[117] Above, pp. 33, 41.   [118] *Selected Readings on Magna Carta*, p. 248.

[119] One fifteenth-century reader took the trouble to list the statutes referring to due process but did not comment on them: ibid. 251.

[120] Ibid. 251. See further above, pp. 39, 41.

their peers was generally reinterpreted – realistically,[121] but clean contrary to the common understanding of 'peers' in chapter 29 – to mean
amercement by the barons of the Exchequer. No reader sought to
explain in what sense those officials could be considered peers of the
nobility, since they were not at that date even knighted. It was a mere
coincidence of nomenclature, which inevitably raised the question
whether barons of the Exchequer could be the peers of earls as well as
barons.[122] There is no indication in any of these expositions of a clear
constitutional understanding of 'peers', though an eccentric Lincoln's
Inn reader of the 1450s ventured the proposition that commoners
should also be tried by their peers under the statute; he also denied
the doctrines about barons of the Exchequer, and about right and
justice, but his lone voice seems not to have shaken the orthodox
teaching.[123] The notion that 'of his peers' in chapter 29 applied only
to peers of the realm was still current in Coke's time,[124] notwithstanding that 'by his peers' in chapter 14 was at the same time clearly
understood to mean 'by his equals'.[125]

The words 'to no one shall we sell right or justice' were construed,
not just narrowly, but with a narrowness bordering on perversity, to
mean merely that no fine could be charged for a writ of right or a writ of
justicies. Thus, far from being given expansive or even ordinary
meanings, 'right' and 'justice' were held not to apply to the king's
central institutions at all: they were confined to writs of right, which
conferred jurisdiction on lords in their seignorial courts, and writs of
justicies, which conferred jurisdiction on sheriffs in their county courts.
This was an exercise in word association rather than rational jurisprudence. Yet if the words were to be given a broader meaning, as
one reader pointed out, it would render illegal the fines which were
regularly taken for other original writs according to the custom of

---

[121] It reflected the practice since the time of Magna Carta itself: *Bracton*, ii. 334; Holt,
    Magna Carta, p. 280; L. W. Harcourt, 'The Amercement of Barons by their Peers' (1907)
    22 EHR 732–40, at pp. 735–7.
[122] *Selected Readings on Magna Carta*, p. 159.
[123] Ibid. 249; below, Appendix 1, p. 452. A slightly later Lincoln's Inn reading reverted to the
    earlier learning, as did the early sixteenth-century Chaloner text: *Selected Readings on
    Magna Carta*, pp. 170*bis*, 252.
[124] See Coke's memorandum on c. 29 (1604) below, p. 509; Co. Inst. ii. 48–50; above, p. 65.
[125] Co. Inst. ii. 28. This was not a new interpretation. In the context of a court leet, it was
    held to mean the suitors rather than the lord's steward: *Selected Readings on Magna
    Carta*, p. 341, *per* Brudenell (*c.* 1505/15).

the Chancery.[126] St German, writing in the 1530s but imbued with the same common learning, still associated 'right' with the writ of right and 'sell' with the availability of the writ without fine.[127] The traditional doctrine lived on even as right and justice were achieving a more generous interpretation.[128] A century later, Coke referred without explicit disapproval to the 'old readers' who 'supposed' that 'right' here meant the writ of right, though he treated this as a secondary meaning.[129] Delaying justice was treated by the old readers with a corresponding minimalism, as being solely concerned with abuses of the procedure for praying aid of the king.[130]

It seems strange with hindsight that such narrowly technical meanings were given to words which seem so naturally expansive. Perhaps the explanation is that positive remedies against the crown were so unthinkable and unheard of, before the sixteenth century, that it could safely be assumed they were not intended. Several readers pointed out that chapter 29 provided no new remedies, though there was occasional speculation that an action might be founded on the statute despite the absence of an express provision for one.[131] In fact there was an express general provision in chapter 5 of the Statute of Marlborough 1267 that writs should be freely granted against those who contravened Magna Carta,[132] and there was a writ in the Register

---

[126] Ibid. 250; below, Appendix 1, p. 453. The reader, unconventionally, held that such fines were indeed illegal. But that question had been laid to rest in the fourteenth century: above, p. 47.

[127] *Doctor and Student*, 91 SS 65.

[128] See James Morice's reading (1578), fo. 14: 'By force of which statute it hath been ever since used that a writ of right should be freely granted to the subject without paying any fine for the same in the king's Chancery, as by his royal prerogative for other writs is accustomed.' Morice did, however, deduce from this the constitutional principle that royal prerogatives could be taken away by Parliament.

[129] Co. Inst. ii. 57. He did not deal with this branch of c. 29 in the memorandum of 1604.

[130] This was in the Ordinary Gloss and still repeated in a reading of 1544: *Selected Readings on Magna Carta*, pp. 249, 256. The remedy which they derived from c. 29 was the *procedendo in loquela*, or (after judgment) the *procedendo ad judicium*. One more imaginative reader also thought the petition of right was a direct result of the same clause: ibid. 250; below, Appendix 1, p. 453.

[131] E.g. *Selected Readings on Magna Carta*, p. 247. The Chaloner manuscript, ibid. 254, contains the only reference in a reading to a real example, identifiable as *Abbot of Bury* v. *Adams* (1514–17) KB 27/1011, m. 33d; below, p. 461. Note also C. St German, *Litle Treatise on the Subpena*, ed. J. Guy (6 SS Suppl. Series, 1985), p. 121), perhaps alluding to *Parnell* v. *Vaughan* (1533) KB 27/1082, m. 37; below, pp. 98, 462.

[132] Statute of Marlborough 1267, c. 5.

founded on another chapter of Magna Carta.[133] But little or nothing was made of this in the readings on either statute. The introduction around 1501 of an action for damages based on chapter 29 therefore owed no debt to the common learning of the inns of court, and in any case the experiment was short lived.[134] Nor did chapter 29 infiltrate the constitutional or juristic arguments of the fifteenth-century Bench and Bar. Sir John Fortescue's works, including his encomium of English law, and his treatise on constitutional monarchy, written in the mid fifteenth century, contain no mention of it.[135] Even in the 1520s Christopher St German could write a treatise on the basic principles of the laws of England (*De Fundamentis Legum Angliae et de Consciencia*)[136] without so much as hinting at any connection between those fundamentals and Magna Carta.

Stirrings of Change

The disdain shown by the late-medieval readers for the important Edward III statutes of due process might seem to modern eyes perplexing. It is a fair conjecture that, even if they had chosen to lecture on due process, the readers would have done no more than list the myriad forms of procedure required in different cases. But it was simply not the custom to lecture on the *Statuta Nova* – the 'new' statutes passed after the reign of Edward II – which were usually separated in the statute-books from the *Statuta Vetera*, the old testament of English law. The newer style of legislation, with preambles and detailed provisions, was less amenable to critical analysis of the traditional kind. It was more profitable, for teaching purposes, to introduce students to the broad and often obscure language of the foundational texts. When recent statutes did enter the curriculum, in

---

[133] The writ *de moderata misericordia* recited the wording of c. 14. This was pointed out by counsel in *Waterhouse* v. *Mady* (1606) CUL MS. Gg.2.23, fo. 26, as proof that an action could be founded on a statute containing a general prohibition.

[134] See below, pp. 97–9, 456–62.

[135] It is fair to add that Fortescue did not cite legal authorities at all in these works, which were not addressed to lawyers. His defence of constitutional monarchy was primarily based on economic arguments. The absence of any reference to Magna Carta does not indicate that it had no influence on his thinking, only that it was not yet the scriptural authority that it became.

[136] First published with this title in 1528. It was enlarged in the 1530s and became *Doctor and Student*.

the Tudor period,[137] a new kind of pedantry would indeed take over.[138] But by then Magna Carta and its progeny had been consigned, for the time being, to history. It was no longer on the regular curriculum.

There are glimmerings of a new approach, albeit still heterodox, in the prefatory lecture given by Richard Hesketh, of Gray's Inn, in his reading on the *Carta de Foresta*.[139] Forest law was still of practical usefulness, and the two Tudor readings by Hesketh (*c.* 1506) and George Treherne (1520) remained standard works of authority into the seventeenth century. Hesketh regarded the forest charter as a royal grant rather than a statute, but he held that (as in the case of the great charter) it had been turned into a statute as a result of parliamentary confimations, beginning with Marlborough. More significantly, he held that it should be interpreted expansively against the crown, 'in favour of liberty'. This principle of interpretation was, as Hesketh pointed out, contrary to the usual rule that grants by the king were construed in favour of the king, and contrary to the doctrine that statutes touching the king, such as *Prerogativa Regis*, should be construed equitably in support of the rights of the crown. It was also, of course, a complete reversal of the approach embodied in the Ordinary Gloss a century before.[140] The departure, according to Hesketh, was justified by the manifest intention of remedying the previous grievances of the subject.[141] Although Hesketh was referring directly only to the forest charter, his argument would have applied with at least equal force to the great charter of liberties. Perhaps here we see Magna Carta just beginning to enter its new career as a statute of unique status, foremost among statutes not merely for rhetorical purposes but for purposes of legal argument as well.

---

[137] The earliest known reading on a recent statute was that by Gregory Adgore (*c.* 1490), but it was not until the 1530s that it became common to lecture on Tudor legislation: *Readers and Readings*, pp. 35, 69, 79.

[138] See the complaints of William Fleetwood and Sir Edward Coke, below, p. 238.

[139] Printed in *Selected Readings on Magna Carta*, pp. 362–3. The precise date is unknown, but there is an internal precedent of an indictment dated 1506. See also *Readers and Readings*, p. 29.

[140] Hervy, only a few years earlier, held that the king was not bound by c. 11 because he was not mentioned: *Selected Readings on Magna Carta*, p. 50. Cf. the reading on Marlborough, c. 5, which said that Magna Carta bound the king as well as the commonalty: Gray's Inn MS. 25, fo. 117.

[141] As another reader pointed out, not all the provisions of Magna Carta concerned the liberties of the subject. Some, such as c. 36, prohibiting alienations in mortmain, actually restrained previous liberties: Thompson, p. 193.

Around this time there arose a practical interest in the possibility of a remedy founded on chapter 29. A trickle of about a dozen trespass actions reciting the 1225 charter may be found in the King's Bench rolls between 1501 and 1532, some resulting in awards of damages,[142] and a few occur also in the Common Pleas records.[143] The plaintiffs nearly all complained of a summons by writ of privy seal to appear before the king and his Council, and that they had duly attended upon councillors at Westminster in obedience to the writ. The first of them was the most far-reaching, in that damages were recovered (by default) for a suit before the lord keeper and other members of the Council in a matter belonging to the common law. Perhaps the legal profession generally was becoming alarmed by the king's avaricious manipulations of the law,[144] and it seems possible that the progressive chief justice of England, Sir John Fyneux, supported these attempts to restrain sub-conciliar jurisdiction.[145] But for the most part these actions were not challenges to the government or the King's Council itself. When the details are examined, nearly all of them are found to have arisen from proceedings in the Court of Requests, the last being a complaint that a party had been forced into arbitration by the recently discredited Dr Stokesley.[146] The actions were not brought against the councillors, but against the plaintiffs who had sued in the Requests. Two others arose from proceedings before Richard Empson, brought the year after his execution in 1510. In one of them a plaintiff was awarded £30 damages after he had been summoned before Empson at Westminster to answer an accusation of theft, 'without any presentation before justices, or matter of record, or due process or original writ according to the ancient law and custom of the lord king's realm of England', and compelled to attend from day to day until he was forced to pay

---

[142] *Spelman's Reports*, ii. 72; OHLE, vi. 192–3. Those which have been noticed are calendared below, pp. 456–62. It is possible that more might be discovered on a fuller search.

[143] *Younghusband* v. *Prior of Tynemouth* (1510) CP 40/991, m. 529 (which was known to Coke: 132 SS 397); *Brandelyng* v. *Prior of Tynemouth*, ibid., m. 538 (also known to Coke: Co. Inst. ii. 33); *Saunders* v. *Broke* (1524) CP 40/1044, m. 280.

[144] John Spelman of Gray's Inn wrote in his private notebook that Henry VII was 'covetous and of great riches' and that Empson and Dudley strove against the common good to enrich him: *Spelman's Reports*, i. 175.

[145] OHLE, vi. 194.

[146] *Butler* v. *Fuller* (1523–5) KB 27/1048, m. 75. For complaints about Dr Stokesley, and his removal from office, see OHLE, vi. 205. An action was also brought on the 1368 statute in respect of one of his cases: *Pomerey* v. *Bucland* (1523) KB 27/1050, m. 47.

Empson £20.[147] The last action in the series was brought in 1532 to challenge an imprisonment by Sir Thomas More, as lord chancellor, in a suit which had been commenced before his predecessor, Cardinal Wolsey.[148] It arose from a complex and notorious commercial case, at the conclusion of which the unsuccessful plaintiff accused More of accepting a bribe, though the King's Bench action does not seem to have reached a conclusion.[149] Thereafter, perhaps because of a return to greater regularity in the Requests after Stokesley's removal,[150] and because attacks on the Chancery were deemed to be out of bounds, the actions disappeared from sight until 1595.[151]

The writs all recited that, by virtue of the great charter of the ninth year of King Henry III, 'according to the law and free custom of the realm of England every free man ought, in common pleas, to implead and be impleaded by original writs under the lord king's great seal' in the Common Bench or King's Bench, and more than half of them described the 1225 charter as 'the statute concerning those who sue writs under the privy seal which touch the common law'. Neither of these notions was in fact specifically expressed in the charter of 1225. The first was derived from a statute of 1368, and the second from one of 1328.[152] At first glance, this looks like careless draftsmanship. But the explanation may be that the statutes of Edward III were not seen as introducing new law, or even as having independent authority, but were merely explanations of what was already present in the enigmatic wording of the original

---

[147] *Speccote* v. *Frye* (1511) KB 27/997, m. 37 (on 42 Edw. III, c. 3); *Vyseke* v. *Frye* (1511) KB 27/1000, m. 28 (on Magna Carta, c. 29).

[148] *Parnell* v. *Vaughan* (1532) KB 27/1082, m. 37 (claiming 2,000 marks damages). There is a possible allusion to the case in the *Little Treatise on the Subpoena* [c. 1532]: *St German on Chancery and Statute*, ed. J. A. Guy (6 Selden Soc. Suppl. Series, 1985), p. 121, where the author noted an unsettled controversy as to whether an action would lie on Magna Carta for suing in Chancery in a matter belonging to the common law.

[149] The story is unravelled, from the Chancery records, in J. A. Guy, *The Public Career of Sir Thomas More* (Brighton, 1980), pp. 75–7. The accusation was investigated by the Council in 1534, seemingly without result. Guy exonerates More.

[150] He was succeeded by a series of common lawyers: *OHLE*, vi. 205. The Civilians regained control later in the century.

[151] Below, p. 277. There may be more in the rolls between Henry VIII and 1595, which no one has read, but none has been encountered in the much fuller law reports of the period.

[152] 42 Edw. III, c. 3 (above, p. 50); 2 Edw. III, c. 8 (above, p. 52). Neither statute mentioned common pleas, or the benches, but this was a further implication from the phrase 'original writ' in the statute of 1368. One plaintiff framed his action on the 1368 statute, but referred to it in the sense of the 1328 enactment: *Speccote* v. *Frye* (1511) KB 27/997, m. 37.

charter. This, again, might be taken as evidence of the overriding importance attached to Magna Carta in comparison with the minutiae of the *Statuta Nova*.

Alive to this ripple of protest against abuses of due process by Henry VII's councillors, the new King Henry VIII was advised to invoke Magna Carta, immediately after his accession in 1509, in order to restore confidence in the government after the rapaciousness of his father's last years.[153] The nationwide commissions of oyer and terminer issued in the first year of the reign included, for the first time, 'trespasses, contempts and offences against the form of the statute of Magna Carta concerning the liberties of England'.[154] At least one of the indictments reached the King's Bench rolls and was cited by Coke.[155] The commissions, which were revoked later in the year, were chiefly aimed against Empson and Dudley, and offences against chapter 29 of the charter featured in the indictments which were collected against them and others.[156] Some of the complaints were very similar to those in the statutory actions, and evidently arose from similar proceedings in the new tribunals which had sprung up without statutory authority in the previous reign. It was in the same context that the new king agreed to the repeal of the statute of 1495 which had introduced summary trial for misdemeanours, on the grounds that it had been used as a means of extortion:[157] 'A good caveat to Parliaments', as Coke later wrote, 'to leave all causes to be measured by the golden and strait metwand of the law,

[153] J. Cooper, 'Henry VII's Last Years Reconsidered' (1959) 2 *Historical Journal* 103–29, at pp. 117–23.

[154] G. R. Elton, *Studies in Tudor and Stuart Politics and Government* (Cambridge, 1974–92), i. 88–9; Cooper, 'Henry VII's Last Years', pp. 117–18.

[155] *R. v. Phillip* (1511) KB 27/999, Rex, m. 5; below, pp. 460, 503. Phillip was indicted before commissioners in Sussex on 17 August 1509, and the indictment was moved into the King's Bench so that the attorney-general could confess his plea of not guilty. He had obtained the royal favour, being a yeoman of the crown. Note also *R. v. Chancey* (1509) in Catlyn CJ's precedent book, Alnwick Castle MS. 475, fo. 24; the bill of indictment (in French), presented before commissioners, was for suing a false action before Sir Robert Sheffield, contrary to the statute 42 Edw. III, c. 3; this was also dated 17 August 1509.

[156] E.g. the indictment of Empson (excerpted in Co. Inst. iv. 198) as given in Cooper, 'Henry VII's Last Years', p. 120, citing KB 9/453/469. The indictment of Empson as printed in 1 And. 156 alleged, inter alia, that he had caused subjects to be (tr.) 'imprisoned in various prisons without any process according to the law of the land ... and so detained them that they could not answer such false indictments according to the law of the realm'; but there is no express recital of c. 29.

[157] 11 Hen. VII, c. 3; 1 Hen. VIII, c. 6. Coke thought this was in deference to c. 29: Co. Inst. ii. 51. See also Cooper, 'Henry VII's Last Years', at p. 125.

and not to the uncertain and crooked cord of discretion.'[158] The same Parliament also reformed the procedure used in inquisitions into crown titles, and in granting liveries of land to heirs, reciting the abuses committed by Empson and Dudley.[159] The Council Learned in the Law, a committee of the Council dominated by that over-zealous pair, in concert with the law officers, with the principal object of increasing the royal revenue, was discontinued.[160] On the other hand, the king rejected the advice of the judges in the Star Chamber to abolish all 'petty' courts which were not of record, meaning the new sub-conciliar tribunals,[161] and refused his assent to a bill which had passed both houses of Parliament to abolish proceedings by subpoena under the privy seal except in the Council of the Marches of Wales.[162] That would have done away with the Requests altogether, a drastic measure not achieved until the 1640s.

This short-lived resurgence of chapter 29 in 1509 was of limited effect. It was not deployed against the king. Indeed, it was the king or his close advisers who had invoked it against fallen ministers and officials, not subjects complaining about the government of the day.[163] The same is true of the complaint said to have been made against Wolsey in 1529, at the time of his fall, that he had stayed the common law by injunctions, contrary to Magna Carta.[164] Even the accuracy of this recollection is uncertain, since the formal articles against Wolsey, signed by Sir Thomas More and numerous peers and judges, did not in fact mention Magna Carta.[165] But an entirely different kind of case arose in the King's Council in 1532, after Humphrey Browne, a serjeant at law and later a judge, was committed to the Tower by the king and then released without charge. When he subsequently complained,[166] all the judges were summoned before the Council to say whether the king could send people to prison at

---

[158] Co. Inst. iv. 41. A metwand was a measuring rod, or ruler.

[159] 1 Hen. VIII, c. 8, 12; Co. Inst. iv. 196–8.   [160] OHLE, vi. 193–4.   [161] Ibid. 194–5.

[162] Journals of the House of Lords, ii. 5–7. For the Council in the Marches see below, pp. 209, 302, 346.

[163] Cf., on a lower plane, Anon. (1518/29) C1/600/29 (a complaint of imprisonment in the city of London, at the suit of one Semer, contrary to Magna Carta; the plaintiff's name is illegible).

[164] This was Stephen Gardiner's recollection in 1547, quoted by Foxe: Thompson, Magna Carta, p. 142 ('And upon that occasion Magna Carta was spoken of, and it was made a great matter, the stay of the common law'). A. F. Pollard, Wolsey (1929), p. 259, suggested that it was c. 1 which Wolsey was alleged to have infringed.

[165] The text was printed in Co. Inst. iv. 89–95, from the original manuscript on vellum (as to which see below, p. 213).

[166] It was not a habeas corpus case, since he was no longer in custody.

his discretion. And the judges advised that, although the king's discretion could no more be questioned than that of an ordinary judge, the cause of imprisonment could be examined to see whether it was lawful; and this was because it appeared from chapter 29 of Magna Carta that the king could not treat his subjects contrary to the law.[167] This notable pronouncement was perhaps the bravest application of Magna Carta before the reign of James I, since it was aimed directly against the king or his chief ministers. It did not, however, establish a substantive remedy, and in any case the only known report of the proceedings was not published until 1977.[168] Nor did it begin a new judicial approach to the king's prerogative. Henry VIII was not easily challenged.

The last known reading on Magna Carta of the old kind was that given in 1544 by Richard Blackwall in Clement's Inn, one of the inns of Chancery where younger students were prepared prior to attending the inns of court.[169] He recognised that in some situations an action could be founded on Magna Carta. But otherwise he showed no awareness of new trends, and in his exposition of chapter 29 he continued the restrictive tradition by treating *capiatur* as applying only to the improper use of writs of *capias*, and *disseisiatur* as applying only to improperly obtained writs of *habere facias seisinam*. He did not mention its potential application to extrajudicial infringements of liberty, such as that in Serjeant Browne's case.

A Reading on Constitutional Law in about 1529

Although Magna Carta disappeared from the regular curriculum of the Tudor inns of court, and also (it seems) from the courts of law, a new interest in constitutional matters may be detected around 1530. The proceedings of the Reformation Parliament, which commenced in 1529, and grumbles about the growing activity of the Court of Chancery under Wolsey and More, were giving rise to keen debate within the

---

[167] *Serjeant Browne's Case* (1532) *Spelman's Reports*, i. 183–4 (there misdated 1540); *OHLE*, vi. 91.

[168] When Browne was locked up again, in 1540, for advising clients on the avoidance of feudal incidents, there was no suggestion of a remedy. But he was then one of the king's serjeants, and for king's counsel to advise on tax avoidance was no doubt considered a misdemeanour: *OHLE*, vi. 681.

[169] *Selected Readings on Magna Carta*, pp. 255–6. Blackwall was a barrister of the Inner Temple. For the inns of chancery see J. [H.] Baker, *The Inns of Chancery 1340–1640* (19 SS Suppl. Series, 2017); *Readers and Readings*, pp. 187–90.

profession which supplied so many members of the House of Commons. It was in this context that one innovative reader of Gray's Inn was emboldened to explore the question how far the king could interfere with the common law through the exercise of his royal prerogative. The reading has not been noticed before but deserves some attention.[170] It was written at the end of a volume containing transcripts of Gray's Inn readings from 1530 to 1547,[171] and was copied by Christopher Yelverton as an addition to the main text, using the minute hieroglyphics in which he wrote rough notes. The table of contents, written by the copyist's son Sir Henry Yelverton (d. 1630), justice of the Common Pleas, did not even recognise it as one of the readings.[172] That it was indeed a reading is shown by its similarity in form to the other contents of the volume, and also by a reference to 'the statute' in one of the headings. Neither the reader nor his inn is named, but the citation of a case dated in the margin as '21 H. 8', and references to the pope, abbots and monks as part of the legal landscape, indicate a date between 1529 and 1534, though it could be slightly earlier.[173] The most likely candidate is Richard Sackvile, who read in Gray's Inn in Lent 1529, the year before the earliest of the dated readings in the volume.[174] The statutory text on which the reading was given is not set out or glossed verbatim, but it was evidently the statute of 1340 which enacted that the justices should not 'leave aside doing common law' by reason of the king's commands under the great seal or privy seal.[175]

The reason for this apparently unique choice of text could be that the reader was primarily interested in the debate over Chancery jurisdiction, which was being aired at the same period by Christopher St German, and which was dependent on injunctions to stop the justices from applying

---

[170] BL MS. Hargrave 92, fos. 119–131v.

[171] Cf. BL MS. Hargrave 88, which also belonged to Yelverton, and has Gray's Inn readings from 1530 to 1542. For the two manuscripts see *Readers and Readings*, pp. 326–8, 330–3.

[172] These factors explain why it was overlooked in *Readers and Readings*.

[173] The case dated 21 Hen. VIII (on fo. 126) seems in fact to be the well reported case decided by the Exchequer Chamber in June or July 1527: YB Trin. 19 Hen. VIII, fo. 9, pl. 4; *Reports temp. Henry VIII*, i. 60; ii. 260, 361. It is conceivable that Yelverton misread xix as xxi.

[174] Three junior benchers of Gray's Inn were elected to serve in the parliament summoned in August 1529: John Hynde (reader in Lent 1527), Robert Wroth (Autumn 1527) and Richard Sackvile (Lent 1529).

[175] 14 Edw. III, stat. 1, c. 14 (tr.). Cf. the heading on fo. 127 of the reading: (tr.) 'the statute is that the justices should go on and hold their courts as if no such writs had come'. This is, however, a paraphrase rather than a quotation.

the common law.[176] A considerable portion of the reading was devoted to the Chancery. Only in the previous generation it had been taught that the English-bill procedure of the Chancery was no part of the *lex terrae*,[177] and the position of the King's Council was even more dubious.[178] The reading shows that the equitable jurisdiction of the Chancery was now tacitly assumed to be part of the law of the land,[179] yet firmly circumscribed by the law. It could not meddle directly with the common law. For instance, if the Chancery were to decree that a penal bond was void, or ought to be cancelled on equitable grounds, an action at law could still be brought on the bond and the decree could not be pleaded. This was orthodox learning, because the chancellor's jurisdiction was solely *in personam*.[180] The equitable remedy was for the Chancery to stop the action being pursued, contrary to good conscience, by means of an injunction. Many detailed examples were given in the reading to clarify the limits of this power, with lectures under the headings 'What decrees given in court of conscience before the chancellor are void, and what not'; 'Where a man may have a right in conscience and yet no remedy in the Chancery'; 'For what causes the chancellor may grant an injunction, and for what not'; and 'Where a man shall have a subpoena in lieu of common actions where he has no remedy at common law, and where not'. The reader stopped short, however, of venturing onto the authority of the newer conciliar courts.

Although the Chancery may have been at the heart of the exercise, the reader nevertheless tackled his subject with thoroughness. Since the statute began by referring to petitions in Parliament, he began with Parliament.[181] The opening lecture, on the procedure for passing

---

[176] *OHLE*, vi. 39–46, 175–8; D. E. C. Yale, 'St German's Little Treatise concerning Writs of Subpoena' (1975) 10 *Irish Jurist* (New Series) 324–33; J. Guy, *Christopher St German on Chancery and Statute* (6 SS Suppl. Series, 1985).

[177] Reading on Magna Carta (Lincoln's Inn, *c.* 1491/1508), below, pp. 454–5. In 1297 the people of Ireland had asked for a grant of Magna Carta, and for procedure before the justiciar to be commenced by writ rather than by bill, suggesting that this was seen as the hallmark of due process: SC 8/53/2643.

[178] Kidwelly did not include it in his list of royal courts at all, and its coercive powers were arguably illegal: see above, pp. 97–8.

[179] Francis Ashley admitted in 1616 that the *subpoena* could not be traced before the reign of Henry IV, but said it had become *lex terrae* as a result of parliamentary confirmation: CUL MS. Ee.6.3, fo. 121.

[180] I.e. the chancellor could coerce the conscience of the party by threat of imprisonment, but could not decide questions of property or legal obligation.

[181] Several readers in Elizabeth's reign prefaced their readings with a lecture or two on Parliament, discussing how it could be summoned and what assents were necessary for a valid Act: e.g. (in Gray's Inn) John Kitchin (1564) BL MS. Lansdowne 1134, fos. 43v–47;

legislation, is not unlike Kidwelly's and refers to the same year-book case, but it is much less detailed. The second lecture raised the novel question, 'What Acts of Parliament may lawfully be observed and performed, and what not'. Some of the examples were of factual impossibility, but they extended to legal absurdity, such as a statute ordering one man to kill another,[182] or granting land with no tenure. The only other known discussion of such questions in this period was that already mentioned as having taken place in Gray's Inn while Christopher Hales was solicitor-general and Richard Broke was chief baron (both 1526-9),[183] and it seems highly probable that it occurred at the same reading. The exact date is obscured by the apparent citation of a case dated 21 Hen. VIII, which does not quite coincide with those participants,[184] but the date may have been an error for 19 Hen. VIII.[185] The discussion was not, however, about judicial review of legislation, which was beyond the competence of ordinary courts of law. It was about how to deal with legislation which seemed not to make sense. There was no mention of fundamental law, no hint that a statute contrary to natural law or Magna Carta might be invalid.

The explanation for this new interest in the question of legislative competence may well have been that minds were turning to the ability of Parliament to reform the Church. The very next lecture was on the subject, 'What laws Parliament may make to bind the spiritualty, and how they shall be bound'. It began by asserting the authority of Parliament to override canon law, choosing an example which had divided the spiritualty and laity since Richard Hunne's case and was addressed in the 1529 parliament:[186] Parliament could abolish mortuaries. Parliament could grant tithes to a layman.[187] It could forbid abbots or deans to serve

---

Richard Chisnall (1565) ibid., fos. 31v, 33; Humphrey Purefoy (1578) HLS MS. 1180(1), fo. 347.

[182] Here (fo. 119) a distinction is drawn between law and morality: (tr.) '[If] it is enacted that John Style should kill John Dale, this Act ought not to be observed, but if he does it he is not punishable.'

[183] BL MS. Add. 35939, fo. 269; tr. in Baker, *Collected Papers*, ii. 942-4. For this discussion see above, p. 90.

[184] The regnal year 21 Hen. VIII commenced on 22 April 1529, after the Lent vacation (when Sackvile read), whereas Broke died in May 1529 and Hales ceased to be solicitor-general on 3 June 1529, before the autumnal reading.

[185] See above, p. 102 n. 173.   [186] Below, p. 123; 21 Hen. VIII, c. 6.

[187] This became of fundamental importance when the monasteries were dissolved in the 1530s. A dissolution of at least some monasteries was already under consideration in 1529.

for more than ten years. But there was no suggestion as yet that Parliament was omnicompetent.[188] It could not impose a limit of tenure on bishops or priests, presumably because it could not override or qualify consecration or ordination. It could not require the ordinary to give holy orders to anyone who sought them, though it could require him to give orders to anyone qualified. If Parliament enacted that the pope should not give benefices by provision, or take annates, that would not bind him; but that was only because he was foreign. Parliament could instead forbid English priests to receive benefices by provision, or English bishops to pay annates to the pope, and this would achieve the same result. The geographical reach of parliamentary legislation was pursued further in the fifth lecture. It was, according to the reader, a matter of jurisdiction rather than direct representation. Wales, and the palatinates of Chester and Durham, were bound by Acts of Parliament, even though they sent no members to Parliament, since they were part of the realm, whereas Irish people were bound only when they visited England.[189] The reader then discussed cases where foreigners were or were not bound by English statutes.

The next section of the reading addressed the topic, 'What laws the king may make without Parliament'. A distinction was here drawn between acts of the commons, lords and king (*jus politicum et civile*), acts of the king and his Council (*jus regale et politicum*), and acts of the king alone (*jus regale tantum*).[190] The king by himself could appoint laws for newly conquered regions,[191] and he could do certain things by proclamation, such as altering the currency, but not imprisoning people contrary to law.[192] The clear implication is that the king could not alter

---

[188] Serjeant Fleetwood asserted in the 1580s that 'no Act of Parliament made repugnant to the word of God is of any force': *Dolman* v. *Bishop of Salisbury* (1583) in his 'Notes for Arguments', fo. 306. The word of God was not, of course, synonymous with man-made canon law.

[189] Ireland was a lordship united to the crown of England but not part of the kingdom: *OHLE*, vi. 108–11. Cf. the reverse case in Richard Chisnall's reading in Gray's Inn (1565) BL MS. Lansdowne 1134, fo. 32v: if the lords and commons of Scotland, Ireland or Wales were summoned to a parliament in England and they made a statute affecting England, it would not be a valid statute.

[190] Sir John Fortescue, in the previous century, had distinguished *jus regale* from *jus politicum et regale* as indicating two distinct forms of monarchy: J. Fortescue, *The Governance of England*, ed. C. Plummer (Oxford, 1885), pp. 114–15. The reader's analysis, which added *civile*, was threefold.

[191] This did not, according to the reader, include Wales. English law was extended to Wales by Act of Parliament in 1536: 27 Hen. VIII, c. 26.

[192] A distinction is here made (fo. 120, tr.): 'The king makes proclamation that John Style should arrest John Dale and put him in prison, and he does it: false imprisonment lies

the law by proclamation.[193] Superior orders from the king did not always constitute a defence. If the king sent a writ to bring a debtor before himself rather than a judge, false imprisonment would lie against the person who carried out the command. And no command from the king could be relied on in law unless it was in writing. The doctrine that the king could do no wrong had evidently become part of the common learning.[194] Considerable attention was then given by the reader to royal licences and pardons, which could not be granted so as to prejudice individuals or subvert the law. Thus, a licence to dig for treasure trove or minerals did not entitle the licensee to dig on private land without permission, unless there was a custom to do so. Nor, it seems, could licences be used to evade laws made in the public interest: if, for instance, the king licensed a surgeon to practise without the statutory qualification, this would be invalid.

Before turning to the Chancery, the reader gratuitously inserted a lecture on 'What laws the clergy may make in their Convocation to bind the king's subjects'. It is not clear how this related to the statute of 1340, though it is clear enough why it would have interested lawyers and law students around 1529.[195] The most important lesson taught on this occasion was that the clergy could not deal with temporal matters, such as payments of money. They could not, for example, impose a monetary penalty for not observing a holy day, though they could impose a penance. They could not even impose a tax of twopence a year on priests. They could, however, assess a fine on someone who abjured heresy in Convocation, and collect it through the Exchequer. The reading ended with an interesting discussion of who were the 'justices' intended by the statute. This permitted some indulgence of a common lawyer's humour, in the proposition that infants, lunatics and doctors of civil law could not be judges. More to the present purpose was the assertion that the king could act as a justice between party and party, and his judgment would be binding, provided the case did not concern his person or his crown. The lecture generally resembles that found in an Inner Temple reading of

against him and this proclamation is not pleadable ... But if John Dale is a suspected felon, and proclamation is made that he should be arrested, the person who arrests him may justify it.'

[193] This was clearly understood in 1539 when Parliament refused to give the king even a statutory power to legislate by proclamation: *OHLE*, vi. 64. For proclamations see further below, pp. 151–4, 390–6.

[194] For the doctrine see above, p. 45.

[195] The convocation of Canterbury met simultaneously with the parliament in 1529.

1512, on chapter 11 of Magna Carta, including similar assertions about the king's role in relation to certifying deaths on the field of battle or while fleeing from the field.[196]

Towards the end of his course, the reader returned to the main point of the statute, royal interference with litigation. This had already been considered in relation to injunctions, but it still remained to treat of writs of privilege, original writs issued where there was no jurisdiction,[197] and writs of protection. The *supersedeas* of privilege stopped a lawsuit, but only on the basis that the defendant should properly have been sued in the court where he was an official or litigant. The writ of protection took several forms, and the reader's account is broadly similar to that in Fitzherbert's *Novel Natura Brevium* (1538). The protection with the clause *nolumus* was designed to safeguard the property of religious houses 'or other simple people' in fear of their persons or property.[198] It was no longer in use, because justices of the peace could give a remedy by surety of the peace. The writ with the clause *volumus* could stay a lawsuit for a year where the defendant was on royal service abroad, or about to go on such service, and the reader thought it was limited to functions relating to war. There was also a prerogative protection for someone indebted to the king,[199] and another (not mentioned by Fitzherbert) for the nurse of the king's son. The scope of these writs had been repeatedly circumscribed by judicial decisions, beginning in the fourteenth century, and there were over one hundred cases on the subject in Fitzherbert's *Graunde Abridgement* (1514–16). There were a number of actions in which they could not be pleaded, and they could never delay proceedings for more than a year.[200] Some, but by no means all, of this medieval learning was collected in the reading.

In these hieroglyphic pages, preserved for us only by an afterthought of Christopher Yelverton's, we have the earliest detailed lecture in an inn

---

[196] Edward Hales's reading (Inner Temple, 1512) *Selected Readings on Magna Carta*, pp. 148–9; above, p. 55.

[197] The reader took the view (fo. 129) that if an action on the case was brought against an innkeeper in the King's Bench, the writ could be ignored, because it was a common plea (and therefore contrary to Magna Carta, c. 11). This was also the view of Edward Hales (previous note): *Selected Readings on Magna Carta*, p. 151; cf. *Spelman's Reports*, ii. 58.

[198] See, e.g., the writs of protection issued for the chancellor and proctors of Cambridge University against the town: HLS MS. 26, fo. 242v; Cambridge University Archives, Misc. Collect. 4, fo. 123.

[199] Below, pp. 174–9.

[200] In 1461 the Common Pleas rejected a protection granted for three years: YB Hil. 39 Hen. VI, fo. 38, pl. 3.

of court on practical constitutional law. The focus was entirely different from that of the readings on *Prerogativa Regis*, which were concerned with the feudal revenues of the crown.[201] Several of the topics addressed, perhaps for the first time in a reading, would become burning issues by the end of the century and will be returned to later in this volume. As usual with readings, the connecting theory is not spelt out but has to be deduced from the strings of illustrative cases. What is especially remarkable, however, is that there was not a single mention of Magna Carta. Far from being the focus of constitutional thinking, it was seemingly irrelevant.

If readers had continued to develop the same themes over the next fifty years, the present book would have been easier to write, because the revival of Magna Carta would have been made explicit; but the innovation in legal education was short lived. In 1540 the lord chancellor, doubtless acting on royal instructions, called all the readers of the inns of court into the Star Chamber and threatened them with 'the king's majesty's high indignation and displeasure, and the danger of the laws', if they did not 'truly and justly' expound the statutes, especially those made for the king's rights and prerogatives, without 'subtle imagination'.[202] This would have been understood to refer primarily to prerogatives of the fiscal kind. The government was desperately worried about a particular brand of subtle imagining which had found effective ways around the Statute of Uses 1536, and it is clear that the principal concern behind the rebuke was the discouragement of tax avoidance.[203] But the threat of Henry VIII's displeasure was frightening enough to freeze, for the time being, any desire to introduce public law into the curriculum.[204]

It has been said that 'but for the corporate solidarity of the English Bench and Bar, centering in the Inns of Court, the conception of a

---

[201] For these see M. McGlynn, *The Royal Prerogative and the Learning of the Inns of Court* (Cambridge, 2003); *Prerogativa Regis: Tertia Lectura Roberti Constable de Lincolnis Inne Anno 11 H. 7*, ed. S. E. Thorne (New Haven, CT, 1949).

[202] Proceedings of 23 February 1540, *Spelman's Reports*, ii. 351.

[203] *OHLE*, vi. 679–81. Several benchers were sent to the Tower until the devices had been checked by the Statute of Wills 1540.

[204] There were later comparable incidents. William Thornton of Lincoln's Inn was sent to prison in 1566 for debating the title of Mary, queen of Scots: *Readers and Readings*, p. 126; J. E. Neale, *Elizabeth I and her Parliaments 1559–81* (1952), p. 133. And in 1640 Edward Bagshaw was in trouble for questioning the jurisdiction of the High Commission: E. Bagshaw, *A Just Vindication of the Questioned Part of the Reading of Edward Bagshaw* (1660), pp. 211, 214–15; W. R. Prest, *The Rise of the Barristers* (Oxford, 1986), p. 23; J. Rose, *Godly Kingship in Restoration England* (Cambridge, 2014), pp. 70–3.

"higher law" of liberty would in all probability have been lost to ... England'.[205] This was a pleasant transatlantic compliment to the inns of court, but it must have referred to a later period than that under consideration in this chapter. On the previous page, the same author wrote that, 'Under the later Plantagenet and the early Lancastrian monarchs Magna Carta took on the semblance of a written constitution even as we know such instruments.' This, however, is not borne out by the legal sources. There is nothing in the way of a higher law of liberty in the readings on Magna Carta before the reign of Elizabeth I, or in the law reports, little or nothing resembling a constitutional interpretation, and no especial reverence shown to its words. The inns of court did not constitute a school of government or politics, let alone a history faculty. They were not interested in uncovering the original intent behind the charter, for which but limited means were available to them anyway, and would not have presumed to lecture anyone on the *arcana imperii* which belonged to the king and his ministers. They were teaching law students a critical appreciation of written legislation and its limitations, and using broadly worded statutory texts as a framework for disputations on difficult points of law. For that purpose, Magna Carta was just another statute, and a largely obsolete one at that.

---

[205] E. S. Corwin, *Liberty against Government* (Baton Rouge, LA, 1952), p. 170. Corwin was Professor of Jurisprudence at Princeton University.

4

Personal Liberty and the Church

Since a significant element in the story of Magna Carta and its reincar-
nation in the later sixteenth century is related to the Church and its
disciplinary jurisdiction, it is necessary to set that part of the scene by
making an excursion away from the secular world of the inns of court
and Westminster Hall to the ecclesiastical sphere, which was governed
by a different system of thought. The spheres were separated intellec-
tually by educational processes and career patterns which were all but
mutually exclusive.[1] At the level of terrestrial justice, there were two
parallel legal systems operating independently in the same kingdom
according to different norms, each perceived by its exponents to be
legally supreme for its own purposes. Common lawyers had no rights
of audience in the Church courts, which were managed by a completely
separate profession. The senior professors of the canon law, who acted as
advocates and judges in the ecclesiastical tribunals, were law graduates
educated in the university law schools and almost invariably (until 1545)
ordained clergy.[2] Their law was not concerned with personal liberty in
the corporeal sense, and was positively opposed to anything resembling
individual rights in the spiritual context.

Magna Carta, in its opening chapter, guaranteed the liberties of the
English Church, which included its separate jurisdiction, but there was
nothing in the charter guaranteeing liberty of religious belief or expression, which would have been an unthinkable concept in the thirteenth

---

[1] There are very few known examples of trained common lawyers becoming ordained, and
probably none of them had been called to the bar: *The Men of Court*, i. 34–5. No common
lawyer is known even to have had a law degree before the later sixteenth century, and it
was rare before the nineteenth century.

[2] G. D. Squibb, *Doctors' Commons* (Oxford, 1977), pp. 25–8; *OHLE*, vi. 236. The statute 37
Hen. VIII, c. 17, enabled laymen to exercise ecclesiastical jurisdiction, provided they were
doctors of law. According to Squibb, the first non-ordained advocate in the Court of
Arches was Thomas Legh DCL (Cantab.) (admitted 1531), and the last ordained clerk
admitted as an advocate was Oliver Lloyd DCL (Oxon.) (1609).

century. The statute was not, in any case, on the curriculum of the university law schools.[3] Those who attended the inns of court in later medieval times would have been taught that this first chapter confirmed the exemption of the clergy from capital punishment for murder and felony. But the inns of court lecturers were more interested in the practicalities which enabled its allowance to laymen, wallowing in the absurdities of the canon law of bigamy through which a felon could be hanged if he had lawfully married a widow but reprieved if, when he went through the marriage ceremony, he was already married to someone else.[4] Useful this learning may have been, in its way, but it had nothing to do with religious freedom and there was no way that chapter 1 could possibly be interpreted to liberate individuals from the chains of obedience to canonical authority. There was only one catholic Church, from which no one was free to resign or dissent. That was equally the case after the break with Rome, since the Church of England was seen as the ancient *Ecclesia Anglicana* of St Edward the Confessor and Magna Carta, finally liberated from interference by foreign potentates and the *Ecclesia Romana*, but still a part of the one catholic and apostolic Church.[5] That Church, whatever its theological complexion, did not allow liberty of conscience to the Christian population. Other religions were beyond its concern, since it did not exert jurisdiction over them. The Jews, while present in England, were free to follow their own religion. The expulsion of the Jews in 1290 – as of the Gypsy immigrants in 1531 – was justified at the time in secular terms and was achieved by secular legislation.[6] It was certainly discriminatory, and therefore contrary to common-law ideology as later understood,[7] but it was presented as resolving social problems and not as being about religious belief as such. Any

---

[3] For Wycliffe's comment that it ought to be, see above, p. 66.

[4] He who married a widow was *bigamus* and incapable of ordination: above, p. 83. But if the marriage with the widow was bigamous in the modern sense, it was void; therefore the bigamist was not canonically *bigamus*, and could in theory be ordained. For this very case in real life see *R. v. Bagnall* (1527) KB 27/1065, Rex, m. 9; *OHLE*, vi. 534. The pope could dispense with the impediment of bigamy, but the English courts could take no notice of such a dispensation: Baker, *Collected Papers*, i. 373 (citing a fifteenth-century reading on the statute *De Bigamis*).

[5] 24 Hen. VIII, c. 12.

[6] In the case of the Jews by royal edict (no text of which survives); in the case of the 'Egyptians' by Act of Parliament (*OHLE*, vi. 615). Gypsies somehow crept back in. For a Privy Council instruction to torture Gypsies to uncover their lewd behaviour and name their ringleaders see 26 APC 325.

[7] Coke said that the statute of 9 Hen. IV requiring all Irish to leave the realm on pain of death was 'utterly against the law': 12 Co. Rep. 76. No such statute can be found, but that does not affect the principle.

theoretical legal prejudice against Muslims, whose presence in England must have been very rare,[8] arose chiefly from their being enemy aliens.[9] There was indeed a scruple about their giving evidence, but for the technical reason that oaths could only be taken on the Bible, a position which was first doubted in the seventeenth century but not clearly abandoned until the eighteenth.[10] It was also said that English subjects could not trade with infidels overseas without a royal licence, but since licences could be purchased this had more to do with royal revenue than religion.[11] The doctrine that Jews and Turks could not perform the feudal service of castle-ward,[12] though hardly to their disadvantage, was doubtless connected more with allegiance than with religion. Since aliens could not own freehold land anyway, the point was purely academic. Generally speaking, then, the common law was blind to religious difference. There is little or no case-law on the subject, but it was not thought absurd for early-Tudor lecturers in the Inner Temple to teach that even the benefit of clergy – in its fictitious form – could be allowed to Jews and Muslims.[13] The only truly religious intolerance was that bestowed by the canon law on Christians.

---

[8] The Gypsies who arrived in England in the sixteenth century either conformed to Christianity or kept their religion to themselves. Negroes were another matter. In 1597 complaint was made that there were too many black immigrants, who were taking employment from subjects, and an order was made to transport some of them to Spain: 26 APC 16–17, 20–1. Their religion is not recorded.

[9] Sir Robert Brooke held in his reading (Middle Temple, 1551) on Magna Carta, c. 17, that it was permissible to kill a Turk or a Jew who came with no safe conduct because they were not Christians: *Selected Readings on Magna Carta*, p. 190. There was no authority for that in English law. Enemy aliens could be killed on the field of battle, but not otherwise.

[10] Coke's opinion that infidels could not be admitted as witnesses, because they could not swear a valid oath, was doubted by Sir Matthew Hale (d. 1676) in *Historia Placitorum Coronae*, ed. S. Emlyn (1736), ii. 279, and finally rejected in *Fachina* v. *Sabine* (Privy Council, 1738) 2 Stra. 1104 (Muslim) and *Omychund* v. *Barker* (1744–5) 1 Atk. 21, Willes 538 (Hindu).

[11] *Michelborne* v. *Michelborne* (1610) 2 Br. & G. 296, *per* Coke CJ. It seems from another report that the prohibition was geographical rather than personal. See BL MS. Harley 1575, fo. 73v: (tr.) 'Coke CJ cited a record in the time of Edward III that no man might travel to any infidel country without the king's licence; and Sir Edward Michelborne had one, who travelled in the Indies.'

[12] *Selected Readings on Magna Carta*, p. 231.

[13] Richard Littleton's reading (1493) on Westminster II, c. 12 (as to Jews), and Richard Snede's reading (1511) on Magna Carta, c. 1, which held not only that Jews and Saracens could claim clergy but also that they were exempt from paying mortuaries, since they did not benefit from the parish priest's services: *OHLE*, vi. 533; *Rights and Liberties*, pp. 116, 122. The orthodox learning, however, excluded infidels (meaning Muslims) from benefit of clergy: *Spelman's Reports*, ii, introduction, p. 331. This became the settled common law: *Powlter's Case* (1610) 11 Co. Rep. 29; Hale, *Historia Placitorum Coronae*, ii. 373.

It is often supposed that English law was somehow based on the law and teaching of the Christian Church, but this is deeply misleading. Those who created and nurtured the common law were, of course, brought up as Christians and influenced in a general way by Christian morality. The canonists in the twelfth-century universities had also led the way in developing a coherent body of detailed jurisprudence, inspired ultimately by the jurists of ancient Rome. But the basic ideas of property and obligation were secular, and the principles were worked out differently in different jurisdictions without any reference to Christian thought in particular. For example, medieval forms of land tenure and their incidents were of no concern to theologians or canonists, and yet they were central to the common law. Since the two English universities declined to countenance the study of domestic law, which they disdained as a kind of local custom, the law of the land was developed by graduates of a different university, with their own distinct schemes of thought.[14] The English common lawyers borrowed from the canonists a few broad ideas which made sense, such as *mens rea* and *aequitas*,[15] but they were very few. Roman law, whether civil or canon, was usually dismissed with a hint of contempt as 'lour ley' – their law, not ours.[16] 'Lour ley' belonged, in medieval times, to the universe dominated by the clergy. 'Nostre ley' was nurtured in the king's courts of law, and in the inns of court, by men of common sense, men of the world who married and had children and learned about human nature from people rather than scholastic books, men who engaged in rational debate and listened to both sides: 'the great mediators between life and logic, a reasoning, reasonable element in the English nation'.[17] The common law did not sentence people to be burned alive for refusing to believe (or to profess belief) in abstractions; it would not so much as fine them for refusing to believe in the undeniable and verifiable truths of feudal tenure. It did not try people without telling them the case

---

[14] See Chapter 3, above.

[15] Not what is now called equity, but the equitable principles of statutory interpetation. Although the Court of Chancery used the inquisitorial procedure, and many of the medieval chancellors were ecclesiastical lawyers by background, the equity of the Chancery was not derived in any specific way from canon law: *OHLE*, vi. 179–82.

[16] There are many examples in the year books, and the usage became commonplace. In an early sixteenth-century Gray's Inn reading on Magna Carta, c. 1, examples are given of the many cases in 'their law' which do not hold in 'our law': *Rights and Liberties*, p. 85. Cf. J. Baker, 'Roman Law and the Third University of England' in *Collected Papers*, i. 367–93.

[17] F. W. Maitland, *Year Books of Edward II* (17 SS, 1903), introduction, p. lxxxi.

against them, or force them to accuse themselves by disclosing their private thoughts upon oath. But the common law did not run in the courts of the Church.

Heresy

The Church had no equivalent to Magna Carta, in the sense of a document protecting the liberties of individuals against its power. Nor did it consider itself bound by chapter 29 of the charter itself, in exercising in England the jurisdiction impliedly confirmed to it by chapter 1.[18] Its immense power was in theory exercised over the mind rather than the body or temporal things. It was not permitted to fine or imprison laymen,[19] except with statutory authority,[20] and as far as English law was concerned it could not override the law of the land.[21] Secular assistance was nevertheless provided to imprison those who were excommunicated,[22] or to set fire to those condemned for heresy, without an independent investigation of the merits. The burning of heretics had an uncertain foundation in England,[23] but was confirmed in certain cases – in return for a large clerical subsidy – by a statute of Henry IV.[24] With pious hypocrisy, the ecclesiastical judges did not themselves mention death or burning in the sentence for heresy, but

---

[18] See further below, p. 274.

[19] See above, p. 106. It could imprison criminous clergy, including laymen who had successfully pretended to be clergy in order to escape the death penalty.

[20] A statute of 1401 (2 Hen. IV, c. 15) introduced fines and imprisonment for impugning the orthodox teaching of the Church. The validity of this statute (for which see also below, n. 24) was later questioned on the grounds that the Commons had not properly assented: below, p. 294 n. 109. It was in the form of a Latin petition from the prelates and clergy, to which only the king and lords gave their formal assent; but the petition stated obiter that the commons were associated with it.

[21] In his Inner Temple reading (c. 1475) Thomas Kebell said that 'if all the prelates were to make a provincial constitution it would be void, for they cannot change the law of the land': BL MS. Hargrave 87, fo. 304v (tr.); *Rights and Liberties*, p. 26.

[22] By the writ *de excommunicato capiendo*, addressed to the sheriff. Until 1563 this writ was not returnable in any court, and this was said to have rendered it largely ineffective: 5 Eliz. I, c. 23.

[23] It had been acknowledged in theory in the thirteenth century, but the writ *de haeretico comburendo* was not used before 1401: F. Pollock and F. W. Maitland, *History of English Law before the Time of Edward I* (2nd edn, Cambridge, 1898), ii. 547–52.

[24] 2 Hen. IV, c. 15. This statute required sheriffs to cause unrepentant convicts to be burned *in eminenti loco*, (tr.) 'to strike fear into the minds of others so that no such wicked teaching and heretical and erroneous opinions . . . may be upheld or in any way suffered'. It did not, as is often supposed, impose this fate on heretics in general, but referred only to those who preached or wrote against the faith, or held schools or conventicles for the purpose, or favoured those who did such things.

merely – 'with sorrow and bitterness of heart'[25] – left the convicted heretic to receive his due from the secular authorities. Yet only Church courts could give the fatal judgment. And the decisions of those courts, however unfair, could not be reviewed by royal judges. Ecclesiastical judges could be restrained by writs of prohibition from straying outside their jurisdictional bounds; but heresy was exclusively within the spiritual jurisdiction, and therefore secular control was limited to placing some obvious restrictions on what kinds of unorthodoxy could be treated as heresy.[26]

The two legal societies in the Temple are the indirect beneficiaries of the vicious papal inquisition of 1309 whereby the original occupants were dispossessed for supposed heresy.[27] But the law against heretics found its teeth in England in the persecution of the so-called Lollards at the end of that century and the beginning of the next. The label itself was calculated to marginalise them as a heretical sect. In fact they were just people who dared to think about religion, to question the super-natural powers claimed by priests, and to challenge other speculative innovations which were taking theology in puzzling new directions.[28] Since the questioning of official doctrine was absolutely forbidden, the full might of the Church was brought to bear on them. In 1377 Pope Gregory XI – a canonist, and dedicated to the use of severe measures against intellectuals – sent bulls to the University of Oxford fulminating against John Wycliffe and other Oxford professors for teaching in contempt of the 'Roman' Church, ordering them to stop such teaching and to arrest Wycliffe and other deviants and send them to the arch-bishop of Canterbury or the bishop of London. The university declined to comply with this piece of effrontery.[29] The law of the land did not

---

[25] The phrase 'cum dolore et amaritudine cordis' is found in the sentence upon Sir John Oldcastle: Rymer's *Foedera* (below, n. 39), at p. 64.

[26] This seems not to have been attempted before *Kayser's Case* (1465) below, p. 120.

[27] The knights Templar were not convicted, but forced to confess by the use of severe torture: below, p. 117 n. 37. After the dissolution of their order, the New Temple in London was granted to the Knights Hospitaller of St John of Jerusalem, who by the 1340s had let it to the lawyers.

[28] In his Middle Temple reading of 1641 Edward Bagshaw praised King Edward III for supporting Wycliffe, 'the maintainer of the doctrine of the Lollards and Waldenses, being the same in substance which protestants now possess': BL MS. Stowe 424, at fo. 4, quoted by W. R. Prest, *The Inns of Court 1590–1640* (1972), p. 214. He did not foresee the secular age, in which most people would share the scepticism of the Lollards without being Christians at all.

[29] The documents are set out in W. Prynne, *Brief Animadversions on the Fourth Institute* (1669), pp. 222–3.

allow the Church a power of arrest, and a foreign bishop – even one who had supreme authority to determine questions of canon law – could have no jurisdiction of that nature over people in England.[30] King Richard II, who succeeded to the throne shortly afterwards, was persuaded instead to obtain a 'statute' in Parliament, without the consent of the Commons, authorising him to issue commissions to arrest preachers and supporters of the new heresies on the accusation of bishops. The commissions, in which the king was styled 'defender of the faith', threatened the preachers, and even those who listened to them, with forfeiture of everything which they could forfeit. When the next Parliament met in 1382, the Commons petitioned that the parent 'statute' be annulled, since they had never given their assent to it and did not wish to give such power to bishops. Although the king gave way, he nevertheless issued further commissions in 1388, clearly contrary to Magna Carta; but there was no remedy at that time.[31]

The persecution of Lollards continued into the fifteenth century.[32] If someone was suspected of heresy he was arrested and his house searched to see whether he had any books written in English. Possession of such books was prima facie evidence of heresy, especially if they included a bible.[33] People who read bibles might find out how little of the Church's new teachings were to be found there,[34] a theological difficulty which only the clergy were trained to explain away. But there were many other suspicious signs to look out for, such as vegetarianism,

---

[30] *Sonde* v. *Peckham* (1484–9) YB Mich. 2 Ric. III, fo. 22, pl. 51, *per* Huse CJ; *OHLE*, vi. 238.

[31] Prynne, *Animadversions*, 395–8; Rot. Parl. iii. 141, no. 53; 12 Co. Rep. 57–8. Coke (loc. cit.) said that the statute of 1382, annulling the pretended statute of 5 Ric. II, 'hath by the craft of the prelates been ever from time to time kept from the print'. It was known by 1607, from the rolls in the Tower: Fuller, *Argument*, p. 8.

[32] The following details are based on J. A. F. Thomson, *The Later Lollards 1414–1520* (Oxford, 1965), pp. 224–35; I. Forrest, *The Detection of Heresy in Late Medieval England* (Oxford, 2005). For the procedural context see also H. A. Kelly, 'Inquisition and the Prosecution of Heresy: Misconceptions and Abuses' (1989) 58 *Church History* 439–51; 'Trial Procedures against Wyclif and the Wycliffites in England and at the Council of Constance' (1999) 61 *Huntington Library Quarterly* 1–28; *Inquisitions and other Trial Procedures in the Medieval West* (Aldershot, 2001).

[33] This was usually just a ground for suspicion, but in 1428 Archbishop Chichele tried someone for having an English new testament: Forrest, *Detection of Heresy*, p. 186.

[34] One early-fifteenth-century writer said the chief reason why the friars disliked vernacular scripture was that 'if the truth of God's law were known to the people, they should lack much of their worldly worship and of their lucre both': A. Hudson, *Lollards and their Books* (1985), p. 157 (spelling modernised), citing also a reference in 1389/90 to the persecution of those who read the bible in English.

or a tendency to be kind to inferiors.[35] The accused was cited to appear, and if he failed to do so could be tried for his life in his absence. He was not entitled to know the names of his accusers, the witnesses did not have to meet the usual standards of probity, and the trial could be in secret. There was no indictment specifying what particular heretical beliefs he was alleged to hold. And he was not allowed to defend the beliefs which he did hold, because the intellectual cogency of his personal views was irrelevant. A heresy trial was not a theological debate. The defendant was simply interrogated at length, and if his interrogators found him unsound – and he declined to recant – he was pronounced a heretic. According to the articles drawn up by an English canonist around 1430 for the examination of suspected heretics, there were forty points on which they could be tested, nearly all of them relating to relatively recent theological inventions which the faithful were expected blindly to accept.[36] Torture could in theory be used at this stage, since the canon law followed Roman civil law in treating it as a normal part of pre-trial procedure, and it was used with inhuman sadism on the knights Templar.[37] It was nevertheless generally considered too Roman for English taste, being foreign to the law of the land, and was probably not thereafter used at the investigative stage. The main object of prosecution was to force the suspect to recant, under threat of death, in which case he might be absolved after a good flogging, perhaps on condition of wearing an embroidered faggot on his sleeve to warn him against relapse. It did not, apparently, matter that this recantation was made under extreme duress. Duress, according to the canonists, would avoid contracts and grants – even Magna Carta – but it seems that this doctrine did not extend to false professions of belief. The Church could not, of course, control what people actually believed, any more than people could themselves. It wanted abject obedience. So it compelled people to choose between lying on oath or

---

[35] These were mentioned in William de Pagula's *Summa Summarum* (c. 1320): Forrest, *Detection of Heresy*, p. 76.

[36] 'Articuli super quibus heretici vel Lollardi debent examinari concepti per juristam', printed in Hudson, *Lollards and their Books*, pp. 133–4 (and cf. 21 articles composed 'per theologos', ibid. 135).

[37] The lawyer Pope Clement V personally put great pressure on King Edward II to allow it to be used, as a requirement of canon law, though the king had protested that it was unknown to English law: see M. Barber, *The Trial of the Templars* (Cambridge, 1978), pp. 197–9; H. Nicholson, *The Knights Templar on Trial: The Trial of the Templars in the British Isles 1308–11* (Stroud, 2009), p. 99. In France many knights were killed in a hideous manner during the process of examination.

suffering death for the crime of failing to achieve the impossible.[38] Most people, needless to say, went along with whatever the Church demanded of them.

One of the Lollard martyrs was Sir John Oldcastle, Lord Cobham (*jure uxoris*), whose trial took place in October 1413.[39] He had been charged vaguely with supporting and protecting Lollard preachers, but his trial was about his own personal beliefs. In answer to the usual interrogatories, he answered, firstly, that the sacrament of the altar was Christ's body in the form of bread, but that material bread remained after consecration; secondly, that although penance was needful, confession to a priest was not necessary; thirdly, that images might be used as teaching aids for laymen but not worshipped, adoration being reserved for Christ alone; and, fourthly, that life was a pilgrimage, but it was not necessary to go to Rome or Canterbury or any other particular shrine. On being further pressed, he said that if the Church held otherwise it was not warranted by scripture, and that it was not within the competence of popes and bishops to declare such things necessary for salvation when they were not revealed by God. This last opinion was probably regarded as the most heretical at all. Christian doctrine could not be allowed to rest on evidence. The archbishop of Canterbury pronounced him a heretic and, since he declined the opportunity to recant, he was sentenced to death. Having nothing to lose, he escaped from the Tower and became involved in rebellion, with the eventual outcome that he suffered the pains of a traitor and a heretic simultaneously. Conveniently for the government, Lollardy had become inextricably linked with treason, perhaps even with a serious fear of popular revolution, and much treasure was collected by the crown from forfeitures and pardons.[40] Thinking about religion was driven firmly underground.

Although executions for heresy were carried out by the sheriff, this was essentially an administrative activity outside the common law.[41] The

---

[38] I.e. believing something which the condemned person did not and could not believe.

[39] For what follows see J. H. Wylie, *The Reign of Henry the Fifth* (Cambridge, 1914), iii. 250–4. The full Latin text of the ecclesiastical process against Oldcastle is printed in T. Rymer ed., *Foedera, Conventiones, Literae*, ix (1729), at pp. 61–6. The case, or one very like it, was alluded to by Coke in *The Case of Heresy*, 12 Co. Rep. 58.

[40] See M. Jurkowski, 'Henry V's Suppression of the Oldcastle Revolt' in G. Dodd ed., *Henry V: New Interpretations* (York, 2013), pp. 103–29.

[41] The suggestion (Forrest, *Detection of Heresy*, pp. 105–6) that the statutes of 1401 and 1414 were on the curriculum of the inns of court is incorrect. They occur in some statute-books and registers of writs, but they were never made the subject of readings.

secular law itself was not concerned with heresy. In fact it conferred elementary legal protection on convicted heretics before the day of execution,[42] and some lawyers held benefit of clergy to be available to an alleged heretic, provided he had not already been condemned.[43] But neither the common law nor Magna Carta could as yet protect people against the Church in the exercise of its terrible jurisdiction. In declaring that the English Church should be free, chapter 1 had confirmed its freedom to send to the flames those who obstinately declined to agree with its teaching. The charter did state expressly that its provisions bound the clergy, and this included chapter 29, but they were only bound with respect to their men (*erga suos*): in other words, only in their capacity as temporal lords.[44] The Church courts did not in spiritual matters follow the due process of the common law, because they used the inquisitorial procedure. The inquisition system had more merits than its sanguinary reputation allows, and canonists had worked out various procedural safeguards, but the Holy See decreed that they should not be applied in heresy cases: it was better to execute innocent people than let a few guilty go free.[45] Instead of following the usual canonical practice of charging the defendant with a particular crime, and giving him the opportunity to defend himself, it became standard practice that 'the inquisitors would make the defendant guess why he had been summoned and would question him on his beliefs and actions'.[46]

The Church was not, therefore, wedded to the idea of due process when its authority was at stake. No more did it believe in constitutional monarchy. Roman law taught that what pleases the prince has the force

---

[42] Thomas Marow, reader of the Inner Temple in 1503, held that a convicted heretic was entitled to ask for surety of the peace against someone who threatened him: B. H. Putnam, ed., *Early Treatises on the Practice of the Justices of the Peace in the Fifteenth and Sixteenth Centuries* (Oxford, 1924), p. 323. This was repeated in Thomas Harlakenden's reading of 1525 in Gray's Inn: *Selected Readings on Magna Carta*, p. 300. A heretic was also entitled to sanctuary, since the privilege belonged to the place, not the person: anonymous reading in *Rights and Liberties* p. 94; but cf. ibid. 110, 130, to the contrary.

[43] Thomas Kebell's reading on Westminster I, c. 1, printed in *Rights and Liberties* at p. 27. See further *Spelman's Reports*, ii, introduction, p. 331.

[44] Magna Carta, following c. 37: (tr.) 'Furthermore, all these... liberties which we have granted to be kept in our realm (in so far as it belongs to us) with respect to our own men, shall be observed by all those of our realm, both clerical and lay, with respect to their men (*erga suos*)'.

[45] Pope Boniface VIII (d. 1303) ordered heresy trials to be conducted without the usual formalities, and without the possibility of appeal: Kelly, 'Inquisition and the Prosecution of Heresy', pp. 443, 445.

[46] Ibid. 449.

of law,[47] and popes trained in Roman law were not slow to apply the same principle to themselves. The first major exponent of the doctrine of absolute power for the papacy was the lawyer Pope Innocent III, the same pope who annulled King John's charter of liberties.[48] His successor Pope Clement V, also a lawyer, purported to strike down Magna Carta in 1305 as endangering absolutism.[49] Well might popes fear the corrosive effects of liberty. The great charter of Henry III, confirmed by Edward I, seemed to threaten radical possibilities even in the ecclesiastical sphere. Wycliffe, it may be recalled, regarded the freedom guaranteed by Magna Carta to the *Ecclesia Anglicana* as including a freedom from undue interference by the Roman Curia.[50] Needless to say, the Church authorities could not stomach that kind of thing.[51] Although Wycliffe died naturally, his remains were exhumed and cremated for heresy in 1428.

The boundary between the spiritual and temporal jurisdictions was always defined, in real life, by the king's temporal courts, and in that context an important precedent was set in *Kayser's Case* in 1465.[52] Kayser, an executor, had been sued in the Audience Court of Canterbury for a customary 'reasonable share' of his testator's goods, and had argued that this was a matter for the secular courts. Reasonable shares were recognised by chapter 18 of Magna Carta and governed by local custom, not canon law.[53] His contention was therefore undeniably correct at common law. Threatened with excommunicaton, Kayser said he did not care, since it would have no effect, and for this he was charged with heresy so that he could be imprisoned. The King's Bench granted a writ of privilege, which was a species of *habeas corpus* to protect its litigants, and released Kayser on bail. Eventually the archbishop backed down. The case was unreported, but in the next century the record came to the

---

[47] Cf. below, p. 145.

[48] See K. Pennington, 'Innocent III and the Divine Authority of the Pope' in *Popes, Canonists and Texts 1150–1550* (Aldershot, 1993), iii. 1–32. Huguccio of Pisa (d. 1210) may, however, have been the first canonist to make an explicit link between the papal *potestas absoluta* and the Roman maxim *Quod principi placuit legis habet vigorem* (Justinian's *Digest*, 1.4.1; *Institutes*, 1.2.6).

[49] Above, p. 9.   [50] See above, p. 66.

[51] One of the articles for examining Lollards was 'whether it is necessary to believe the Roman Church to be supreme among other churches': Hudson, *Lollards and their Books*, p. 133, no. 21. The bull which Gregory XI sent to Oxford had referred to contempt of the *Roman* Church, indicating that it was somehow distinct from the English Church.

[52] *Kayser's Case* (1465) KB 27/818, m. 143d; summarised in *Dyer's Notebooks*, i. 108.

[53] For discussion see Baker, *Collected Papers*, iii. 1368–70; *Selected Readings on Magna Carta*, pp. 196–216.

attention of Catlyn CJ and Dyer CJ,[54] and it was thereafter hailed as an inveterate authority for the jurisdiction of the royal courts to discharge prisoners of the Church.[55] For the time being, however, its scope was limited to jurisdictional disputes.

The Defence of the Faith and Sir Thomas More

Another wave of persecution gained momentum in the early sixteenth century. Henry VIII, as defender of the faith,[56] was determined to suppress deviants from catholic orthodoxy, and Sir Thomas More was pleased to help him by establishing a network of informers to uncover and hunt to the kill those who did not toe the theological line.[57] The Lollards had not been completely exterminated, but the new arch-enemy was Martin Luther. People could on no account be allowed access to Luther's works, which too many readers were finding persuasive, or at least conducive to doubt. Reading about religion had to be stopped, and More pursued the Benedictine monk Richard Bayfield to an agonisingly slow death by fire at Smithfield after he was caught importing Lutheran books in 1531. Even the universities could not be allowed access to sceptical arguments, lest they proved convincing, and this time Cambridge was the main target.[58] Cambridge University was forced to arrange a ceremonial bonfire of Lutheran

---

[54] *Dyer's Notebooks*, i. 108; Catlyn's notebook, Alnwick Castle MS. 475, fo. 30. Coke learned about it from Dyer's manuscript: Co. Inst. iii. 42; 2 Bulst. 200. Selden also had a copy: LI MS. Hale 32(5).

[55] E.g. Coke's memorandum on c. 29 of Magna Carta (1604) below, p. 506; *Maunsell's Case* (1607) below, p. 523, *per* Yelverton J.; *Sir William Chauncy's Case* (1611) BL MS. Add. 48186, fo. 201; *Ruswell's Case* (1615) BL MS. Add. 35957, fo. 2v; *Bradstone's Case* (1614) 2 Bulst. 300; Co. Inst. ii. 55; Co. Inst. iii. 42.

[56] The title was conferred on him by Pope Leo X in 1521. It had, however, been used by earlier kings: see above, p. 116.

[57] For what follows see W. A. Clebsch, *England's Earliest Protestants* (New Haven, 1964; reprinted, Westport, CT, 1980), pp. 100–7, 277–86; J. Guy, *The Public Career of Sir Thomas More* (Brighton, 1980), pp. 155, 164–74; J. Guy, ed., introduction to *The Debellation of Salem and Bizance* (10 *Complete Works of St Thomas More*, New Haven, CT, 1987), pp. xlvii–lxvii; D. Oakley, 'English Heresy Procedures in Thomas More's *Dialogue concerning Heresies*' (2008) 3 *Thomas More Studies* 70–80; R. Rex, 'Thomas More and the Heretics: Statesman or Fanatic?' in G. Logan ed., *The Cambridge Companion to Thomas More* (Cambridge, 2011), pp. 93–115; D. Loewenstein, *Treacherous Faith: The Specter of Heresy in Early Modern English Literature and Culture* (Oxford, 2013), pp. 26–53.

[58] One of the articles against Wolsey, which More signed in 1529, was that he had stopped an enquiry into Lutheran errors which were said to 'reign amongst the students and scholars' at Cambridge: Co. Inst. iv. 94, no. 43.

literature which had been obtained by the University Library. Meetings to talk about religious questions were banned. The scholarly Thomas Bilney, bachelor of canon law, who attended the theological discussion group in the White Horse near St Catharine's College, fell foul of More's police and was burned to death in the Lollards' Pit at Norwich. The inns of court were also put under watch. One Baynham, of the Temple,[59] was imprisoned by More in his house, interrogated, and urged to betray fellow Templars – barristers, perhaps, like Christopher St German of the Middle Temple, who had dared to take on More in print. St German managed to escape with his life by remaining doctrinally orthodox, but Baynham was burned at the stake in 1532. John Frith was another of More's victims. He had argued that Christ's physical body could not be in heaven and in the eucharist at the same time, and that purgatory was an imaginary state. Even his accusers accepted that neither transubstantiation nor purgatory had any scriptural foundation, but that was beside the point; faith did not depend on evidence. Frith did not claim that he was right, only that the Church had no authority to turn the doctrinal inventions of academic scholars into essential articles of faith. That was what really sealed his fate. Pursued by More's secret police, he was burned at the stake in 1533.

More's writings show that he was proud of his police activities, which were in no way connected with the functions of a lord chancellor. Following the medieval teaching of the militantly intolerant Aquinas,[60] he regarded the unorthodox as vermin to be hunted down and destroyed. He famously wrote that if one were to require open accusations, or exclude the evidence of tainted witnesses, the streets would be swarming with heretics.[61] He defended the refusal of bail, on the grounds that heretics might abscond, and was against allowing defence

---

[59] There is some doubt as to his identity. Foxe said he was of the Middle Temple, for which the admissions records at this period are lost, but there was a James Baynham in the Inner Temple: *The Men of Court*, i. 285 (expelled for not paying his dues).

[60] For the theology of hate see A. Walsham, 'The Theology of Religious Intolerance' in *Charitable Hatred: Tolerance and Intolerance in England 1500–1700* (Manchester, 2006), pp. 40–9.

[61] For this favourite figure of speech, which he had used in his *Apology*, see More, *The Debellation of Salem and Bizance* (above, n. 57), pp. 85, 89, 101, 102, 104, 105. (Elsewhere he denied that there were many heretics in England.) A detailed defence of More's approach to heresy trials (as opposed to the persecution of heretics) is made by H. A. Kelly, 'Thomas More on Inquisitorial Due Process' (2008) 123 EHR 847–94. The defence case requires rejection of the contemporary testimony of common lawyers such as St German and Hall, and the members of the 1529–36 parliament collectively, as to a widespread public perception of unfairness.

witnesses because they might lie.[62] He was even in favour of punishing suspects whose guilt could not be proved, since giving rise to suspicion was itself reprehensible.[63] It is evident from his writings that he was motivated by a strong personal hatred of the unorthodox, even when they had law on their side.[64] The foremost instance of this was his scathing attack on Richard Hunne, who was tried and burned posthumously for heresy in 1515 after being allegedly murdered in the bishop of London's prison. Hunne's core 'crime' was arguing that his dead infant son's winding-sheet, which the rector had claimed as a mortuary, was not liable to seizure because it had never belonged to the little boy, a contention which seems irrefutable.[65] It had, moreover, been judicially decided in 1496 that denying ecclesiastical jurisdiction was not heresy within the meaning of the statute of 1401.[66] To bolster their case, the prosecutors had rummaged through Hunne's books and found what they alleged to be heretical notes written in an English bible, an allegation which, being dead, he was not in a position to answer.[67]

More still has his admirers, but the defence case is difficult to grasp. Perjury was a sin, and yet he would force people to abjure, that is, to aver on oath that they did not believe things which in their inner hearts they did, or vice versa, on pain of death. Religion was thus a two-edged sword, offering a choice between the sin of perjury and extermination as a heretic.[68] It was not a matter of belief, in the sense of intellectual persuasion, or of conscience, but of obedience. An analogy was drawn with civil allegiance, which was likewise a matter of birth rather than of choice. Heresy was seen by More as a kind of

---

[62] Kelly, 'Thomas More on Inquisitorial Due Process', pp. 861, 891–2.

[63] More, *The Debellation of Salem and Bizance* (above, n. 57), pp. liii–lv, 82–3, 111–13, 271–2. One instance of this, the punishment of Thomas Philips (who was prosecuted and put in the Tower by More), was taken up in Parliament in 1534: ibid. lxii. Philips's lawyers tried unsuccessfully to obtain a *corpus cum causa* (a species of *habeas corpus*) after More ceased to be chancellor, to remove the case into Chancery: ibid. lxiii.

[64] Particularly Thomas Philips (previous note) and Richard Hunne (next note).

[65] *OHLE*, vi. 241, and the references there. Richard Snede, in his Inner Temple reading of 1511, said that the custom of London excluded mortuaries anyway: *Rights and Liberties*, p. 122.

[66] *Warner v. Hudson* (1495–7) YB Hil. 10 Hen. VII, fo. 17, pl. 17; CP 40/934, m. 327; cited by Coke CJ from the record, 2 Bulst. 300; Coke's copy of the record is in YLS MS. G.R24.1, fo. 111; Selden's copy is LI MS. Hale 32(3).

[67] According to More, who attended the trial, he was convicted on this evidence of questioning the doctrine of transubstantiation ('misbelief toward the holy sacrament'): Kelly, 'Thomas More on Inquisitorial Due Process', pp. 864–5.

[68] This was, ironically, More's own complaint about the statute under which he was condemned to death for treason.

spiritual treason against the faith of one's forebears. It did not matter whether the Church was demonstrably right: it had to be obeyed, to prevent diversity of opinion. More's extreme intolerance has long been a puzzle, given his earlier interest in humanist scholarship, with its emphasis on evidence and reasoning, his education in the inns of court and his literary invention (while reader of Lincoln's Inn)[69] of a *Utopia* in which there was complete freedom of belief. Intolerance was not the prevailing intellectual ethos in the common-law world. Christopher St German, a barrister of the Middle Temple, was one of those who favoured moderation. Edward Hall, a bencher of Gray's Inn, was another; he reported that fellow members of the Commons in 1532 – many of them common lawyers – 'sore complained of the cruelty of the ordinaries, for calling men before them *ex officio*'.[70] It was a key issue in the break with Rome, which More's ruthless activities had inadvertently facilitated. Although Henry VIII himself remained doctrinally orthodox, a major concession wrung from him by Parliament was a statute of 1534 which provided that no one should be accused of heresy at the behest of a bishop alone, but only upon due accusation and presentment; suspects were to be allowed bail; and the trial was to be in open court. Whether or not such measures addressed real problems,[71] they were a conscious echo of chapter 29 of Magna Carta, which was cited in the Commons and recited in full in the draft bill, though the reform was limited to procedural safeguards rather than religious freedom.[72] Henry VIII had no interest in a reformation of religion.

---

[69] He read in Lent 1515, though the subject of his lectures is unknown. *Utopia* was first published in 1516.

[70] *Hall's Chronicle* (1809 edn), p. 784. He was referring to the 'Supplication against the Ordinaries', which complained of (i) summons without lawful accusation or credible fame; (ii) imprisonent without bail; and (iii) self-incrimination on interrogation under the oath *ex officio*. See A. Ogle, *The Tragedy of the Lollards' Tower* (Oxford, 1949), pp. 324–30; G. R. Elton, 'The Commons' Supplication of 1532' (1951) 66 EHR 507–34; J. Cooper, 'The Supplication against the Ordinaries Reconsidered' (1957) 72 EHR 616–41; S. E. Lehmberg, *The Reformation Parliament 1529–36* (Cambridge, 1970), pp. 138–42, 145–7.

[71] It has been argued that the Commons and Lords were mistaken about the canon law, and that their perception of unfairness was imaginary: Kelly, 'Thomas More on Inquisitorial Due Process' (above, n. 61).

[72] 25 Hen. VIII, c. 14; Guy, introduction to *The Debellation of Salem and Bizance* (above, n. 57), pp. lvii–lxvii. The bill had first been drawn in 1529.

Religious Change and Treason

The persecution of supposed heretics was renewed with increased fervour in the time of Mary I, who restored Roman authority over the Church and repealed the due-process statute of 1534. The cruelty of the Marian religious regime was relentless and unpopular. Sheriffs were punished for showing mercy to those condemned by Holy Church, and in the end burnings were carried out in private, lest young people be turned against the faith out of sheer revulsion.[73] Once Mary I was dead, however, the executions for heresy virtually ceased and there were signs that England might have become a country of comparative religious tolerance.[74] Outward conformity was still required; but no one was going to be burned to death for believing in transubstantiation or purgatory, even if those were errors equal in weight to not believing in them, depending on one's point of view.[75] As was said in the House of Commons in 1571, it was 'not convenient to enforce consciences'.[76] However distasteful it was to some to accept a uniform common worship with elements of compromise, there was no need to make windows into men's hearts and secret thoughts.[77] The humane and sensible men of the inns of court and serjeants' inns, who had lived through the changes of regime, were typically tolerant of religious differences. In the 1560s a bishop was even driven to complain that the assize judges 'show themselves not favourable to *any* manner or cause of religion'.[78] In the same decade, some leading judgments on *habeas corpus*

---

[73] *OHLE*, vi. 252; 109 SS lxxiv, 13; G. Alexander, 'Bonner and the Marian Persecutions' in *The English Reformation Revisited*, ed. C. Haigh (1987), pp. 157–75.

[74] For what follows see also J. Baker, 'Religion and the Law' in *Dyer's Notebooks*, i, introduction, pp. lxvii–lxxv.

[75] According to Edward Bagshaw (below, p. 375 n. 214), at pp. 27–8, it was decided in *Viner and Pelling's Case* (1611) Trin. 9 Jac. I, rot. 2248, that heresy could no longer be committed in respect of matters not revealed in holy scripture. For this case cf. below, p. 311 n. 173.

[76] *Proc. Parl. 1558–81*, p. 206, *per* Edward Aglionby MP. Cf. ibid. 98 (1563), *per* Robert Atkinson MP, of Lincoln's Inn ('religion ... must sink in by persuasion; it cannot be pressed in by violence').

[77] This figure of speech was attributed by Francis Bacon to Elizabeth I, though various forms of it were in circulation and it is not clear who first used it: see *Proc. Parl. 1558–81*, p. 241, *per* Thomas Norton MP (1581); *Proc. Parl. 1584–9*, p. 46 ('they enquire into the secrets of men's hearts', 1585); J. E. Neale, *Elizabeth I and her Parliaments* (1953), i. 391 (Elizabeth I); cf. below, pp. 260, 354.

[78] J. S. Cockburn, *A History of English Assizes 1558–1714* (Cambridge, 1972), p. 192, quoting John Best, bishop of Carlisle (emphasis added). The judges on the Northern circuit then were both serjeants at law (Powtrell and Walsh).

were given in the interests of Roman Catholic recusants.[79] And several times in the later sixteenth century the judges held that it was not actionable defamation to call someone a papist, since this might refer only to 'frivolous ceremonies' or superstitious beliefs (such as the real presence in the mass) rather than treasonable proclivities.[80] These decisions were still remembered, and followed, in the next century.[81] Sir Roger Owen, writing around 1615, could claim it as a principle of the common law itself that 'weapons have no . . . force over the soul'.[82]

Reading books was now permitted. When in 1569 the chaplain and six members of Lincoln's Inn were prosecuted for importing seditious papist literature from the Continent, the judges held that it was no offence merely to read subversive literature. The Star Chamber, however, discovered that they had not merely read the books but distributed and commended them to others; this merited imprisonment, and also expulsion from Lincoln's Inn.[83] These were milder times, indeed; there was no threat of immolation at the stake. Instead, the inns of court were ordered to put out of commons those members who did not conform, and to exclude them from practice. Prominent among those whom Lincoln's Inn was ordered to expel was Thomas Egerton, who promptly conformed and eventually became lord chancellor.[84] Two years later Archbishop Parker threatened the worryingly tolerant inns of court

---

[79] See below, pp. 158–60.

[80] *Anon.* (*c.* 1577) HLS MS. 2071, fo. 81; *Yardley* v. *Hudson* (1580–1) 101 SS xci, 79; variant texts in 109 SS lxxii n 6; *Savage* v. *Cook* (*c.* 1585) cited in Cro. Eliz. 192.

[81] *Ireland* v. *Proctor* (1612) BL MS. Add. 25232, fo. 65v: (tr.) 'Coke [CJ] said that this word "papist" will not bear an action, and so it was adjudged by Catlyn CJ and, it seems, Wray CJ . . . Warburton J. further said that this word "papist" denotes only an error in religion and is no defamation; and Winch J. agreed. But he said that if a man calls a spiritual person or a bishop a papist, an action well lies, because religion is his profession.' Serjeant Hutton cited *Knighton* v. *Hall* (1605) to the same effect.

[82] Owen, *Common Law*, BL MS. Harley 6604, fo. 95: 'the common law holds that weapons have no more force over the soul than the surgeon's razor over the man's understanding that guides it. It is the phrase of St Paul, "We domineer not over your faith; it is the gift of God" . . . Consequently it cannot be given, much less coactively imposed.'

[83] *Att.-Gen.* v. *Cooke and others* (1569) *Dyer's Notebooks*, i. 161; Dyer 282. These texts correct very significantly the imperfect note from the record in BL MS. Harley 2143, fo. 14, where it is said that Cooke was committed to the Fleet and fined for buying, reading and keeping seditious books 'against the religion professed'. The prosecution was brought upon the statute of 5 Eliz. I, c. 1.

[84] *Calendar of Inner Temple Records*, i. 252–4; *Black Books of Lincoln's Inn*, i. 370–2; Beale papers, BL MS. Add. 48064, fo. 205v; IT MS. Petyt 538.47, fo. 47. His answers to the interrogatories are in SP 12/60, fo. 202.

with action by the High Commission if they did not do more to enforce the 1569 decree and to correct the 'over bold speeches and doings touching religion used by some of the same houses without control-ment'.[85] He was supported in this by the Star Chamber.[86] The inns were obliged to take appropriate measures, but even expulsion seems to have had limited effect. Two busy counsel practising at the Bar in the last quarter of the sixteenth century (Robert Atkinson and Richard Godfrey) were men who as Roman Catholics had been formally dis-barred – and actually expelled from their inns – for recusancy.[87] Edmund Plowden, another recusant with a substantial practice, was denied public office but oversaw the building of the new Middle Temple hall and was allowed the most sumptuous of all the monuments in Temple Church after his death in 1585.

Attitudes necessarily stiffened after the Northern Rebellion of 1569, and the issue of Pope Pius V's bull *Regnans in Excelsis* in 1570, which purported to deprive the queen of her 'pretended' right to the realm and to dissolve the allegiance of her subjects. This purported deposal of a reigning queen by a foreign potentate was virtually a declaration of war, which turned adherents of the pope into potential traitors.[88] Religious difference was no longer merely a matter of private belief. Coke would later make the claim that until 1570 there were no recusants,[89] and that

---

[85] Letter to Cecil, BL MS. Lansdowne 13, fo. 196 (17 June 1571). This followed a letter of the same date from the Privy Council to Parker (and to the archbishop of York) to take steps to enforce the 1569 order: IT MS. Petyt 538.47, fo. 38 (unsigned copy).

[86] The Star Chamber decree is referred to with approval in *Proc. Parl. 1558–81*, pp. 240–1, *per* John Agmondesham MP, of the Middle Temple (1571).

[87] F. A. Inderwick, ed., *Calendar of Inner Temple Records*, vol. i (1896), pp. 266–7. Com-plaint was made in Parliament in 1626 that popish lawyers living outside the inns of court were continuing to practise: *Proceedings in Parliament 1626* ed. W. B. Bidwell and M. Jansson, vol. iii (New Haven, CT, 1992), p. 312.

[88] A further bull against Elizabeth I was issued by Pope Sixtus V in 1588, following the execution of Mary, queen of Scots. Since Mary had been convicted on clear evidence of plotting to assassinate Elizabeth, this reaction made plain beyond question the papal sanctioning of regicide.

[89] *Att.-Gen. v. Pounde* (1603) Hawarde 182 at p. 183 ('Mr Attorney did shew that at the beginning of her reign there were no recusants, but all went to church until the 9th [*sic*] year of her reign that Pope Pius Quintus sent his bull and absolved them from their obedience, and after sent their priests and seditious books'); 5 Co. Rep., part 1 (1605), in the notes to *Cawdray's Case*, at ff. 34v–35 ('until the 11th year of the late Queen Elizabeth's reign no person of what persuasion of Christian religion soever at any time refused to come to the public divine service celebrated in the Church of England'); *JHC*, i. 302 (29 April 1606).

the queen had seen no need to meddle with papists.[90] This was a rose-tinted recollection of what in retrospect seemed to have been calmer times. But England certainly changed. Previously the enforcement of conformity had been limited, and had been more the concern of the High Commission than the assizes and quarter sessions.[91] Thereafter there was a real fear that undercover papal agents were actively plotting to murder the queen and overthrow the state, and several plots were uncovered. Parliament was led by this fear into passing some repressive legislation in 1581, which even made it a capital felony to import books with treasonable content.[92] Saying and hearing mass were made punishable by fine and imprisonment.[93] This was undoubtedly an infringement of religious liberty, but the mass was thought to perpetuate the belief that priests had supernatural powers, whereby they acquired an undue and malign influence over the susceptible.[94] The judges, in applying the new legislation, were careful not to stretch statutes beyond their words. Parliament could legislate on religious matters, but it had better do so with clarity.[95] For example, when Francis Tregeon was indicted in 1578 upon the Elizabethan statutes of *praemunire* for aiding Cuthbert Mayne, knowing him to a maintainer of the pope, the Queen's Bench held the indictment bad because mere knowledge was not enough; the indictment should have said 'upon purpose and intent to set forth and extol the authority of the bishop of Rome'.[96] In 1581, Wray and Dyer CJJ advised that Jesuits and seminary priests could not be indicted under a statute of 1571 unless they imported written bulls or documents as their authority,

---

[90] *R. v. Fawkes and others* (1605) Hawarde 251 at p. 255 ('she never meddled with any of them before Impius, and not Pius, quintus sent over his bills in 13th of her reign, whereby he did excommunicate her and absolve her subjects from their obedience to her'); *R. v. Garnet* (1606) 2 St. Tr. at col. 245. Even Garnet admitted that most Roman Catholics went to church before the bull (ibid. 239).

[91] Cockburn, *History of English Assizes*, pp. 193–5.

[92] 23 Eliz. I, c. 2. Superstitious beliefs, however, never in themselves amounted to treason. Cf. 3 Jac. I, c. 5, which made it finable to import, print or sell any popish book.

[93] 23 Eliz. I, c. 1.

[94] At the beginning of the reign, there had been moves to prosecute priests for unlawful magic in connection with the mass: *Dyer's Notebooks*, i. lxix–lxx.

[95] Cf. Coke's strong protest against the exploitation of obscure statutes concerning religious questions: Co. Inst. iv. 42.

[96] *R. v. Tregeon* (1578) Dyer 363; *Dyer's Notebooks*, ii. 368; CUL MS. Gg.5.4, fo. 106. They held, however, that they could not give judgment in his absence (in prison in Cornwall). He was later indicted more effectively and attainted: Coke's notebook, BL MS. Harley 6687B, fo. 45v.

according to the words of the statute,[97] because penal laws had to be construed strictly.[98] And in 1584 a clergyman of a different persuasion, indicted for the offence of omitting the sign of the cross in baptism, was discharged on the grounds that the indictment failed to allege that he had persevered in his obstinacy, as the statute required.[99] Though hardly evidence of a liberal approach to religion, it may be noted that the 1581 Act was applied to extreme Puritans as well as to Roman Catholics.[100]

More serious by far than these misdemeanours were the offences concerning temporal allegiance and the desire to depose the queen.[101] At the trial of Alfield, the Jesuit, for importing copies of Cardinal Allen's *Modest Defence of English Catholiques* (1584),[102] contrary to the statute of 1581, Alfield asserted that the pope had authority to depose any king with force, because he had regal power. William Fleetwood, the recorder of London, told him that they were not there to try matters of religion but only a question of fact, though he could not help reminding Alfield of Christ's teaching that Caesar should be obeyed.[103] As recorder, Fleetwood was at the forefront of police work in Elizabethan London detecting Jesuits and 'seminary priests',[104] and it might be tempting to draw a parallel with More. The fervour had superficial echoes of the 1530s, and there may have been an element of retribution: Fleetwood's Middle Temple friend Bartholomew Green had been burned at the stake for heresy under Mary.[105] Yet this was not a matter of hounding people for their beliefs alone, and even in treason cases Fleetwood believed in giving people a fair hearing.[106]

[97] 13 Eliz. I, c. 2, referring to any 'bull, writing or instrument written or printed of absolution or reconciliation'.

[98] *Question concerning Jesuits* (Hil. 1581) *Dyer's Notebooks*, ii. 390; but cf. Sav. 3 (Mich. 1580). The lacuna was closed by the statute of 1581.

[99] *Anon.* (1584) CUL MS. Ii.5.38, fo. 189. Cf. *Anon.* (1587) Godb. 118.

[100] Collinson, *Bancroft*, p. 125.

[101] These were also dealt with in 23 Eliz. 1, c. 1. Coke argued that this was declaratory of the common law of treason: 5 Co. Rep., part 1 (1605), in the notes to *Cawdray's Case*, fos. 38–9.

[102] Written as a response to *The Execution of Justice* (attributed to Lord Burghley), which made the case that the punishment of Roman Catholics was not for their religion but for treason.

[103] *R. v. Alfield* (1585) as reported in Burghley's papers, BL MS. Lansdowne 45, fos. 162v–163. The biblical text is *Matthew*, xxii. 21: see *Selected Readings on Magna Carta*, p. 114 n. 7.

[104] Below, pp. 217, 263.

[105] J. Foxe, *Acts and Monuments* (1563), p. 1465. *ODNB* mistakenly placed him in the Inner Temple. See *The Men of Court*, ii. 773–4.

[106] *Hale and Fleetwood on Admiralty Jurisdiction*, ed. M. J. Prichard and D. E. C. Yale (108 SS, 1993), p. xxi.

It was important not to treat all Roman Catholics as traitors. Jesuits and seminary priests were the main target. Whether or not they could be proved to be plotting specific acts of murder, they were deemed to be engaged in seducing subjects from their allegiance, by teaching that the pope had rightfully deposed the queen and released her people from obedience.[107] In 1585 they were forbidden by Parliament to enter or remain in England on pain of suffering as traitors, and those who harboured them were liable to execution as felons.[108] On the other hand, it was acknowledged that there were also groups of ordinary, peaceful people who wished only to follow the religious observances of the past. There was an insuperable difficulty in that they could only do so, according to their inherited beliefs, through the mediation of a mass priest. Fleetwood and Egerton nevertheless both signed a paper in 1588 suggesting a way of distinguishing 'those that carry traitorous and malicious minds against her majesty and the state from them whose simplicity is misled by ignorant and blind zeal'.[109]

Despite his youthful flirtation with Rome, Egerton was involved as solicitor-general in the prosecution of several Roman Catholic offenders, including Lord Vaux and Edmund Campion (1581), Mary, queen of Scots (1586), the earl of Northumberland (1585), the Babington conspirators (1586), the earl of Arundel (1589) and Sir John Perrot (1592). In due course he veered personally towards Calvinism, declaring himself implacably imposed to 'the devilish doctrine of Rome'.[110] Yet he always maintained the same distinction between papists: 'some are simple and led by error – those he pitied and was not forward to punish – others dangerous, wilful and seditious'.[111] He reminisced in 1606 that the late queen 'would never have had any die but to prevent the danger of the state and common wealth, and to preserve them in safety, and that was never done but with great grief and almost tears'.[112] Coke, likewise, when he was attorney-general, said that 'in very truth was not any one in all

---

[107]   Coke advised Lord Keeper Puckering in 1593 that Jesuits could be prosecuted under the Statute of Treasons 1350 for levying war and compassing the queen's death: SP 15/32, fo. 171 ('25 E. 3' is misread in the calendar as 25 Eliz.).

[108]   27 Eliz. I, c. 2.   [109]   PRO, SP 12/212, fo. 120 (20 July 1588).

[110]   H. E. Huntington Library, MS. EL 459, fo. 1. The dowager Lady Russell reported that many thought him 'an arrant hypocrite and deep dissembler': Huntington Library, MS. EL 46, fo. 1. See *ODNB*.

[111]   *Att.-Gen.* v. *Carewe* (1603) Hawarde 162 at p. 164. The same distinction had been made by the Privy Council in *R.* v. *Willoughby* (1575) 8 APC 331. It was also set out in a proclamation of 1582: Youngs, p. 234.

[112]   *Kennell* v. *Gawen* (1606) Hawarde 264 at p. 270.

Queen Elizabeth's time that suffered death for religion or conscience, but for treason to the person of the prince or state, or withdrawing or seducing the people from their obedience'.[113] No Roman Catholic was ever executed for heresy, since in practice that fate was reserved for extreme nonconformist sectaries.[114] Indeed, Francis Bacon said in Parliament in 1606 that 'novelists' were a greater danger than old papists.[115] Although heresy remained within the exclusive jurisdiction of the Church, the common-law judges were most unwilling to see it resurrected in practice. Sir Roger Owen reported that in the time of Popham CJ (1592–1607) a man was proceeded against as a heretic merely for saying, with reference to excommunication, 'I respect not the bishops' thunderbolts, they are but dare-words', but the judges discharged him on *habeas corpus*.[116] The last execution for heresy, in 1612, was carried out contrary to Coke CJ's advice to the law officers.[117] Whatever view is taken of the severe measures taken by Parliament against the Roman priests, which some contemporaries tried to moderate in practice,[118] this was a major shift in attitude. It was now axiomatic in England that no one should be persecuted for their private beliefs alone.

The distinction between treason and religion could not be drawn precisely in real life, but there was nothing imaginary about the dangers. The worst fears were almost realised in 1605, when some pious English gentlemen under the influence of Jesuits schemed to murder King James I,

---

[113] *Att.-Gen.* v. *Pounde* (1603) Hawarde 182 at pp. 183–4. The penalties were imposed under the statute 23 Eliz. I, c. 1.

[114] There were four executions for heresy in Elizabeth's reign, all for Arianism or Anabaptism. In 1581 there was a long debate in the House of Commons (not reported) as to whether the 'Family of Love' was a heresy punishable by death: *Proc. Parl. 1558–81*, p. 539; Neale, *Elizabeth I and her Parliaments 1559–81*, pp. 410–11. But its members practised outward conformity and escaped punishment. Owen maintained that Roman Catholics were not heretics in English law, because Parliament had never defined heresy: *Common Law*, LI MS. Misc. 209, fo. 8.

[115] *JHC*, i. 215 (7 February 1606): 'Papists, old, rooted and rotten. Novelists, the greatest danger.' By old papists he did not, of course, mean to include Jesuit activists. See also the remarks of Williams J. in *Maunsell's Case* (1607) below, p. 525, treating 'these novelists' and 'our own schismatics' as more objectionable than papists.

[116] Owen, *Common Law*, BL MS. Lansdowne 646, fo. 158. This would have been justified by *Kayser's Case* (1465) above, p. 120.

[117] *Wightman's Case* (1612) below, p. 295.

[118] Some priests were banished from the realm instead of facing prosecution: e.g. 32 APC 299–301, 316; 33 APC 95–6. In 1607 it was said that justices of assize who executed priests in accordance with the statutes (i.e. did not recommend pardons) were 'blamed, unless it is a case of an obstinate and wilful papist who inclines others to his superstition and refuses the oath of allegiance': Wilbraham, *Journal*, p. 97 (tr.).

the peers, the members of Parliament and the judges assembled at Westminster, a plot which very nearly succeeded. That would have been a more appalling crime than any ever committed on British soil in time of peace, and the day of deliverance from the Gunpowder Plot – 5 November – has been celebrated ever since.[119] When Guy Fawkes was asked by the king why he tried to kill him, he replied, 'Because you are excommunicated by the pope'.[120] Since the pope pronounced regular excommunications upon all who did not render obedience to him,[121] this understanding of canon law – propagated in a more nuanced form by the Spanish Jesuit theologian Francisco Suárez[122] – could easily have encouraged militant Roman Catholics to engage in a holy war against other Christians. But treason and conspiracy to murder, however motivated, are temporal crimes to which sincere religious belief can never be an acceptable defence. As Coke wrote earlier in 1605, 'these Jesuits and Priests are not condemned and executed for their priesthood and profession, but for their treasonable and damnable persuasions and practices against the crowns and dignities of monarchs, who hold their kingdoms and dominions . . . directly of Almighty God, and are not tenants of their kingdoms (as they would have it) at the will and pleasure of any foreign potentate'.[123] It was the king's personal wish that the gunpowder terrorists be tried by jury according to the ordinary course of law and not attainted by Parliament without trial.[124] This is not, however,

---

[119] Originally by command of Parliament: 3 Jac. I, c. 1.

[120] Coke's reminiscence in *Sympson's Case* (1615) Godb. 264. Coke had been involved in the interrogations as attorney-general.

[121] Ibid. When the king asked Fawkes how he came to be excommunicated (a fact of which he had been unaware), Fawkes answered, 'Every Maundy Thursday the pope doth excommunicate all heretics who are not of the faith of the Church of Rome'. Under Roman canon law, heretics still incur automatic excommunication, but this is immaterial to them if it does not carry a death sentence.

[122] In 1614 an Irish barrister was prosecuted in the Star Chamber for maintaining the doctrine of Suárez: *Att.-Gen. v. William Talbot* (1614) 2 St. Tr. 778 (Bacon's speech for the prosecution). His defence was that it was a matter of faith, on which he deferred to the Roman Church. He was fined £10,000, but doubtless did not pay. He returned to Ireland, and in 1623 was created a baronet: *ODNB*.

[123] 5 Co. Rep., part 1 (published in 1605), in the notes to *Cawdray's Case*, at fo. 39. Cf. Owen, *Common Law* (*c.* 1615) LI MS. Misc. 207, fo. 7v: 'The papists complain that . . . we put them to death, namely their priests, for religion's sake only, which is remarkably false. Queen Elizabeth and King James are as far from the infamy of persecution as these messengers of Satan from the glory of martyrdom.'

[124] *R. v. Garnet* (1606) 2 St. Tr. at col. 228, *per* Coke Att.-Gen. Coke had argued in the House of Commons for an attainder, in some cases posthumously, in order to define what property was forfeited: *JHC*, i. 301 (29 April 1606).

unequivocal evidence of James's obeisance to Magna Carta, since it had the advantage of enabling Coke, as attorney-general, to relate their planned atrocities in public.

Treasonable activities, even when motivated by religion, were dealt with by the secular law. This meant that the trials were conducted by laymen and the outcome decided by laymen, not by bishops or ecclesiastical lawyers. Whether or not they were tainted by religious bias, they were not within the control of the Church. The principal threat to liberty posed by the English Church in the later sixteenth century was seen to be concentrated rather in the jurisdiction of the high commissioners in ecclesiastical causes. This was not a matter of life and death, though it could affect lives and livelihoods in serious and contentious ways and raised anxieties about a creeping reversion to the dirigisme of the late-medieval Church. As will be seen in subsequent chapters, the adverse reaction by Bar and Bench to the burgeoning jurisdiction of the so-called High Commission was in large part responsible for the initial development of *habeas corpus* and the reinvigoration of Magna Carta.

The High Commission

The ecclesiastical commissions were authorised by the first statute of Elizabeth's first Parliament, in 1559, as a means of removing – though not burning – the bishops and senior clergy who had sought to lead the Church back to Rome under Mary I.[125] But the commissions remained in place long after the legislative purpose was achieved, their terms were steadily enlarged, and their members assumed an ever-increasing extraordinary jurisdiction over relatively ordinary cases. The commissioners were much concerned in the 1560s and 1570s with punishing recusancy in the papist laity, though an entirely different target was presented to them by 'sectaries' (nonconformists) who did not think the reformation of the Church, and the extirpation of ritual, had

---

[125] 1 Eliz., c. 1. About twenty bishops were deprived. In 1597 Parliament thought fit to confirm the deprivations by statute: 39 Eliz., c. 8. The history of the High Commission was traced in R. G. Usher, *The Rise and Fall of the High Commission* (Oxford, 1913), but the account was very one-sided. Usher had no time for the common lawyers' arguments and paid little attention to reported cases. He even accused Coke of fabricating precedents (without checking the roll references which Coke gave), and rejected the value of the authentic reports from Dyer's notebooks because they were not printed: ibid. 191–2 n. 2. See now Smith, *Sir Edward Coke*, pp. 176–212; below, pp. 289, 353.

proceeded far enough.[126] The extreme Puritans wanted a more demo-cratic form of Church government, without bishops or lay patronage, and did not believe in prescribed forms of worship or clerical dress. There were many more who objected to parts of the Book of Common Prayer, to usages which they considered superstitious (such as the sign of the cross in baptism, or the use of the ring in marriage), and to some of the articles of religion to which ministers were required to assent. True Puritans were seen as dangerously subversive, but the moderate wing enjoyed sympathy in high places, particularly with legally educated ministers such as Lord Keeper Bacon and Lord Treasurer Burghley, and had considerable influence in the inns of court.[127] Nonconformist clergy also had lay support in many parts of the country and were increasingly being presented to livings. In consequence, they were feared by the episcopal hierarchy as threatening the delicate Anglican settlement. Different forms of divine service were being used in different parishes, supposedly leaving some parishioners in a dilemma whether it was proper for them to attend church or not.[128] Measures were taken against nonconformist clergy-men in the 1560s by Matthew Parker, as archbishop of Canterbury, and in 1571 it was enacted that ministers could be deprived of their benefices for persistently maintaining doctrines contrary to the articles of religion, or failing to subscribe to them.[129] A more concerted and divisive campaign was launched in 1581, with a parallel secular dis-ciplinary jurisdiction conferred on the assizes and quarter sessions,[130] and this was reinforced in the High Commission after John Whitgift became archbishop of Canterbury in 1583.[131] At first operating as 'the ecclesiastical arm of the Privy Council', the Commission became, around the time Richard Bancroft joined it in 1587, 'a court of equity

---

[126] This was partly regional. The northern commission, based in York, continued to be focused on papists into the 1580s, whereas Puritanism became the predominant concern of its southern counterpart: Collinson, *Bancroft*, p. 48.

[127] Prest, *The Inns of Court*, pp. 187–219. There were papists also in the Elizabethan inns of court, but chiefly among the non-vocational elements: ibid. 174–86.

[128] *Proc. Parl. 1558–81*, pp. 205–6.   [129] 13 Eliz. I, c. 12.

[130] 23 Eliz. I, c. 1. Common informers were encouraged by giving them one third of the penalties recovered, though this had been opposed by Fleetwood in 1571, as giving 'private gain to the worst sort of men': *Proc. Parl. 1558–81*, p. 201. For enforcement of uniformity at the assizes see Cockburn, *History of English Assizes*, pp. 189, 202–9.

[131] According to Usher, *High Commission*, p. 124, the first 'quasi-legal assault' on the High Commission by the Puritans was in 1584. But there had been skirmishes since the 1560s: below, pp. 159–61.

for ecclesiastical affairs' wielding 'coercive force of unlimited amount'.[132]

As a result of its transformation, the activities of the High Commission were no longer by the 1580s confined to deviant ministers and recusants of various persuasions. The commissioners had begun to punish the laity as well as the clergy for everyday offences not involving religious worship, such as 'incontinency' (sexual misconduct), defamation and usury, thereby displacing the traditional jurisdiction of the bishops' courts. The main justification for these innovations was that a bishop's court had no jurisdiction beyond his diocese, and so a mobile defendant could easily remove himself from its reach, and also that it had no coercive powers of fine or imprisonment.[133]

Such innovations upon the legal system were open to several objections. For one thing, the commissions were not enrolled in Chancery, so only insiders knew what was in them.[134] Coke later wrote that the commissions had been kept secret because the commissioners knew the weakness of their authority, 'so as the subject lived under an unknown commission and authority'.[135] This secrecy contrasted with the age-old practice whereby secular judicial commissions, such as those of the assize judges, were produced and read out in public before the judges took their seats.[136] The commissioners made people travel long distances to appear before them,[137] whereas this was not the case

---

[132] Usher, *Reconstruction*, i. 101–9.

[133] These were the arguments presented to James I at the Hampton Court conference in 1604: Usher, *Reconstruction*, i. 328. Usher said that the bishops at the conference would have agreed to curtail the powers of the commission if they had themselves been given the power of fining and imprisonment: ibid. 340.

[134] This was complained of as late as 1605 in *Needham* v. *Price* (1605) BL MS. Add. 35954, fo. 418, *per* Fenner J. (tr. 'they have a commission to proceed according to their instructions, but what those instructions are no one can know; also no one can see what is their commission, for it is not enrolled, which seems to me a great abuse').

[135] Co. Inst. iv. 326, 332. He noted that the first commission was said to be lost, and that none of the commissions before Lord Ellesmere's time had been enrolled, 'so as no man could know what instructions they contained': autograph note in the margin of BL MS. Add. 58218, fo. 11v. He omitted to mention that he had drawn at least one of them himself, as attorney-general.

[136] This practice was observed until the abolition of the assizes in 1971.

[137] In *Vinor* v. *Pelling* (1611) BL MS. Add. 9844, fo. 42, Coke CJ pointed out that a statute of 1531 (23 Hen. VIII, c. 9) protected people from being drawn into ecclesiastical courts out of their own dioceses. He added, (tr.) 'If we were to drag those who are at Berwick to St Michael's Mount in Cornwall, what inconvenience might follow?'

with diocesan courts or the courts of common law. Whitgift retorted that in a civil action, such as debt, a man might be called from Carlisle to Westminster Hall;[138] but this was disingenuous, because the defendant at common law could appear by attorney. The commissioners assumed the power to fine and imprison, a power which had never been available to ordinary Church courts without parliamentary sanction.[139] They incarcerated people for long periods without bail, a practice which Whitgift defended on the grounds that the imprisonment was for punishment rather than for safe custody;[140] the 'punishment', however, was for contempt of the commissioners' mesne process, not for a substantive spiritual offence. And imprisonment was sometimes imposed for trivial offences. One extreme example given in the House of Commons was that of a Mrs Marion, who was kept in irons for declining to be churched after the birth of her baby so that she could stay at home and nurse the child and her sick husband.[141] Whitgift's general response to such complaints was that any contempt of the jurisdiction, even in minor cases, was a major matter.[142] Another objection was that this was the only first-instance tribunal in the land from which there was no appeal.[143] Worst of all, the commissioners forced people to incriminate themselves by means of the oath *ex officio*,[144] without showing them the questions in advance,[145] a procedure which was not mentioned in the original commissions but had been reintroduced under Whitgift.[146] The oath was seen by many as a

---

[138] *Proc. Parl. 1584–9*, p. 442.

[139] This was questioned as early as 1577, when four judges and the law officers gave an opinion that there was a power to fine in cases of recusancy: Usher, *High Commission*, p. 158.

[140] *Proc. Parl. 1584–9*, pp. 443, 463.   [141] Ibid. 447–8.

[142] Ibid. 51, 454. His particular response was that it was no business of Parliament anyway.

[143] The point was made by Coke, as counsel, in *Anon.* (1582) BL MS. Lansdowne 1078, fo. 57; *R. v. Manning* (1590) BL MS. Add. 35949, fo. 107v. See also *Th'Appellation of John Penri unto the Highe Court of Parliament from the ... High Commission* (1589/90). It was even more frequently made by Coke as a judge: below, pp. 377–8, 388.

[144] See C. M. Gray, 'Self-Incrimination in Interjurisdictional Law: the Sixteenth and Seventeenth Centuries' in *The Privilege against Self-Incrimination: Its Origins and Development*, ed. R. H. Helmholz and others (Chicago, 1997), pp. 47–81; E. H. Shagan, 'The English Inquisition: Constitutional Conflict and Ecclesiastical Law in the 1590s' (2004) 47 *Historical Journal* 541–65; Smith, *Sir Edward Coke*, pp. 185–90.

[145] Whitgift's defence was that defendants should not be allowed time to think, 'lest they seek through counsel by evasions to delude the truth': *Proc. Parl. 1584–9*, pp. 442, 463.

[146] It was not mentioned until the sixth version in the 1580s: see Robert Beale's tract of 1591 in BL MS. Add. 48039, fo. 84.

reversion to the evil foreign ways of the past.[147] These were the bones of contention which caused constant rifts between the ecclesiastical hierarchy and the judiciary for over fifty years.

It was asserted in 1571 by Christopher Wray (the future lord chief justice), as speaker of the Commons, that the queen's power in ecclesiastical matters was absolute.[148] But the extent of this absolute power was much controverted. The chief concern of the judges was to uphold the rule of law and to prevent too much unbridled coercive power being exercised by the Church, independently of Parliament, under the aegis of the prerogative. The archbishops, on the other hand, wanted the absolute power to be exercised so as to impose a middle way in religion which might in time become tolerable to all sides. They were therefore inclined to favour the strict and effective enforcement of religious conformity at the expense of due process. Freedom of conscience, or of religious observance, could hardly be extended to the clergy, since they were ordained and beneficed of their own volition, had public duties in relation to their flocks, and owed obedience to the hierarchy of the day. And outward conformity, at least, was expected from the laity. In enforcing this policy the ecclesiastical regime was supported at the highest level. The Star Chamber in 1577 sentenced Leonard Babthorpe, a barrister of the Middle Temple, to be sequestered from the Bar, to pay £100 and to confess his faults at the next assizes; his instructing attorney was sent to the pillory and disqualified for life. Babthorpe had been of counsel with a woman indicted before the Council in the North for not going to church and had advised her, firstly, that she should seek a copy of the indictment; secondly, that she could not answer without her husband; and, thirdly, that the process was defective. When all these points were rejected by the councillors, Babthorpe in exasperation said they were denying law and justice. The councillors thought his insolence had given rise to a rumour in Yorkshire that there was no law to touch papists, especially women. But the truth is that, although Babthorpe committed a

---

[147] It was thought to be a good argument against the oath that Thomas More had been in favour of it: Robert Beale's treatise (1591) BL MS. Add. 48039, fo. 83. Henry Finch and Nicholas Fuller argued in *Maunsell's Case* (1607) below, Appendix 9, that the oath was derived from 'foreign law' (p. 521) or 'foreign authority' (p. 527). On the other hand, Lord Ellesmere told the king at the Hampton Court conference in 1604 that the oath was very necessary: Usher, *Reconstruction*, i. 328.

[148] *Proc. Parl. 1558–81*, p. 198. This has been described as 'a piece of crown aggression' against Parliament: A. Cromartie, *The Constitutionalist Revolution* (Cambridge, 2006), p. 115 (where the speech is attributed to the lord keeper).

contempt in saying what he did in open court, the law was on his side. Dyer CJ reported the incident without comment, but it is unlikely that he felt comfortable with it.[149]

The Bar were not to be so easily cowed. Edward Coke was prominent as counsel in legal challenges to the High Commission as early as the 1580s. For example, he represented the notorious Calvinist minister Melancthon Jewell[150] upon his indictment for not saying the common prayer in the prescribed form, by omitting the litany and the Athanasian creed, and substituting Geneva psalms for the Psalms of David. Coke's first line of defence was that Jewell was only preaching on the day in question, not conducting the offices, and it was not a wilful deviation, but Gawdy J. interjected impatiently: 'such seditious persons shall have no favour, for they are authors of the schisms which the statute of 1 Eliz. intended to avoid'. Coke then secured Jewell's discharge on technical grounds.[151] The following year Coke obtained a prohibition where a party was asked, upon an interrogatory, whether or not he was guilty of an offence, for by such means (as he said) anyone might be compelled to accuse himself.[152] The year after that, where a party charged with sexual incontinency had been asked directly about his relations with a particular woman, Coke argued successfully that 'the law in this case has a care of souls and will not tempt anyone to forswear himself', citing the maxim *Nemo tenetur seipsum prodere*.[153] The care of souls was no longer, it seems, a monopoly of the clergy, who were inclined to endanger them. Coke was soon afterwards involved, as a magistrate, in the indictment of Dr John Hunt, an ecclesiastical judge in

---

[149] *Att.-Gen. v. Babthorpe and Launder* (1577) *Dyer's Notebooks*, ii. 361, and the variant reports printed there. Dyer CJ had held public office under Edward VI, Mary I and Elizabeth I.

[150] Jewell was a basket-maker and wandering preacher who was prosecuted before the High Commission two years later: Collinson, *Bancroft*, p. 105.

[151] *Jewell's Case* (1588) BL MS. Harley 1331, fo. 52v (tr.); CUL MS. Ii.5.38, fo. 203v. A few terms earlier he had argued successfully against Nicholas Fuller in a similar case (MS. Harley 1331, fo. 40; Godb. 118, dated 1587).

[152] *Anon.* (1589) BL MS. Harley 1633, fo. 68v. It seems the argument was successful: Gray, *Writ of Prohibition*, ii. 322. Cf. a similar case in the Common Pleas the same year, in which the judges apparently declined to give relief: *Anon.* (1589) Moo. 906; BL MS. Lansdowne 1073, fo. 108; MS. Add. 25194, fo. 6v; MS. Add. 25196, fo. 199v; Gray, *Writ of Prohibition*, ii. 317–22.

[153] *Collier* v. *Collier* (1590) CUL MS. Ff.5.20, fo. 39 (tr.); MS. Ll.3.9, fo. 95; BL MS. Add. 24845, fo. 200; Cro. Eliz. 201; Moo. 906. According to the version in MS. Ll.3.9, (tr.) 'The court said they would be advised until the next term, but I do not remember that this case was moved again' (cf. 4 Leo. 194). But Croke and Moore say the prohibition was granted.

Norwich, for excommunicating a party who had refused to take the oath *ex officio*. The queen was displeased by this, and insisted that in future grand juries should not be charged to enquire into ecclesiastical proceedings.[154] But in a civil action against Dr Hunt by the same party, Fenner J. held that 'their law may admit the party to purgation by oath, if the party wishes, but may not force the party to accuse himself'.[155] 'Their' law, the canon law, was now subject to 'our' law when it impinged on liberty.

Coke was involved in a more serious challenge to the High Commission which began in 1584.[156] It had nothing to do with religious liberty, or uniformity of worship, but it raised a fundamental question about the commissioners' jurisdiction. The plaintiff Cheney, a clergyman, had been sentenced in the bishop's court for adultery, having failed his purgation, but the sentence had been reversed on appeal to the Court of Audience. He was then prosecuted in the Court of Arches on the same charge, and while that case was pending he was brought before the High Commission, put to his purgation again, and deprived of his living. It was a serious case of double, if not triple, jeopardy. This was not at all acceptable to practising ecclesiastical lawyers, and was arguably contrary to canon law.[157] But there was no regular appeal from the High Commission, and Cheney was advised that his best course was to bring an action of trespass against the new incumbent in the Common Pleas, for taking the tithes. His action failed, but the case attracted wide notice when it was reargued on a writ of error in the King's Bench. Cheney's chief point was that adultery was not within the terms of the Act of 1559, being a matter for the ordinary episcopal courts, and that the proceedings were objectionable because there was no appeal. Coke was retained by the defendant, and

---

[154] Gray, *Writ of Prohibition*, ii. 321–2; Brooks, *Law, Politics and Society*, pp. 104–5. The charge to the grand jury had been delivered at the quarter sessions by Wyndham J. and Coke JP.

[155] *Benington* v. *Hunt* (1590–91) BL MS. Add. 35948, fo. 53; also reported in Cro. Eliz. 262; MS. Lansdowne 1057, fo. 145; CUL MSS Ii.5.16, fos. 101v–102; Ll.3.9, fo. 100.

[156] *Cheney* (or *Cheyny*) v. *Frankwell* (1584–8) 2 Leo. 176 (dated 1588); Coke's notebook, BL MS. Harley 6687D, fo. 730 (1587); BL MS. Hargrave 15, fos. 134v–135 (1584); CUL MS. Ii.5.38, fo. 153 (dated Mich. 1584 and Pas. 1585); MS. Hh.2.9, fos. 359v–360 (Trin. 1587, and later); BL MS. Add. 35945, fo. 47. Cf. Sav. 82, pl. 162; ibid. 114, pl. 186 (an identical report which adds that the question arose in the Exchequer when the fine for fornication was estreated).

[157] That point had been argued by Dr Clarke in *Anon.* (1582) BL MS. Lansdowne 1078, fo. 57, though he admitted that the judgment would be voidable rather than void, and therefore there was a doubt how it could be reversed. He suggested a *supplicavit* to appoint a commission, following the procedure in France.

argued that adultery was a cause of deprivation under the canon law and was a spiritual matter, being against the law of God, and could therefore be tried by the commissioners. It was not quite the last time he spoke in favour of the Commission,[158] but – doubtless to his later regret – he won. The King's Bench upheld the decisions of the Commission and the Common Pleas, and the judgment was upheld again by the Exchequer Chamber in 1588. Wray CJ said the High Commission was made for two reasons, namely to expedite cases depending in the spiritual courts and to punish spiritual offences by fine and imprisonment, whereas before they could only excommunicate.[159] It would take much legal debate, brought to a head when Coke was chief justice, to overturn this thinking. It seems that Coke may have foreseen the difficulties ahead, for the report which he wrote in his notebook at the time shows some ambivalence and was reworked later, with interlineations and corrections. He not only omitted to mention his own involvement as counsel but managed to detect an important qualification in the decision which other reporters missed. On the point of substance, according to Coke's unpublished report:[160]

> It was resolved by the whole court that the high commissioners ought not to have determined a thing for which the party could have an ordinary remedy ... for they only have power to determine according to the law ecclesiastical. [But] note well that the statute has reference to the letters patent [of commission] and confirms and corroborates them. If, therefore, the high commissioners have power by the Act and by the letters patent to determine the offence,[161] then, even though the matter depends in court Christian by ordinary course of the Civil law, this judgment is not void but stands in force until it is annulled and reversed by a higher court, and that can only be in Parliament or by a commission of review. But they could be prohibited before the deprivation, for it takes away the [? freehold] of the party, which is his birthright.[162]

In other words, the High Commission were in the wrong, but no remedy could be given in an action of trespass at common law. The principle of judicial comity required the secular courts to accept the ecclesiastical

---

[158] See *Cawdray's Case* (1595) below, pp. 141–3.

[159] According to Nicholas Fuller, 'ecclesiastical persons should in their government use only the spiritual sword of exhortation, admonition and excommunication': *Proc. Parl. 1610*, ii. 407.

[160] BL MS. Harley 6687D, fo. 730 (tr.).

[161] The commission did refer to adultery, though this was not an offence mentioned in the Act.

[162] The last sentence is an interlineation and is difficult to decipher as a result of alterations.

judgment unless and until it was duly reversed.[163] But that principle applied only to final determinations. Coke's qualification of the decision, apparently an afterthought, made the vital point that the common-law court could have stopped the suit while it was depending, by a writ of prohibition. That was to be the future weapon of choice, together with *habeas corpus*.

More judicial support for the High Commission came in 1587, when all the judges were assembled in Serjeants' Inn, Fleet Street, to consider whether the commissioners had the power to fine for moral offences.[164] One of the queen's servants had been fined 200 marks for fornication with his fiancée in Greenwich House before marrying someone else.[165] When the fine was estreated into the Exchequer, objection was taken that the fine had been imposed without authority. The submission was rejected. By a majority, the judges held that the statute gave the queen a broad discretionary power under which her commissioners could punish by fine or imprisonment all offences corrigible by the ecclesiastical jurisdiction. The fine was therefore properly imposed. They said their minds were reinforced in so deciding because fornication was such a detestable offence, though they added a cautionary note that the fines imposed by the commissioners had to be reasonable, and any imprisonment limited to a suitable time, since there was no appeal. It was an instance of a bad case making bad law, and the judges were careful not to refer to it again.

The power to deprive clergy of their benefices was revisited in *Cawdray's Case*, reported at length by Coke – though his amplified version was not produced until ten years after the event[166] – and also by

---

[163] Coke had made the same argument with success in *Bunting* v. *Leppingwell* (1585) Coke's notebook, BL MS. Harley 6687D, fo. 710; 4 Co. Rep. 29; J. Baker, 'Some Elizabethan Marriage Cases' in *Studies in Canon Law and Common Law in Honor of R. H. Helmholz*, ed. T. L. Harris (Berkeley, CA, 2015), pp. 181–211, at pp. 197–9. That case concerned a decree of divorce obtained contrary to natural justice.

[164] *Anon.* (1587) Sav. 83, 115 (two versions of the same report); Clench's reports, BL MS. Harley 4556, fos. 195–6. The case stated, in English, is set out verbatim in both reports.

[165] The fine seems nevertheless to have primarily, if not solely, for the fornication rather than the breach of promise.

[166] *Cawdray* v. *Acton*, sub nom. *Caudrey's Case* (1594–5) 5 Co. Rep., part 1 (with a substantial historical commentary appended: below, p. 295); there is a shorter contemporary report in Coke's notebook, BL MS. Harley 6686A, fos. 109v–111. Cawdray so spelt his own name, and that spelling is adopted here, though Coke rendered it Caudrey. Most accounts of the case are based solely on Coke's report. For comment see J. Guy, 'The Elizabethan Establishment and the Ecclesiastical Polity' in J. Guy, ed., *The Reign of Elizabeth I* (Cambridge, 1995), at pp. 131–6; Smith, *Sir Edward Coke*, pp. 190–4.

others.[167] Robert Cawdray, a Norfolk minister with a wife and eight children, had been deprived of his living in 1587 by the ecclesiastical commissioners for the usual Puritan offences of impugning the Book of Common Prayer in a sermon, omitting the sign of the cross in baptism, and omitting the ring at weddings. His case was taken up by the progressive barristers James Morice, Nicholas Fuller and George Croke, who signed a joint opinion in 1591 that the deprivation was not warranted by the Act of 1559 because it was only a first offence and there should have been a prior indictment.[168] Morice admitted privately that it was a hopeless case, and that he was under criticism from on high, but wrote to Burghley that 'seeking to help the wronged, to maintain law and justice, and to make ecclesiastical judges more careful hereafter, I think it unseemly in a man of my profession to be afraid of every frown'.[169] When the matter was brought before the King's Bench in 1594, similar arguments were presented on Cawdray's behalf by Matthew Dale and Henry Finch, on successive occasions. None of these counsel chose to rely on Magna Carta, as they might have done,[170] preferring to present the matter as a question of statutory interpretation. But the arguments failed. The defendants were represented by Richard Hutton, Francis Gawdy and Edward Coke (now the queen's attorney-general), who made two successful responses. The first was that, if the sentence of deprivation was erroneous on technical grounds, it was only voidable rather than void, and had therefore to be recognised by the secular courts until it was duly reversed.[171] The second was that the commissions were not circumscribed by the wording of the statute because they were granted by the queen under the prerogative, as supreme governor of the Church, and there was a pre-existing canon law jurisdiction to punish spiritual offences. The Act of 1559 was 'not a statute introductory of new law but declaratory of the old', and the queen could have granted the commissions even if the Act had not been made. Popham CJ (himself a high commissioner), after consulting all

---

[167] E.g. BL MS. Harley 1697, fos. 25, 40v–41; MS. Harley 4998, fos. 74–75; MS. Lansdowne 1084, fo. 109.

[168] BL MS. Lansdowne 68, fo. 104. Edward Phelips subscribed his opinion to the same effect, adding 'if the deprivation grow upon the statute'. There are also longer opinions given by Morice alone: ibid. 106; MS. Lansdowne 115, fos. 31–32. These all date from 1591.

[169] BL MS. Lansdowne 68, fo. 125 (letter of 3 July 1591).

[170] The applicability of c. 29 to the proceedings of the High Commission had been explored in the 1580s: below, pp. 255–61.

[171] They cited Cheney v. Frankwell (1588) and Bunting v. Leppingwell (1585), above.

the judges, held it to be clear that the authority of the commissioners did not rest solely on the statute.

The decision in *Cawdray's Case* did not prevent prohibitions in appropriate cases,[172] and they continued to be granted on due-process grounds. In 1596, when another Norfolk minister was convented before the commissioners for saying of a fellow minister that he was 'fitter to stand in the pillory than to preach in the pulpit', the King's Bench granted a prohibition on the grounds that such defamatory words could be remedied by an action at common law, and also because the minister had been forced to incriminate himself on the oath *ex officio*.[173] Shortly afterwards a barrister of the Middle Temple was released on *habeas corpus* after having been committed for refusing to answer interrogatories concerning sexual incontinency.[174] Counsel in that case said that, by the constitutions of the English Church, a person could excuse himself by his oath, but not accuse himself. The decisions in *Cheney v. Frankwell* and *Cawdray's Case* were nevertheless seen by some lawyers as dangerous, in so far as they seemed to sanction an absolutist form of royal supremacy over the Church. The queen herself viewed the supremacy as one of her absolute prerogatives, and forbade the House of Commons to meddle with it. And yet, when the High Commission disseised ministers of their freeholds, and fined or imprisoned offenders without formal presentments or jury trial, it was exercising a temporal authority which was arguably at odds with the liberties granted by the great charter. The point has already been made that in none of the reported cases so far was reliance placed on Magna Carta. But, as will be seen later, grievances about the High Commission were foremost in the thoughts of those who set about to resuscitate chapter 29 in the 1580s and 1590s.[175]

---

[172] See James Whitelocke's note in Mich. 1597, CUL MS. Dd.8.48, fo. 8 (tr. 'It was held that the high commissioners may not punish otherwise than as ordinaries could have done before, unless the statute and commission give other authority, and, [if] they do, prohibition lies').

[173] *Parlor* (or *Partlet*) v. *Butler* (1596) BL MS. Harley 1631, fo. 148v; BL MS. Lansdowne 1059, fo. 256; MS. Add. 25198, fo. 170; CUL MS. Ii.5.26, fo. 147; sub nom. *Barlam's Case* (1597) BL MS. Lansdowne 1061, fos. 28v–29; more briefly in Moo. 460; Gray, *Writ of Prohibition*, i. 148–9; ii. 186–7 (where this is treated as the first prohibition to the High Commission). Cf. *Anon.* (Pas. 1599) BL MS. Lansdowne 1065, fo. 10v (prohibition refused in a case of laying violent hands on a clerk).

[174] *Gawin's Case* (1598) James Whitelocke's reports, CUL MS. Dd.8.48, p. 35. Popham CJ 'greatly misliked' this, because of Gawin's ill fame, but Coke, Tanfield and Foster (as counsel) insisted on *Hynde's Case* (1576) below, p. 161.

[175] Below, pp. 255–61, 270–5.

5

Royal Prerogative and Common Law
under Elizabeth I

The virtual absence of public law from the teaching in the inns of court reflected the irrelevance of the subject for legal practitioners. English lawyers were not much given to speculating openly about the constitutional powers of the king before the late Tudor period. Some materials were to hand, in the form of *Bracton* (first printed in 1569) and the works of Fortescue (one of which was printed in the mid-1540s), but sophisticated theories were not required for practical purposes. By the end of the sixteenth century, however, the climate was changing and lawyers were beginning to discuss prerogative powers openly. It was already standard learning that the king's prerogatives were of two kinds.[1] As Edward Coke wrote in his notebook in 1594, shortly before becoming attorney-general to Elizabeth I, one kind was ordinary and the other absolute.[2] The ordinary kind, meaning that branch of the prerogative which was governed by law and controlled by the judges, was represented in part by the pseudo-statute *Prerogativa Regis*. It was the subject of readings in the inns of court and the treatise of 1548 by William Staunford,[3]

---

[1] See W. S. Holdsworth, 'The Prerogative in the Sixteenth Century' (1921) 21 *Columbia Law Review* 554–71; F. Oakley, 'Jacobean Political Theology: The Absolute and Ordinary Powers of the King' (1968) 29 *Journal of the History of Ideas* 323–46; G. Burgess, *Politics of the Ancient Constitution 1603–42* (1992), pp. 139–62.

[2] BL MS. Harley 6686A, fo. 95. His authorities were *Bracton* and Sir Thomas Smith. The passage is discussed in Smith, *Sir Edward Coke*, pp. 256–9. Cf. Crompton, *Courts*, fo. 78v, citing a dictum of Catlyn CJ in 1565 (tr. 'he excepted the absolute power of the queen of England, and spoke of her ordinary power as to the execution of justice'); John Dodderidge (*c.* 1600) BL MS. Harley 5220, fo. 9v ('the power of the supreme potentate and monarch of England is double and divided into two branches, the one absolute and the other ordinate'); *Coke v. Old* (1601) BL MS. Add. 25215, fo. 3, *per* Hesketh (quoted below, p. 183).

[3] W. Staunford, *An Exposicion of the King's Prerogative* [1548] (1567). This was a simplified version, in English, of the common learning found in the readings, with some antiquarian embellishments: M. McGlynn, *The Royal Prerogative and the Learning of the Inns of Court* (Cambridge, 2003), pp. 224–35. William Staunford (d. 1558), a bencher of Gray's Inn, became JCP in 1554.

it was justiciable in the courts, and it was mostly concerned with feudal rights and revenues rather than powers and authorities; it had little or no connection with the subjects of this chapter.[4] The other, which included making treaties, declaring war, summoning parliaments, and so forth,[5] was a transcendent mystery of state beyond the reach of the courts and not mentioned in the law books.[6] Unlike 'ordinary' prerogatives,[7] it was inseparable from the crown and not delegable to subjects.[8] It was also not justiciable. Coke explained the distinction between the two types of prerogative more expansively in 1600, when still attorney-general:[9]

> The queen has two kinds of prerogative, the one absolute and the other ordinary. In the first, the king's [*sic*] command is to be obeyed without dispute, and the pleasure of the prince has the force of law and the king's letters have the strength of law (*Principis placitum legis vigorem habet, et epistola regis vim habet legis*).[10] The other is ordinary and may be disputed, for it is to be decided by the laws of the realm. Of the former kind are setting values to her coin, levying, directing and finishing her wars, and such like. These belong to the absolute prerogative of the king, which no subject ought to dispute; and these high matters of state are not

---

[4] The readings on *Prerogativa Regis* did not deal with the absolute prerogatives or theorise about the nature of the prerogative: McGlynn, *Royal Prerogative and the Inns of Court*, p. 258.

[5] For these absolute prerogatives see T. Smith, *De Republica Anglorum* (1583), pp. 43–5; Hake, *Epieikeia* (1603), pp. 77–8 (commenting on Smith). For the prerogative of regulating the coinage by proclamation, which still exists, see also Youngs, pp. 104–10.

[6] Morice's reading (1578), fo. 21; *Att.-Gen. v. Bate* (Exchequer, 1606) as reported in BL MS. Harley 37, fo. 175v, and MS. Hargrave 34, at fo. 61v, *per* Hitchcock: (tr.) 'The other kind of prerogative is transcendent and not bound by common law or statute ... termed by state writers *arcana imperii* ... whereof no mention is made in our law books as cases coming under the judgment of any court, and therefore I will not meddle with them.'

[7] As Coke CJ pointed out in a speech to the Lords, no prerogative was delegable in its entirety, but individual prerogative rights (such as particular wardships) could be granted to subjects because they were 'flowers of the crown': *Proc. Parl. 1610*, i. 64–5.

[8] Cf. Lord Ellesmere's brief tract on the royal prerogative, which treats judicature as an 'absolute prerogative' which (unlike discretionary royal powers) could be delegated, though only in accordance with the law: BL Cotton MS. Vespasian C XIV(2), fo. 176; printed from HLS MS. 4006 in L. A. Knafla, *Law and Politics in Jacobean England* (Cambridge, 1977), p. 197.

[9] *Earl of Essex's Case* (1600) in Coke's autograph notebook, BL MS. Harley 6686B, fos. 409v–410 (tr.). The context was the decision that the queen's signet letters, in relation to the conduct of the war in Ireland, prevailed over a general commission under the great seal: below, p. 337.

[10] For the maxim of Roman law see above, p. 120 n. 48; below, p. 340. Fortescue had denied absolutely that it had any application in England, not mentioning the concept of absolute prerogatives: *De Laudibus Legum Anglie* [c. 1470], ed. S. B. Chrimes (Cambridge, 1942), pp. 25, 79.

to be directed by the ordinary rule of the common law, but therein the queen's command ought to be obeyed.

The distinction was restated and explained a few years later by Fleming CB in the great case concerning impositions on currants:[11]

> The king's power is of two kinds (*duplex*), ordinary and absolute, and they have several ends. The ordinary power tends to the utility of every private subject by punishing offences[12] and maintaining *meum et tuum*, and it is exercised by equity and justice in ordinary courts.[13] The Civilians call it private law (*jus privatorum*)[14], though in truth it is the common law itself, in which every man has an interest and an inheritance; and it may not be changed without the consent of the subject through Parliament. Although their form and course may be changed and interrupted, nevertheless they may never be changed in substance.[15] The absolute power of the king aims and tends to the good of the people (*ad salutem populi*), as an entire kingdom and one body, whereof every subject is a member and the king is the head; and it is not ruled by the rules of the common law but by rules of state and policy whereby the common wealth may be the better governed, not respecting private right but common good and public utility.[16] And just as matters of state vary,[17] so [this absolute law varies][18] according to the wisdom of the king, for the common good. These are true positions, and whatever is done by any of these powers is lawful.

---

[11] *Att.-Gen.* v. *Bate* (1606) as reported in BL MS. Harley 37, fo. 182, and MS. Hargrave 34, fo. 70 (tr.). A slightly abridged and garbled English version of this passage is printed in Lane 27 (from which it is usually quoted; reprinted in 2 St. Tr. 382 at col. 389). Burgess noted a parallel passage in the writing of Alberico Gentili, but concluded that this cannot have been the source: *Absolute Monarchy and the Stuart Constitution*, (New Haven, CT, 1996), pp. 81–3. For *Bate's Case* see below, pp. 328–31.

[12] Cf. Lane 27: 'for the execution of civil justice'.

[13] Variant reading from Lane 27; also in BL MS. Add. 24846, fo. 158 (tr.). The other manuscripts read: (tr.) 'this power is by the laws of equality and put in ure in the common courts'. Cf. the different version in BL MS. Hargrave 34, fo. 59: (tr.) 'the ordinary power ... is executed by the common law, and he may not execute this power except in the form which the common law has appointed to him, or by Parliament by consent of the subjects, who have an inheritance in this law'.

[14] Literally, the law of private individuals.

[15] This sentence is from Lane 27; CUL MS. Gg.2.23, fo. 30v; MS. Gg.4.9, fo. 230v. The Harleian and Hargrave texts read: (tr.) 'Although the king may alter the form of the laws, nevertheless he may not alter the substance of them.'

[16] Cf. the different report of the speech in BL MS. Hargrave 34, fo. 59: (tr.) 'The extraordinary or absolute power tends to the preservation of the whole kingdom, and is governed not by rules of equity and justice but by policy.'

[17] Cf. Lane 27: 'the constitution of this body varieth with the time'.

[18] Lane 27. The Harleian and Hargrave texts read: (tr.) 'the laws vary'.

This was an uncontroversial statement. It was in fact based on the submission made by the losing side,[19] and it remains to some extent true even today, since the exercise of some prerogative powers – for instance, to conclude treaties or declare war – cannot be challenged in the courts. The legal difficulty lay in deciding which prerogatives fell into the absolute category. And the important subtext beneath the statement was that this decision belonged not to the king himself but to his judges,[20] a principle which Serjeant Fleetwood had explicitly enunciated in 1582 when addressing the King's Bench:[21]

> If a prerogative granted by the king or a custom is pleaded, and thereupon a demurrer joined, you who are judges of the law, and in whom the law is a speaking law, shall judge whether it is a good grant, or a good prerogative, or a good custom, and your judgment is grounded upon and understood through the knowledge of the law ... [For] the kings of England ... wish their grants and prerogatives to be directed and adjudged according to the law... and you who are judges do so adjudge them, and have so adjudged and given judgment.

He reinforced this by asserting that the Roman maxim which gave the king's pleasure the force of law was not a rule followed by English judges.[22] He also related the story of King Antigonus, who in response to a flatterer telling him that 'all things are honest and lawful for kings', said: 'That is only for such kings as are barbarous beasts and without humanity, whereas for true and good princes nothing is honest but that which is honest in fact, and nothing is just but that which is just in fact.' The principle was nowhere stated in Magna Carta, and it did not extend to the exercise of the absolute prerogative,[23] but it rested on the same foundation: that the king was subject to the law of the land. Fleetwood had managed to read this into Magna Carta.[24] But it was not a commonplace of legal argument for most of Elizabeth's reign.

---

[19] See below, p. 330. The argument, which did not succeed, was that impositions did not fall under the absolute prerogative.

[20] See *Waram's Case* (1587) below, p. 177.

[21] Notes of argument in *Att.-Gen.* v. *Joiners' Company of London* (1582) below, Appendix 5, p. 472 (tr.). Cf. *Proc. Parl. 1558–81*, p. 210, where he argued in 1571 that the House of Commons could not discuss the prerogative without permission.

[22] Below, p. 473. For the Roman principle see above, p. 120. Its inapplicability in England was recognised in the fifteenth century: see Fortescue, *De Laudibus Legum Anglie*, p. 25; J. Fortescue, *The Governance of England*, ed. C. Plummer (Oxford, 1885), pp. 112, 117.

[23] Coke said as much in the *Earl of Essex's Case* (1600) above, p. 145.

[24] Below, p. 463 (making a clear allusion to the Roman maxim).

Many of the new problems confronting the courts in the Elizabethan and early Stuart period arose along the boundary between the two kinds of prerogative. They were occasioned by the creation of new jurisdictions and authorities which did not follow the common law, the granting of monopolies which impinged on individual freedom of trade,[25] assisting favoured parties to evade legal proceedings, and imprisoning people without trial on specious grounds of state. The courts also became concerned with urban authorities, operating under royal charters and customs, which tended to see themselves as miniature civic states independent of central government. None of these perceived encroachments upon the old law were attributed to the queen personally, nor was she suspected of favouring absolutism or of wishing to enlarge the prerogative in any essential respect, though she was very touchy about any discussion of its boundaries. The judges, even the chief justices, did not have direct access to the queen, and yet until the end of her reign they felt sure – perhaps naively – that if only she were accurately informed of improper innovations she would put things right.[26]

When Coke became attorney-general in 1594, he was summoned into the queen's presence and commanded to kneel, whereupon she addressed him as follows:[27]

> I charge thee in exercise of that office, that if thou shall perceive that in any case which concerneth me rigour of law should give me more than equity, good conscience would that I may have no more than that which I may safely enjoy both by law with a good conscience. And yet hereof I mean not to make thee a chancellor in those cases, but when such cases do fall out that thou dost inform me and I will moderate the same according to justice and equity. But in matters doubtful, when the cause resteth *in aequali jure*, then it is no reason but that I should be preferred according to my prerogative royal. Secondly, I charge thee that my subjects receive at thy hands that which to them appertaineth according to law: Justice. For a better prince hereafter you may have when I am

---

[25] Below, pp. 187–99.

[26] E.g. in 1587 Wray CJ said he would report a novel form of protection to the queen (below, p. 178), and in 1592 the judges sought to inform the queen of abuses of imprisonment by privy councillors (below, p. 166).

[27] Coke's autograph notebook, BL MS. Harley 6686A, fo. 86. Cf. his reminscence in 1615 (3 Bulst. 44): 'When I was the queen's attorney, she said unto me, "I understand that my counsel will strongly urge *praerogativa reginae*, but my will is that they stand *pro domina veritate* rather than *pro domina regina*, unless that *domina regina* hath *veritatem* on her side"; and she also used to give this in charge many times, when anyone was called to any office by her, that they should ever stand *pro veritate* rather than *pro regina*.'

gone, but never any that have a more fervent desire to execute justice, and to do right to all, and see that my subjects have justice with expedition and with as small charge as conveniently may be.

No doubt she was referring here to the ordinary prerogative, but any decision as to the boundaries of the just and lawful rights of the crown, and of the manifold authorities exercised in the name of the queen, would necessarily impinge on the absolute power. In so far as the boundary disputes could be resolved formally, the decision rested in practice with the queen's chief ministers, the queen's judges and the queen's law officers,[28] rather than with the queen herself. And, in resolving them, Magna Carta would increasingly be prayed in aid of the subject, to the point where reference to chapter 29 became instinctive.[29] In the last year of the queen's life, Coke wrote:[30]

Bless God for Queen Elizabeth, whose continual charge to her justices, agreeable with her ancient laws, is that for no commandment under the great or privy seal, writs or letters, common right be disturbed or delayed; and if any such commandment (upon untrue surmises) should come, that the justices of her laws should not therefor cease to do right in any point.[31] And this agreeth with the ancient law of England, declared by the great charter, and spoken in the person of the king, *Nulli vendemus, nulli negabimus aut differemus justiciam vel rectum.*

For the queen's attorney-general thus to affirm the principles of constitutional monarchy, in her name, was significant. It was a rhetoric adopted even by Lord Keeper Egerton in this period. When he was sworn in as lord keeper, in 1596, he spoke of

the religious and grave exhortations made to him by the queen at several times, namely when he was made solicitor, attorney, and master of the rolls, and now lord keeper, the sum whereof was that he should serve her

---

[28] The attorney-general did have access to the sovereign. Elizabeth I told Coke in 1594, 'Thou shalt have free access to my person, and thus I will assure thee that I will never credit any report of thee before I have called thee to thine answer and hear thyself to defend thyself': BL MS. Harley 6686A, fo. 87.

[29] See Chapter 7, below.

[30] *Le Second Part des Reportes del Edward Coke Lattorney Generall de Roigne* (1602), preface, sig. ¶v. There is a similar encomium in Hake, *Epieikeia* (1603), p. 84. Hake said her reign had been 'one of the most blessed patterns of just government in the world', since she had never acted contrary to law. She did, nevertheless, show a propensity to authorise summary martial law in suppressing popular disorder: below, p. 431 n. 114.

[31] This was far from being merely a speculative possibility: see below, pp. 181, 424. Christopher Wray, as speaker of the Commons in 1571, had praised the queen for the same reason, perhaps hoping to ward off any reversion to this practice: *Proc. Parl. 1558–81*, p. 199.

in the fear of God, without which all learning, eloquence, wisdom and other gifts are but as a sword in the hand of a madman, and particularly at this time that he should administer justice indifferently to all, without fearing the might of any man; and he protested that if any injury or injustice is done to any of her subjects the fault is in us (who are her officers and ministers of justice), and she is spotless — and he said this that all the realm might know it.[32]

Whether these encomiums were fully justified by the reality is beside the point. There was at least a public commitment to the rule of law, which could only benefit from such proclamations of the queen's impartiality and commitment to justice. Coke's allusion to Magna Carta was a sign of its recent revival, which will be traced in later chapters. But the rule of law itself, even if that terminology was yet to be invented, was no innovation.[33] The royal judges had already before this time made considerable headway in the defence of individual liberties using common-law tools. Their inventions would later be attributed to the great charter, but they seem not to have been consciously inspired by it. The golden principle was that the king could not use his prerogative so as to wrong a subject.[34] That was, no doubt, the principle underlying chapter 29, but Tudor lawyers did not at first make the association explicitly. It was, rather, an application of the late-medieval legal principle that the king could do no wrong.[35] In order to pinpoint the reinvention of Magna Carta, and in particular chapter 29, it is necessary first to assess the extent of the common-law developments which preceded it, and to note how rarely it was mentioned in discussions of individual liberty and the rule of law until the 1580s.

---

[32] BL MS. Lansdowne 1061, fo. 25v. Cf. his remarks in Hawarde 52 ('her whole care is that truth, equity and justice should be with equal hand ministered unto all her subjects', 1596), p. 93 ('it is her majesty's daily commandment to do justice to all sorts, and [i.e. even] if her self be a party', 1597), p. 100 ('it is her continual charge [to] do justice equally to all my subjects in the fear of God', 1598).

[33] For the early Tudor period see *OHLE*, vi. 63–73.

[34] *Willion v. Lord Berkeley* (1562) Pl. Com. 223 at fo. 236 (tr. 'although the king has many prerogatives ... the law has nevertheless so admeasured them that they cannot take away or prejudice anyone's inheritance'); *Manser v. Annesley* (1575) as reported in HLS MS. 2071, fos. 65v–69, at fo. 67v, *per* Harpur J.; *Fortescue's Case* (1586) BL MS. Harley 1331, fo. 1, at fo. 4, *per* Anderson CJ (tr. 'the king shall not have a prerogative whereby a subject would be wronged'); *Waram's Case* (1587) Moo. 239 (tr. 'a prerogative which tends in high prejudice of the subject is not allowable'); H. Finch, *Law, or a Discourse Thereof* [c. 1595/1600], ed. D. Pickering (1759), pp. 82–5.

[35] For the general principle see above, p. 45; and *Darcy v. Allen* (1602) below, p. 322, *per* Popham CJ. Cf. *Willion v. Lord Berkeley* (1562) Pl. Com. 223 at fo. 246 (tr. 'the king cannot do wrong, nor will his prerogative be any warrant for him to injure another').

Legislation by Proclamation

A preliminary matter to consider briefly, because of its later significance, is the controversy over the extent to which the queen was able to effect changes in the law of the land by proclamation. Royal proclamations were issued very frequently under the Tudors, for the most part on the initiative of the Privy Council.[36] They were, and to some extent still are, the proper form of instrument for exercising absolute prerogative powers, such as announcing the accession of a new monarch, making innovations in or revaluations of the coin of the realm,[37] varying the royal style and titles,[38] and declaring war.[39] They were also used to support parliamentary legislation, by commanding obedience and threatening punishment for the disobedient, and occasionally to suspend the enforcement of a statute pending amendment. Sometimes they sought to explain statutes, or even to supply punishments not specified in statutes,[40] and in such instances the government seemed to be asserting a legislative power. The law was clear, however, that the queen could not herself alter the law or impose penalties without Parliament. It could not be done by letters patent; no more could it be done by proclamation.[41] The Commons had insisted in 1539 that Henry VIII's controversial Statute of Proclamations should make it clear that no proclamation could affect a person's legal rights, and this proviso was remembered and cited as an authority long after the repeal of the statute.[42] The assembled judges had made the legal position plain in 1556:[43]

---

[36] Cf. proclamations made by courts, e.g. in the levying of final concords, or adjourning the term because of plague.

[37] Staunford J. in 1556 denied that this extended to debasement of the coinage, which would prejudice people: *The Reports of William Dalison 1552-1558*, ed. Sir John Baker (124 SS, 2007), pp. 101-2; *OHLE*, vi. 64-5.

[38] E.g. *Dyer's Notebooks*, ii. 401 (Philip and Mary); this was also notified to the judges by writ, KB 27/1178, m. 20.

[39] Cf. the 'proclamation of enmity' against specific Scottish lords who had received fugitive English rebels in 1571: *Dyer's Notebooks*, ii. 238.

[40] Cf. Egerton's classification of proclamations as (i) mandatory, (ii) prohibitory, (iii) declaratory (or explanatory), and (iv) dispensatory: H. E. Huntington Library MSS EL 438-439; cited in Youngs, p. 17.

[41] This was settled, after some difference of opinion, in the time of Henry VIII (above, p. 106; *OHLE*, vi. 64-5; Youngs, pp. 27-9).

[42] E.g. it was cited in the Commons in 1607: R. W. Heinze, 'Proclamations and Parliamentary Protest 1539-1610' in *Tudor Rule and Revolution*, ed. D. J. Guth and J. W. McKenna (Cambridge, 1982), pp. 237-59, at p. 243. See also Crompton, *Courts*, fo. 14; 12 Co. Rep. 75.

[43] *Dalison's Reports*, p. 101. Note also *Att.-Gen. v. Cioll* (1559) Co. Inst. ii. 62-3, where there was a demurrer to an information founded upon a proclamation of 1558 forbidding the

> The king may make a proclamation to his subjects *quoad terrorem populi*,
> to put them in fear of his displeasure and indignation, but not upon any
> certain penalty, such as forfeiture of lands or goods, or making fine, or
> suffering imprisonment, or other penalties, for no proclamation in itself
> may make a law which was not law before; for a proclamation is only to
> confirm and ratify a law or statute, not to change law or make new law.
> Although several precedents to the contrary were found and shown ...
> the justices paid no regard to them.

Such was the distrust of proclamations that some members of the
Elizabethan House of Commons even opposed a bill which would have
authorised delegated legislation by proclamation.[44] The topic was sometimes addressed by the readers in the inns of court. Fleetwood, in his
treatise on statutes, recalled that, although 'therein hath been doubted of
what effect such proclamations have been, and what pain he that break-
eth them should have', the readers had affirmed that a proclamation was
good if it was 'in supplement or declaration of a law', but bad if it was 'in
alteration or abridgment of the common law'.[45] James Morice, in his
reading of 1578, said that proclamations were binding as law only so far
as they were 'agreeable to the word of God, not repugnant to the laws of
the realm, impossible to be performed, or injurious to the subject'.[46] This
teaching appeared to allow them some legislative potential, analogous to
that exercised by towns in making bye-laws for the public good. But
'injurious to the subject' prevented any unilateral burden being imposed,
and so, according to Morice, the king could not without the authority of
Parliament command subjects to find men at arms or armour for the
defence of the realm, or to go abroad on active service, or afforest
the lands of subjects, or levy taxes or take goods for the necessary affairs
of the realm.[47]

An extensive analysis of the proclamations issued by Mary and
Elizabeth, and of recorded instances of their enforcement, led their
historian to conclude that it is 'certain that proclamations legislated,

---

importation of French wine; there was no recorded judgment, but Coke offered his own
explanation why the proclamation was illegal.

[44] Heinze, 'Proclamations and Parliamentary Protest' (above, n. 42), at pp. 239–40 (where
some examples of delegated legislation are given). Perhaps because of this legacy,
delegated legislation in modern times is usually effected through Orders in Council rather
than proclamations.

[45] *Discourse upon Statutes*, pp. 103–5; cf. the badly garbled early version in LMA, CLC/270,
MS. 86, fo. 1, which supplies the words 'of the common law'. For the authorship see
below, pp. 232–6. Cf. the reading of *c.* 1529, above, pp. 105–6.

[46] BL MS. Egerton 3376, fo. 23. [47] Ibid. 21–3; MS. Add. 36081, fos. 253v–257.

but it is just as clear that this legislation had three characteristics: it was temporary, it was limited, and it was inferior to and not in conflict with Parliament's legislation'.[48] Despite these qualifications, proclamations would still be in conflict with the rule of law if they were penal, as some undoubtedly were. It was not, however, made a constitutional issue at the time. Even Coke accepted, when he was a law officer, that the queen could prohibit anything 'hurtful or prejudicial to the common wealth of the state, albeit the same be not prohibited by law'.[49] No one was ever executed for breach of a proclamation, and it seems that lesser penalties threatened by proclamations *in terrorem* were not usually imposed in fact.[50] No reported challenge was made to a proclamation in the Elizabethan courts of law on the grounds that it encroached upon the common law. The most notorious opportunity for doing so was the case of Lord Vaux and others, who were prosecuted in 1581 for receiving in their houses Edmund Campion and other priests.[51] The receiving was charged to have occurred before the statute of 1581 which clarified the position,[52] but a proclamation of 10 January 1581 had declared that those who received, maintained or concealed any seminary priests should be reputed as maintainers and abettors of seditious persons, and the charge was based on this proclamation. When the defendants were questioned upon interrogatories by the Privy Council, they refused to answer, on the grounds that they might incriminate themselves. They were thereupon prosecuted in the Star Chamber, and heavily fined for their contempt in not answering.[53] The case was considered by the assembled judges at Serjeants' Inn, Fleet Street, but the sole difficulty was whether the defendants were protected by the nascent privilege against

---

[48] Youngs, p. 54.

[49] Burgess, *Absolute Monarchy*, p. 201, quoting PRO, SP 12/276/81–2 (written *c.* 1600).

[50] Youngs, p. 55.

[51] *Att.-Gen. v. Lord Vaux, Tresham, Catesby and others* (1581) Sav. 4 (110 SS 391); BL MS. Lansdowne 1101, ff. 3v–4 (a variant of Savile's report); *Dyer's Notebooks*, ii. 397; Youngs, pp. 233–7. Dyer CJ referred to Campion, the prominent Jesuit, as a 'wry, seditious and traitorous person, a mover and a withdrawer of the queen's subjects from their obedience and allegiance ...'. Campion was one of several priests convicted of treason and sentenced to death in 1581: 110 SS 390; KB 27/1279, Rex, mm. 2–3 (fourteen defendants convicted, one acquitted).

[52] Above, p. 128.

[53] The reports indicate that they were punished for the contempt, not for the substantive offences which they had declined to confess. The decree, however, suggests that they were deemed guilty of receiving as well: *Dyer's Notebooks*, ii. 397–8; see also A. G. Petti, *Recusant Documents from the Ellesmere MSS* (60 Catholic Record Society, 1968), pp. 5–9.

self-incrimination.[54] No mention is made in the reports of any objection to the possible extension of criminal law by proclamation, or to retrospective penal law, perhaps because the proclamation was seen merely as a declaration of the law of sedition in accordance with the judges' own understanding. Misdemeanours were ill defined and could be enlarged or even invented by the Star Chamber.[55] Four years later Sir John Arundel was fined 1,000 marks by the Star Chamber for contempt against a different proclamation concerning the receiving of seminarians.[56] It would have been another matter if an attempt had been made to enlarge treason or felony by proclamation.

By the end of the century, nevertheless, some misgivings were arising among lawyers over the authoritarian tendencies of the Privy Council. In 1597, on the occasion of a prosecution of engrossers by Coke, Bacon sparked off an alarmed reaction when he said that Egerton and the Privy Council were minded to legislate by proclamation. The reporter Hawarde protested:[57]

> For the lord keeper and others of the queen's Council, and the judges also, being so instructed, intend redress for such offences (and many others in the common weal) by the queen's prerogative only ... and thus their decrees and councils, proclamations and orders shall be a firm and forcible law, and of the like force as the common law or an Act of Parliament. And this is the intent of the privy councillors in our day and time, to attribute to their councils and orders the vigour, force and power of a firm law, and of higher virtue, force, jurisdiction and pre-eminence than any positive law, whether it be the common law or statute law. And thus in a short time the privy councillors of this realm would ... have the majesty of prince and ruler of the greatest reverence in all the world.

In the next decade this would become an acknowledged grievance.[58]

---

[54] For its emergence see above, pp. 124, 136–9; below, p. 160.

[55] In *Att.-Gen.* v. *Lady Gresham* (1596) Hawarde 64, at p. 65, Egerton LK said in the Star Chamber that 'we ought to make laws according to men's offences'. In his tract on Magna Carta, c. 29, Coke wrote in 1604 that the Star Chamber could punish offences which were not known at common law: below, pp. 501–2. There was, in any case, no finite list of misdemeanours at common law.

[56] *Att.-Gen.* v. *Arundel, Tresham and others* (1585) BL MS. Harley 2143, fo. 42 (from the lost order book). Sir Thomas Tresham, who had been fined 1,000 marks in the 1581 case, was this time fined £500.

[57] *Att.-Gen.* v. *Parker and others* (1597) Hawarde 78–9. He also complained that Orders in Council were not always widely known in the country, and yet ignorance of the law was no excuse.

[58] Below, pp. 390–6.

Imprisonment and *Habeas Corpus*

The 'liberty of the subject', a concept which by the end of the sixteenth century was common currency,[59] at least in connection with freedom of trade,[60] is not much to be found in the medieval legal sources.[61] Imprisonment by a lesser official could be redressed by an action of false imprisonment – which lay also against the arresting officer and the gaoler[62] – but this gave only damages after the event. However, whether or not it was lawful, kings and their councillors could in practice send people to prison without risk of any formal challenge. Even at the dawn of the Elizabethan age, someone whose sole offence was a birth which made her very existence dangerous to the royal succession could be imprisoned, albeit in comfort, without trial.[63] Coercive imprisonment by privy councillors, without a formal charge, still occurred throughout the reign of Elizabeth I, and the queen herself had no hesitation in sending even members of Parliament into custody if they spoke too boldly on forbidden subjects.[64] But the legal climate was undergoing a change as a result of the writ of *habeas corpus*, which the judiciary were

---

[59] An early instance is *Att.-Gen.* v. *Donatt* (1561) as reported in BL MS. Hargrave 37, fo. 87, *per* Gerrard Att.-Gen. (tr. 'it is the liberty and part of the inheritance of every subject to be of what mystery he will'); and see *Davenant* v. *Hurdys* (1599–1600) as reported by Coventry, BL MS. Add. 25203, fo. 92, *per* Coke Att.-Gen.; *Cleygate* v. *Batchelor* (1601) Owen 143 (liberty of a free man); *Davies* v. *Cornelius* (1607) CUL MS. Gg.2.23, fo. 108, *per* Montagu, recorder of London. These cases all concerned freedom of trade. Cf. also James Morice's reading in the Middle Temple (1578), quoted below, p. 257; and his *Briefe Treatise of Oathes exacted by Ordinaries* (Middleburg, c. 1591), pp. 57–8.

[60] But note the 'liberty of a free man' in *Paramour* v. *Verrall* (1599) 2 And. 151, at p. 153 ('liberty de frankhome'). For 'the liberty of the subject' in relation to imprisonment see also *Whetherly* v. *Whetherly* (1605) below, pp. 309, 513, *per* Yelverton J.; *Maunsell's Case* (1607) below, pp. 518, 520, *per* Fuller. These were probably allusions to Magna Carta, c. 29.

[61] Cf. *Abbot of Westminster's Case* (1462) YB Mich. 2 Edw. IV, fo. 23, pl. 21, *per* Choke J. (tr. 'every subject (*lige*) is inheritable to sue here in the king's court, and no one shall be suffered to prescribe against this; but I quite agree that a man may prescribe to hold plea above 40s. in his court, for that does not restrain the liberty of the king's subjects (*liberty de ses liges*)').

[62] See *Anon.* (1587) BL MS. Lansdowne 1061, fo. 63v: (tr.) 'One was committed to the Fleet by Sir Owen Hopton [lieutenant of the Tower], without cause, and the court said to him, "You may sue a writ of false imprisonment against Sir Owen Hopton or whoever else commits you without cause, and also against the pursuivant and the warden of the Fleet who detains you."'

[63] This was the plight of Lady Katherine Grey (1563): *Dyer's Notebooks*, i. 80–3. She died while still under house arrest in 1568: ibid. 92.

[64] For examples see below, pp. 169, 274. Crompton, *Courts* (1594), fo. 16v, glossing Staunford, said the queen by her 'absolute authority' could imprison during her pleasure.

developing together with a growing confidence in their authority to question abuses of power by the highest in the land.

Old accounts of *habeas corpus*, relying on the printed law reports, traced the first signs of this judicial activity to the 1580s and placed its firm establishment in the seventeenth. But it is now known that a prominent actor in the story was Sir James Dyer, chief justice of the Common Pleas, who died in 1582.[65] Only a year after he was appointed chief justice in 1559, he was confronted with the disturbing case of Alexander Scrogges, an attorney of the Common Pleas who had become embroiled in a controversy over the exigentership of London and Middlesex.[66] The office had been unlawfully granted by Mary I as a favour to the young courtier Robert Colshill, while the chief justiceship was vacant in 1558, but the court had rejected the grantee as an untrained layman and admitted Scrogges.[67] Improper influence, attributed in Dyer's original notebook to the earl of Bedford and Lord Dudley,[68] was then used to procure a special commission to the marquess of Northampton, Sir Thomas Parry, and others (including two judges), to determine the title, with power to commit Scrogges if he refused to answer.[69] Scrogges demurred to the bill of complaint, and was thereupon committed to the Fleet prison for contempt. He applied to the Common Pleas for his release, and Dyer CJ considered using a general *habeas corpus*, following a precedent which he found in his former pupil-master's book of entries,[70] and which he considered could be issued under the inherent jurisdiction of the court; but it was decided to rely instead on Scrogges's privilege as an attorney, and to release him on a writ of privilege (a special form of *habeas corpus*), laying stress on the need for his attendance to serve his clients.[71] Scrogges was released but immediately rearrested by the commissioners, 'to be kept in close

---

[65] For what follows see also J. H. Baker, 'The Rise of Habeas Corpus' in *Dyer's Notebooks*, i, introduction, pp. lxxvii–lxxxiii.

[66] The exigenters were Common Pleas clerks who made out process of outlawry.

[67] *OHLE*, vi. 134; *The Men of Court*, ii. 377. Scrogges was a nephew of Sir Anthony Browne, Dyer's predecessor as CJCP.

[68] *Dyer's Notebooks*, i. 34 (omitted from the printed report in Dyer 175). Robert Dudley was already a close friend of the queen.

[69] *Scrogges' Case* (1559–60) Dyer 175; *Dyer's Notebooks*, i. 34, 54–7. In his answer, Scrogges relied on Magna Carta, c. 29: BL MS. Lansdowne 1057, fo. 3.

[70] John Jenour's book of precedents, Library of Congress MS. Phillipps 26752, fo. 23v; *Dyer's Notebooks*, i. 54. This probably dates from the time of Edward IV.

[71] There is a precedent for such a writ in BL MS. Harley 1715, fo. 191 (*c.* 1510/25).

prison': a move calculated, as Dyer put it, as 'a check to the law'. He remained in the Fleet for over five weeks before he was released by Lord Keeper Bacon, who intervened to end the dispute. Scrogges was allowed to keep his office, but had to pay £200 for it. The judges regarded the commission's behaviour as a major affront, and (according to Saunders CB) held the commission void in law, so that everything which the commissioners did was *coram non judice*. The chief baron wrote with some feeling about the case, concluding that 'all such of the judges of the Common Pleas as did learnedly and willingly agree to the awarding and executing of the same writ of privilege deserved the immortal fame of honourable and good judges'.[72] Nevertheless, the incident had brought home to them – at the very beginning of the new reign – how troublesome it might be to give effect to the law in the teeth of powerful courtiers who cared little for inidivual rights or due process. This may be one of the reasons why, as early as the 1560s, Dyer was collecting pertinent precedents of general *habeas corpus*, and these are of considerable interest, since they were unknown to Selden (when collecting similar materials in 1627), though they became known to Coke after he came into possession of Dyer's notebooks.[73] Coke also found many more himself,[74] some of them older.[75] The Court of Common Pleas could not itself award writs of *habeas corpus*, except in cases of privilege,[76] and yet it was a chief justice of that court whose researches laid the foundations of the remedy.

The first of Dyer's precedents was from 1518, when Thomas Apryse was detained by command of Cardinal Wolsey, but later released by *habeas corpus* in the King's Bench (under Fyneux CJ) because the attorney-general could not support the detention.[77] Apryse may have been implicated in the feud between Wolsey and Sir Robert Sheffield, bencher of the Inner Temple, whose *habeas corpus* in the same roll is

---

[72] Saunders' reports, BL MS. Hargrave 9, fo. 22v. Saunders had been CJKB from 1557 until January 1559, when he was demoted to chief baron.
[73] They were also known to Yelverton J: see *Maunsell's Case* (1607) in Appendix 9, p. 524.
[74] Memorandum on c. 29 of Magna Carta (1604) below, p. 505. In the *Case of the Lords Presidents of Wales and York* (1608) 12 Co. Rep. 50 at fos. 54–5, he cited cases from the 1560s and 1570s from the controlment rolls, and said he had collected precedents in a *Liber de Habeas Corpus*.
[75] E.g. *Bothe's Case* (1494) KB 29/124, m. 14; *Selected Readings on Magna Carta* (a Cambridge scholar committed by the king's command, and for no other cause; bailed).
[76] It did not begin doing so until around 1605–7: above, p. 354. Cf. Halliday, *Habeas Corpus*, p. 76 (dates it to the 1660s).
[77] KB 29/150, m. 34; *Dyer's Notebooks*, i. 77.

returned 'by command of the king alone'.[78] Sheffield was accused by Wolsey of harbouring two murderers, Milner and 'Rice' (Apryse), though he claimed that the accusation was motivated by malice. The writ did not avail Sheffield himself, who was remanded to the Tower and died there later in the year. The merits of his case are elusive at this distance, though it seems probable that he had been persecuted for defending the rule of law against Wolsey.[79] The second of the precedents was from 1546, when John Hogges and Thomas Heyth, after being committed to the Tower by order of the King's Council, were removed into the King's Bench by *habeas corpus*.[80] They seem to have been common criminals; at any rate, they were sentenced to death the same term for receiving a thief.[81] But that was not stated in the return, and (as Dyer noted) the legal significance of these precedents was that they established the authority of the King's Bench to examine the cause of imprisonment of any prisoner in the realm, and to commit, bail or enlarge him as they thought expedient.[82] Whatever specific reason caused Dyer to search these out in 1562, we may guess that the case of Scrogges had proved not to be an isolated incident. In the same year the King's Bench granted an immediate discharge to a gentleman who had been committed to custody by Sir Ambrose Cave, chancellor of the duchy, 'for various contempts'. There is obviously more to that case than is revealed by the record; but it provides another clear example of discharge without bail.[83]

Two important cases occurred in 1565 in connection with jurisdictional disputes, in each of which the courts acted to protect Roman Catholic recusants. First, there was the case of John Lamburne (or Lambert), imprisoned by the Council of the North at York.[84] The sheriff returned to the writ of *habeas corpus*, in the King's Bench, that he had sent his deputy to York Castle to take the body, and was told by

---

[78] KB 29/150, m. 18 (tr. 'committed by command of the lord king alone, and this is the cause and no other'); *Dyer's Notebooks*, i. 78; cited in *Darnell's Case* (1628) BL MS. Hargrave 27, at fo. 97 (misdated 18 Hen. VIII).

[79] J. A. Guy, *The Cardinal's Court* (1977), pp. 76–8; *The History of Parliament: the House of Commons 1509–1558*, ed. S. T. Bindoff (1982), iii. 305; *Dyer's Notebooks*, i. lxxviii n. 47; *OHLE*, vi. 93, 538. Sheffield had fallen foul of Wolsey for supporting the reform of fictional benefit of clergy, so as to prevent it being claimed for murder by non-clerics.

[80] KB 29/179, m. 13; *Dyer's Notebooks*, i. 78.

[81] KB 29/179, m. 4d; *Dyer's Notebooks*, i. lxxviii n. 50.   [82] *Dyer's Notebooks*, i. 78.

[83] *Robert Cooke's Case* (1562) KB 29/196, m. 19. Cooke was nevertheless ordered to appear in the King's Bench *de die in diem*.

[84] For the Council in the North see further below, pp. 305–6, 379–82.

the gaoler that he would not release the prisoner without leave of the archbishop of York, president of the Council in the North, and the other members of the Council; the sheriff thereupon went to the archbishop (Thomas Young), who told him that the prisoner was 'incarcerated by command of him the said archbishop and others of the lady queen's Council', that he was not the sheriff's prisoner, that he had written to the queen for a pardon, and that until he heard from the Privy Council concerning the pardon he would not release him; the archbishop then sent his secretary to the gaoler, commanding him not to deliver the prisoner when he received the queen's writ. For this affront, the King's Bench not only ordered an *alias habeas corpus*, but (on the motion of a queen's serjeant) ordered a writ of attachment against the archbishop and the gaoler.[85] Catlyn CJ was reported as saying:[86]

> In this court we hold we hold pleas before the queen herself, because this is the queen's highest court – whatever those of the Chancery might say – and [it] is of such dignity that, in whatever prison a man may be, we may command the officer to bring him here. Even if he is a prisoner in the Tower by command of the Council, we may send for him here by writ of *corpus cum causa*[87] directed to the constable of the Tower ... And [we] do not use to set out in the writ why we send for anyone, but reserve that in our breast, since it may be for treason or great conspiracy.

This passage was to inspire Sir Edward Coke forty years later.[88]

The other case in 1565, which was noted by Dyer but omitted from his printed reports, provides the first instance of *habeas corpus* for a prisoner of the High Commission. Edward Mytton, a Shropshire gentleman, was imprisoned for hearing mass (now an indictable misdemeanour), and it was argued for the commissioners that they had the power to imprison at their discretion, without bail or mainprise. Although the prisoner was released by the King's Bench, he was promptly rearrested on the order of the commissioners. This further example of high-handedness was 'much

---

[85] *John Lamburne's Case* (alias *Lambert*) (1565) KB 29/199, m. 31. The case was noted as a precedent by Coke: memorandum on c. 29, below, p. 506; 12 Co. Rep. 54. Lambert's offence is not specified, but he was doubtless one of the many recusants in Yorkshire.

[86] Crompton, *Courts*, fos. 78v–79, presumably from a manuscript report (tr.). He cited the case of the imprisonment by Cardinal Wolsey when Fyneux was CJKB, and Whiddon J. referred to the story of Prince Henry (later Henry V) being committed to prison by Gascoigne CJKB.

[87] I.e. *habeas corpus*.   [88] Below, pp. 387 n. 277, 504.

debated' by the judges, apparently without a resolution.[89] It was on this occasion that the valuable precedent of 1465 was discovered in the plea rolls, showing that *habeas corpus* (albeit in the form of a writ of privilege for a litigant) could be used to discharge prisoners of the Church.[90] Three years later, in 1568, the Common Pleas released a prisoner of the High Commission who had refused to incriminate himself upon the oath *ex officio*. Here, as in Scrogges's case, the prisoner was an attorney entitled to privilege, and this provided the formal justification for the judgment. It was also the first clear decision affirming the privilege against self-incrimination.[91] Thereafter the common-law courts were consistently opposed to the use of the oath in the case of laymen.[92] The King's Bench did not need to rely on privilege as a justification in granting *habeas corpus*, and in the same year (under Catlyn CJ) it bailed Mary Wilkinson, doubtless a recusant, who had been placed under close arrest by the High Commission.[93]

The courts of common law did not aim to thwart the Commission at every opportunity, but insisted on giving every prisoner a day in court and an opportunity to challenge the grounds of committal.[94] Committals by the high commissioners over the next few years were still sometimes

---

[89] *Mytton's Case* (1565) KB 29/199, m. 31 (the same roll as Lambert); *Dyer's Notebooks*, i. lxxix, 107. Mytton was subsequently indicted at common law, but died in 1568 before trial. Cf. *Edmund Bonner's Case* (1565) KB 29/199, m. 34; Dyer 234. Bonner, formerly bishop of London, had been committed by the High Commission for offences against the Act of Supremacy. An imprisonment by order of Bonner himself had been challenged only four years earlier: *Poynton's Case* (1561) KB 29/195, m. 29 (bailed).

[90] *Kayser's Case* (1465) KB 27/818, m. 143d; above, p. 120. Coke knew of the case, which he learned about from Dyer's notebooks. Note also *Russel's Case* (1482) below, p. 288 n. 65, where it was said that a *habeas corpus* of privilege could be awarded to release a prisoner of the Chancery.

[91] *Thomas Lee's Case* (1568) *Dyer's Notebooks*, i. 143; copy of the *habeas corpus*, tested by Dyer CJ, in BL MS. Harley 7648, fo. 267v; noted by Coke, commentary on c. 29, below, p. 506. It was frequently cited by Coke CJ in the following century: below, pp. 358 n. 122, 372, 529 n. 46.

[92] Above, pp. 136, 143. The clergy were not so fortunate: below, p. 358.

[93] *Wilkinson's Case* (1568) KB 29/202, m. 83d (later pardoned). This was discovered by, or for, Coke: YLS MS. G.R24.1, fo. 106.

[94] On the same page of Coke's precedents (Yale MS., previous note) was the case of Dame Martha Carew, a well-known recusant, who had been imprisoned under a similar warrant, though she was committed to the marshal before being pardoned: KB 29/202, m. 107d. The widow of Sir Wymond Carew (d. 1549) of Anthony, Cornwall, she had been arrested by order of the commissioners in 1562 and punished after refusing to take the oath *ex officio*: ODNB. Cf. Thomas Carew, the Presbyterian curate of Hatfield Peverel, Essex, who also took a stand against the oath *ex officio* (in 1584): Usher, *High Commission*, p. 129; brief note in ODNB.

returned to writs of *habeas corpus* without showing the cause, though bail was generally given by the King's Bench.[95] In 1577, however, the Common Pleas showed more boldness in rejecting a general return completely. Dyer's report of the case has not survived, but only a marginal cross-reference.[96] Some reliance was placed on this cross-reference in the 1590s, in the controversy over the oath *ex officio*, occasioning Dr Cosin to protest that the report did not appear to be by Dyer or to mention a committal by the commissioners; but Cosin was either being disingenuous or displaying a casual ignorance of the facts of a notorious case occurring only fifteen years before he wrote.[97] The case is reported in several manuscripts by other hands, and the outcome is clear even if some of the details are not. John Hynde, a litigant in the Common Pleas, had been committed by the commissioners on suspicion of usury 'and other causes', but this was not stated in the return to the *habeas corpus*, and the judges disapproved the general return. Hynde's having privilege of the Common Pleas, as a litigant, was once again the stimulus which emboldened them to give relief, though the principle was stated in wider terms. After this date, returns to *habeas corpus* by order of the High Commission began to specify causes, though this still did not prevent the King's Bench granting bail.[98] The same principles were applicable to the King's Council. One of the reports of Hynde's case preserves a reminiscence by Dyer that, when he was a student, the judges of the Common Pleas had disallowed a general return of a committal to the Tower by Thomas Cromwell as a member of the Council.[99] The court now said that it would allow a general

[95] See the cases summarised in *Dyer's Notebooks*, i. lxxix n. 57 and *Smythe's Case* (1584) KB 29/221, m. 34d. Cf. *Beconshawe's Case* (1584) KB 29/220, m. 124 (committed by the High Commission for ecclesiastical causes unknown to the sheriff; remanded because of an indictment); he was a Roman Catholic recusant.

[96] *Hynde's Case* (1576-7) Dyer 175, margin; *Dyer's Notebooks*, ii. 355-61; reported in 4 Leo. 21; BL MS. Hargrave 373, fo. 226; CUL MS. Ll.3.8, fo. 275v; Exeter College, Oxford, MS. 119, fo. 39; HLS MS. 2071, fo. 88. The case was much cited in the following century.

[97] R. Cosin, *An Apologie for Sundrie Proceedings by Jurisdiction Ecclesiasticall* (1593), part 3, pp. 83-4. Cosin was a Civil lawyer.

[98] E.g. *Thomas Metham's Case* (1578) KB 29/214, m. 39d (clergyman committed to the Tower for offences against the Statute for Uniformity of Prayer; bailed). Metham was one of the first seminary priests to arrive in England from Douai; he died in custody in 1582. He was doubtless related to the knight of the same name who was a notorious recusant and died in York Castle in 1573.

[99] Tr. in *Spelman's Reports*, ii. 74. This may be *Foster's Case* (1541) KB 29/174, m. 38 (committed by the late Lord Cromwell; bailed); noted by Coke, *Selected Readings on Magna Carta* p. 399. Dyer was probaby a barrister by this date: *Dyer's Notebooks*, i. xxiii.

return only in the case of a committal by the whole Privy Council, which might have secret reasons which it would be unsafe to make public;[100] but an individual privy councillor had no power of committal without express cause.[101] Even in the case of committal by the whole Council, the King's Bench would sometimes allow bail.[102]

At the same period we find the courts of law approving *habeas corpus* to release or bail prisoners of the Chancery,[103] and (a little later) of the Court of Requests,[104] thus anticipating Coke by forty years. The usual context of these cases, as in Coke's time, was the use of injunctions to interfere with the courts of law.[105] In 1562 Dyer CJ was moved to describe a Chancery injunction (though issued under the authority of the sign manual) as clean contrary to law,[106] and in 1566 his court disregarded a Chancery injunction on the grounds that 'otherwise all actions pending in the same place would be removed by injunction, in retardation of justice, which is a great mischief'.[107] In 1571 the Common Pleas rejected an injunction from the Court of Requests to restrain execution of a judgment as 'utterly void, tending to the subversion of the common law', and relievable (in case of imprisonment) by *habeas corpus*.[108]

---

[100] HLS MS. 2071, fo. 88; quoted in *Dyer's Notebooks*, i. lxxx n. 61. Cf. 4 Leo. 21 ('because it may concern the state of the realm, which ought not to be published'). An example is *Hyde's Case* (1585) KB 29/221, m. 118d (committed by special command of the lords of the Privy Council 'for causes to him then unknown').

[101] An example of a committal by a minister is *Travers's Case* (1565) KB 29/199, m. 34d (by order of Sir William Cecil PC).

[102] *Mytton's Case* (1565) *Dyer's Notebooks*, i. lxxix, 107.

[103] *Astwick's Case* (1567) cited in Moo. 839; BL MS. Add. 25211, fo. 146; MS. Lansdowne 1110, fo. 27, *per* Coke CJ (committed by Lord Keeper Bacon for contempt of the Chancery; bailed); *Humfreys' Case* (1572), below; *Mychell's Case* (1577) KB 29/212, m. 77 (committed by Lord Keeper Bacon, no cause being mentioned; bailed); cited in *Ruswell's Case* (1615) Moo. 839; Calth. MS. i. 374v, *per* Coke CJ. An earlier precedent is *Ley's Case* (1549) KB 29/182, m. 32 (committed to the Fleet by the lord chancellor; bailed, and later discharged).

[104] *Clerke's Case* (1584) KB 29/221, m. 34d (committed to the Fleet for scandalous words spoken of the masters of Requests; bailed, and afterwards discharged); *Brystowe's Case* (1585) KB 29/221, mm. 59, 91 (committed to the Fleet for contempt of a decree of the Requests; bailed).

[105] See further below, pp. 208, 212–14.

[106] *Lord Grey* v. *Earl of Arundel* (1562) *Dyer's Notebooks*, i. 109. In suitable cases, however, Dyer CJ actually invited the Chancery to stay suits by injunction: W. J. Jones, *The Elizabethan Court of Chancery* (1967), p. 468.

[107] *Anon.* (1566) CUL MS. Gg.6.2, fo. 204.

[108] *Humfreys' Case* (1572) BL MS. Add. 35941, fo. 30 (French text in *Dyer's Notebooks*, i. lxxxi n. 67; MS. Harley 2036, fo. 33; MS. Add. 24845, fo. 83; CUL MS. Ll.3.8, fo. 137v; Dal. 81; 3 Leo. 18. Sir Julius Caesar was therefore wrong to say that conflict began in

In the same case Serjeant Bendlowes said, and it was not denied, that a *habeas corpus* would be awarded if the Chancery arrested someone to enforce an injunction after judgment had been given at common law. This was to become one of the burning issues of Coke's chief justiceship.[109]

The writ of *habeas corpus* was usually returned before the courts in banc, but its availability was not so limited. Dyer noted in 1573 that, as a justice of assize, he had followed a precedent of 1523 authorising a *habeas corpus* to remove a prisoner before the chief justice at his house in the country during the vacation; the reason for doing this is not stated, but the precedent was of value as showing that the writ could be used out of term or in chambers.[110] The practice seems to have been common before 1573,[111] and there was an equally well established practice of making such writs returnable before a judge in one of the serjeants' inns;[112] but the controlment rolls suggest that the practice of returning *habeas corpus* before individual judges in vacation became more common during the Elizabethan period. Many of the instances look like routine criminal proceedings, which were not regulated by the law terms, but the under- lying principle was of constitutional importance: liberty could not be constrained by the calendar of Westminster Hall.

Imprisonment was from time to time the occasion of jurisdictional and procedural wrangles of a different kind. By the 1570s *habeas corpus* was being used to challenge customary claims by municipal authorities to imprison for disciplinary purposes.[113] Then there were jurisdictional disputes between royal courts and tribunals of various kinds. On several occasions Dyer reported cases concerning gaolers and their responsibility for the custody of prisoners as between the central courts, most of them arising from a minor feud between the Exchequer and the

---

1591: Lambarde, *Archeion*, p. 167. But prohibitions to the Requests began in earnest in the 1590s.

[109] Below, pp. 410–22.   [110] *Howkyns' Case* (1573) *Dyer's Notebooks*, ii. 287.

[111] E.g. KB 29/189, m. 58d (writ returned before Portman CJ, 1556); KB 29/193, m. 33 (before Catlyn CJ at his town-house in the parish of St Bartholomew-the-Great, 1560); KB 29/195, m. 63d (before Catlyn CJ at home, 1562); KB 29/200, m. 25d (before Southcote J. at his house in Carter Lane, 1566); KB 29/203, m. 117d (before Catlyn CJ at his house at Newnham, Beds, 1569).

[112] E.g. KB 29/180, m. 4d (writ returned before Lyster CJ in Serjeants' Inn, Chancery Lane, 1547); KB 29/187, mm. 20, 38d (before Bromley CJ at his chamber in Serjeants' Inn, Chancery Lane, 1554). It was thereafter very common.

[113] *Marshall's Case* (1572) BL MS Hargrave 8, fo. 163. For this and other similar cases, in which Magna Carta was cited, see below, pp. 201–2, 250.

King's Bench.[114] Later in the century, anger was expressed at the assumption of powers of imprisonment by lay commissioners proceeding outside the common law. In 1595 the commissioners for stalling the debts of poor people had directed a pursuivant to arrest a creditor wherever they could find him, and they arrested him in his counsel's chambers in the Temple, adding insult to injury by demanding fees before releasing him. Popham CJ directed the pursuivant to repay the fees, released the prisoner and ordered the commissioners to attend at the bar, 'when they were greatly checked by all the justices'.[115]

Another series of cases concerned the liability of the warden of the Fleet prison and the marshal of the Marshalsea of the King's Bench in respect of prisoners given leave to go at large without bail.[116] The warden was liable to an action of debt by a creditor whose debtor escaped from his custody,[117] and it was argued that licensing prisoners to go at large amounted to a constructive permission to escape. However, the practice of permitting prisoners for debt to go around with a tipstaff, in order to attend to their own affairs, seems to have become very common in the sixteenth century, and was even alleged to be a custom of London,[118] despite a well known Star Chamber ruling in 1532 that it was unlawful.[119] It made some practical sense, in so far as

---

[114] See the cases in *Dyer's Notebooks*, i. lxxxii.

[115] *Anon.* (1596) HLS MS. 110, fo. 187 (tr.).

[116] Warden of the Fleet: *Thurland's Case* (1558) Dyer 162; *Pledall v. Annesley* (1570) Dyer 296; *Dyer's Notebooks*, ii. 271; *Paine v. Puttenham* (1571) Dyer 306; *Manser v. Annesley* (1575) *Dyer's Notebooks*, ii. 349; Benl. 238. Marshal: *Gawdy's Case* (1568) Dyer 278; *Vast v. Gawdy* (1582) Cro. Eliz. 5.

[117] Statute of Westminster II, c. 11; 1 Ric. 11, c. 12. Other gaolers were held to be within the equity of the statutory provision: *The Notebook of Sir John Port*, ed. J. H. Baker (102 SS, 1986), p. 115.

[118] *Case of Ludgate Prison* (1568) CUL MS. Ll.3.14, fo. 177v (custom held bad); *Gaoler of Ludgate's Case* (1579) BL MS. Harley 1699, fos. 53v–54v, 107; MS. Hargrave 4, fos. 57v–58 (custom thought bad, but judgment deferred); *Mackwilliams v. Sheriffs of London* (1580-2) BL MS. Hargrave 9, fos. 110v–111v; LI MS. Misc. 487, fos. 107v–109v; MS. Misc. 488, 65–6; *Anon.* (Exchequer, 1582) BL MS. Lansdowne 1101, fo. 21, *per* Fanshaw, queen's remembrancer (a prisoner for the queen's debt may go with a keeper to his counsel, because if he escapes he may be rearrested, but a private debtor may not). Cf. *CPR 1553-4*, p. 73 (commission to examine the complaints of the prisoners in Ludgate, authorising the sheriffs to allow prisoners to go at large with keepers to collect their debts).

[119] Order cited in Saunders's reports, BL MS. Hargrave 9, fos. 33v–34; BL MS. Lansdowne 1057, fo. 16v; cited in *Worlay v. Harrison* (1566) Dyer 249; and in *Manser v. Annesley* (1574) LI MS. Maynard 73, fo. 22v, *per* Mounson J.; *Mackwilliams v. Sheriffs of London* (1580) LI MS. Misc. 488, 66, *per* Plowden.

it might enable prisoners to raise the money to pay off their debts; but the courts continued to disapprove of it. The policy which prevailed was that the best incentive to the payment of debts was strict imprisonment.[120] Moreover, a gaol was held to be a physical place; it did not follow the person of the gaoler. Therefore, if a gaoler allowed the prisoner such liberty, even though he remained in his custody, it was considered in law to be an escape from the gaol.[121] This was finally settled in 1575, when the warden of the Fleet, Brian Annesley, was himself held liable for a debt in such circumstances. Annesley was reportedly disgruntled, and later came with the attorney-general (Gerrard) to ask the court to respite judgment on the ground that the judgment was contrary to law; but Dyer CJ responded, with a note of anger, 'Fiat justicia'.[122] The warden was not on the best terms with the judges, since he had failed to keep Westminster Hall in a salubrious state.[123] Five years later, Dyer remarked pointedly that he would think twice before permitting his prisoners such liberty again, since he had recently been 'in the lurch'.[124]

Imprisonment by privy councillors became a matter of regular complaint in the later 1580s. In 1587 the King's Bench was minded to release a prisoner who had been committed to the marshal by Lord Hunsdon, the lord chamberlain, since no cause was returned to the *habeas corpus*. The judges drew the same distinction as in *Hynde's Case* between committal by a single councillor and committal by several of the Council, for in the latter case it was 'presumed to be of the same effect as if the queen herself had committed him'. The lord chamberlain, on being invited to show the authority under which he committed the prisoner, 'was not well pleased with this, or with the scanning by what authority he did it, and said that as soon as they enlarged him he would commit him again'. The impasse was resolved by a submission to arbitration.[125] Later the same

---

[120] *Manser v. Annesley* (1575) *Dyer's Notebooks*, ii. 349; *Gaoler of Ludgate's Case* (1579) BL MS. Hargrave 4, fos. 57v–58, *per* Wray CJ (tr. 'the matter which should cause them to discharge their debts is strait imprisonment'). Cf. to the same effect, *Small's Case* (1613) 2 Bulst. 148, *per* Coke CJ (concerning the marshal of the Marshalsea).

[121] *Bamburgh v. Shepherd* (1575) *Dyer's Notebooks*, ii. 467.

[122] *Manser v. Annesley* (1575) as reported in BL MS. Hargrave 9, fo. 232v (French text in *Dyer's Notebooks*, i. lxxxiii, n. 81). For more of this case, see below, pp. 179–81.

[123] *R. v. Ansley* (1579) KB 29/215, m. 9 (indictment for nuisance caused to the judges and the public by reason of his neglect).

[124] *Bird v. Davyes* (1580) BL MS. Hargrave 4, fo. 72. The case is reported, without this remark, in Dyer 364.

[125] *Anon.* (1587) BL MS. Harley 5030, fo. 74 (quotations tr.). The case has not been found in the controlment roll, but cf. *Wolryche's Case* (Mich. 1587) KB 29/224, m. 39d (committal

year, the court rejected a general return that a prisoner had been committed by Sir Francis Walsingham, the queen's principal secretary and a privy councillor, without disclosing the cause. The return was thereupon amended to say that the prisoner was committed by command of the whole Privy Council, 'and therefore I cannot have his body'. This was again rejected, because although no cause had to be shown in such a case, it was always necessary to bring the body before the court.[126] The councillors did not much care for these judicial checks, and they admonished the judges not to release prisoners committed by individual councillors without first giving notice to the councillor concerned.[127]

A more serious confrontation occurred in 1590 when John Agmondesham, a senior bencher of the Middle Temple, and a Puritan member of Parliament, was committed to prison by Lord Hunsdon and told he would be detained until he released a lawsuit which he had brought against a minor royal servant. This time all the judges of England were assembled to consider the matter, and they agreed that it was against the law and statutes of the realm to deprive subjects of the benefit of the law.[128] Only the Council as a whole could commit without cause, because in that case it would be deemed to be a matter of state. They resolved to prepare a document setting out the recent abuses, and the legal position, and to present it to the queen herself through the medium of the lord chancellor (Sir Christopher Hatton) and Lord Treasurer Burghley. The judges were also prepared to attend the queen themselves. The following term they released another prisoner committed by Lord Hunsdon, and in Trinity term an attorney committed by Lord Howard, because the returns were too general.[129] There was another similar case in 1592 arising from an imprisonment by Sir Thomas Heneage,

to the sheriff of Suffolk by Lord Hunsdon, as lord lieutenant, for various contempts and misdeeds; bailed); *Parker's Case* (Mich. 1588) KB 29/225, m. 35 (committal to the Marshalsea by Lord Hunsdon, chamberlain of the household; no cause stated; bailed).
[126] *Howell's Case* (1587) 1 Leo. 70; less fully reported sub nom. *Hellyard's Case*, 2 Leo. 175; 15 APC 349–50; Dawson, 'Privy Council', p. 640.
[127] 16 APC 48.
[128] *Agmondesham's Case* (Hil. 1590) BL MS. Harley 4998, fo. 26; printed in translation below, Appendix 6, pp. 495–6.
[129] *Keble's Case* (1590) KB 29/226, m. 116; as reported in BL MS. Add. 35949, fo. 208v: (tr.) 'and thus Hide was delivered, being imprisoned by command of the lord chamberlain, namely the Lord Hunsdon, last term, and in the case of the marquess of Winchester likewise'. The prisoner in the principal case, a King's Bench attorney, was committed for contempt in that he had sued Lord Howard for false imprisonment in respect of an order of the Court of Admiralty.

vice-chamberlain of the Household, for infringing a patent of monopoly.[130] In two other cases in 1592, the Privy Council ordered the deputy keeper of the Marshalsea not to release prisoners but to return to any writs of *habeas corpus* that they were committed by special command of the Council.[131]

It was not until Easter term 1592 that the judges produced their report, having evidently been further harassed in the interim.[132] That they wrote it at all is testimony to the strong feelings which had been engendered by these cases,[133] since it was unprecedented for the judges to write such a memorial. There is a preamble to the document complaining that the judges had been subjected to commands procured by 'divers great men' not to set prisoners at liberty, even though they were imprisoned upon pleasure and without cause. The document itself was signed by all the judges of both benches and barons of the Exchequer, though it was addressed, not to the queen, but to the lord chancellor and lord treasurer, at whose instance it purported to have been written. They desired that some order might be taken to prevent subjects being imprisoned by command of any nobleman or privy councillor against the laws of the realm, and that the judges might have access to the queen 'to become suitors to her for the same'. It was a particular grievance that plaintiffs had been incarcerated for bringing actions at law, even after they had obtained judgments, in order to make them withdraw the suits or executions.

---

[130] *Langley v. Heneage* (1592), *Selected Readings on Magna Carta*, p. xciii (cited in Francis Ashley's reading). It may not have been a judicial decision, because Ashley said only that (tr.) 'the opinion of several learned in the law concurred that the imprisonment was not lawful'.

[131] *Goward Vanderhagin's Case* (1592) 23 APC 95; *Jasper Swift's Case*, ibid. 330. Vander-hagin seems to have been interfering with a glass-making monopoly. Swift was probably the Admiralty marshal of that name.

[132] It is best known from the copy in the reports of Anderson CJ, 1 And. 297–8; BL MS. Harley 4817, fos. 99v–100. There are also copies in BL MS. Harley 37, fos. 112–116; MS. Lansdowne 1062, fos. 224v–225; SP 12/261, fos. 137–41. Coke CJ said in 1615 that the original still remained in the Council Chamber: 1 Rolle Rep. 192 (dated '36' Eliz.). In 1627 he apparently rejected it as apocryphal: *The Five Knights' Case* (1627) 3 St. Tr. 1 at col. 82. But Sir Edward Littleton and Hyde CJ both said they had seen and copied it from Anderson's autograph: CUL MS. Ee.6.63, fos. 116, 193. MS. Harley 37 contains a lengthy interpolation, with a lucid account of the remedies for securing personal liberty, but it seems to belong to the reign of James I. The extended text is printed below, pp. 496–9.

[133] Cf. Dawson, 'Privy Council', pp. 640–1, 648–50, where the impetus is said to have been disgruntlement at the commissions issued by the Council to relieve poor prisoners for debt. In 1587 some of the commissioners had been prosecuted in the Common Pleas for a *praemunire*: ibid. 648.

The judges also complained that, when they had released prisoners upon *habeas corpus*, the prisoners had been rearrested and sent to prison in secret places so that no one knew to whom a second *habeas corpus* could be sent. Another grievance was that the sheriffs' officers in London had been themselves committed to prison for lawfully executing the queen's writs. They then set out the principles of law. If someone was committed by the queen in person, or the Council Board, or for treason, the courts could not deliver them before a jury trial and acquittal. Even in those cases, however, the prisoners were entitled to bring *habeas corpus* so that the lawfulness of the imprisonment could be examined upon the return.[134] Although it was not explicitly spelt out, it was the obvious implication that those were the only cases in which the courts could not deliver prisoners.[135] There is no record that the judges ever gained access to the queen to put their case, but it was reported that afterwards 'did follow more quietness than before in the cases before mentioned'. When, in 1599, the lord mayor of London, Sir Henry Soame, was reported to have said that 'even if twenty *habeas corpus* came he would not obey them', the whole court of Common Pleas agreed that, if those words could be proved, he would 'lose as much as he was worth'.[136]

The writ of *habeas corpus* had thus, within half a century, achieved its sacrosanct status. It was the most expansive remedy of the common law, available whenever a person was detained anywhere in the king's dominions,[137] without any restrictions.[138] No gaoler was privileged by higher authority from the duty of bringing in the body with a return.

---

[134] An example which Coke CJ cited in 1615 (below, p. 401) was *Harcourt's Case* (1598) KB 29/235, m. 62, where Edward Harcourt, who had been committed by command of the Privy Council, was moved to the Marshalsea and later bailed: Moo. 839; *Cases Concerning Equity and the Courts of Equity, 1550–1660*, ed. W. H. Bryson, vol. ii (118 SS, 2001), pp. 457, 464–5.

[135] In *The Leathersellers' Case* (1595) BL MS. Hargrave 26, fos. 51v–52, the parties were committed by the Privy Council for resisting a new monopoly for sealing leather. It was held that those committed by the body of the Council for matter of state were not bailable, though it was otherwise of a committal by an individual councillor. But Walmsley and Owen JJ (Anderson CJ *absente*, Beaumont J. *silente*) thought *habeas corpus* should be granted, apparently because they had privilege as litigants.

[136] *Deane's Case* (1599) BL MS. Add. 25223, fo. 68.

[137] It was decided as early as 1540 that it would lie to the Cinque Ports: *Spelman's Reports*, i. 186. Coke found a precedent of *habeas corpus* to Guernsey in 1565, though the roll has not been found: below, p. 505.

[138] Coke's memorandum on c. 29 (1604) below, p. **; Halliday, *Habeas Corpus*, pp. 259–62. Cf. *Maunsell's Case* (1607) BL MS. Add. 11681, at fo. 45v, *per* Yelverton J. (tr. 'It is presumed that the king sits here in his own person, and he is to have an account why any

The procedure had become so well established that it was even deemed by some to be immemorial.[139] Yet it is notable that neither the judicial resolutions of 1592 nor the arguments in the other cases mentioned above made any mention of chapter 29 of Magna Carta.[140] The connection between the new addition to the immemorial armoury of the common law and its ex post facto explanation did not take root quickly.[141] Moreover, the substantive law as to the deprivation of liberty by the government, in the absence of a general principle, was still unsettled. The acknowledgement of the queen's prerogative power to imprison without showing cause, which had been questioned by James Morice in 1578[142] but affirmed by the resolution of 1592, left a gaping chasm in the remedy. There was still no compunction about locking up members of Parliament, even distinguished lawyers, for political reasons.[143] Nor, despite the medieval authorities,[144] does there seem to have been much questioning of the prerogative power to conscript seamen and soldiers to serve outside the realm under commissions of impressment, prerogative acts which effectively took away their liberty without redress.[145] On the contrary, Sir John Smith was committed to the Tower and interrogated in 1596 after allegedly informing a parade of

---

of his subjects are imprisoned. For this reason the judges of this court may send for any prisoner to any prison in England without showing the cause why they send for him').

[139] *Maunsell's Case* (1607) BL MS. Add. 11681, at fo. 46, *per* Williams J. (tr. 'I will not make any an apology for prohibitions and *habeas corpus*. They were before the Conquest'). Yelverton J. (fo. 45v) agreed that they were (tr.) 'by the common law of great antiquity'.

[140] There is an exception in Scrogges's pleading of 1559: above, p. 156 n. 69.

[141] For the connection see below, pp. 250, 261.   [142] Below, p. 257.

[143] E.g. James Morice MP, bencher of the Middle Temple, in 1593 (below, p. 274), and James Whitelocke MP, bencher of the Middle Temple, in 1613 (below, p. 400–1). See further J. E. Neale, *Elizabeth I and her Parliaments 1584–1601* (1957), pp. 157–8, 164–5, 174–5, 255–6, 259–66, 274–6, 277, 278. Sir John Neale was inclined to defend the queen's disciplinary jurisdiction over members, despite it seeming in modern eyes tyrannical (ibid. 174).

[144] Thirning CJ said in 1405 that the king could not compel subjects to go out of the realm: YB Mich. 7 Hen. IV, Fitz. Abr., *Protection*, pl. 100; cited with approval in Morice's reading (1578), fo. 20v. And Parliament enacted in 1327 that men could not be compelled to go out of their shire except in times of necessity when there was a sudden invasion: 1 Edw. III, stat. 2, c. 5.

[145] The power was assumed to exist by Parliament: 2 & 3 Phil. & Mar., c. 16 (imposing a penalty for absconding in time of a commission of pressing); 4 & 5 Phil. & Mar., c. 3; 5 Eliz. I, c. 5, s. 43. See also *Att.-Gen.* v. *Gresham* (1596) Hawarde 32. For examples of commissions to press loose and masterless men to serve overseas see 24 APC 97 and 25 APC 47 (for Normandy, 1592); 27 APC 290 (for Picardy, 1597); 32 APC 27–8 (for Ostend, 1601).

pikemen that by the laws of England no one could be ordered to serve the queen overseas.[146] The Privy Council nevertheless recognised certain exemptions from conscription, for instance on grounds of age or substance.[147] A similar power of impressment was used to conscript boys to sing in the chapel royal, though the commissioners were brought to heel by Coke in the Star Chamber when they overstepped the mark by kidnapping a gentlemen's son to become a mere stage-actor.[148] These issues were not resolved until later, when the assistance of Magna Carta would be needed to overturn the Tudor learning.

Torture

Torture is the most extreme infringement of personal liberty, and there is no doubt that it was used in the reign of Elizabeth in the investigation of terrorist plots and networks, and occasionally in less serious cases as well. Indeed, there are sixty-five documented cases during the reign, more than in any other period of English history, and this is not the complete figure.[149] It was inflicted officially, insofar as the authorisation was often recorded in the registers of the Privy Council. What is more, the register in 1587 casually referred to the rack as the 'accustomed torture'.[150] And yet, whereas torture was an accepted feature of regular criminal procedure on the Continent, the subject of learned treatises by Civilians, it was

---

[146] 25 APC 459, 501–2, 506–7. He said he had learned this from two local lawyers.

[147] *Edward Bateman's Case* (1598) 26 APC 631. Bateman complained of being impressed as a soldier to serve in Ireland despite his years and the fact that he was a good taxpayer. Impressment seems usually to have been restricted to the unemployed, and was seen to have social benefits in removing them from towns.

[148] *Att.-Gen. v. Evans* (1601/2) IT MS. Petyt 511.13, fo. 149. Henry Evans was deputed by a patentee to 'take up' children for the chapel, and by virtue of this authority took a gentleman's son, an heir apparent from Norfolk, set him on the stage at the Blackfriars playhouse (recently revived), and kept him there as a player. For this he was fined £200, imprisoned, and ordered to stand on a pillory on the theatre stage. The offence, it seems, was not in pressing a boy as such, but in pressing a gentleman's son, and doing so for the purpose of acting rather than singing.

[149] J. H. Langbein, *Torture and the Law of Proof* (Chicago, 1977), pp. 81–123; J. Guy, *Tudor England* (Oxford, 1988), p. 318. It is evident from the case of 1589 discussed below that there were more instances in fact than the surviving warrants indicate.

[150] 15 APC 51; cf. 25 APC 179 ('ordinary' torture). The ordinary form seems to have involved the use of manacles: 25 APC 73, 251; 26 APC 325, 374, 457; 27 APC 38; 28 APC 165, 187, 407; 29 APC 428; 31 APC 281. In 1597 torture with the manacles was authorised against Richard Anger of Gray's Inn, suspected of murdering his father, a bencher: 28 APC 187 (also against the porter of the inn).

never recognised as permissible by the common law. It had, indeed, been made felony by a statute of 1340 to induce someone by torture to accuse another of felony.[151] It does not seem, however, despite Coke's assertion to the contrary,[152] that its apparently increased used in the sixteenth century was a conscious reception of Roman law.[153] No one tried to justify it on legal grounds at all. It was done outside the law, under the absolute royal prerogative, on grounds of national emergency. Whether a warrant from a secretary of state, or law officer, would have provided a defence to a gaoler in an action for battery was never tested in court. Nor was occasion ever taken in public to challenge the presumably illegal written instructions of 1602 for the Council of the Marches in Wales, whereby the president or vice-president and any two or more councillors were given 'full power ... upon sufficient ground, matter and cause to put any person that shall commit, or which shall be vehemently sus-pected to have committed, any treason, murder, rape, burglary or other felony ... to tortures, when they in their wisdoms and discretions shall think convenient and the cause shall apparently require the same'.[154] This was notoriously and uniquely irregular, and Dr Cosin (in defending the High Commission) claimed it as proof that the queen could grant a commission contrary to the common law.[155]

The judges never formally decided whether a confession extracted under torture was admissible in evidence. In principle it should not have been,[156] but it was not a question of law. The only known discussion of the matter occurred in 1589. Thomas Smyth, a servant, was accused of murder and said he had done the deed by the procurement of his master, Lewis Grevyll. Grevyll, a Warwickshire esquire, was a notorious ne'er-do-well,[157] and the investigation was taken over by the Privy Council with the assistance of the law officers (Popham and Egerton). When the case came before the King's Bench, Smyth claimed that he had been racked in the Tower and had

---

[151] 14 Edw. III, stat. 1, c. 10.

[152] Coke wrote that torture had been introduced in the fifteenth century, by the duke of Exeter, in imitation of the Civil law: Co. Inst. iii. 35. There are scathing remarks about torture under French law in J. Fortescue, *De Laudibus Legum Anglie*, ed. S. B. Chrimes (Cambridge, 1942), pp. cvi, 46–51; cf. the statute 28 Hen. VIII, c. 15 (referring to torture under the Civil law as used in the Admiralty courts).

[153] Langbein, *Torture and the Law of Proof*, pp. 131–4.   [154] BL MS. Add. 25244, fo. 37.

[155] R. Cosin, *An Apologie for Sundrie Proceedings by Jurisdiction Ecclesiasticall* (2nd edn, 1593), p. 110.

[156] Sta. P.C. 142C, held that a judge should not accept a confession (meaning a plea of guilty) if it was obtained by fear, menace or duress.

[157] For his other activities see *Dyer's Notebooks*, ii. 225, 226, 293–4, 389.

implicated Grevyle in his confession to Popham and Egerton through the extremity of his torture, 'and that if he were put again to the same torture he would accuse his own father, or the chief justice, or anybody else'. He was allowed to put his defence to the jury, who nevertheless convicted him, and he was sentenced to death.[158] Grevyle refused to plead unless and until the person who had made Smyth accuse him on the rack was tried as a felon under the statute of 1340. He was therefore pressed to death for standing mute of malice.[159] These judgments were not an endorsement of torture, because English law – unlike the Civil law – did not require a formal confession of guilt. Indeed, since jurors were deemed to have local knowledge, it was arguably not necessary to produce any evidence in court at all, although it was usual.[160] Exclusionary rules of evidence lay in the future. The validity of a confession was therefore not a matter of law. The defendant was allowed to deny the confession at his trial, and its evidential weight was a question of fact for the jury alone to decide. Here, then, was a supposed prerogative which lay beyond direct judicial challenge, albeit in the last resort jurors were free to express disapproval by a verdict of acquittal. Its ambivalent nature may be gathered from the irony that, whereas Sir Edward Coke as attorney-general was named in six torture warrants between 1593 and 1603, and took part in the racking of Guy Fawkes in 1605 under the king's personal directions, Sir Edward Coke the jurist wrote in his old age that 'there is no law to warrant tortures in this land, nor can they be justified by any prescription, being so lately brought in'.[161] It was, in his mature view, contrary to Magna Carta.[162] But that was new learning.

---

[158] R. v. *Smyth* (1589) Bodl. Lib. MS. C.85, fo. 50 (tr.); KB 29/226, m. 33d; Baker, *Collected Papers*, ii. 1068. The return to Smyth's *habeas corpus* said he was committed to the Gatehouse by John Popham Att.-Gen., by command of the Privy Council. No torture warrant is recorded in APC.

[159] R. v. *Grevyle* (1589) ibid.; J. Stow, *The Annales of England* (1592), pp. 1286–7; W. Dugdale, *The Antiquities of Warwickshire* (2nd edn, 1730), ii. 710–11. Pressing (the 'peine forte et dure') was the mandatory penalty for refusing to plead, under a statute of 1275 (Westminster I, c. 12).

[160] Baker, *Collected Papers*, ii. 1051 n. 140.

[161] Co. Inst. iii. 35. The known warrants are calendared in Langbein, *Torture and the Law of Proof*, pp. 114–19. Coke wrote in 1612 that 'for the honour and reverence which the law gives to nobility, their bodies are not subject to torture' in cases of treason: 12 Co. Rep. 96. That passage suggests he had not yet come to the conclusion that torture was altogether illegal: see Francis Hargrave's annotation in 2 St. Tr. 774.

[162] Co. Inst. ii. 48 gl. *destruatur*. He had earlier collected references to its use, citing Fortescue as an authority that it was against the common law: BL MS. Marley 6687A, fo. 12.

Lesser torments, in the form of unduly harsh punishment, were more amenable to challenge and disapproval. The general principle, as stated by James Morice, was that imprisonment was intended 'to restrain, not to destroy; safely to guard, not sharply to punish'.[163] Coke found authority for the same notion in *Bracton*: gaolers were not allowed to keep prisoners in shackles, because a gaol ought to be for containment and not for punishment.[164] This was clearly accepted with respect to prisoners in civil cases, who were entitled to a certain amount of leisure and even to play bowls.[165] Abusing a power of imprisonment was a punishable misdemeanour. In 1577 Simon Harcourt, a justice of the peace, was put out of the commission and fined £200 by the Star Chamber for arresting a man on horseback, taking him bareheaded to his own house, pinioning him on his back in stocks for three or four hours, and then putting him in the common cage.[166] In a worse instance, to be encountered later, the gatekeeper of the Council in the Marches imprisoned a party to a civil suit in a noisome prison without access to his friends, prevented food from being delivered to him and failed to provide sustenance, so that he was compelled to drink his own urine; for this he was fined £100.[167] But harsh imprisonment, amounting to torture, was sometimes considered acceptable as a way of coercing people to comply with the law.[168] The 'loathsome' and cramped cell in the Tower of London called 'Little Ease', in which prisoners could neither stand nor lie down, was used even by the House of Commons in 1604, perhaps with a note of cruel irony, to force the warden of the Fleet

---

[163] Morice's reading (1578), fo. 27. For the doctrine that imprisonment itself was not a valid form of punishment at common law see also *Att.-Gen.* v. *Skynner and Catcher, sheriffs of London* (1588) below, p. 269.

[164] Co. Inst. iii. 34–5; *Bracton*, ii. 299, 385; Sta. P.C. 78A. Cf. *Scriven* v. *Wright* (1611) 1 Bulst. 145; BL MS. Add. 24846, fos. 324v, where Williams J. said felons could be put in fetters but not prisoners for debt. Chains and irons could be used to restrain unruly prisoners: *Anon.* (1615) Calth. MS. i. 345v. Prisoners other than peers were normally shackled on committal and arraignment: Sir Roger Owen's treatise on the common law (*c.* 1615), BL MS. Harley 6605, fo. 299v ('in all ages, for ought that I remember').

[165] *Scriven* v. *Wood* (1611) BL MS. Add. 24846, fo. 324v; MS. Hargrave 32, fo. 50v.

[166] *Buttle* v. *Harecourt* (1577) BL MS. Harley 2143, fo. 33. Harcourt died later in the year from gaol fever, caught at the Oxford assizes: *HPHC 1558–1603*, ii. 250.

[167] *Whetherly* v. *Whetherly* (1605) below, p. 310.

[168] E.g., from the next reign, *Att.- Gen.* v. *Glanvile and Allen* (1616) Hob. 115, where defendants who refused to answer Star Chamber interrogatories were ordered to be put in irons 'and so more and more clogged till they answered' (presumably on the analogy of the *peine forte et dure*).

Prison to disgorge one of his own prisoners.[169] The absence of any fixed punishment for misdemeanours also gave the courts leeway to impose various kinds of corporal punishment[170] and public humiliation, even for relatively minor offences. The most extreme example was the amputation of a hand, a sentence imposed by the King's Bench on a Puritan barrister in 1579 for writing against a rumoured marriage proposal between the queen and the duc d'Alençon. This was supposedly authorised by a statute of Mary I, which had been renewed in 1559, but it was uncertain whether it applied to the case in question and the incident caused considerable consternation. A Common Pleas judge, Robert Mounson, was imprisoned and effectively forced out of office for objecting to this display of official savagery.[171] It was perhaps the worst instance of interference with judicial independence in Elizabeth's reign.

Prerogative Protections

Besides powers of imprisonment, another issue which concerned the courts in the early years of Elizabeth's reign was the undue exercise of the prerogative power of protection. The common law had long recognised the power of the crown to put a person temporarily outside the reach of the courts of law in certain limited cases. The ordinary writ of protection was restricted to persons on military or government service outside the realm, or about to go on such service, and was limited in duration to one year.[172] Protections which did not conform to the

---

[169] Langbein, *Torture and the Law of Proof*, p. 190 n. 26. The warden complied within two days.

[170] The Star Chamber and Privy Council were sometimes more severe in punishment than lesser courts. In 1593 the Council sentenced a person to be chained in the galleys for a misdemeanour: 24 APC 486–7.

[171] *R. v. Stubbe* (1579) KB 29/215, m. 20. John Stubbe was a barrister of Lincoln's Inn, and Coke's brother-in-law. Mounson, a former treasurer of that inn, was sent to the Fleet and then kept under house arrest until he resigned his judgeship in 1580. James Dalton, a bencher of Lincoln's Inn, was sent to the Tower for his opposition to the sentence. See *Dyer's Notebooks*, i. lxv–lxvi; N. Mears, 'Counsel, Public Debate and Queenship: John Stubbs's *Discoverie of a Gaping Gulf*, 1579' (2001) 44 *Historical Journal* 629–50; ODNB.

[172] See above, p. 107. In *Osborne v. Kirton* (1588) BL MS. Hargrave 5, fo. 99, a protection was produced for someone about to stay in Wlissingen (Flushing) in the parts of Zeeland, in the company of Lord Willoughby, and it was objected (inter alia) that giving aid to foreign princes did not fall within the protection of royal service; no judgment is reported.

common-law requirements were rejected as void.[173] And, according to a decision of 1558, a protection could not be used to secure the release of someone already in custody at the suit of a subject.[174] Besides the ordinary writs there was also an established species of protection *quia indebitatus nobis*, used to protect the king's debtors from losing their assets to creditors until the king's debt had been paid.[175] Fitzherbert and Dyer referred to this as a writ of the king's prerogative.[176] This characterisation of the writ may have inspired the notion that there was an absolute prerogative power of granting protection from legal action. In early Tudor times the practice grew up of issuing similar protections under the great seal, without any cause shown,[177] 'by reason of our royal prerogative, which we do not wish to be disputed'. The reason for introducing such arbitrary exemptions from the law is not clear, especially since they were apparently forbidden by statute,[178] but presumably they were obtained from ministers or courtiers either for profit or as favours. In 1495,[179] and again in 1515,[180] the Common Pleas had adjudged the new kind of prerogative protections to be invalid. Indeed, in the 1515 case, the court fined the sheriff for obeying the prerogative writ and in consequence failing to execute its own judicial writ of exigent. The writs seem then to have been less frequently used for a time, and

---

[173] Fleetwood, *Discourse on Statutes*, p. 107, cited a reading on *De Bigamis* to this effect. The various limitations were discussed in the fifteenth-century reading 'De protextione' in BL MS. Lansdowne 1138, fo. 16, and in the reading of *c.* 1529 discussed above, p. 107.

[174] *Anon.* (1558) Dal. 23; BL MS. Add. 24845, fo. 3v; Dyer 162. Cf. *Thurland's Case* (1558) Dyer 162, where a prisoner obtained a licence under the signet seal to go at large. In *Osborne* v. *Kirton* (n. 172, opposite) it was objected that, since the party was already in execution and on bail, the assertion that he was abroad was contrary to the record.

[175] *Registrum Omnium Brevium*, fo. 281v (for Lombard merchants); Morice's reading (1578), fo. 15v; Co. Litt. 130–1.

[176] FNB 28B; *Stringfellow* v. *Brownesoppe* (1549) Dyer 67.

[177] Cf. a different formula, without the prerogative clause, in *Registrum Omnium Brevium*, fo. 262; a marginal note says (tr.) 'But this is not granted except in time of insurrection or for a similar cause'.

[178] 25 Edw. III, stat. 5, c. 19; *Kainesham* v. *Wilkes* (1565) *Dyer's Notebooks*, i. 120.

[179] *Devykke* v. *Halman* (1495) CP 40/934, m. 124; noted by Dyer in *Dyer's Notebooks*, i. 153. No reason is recorded, but Coke (who learned of the case from Dyer's notes) later attributed the decision to the *nulli differemus* clause of Magna Carta, c. 29: Co. Inst. ii. 56. The recipient of the protection, John Halman, was a London vintner. In 1500 Halman had an ordinary protection, as being in the company of Lord Daubeney in Calais: *Fitzherbert* v. *Alman* (1500) KB 27/955, m. 39.

[180] *Isaac* v. *Camden* (1495) CP 40/1010, m. 66d; noted by Dyer his in notebooks, i. 152. The defendant Richard Camden, fishmonger (and a groom of the king's chamber), had obtained a protection for four years, but the writ which he produced in court was only for one.

Dyer remarked in 1568 that during his first ten years as chief justice only four protections (even of the regular kind) had come to his notice in the Common Pleas.[181] But there was a marked increase in the number of prerogative protections enrolled on the patent rolls in the 1560s, many of them in the *indebitatus* form, but some in the general form.[182] The Privy Council also granted protections for those on royal service within the realm. When the general prerogative protections began to be produced in the courts they were seen as a grievance, and several challenges to them are mentioned in Dyer's reports. In 1565 and 1568 the judges seemed loath to disobey the express command not to dispute the prerogative, and unwilling formally to determine the question of validity,[183] though Dyer CJ held in the 1568 case that such protections were invalid.[184] In 1572 the court went so far as to reject one, with Manwood J. alone dissenting.[185] Dyer, who had by then become aware of the earlier precedents, affirmed that no prerogative protection had ever been allowed,[186] and apparently regarded such writs as contrary to the statutes of due process. The protection in that case had been obtained by a defendant after issue joined, and the court proceeded to take the verdict of the jury *de bene esse*, at the plaintiff's 'risk'; judgment was then deferred for advisement. The following term, Dyer received a direct order from the Privy Council to 'forbear all intermeddling' in the case until it had been considered at a conference in the Star Chamber.[187] The court in the mean time required

---

[181] *Lacye's Case*, probably the same as *Eliott's Case* (1568) BL MS. Hargrave 15, fo. 16v; printed in *Dyer's Notebooks*, i. 152 (tr. 'as I remember, in all the time of this queen I have only seen four protections brought in this court').

[182] E.g. William Wilkes's protections of 1563–8: *CPR 1563–8*, pp. 175, 319; *CPR 1566–9*, pp. 70, 328; *Dyer's Notebooks*, i. 120. See also Dawson, 'Privy Council', p. 413, who described them as being 'on the verge of legality'.

[183] *Kainesham v. Wilkes* (1565) *Dyer's Notebooks*, i. 120; *Eliott's Case* (1568) ibid. 151; Co. Inst. ii. 56; BL MS. Hargrave 15, fo. 16v.

[184] BL MS. Hargrave 15, fo. 16v.

[185] *Alcock d. Moyle v. Hitchcock* (1572) BL MS. Add. 25211, fo. 23v; abridged in BL MS. Add. 48186, fo. 435; next note. The report ends (tr.) 'And as the cobbler's crow said, *opera et impensa* Alcock *periit* [Alcock lost his labour and costs].' For the story of the cobbler's crow see *Euphues: The Anatomy of Wit and Euphues his England*, ed. M. Croll and H. Clemens (New York, 1964), p. 236. Alcock was a member of Gray's Inn.

[186] *Alcock d. Moyle v. Hitchcock* (1572) BL MS. Hargrave 374, fo. 122v, corrected from CUL MS. Ll.3.8, fos. 145–148; *Dyer's Notebooks*, i. 152, 154. The dispute concerned the manor of Caversfield, Bucks, which was granted to Hitchcock by the queen in 1563 and first litigated with Moyle in Chancery.

[187] Copy letter to Dyer CJ dated 1 February 1573, BL MS. Add. 32323, fo. 114; cf. 8 APC 86 (Dyer ordered to inform the Council of the order made in Star Chamber).

the defendant to give security not to commit waste on the land in question while the decision was pending. We have no clear account of what transpired in the Star Chamber,[188] but Dyer's view seems to have prevailed; the Common Pleas record shows that two terms later judgment was given for the plaintiff.[189] This did not put an immediate end to the issue of prerogative protections,[190] but doubtless emboldened the judges to kill them off. In 1581 Dyer's court again formally disallowed one,[191] and in 1583 the judges had to confront a particularly fierce protection which threatened imprisonment for anyone who dared to vex the party or for any counsel who dared to argue against it. Although the court held it void, the beneficiary of the protection then had Hugh Hughes of Lincoln's Inn arrested for speaking against it.[192] This the court could not tolerate, and it not only released Hughes but ordered the arrest of the officer who had arrested him.[193] There was a similar clash in 1587 between the Common Pleas and the Privy Council over a protection with power to imprison anyone who imprisoned the protected party.[194]

Those responsible for issuing protections were not easily deterred, and a new variety was tested in the King's Bench in 1587. Richard Waram, a merchant, had been ruined by 'losses of the sea' amounting to £3,000, and obtained a writ of protection under the great seal reciting his

---

[188] According to the report in BL MS. Add. 48416, the lords of the Council ordered the plaintiff's lessor to bring a new action, (tr.) 'and so the hands of the justices were closed'.

[189] CP 40/1299, m. 342; *Dyer's Notebooks*, i. 153.

[190] See *Christmas's Case* (1576) in C. Monro, *Acta Cancellariae* (1847), p. 435 (prerogative protection entered verbatim in the Chancery decree books, but not said to have been allowed); *Locke's Case* (1578) 10 APC 423 (granted to the treasurer of Frobisher's expedition, after its conclusion). There are numerous examples of protections against creditors in the APC after this date, though the form is not set out.

[191] *Countess of Derby's Case* (1581) *Dyer's Notebooks*, ii. 395; probably the case reported anonymously in BL MS. Hargrave 37, fo. 16.

[192] The report does not give the forename, but this must be Hugh Hughes, called to the Bar in 1580 and to the bench in 1594. He was attorney-general for North Wales from 1596 and a member of the Council in the Marches from 1601: *Readers and Readings*, p. 132.

[193] *Hunt v. Woodcock* (1583) BL MS. Lansdowne 1119, fos. 119–118v (reversing); MS. Lansdowne 1078, fo. 60v (same); MS. Add. 35942, fo. 52 (same); CUL MS. Ii.5.38, fos. 98v–99. Cf. BL MS. Hargrave 37, fo. 63: (tr.) 'Fleetwood sjt showed a protection granted by the queen to one Woodcock and Napton and another for the space of one year, and prayed that it might be enrolled. The lord Anderson, Mead and Peryam said it should not be, because it does not come into the court by way of pleading'.

[194] *Searche's Case* (Mich. 1587) 1 Leo. 70; Dawson, 'Privy Council', pp. 640, 649. The protection was for John Mabbe, identifiable as the Cheapside goldsmith who provided jewellery for the queen.

misfortune, but no other cause, unless perhaps that he was indebted to the queen,[195] and containing the peremptory clause forbidding argument. Wray CJ said circumspectly that, 'although the absolute prerogative is great, and of such pre-eminence that it is not suitable for an inferior counsellor to make a public argument in derogation of it, nevertheless the justices themselves by virtue of their proper office ought to consider the true prerogative, so that it should not be allowed to the prejudice of the subjects'. It was reaffirmed that protections could only be allowed for those overseas, or going overseas, in royal service, and then for one year only.[196] The court 'greatly misliked' both the protection and Serjeant Fenner, for proffering it, and in handing it back to him said they would acquaint the queen with it.[197] It was nevertheless not the last of its kind.[198] In 1590 a protection was granted to Sir William Heydon, apparently for good service in the past, with a letter to his creditors, their attorneys, counsel and solicitors, not to pursue further any suit against him.[199] Another kind of protection appeared in 1592, when the Privy Council granted a warrant of protection to Captain Woodhouse, who was needed as a prosecution witness in Sir John Perrot's case.[200]

The court was still rejecting the occasional illegal protection in the 1590s,[201] but then the law reports are silent on the subject.[202] The 'writ of prerogative' continued to be issued by the Exchequer as of course to prevent a creditor recovering against a debtor until the debtor had paid his debts to the king,[203] while the Privy Council continued to issue

[195] This is mentioned only in BL MS. Add. 35949, fo. 62v.

[196] *Waram's (or Wharam's) Case* (Pas. 1587) BL MS Harley 4562, fo. 78v (tr.); MS. Add. 35943, fo. 134 (same); also reported in CUL MS. Ii.5.38, fo. 237; MS. Dd.11.64, fo. 61 (same); Moo. 239. There was a precedent the previous year when Robert Barnaby was granted a protection by reason that he was 'decayed by losses at sea': 14 APC 268.

[197] BL MS. Add. 35949, fo. 62v (tr.).

[198] See, e.g., 15 APC 358 (protection to be granted by the lord deputy of Ireland to Donoghe Offalie, professor of Civil law, whose substance had been wasted by the rebels in Munster, 1587); 16 APC 259 (protection for distressed merchants, 1588).

[199] PC 2/18, fos. 154–5.

[200] *Woodhouse v. Barney* (1592) BL MS. Harley 2143, fo. 54 (where the defendant was committed close prisoner by the Star Chamber for contempt in pursuing a suit in London, knowing of the protection); 22 APC 441, 452, 485. It seems the defendant's suit was thought to be a ploy to put the witness in prison.

[201] *Abdie's Case* (1596) BL MS. Add. 48186, fo. 435.

[202] Prerogative protections were not among the species of legal protection enumerated by Coke, whose over-generous recollection was that Elizabeth I had issued very few protections even of the regular kind: Co. Litt. 131.

[203] E.g. *Anon.* (1609) BL MS. Add. 25207, fo. 7v.

protections – or letters in the nature of protections – in connection with its assumed jurisdiction to assist debtors in trouble.[204] But the noble campaign by the judges against prerogative protections, led by the Common Pleas under Dyer CJ and Anderson CJ, though no doubt inspired by general notions of due process and the rule of law, was largely over before the resurrection of Magna Carta. It did not occur to counsel or judges to rely on the *nulli differemus* clause of chapter 29, a connection which would come to seem as obvious to Coke as it had been to Bereford.[205] More directly in point, it seemed, was the legislation of Edward III instructing the judges to ignore the king's letters if they hindered common right, a prohibition which was still embodied in the judicial oath.[206] This bound the king and could not be dispensed with.[207] It was held in the 1590s that the judges' sworn duty prevented them from obeying a letter from the Privy Council to stay a suit against an English ambassador, instead of using a protection or an essoin of the king's service, an irregular course which they 'greatly misliked'.[208] It was only at the very end of the reign that Edward Hake could condemn all prerogative protections as contrary to chapter 29,[209] but they would actually increase in number under James I.[210]

Other Stays of Justice

The case of Brian Annesley, warden of the Fleet, has already been mentioned in connection with the gaoler's liability for a constructive escape.[211] It also raised the constitutional question whether there was a prerogative power to interfere with the execution of a judgment in a private suit. The complex pleadings revealed that a debtor had been committed to the Fleet by the barons of the Exchequer, for the queen's

---

[204] Dawson, 'Privy Council', pp. 413, 631, 650–1.

[205] Co. Inst. ii. 56, citing the records of 1495 and 1515. For Bereford CJ's decision of 1311 see above, p. 47.

[206] See above, p. 52.

[207] Morice's reading, fo. 15v, referring to 2 Edw. III, c. 8 ('which statute, reforming the abuse in deferring justice, crept in as prerogative, is also restrictive and bindeth the king'). Morice was careful to add that it did not extend to ordinary prerogative writs of protection.

[208] *Sir William Bowes' Case* (c. 1596) BL MS. Add. 25199, fo. 3. Bowes was ambassador to Scotland. The justices said that if there was a protection or essoin their consciences would be discharged if they stayed the cause, but not otherwise.

[209] Hake, *Epieikeia*, pp. 74–6.   [210] Dawson, 'Privy Council', pp. 413, 650–1.

[211] Above, p. 165.

debt, on the same day that he had been committed to the Fleet by a *capias ad satisfaciendum* from the Common Pleas, at the suit of a party, and that the barons had later ordered his release so that he could collect his debts and see to other business, the better to be able to pay his debt to the queen. However unlikely the coincidence, this dual imprisonment had to be accepted as fact since neither party's assertion was factually disputed. The Common Pleas took the view that its own process took precedence, so that the debtor was in its custody; on that footing, the question was whether, in order to protect the queen's debt, the plaintiff could be prevented by the Exchequer from pursuing execution to recover his own debt. Dyer CJ and all his brethren showed little sympathy with the proposition that he could.[212] Manwood J. said that a prisoner could only be discharged by justices sitting in court, 'and this ought to be for the advancement of justice and not to defeat justice', for *justicia est suum cuique tribuere*,[213] and justice could not be achieved without execution, 'for execution is the fruit of the law'. Dyer doubted whether even the Privy Council could release someone from execution in a private suit on account of the queen's interest. He recalled that in Mary's reign the court was requested by the Council to release someone 'by baston' to serve the queen at Berwick, but the court answered that they could not do it without the plaintiff's consent, and so he remained in prison. The reporter here noted that Brograve of Gray's Inn, while walking with him in the fields, remembered another case, in the time of the present queen, where a privy seal was sent to release someone from execution in order to survey the queen's mines, but it was refused. The judges all agreed that the queen could not by her prerogative release anyone from execution. They were sworn to uphold the prerogative, but only in accordance with the law, for – as Dyer said, in another quotation from *Bracton* – 'The king may only do what by right and law he may do'.[214] Mounson J. did draw attention to chapter 29 of Magna Carta (the *nulli differemus* clause), along with several other statutes and cases, about which there was much discussion and scratching of heads.[215] But the eventual decision was to disallow the order from the Exchequer as illegal,

---

[212] The following quotations are from *Manser v. Annesley* (1575) BL MS. Hargrave 9, at fo. 230 (tr.). For other manuscript reports see *Dyer's Notebooks*, ii. 349.

[213] Cf. *Bracton*, ii. 25 (from Azo). This was not a definition of justice, but one of Ulpian's three precepts of the law (*praecepta juris*).

[214] *Bracton*, ii. 305 (tr.).

[215] The reporter said of one case, 'Manwood et Dier esbraule lour test, quasi ne serra ley' (i.e. scratched their heads, as if to say that it was not law).

so that the warden was liable for the private debt, and this was affirmed on a writ of error.[216]

These were not the only ways in which justice might be interfered with under the cloak of the royal prerogative. The other principal ways were aid prayer of the queen, writs of search, and writs of *non procedendo rege inconsulto*, none of which had been inhibited in the slightest by Magna Carta, though the most dilatory aspects of aid prayer and search had been removed by statute in 1276 and 1340.[217] Both procedures were predicated on the need for the king to be brought in if he had interest in a suit, so that the case could be transmitted to the Chancery for a search of records touching the king's title, and then remitted to the common-law court. The procedure more often benefited the defendant than the crown, and it operated as a delay of justice, but it was a delay permitted by the law of the land for good reason. Delay was not always a bad thing.[218] The problem was that, in the event of abuse, there was no remedy in the courts.[219] In 1595 the King's Bench received a *supersedeas* commanding them not to proceed *regina inconsulta* in an ejectment action – a form of trespass action to recover possession of land – because the queen was entitled to the land in remainder.[220] Serjeant Glanville raised a fundamental objection to this course. A statute of 1328 provided that common right should not be disturbed or delayed by any command under the great or small seal, and that if any such command came to the justices

---

[216] *Dyer's Notebooks*, ii. 351.

[217] 4 Edw. I, stat. 3 (called *De Bigamis*), cc. 1–2 (as to aid prayer); 14 Edw. III, stat. 1, c. 14 (as to writs of search upon a petition of right). The 1276 statute was the subject of a detailed reading by George Bromley in the Inner Temple in 1568: BL MS. Hargrave 33, fos. 160–173. Cf. Co. Inst. ii. 268–70.

[218] In 1588 Serjeant Fleetwood argued that 'all delays are odious to the king' (*omnes dilationes sunt odiosae regi*), but he was answered by Anderson CJ that it is better to suffer a delay than an injustice: *Horslye's Case* (1588) BL MS. Lansdowne 1059, fo. 74; sub nom. *Horsey's Case*, LI MS. Misc. 361, fo. 121 (same report).

[219] The only remedy lay in Parliament, or in the king's grace. In *Grey v. Mautravers* (c. 1330) SC 8/48/2400, a petitioner asked the king to order the judges to proceed in such a case, lest he be disinherited contrary to Magna Carta; for this case see also *The Eyre of Northamptonshire 1329–30*, ed. D. W. Sutherland (97 SS, 1981), pp. 470–1. A later example of improper use is *Melton v. Earl of Northumberland* (1535), where a suit was stayed so that retrospective legislation could be passed before judgment was given: Baker, *Collected Papers*, iii. 1392–4.

[220] *Sale d. Nevill v. Barrington* (1595) Cro. Eliz. 417; CUL MS. Dd.10.51, fos. 112v–113; MS. Gg.5.3, fos. 67v–68v; MS. Ll.3.9, fos. 481v–482; BL MS. Hargrave 356, fos. 87v–88, 127; MS. Add. 25198, fo. 100 (same); MS. Harley 4814, fo. 48 (same); MS. Harley 1624, fos. 269, 297; CUL MS. Gg.6.29, fos. 37 (Mich. 1595), 48v (Trin. 1596); HLS MS. 110, fos. 162v–163.

they should ignore it.[221] The *supersedeas* was a delay of justice, and it did not protect any royal interest in the present case because it was a personal action by a lessee and could not prejudice the queen's ultimate remainder, which was separated from the lease by several intermediate remainders. It had, however, already been decided by all the judges in 1592 that *regina inconsulta* lay in a personal action.[222] This enabled Coke, as attorney-general, to argue successfully that the queen's interest was no less in an ejectment than in a real action. The court agreed that the procedure had always been allowed by law, just as delays by protections and essoins had been, and that it was allowable in the case at the bar because the queen could possibly be prejudiced in future by the verdict. When the case was moved again a year later, Popham CJ blamed the plaintiff for not removing it into Chancery for the requisite search of records, so that it could proceed, remarking tartly that the court's hands were closed and that 'by this ignorance of Nevill's counsel it might depend for seven years here without proceeding, for until the record is removed into Chancery no *procedendo* can ever be granted.'[223] The only qualification agreed by the courts was that aid of the queen would not be allowed in an action for personal chattels if the queen's title was not set out.[224]

In the same year the Common Pleas was presented with a new kind of *supersedeas*,[225] where no aid was prayed and there was no writ of *non procedendo regina inconsulta*, in an attempt to halt an action by Mary Arden on the ground that her father had been attainted of treason. The writ was disallowed by the whole court because it did not set out the inquisition whereby the queen was entitled through the attainder. A mere surmise was insufficient. By such means, said the judges, all real actions for any lands in England might be stopped, and this would be against the judges' oath not to delay justice by reason of the great or

---

[221] Above, p. 52. Glanville also relied on the statute of 1346 cited ibid.

[222] *Blofield* v. *Havers* (1592) 1 And. 280; Co. Inst. ii. 269. Coke said in *Sale* v. *Barrington* (1595) Cro. Eliz. 417 that it had been referred to all the judges.

[223] CUL MS. Gg.6.29, fo. 48v (Mich. 1596). Cf. Co. Inst. ii. 270, where Coke says that writs of search were only allowed upon petitions of right, and not in the case of aid prayer or *rege inconsulto*.

[224] *Foxley* v. *Annesley* (1599–1601) 5 Co. Rep. 109; Cro. Eliz. 693; Moo. 572 (trover for sheep claimed as waif); Co. Inst. ii. 269.

[225] Cf. *Lord Powis's Case* (1558) Dyer 170, where it was held that an escheator should not obey a writ of *supersedeas* which obstructed a party's right. For objections to writs of *supersedeas* from the Chancery in support of the equitable jurisdiction see Smith, *Sir Edward Coke*, p. 233.

little seal.[226] One reporter noted that the defendant Darcy was in great favour with the queen – he must be the same Darcy who earned unworthy fame as monopolist[227] – and for that reason Mary's husband would not trust anyone to act as his counsel but argued the case in person.[228] Reliance was again placed on the statute of 1328, apparently without success.

Coke once again had to defend the prerogative power of *supersedeas* in 1601, when he was still attorney-general. The question was raised in the Court of Wards whether it could be used to quash an inquisition *post mortem*.[229] After Coke had deftly distinguished the adverse precedents and 'alleged the queen's prerogative *ultra legem*', the case was argued by Thomas Hesketh, attorney-general of the Court of Wards. Hesketh argued that writs were issued by the Chancery under two different authorities, *potestas ordinata* and *potestas absoluta*. Under the former, the Chancery awarded process at common law to the sheriff or escheator, such as the writs ordering inquisitions *post mortem*. But the *supersedeas* was issued under the absolute power, and to prove that the queen was not tied to a strict observance of the law he cited Frowyk's reading on the prerogative 'enrolled in the Petty Bag'.[230] The contrary case, he said, rested on a misunderstanding of the statute of 1328. Sir Robert Cecil, master of the Wards, said there were so many precedents over such a long time that he did not need to call on the judges for their assistance. The *supersedeas* was therefore awarded, 'both by law and by the discretion of the court'.

These cases raised some important questions but were of limited impact. As Coke had argued, it was both lawful and reasonable for the queen's prerogative rights to be protected, provided that the subject was not thereby wronged. The procedures delayed justice, but for good reason and without denying it. None of the reported cases turned on egregious

---

[226] *Arderne v. Darcy* (1595) CUL MS. Ii.5.24, fos. 67v–68; 1 And. 281; sub nom. *Arden v. Darcy* (1596) Warburton's reports, CUL MS. Ii.5.25, fos. 38v–39v.

[227] Darcy was a groom of the privy chamber and a kinsman of Sir Walter Raleigh. His playing-card monopoly (below, p. 319) was granted as partial compensation for giving up his leather-searching monopoly (below, p. 196), which had caused an outcry: see N. Tyacke, *The English Revolution c. 1590–1720* (Manchester, 2007), pp. 15–16.

[228] BL MS. Add. 25199, fo. 6.

[229] *Coke v. Old* (1601) BL MS. Add. 25215, fos. 2v–3 (quotations tr.).

[230] For this reading of 1495 see M. McGlynn, *The Royal Prerogative and the Learning of the Inns of Court* (Cambridge, 2003).

abuses of the procedures. The principal question was whether the delaying powers could be reconciled with the legislation of Edward III. Magna Carta did not yet feature in the arguments.[231]

Revenue and the Prerogative

Although it was maintained by James Morice that the queen had no power to levy money or take goods from her subjects for the necessary affairs of the realm except by Act of Parliament,[232] there had always been several sources of extra-parliamentary revenue, such as feudal wardships, rents from crown estates, and customs duties. The regular revenues were nevertheless insufficient to support the activities of government, and so new ways of raising money, without dependency on Parliament, were constantly being sought. The most controversial of them were impositions, forced loans, purveyance and monopolies.

The crown had been entitled since medieval times to certain customary impositions in the form of import duties on wool, woolfells and leather (the great customs and the petty customs) and on wine (prisage) and to similar duties on exports,[233] besides other statutory levies, but it was now claiming the right to levy other impositions on both imports and exports under the prerogative. In the first year of Elizabeth's reign the judges met several times to consider the lawfulness of a new export duty on cloth, which was 'not granted by Parliament but assessed by Queen Mary of her absolute power'. The principal justification for it, with respect to denizen merchants, was that any subject could be forbidden to go out of the realm by the writ *ne exeat regno*, and this would prevent him exporting his goods without permission, though this was convincingly refuted by Plowden with respect to merchants, citing statutes from the

---

[231] Cf. Plowden's argument in Fleetwood's reading (1569) that a *supersedeas* in a suit between private persons would be contrary to c. 29 ('we shall not deny right or justice'): Fleetwood, 'Miscellanea', fo. 161.

[232] Reading in the Middle Temple (1578) BL MS. Egerton 3376, fo. 22v; MS. Add. 36081, fo. 256.

[233] These were held by Dyer to be an inheritance of the king at common law: *Anon.* (1538) Dyer 43; *Anon.* (1553) Dyer 92. Others denied this: see *Proc. Parl.* 1610, ii. 230–1, *per* Heneage Finch ('The truth is, proof can be made of neither side'); *Proc. Parl.* 1614, p. 260, *per idem*; Co. Inst. ii. 58–9. Plowden (n. 235, opposite) said that no customs were payable at common law by English merchants, though export duties had been introduced by statute.

fourteenth century.[234] Plowden also argued that the various statutes approving new imposts would have been unnecessary if the king could have introduced them without Parliament.[235] No clear conclusion is recorded, leaving posterity to interpret the case in different ways, though it seems to have had no inhibiting effect on impositions.[236]

The crown had also resorted for well over a century to extra-parliamentary subsidies in the form of forced loans or benevolences. A celebrated statute of 1484, the second of Richard III's reign,[237] had blamed their introduction on Edward IV. Reciting the great thraldom and unbearable charges imposed on subjects by new inventions under Edward, 'and in especial by a new imposition called a benevolence', whereby subjects paid great sums of money against their wills, it enacted that 'the commonalty ... from henceforth in no wise be charged by none such charge, exaction or imposition called a benevolence, nor by such like charge, ... but it shall be damned and adnulled for ever'. This was Richard III's Magna Carta, and it was not forgotten.[238] But forced loans were promptly reintroduced by Henry VII, and they became a major source of revenue in the sixteenth century.[239] The legal profession was particularly disgruntled in 1523 about the forced loan initiated by Wolsey.[240] The word 'loan' was a euphemism, since the lending was more or less compulsory and no one expected the money to be repaid.[241] It has been said that crown used persuasion rather than

---

[234] 38 Edw. III, stat. 1, c. 2; 5 Ric. II, c. 2. Cf. BL MS. Harley 1575, fo. 77v (c. 1610): (tr.) 'Note by the court, a *ne exeat regnum* shall not issue unless the party will do some notable mischief beyond the sea or adhere to the king's enemies.'

[235] 'How and in what manner the custom that is due unto the queen's majesty for cloths carried out of the realm by English merchants did commence, and whether the queen's majesty may increase the same at her pleasure', BL MS. Hargrave 27, fos. 84–85v. Another hand has added in the margin, 'Mr Plowdens argument 1 Eliz.'.

[236] *Case of Impositions on Cloth* (1559) Dyer 165; G. D. G. Hall, 'Impositions and the Courts 1554–1606' (1953) 69 LQR 200–18, at pp. 209–10. See further below, pp. 328–34.

[237] 1 Ric. III, c. 2.   [238] See below, p. 407.

[239] F. C. Dietz, *English Government Finance 1485–1558* (2nd edn, 1964), pp. 52, 92–7, 164–6. The 'loans' of 1542 and 1545 generated over £100,000 each.

[240] *Hall's Chronicle* (1809 edn), pp. 698–9; *Spelman's Reports*, i. 169. It was the first time the judges, serjeants, members of the inns of court and chancery, and officials of the courts, were assessed separately for a tax: *The Men of Court*, i. 51.

[241] Cf. R. Schofield, *Taxation under the Early Tudors 1485–1547* (Oxford, 2004), p. 202, where it is said that the loans were usually paid back, except in military emergencies. But some of the loans were written off by statute: 11 Hen. VII, c. 10; 21 Hen. VIII, c. 25; 35 Hen. VIII, c. 12; 37 Hen. VIII, c. 25.

compulsion to secure the loans,[242] though when an alderman of London questioned the legality of the pressure put upon him in 1545 he was sent to prison.[243] Mary I gave privy seal receipts for loans, but they contained no promise of repayment and no repayment was made.[244] Elizabeth's government continued the practice of demanding loans from time to time. The least controversial version was 'ship money', when it was raised willingly from coastal towns at the time of the Spanish armada in 1588, though attempts to extend it proved less welcome.[245] Large sums were also raised by nationwide loans. The practice was immune to legal challenge because the loans were in form genuine, and the privy seals now contained a promise to repay the money within a certain time. In reality the lender had little choice but to oblige, repayments were often delayed, and there was usually no interest.[246] The practice therefore continued to be a grievance in the later sixteenth century, not least when a benevolence was demanded from the lawyers in 1599.[247]

The prerogative right of purveyance, the compulsory purchase of commodities for the royal household, was of long standing and had been regulated by a series of statutes beginning with chapter 19 of Magna Carta; but it was asserted more oppressively in the sixteenth century and was said to be worth perhaps £37,000 a year to the queen.[248] The grievance was that purveyors did not pay the full market rates for the commodities which they seized, and various measures had to be introduced to make up the

---

[242] Schofield, ibid.

[243] Dietz, *English Government Finance*, p. 166. Another alderman who refused to pay, Richard Rede, was sent to serve in Scotland, where he was taken prisoner and had to pay ransom.

[244] Ibid. 211.

[245] A. H. Lewis, *A Study of Elizabethan Ship Money* (Philadelphia, 1928); D. L. Keir, 'The Case of Ship Money' (1936) 52 LQR 546. In 1596 the Privy Council threatened defaulters with unspecified sanctions: 25 APC 496 ('let them know from us that we will not fail to take order to reform their disobedience').

[246] See the specimen privy seal printed in G. R. Elton, *The Tudor Constitution* (2nd edn, 1982), p. 59, no. 28a (1591). This contained a promise to repay within one year, but the receipt shows that it was not in fact repaid for three years.

[247] *Letters written by John Chamberlain during the Reign of Queen Elizabeth*, ed. S. Williams (Camden Soc., 1861), pp. 44–5 (referring in February 1599 to a 'benevolence demanded of the lawyers, not only of the inns of court, but all manner officers and clerks ... not forgetting the poor doctors of the Arches ... Whether from them it shall proceed all over England it is doubtful').

[248] Guy, *Tudor England*, pp. 397–9. See also A. Woodworth, *Purveyance for the Royal Household in the Reign of Elizabeth* (Philadelphia, 1945).

difference from local rates. The measures did not operate effectively or fairly, and abuses by the purveyors were complained of in the House of Commons throughout the reign, albeit without effect.[249]

Monopolies

The festering grievance of monopolies in the later sixteenth century is apparent from the proceedings in the Elizabethan House of Commons, and much of the story is well known.[250] There were two principal forms. The first depended on the prohibition by statute of a particular branch of trade, usually in relation to importing or exporting commodities; an individual was then licensed by patent to carry on the trade, notwithstanding (*non obstante*) the statute, on the footing that the queen was not bound by it. The second form had no statutory sanction behind it. The crown assumed a power under the prerogative to grant to individuals, by letters patent, the sole right to import, work or sell particular commodities, and such a right (to have any practical meaning) necessarily included a power to prevent others from competing with them. Both forms raised questions about their validity at common law, long before legislation was introduced under James I. The first question was the extent to which the king could dispense with Acts of Parliament, and the second was the extent to which people could be prevented from carrying on the trades of their choice in order to enforce monopolistic rights created solely under the royal prerogative.

As a general principle, although the king could not make grants contrary to law, he could in certain circumstances set aside the effect of Acts of Parliament made solely for his benefit, such as revenue legislation. Well-established examples were licences to alienate in mortmain and (more recently) export licences. The reason was that the king was not bound by statute 'in a point which touched his prerogative', in the absence of express words.[251] The late-medieval case-law indicated that

---

[249] Neale, *Elizabeth I and her Parliaments 1559–81*, pp. 122–3; 219–20 (1563 and 1571); *Proc. Parl. 1558–81*, p. 202 (1571); *Proc. Parl. 1584–9*, pp. 392 (1587), 496 (1589). Smith, *Sir Edward Coke*, p. 69, cites a letter from Wray CJ to Anderson CJ on the subject in 1586 (BL MS. Lansdowne 43, fo. 193). James Morice complained in 1592 of the practice of compounding for purveyance: 23 APC 364. See further below, pp. 324–8.

[250] See Neale, *Elizabeth I and her Parliaments 1584–1601*, pp. 352–6, 376–93; M. B. Donald, *Elizabethan Monopolies* (Edinburgh, 1961); Guy, *Tudor England*, pp. 399–403.

[251] *Willion v. Lord Berkeley* (1561) as reported in *Dyer's Notebooks*, i. 59; *Discourse upon Statutes*, pp. 110 n. 5, 179–80; Morice's reading (1578), fos. 16–19.

the king could waive future taxes which might become due to the crown from a particular patentee,[252] and that he might license certain activities prohibited by statute; but such licences with the clause *non obstante* were valid only if they did not prejudice other individuals or sanction the commission of a wrong which was inherently bad (*malum in se*).[253] Legal logic went so far as to allow that the king could in some cases grant charters *non obstante* a statute forbidding the grant of such charters,[254] even if the statute expressly forbade charters with a *non obstante* clause, because the statute (however explicitly worded) could not bind the crown.[255] In the early sixteenth century, the doctrine as to waiving taxation was questioned on the ground that a waiver of future income could only operate as a promise, rather than a grant, and a promise could not bar the crown since an action of covenant would not lie against the king.[256] It was an unconvincing quibble, since the only question was whether the promise could be pleaded by way of defence, not whether it would support an action for damages. A new line of reasoning appeared in 1542, when the Common Pleas considered a licence to export bell-metal *non obstante* the statutes already made 'and thereafter to be made'. Two of the judges held that, although the king could grant a discharge from future taxation, he 'could not dispense with a new law to be made

---

[252] *Rector of Edington's Case* (1441) YB Pas. 19 Hen. VI, fo. 62, pl. 1; *Bishop of Salisbury's Case* (1459) YB Mich. 38 Hen. VI, fo. 9, pl. 20, at fo. 10. A number of such grants were made to religious houses and municipal corporations in the fourteenth and fifteenth centuries: R. Schofield, *Taxation under the early Tudors 1485–1547* (Oxford, 2004), pp. 65–8.

[253] *Dyer's Notebooks*, i. lii. For the earlier history see also P. Birdsall, '"Non Obstante" – A Study of the Dispensing Power of the English Kings' in *Essays in History and Politics in Honor of C. H. McIlwain* (Cambridge, MA, 1936), pp. 37–76. In 1614 Serjeant Montagu argued that the distinction was between negative statutes, which could be dispensed with, and affirmative statutes: *Proc. Parl. 1614*, p. 111.

[254] Morice's reading (1578), fo. 16 (grant of a pardon *non obstante* the statute of 2 Edw. III, c. 2). Morice held the prerogative of mercy to be so unrestrainable that, even if Parliament forbade all pardons, the king could still grant them *non obstante* the statute. As late as 1607 it was apparently agreed by the judges and the House of Commons that a statute taking away a 'necessary prerogative', such as purveyance, would be void: Wilbraham, *Journal*, pp. 83, 84.

[255] *Earl of Northumberland's Case* (1487) YB Mich. 2 Hen. VII, fo. 6, pl. 6, pl. 20 (grant of the office of sheriff *non obstante* the statute of 23 Hen. VI, c. 7); 64 SS 126; cited without demur by Henry Finch, *Law* (c. 1595/1600) CUL MS. Ll.3.6, fos. 41v–42, and by Coke Att.-Gen. in *Darcy v. Allen* (1602) BL MS. Add. 25203, fo. 547.

[256] *Spelman's Reports*, i. 152 (undated). Thomas Egerton held in his reading (Lincoln's Inn, 1582) that 'a *non obstante* may dispense with a thing which is then in being, but not with a future thing': BL MS. Harley 5265, fo. 133 (tr.).

by Act of Parliament, before the Act be made'. Dyer's report ends, 'therefore query'.[257] Dispensation from pre-existing penal or fiscal statutes was less controversial as a matter of law,[258] though licences *non obstante* were already a popular grievance by the start of Elizabeth's reign. A bill was presented in the parliament of 1559 to abolish them, but it went nowhere.[259] Robert Bell of the Middle Temple complained about them in the 1571 parliament, saying that 'by licences a few were enriched and the multitude impoverished', and the queen promised in response to be more careful in granting them.[260] Bell's speech was nevertheless misrepresented to the queen as an assault on her prerogative, and he was in trouble for it.[261] Challenges were also made in the courts, and Dyer noted three Elizabethan decisions. In 1568 the judges held that a Marian licence to retail wine notwithstanding a statute was operative during the queen's pleasure only, and was therefore determined by Queen Mary's death.[262] And in 1571 they avoided giving effect to a *non obstante* in a Marian patent issued in contravention of a statute requiring such patents to be warranted by the lord treasurer.[263] In the third case, however, the judges assistant to the Court of Wards held in 1574 that the king could by dispensation waive his future entitlements under the Statute of Wills 1540.[264] It remained the law that the queen could not dispense with any law made for the public good, such as the statute requiring an inquisition to establish the queen's title to land before it was granted to a subject.[265] A fortiori, the queen could not dispense with the common law, for instance

---

[257] *Att.-Gen.* v. *Richards* (1542) Dyer 54.

[258] *Anon.* (1553) Dyer 92; Gell's reports, i, Library of Congress, Law MS. 15, Mich. 1 Mar.; *Anon.* (1559) Gell's reports, ii, Derbyshire Record Office MS. D3287, fos. 74–5; *Anon.* (1568) Dyer 270.

[259] Elton, *Parliament of England*, p. 280. See also J. Loach, *Parliament under the Tudors* (1991), pp. 132–4.

[260] *Proc. Parl. 1558–81*, pp. 202, 207, 238; J. Neale, *Elizabeth I and her Parliaments 1559–81*, pp. 218–19.

[261] *Proc. Parl. 1558–81*, pp. 224, 248. Bell was shortly afterwards elected speaker of the Commons, and was particularly emphatic about the liberty of free speech in the House: ibid. 264.

[262] *Anon.* (1568) Dyer 270.   [263] *Northcote* v. *Ward* (1571) Dyer 303.

[264] *R.* v. *Powlett* (1573) *Dyer's Notebooks*, ii. 274. But in 1555 the crown was advised against granting a tenant power to subinfeudate, notwithstanding the statute *Quia Emptores*, because it would prejudice the king and be a bad example: *Lord North's Case* (1555) *Dyer's Notebooks*, i. 14.

[265] *Anon.* (c. 1582) BL MS. Harley 5030, fo. 37 (printed in *Dyer's Notebooks*, i. liv n. 62). Cf. *Att.-Gen.* v. *Kinge* (1582) BL MS. Lansdowne 1101, fo. 17, where the Court of Exchequer upheld a crown lease to the vicar of West Ham, made *non obstante* the statute of 21 Hen. VIII, c. 13.

to validate a grant which she was not entitled at law to make.[266] Moreover, the prerogative was non-delegable, and so the grantee of a licence *non obstante* could not license others to infringe the statute;[267] if he did so, claiming such authority, it was punishable in the Star Chamber.[268]

Monopolies of trade and industry were more legally troublesome, and the courts were consistently hostile to their extension. At the beginning of the reign, when some of Mary I's patents came into question, the judges were asked to rule on a Marian patent granting that all imported malmsey wines should be landed solely at Southampton, on pain of paying treble the custom.[269] The attorney-general, Gilbert Gerrard, informed in the Exchequer against some Venetian merchants who had landed malmseys in Kent and taken them by water to London. The information was contested by Christopher Wray as counsel for the merchants, and the case was argued before all the judges of England in the Exchequer Chamber and Serjeants' Inn.[270] Wray's argument was that the patent prejudiced the queen's subjects, because it was everyone's liberty to follow what trade he wished, and to use it to his best advantage, and it was the liberty of merchants to bring their merchandise to whatever place they would. He recalled from his own time the opinion of all the justices concerning a patent for sole printing, which they held void because it was 'against the liberty and freedom of everyone of the same mystery, which was that anyone who pleased might print every book, and also to the great damage of other printers and of every other man'. If the grant were good, he argued, it would follow that the king might grant a monopoly of printing to one man, which would be against reason.[271] He also argued that a grant to a particular person, in this case

---

[266] *Futter* v. *Bozoun* (1585) 4 Co. Rep. 34. Coke was counsel in this case, which was in a missing portion of his autograph notebook.

[267] *Shaw* v. *Harries* (1606) BL MS. Add. 35954, fos. 441–2v. The same point is reported anonymously in 'Penal statutes' (1605) 7 Co. Rep. 36, where it is said to have been referred as a question to the judges and resolved in a written opinion.

[268] *Att.-Gen.* v. *Eversides* (1562) BL MS. Harley 2143, fo. 21 (abridged from the lost register, fo. 148).

[269] *Att.-Gen* v. *Donatt* (1561) *Dyer's Notebooks*, i. 49; BL MS. Harley 1057, fos. 154–156v; MS. Hargrave 37, fos. 85–89; MS. Lansdowne 1067, fos. 131v–134 (same); other MSS. noted in 69 LQR 207 n. 43; record, E 159/340, Communia, Trin. 1 Eliz., m. 73 (printed with translation in *Dyer's Notebooks*, i. 51–3). For the background to the case see Hall, 'Impositions and the Courts', pp. 206–8.

[270] For Wray's reliance on Magna Carta, cc. 29 and 30, see below, p. 250.

[271] The case has not been identified, but see L. Patterson, 'The Printing Patent and the Royal Prerogative' in *Copyright in Historical Perspective* (Nasvhille, TN, 1968), pp. 80–90. In 1593 the Privy Council acted to protect the law-printing patent: 24 APC 369–70. In

the corporation of Southampton, could not prejudice strangers who were not party to the grant. Serjeant Carus argued rather feebly in support of the patent that it only prejudiced foreigners, who were not favoured in law. The judges accepted Wray's argument and held the patent 'utterly against the law', though no judgment was entered.[272] Deferring to the judges' opinion, Southampton obtained an Act of Parliament to reinstate their privilege.[273] The judicial ruling, though ineffective in practice, was significant as confirming the authority of the judges to determine the limits of the royal prerogative beyond the sphere of private property.[274] Dyer's report of the case was omitted from his printed reports, perhaps because it was too controversial, but it was cited in the Commons in 1571,[275] and in a case of 1582,[276] and was still known in the next century.[277] The decision was probably the principal authority for James Morice's assertion at his reading (1578) that the king could not grant a monopoly in a common trade or traffic, or make any mystery or occupation private unto a few,[278] with certain exceptions.[279] And it was

---

Darcy v. Allen (1602), below, p. 319, counsel on both sides accepted that the printing monopoly was in the public interest.

[272] Egerton says that, after long arguments at the bar, the merchants were discharged without any argument by the barons: autograph note in a printed year book, H. E. Huntington Library, PB 61062 (printed in *Dyer's Notebooks*, i. 50).

[273] Co. Inst. iii. 182. This was taken as proof that the patent was invalid: see *Proc. Parl. 1558–81*, p. 210, *per* Francis Alford MP (1571); note of argument, probably by Fleet-wood, in *Att.-Gen. v. Joiners' Company of London* (1582) below, p. 474 ('they could not enjoy it before they had a confirmation by Parliament').

[274] Cf. A. Cromartie, *The Constitutionalist Revolution* (Cambridge, 2006), pp. 105–6.

[275] *Proc. Parl. 1558–81*, p. 211, *per* John Popham MP, of the Middle Temple, who said the principle was attributed by the learned to Magna Carta.

[276] *Att.-Gen. v. Joiners' Company of London* (1582) below, p. 474; but it was distinguished as applying only to merchants, by virtue of the law of nations and Magna Carta, c. 30. It was also cited in Daniel's argument in the same case, below, p. 472.

[277] Coke knew it from Dyer's notebook: Co. Inst. ii. 61; Co. Inst. iii. 182. It was cited in the Commons in 1614: *Proc. Parl. 1614*, pp. 95, 149.

[278] BL MS. Egerton 2376, fos. 18v–19. Fleetwood challenged the reader, arguing that the queen could by prerogative govern the persons of her subjects but not their inheritances, though the reporter thought he had been unwilling to give his real opinion: BL MS. Add. 16169, fo. 40 (tr. 'query, for he seemed the contrary but dared not utter as much for the check that he had received earlier [from the queen's counsel], as it seemed to me from his speech amongst us afterwards').

[279] E.g. that since the king could restrain the liberty to export goods he could grant a monopoly of exporting certain categories of goods: BL MS. Egerton 2376, fo. 19. He mentioned the recent patent to export shreds (of cloth). He also allowed printing monopolies, perhaps because they were of long standing.

approved by the King's Bench in 1590, by which time Wray had become chief justice.[280] In the 1590 case it was argued that the king could not restrain his subjects in such a manner without an Act of Parliament, for otherwise he might just as well grant that no one but Foster should plead in the King's Bench and no one but Chidley in the Chancery. Wray CJ, not surprisingly, assented to this argument with alacrity.[281] Such monopolies could exist by immemorial custom, but they could not be created by the king's grant.[282] The decision was further followed by the Common Pleas in 1599,[283] and in the 1620s Coke hailed it as an important decision against monopolies and a clear application of chapters 29 and 30 of Magna Carta.[284] Those chapters had indeed been relied on by Wray in argument, though they are not mentioned in Dyer's report of the decision. The argument was focused on the rights of merchants rather than more sweeping notions of individual liberty and restraint of trade.

The age of exploration brought into being the companies of merchant adventurers, who were granted monopolies of trade in defined foreign regions; but it was held that even these were invalid without an Act of Parliament, such as that obtained by the Muscovy merchants in 1566.[285] The merchants had been given a monopoly of fishing and trading in the Arctic regions, with a penalty for infringement. In 1609 the company sued one Jones in the Admiralty to recover a penalty for killing 'sea-horses'[286] (walruses) on Cherry Island,[287] within the area of their

---

[280] *Fermour v. Brooke* (1589–90) as reported in 1 Leo. 142 at p. 143; BL MS. Add. 35941, fo. 286; MS. Add. 35949, fo. 105v.

[281] The report in the Add. MSS. attributes this remark to counsel, but Leo. attributes a similar remark to Wray CJ himself.

[282] See further *Case of the City of York* (1568) Dyer 279; *Wagoner's Case (Waggoner v. Fish)* (1610) 8 Co. Rep. 121.

[283] *Waltham v. Austin* (1599) Coke's notebook, BL MS. Harley 6686B, fo. 352v; cited in 8 Co. Rep. 125, at fo. 127, as being 'in the Fifth Part of my Reports'; Co. Inst. ii. 47. It is not in 5 Co. Rep. (Coke was probably thinking of *The Chamberlain of London's Case* (1590) 5 Co. Rep. 62.)

[284] Co. Inst. iii. 182. The link with Magna Carta was not his invention, because both chapters had been cited by Wray in argument: below, p. 250.

[285] *Att.-Gen. v. Joiners' Company of London* (1582) below, p. 472 (note for an argument, probably by Fleetwood). The decision cited in the argument seems not to be reported; perhaps it was an opinion by the law officers.

[286] 'Sea-horses' is attested elsewhere for walruses, though perhaps it was more properly sea-morses.

[287] So named in 1603 after Sir Francis Cherry, but now more usually called Bear Island. The recorder of London argued that it belonged to the crown as a new discovery by the company, though it is now part of Norway.

privilege, and indeed almost wiping out the walrus population there in order to get their 'teeth' (tusks) and oil.[288] Williams J. said that by the law of nature any one could work or fish anywhere, but this liberty had been restrained by the statute, which gave the company a means of protection by way of an action of debt for the penalty. Although the statute was ambiguous, the general rule was that debts could only be recovered at common law. In any case, walruses were not fish. The judges unanimously granted a prohibition.[289]

Another kind of monopoly was that claimed by the crown in certain minerals, wherever they were found. Some readers in the early sixteenth-century inns of court had recognised a prerogative right to take gold and silver from private land,[290] though in 1555 the assembled judges had advised that there was no such right; unmined gold and silver ore was not treasure trove but part of the land.[291] In 1568 the decision was formally overturned by another assembly of all the judges and barons, who held that the crown was entitled not only to gold and silver but to all ores of base metal which contained gold or silver, and that the queen could sever these 'mines royal' from the crown and grant them to a subject.[292] The judges affirmed that mines containing only copper, tin,[293] lead or iron belonged to the owner of the soil. But a question remained whether the crown could claim newly discovered categories of mineral and grant them out to prospectors. In 1565 a patent was granted to mine calamine stone,[294] and its validity was debated for three hours at a conference in

---

[288] Nearly a thousand walruses had been killed on a single expedition to the island in 1608: G. Jackson, *The British Whaling Trade* (2005), p. 3.

[289] *Jones v. The Muscovy Merchants* (1609) BL MS. Harley 6713, fo. 27; MS. Hargrave 32, fo. 16v; MS. Lansdowne 1075, fo. 319; CUL MS. Ii.5.14, fo. 15v (all the same); CUL MS. Mm.6.69, fo. 129 (a fuller report).

[290] Bro. Abr., *Prerogative*, pl. 134, apparently citing (but with a query) the reading of John Fitzjames, junior, in the Middle Temple in the time of Henry VIII. Richard Hesketh made the same point in his earlier reading (c. 1506) on the *Carta de Foresta*, in relation to private land within forests: Pl. Com. 321. Cf. the reading of c. 1529 discussed above, p. 106, which referred only to treasure trove and minerals in general (not mines of gold).

[291] *Case of Gold and Silver Mines* (1555) *Dyer's Notebooks*, i. 14. This may have been connected with the grant to Burchart Kranich in 1554 to search for and mine all manner of minerals.

[292] *Att.-Gen. v. Earl of Northumberland* (1568) Pl. Com. 310.

[293] In Cornwall, however, the king had a prescriptive right to the pre-emption of tin: *Case of the Stannaries* (1606) 12 Co. Rep. 202; *JHC*, i. 295 (much disputed in the Commons, 9 April 1606).

[294] Calamine, an ore of zinc, was used in making brass.

Serjeants' Inn in February 1568. The solicitor-general and king's serjeants maintained that it was valid, because 'it did not prohibit any man of any thing before known or used within this realm, whereby any occupation or liberty of art was infringed'. This was countered by Plowden, who argued that the king could not take from a man any part of his inherit-ance, and that a man owned all the minerals in his own land. It did not occur to him to cite Magna Carta, which would surely have been used to buttress such an argument twenty or thirty years later. No agreement was reached,[295] and the patent was still litigious in 1597.[296] The commissions to dig for and extract saltpetre in private soil, first granted in 1589 following the defeat of the Armada,[297] were justified not on the grounds that the king owned the saltpetre but that it was a form of purveyance necessary in making gunpowder for the defence of the realm.[298]

Despite the judicial opinions limiting monopolies, patents of monop-oly were granted with ever-increasing frequency in the Elizabethan period. Over twenty were granted in the 1560s, about half of them for the extraction of minerals, others for newly invented processes.[299] The earliest was that granted in 1563 to Jasper Seler and Peter de Ruse for making white salt, to last for twenty years.[300] It recited that Seler, a German, 'by long travail and industry, and by sundry uses and experi-ences, to his great cost and charge many years sustained, hath found out the feat and way of making white salt without any kind of fire or other kind of fuel, or any manner of salt to be used', and that such salt was far cheaper than that produced the old way. It threatened any subject who presumed to infringe the monopoly with one year's imprisonment, and a

---

[295] Letter from William Humfrey to Sir William Cecil, SP 12/46, fo. 75; discussed in Donald, *Elizabethan Monopolies* (n. 250, above), pp. 86–94. Plowden mentioned calamine in Pl. Com. 339 (tr. 'whereof there is great abundance in this realm, as I have heard').

[296] *Company of Mineral and Battery Works* v. *Brode* (1597) 27 APC 235.

[297] 20 APC 21; Youngs, pp. 145–6.

[298] *Case of Saltpetre* (1606) below, p. 327. The judges took notice that gunpowder was invented in the time of Richard II, and therefore the claim could not be based on prescription.

[299] E. W. Hulme, 'The Early History of the English Patent System' in *Select Essays in Anglo-American Legal History* (Boston, MA, 1909), iii. 117–48.

[300] The original patent under the great seal, dated 13 March 1563, is in the writer's collection (JHB MS. 2155). It also granted denization to Seler. There was another similar patent, granted to Seler alone, on 15 January 1564: *CPR 1563–6*, p. 119, no. 487. There seem to be two other exemplifications of the patent under the great seal: Folger Shakespeare Library MS. Z.c.44(3); University of Chicago Library MS. 4504.

fine of 100 marks for every 'attempt', half of which was to go to Seler and half to the queen. This grant is known to have been obtained through the intervention of Sir William Cecil, who was doubtless the mastermind behind the Elizabethan monopoly project.[301] The reason why such patents were thought immune to challenge is that the legal objections to monopoly did not extend to the exploitation of inventions or new-found imports from abroad. In such cases monopolies might encourage entrepreneurship in the public interest, as well as enriching the crown or its beneficiaries. The distinction was formally recognised in 1573 when the assembled judges decided in the Exchequer Chamber that, although monopolies could not be granted so as to restrain an existing trade or manufacture, they could validly be granted to protect and exploit a new invention. For this purpose the invention had to be essentially and substantially new, and not merely an improvement which made it more profitable.[302] This important case has not yet been found in law reports, but it concerned the German mining engineer and physician Burchard Cranach or Kranich (d. 1578), sometimes known as Dr Burcot, who brought over to England from Germany the technology of water-powered blast furnaces and attracted investors by dabbling as a sideline in alchemy.[303]

Some of the patents granted later in the reign strained the concept of novelty to the limits, or beyond, since they included the making of drinking glasses, of sackbuts and trumpets, of starch, of mathematical instruments and of playing cards, and the teaching or publication of guides to shorthand writing. The penal sanctions also raised potential legal questions, since they involved imposing fines and imprisonment

---

[301] SP 14/33, 234 (articles for the patent, and for an accompanying indenture imposing obligations on Seler, January 1563); SP 14/28, fo. 17 (copy letter from Cecil to Seler, in Latin, 13 March 1562/3, reporting that he has obtained the grant for him). See further E. Hughes, 'The English Monopoly of Salt in the Years 1563–71' (1925) 40 EHR 334–50 (who wrongly dated the patent to 1564).

[302] Sub nom. *Bircot's Case* (1573) Co. Inst. iii. 184 (where a new method of smelting lead was held not to be a new invention, for it was 'but to put a new button to an old coat, and it is much easier to add than to invent'). Francis Moore asserted in 1614 that monopolies could only be granted to inventors of things, not of the means of making them: *Proc. Parl. 1614*, p. 134. But that had long been a lost cause.

[303] Hulme, 'Early History of the English Patent System', at p. 121 (his original patent of 1554, which was for six years), 124 (a different patent of 1563 for an engine for draining waters from mines); M. B. Donald, 'Burchard Kranich' (1950) 6 *Annals of Science* 308–22; *ODNB*, sub nom. Burchard Kranich. None of these mentions the case. The Kranich invention seems also to have been the subject of litigation in *Zouch* v. *Tracy* (1582): Donald, *Elizabethan Monopolies*, pp. 167–75.

without parliamentary authority. But an effective monopoly was dependent on the sanctions, and they seem not to have been objected to on constitutional grounds. Even the enforcement of a statute against monopolies might be granted as a monopoly.[304] An argument in court in 1582, probably by Serjeant Fleetwood, acknowledged that punitive sanctions were permitted and suggested that the restrictive conditions laid down by the Exchequer Chamber had not taken root:[305]

> Privileges granted to those who have been the inventors of any art or science which is beneficial for the common weal, and which was not before, or which make things more readily available with less charge and more profitably for the common weal, have allowance in law ... These privileges are maintained in the Exchequer, and punishments inflicted on those who offend against the privileges.

The reason given was that, in the case of an invention, 'everyone benefits from it and has *quid pro quo*'. There was no other plausible ground for restraining liberty of trade. A monopoly which did not benefit the public was therefore indefensible. The distinction was applied in the Court of Exchequer around the same time, in declining to enforce a patent of 1567 for the sole making and selling of 'frisadoes' (a kind of baize) as made in Haarlem and Amsterdam.[306] Resort was sometimes had to the Privy Council or the Star Chamber in enforcing monopolies, and the method was to punish infringers for a vague offence of 'contempt' against a patent. The judges were uneasy about supporting royal grants in this way, and by 1595 the Common Pleas could contemplate releasing on *habeas corpus* a member of the Leathersellers' Company who had been committed for infringing Edward Darcy's patent of monopoly for sealing leather.[307] The problems were exacerbated by the difficulty of applying the legal distinctions in particular cases, and consequent pressures to exploit the

---

[304] SP 12/90, fos. 108–29 (1572), a draft patent for enforcing the statutes against regraters and forestallers, with a share of the penalty; it seems not to be in *CPR*.

[305] *Att.-Gen.* v. *Joiners' Company of London* (1582) below, p. 474.

[306] *Hastings' Case* (c. 1582) cited by Nicholas Fuller in *Darcy* v. *Allen* (1602) Noy 173 at p. 182 ('about 20 years past'), BL MS. Add. 25203, fo. 583, and in *Proc. Parl. 1610*, ii. 158 (where he claimed credit for the successful argument); and by Serjeant Montagu in CUL MS. Mm.1.21, fo. 184v (1611); 45 *Emory Law Journal* 1304 n. 154. Fuller cited three other undated cases to the same effect (Noy 183). ·

[307] *Leathersellers' Company* v. *Darcy* (1595) 25 APC 106–7; BL MS. Hargrave 26, fos. 51v–52, *per* Walmsley and Owen JJ (Anderson CJ *absente*, Beaumont J. *silente*); Wright, 'Nicholas Fuller and the Liberties of the Subject', pp. 179–80. The justification for the Common Pleas jurisdiction was that the prisoners had privilege as litigants.

uncertainty with more and more audacious monopolistic schemes. By the end of the century the problems were mounting up to a crisis.

In 1597 the Commons presented a petition to the queen against monopolies. According to the tactful speech by Christopher Yelverton of Gray's Inn, as speaker, the Commons were not complaining about the queen, for she must surely have been misled by the patentees' representations that their monopolies would serve the public good.[308] Misinformation of the crown was a good ground for rescinding patents. The queen's response, while protesting that the prerogative of granting monopolies was 'the principal and head pearl in her crown or diadem', was to promise that the patents would be 'examined, to abide the trial and true touchstone of the law'.[309] Coke, as attorney-general, immediately launched a series of *quo warranto* informations in the Exchequer, and six patents were cancelled in Michaelmas term 1597 as illegal and 'against the liberty of the subject'.[310] This was nevertheless only the tip of the iceberg, and the grievance remained at the forefront of politics.[311] When a bill was read in the 1601 parliament for their regulation, Francis Bacon, now the queen's counsel extraordinary,[312] displayed his readiness to defend the prerogative from parliamentary scrutiny:

> For the prerogative royal of the prince, for my own part I ever allowed of it, and it is such as I hope I shall never see discussed. The queen, as she is our sovereign, hath both an enlarging and restraining liberty of her prerogative; that is, she hath power by her patents to set at liberty things restrained by statute law otherwise;[313] secondly, by her prerogative she may restrain things which be at liberty . . .

After giving various examples of monopolies which were permitted by the law, he tried to end the debate by reporting that the queen had

---

[308] *Proc. Parl. 1593–1601*, p. 203 (9 February 1598). Yelverton said she had, 'before we had any thought of it', commanded 'reformation in [the] courts of justice of the strange and exceeding abuses of the patents of privilege commonly called monopolies'.

[309] *Proc. Parl. 1593–1601*, p. 242, *per* Egerton LK (9 February 1598).

[310] They are all noted, with the roll references, in Coke's copy of *Magna Carta cum Statutis* (1556), bound in crimson velvet, now at Holkham Hall, on additional fos. iii–iv. He said that (tr.) 'all these informations were preferred in the Exchequer and resolved there, and Popham CJ was of clear opinion against all these monopolies': ibid. fo. iv. He noted four more similar decisions in Mich. 1602, the implication being that nothing was done between 1597 and 1602.

[311] Guy, *Tudor England*, pp. 401–2.

[312] Baker, *Collected Papers*, i. 125; Hawarde 78 ('counsel at large to the queen'). He was the first known holder of the office, granted informally in 1594.

[313] This refers to the dispensing power.

already commanded the attorney-general (Coke) to bring several of the monopolies to trial upon *quo warranto*, as a result of which at least fifteen patents had been repealed after trial in the Exchequer.[314] In other words, nothing more needed to be done. Francis Moore, of the Middle Temple, found Bacon's subservient complacence intolerable:[315]

> I know the queen's prerogative is a thing curious to be dealt withall, yet all grievances are not comparable. I cannot utter with my tongue or conceive with my heart the great grievances that the town and country for which I serve suffer by some of these monopolies. It bringeth the general profit into a private hand, and the end of all is beggary and bondage to the subject ... there is no act of [the queen's] that hath been or is more dangerous to the common wealth than the granting of these monopolies.

A few days later Thomas Fleming, the solicitor-general, gave an account of the queen's command earlier in the year to himself and the attorney-general (Coke), concerning monopolies, but admitted – seemingly in contradiction of Bacon – that they had been too busy to do anything. Sir Robert Wroth, a member of Gray's Inn, rose to ask why action had not been taken earlier, and why it was necessary to resort to the 'stir' of *scire facias* and *quo warranto* when the patents contained a revocation clause and could simply be called in.[316] He complained that the most recent grants were worse than ever, and read a list of over thirty currently in being.[317] William Hakewill, of Lincoln's Inn, stood up to ask sardonically why bread was not yet on the list, saying that if some order were not taken it would be there before the next parliament.[318] Much debating and committee work followed, but all the Commons won was another promise from the ageing queen, albeit a famously ornate and moving promise:[319]

> I must say this, I was never any greedy, scraping grasper, nor a strait, fast-holding prince, not yet a waster. My heart was never set on worldly goods, but only for my subjects' good. What you do bestow on me, I will not hoard it up, but receive it to bestow on you again ... Since I was queen, yet did I never put my pen to any grant but that upon pretext and

---

[314] *Proc. Parl. 1593–1601*, pp. 372–3. He said that several had also been tested in actions of trespass in the Common Pleas.

[315] *Proc. Parl. 1593–1601*, pp. 374–5.   [316] *Proc. Parl. 1593–1601*, pp. 380–1.

[317] Cf. Robert Cecil's list of nearly forty granted since 1574: *Proc. Parl. 1593–1601*, pp. 388–90.

[318] Ibid. 381. Hakewill was not called to the bar until 1606. This was his first parliament.

[319] The queen's 'Golden Speech', *Proc. Parl. 1593–1601*, pp. 412–14. There is a slight doubt whether all of it was delivered: ibid. 251.

semblance made unto me that it was both good and beneficial to the
subject in general, though a private profit to some of my ancient servants
who had deserved well ... If my kingly bounty have been abused, and my
grants turned to the hurt of my people, contrary to my will and meaning,
or if any in authority under me have neglected or perverted what I have
committed to them, I hope God will not lay their culps and offences to my
charge ... I know the title of a king is a glorious title, but assure yourself
that the shining glory of princely authority hath not so dazzled the eyes of
our understanding but that we well know and remember that we also are
to yield an account of our actions before the great Judge. To be a king and
wear a crown is a thing more glorious to them that see it than it is pleasing
to them that bear it. For myself, I was never so much enticed with the
glorious name of a king or royal authority of a queen, as delighted that
God hath made me his instrument ... And though you have had and may
have many princes more mighty and wise sitting in this seat, yet you never
had nor shall have any that will be more careful and loving.

Thus was the matter of monopolies eloquently deflected until the
following reign.

A related question was raised by Elizabeth's device of raising revenue
by granting to subjects the right to enforce penal statutes by compounding with offenders in return for money. Not surprisingly, the informers
took most of the money for themselves. A statute of 1576 brought them
under a degree of control, and forbade the composition of offences prior
to a hearing in court and without a court order.[320] Nevertheless,
although compounding with offenders was punishable in the Star
Chamber as extortion, before and after the statute, it seemed to be
ineradicable.[321] The device was therefore widely disliked, even by the
law officers. Thomas Egerton, as solicitor-general, did not mince his
words in condemning informers as caterpillars and blood-suckers of the
common wealth.[322] An alternative strategy was to cut out the freelance
prosecutor by granting monopolies of prosecution to particular
grantees.[323] Other forms of revenue collection were privatised in the

---

[320] 18 Eliz. I, c. 5; Youngs, pp. 137–8.
[321] *Att.-Gen.* v. *Askewe* (1569) BL MS. Harley 2143, fo. 26; *Att.-Gen.* v. *Crapnell* (1587) ibid.
fo. 26v; *Att.-Gen.* v. *O'Parsons* (1605) BL MS. Harley 639, fo. 104v. Crapnell was said to
have exhibited seventy informations and brought only one to trial.
[322] *Proc. Parl. 1584–9*, p. 120. He referred to 'promoters', which from the conext evidently
meant informers rather than monopolists. A bill was introduced in 1589 to prevent
criminals and people of little substance from being informers: *Proc. Parl. 1584–9*,
p. 494.
[323] The strategies, and their effects, were fully examined in D. R. Lidington, 'The Enforcement of the Penal Statutes at the Court of Exchequer c. 1558–c. 1571' (Cambridge PhD

same way,[324] such as Sir Henry Lee's privilege of manumitting such of the duchy of Lancaster villeins as could afford to buy their liberty.[325] Particularly grievous to landowners were patents to investigate concealments of crown titles, the first of which, according to Coke, was granted in the time of Mary. Since time did not run against the king, old titles could be unsettled by these means, particularly when loopholes could be found in complex grants of monastic lands.[326] Coke recalled that few landowners had been immune, and that no one who found his property so threatened had been able to sleep at night. In 1572 the queen revoked all the existing commissions for concealments because of abuses, though she did not renounce the crown's rights to concealed lands and the problem continued.[327] To his credit, Coke as attorney-general intervened to save the bishop of Norwich from a serious loss through the 'fraud and falsehood of the concealers', by helping him to obtain an Act of Parliament in 1597 to settle his titles.[328] The dean and chapter of Norwich lost nearly all their possessions around the same time through the efforts of 'greedy and indigent persons' who had obtained a patent of concealment, though again Coke came to the rescue, apparently with the queen's personal approval.[329] While it is noteworthy that the queen's

dissertation, 1988). Dr Lidington counted 18,760 Exchequer informations in this period: ibid. 41.

[324] E.g. Thomas Lichfield's grant (1569) of a share of money recovered in the Exchequer: *Dyer's Notebooks*, i. 189; 12 Co. Rep. 117.

[325] See I. S. Leadam, 'The Last Days of Bondage in England' (1893) 9 LQR 348–65; A. Savine, 'Bondmen under the Tudors' (1902) 17 *Transactions of the Royal Historical Society* (2nd series) 235–89. Lee's patent was granted in 1575, and an original commission of that year, granted by Lee under the patent, is in the writer's collection: JHB MS. 765(1). The last manumission under the scheme was in 1599. Villeinage was by then almost defunct. A late example of an action *de nativo habendo* is *Bartholomew* v. *Deighton* (1600) BL MS. Lansdowne 1088, fos. 21v–22, 78; and on a writ of error, sub nom. *Dighton* v. *Bartholomew* (1602) Cro. Eliz. 853, 881; Yelv. 2.

[326] For the background see C. J. Kitching, 'The Quest for Concealed Lands in the Reign of Elizabeth I' (1974) 5 *Transactions of the Royal Historical Society* (5th series) 63–78; Youngs, pp. 139–41; Boyer, *Coke and the Elizabethan Age*, pp. 75–8. Over a hundred patents were granted in the first thirty years of Elizabeth's reign: BL MS. Lansdowne 59(39).

[327] E.g. *Vowe* v. *Smith* (1580) 10 Co. Rep. 110; 2 And. 19; *Shane's Case* (1596) 10 Co. Rep. 112; Moo. 417.

[328] 39 Eliz. I, c. 22; Co. Inst. iv. 257. Coke called the patentees *helluones*, or squanderers: Co. Inst. iv. 76, 257. Cf. *Legat's Case* (1612) 10 Co. Rep. 109, which he subtitled 'In subversion of pestilent patents of thievish concealers'.

[329] *Downing* v. *Dean and Chapter of Norwich* (1599) 3 Co. Rep. 73; Boyer, *Coke and the Elizabethan Age*, pp. 75–8. The judges here, advising the Chancery, found a solution through a benevolent interpretation of two existing statutes.

principal law officer actively opposed such attempts to exploit the prerogative, albeit he was motivated by his Norwich connections,[330] legislation was the only safe remedy for such abuses.

Urban Oligarchies Created by Charter

Monopolies conferred on individuals were not the only grievance associated with royal charters. The sixteenth century saw a threefold increase in the number of chartered urban corporations,[331] each of which was under the almost unfettered control of a small group of aldermen under the presidency of a mayor. Many older corporations received new charters as well, during the same period, with ever-increasing powers of self-government and regulatory legislation.[332] These urban oligarchies were composed chiefly of uneducated tradesmen, who sometimes showed scant regard for the niceties of law and due process, and there were frequent wrangles with local lawyers, at times resulting in litigation.[333] Mayors resorted to imprisonment to maintain their authority, leading to challenges by actions of false imprisonment, or *habeas corpus*.[334] The case most often cited, and perhaps the first, was an action against the mayor of Barnstaple in 1587.[335] The mayor had imprisoned the plaintiff for calling him a fool; but the plaintiff recovered damages for false imprisonment, with the result that (as Wray CJ quipped

---

[330] Coke's grandfather had been a Norwich attorney, and he had himself attended Norwich school. He was recorder of Norwich from 1586 to 1592.

[331] From 38 in 1500 to 130 in 1600: P. Withington, *The Politics of Commonwealth: Citizens and Freemen in Early Modern England* (Cambridge, 2005), p. 18.

[332] Local authority at county level belonged to the justices in their quarter sessions. Their doings were subject to survey by the assize judges, or by the use of *certiorari* returnable in the King's Bench: Henderson, *Foundations*, pp. 93–101; Baker, *Collected Papers*, ii. 956–8.

[333] C. W. Brooks, *Pettifoggers and Vipers of the Commonwealth: the 'Lower Branch' of the Legal Profession in Early Modern England* (Cambridge, 1986), pp. 220–3. Note also Henderson, *Foundations*, pp. 35–45; R. Tittler, *The Reformation and the Towns in England: Politics and Political Culture c. 1540-1640* (Oxford, 1998), pp. 199–203, 331–3.

[334] *Deane v. Jarret* (1599) BL MS. Add. 48186, fos. 162v–163; MS. Lansdowne 1065, fo. 15v; BL MS. Add. 25202, fo. 6 (calling Sir Thomas Jarret, alderman of London, a knave and a companion with drunkards; bailed on *habeas corpus*). Note also the case of 1591 which was mediated by an assize judge after the issue of a *habeas corpus*: *Records of Early English Drama: Shropshire*, ed. A. Somerset (Toronto, 1995), pp. 398–404.

[335] *Simons v. Swette* (1587) Cro. Eliz. 78; identified by name in CUL MS. Hh.2.9, fo. 388v; BL MS. Harley 4779, fo. 250v. Wray CJ's quip was in *Deane v. Jarret* (previous note). Cf. *Jerome v. Neale and Pleere* (1588), below, pp. 262, 481 (an action of trespass).

afterwards) the mayor had managed to prove himself a fool of record. Sometimes the Privy Council had to intervene in such cases and impose mediation.[336] There was a growing worry, as Walmsley J. observed early in the following reign, that 'corporations are too proud and exercise more authority than subjects ought'.[337] The power to make bye-laws for the public good was arguably incident to any corporation, without the need to show a charter or immemorial custom.[338] And yet a bye-law could not be allowed to take away a man's common-law rights. As the Common Pleas said in 1590, 'by no means is it reasonable for subjects to make laws, for that belongs solely to the king and prince, and is one of the roses of the crown; and it is impertinent for subjects to make laws, the queen not being privy, to take away any man's inheritance'.[339] Bye-laws interfering with freedom of trade were likewise open to challenge on that ground.[340]

Even the city of London, which claimed extensive liberties and privileges under the protection of chapter 9 of Magna Carta, was not immune from challenges to its authority. The city could enact bye-laws and enforce them by fines, recoverable by actions of debt in the city courts.[341] But in 1586 an objection was made in the Common Pleas to an Act of Common Council forbidding anyone to sell sand in London unless taken out of the Thames, on pain of forfeiting £10 for a second offence, to be recovered in an action of debt in which no essoin, protection or wager of

---

[336] Henderson, *Foundations*, pp. 72–4. In *Lumbard* v. *Holland* (1598) 29 APC 296, the Privy Council ordered the King's Bench to stay a frivolous action of false imprisonment against a former mayor of Dartmouth.

[337] *Gibbins* v. *Bailiffs of Shrewsbury* (1606) BL MS. Add. 25205, fo. 40v (tr.).

[338] *Chamberlain of London's Case* (1590) 5 Co. Rep. 63; 3 Leo. 265. Coke was at this time recorder of London.

[339] *Laton* v. *Yerbery* (1590) YLS MS. G. R29.8, fo. 196 (tr.); differently reported in 1 And. 234; BL MS. Harley 4812, fo. 80; BL MS. Harley 1588, fo. 28. This case concerned manorial bye-laws.

[340] E.g. *Case of Buckingham Town* (1587) cited by Tanfield in *Davenant* v. *Hurdys* (1599) BL MS. Hargrave 5, at fo. 76v (monopoly of shipping skins granted to the town's glovers); *Weavers of London* v. *Browne* (1601) BL MS. Add 25213, fo. 1 (London bye-law in restraint of trade held void); *Case of the Car-Men of London* (1601) 32 APC 100–01, 421–3 (where the Privy Council sided with the city against the King's Bench).

[341] *Chamberlain of London's Case* (1590) 5 Co. Rep. 62; *Wilford* v. *Massam* (1596) BL MS. Harley 1624, fo. 299v; HLS MS. 110, fo. 195v. The latter was an action by the chamberlain of London to recover a fine for selling unwholesome drugs; it was removed into the King's Bench by *corpus cum causa*, but Coke (being recorder of London) successfully moved for it to be sent back. Fenner J. (dissenting) thought the fine illegal, and that bye-laws could only be enforced by disfranchisement.

law should be allowed. Thames sand was said to be much worse than land sand, yet more expensive. Anderson CJ and his brethren 'did greatly speak against the said Act ... that it is against reason that any freeman should be so restrained from merchandising and selling, and also it might concern the inheritances of some who might have sand in their lands'. They also said that 'they were very presumptuous in making Acts so Parliament-like, viz. that no essoin, protection or wager of law should be allowed, and that they did arrogate to themselves too high authority'. Their indignation fully aroused, the judges went on to suggest that the plaintiffs should 'shake their liberties' by exhibiting a bill against the city in Parliament, and by suing them in the King's Bench 'for their presumption and insolency ... for such were the misdemeanours of Empson and Dudley'.[342] Ten years later the King's Bench held that, even though the privileges of London had been confirmed by Act of Parliament, and they had the power to make bye-laws,[343] they could not make bye-laws which contradicted the common law. Therefore, although they could make it an offence to take aliens – or even northerners – as apprentices, they could not enact that an indenture of apprenticeship for an alien should be void.[344] This was obvious Magna Carta territory,[345] though it seems not to have been mentioned on either side.

Another development which began before it was attributed to Magna Carta was the use of writs of restitution – later called *mandamus*[346] – to restore aldermen, officials and freemen who had been removed from their places contrary to natural justice. The writ was not new, since there there were precedents of a kind in the fourteenth century – in 1313[347] and 1381[348] – but it had been used very sparingly. Only one example has

---

[342] *Anon.* (1586) Godb. 106.

[343] See *The Chamberlain of London's Case* (1590) above, p. 29.

[344] *Doggerell* v. *Powkes* (or *Pooks*) (1595) Moo. 411; Owen 66; more fully reported in BL MS. Harley 4998, fo. 77; MS. Harley 6745, fo. 161 (also MS. Hargrave 50, fo. 169v); MS. Harley 1697, fo. 89; MS. Add. 25198, fo. 101; MS. Add. 25199, fo. 35; CUL MS. Ii.5.24, fo. 169v; HLS MS. 110, fo. 163v. The record was cited as Trin. 37 Eliz., rot. 1076.

[345] Below, pp. 311–18.

[346] It was referred to in 1619 as a mandatory writ: *Case of Sutton Valence* (1619) HLS MS. 2072, fo. 88v. The word *mandamus* occurred in the earlier writs of restitution, but it was also used in several other types of writ.

[347] *Randolf's Case* (1313), cited in Vaillant's notes to Dyer 332; cf. Henderson, *Foundations*, pp. 66–8 (unidentified). For the background see S. K. Cohn, 'The Bristol Revolts 1312–16' in *Popular Protest in Late Medieval English Towns* (Cambridge, 2013), pp. 133–40.

[348] An undated writ of *mandamus* to the bailiffs, aldermen and burgesses of Cambridge to admit Richard Maisterman as mayor, having been elected to that office, is transcribed in

been noted from the fifteenth century,[349] and there was another in Henry VIII's reign.[350] In 1574 some of these precedents were unearthed, and the remedy was sanctioned by Dyer CJ in the Common Pleas as a means of restoring a citizen of London to his freedom and to his shop,[351] though the writ of restitution itself is said to have issued from the King's Bench.[352] In about 1604 Coke, as attorney-general, and Popham CJ, advised the Privy Council that the same remedy was available for an office-holder. Sir William Dethick had been removed from the office of Garter King of Arms for supposed insolence while on an embassy with Lord Spencer in 1603.[353] The advice they gave was that his alleged misbehaviour did not amount to a cause of forfeiture, and so he was entitled to be restored; but in the event he was persuaded to accept an annuity from his successor in return for his resignation.[354] The following year it was said by Popham that the writ would lie from the King's Bench or the Chancery whenever a member of a company or fraternity was removed without just cause.[355] The writ operated in a similar way to *habeas corpus*, by requiring the recipient to return a cause of dismissal for the court to review.[356]

LI MS. 83, fo. 124 (wrongly catalogued as Canterbury). The circumstances, and the date, are given in *HPHC 1386–1421*, iii. 670; cf. *CPR 1381–5*, p. 179 (writ of aid commanding the bailiffs, alderman and burgesses to be obedient to him as mayor).

[349] *Anable's Case* (?1416), cited in Dyer 332 (translated in Henderson, *Foundations*, 175–6). Dyer prints the writ, supposedly witnessed by Sir John Fortescue (CJKB 1442–61), but this must be a mistake. The case seems to have been in 1416, when Hankford was CJKB: *City of London Letter Book I*, pp. 156–7 (writ of *pluries* to the mayor, writ of attachment, and *supersedeas*).

[350] Peryam J. said in 1584 that he had seen a record in Henry VIII's reign where a citizen of London was disfranchised and the court directed a writ of restitution to the mayor and aldermen and set a fine of 100 marks on those who had been party to the decision: Cro. Eliz. 33.

[351] *Middleton's Case* (1574) Dyer 332 (writ of restitution to the freedom of London and to his shop).

[352] Treby's notes to Dyer 332, citing Dodderidge J. In BL MS. Add. 35950, fo. 83v (1595), the writ in *Middleton's Case* was said to have been sent from the Chancery.

[353] They were sent to confer the Garter on the duke of Württemberg, and Dethick was alleged to have ruffled the smoothness of the proceedings by claiming equality in the commission with Lord Spencer. The real underlying problem was discord within the College of Arms: see *ODNB*.

[354] These details are from the recollections in *Bagg's Case* (1615) as reported in 1 Rolle 224 at fo. 225, *per* Coke CJ; MS. Add. 35957, fos. 6v–7v (tr. 'otherwise by the law Dethick ought to have been restored'). For *Bagg's Case*, see below, p. 396.

[355] *Att.-Gen. v. Glover* (1606) Hawarde 302 at p. 306.

[356] It is not clear to whom the writ could have been addressed in Dethick's case, since he was removed by the king.

Although the only known judicial decision to issue *mandamus* in Elizabeth's reign was that of 1574, there was a stream of examples from 1605 onwards, in a variety of contexts. The way was paved by the Puritans, who were astute to add a new remedy to their armoury of *habeas corpus* and prohibition, and in 1605–6 obtained several writs of *mandamus* to restore parsons to their benefices.[357] But the main context was urban politics. In 1606 a bailiff of Cambridge was restored because he had been dismissed without cause.[358] In 1608 a shopkeeper of London was restored to his freedom after being released from imprisonment by *habeas corpus*.[359] In 1609 an alderman of Stamford complained that he had been disfranchised by the other aldermen for stirring up dissension between the aldermen and others of the corporation, saying that if they checked their accounts they would find they had been horribly cheated;[360] these were held not to be causes of disfranchisement. Another cause returned was that he, being a justice of the peace, had gone into an alehouse where many were drinking and stayed until many of them were drunk without committing any of them to prison. It was held that this was not a good cause either, because perhaps he was unaware of them, or was in another room and could not imprison them. In any case, an alderman could not be disfranchised for so slight an offence, even if he was drunk himself. The last causes alleged were that he was contentious, seditious, a common haunter of taverns and incontinent with women; but these were held to be alleged too generally. The recorder, Matthew Dale of the Middle Temple, urged that the aldermen and burgesses were the best judges of the reasonableness of the cause, but the court rejected this argument, on the grounds that they would then be able to displace anyone at their pleasure out of spleen. The case was adjourned without a

---

[357] Halliday, *Habeas Corpus*, pp. 78, 365 n. 63. Other examples are *Hodkinson's Case* (1605–6) below, p. 298 (from London); *Waters v. Goodacres* (1606) in C. Monro, *Acta Cancellariae* (1847), pp. 59–61 (from Sussex).

[358] *Tompson v. Edmonds* (1606) KB 29/246, m. 125; 1 Rolle Abr. 456, pl. 4; Dyer 332, note in the 1688 edn; Henderson, *Foundations*, pp. 50–3, 62–3, 163–7 (said to be the earliest writ of restitution in the King's Bench controlment rolls). Tompson had been arrested while on his way to Westminster to take counsel in a King's Bench case, and imprisoned in the Cambridge Tolbooth; his release was also ordered. The special writ 'combined habeas corpus and mandamus': Halliday, *Habeas Corpus*, 78–9. As Henderson pointed out, it could also be viewed as a writ of privilege for a litigant.

[359] *Farndon's Case* (1608) KB 29/249, m. 16: Henderson, *Foundations*, pp. 58–9, 63–4, 167–71.

[360] The finances of Stamford had been in contention since the late 1580s: Henderson, *Foundations*, p. 75.

reported resolution.[361] In the same year, however, the Common Pleas restored an alderman of Kings Lynn who had been disfranchised as a common barrator and haunter of taverns, on the ground (amongst others) that he had not been convicted after a trial on indictment.[362] There was a third case, of a similar kind, from St Albans.[363] The writ had therefore become generally available to impose on urban authorities the requirements of due process, albeit that difficult questions could arise if a new alderman or officer had been elected in place of the one who had been expelled.[364] It was not yet clear how far *mandamus* could be used beyond the sphere of restitution to an office or position.[365] But it had become firmly established as one of the prerogative writs, available for the protection of what later lawyers would call the principles of natural justice. It was achieved without reference to Magna Carta, though a connection with chapter 29 would be made by Coke.[366]

Prerogative Jurisdictions

Some of the most persistent legal complaints about prerogative authority in the Elizabethan and Jacobean periods were consequent upon the rise of new jurisdictions created under the prerogative. The most important of these were the High Commission, the Court of Requests, the Council

---

[361] *Loveday's Case* (1609) CUL MS. Mm.6.69, fo. 113, 117v–118, sub nom. Loveden. This is identifiable as *R. v. Stamford*, ex parte *Loveday* (1608) KB 29/249, m. 138d; Henderson, *Foundations*, p. 59 n. 19.

[362] *Baker's Case* (1609) BL MS. Add. 25215, fo. 78v. This is identifiable as *R. v. Kings Lynn*, ex parte *Baker* (1608) KB 29/249, m. 108d; Henderson, *Foundations*, p. 59 n. 19. The outcome is mentioned in 1 Rolle Rep. 173.

[363] *R. v. St Albans*, ex parte *Robinson* (1608) KB 29/249, m. 101; Henderson, *Foundations*, pp. 59 n. 19, 171–5.

[364] *Shuttleworth's Case* (1613) Calth. MS. i. 92 (sub nom. Shettleworth); ii. 115; 2 Bulst. 122; sub nom. *Wharton's Case*, BL MS. Harley 4948, fo. 46. Edmund Shuttleworth had been removed as alderman and town clerk of Lincoln: KB 29/254, m. 116; Henderson, *Foundations*, pp. 60 n. 23, 75–6. See also *Anon.* (1613) Calth. MS. i. 116, arising from the removal of the mayor of Lostwithiel, Cornwall, and the election of a successor; here the return seems to have been accepted and so restitution was refused (cf. the *habeas corpus* against the mayor on fo. 125); and *Middlecote's Case* (1615) Calth. MS. i. 353v, concerning the purported resignation by an alderman of Boston. An anaologous problem arose in the case of Garter King of Arms (1603) above, p. 204.

[365] For its extension to ordering the performance of public duties, see *Re the Parish of Sutton Valence* (1619) 2 Rolle Rep. 106; Palm. 50; Henderson, *Foundations*, pp. 127–8. Reference is there made to earlier precedents of writs ordering the mayor of Oxford to enrol a will and to the lord of a manor to hold a court.

[366] Below, p. 396.

in the Marches of Wales, the Council in the North at York and the Court of Marshalsea. Mention has already been made of the first.[367] The commissions for ecclesiastical causes were introduced under a statute of 1559, but steadily enlarged on the footing that the queen's prerogative as supreme governor empowered her to direct the enforcement of Church discipline and to rearrange ecclesiastical jurisdiction without parliamentary sanction.[368] The others were offshoots of the King's Council.[369] The Requests was originally set up to dispatch the petitions of poor people, while the provincial councils sitting at Ludlow (in Shropshire) and York exercised prerogative jurisidiction devolved, in effect, from the Chancery and Star Chamber at Westminster.[370] The Marshalsea had a limited jurisdiction within the verge of the royal household, though it was becoming a court of regular resort for small suits in the metropolis.[371]

The complaints about these innovations were not so much about arbitrary tendencies in the central government as about certain troublesome aspects of new tribunals which did not follow the common law. In so far as the ecclesiastical commissioners dealt with questions of heresy and schism, which were beyond the purview of the secular courts, and the secular conciliar jurisdictions relieved the central courts from dealing with suits of lesser importance, there was little to quarrel with. It may be that they proceeded in a less professional and impartial manner than the courts in Westminster Hall, but that was not itself a formal objection. Litigants were ever astute to complain of jurisdictional transgressions, and it is impossible today to second-guess the courts of the day as to the quality of justice administered by the councillors. What is clearly observable as fact, however, is that the King's Bench and Common Pleas were already very receptive to jurisdictional complaints against these courts in the generation or two before Coke became chief justice.[372] The underlying grievances were of the same kind as those

---

[367] Above, pp. 133–43.   [368] This was controversial: above, pp. 137–43; below, pp. 291–3.

[369] Lambarde thought they had all been introduced under Henry VIII: *Archeion* (1579 draft) BL MS Harley 4717, fo. 24v. They in fact began in the fifteenth century but increased their business dramatically in the sixteenth: see *OHLE*, vi. 203–7.

[370] For their relationship to the central courts see Jones, *Elizabethan Chancery*, pp. 348–77.

[371] Walmsley J. was moved to protest about this, saying that if the steward of the court was more learned he would not be entertaining pleas of debt, since such proceedings were *coram non judice*: Anon. (1601) YLS MS. G.R19.16, fo. 25v. See *The Case of the Marshalsea* (1612) 10 Co. Rep. 68; below, pp. 389–90.

[372] There was also long-standing friction between the assize judges and the two provincial councils: J. S. Cockburn, *A History of English Assizes* (Cambridge, 1972), pp. 36–8, 40–2, 220–1.

which would be spelt out more clearly in Coke's time.[373] These were all courts of first instance,[374] and yet there was no appeal from their decisions. They asserted the power to prevent parties from using regular courts which were often more suited to their causes – for ecclesiastical causes the bishops' courts, and for lay causes the courts of common law. Their procedures were not those of the common law, there were no juries, and parties might be pressed to incriminate themselves upon oath. Parties were often required to travel considerable distances to appear in person, and forced to remain in attendance from day to day at ruinous expense.[375] And yet the jurisdictions rested on shaky legal foundations. The high commissioners and the councillors in the Marches and at York all derived their authority from commissions under the great seal and written instructions, which were not published.[376] Only the commissions for ecclesiastical causes had a statutory basis, but they were also kept secret,[377] and were increasingly widened in scope beyond the wording of the parent statute. The Court of Requests had no written commission at all, and was not old enough to claim a jurisdiction by prescription.[378] The powers of these courts were therefore difficult to square with the fourteenth-century statutes and decisions which denied the king any authority to order departures from the common law by writ or commission under the great or lesser seal.[379] It is noteworthy that Richard Crompton's painstaking treatise

---

[373] See further Chapters 8 and 9. For the High Commission in particular cf. above, pp. 135–6.

[374] The High Commission sometimes took over cases which were depending in the ordinary Church courts, but not by way of appeal.

[375] Defendants in the common-law courts could be represented, in their absence, by attorneys.

[376] Roger Wilbraham in 1607 said that not only were the instructions secret, and sometimes concealed, but sometimes there was a secret intention quite different from that expressed in the instructions: Wilbraham, *Journal*, p. 97 (referring particularly to the Council in Ireland, but in a passage concerning all 'great councils'). Likewise Coke CJ in *Oliver's Case* (1615) Calth. MS. ii. 32v (tr. 'before the time of King James the instructions for York and the Marches of Wales were not enrolled in Chancery as they now are, and so no one could know what their instructions were, *et miserrima est servitus ubi jus est incognitum*': miserable is the slavery where the law is unknown).

[377] Above, p. 135.

[378] In *Anon.* (1589) BL MS. Lansdowne 1087, fo. 96, where an action was brought for slander in saying that the plaintiff was perjured in the Requests, Coke argued that (tr.) 'The Court of Requests is no ancient known court of which this court can take cognizance, for it only began to be a court in the time of Henry VIII'. Cf. below, pp. 484–5.

[379] See above, pp. 52, 102. The principal contrary authority cited was the *Case of Oxford University* (1366) above, p. 60, referring to the early Tudor interpolation.

on the queen's courts, published in 1594, did not deign to mention any of them among their number.

It has already been noticed that the High Commission and the Court of Requests featured prominently as targets in the development of *habeas corpus*,[380] and the writ was deployed in the same period for prisoners of the Council in the Marches[381] and the Council at York.[382] But another weapon available to the two benches in controlling jurisdictions was the ancient writ of prohibition. It had been used since medieval times chiefly against the ecclesiastical courts, and enjoyed a resurgence in the Elizabethan period in tithe cases, which were now frequently litigated between laymen as a result of the dissolution of the monasteries and the creation of lay rectories. The common lawyers, while not wholly unfamiliar with the territory of the ecclesiastical lawyers, had no desire to take it over generally. In the sphere of marriage and divorce, for instance, the judges were scrupulous in protecting the exclusive jurisdiction of the bishops' courts.[383] Tithes were more contentious, since they affected the value of manors to which rectories or advowsons were attached, and claims often rested on prescription. The right to a lay rectory or advowson, and rights based on prescription, were within the exclusive province of the common law.[384] The Elizabethan and Jacobean law reports are full of prohibitions to the ordinary ecclesiastical courts in tithe cases, but they were mostly fought on a very technical level and did not raise constitutional issues.[385] The principal lay tribunal to receive prohibitions before the time of Elizabeth was the Admiralty, and the skirmishing over its jurisdictional ambitions continued throughout the sixteenth and seventeenth centuries. As with the prohibition of Church courts, it was to some degree a conflict

---

[380] Above, pp. 159–61, 162.

[381] *Thomas ap Morgan's Case* (Pas. 1570) and *John Rowland's Case* (Trin. 1578), cited from the controlment rolls in 12 Co. Rep. 55. Coke also discovered an action on the statute of *praemunire* for suing in the Marches after judgment at common law: *Beanes* v. *Lloyd* (1579) CP 40/1367, m. 319; Co. Inst. iii. 124 (writ only).

[382] *John Lamburne's Case* (alias *Lambert*) (Mich. 1565) and *Dawson's Case* (same term), cited from the controlment rolls in *Selected Readings on Magna Carta*, p. 399 and 12 Co. Rep. 55; above, p. 158. *Lambert's Case* was also cited in Crompton, *Courts*, fo. 78v.

[383] J. Baker, 'Some Elizabethan Marriage Cases' in *Studies in Canon Law and Common Law in Honor of R. H. Helmholz*, ed. T. L. Harris (Berkeley, CA, 2015), pp. 181–211.

[384] For prohibition to the High Commission where the title to an advowson was in issue see *Evans* v. *Jeffreys* (1575) cited by Coke in BL MS. Add. 58218, fo. 22v, as Common Pleas, Hil. 17 Eliz., rot. 1402.

[385] They have been the subject of a full analysis, chiefly concerned with procedural questions: C. M. Gray, *The Writ of Prohibition: Jurisdiction in Early Modern English Law* (New York, 1994).

between different professional worlds, between the common lawyers and the Civilians of Doctors' Commons. In 1590 there was a direct confrontation when an attorney of the King's Bench was committed by the lord admiral for contempt in bringing an action of false imprisonment at common law in respect of Admiralty process; the King's Bench bailed and later discharged him. This was one of the irritations leading to the judges' resolutions of 1592 concerning *habeas corpus*.[386] Prohibitions to the Admiralty seem to have increased in the 1590s, with the Common Pleas joining the fray.[387]

During the Elizabethan period writs of prohibition began to be directed also against the new prerogative jurisdictions,[388] and in 1592 complaint was made against the Common Pleas judges in the Privy Council, apparently by the president of the Council in the Marches. Anderson CJ countered that the conciliar jurisdictions now had more causes than the courts of common law, and 'at their pleasure they enjoin parties not to pursue their remedies according to the laws of the land, against various statutes and the public weal of the realm'.[389] He challenged the complainants to show their authority, but they failed to do so and the matter lapsed.[390] These were the stirrings of a major conflict which would become more and more intense over the next twenty-five years.[391] But, as with *habeas corpus*, it was not yet usual to connect the writ of prohibition with Magna Carta.[392]

---

[386] Above, pp. 166 n. 129, 167.

[387] *Hale and Fleetwood on Admiralty Jurisdiction*, ed. M. J. Prichard and D. E. C. Yale (108 SS, 1993), at pp. l–li. The King's Bench judges agreed in 1575 that the Admiralty jurisdiction extended to charterparties made on land and transactions beyond the sea, though this concession proved controversial for almost a century: ibid. xci–xcix. For complaints in the Privy Council of prohibitions from both benches in the late 1590s see 29 APC 367–8; 30 APC 3, 43. The story may be left there for present purposes, since Magna Carta did not feature in the controversies.

[388] Note also *Beanes v. Lloyd* (1579) CP 40/1367, m. 319; cited in Co. Inst. iii. 124. This was a writ of *praemunire* for suing in the Council of the Marches after a judgment in the Common Pleas; only the writ is enrolled.

[389] *Anon.* (1592) 1 And. 279 (tr.).

[390] In 1595 the Requests committed an attorney to prison for pursuing an action in the King's Bench contrary to such an injunction, though he was promptly released on *habeas corpus*: *Cawdry's Case* (1595) BL MS. Hargrave 356, fo. 101; MS. Add. 25198, fo. 80; sub nom. *Cowdry*, HLS MS. 110, fo. 146v; HLS MS. 5066, fo. 53v; BL MS. Harley 1624, fo. 282v (which says he was solicitor for one Malyns).

[391] Below, pp. 302–11, 379–90.

[392] The connection began to be made in reported cases from around 1600: below, p. 292. It was also made by Francis Ashley in his reading of 1616: BL MS. Harley 4841, fos. 4, 40v.

Largely exempt from this new activity, for most of Elizabeth's reign, were the three palatinate jurisdictions of Chester, Durham and Lancaster,[393] which possessed *jura regalia*, and the three highest prerogative jurisdictions, the Privy Council, the Star Chamber and the Chancery.[394] The Council Board and Star Chamber possessed some of the defects of the newer prerogative courts which emulated them. They required attendance from day to day, they interrogated parties on oath as to alleged crimes,[395] and there was no appeal. But they were both derived from the medieval King's Council, and were therefore regarded as immemorial features of the constitution.[396] Although they were dominated by officers of state, they were usually attended by the chief justices and law officers to give legal advice, and it was common to refer petitions to puisne judges for their opinion as to whether they should be struck out.[397] They were not permitted to deal with matters of life and limb, or freehold property. Even if the Star Chamber was sometimes deliberately fierce, and resourceful in discovering new criminal offences,[398] the awesome fines and other frightening tactics were usually directed at fraudsters, troublemakers and malefactors of all kinds, and quietly moderated at the end of term. The Star Chamber was to earn an unsavoury reputation in the time of Charles I, which has clung to it ever since, but to the Elizabethans the court was a guarantee

[393] In 1568, Dyer CJ, Weston and Harpur JJ, in a written opinion delivered to the queen, affirmed the exclusive jurisdiction of Chester: Coke's notebook, BL MS. Harley 6686A, fos. 116–118; Co. Inst. iv. 212–13; BL MS. Add. 25244, fos. 2v–4; and the other MSS. cited in *Dyer's Notebooks*, i. lxxxvi n. 7. Writs of error lay from the common-law courts in the palatinates to the King's Bench. For their equitable jurisdiction see below, p. 387.

[394] Lord Keeper Bacon wrote in 1572 that the Chancery jurisdiction (on the equity side) was warranted by the royal prerogative: *Proc. Parl. 1558–81*, p. 266. Cf. *Martin* v. *Marshall* (1615) Hob. 63, where it was said that equity was not regular law but an 'arbitrary disposition' administered by the king himself and his chancellor, as a special trust.

[395] *Att.-Gen.* v. *Lord Vaux* (1581), *Dyer's Notebooks*, ii. 391, 397 (fined £1,000 and imprisoned for refusing to take the oath); *Att.-Gen.* v. *Henton* (1608) BL MS. Add. 25207, fo. 4 (held that both the Exchequer and the Star Chamber could examine defendants as to fraud).

[396] In 1606 Thomas Richardson of Lincoln's Inn (later chief justice) was 'sharply reproved' by the Star Chamber for questioning its antiquity, and it was noted that the court existed before the time of Henry VII (i.e. before the so-called Act *Pro Camera Stellata*, which in fact had nothing to do with it): BL MS. Lansdowne 639, fo. 75. See further below, pp. 404–5.

[397] There is a collection of their certificates from 1593 to 1595 in BL MS. Add. 37045. Some are from William Mill, clerk of the Star Chamber, and a few are from law officers.

[398] See above, p. 154.

of impartial justice rather than its enemy.[399] It came down particularly hard on men who abused their authority or social standing. For instance, in 1562 Viscount Bindon was fined £100 for reviling a witness, in 1581 a justice of the peace was fined £40 for hitting a poor man, and in 1591 Sir Richard Bulkeley was fined for a similar offence.[400] In an even worse case, in 1588, the sheriffs of London had two gentlewomen arrested in the street, imprisoned in Bridewell, and whipped as prostitutes, without trial; for this grave abuse of their police function they were imprisoned for three months, heavily fined and ordered to pay substantial compensation.[401] The principal complaint about Star Chamber proceedings in the Elizabethan period was that the attorney-general could commence a prosecution by word of mouth (ore tenus), without a written indictment. This was clearly contrary to the concept of due process as clarified in the fourteenth century, but no one could seriously challenge it, and so it was accepted as something established by long usage.[402]

The Chancery was of seemingly equal antiquity, but its relationship with the common-law courts was more problematic because of its injunctive power. The authority of the Chancery to inhibit proceedings at common law by injunction had been a source of intermittent complaint since at least the time of Edward IV,[403] though it was accepted in principle by the common-law courts as a necessary feature of equitable jurisdiction.[404] Lambarde even held that the jurisdiction of the Chancery and Council was a fulfilment of the king's promise in chapter 29 of Magna Carta not to deny justice.[405] It was another matter, however, when serjeants at law were enjoined not to represent their clients in common-law proceedings, contrary to their oaths to serve the queen's people,[406] or when the due process of the

---

[399] See, e.g., Sir Thomas Smith, *De Republica Anglorum* [1583], ed. M. Dewar (Cambridge, 1982), at p. 127; Lambarde, *Archeion* [c. 1591], p. 49.

[400] BL MS. Harley 2143, fos. 21v (Viscount Bindon), 38 (Powell JP), 50v (Bulkeley). In 1595 a JP was fined 3,000 marks and put out of the commission for bribery: ibid. 62.

[401] *Att.-Gen. v. Skynner and Catcher, sheriffs of London* (1588) BL MS. Harley 2143, fo. 44. The Star Chamber held the sheriffs' conduct to be clearly contrary to Magna Carta: below, pp. 266–9.

[402] See Lambarde, *Archeion*, pp. 94–6.   [403] See *OHLE*, vi. 174–9.

[404] For a useful discussion of this see Smith, *Sir Edward Coke*, pp. 224–32.

[405] Lambarde, *Archeion*, 67. He said that a balance was achieved by 'that golden mediocrity which both religion, reason and law do maintain in this point' (p. 66). Note also Robert Snagge's reading of 1581, below, p. 251.

[406] In 1581 Wray CJ agreed with Fleetwood that for him to obey a Chancery injunction directed to counsel would be contrary to his serjeant's oath to serve the queen's people: *Anon.* (1581) BL MS. Lansdowne 1060, fo. 62; MS. Hargrave 9, fo. 142.

King's Bench was stopped by a Chancery *supersedeas*.[407] In 1601 Serjeant Hele was served with an injunction not to represent a litigant in the Common Pleas, and he complained to the court.[408] Walmsley J. said that a serjeant could disobey such an injunction, because it was contrary to his oath as *serviens ad legem* and a breach of his contract to serve his client.[409] Warburton J. said that, even if he did not regard his oath, the judges would obey theirs and do justice.[410] An especial grievance – the same as that voiced against the Council in the Marches – was the use of injunctions to restrain plaintiffs, who had succeeded at common law, from enforcing their judgments.[411] This was directly contrary to the statute of 1402 which enacted that 'after judgment given in the courts of our lord the king, the parties and their heirs shall be in peace thereof until the judgment is annulled by attaint or error, if error there be.'[412] The grievance had formed one of the charges against Cardinal Wolsey in 1529, signed by his successor Sir Thomas More,[413] and it resurfaced at the end of the sixteenth century. In 1566 and 1585 there were

---

[407] *Marshall's Case* (1600) BL MS. Add. 25202, fo. 12. The King's Bench said that, even if it had become the usage, it was not law.

[408] The report says the injunction came from the Exchequer, presumably the Equity Side, which had the same jurisdiction as the Chancery.

[409] Lord Keeper Egerton accepted that, because of the oath, he could not commit a serjeant for breach of an injunction, as he could a junior barrister. But he nevertheless held that he could debar him from practising in Chancery: *Anon.* (*c.* 1600) *Cases Concerning Equity and the Courts of Equity 1550–1660*, ed. W. H. Bryson, vol. i. (117 SS, 2001), p. 291, no. 128.

[410] *Anon.* (1601) YLS MS. G.R.29.16, fo. 21v. Two years later Hele sought a prohibition against counsel, because the party could not be found, and Walmsley J. denied the motion on the same ground: below, p. 283.

[411] The Star Chamber also assumed the authority to grant an injunction after judgment at law: *Tompson* v. *Midleditch* (1593) BL MS. Harley 2143, fo. 56v. But the action at law there was for slander in respect of things said in relation to a Star Chamber suit for perjury.

[412] 4 Hen. IV, c. 23. *St German's Doctor and Student*, ed. T. F. T. Plucknett and J. L. Barton (91 SS), at p. 107, said that the statute provided that judgments could not be examined in the Chancery or Parliament. Crompton, *Courts*, fo. 67, pointed out that the statute did not say that expressly but could reasonably be so intended. Crompton thought it clear that the Chancery was within the statute: ibid. 41v, 58v.

[413] Co. Inst. iv. 91–2, no. 20. The original manuscript on vellum was lent to Coke by Sir Robert Cotton around 1612 but is now lost: C. G. Tite, *The Early Records of Sir Robert Cotton's Library* (2003), pp. 24 (still on loan in 1621), 52, 61; Co. Inst. iii. 124 ('which I have seen in parchment'); Co. Inst. iv. 89 ('which we have seen and had in our custody'). It was also signed by the privy councillors, and by Fitzjames CJ and Fitzherbert J. Coke cited it in the Privy Council in 1616 to justify his saying that Chancery injunctions after judgment would overthrow the common law: CUL MS. Gg.2.31, fo. 202.

indictments in the King's Bench under the statutes of *praemunire*[414] for procuring injunctions after judgments at law, though their outcome is uncertain.[415] In 1588 Coke persuaded the King's Bench that *habeas corpus* would lie to the warden of the Fleet for a prisoner of the Chancery; even if the judges had no power to release him, the body still had to be brought before them with a sufficient return.[416] In the same year John Hele, a bencher of the Inner Temple, counselled a party to reopen a case in Chancery after a judgment in the King's Bench, claiming that there was a precedent for doing so. The court's response was that the precedent was contrary to the statute of 1402, and Hele himself was indicted for a *praemunire*, though he escaped on a technicality.[417] The lord chancellor (Hatton) retaliated by ordering the imprisonment of the barrister who drew the indictment, expressing his amazement at such an attempt to 'blemish and deface the authority of the court'.[418] Battle had commenced. Here, too, it was time for Magna Carta to be brought into play.[419]

The Prolonged Latency of Magna Carta

An obvious conclusion to be drawn from the evidence considered in this chapter is that most of the principles and remedies which seventeenth-century lawyers derived from chapter 29 of Magna Carta were introduced into legal thinking without reference to the wording of

---

[414] Legislation of the fourteenth century which imposed heavy penalties on those who impeached the judgments of the king's courts, the penal proceedings to be commenced by a *praemunire facias*: 27 Edw. III, c. 1. The word *praemunire* ('to warn') came to be transferred to the whole procedure, including the penalties. The legislation was directed against papal juridiction and had been used to bring down Wolsey in 1529: *OHLE*, vi. 241–6.

[415] *Heydon's Case* (1566) and *Dewse's Case* (1585) Co. Inst. iii. 124. Presumably there was no judgment, or Coke would have mentioned it. The statute was also cited by Gawdy J. in questioning the supposed jurisdiction of the lord mayor of London to reopen cases in equity after judgment in the Sheriffs' Court: *Anon.* (1587) Godb. 127.

[416] *Brockhouse's Case* (1588) BL MS. Lansdowne 1095, fos. 61v–62; YLS MS. G.R29.8, fo. 36v.

[417] *Hele's Case* (1588–9) 2 Leo. 115; Coke's notebook, BL MS. Harley 6686A, fo. 226v (cited at the end of *Throckmorton v. Finch* in 1597); Co. Inst. iii. 124; BL MS. Lansdowne 1095, fo. 48v; Crompton, *Courts*, pp. 57–8. Coke said the indictment was specially endorsed that it had been quashed for misnomer 'and not for the matter'.

[418] C. Monro, *Acta Cancellariae* (1846), pp. 5–8. According to Bacon (in a letter of 1616) the judges had answered for it, on their knees, in the Privy Council: below, p. 419 n. 58.

[419] *Throckmorton v. Finch* (1597) below, pp. 284–8.

the charter. Chapter 29 was never forgotten, and it made occasional appearances before the 1580s, but there is no evidence that it was the ultimate source of the principles or the remedies. If it was an inspiration in some subliminal way, no one seems to have been aware of it. The paucity of references, especially in the context of the late-medieval and early Tudor teaching in the inns of court, proves rather that it was not the well from which the legal ideas flowed. There was to be a dramatic change beginning in the 1580s. Before coming to that, however, some account needs to be taken of the transitional writings and speeches of William Fleetwood.

6

William Fleetwood and Magna Carta

In order to situate more precisely the new learning on Magna Carta which exploded on the inns of court in the 1580s, William Fleetwood[1] (d. 1594) deserves particular scrutiny as the author of the principal commentary on the charter before Coke. His commentary was written half way between the late-medieval learning on which it was heavily based and the newer thinking which Coke was to promote, though it was closer in approach to the former. Of considerable interest in its own right, it also interconnects with a group of innovative treatises on statutory interpretation and legal history, and with a collection of draft legal arguments in which the charter features prominently. None of these works has previously been identified as Fleetwood's, and indeed Fleetwood's part in the story of Magna Carta has hitherto been overlooked. An excursus is therefore necessary to establish and explain his authorship of these writings, and to show how they – more than any others in the early-Elizabethan period – reflected a new interest in historical scholarship which assisted the renaissance of the great charter.

Fleetwood was one of the most prominent lawyers in Elizabethan England.[2] His father Robert, a member of the Middle Temple and a Chancery clerk, charged him by his last will (1560) to apply himself diligently to learning 'and to minister true justice and counsel without favour or affection bearing to any party'.[3] William seems to have been little in need of parental encouragement to study, since he was already devoted to scholarship, both legal and historical. After an education at

---

[1] This standardised spelling is adopted here, though the serjeant himself invariably wrote his name 'Fletewoode', and that form was used by his descendants for at least two centuries.

[2] There are summary biographies in *HPHC 1509–58*, ii. 148–9; *HPHC 1558–1603*, ii. 133–8; *Hale and Fleetwood on Admiralty Jurisdiction*, ed. M. J. Prichard and D. E. C. Yale (108 SS, 1993), introduction, pp. xviii–xxv; *ODNB* (by C. W. Brooks); *The Men of Court*, ii. 688–9. Much of the material about Fleetwood in the old *DNB* had been well known since the eighteenth century: see the biography in *Biographica Britannica* (1750), iii. 1958–64.

[3] PCC 23 Loftes; *The Men of Court*, i. 687.

Eton and Oxford, he had become a student of Clifford's Inn in 1543,[4] and around this time enjoyed briefly the patronage of Thomas, Lord Audley (d. 1544), the lord chancellor.[5] He then proceeded to the Middle Temple, where he was called to the bar in the 1550s.[6] He was a keen participant in the exercises of learning there, and said in 1585 that he had been a moot-man for thirty years.[7] He gave lectures on Littleton,[8] presumably in New Inn, and two readings in the Middle Temple (in 1564 and 1569). In Lent 1576 he took over the reading in New Inn 'for his pleasure', a form of pleasure otherwise unheard of in a bencher.[9] Even after becoming a serjeant in 1580, he continued to attend readings, as was the custom.[10] He is best known to posterity for his police activities as recorder of London, which he related in detail in his reports to Lord Burghley,[11]

---

[4] Middle Temple Library MS. 95, fo. 61v. In a letter to Lord Burghley in 1582 he recalled that Sir Thomas Bromley LC, Sir Christopher Wray CJQB, Sir Roger Manwood CB, Sir George Bromley, and he himself, had all been members of the Inn under the principalship of [Thomas] Hanchett, who kept them in good order: BL MS. Lansdowne 37(5); printed in *Queen Elizabeth and her Times*, ed. T. Wright (1838), ii. 188 (misprinted as 'Haachett'). Hanchett was an attorney: *Men of Court*, i. 813.

[5] BL MS. Harley 5194, fo. 2 ('my especial good lord and patron the Lord Audley of Walden and chancellor of England').

[6] *ODNB* says he was admitted in 1547 and called in 1551, though this must be conjecture. The Inn's records, which resume in 1551 after a hiatus, show only that he must have been a member by 1551, when his father was described as 'senior', though he is not himself named before 1556: *MTR*, i. 82, 88, 105. He must have been called before 1558, when he was appointed a common pleader of the city of London and retained as counsel by the duchy of Lancaster. He argued a case in the King's Bench in 1558: below, p. 239.

[7] *Proc. Parl. 1584–9*, p. 127 ('I was a mote man 30 year together'). Some reports he took of readings in the 1550s are in BL MS. Harley 5156; *Readers and Readings*, pp. 291–2. He probably also collected the notes from Middle Temple readings *c.* 1546–50 in BL MS. Harley 4717, fos. 26–112v: below, p. 240. In 1552 he attended Reynold Corbet's reading and wrote in exasperation: (tr.) 'Note well the mystery of this case, for it is too erudite, politic, subtle, and unintelligible' (MS. Harley 5156, fo. 18v).

[8] BL MS. Harley 5158, fos. 8–14v; St John's College, Cambridge, MS. S.28, fos. 70–103; *Readers and Readings*, pp. 293, 564. These fragments are variously described as 'lectures', 'tractatus' and 'observations'.

[9] Coke's notebook, BL MS. Harley 6687, fo. 17; *Readers and Readings*, pp. 210, 300.

[10] *Readers and Readings*, pp. 162–8; Prichard and Yale, *Hale and Fleetwood*, p. xix n. 4 ('I am always at the reading', 1575); *Selected Readings on Magna Carta*, p. lxxxvi (1578). He is reported as having spoken at the readings by Robert Bell (1565), Richard Stephens and Richard Inkpen (1575), James Morice (1578), Richard Crompton (1579), William Peryam (1580, when they were both serjeants-elect), Henry Blanchard (1581), Thomas Bowyer (1586), Thomas Harris (1589) and William Gibbes (1590).

[11] His work as recorder is sketched in H. W. Woolrych, *Lives of Eminent Serjeants* (1869), i. 132–64; E. A. Parry, *Judgments in Vacation* (1911), pp. 165–89; R. Harris, 'William Fleetwood, Recorder of the City, and Catholicism in Elizabethan London' (1963) 7

and that may well have been his chief claim to fame in his lifetime as well. It was said that he was so successful in the post that Queen Elizabeth refused to remove him to the more senior judicial position which was reckoned to be his due. He was at the same time an active member of the House of Commons, which he entered as early as 1558.[12] Given that he also maintained a private practice at the Bar, it is a wonder that he found any time for reading and writing. Indeed, he once complained to Burghley that 'I have not leisure to eat my meat'.[13] He was, for all this, a prodigious historical scholar and writer throughout his life, and can justly be regarded as the first English legal historian.[14] He was about ten years senior to William Lambarde of Lincoln's Inn, whose earliest interests lay in Anglo-Saxon antiquities rather than the common law. He extolled the virtues of great antiquaries,[15] and no doubt considered himself an antiquary, a new word which then had positive connotations.[16] He was perhaps the first English lawyer to collect old legal manuscripts for their historical, rather than their purely forensic, value.[17] A twelfth-century manuscript containing the *Quadripartitus*, which he quoted in his *Of Forests* and again in the *Itinerarium ad Windsor*, was an acquisition in his student days,[18] and over time he amassed an impressive

---

Recusant History 106–22. The autograph reports to Burghley are now among the Lansdowne MSS. See also above, p. 129.

[12] The History of Parliament described him as 'one of the great parliament men of Elizabeth's day': *HPHC 1558–1603*, ii. 133. Professor Loach said that by the 1570s 'the House of Commons felt committees to be incomplete without William Fleetwood, or Thomas Norton': J. Loach, *Parliament under the Tudors* (Oxford, 1991), p. 145.

[13] *HPHC 1558–1603*, ii. 137. Perhaps he was saved by the Long Vacation. In 1575 he wrote to Burghley, 'I have no business, but go as quietly to my book as I did the first year that I came to the Temple': BL MS. Lansdowne 20(8), printed in *Queen Elizabeth and her Times*, ed. T. Wright (1838), ii. 21.

[14] See below, pp. 220–6.

[15] He used this description for John Leland: CUL MS. Dd.9.17, fo. 24v ('antiquariers'; but cf. Fleetwood, *Itinerarium ad Windsor*, p. 136, where in a different manuscript the word is 'antiquary'). And also for Jacob Manlius: *Itinerarium ad Windsor*, p. 151 n. 38.

[16] *Itinerarium ad Windsor*, pp. 24–5, 46 n. 18. For Fleetwood as an antiquary see J. D. Alsop, 'William Fleetwood and English Historical Scholarship' (1994) 25 *Sixteenth-Century Journal* 155–76; *Itinerarium ad Windsor*, Alsop discovered that he was a protégé of Matthew Parker.

[17] *CELMC*, introduction, pp. xlvii–xlviii. For his 'old book of the customs of Normandy' see *ELMUSA*, ii. 275, no. 1130.

[18] Manchester, John Rylands Library, MS. Lat. 420; *Itinerarium ad Windsor*, p. 32. In the dedication of his book on forest law, dated 1571, he says he acquired it twenty years earlier 'by the means of one Mr Badby' in the house of Mr Eyle, an old servant of Lord Chancellor Audley (d. 1544), in Bury St Edmunds: BL MS. Harley 5194, fo. 2. He had

library of medieval statutes and treatises,[19] year books,[20] and – most significant for present purposes – late-medieval and early Tudor readings on statutes.[21] At least one of these came into the possession of his younger acquaintance Francis Tate (of the Middle Temple) in 1599,[22] and it is possible that more of Tate's equally important collection came from Fleetwood than now bear his name.[23]

Fleetwood's own second reading, in 1569, was on a statute of 1536 for recontinuing liberties in the crown,[24] doubtless chosen so as to provide him with a pretext for plenty of historical digression about counties palatine, forest law and the royal prerogative, though only some garbled cases from it survive.[25] In 1577 he told Burghley that he was working day and night on a 'general table for the whole body of the common law, that I may turn to any thing at the first that is set down in our books of the common law', and that he had 'found out such strange and rare things in the law that I never either marked in reading or heard any other tell of'.[26] This presumably referred to his index to the year books of Henry VII and Henry VIII,[27] which was published in 1579. Fleetwood's *Annalium*, as it

---

obtained a fifteenth-century *Natura Brevium*, formerly Spelman's, as early as 1548: YLS MS. G. N21.1; *ELMUSA*, i. 75, no. 202.

[19] The 1774 sale of the Missenden Abbey library included five copies of the *Statuta Vetera* (beginning with Magna Carta): BL, 269.k.5, lots 3603–7. Only one has been traced: HLS MS. 21. There is an illuminated *Statuta Nova* with Fleetwood's signature at Harvard: HLS MS. 48. Perhaps the *Glanvill*, *Bracton* and *Britton* given to the Bodleian Library in 1601 by Edward Fleetwood were his: Bodl. Lib. MS. Bodl. 344, 562, 564. For a list of manuscripts at Missenden which had belonged to Serjeant Fleetwood but had been taken away see Bodl. Lib. MS. Rawlinson D.888, fo. 42v.

[20] Those so far identified are BL MS. Harley 5155; MS. Add. 5925; MS. Add. 37659 (which had belonged to Thomas Marow and Sir John Spelman); CUL MSS. Hh.3.9; Mm.2.17; Free Library of Philadelphia, H. L. Carson Collection, MS. LC.14.11 (*Liber Assisarum*).

[21] CUL MSS. Ee.5.19; Ee.5.20 (Marow); Hh.3.9; Hh.3.10. These do not include any readings on Magna Carta, so he must have had more.

[22] CUL MS. Mm.2.17; *CELMC*, p. 482. Tate was called to the Bar in 1587, thirty years or so after Fleetwood.

[23] For Tate's manuscripts see *CELMC*, pp. xlviii–l. Sir Robert Cotton lent Tate a book of Anglo-Saxon laws in Latin which had been Fleetwood's: C. G. Tite, *The Early Records of Sir Robert Cotton's Library* (2003), p. 34. It is perhaps BL Cotton MS. Domitian VIII(16).

[24] 27 Hen. VIII, c. 24.

[25] Fleetwood, 'Miscellanea', fos. 159–61. He said it had included an exposition of some Anglo-Saxon legal terms, but acknowledged later that it was full of errors, and so he revised it in 1571: HLS MS. 15, fo. 188; Fleetwood, *Of Forests*, fos. 49–59.

[26] BL MS. Lansdowne 24, fo. 198; Prichard and Yale, *Hale and Fleetwood*, p. xxii n. 6.

[27] *Annalium tam Regum Edwardi quinti, Richardi tertii, & Henrici septimi, quam Henrici octavi Elenchus* (1579).

was called, was quite unlike any other year-book index, and far more useful, including anything out of the way which a reader might wish to find,[28] a 'kallender' (with the names of people and places), Latin phrases and maxims, and a table of statutes. The *Annalium*, and his table to Plowden (1578),[29] were in fact his only legal publications printed during his lifetime. His other writings were circulated in manuscript, mostly in the form of tentative or unfinished drafts, and were still being copied in the seventeenth century.[30] Among them were several which have a useful bearing on the study of Magna Carta.

The Beginnings of English Legal History

Fleetwood was at the forefront of a new historical movement in the English legal profession, the chief purpose of which was to uncover the origins of the common law from the best available sources. This may well have owed something to the humanistic humour of the times, though it received a more specific impetus in England from the final rejection of papal authority over the English Church and a consequent desire to explore the status of the early Church in England and its relationship with the monarchy.[31] That impetus drove Richard Gynes to deliver his influential lecture in the Inner Temple in 1568, in which he demonstrated with impressive learning that the kings of England had always exercised a legally recognised temporal headship over the Church within their realm.[32] The topic was addressed again in James Morice's reading in

---

[28] E.g. absurdity, bawdery, beacon, bye-laws, butcher, circuity of action, common-wealth, conscience, coronation, counsel learned, discretion, forest law, Fleet, 'gossiprick', grammarians, laches, lectura (noting the one reading cited in the year books), London, 'May games en amour', maxim, negligent dealing, night-walkers, policy, pope, poverty, precedents, printing, reason, usage, 'zeal de justice'.

[29] In 1575 he said he had almost finished his table to Plowden: CUL MS. Dd.9.17, fo. 20v. It was printed with part II in 1578.

[30] Much of Lambarde's work on legal history in the 1590s similarly circulated in the form of drafts, and the *Archeion* was published posthumously without having been completed by the author. Likewise Sir Roger Owen's treatise (*c.* 1615), none of which was ever printed.

[31] For the importance of history in this connection see also D. C. Smith, 'Remembering Usurpation: The Common Lawyers, Reformation Narratives and the Prerogative' (2013) 86 *Historical Research* 619–37.

[32] BL MS. Harley 813, fos. 111–118v; MS. Add. 11405, fos. 5–13v; MS. Add. 28607, fos. 3–11; LI MS. Hale 80, fos. 188–197; Exeter College, Oxford, MS. 101, fos. 7–13; Folger Shakespeare Library, Washington, MS. V. b. 74, fos. 227v–237. This was the prefatory lecture to a course on tithes, which has not survived.

the Middle Temple in 1578,[33] and it was an interest of Fleetwood's as well.[34] When the question arose in the Common Pleas in 1583 whether the pope had once had authority under English law to grant dispensations to hold benefices in plurality, Fleetwood sought to prove from scriptural authority that the king was supreme head in spiritual and temporal causes within his realm: 'And he said he would not vouch any places of scripture to prove it save those which were vouched by the sage judges of this realm in 26 Hen. VIII, when Cromwell by the king's command assembled the judges and the expert men of this realm to argue this matter'.[35] This suggests that Fleetwood had access to papers relating to the commission for reviewing the canon law.

Fleetwood evidently loved history both for its own sake and for what he saw, perhaps too enthusiastically, as its manifold practical usefulness to a contemporary lawyer. As is evident from his arguments in court and his speeches in Parliament, he never missed an opportunity to relate the history of the matter in hand, even when it did not seem to others to be strictly apposite.[36] Some found these disquisitions instructive, but law reporters – and parliamentary reporters as well[37] – at times found them too divergent from the main line of argument to be worth noting.[38] For instance, in 1584, when Fleetwood appeared for the plaintiff in a celebrated libel case against

---

[33] BL MS. Egerton 2376, at fos. 46–60, in the polished redaction prepared at the instance of Lord Burghley. For this reading see below, pp. 255–8. Cf. Coke's speech as speaker of the Commons in 1593: *Proc. Parl. 1593–1601*, p. 66.

[34] He addressed it in *Dolman* v. *Bishop of Salisbury and Pickaver* (1583): Fleetwood, 'Notes for Arguments', fo. 306. The full speech as delivered is reported in BL MS. Lansdowne 1078, fos. 59, 121v–122v; slightly variant in MS. Harley 1693, fos. 92v–93; MS. Harley 4988, fos. 14v–16v (tr.).

[35] *Dolman* v. *Bishop of Salisbury and Pickaver* [1583]: BL MS. Lansdowne 1078, fos. 59, 121v–122v; slightly variant in MS. Harley 1693, fos. 92v–93; MS. Harley 4988, fos. 14v–16v (tr.). See also Fleetwood, 'Notes for Arguments', fo. 306. Walmsley was prepared to argue for the pope's former authority, but did not dare ('n'osa pas') without the advice of the court. Anderson CJ managed to avoid the issue by deciding that the alleged papal dispensation had not been adequately pleaded.

[36] For his meandering and sometimes irrelevant speeches in Parliament see G. R. Elton, *The Parliament of England 1559–81* (Cambridge, 1981), pp. 204–5, 296, 345. Cf. Neale's remark that, in a speech of 1571, the antiquary in him got the better of the radical: *Elizabeth I and her Parliaments 1559–81* (1952), p. 203.

[37] *Proc. Parl. 1558–81*, p. 313 ('long and tedious talk, nothing touching the matter in question', 1572).

[38] See *Specott* v. *Bishop of Exeter* (1588) 3 Leo. 198 at p. 199 ('It was argued by Fleetwood sjt for the bishop, but to little purpose, and there[fore] I will report but certain passages of his argument'). See also *Collett* v. *Webbe* (1587) below, p. 480 (tr. 'He made a long argument, but he never argued the very point').

the bishop of Coventry, he began with a little digression on the etymology and meaning of 'bishop', and later on referred to an allusion to 'unlawful words' in the articles of the eyre; most reporters ignored these offerings.[39] A case about tenures in 1588 provided him with an excuse to offer his speculative theory about the origin of tenures.[40] His speeches in Parliament often began with Anglo-Saxon laws.[41] And when, as recorder of London, he was asked by Lord Burghley for some practical advice on detecting criminals, he could not resist a historical disquisition beginning with the Book of Sirach and covering the Danish invasion, the division of the country into counties, hundreds and tithings and the provisions of the 'great charter of England' as to tithings.[42] Even at Newgate, prisoners in the dock might find him citing Plutarch and the canon law.[43]

Fleetwood wrote scathingly of lawyers who held it unnecessary to know what the old common law was, once it had been replaced by statute: '[they are] much deceived in their opinion, for without knowledge of the ancient law they shall neither know the statute nor expound it well, but shall (as it were) follow their noses and grope at it in the dark'.[44] It had long been the practice for readers in the inns of court to begin their exposition of a statute by offering a historical explanation of the mischief at which it was aimed. But Fleetwood complained that this was often undertaken without proper research:[45]

> A rule which is much in use among the readers . . . is that, if it be uncertain what the common law was, then by intendment the common law is taken to be contrary to the statute: as rape, they guess, was but trespass at the common law, because Westminster I, c. 13, doth make it felony. But this is an uncertain rule, for they were deceived, as you may easily see in Staunford upon that statute.[46] And therefore the more sure way is that, if it can not be

---

[39] *Boughton v. Bishop of Coventry* (1584) BL MS. Harley 4779, fo. 180; below, p. 239 n. 150; cf. 1 And. 119; *Select Cases on Defamation to 1600*, ed. R. H. Helmholz (101 SS, 1985), p. 86.

[40] *Merifeilde v. Banister* (1588) BL MS. Add. 35944, fos. 31v–32; MS. Hargrave 26, fo. 132v; sub nom. *Meryfield v. Street*, LI MS. Misc. 361, fos. 131–3. Cf. *Ognell v. Umbrell* (c. 1588) MS. Lansdowne 1078, fo. 36 (tr. 'Fleetwood, for the defendant, said that Littleton argued for four kinds of fees').

[41] E.g. *Proc. Parl. 1558–81*, pp. 202 (laws of King Edgar), 236 (laws of King Aethelred).

[42] BL MS. Lansdowne 81, fos. 163–7, dated 12 April 1585. The statute is Magna Carta, c. 35, and Fleetwood suggested that *trithinga* was derived from *trith*, a head, and *tinge*, a court.

[43] The case concerned a woman indicted for picking the pocket of someone with whom she was fornicating in a field: BL MS. Hargrave 4, fo. 44v. Fleetwood also cited Plutarch in the opening sentence of the preface to *Justices*, sig. A2.

[44] *Discourse upon Statutes*, p. 141. For the identification of the author see below, pp. 232–7.

[45] *Discourse upon Statutes*, pp. 141–2.   [46] Sta. P.C. 21v.

gathered by the words of the statute, then to see what ancient writers, as Bracton and Glanvill, those worshipful antiquities of our law, have had [sic] written in their books . . . For the other way, of guessing at the common law, although it be much and almost altogether in use among the readers, yet hath it caused them much to be deceived: as well may be seen upon Merton and Magna Carta, which both statutes for the most part did but affirm and confirm the common law, and yet are taken by them to make a law.

The notion that most of the content of Magna Carta and Merton was not new law was itself an advance in historical understanding, but Fleetwood could not single-handedly and immediately rid history of all its errors. No historian will ever be blessed with that faculty. The earlier history of England was gravely misguided in Fleetwood's day by texts which appeared plausible but had yet to be exposed as false. In particular, the legends of King Brut and King Lucius were still accepted as showing the antiquity of English law and its independence from foreign influence.[47] Indeed, the forged letter from Pope Eleutherius to King Lucius of Britain, supposedly written in the second century,[48] and referring to the law of Lucius's realm, was sufficiently plausible to be accepted as genuine until the seventeenth century.[49] Parliament,[50] the central royal courts,[51] and the common law, all

---

[47] Fleetwood, *Of Forests*, fo. 11v; 'Miscellanea', fo. 60v; *Bishop of Salisbury* v. *Pichaver* (1583) BL MS. Harley 1693, fo. 92v (where Fleetwood quoted part of the Eleutherius letter – next note – to show that 'a bishop of Rome had refused the supremacy tendered to him by King Lucius').

[48] A letter from Eleutherius to this mythical king was mentioned as early as the sixth century, but the forged text was rediscovered in Henry VIII's reign in the London *Liber Custumarum* (dating from the time of King John). See D. J. Knight, *King Lucius of Britain* (Stroud, 2008).

[49] *Rights and Liberties*, p. 139 (laws of Lucius mentioned *c.* 1546/50); W. Lambarde, *Archaionomia* (1568), fo. 131; *Proc. Parl. 1558–81*, p. 198, *per* Christopher Wray MP (1571); *Proc. Parl. 1610*, ii. 152, *per* Nicholas Fuller MP; Co. Inst. iv. 342; below, p. 224. In *Mullins* v. *Dawes* (*c.* 1582/4) BL MS. Hargrave 6, fo. 76v, and MS. Hargrave 8, fo. 261v, Robert Bowyer cited a supposed ordinance of King Lucius to show that tithes were governed by the temporal law.

[50] Fleetwood held that there was a Parliament in the time of King Edgar: *Itinerarium ad Windsor*, pp. 71, 79; cf. *Of Forests* fo. 13 ('the conqueror in a full Parliament holden anno 4 of his reign'). He accepted that the *Modus tenendi Parliamentum* was written in the time of Edward the Confessor: 'Miscellanea', fos. 1–2 ('Order [sic] parliamenti'). Coke (as speaker in 1593) relied on the supposed antiquity of the *Modus* in tracing Parliament to the time of the Heptarchy: *Proc. Parl. 1593–1601*, p. 170. John Dodderidge, a keen legal antiquary, took much the same view: *Proc. Parl. 1610*, ii. 231. On the other hand, a Gray's Inn reader *c.* 1515 had taught that Parliament did not exist at the time of the Conquest: *Rights and Liberties*, p. 131.

[51] He once thought there were originally three royal courts, the Marshalsea, the Chancery and the Exchequer: Fleetwood, *Magna Carta*, fo. 18v, *Selected Readings on Magna Carta*, p. 372. He recognised that the *capitales justiciarii* of Magna Carta, c. 13, were not the chief justices of the benches but justiciars: ibid. fo. 20.

existed in Fleetwood's thinking before the Norman conquest. Parliament could even be traced back to the 'council of thy kingdom' alluded to in the letter supposedly written by Eleutherius to Lucius.[52] The 'original court of the whole realm', he opined, was the Exchequer, out of which developed the Chancery and then the two benches.[53] Fleetwood was quite probably the author of a treatise on the Exchequer, illustrated with diagrams based on the chess-board.[54] This was based on the twelfth-century *Dialogus de Scaccario*, but it offered a brief account of the origins of the royal courts, tracing the Chancery, King's Bench and Common Pleas to a fission of the Exchequer. This was not, however, a new theory. Fleetwood's notions had been long prevalent in the inns of court,[55] and they would still be Coke's assumptions fifty years later. On occasion Fleetwood made less defensible historical errors.[56] Yet, unlike many of his contemporaries, Fleetwood was critical in assessing sources, avowing a preference for contemporary chronicles before retrospective histories, which were more likely to be biased.[57] He became particularly scathing about Polydore Vergil's inaccuracies,[58] though in his earlier days he had accepted him less critically.[59]

---

[52] Fleetwood, *Of Forests*, fos. 3v–4; 'Miscellanea', fo. 60; *Proc. Parl. 1558–81*, p. 236. For this medieval forgery see above, p. 223.

[53] *Liber Fleetwood*, fos. 88, 89v. The same point is made in CUL MS. Dd.9.17, fo. 17, and at his reading in the Middle Temple (1569), when he said that all pleas were at the Exchequer until King John removed common pleas: Fleetwood, 'Miscellanea', fo. 159v. Roger Owen argued that Serjeant Fleetwood was mistaken in this: BL MS. Harley 6605, fo. 65v.

[54] Folger Shakespeare Library MS. V.b.9, fo. 171 (in a copy of the *Liber Fleetwood*); Library of Congress Law MS. Folio 2, fo. 19; BL MS. Lansdowne 170, fo. 47; MS. Add. 48038(2); MS. Add. 48116, fo. 347.

[55] See above, pp. 76–7, 85–6.

[56] E.g. the undated argument, apparently by him, that the statute of Carlisle, 35 ('30') Edw. I, usually titled *De Apportis Religiosorum*, showed that the archbishoprics and ecclesiastical dignities had been founded by the kings and nobles of the realm: 'That the cathedral church of Durham founded by King Henry VIII is not visitable by any Bishop', BL MS. Hargrave 26, fos. 69–71v (ending 'Collect per William Fleetwood serjeant de ley et recorder de London'). The statute recited only that *monasteries* had been founded by kings and nobles.

[57] CUL MS. Dd.9.17, fos. 23v–27.

[58] CUL MS. Dd.9.11, fos. 24v–25 (printed in *Itinerarium ad Windsor*, 136–7). Cf. James Morice's reading (1578), fo. 47, where Polydore is dismissed even more contemptuously as an 'ignorant Italian' and 'a vain man forgetting himself, as oftentimes they do which delight in lies'. Roger Owen was another fierce critic: BL MS. Harley 6605, fo. 5.

[59] There are several citations in his commentary on Magna Carta (*c.* 1558), discussed below.

Treatise on the Origins of English Law

Among the Harleian manuscripts is an imperfect copy of a more detailed draft treatise on the origins of English law.[60] It begins with some general remarks about the various ranks of dignity, and about tenures, a defence of English law against the criticism that it was unwritten, and an enumeration of the different sorts of laws, before coming to the British story with Brutus and Malmutius and proceeding through the Saxon and Danish periods, teasing out the few references to the law in that early period. The copy ends with Henry II and his conquest of Ireland, and therefore does not reach 1215, though a loose connection is drawn in passing between the old laws of Britain and the restatement in Magna Carta, while a marginal note compares Cnut's appointment of judges with the provision for common pleas in chapter 11.[61] The only indication of date is a reference to the queen 'that now is', identified in a marginal note as Queen Elizabeth. It is a remarkable reference, for it says that the queen had 'graced a reading in one of the inns of court with her own presence', presumably meaning a reader's feast.[62] There is no record of such an event before 1661, when Charles II's visit to the Inner Temple attracted much notice, and if it may be assumed that a royal visit could not occur without leaving a trace in the records of the inn concerned, it must have been in Gray's Inn before 1569. It is tempting to see Fleetwood's hand in this treatise. Like much of his work, it appears to be a draft, with a preface in note form.[63] The primacy given to the origin of ranks of dignity is paralleled in his treatise on forest law.[64] The author twice refers to the importance of readings in the inns of court, which was a particular and perhaps peculiar predilection of Fleetwood's and rules out Lambarde.[65] The list of different types of law is matched by a similar list in Fleetwood's *Itinerarium*, though the latter was more specifically English and the former (as the author said) was

---

[60] BL MS. Harley 4317. This is a copy, apparently dating from the seventeenth century, taken from an incomplete exemplar. The copyist wrote at the end: 'Multa desunt'.

[61] Ibid. 6v (text), 11 (margin). An even more strained allusion occurs further down the margin on fo. 11, where a comment is written against a mention of trial by combat: 'This remedy accordeth to Magna Carta'. It is not obvious what part of Magna Carta is here meant.

[62] Ibid. 1.

[63] Ibid. 1: 'Observations for the preface'. The style is reminiscent of Fleetwood's 'Notes for arguments', below, pp. 238–41.

[64] Fleetwood, *Of Forests*, in 'Miscellanea', at fo. 60.

[65] BL MS. Harley 4317, fos. 1, 4; below, pp. 237–8.

'external'.[66] And there are gratuitous references to Magna Carta, another of Fleetwood's interests. At first glance, there are some seeming counter-indications. The author treated the King's Bench and Common Pleas as coeval, without mentioning the Exchequer;[67] but this was only by way of drawing a comparison with the legal system of the British kings, not an account of their origin. He also said that the common law was 'established' by Edward the Confessor, which seems contrary to Fleetwood's conception of an immemorial common law; when, however, the passage is read carefully, it seems rather to say that King Edward abolished various legal accretions which detracted from the common law and thereby purified it.[68] Establishing did not in this passage mean introducing new laws, but rather singling out for confirmation and perpetuation those which were consonant to the laws of reason and nature and good for the community. These passages do not, therefore, stand in the way of supposing that this was one of Fleetwood's early essays on legal history. Although it did not reach the thirteenth century, the omission was partly supplied by his commentary on the great charter, which might be seen as a continuation.

Commentary on Magna Carta

As early as the 1550s Fleetwood embarked on a project to write historical and legal commentaries on the old statutes.[69] It is conceivable that he

---

[66] Fleetwood, *Itinerarium ad Windsor*, pp. 27–8 (law of God, spiritual law, civil law, martial law, forest laws, laws of Oleron or *lex mercatoria*, laws of the March, customary laws, law of the lord steward at coronations, law of Parliament, common law, and laws of the crown). His equation here of the laws of Oleron with the *lex mercatoria* also occurs in his speech in *The Chamberlain of London's Case* (1590) BL MS. Harley 1633, fo. 181. There is a list of nine species in *Specott* v. *Bishop of Exeter* (1588) Fleetwood, 'Notes for Arguments', fo. 325, the first being the law of the crown, the second the law of the land. Cf. the eight species listed in MS. Harley 4317, fo. 3 (*jus gentium, jus civile, jus consulare, jus Quiritum, jus publicum, jum faeciale, jus magistrale* and *jus naturale*); he went on to say that a similar division could be made in England between *jus naturale, jus gentium, lex condita* (statute law) and *mos antiquus* (common law and custom); the author mentioned a case which showed how the law of nature could be of practical relevance in English law, which may be the case of a Mr Bar cited for the same purpose in Francis Rodes's reading of 1576 (Fleetwood, 'Miscellanea', fo. 162v).

[67] BL MS. Harley 4317, fo. 5.

[68] Ibid. 13: 'he caused the unprofitable and unequal laws to be abolished, establishing those only which were consonant to the laws of reason and nature, which he entitled the common laws because they were indifferently grounded for the benefit of the commons'.

[69] Fleetwood, *Magna Carta*, fo. 12, (*Selected Readings on Magna Carta*, p. 368, referring to an intention to write on the Statute of Merton), and fo. 25v (an intention to write on

finished the task, at least in draft,[70] though the only parts to have been discovered are the commentary on Magna Carta,[71] and another on the Carta de Foresta.[72] The full version of the commentary on Magna Carta exists only in one very corrupt copy,[73] though the preface and first chapter occur also in an equally corrupt text found in a miscellany written in the hand of Fleetwood or his clerk.[74] The full copy is linked to Fleetwood by the appearance of his initials on folio 48, and by a note on folio 41 which seems to be in his italic hand. Although the treatise contains obvious Renaissance touches, such as lessons from the classics and from English history, references to other nations,[75] and philological excursions[76] – embellishments of the kind which were coming to be expected in legal writing – no other lawyer of the time, at any rate none of those known to posterity, could have written such a work. It is in the lively style associated with Fleetwood, it contains some out-of-the-way legal history,[77] and it contains tell-tale references to 'the readers'.[78] The law before Magna Carta is not guessed at, in the way Fleetwood deplored, but taken from *Glanvill* and *Bracton*, or the *Dialogus de Scaccario*.[79]

Westminster I). In the preface to Fleetwood, *Justices*, sig. A8; CUL MS. Add. 3295, fo. 178v; he says that he has written a treatise *De Pace*, presumably c. 1 of Westminster I.

[70] Fleetwood, *Statutes*, discussed below, offers the same kind of observations on Merton, Marlborough, Westminster I and Westminster II as it does on Magna Carta, and these last were derived from the Magna Carta treatise: below, p. 233; Appendix 4, p. 466. Most of the references to readers, however, relate to Magna Carta.

[71] This was first identified in *Selected Readings on Magna Carta*, pp. lxxxiii–lxxxv.

[72] HLS MS. 15; *ELMUSA*, ii. 97

[73] CUL MS. Gg.6.18, fos. 3–41v; partly printed (with a translation) in *Selected Readings on Magna Carta*, pp. 366–92.

[74] Fleetwood, 'Miscellanea', fos. 14–17; printed in McGlynn, *Royal Prerogative*, pp. 133–7. It was obtained from the Fleetwood family in 1719 by John Anstis, Garter King of Arms: for its later devolution see J. H. Baker, *The English Legal Manuscripts of Sir Thomas Phillipps* (16 SS Suppl. Series, 2008), p. 196 (where 'MS. 82' should read 'MS. 86'). It also contains, on fos. 14–17, the preface and first chapter of Fleetwood, *Magna Carta*, and on fos. 159–161 a garbled report of some discussions at Fleetwood's Middle Temple reading of 1569: *Readers and Readings*, pp. 474–5.

[75] E.g. the reference to the mourning customs of the Russians: Fleetwood, *Magna Carta*, fo. 13v, *Selected Readings on Magna Carta*, p. 370.

[76] E.g. the citation of Chaucer for one of the meanings of disparagement: Fleetwood, *Magna Carta*, fo. 12v, *Selected Readings on Magna Carta*, p. 368.

[77] E.g. the laws of Canute: Fleetwood, *Magna Carta*, fo. 37, *Selected Readings on Magna Carta*, p. 387.

[78] Above, pp. 222–3. He even omitted the last two chapters because the readers did not deal with them: Fleetwood, *Magna Carta*, fo. 41v.

[79] Fleetwood, *Magna Carta*, fo. 18v, *Selected Readings on Magna Carta*, p. 373.

Moreover, as will be shown, some of the content was worked into the treatise on the interpretation of statutes which is unquestionably attributable to Fleetwood.[80] Unlike Fleetwood's later writings, it is written in French, albeit a degenerate law French which fails to hide the obvious fact the author spoke and thought in English. The badly blundered wording is perhaps attributable to Fleetwood's clerk. But the choice of language shows that the commentary was intended first and foremost as a work of jurisprudence aimed at lawyers, or perhaps merely for private use. The awkwardness of the wording no doubt persuaded Fleetwood that French was not an ideal medium for the English legal antiquary. The tract on the origins of English law, tentatively attributed above to Fleetwood, hinted that it was not ideal for lawyers either.[81] Dislike of French would have been consistent with Fleetwood's view of the Norman conquest as a brutal and unwelcome foreign interruption of English history.[82]

There are a number of internal clues as to the date. Although the author refers throughout to the king, this cannot refer to a king regnant. Lawyers in the reigns of Mary and Elizabeth sometimes referred to the 'king' when making general legal propositions about the monarch and the royal prerogative,[83] and when referring to permanent royal institutions such as the King's Bench.[84] The *terminus a quo* may be inferred instead from the citations: Polydore Vergil (1546),[85] the *Long Quinto*, referred to as the 'new 5 Edw. IV' (1552), *Glanvill* (c. 1554/55) and Staunford's *Plees del Coron* (1557), which are cited throughout with their page or folio numbers, and also a statute of 1554. *Bracton* is frequently cited, but without folio numbers, suggesting that the author was writing

---

[80] Below, pp. 233, 466.   [81] BL MS. Harley 4317, fo. 2v.

[82] This was often given as a reason for attacking the use of law French: J. H. Baker, *Manual of Law French* (2nd edn, Aldershot, 1990), p. 1. Both Fortescue and Polydore Vergil had attributed it to the Norman Conquest.

[83] This seems to be the point of Fleetwood's reference to the king's two bodies in the context of queenship: *Itinerarium ad Windsor*, pp. 36–8. Cf. George Bromley in his Inner Temple reading (1568) BL MS. Hargrave 33, fo. 160: (tr.) 'the king, or to speak more properly according to our times the queen, who is to us as a king and sovereign prince'. It was said that Elizabeth I would refer to 'our king', but could not bear others doing so: *The Diary of John Manningham of the Middle Temple 1602–03*, ed. R. Sorlien (Hanover, NH, 1976), p. 245. In 1613 Coke explained that 'king' in an Act of Parliament included a queen regnant, because the word referred to his politic capacity: 13 Co. Rep. 110.

[84] See *Raven v. Stockdale* (1587) Goulds. 87 ('the queen's majesty's court called the King's Bench'). Coke consistently called it the King's Bench.

[85] Cf. above, p. 224.

before its first printing in 1569, and there are no references to Plowden (1571).[86] The most likely date-range, therefore, is between 1557 and 1569. An argument for its being before November 1558 is that Elizabeth Woodville is referred to as 'the Queen Elizabeth', without distinction.[87] It most probably, therefore, dated from Fleetwood's earliest years as an utter barrister, when he was still immersed in law French. He later acknowledged that some of his other work contained too many errors for it to be printed,[88] and the same might fairly be said of the treatise on Magna Carta, unless the errors are entirely attributable to the copyist. There is no evidence that it circulated. It is nevertheless a work of great interest for present purposes. The content owed a good deal to the common learning of the inns of court, derived from manuscript readings, but also incorporated the result of Fleetwood's researches into histories and the earliest treatises on the common law.

Attention has been drawn elsewhere to the apparent mysogyny betrayed by the author as seemingly inconsistent with what is known of Fleetwood's character.[89] Women, he said, now that the Amazons were all dead, were 'imbecill de nature' (meaning that they were weak);[90] they were easily enticed into betrayal;[91] they could not be relied upon to refrain from marrying aliens, even when it was against the national interest;[92] sisters could not be trusted to bring appeals of felony, for 'such is the inconstancy of sisters, who often bury their grief along with the bodies of their friends';[93] like outlaws and infants, women could not be faithful witnesses because they were unsuitable;[94] and, as if those examples were not enough, there was the story of Queen Elizabeth Woodville, who 'contrary to her oath made to the Lady Margaret, not

---

[86] He made use of a manuscript *Bracton* in his treatise on Admiralty jurisdiction (*c.* 1568): Prichard and Yale, *Hale and Fleetwood*, p. xxv.

[87] Fleetwood, *Magna Carta*, fo. 36, *Selected Readings on Magna Carta*, p. 386.

[88] HLS MS. 15, fo. 188 (referring in 1581 to his treatise on the liberties of the forest, and to his reading of 1569 on liberties); *ELMUSA*, ii. 97; *Readers and Readings*, p. 479. Part of the first lecture on liberties, which is full of verbal errors, is in Fleetwood, 'Miscellanea', fos. 159–1.

[89] *Selected Readings on Magna Carta*, introduction, pp. lxx–lxxi. In *Justices* he removed passages in Marow's reading about the mistreatment of wives but left in the observation that wives could seek surety of the peace against their husbands. The protection of wives, however, was compatible with regarding women as inferior to men.

[90] Ibid. 370. [91] Ibid. [92] Ibid. 372. [93] Ibid. 386.

[94] Ibid. 383. Cf. Morice's reading (1578) in BL MS. Add. 36081, fo. 271, where women are classed with infants and idiots as unable to hold higher judicial office; but the reason seems to be that de facto they cannot become learned in the law.

remembering the murder of her sons, the bastardising of her issue, the slaughter of her brothers, the defaming of her husband, and her own danger, gave her daughter the hand of the cruel tyrant Richard III', a sorry tale which stood in the history books 'to the reproach of all women'.[95] This negative attitude to womankind may have been a passing Middle Temple fashion,[96] but it is strikingly at odds with the case made in Fleetwood's *Itinerarium ad Windsor* (1575) for the acceptability of female rule.[97] It had nothing to do with women's ordinary legal rights, since Fleetwood had no difficulty with the application of Magna Carta to women, and followed the old common learning in holding that *pueris* in chapter 18 and *homo* in chapter 29 were both gender neutral.[98]

The solution to this apparent paradox is itself historical. Fleetwood, in common with other Protestants, regarded the accession of Mary I as a disaster.[99] After the execution of Queen Jane it was a legal *fait accompli*,[100] and thereafter dissatisfaction with the succession could only be expressed in terms of the general unsuitability of women for government, a position supported by Calvinist philosophy and reinforced by the experience in Scotland with Mary of Guise and Mary, queen of Scots.[101]

---

[95] *Selected Readings on Magna Carta*, p. 386.

[96] Plowden, a fellow bencher (but a bachelor), argued that God made women inferior to men and that 'men are for the most part more reasonable than women': *Sharington v. Strotton* (1565) Pl. Com. 298.

[97] In addition to the commentaries in the 2013 edition of the *Itinerarium* see D. Moore, 'Recorder Fleetwood and the Tudor Queenship Controversy' in *Ambiguous Realities: Women in the Middle Ages and Renaissance*, ed. C. Levin and J. C. Watson (Detroit, 1987), pp. 235–51.

[98] Fleetwood, *Magna Carta*, fos. 25, 30v (*Selected Readings on Magna Carta*, pp. 380, 384). On the other hand, *heres* was ambivalent. While *heredes* in c. 6 included females, *heres* in c. 3 did not, because it was qualified by the later words *si ipse fiat miles*, and a woman could not be knighted: ibid., fos. 8, 12, *Selected Readings on Magna Carta*, p. 368; *Discourse upon Statutes*, p. 153; this was affirmed in *Doylie's Case* (1605) BL MS. Hargrave 19, fo. 203v, *per* Warburton J.

[99] See the comments of C. Beem in *Itinerarium ad Windsor*, p. 66.

[100] Mary had nevertheless, for good measure, caused Parliament to declare her a king: see J. Loach, *Parliament and the Crown in the Reign of Mary Tudor* (1986), pp. 96–7; J. D. Alsop, 'The Act for the Queen's Regal Power, 1554' (1994) 13 *Parliamentary History* 261–76; Baker, *OHLE*, vi. 61–2; Fleetwood, *Itinerarium ad Windsor*, pp. 33–6.

[101] See M. Levine, 'The Place of Women in Tudor Government' in *Tudor Rule and Revolution*, ed. De L. J. Guth and J. W. McKenna (Cambridge, 1982), pp. 109–23; C. Jordan, 'Woman's Rule in Sixteenth-Century British Political Thought' (1987) 40 *Renaissance Quarterly* 421–51; A. Shephard, *Gender and Authority in Sixteenth-Century England: The Knox Debate* (Keele, 1994); J. Richards, '"To Promote a Woman to Beare Rule": Talking of Queens in Mid-Tudor England' (1997) 28 *Sixteenth Century Journal* 101–21; A. Cromartie, *The Constitutionalist Revolution* (Cambridge, 2006), pp. 97–8.

The Amazons and Elizabeth Woodville had all featured in the previous political literature,[102] while Fleetwood's point about women marrying foreigners contrary to the national interest was obviously an allusion to Mary I's marriage with Philip of Spain. John Knox carried the argument to its extreme in his *First Blast of the Trumpet against the Monstrous Regiment*[103] *of Women* (1558), since he went so far as to advocate the deposition of female rulers. But Knox, like Fleetwood, actually respected women, and his book turned out to be very badly timed – he never redirected his blast, or issued further blasts, against Elizabeth I, whose accession happily disproved his thesis at the very moment of publication.[104] Once Mary of England was gone, attention could focus on Mary of Scots, and on the importance of preventing any possibility of her accession to the English throne. This resulted in some legal pamphleteering, to which Fleetwood contributed with great effect in the first half of the 1580s, besides pressing in Parliament for Mary's execution. He also composed an imaginary dialogue between two fictitious serjeants at law called Browne and Fairfax, concerning the difference between allegiance and feudal homage, and the nature of the law of succession to the crown.[105] This was intended as a response to the case put by his fellow Middle Templars Edmund Plowden and Sir Anthony Browne, and as a refutation of Mary's claims.[106] Serjeant Browne is presumably a thinly veiled representation of the late Sir Anthony Browne (died 1567), who was a judge but had been a serjeant around the time of Fleetwood's call to the bar, while Serjeant Fairfax is evidently Fleetwood himself, who was probably a serjeant (1580) by the time

---

[102] Elizabeth Woodville's wickedness had been emphasised in the histories by Thomas More, Edward Hall and Richard Grafton: see C. Levin and C. Beem in *Itinerarium at Windsor*, p. 161. Henry Howard, in his manuscript treatise 'A Dutiful Defence of the Lawful Regiment of Women' (1590), felt it necessary to his case to defend her: Shephard, *Gender and Authority*, p. 143.

[103] I.e. rule (*regimen*).

[104] Richards, 'Talking of Queens in Mid-Tudor England', at p. 116. The same was true of Thomas Becon, who had regarded the inheritance of the crown by Mary as a form of divine punishment: ibid. 113–14, 117.

[105] *Certain Errors upon the Statute ... of Children born beyond the Sea, conceived by Serjeant Browne and confuted by Serjeant Fairfax, in Manner of a Dialogue*. The autograph original is CUL MS. Add. 9212 (formerly-Phillipps MS. 2190; purchased in 1993 at the present writer's suggestion); *CELMC*, pp. 653–4.

[106] For the arguments by Plowden and Browne see M. Axton, 'The Influence of Edmund Plowden's Succession Treatise' (1974) 37 *Huntington Library Quarterly* 209–26; *The Queen's Two Bodies: Drama and the Elizabethan Succession* (1977).

he wrote it.[107] The dialogue was a tour-de-force of historical and comparative scholarship and requires further study. Evidently regarded as very important in its time,[108] it has been virtually over-looked until recently.[109]

Discourse on the Interpretation of Statutes

At the end of Fleetwood's treatise on justices of the peace, as printed in '1658' (1657), were appended some 'Instructions how and in what manner statutes are to be expounded'. According to the title-page, this was also by Fleetwood, though it has no relation to the subject of justices of the peace and has not been noticed in modern times as one of his works. The greater part of it is the same as the anonymous text edited by Professor Thorne in 1942 from two Ellesmere manuscripts, though Thorne was unaware of the printed version.[110] Seventeenth-century title-pages are untrustworthy, but the evidence shows that this almost certainly was another of Fleetwood's works. Like the commentary on Magna Carta, it is full of references to 'the readers', and it has the combination of learning and informality of tone which was the hallmark of Fleetwood's writing. There is less history than elsewhere in his work, but it is replaced by a subtle interest in philology.[111] Fleetwood had a particular interest in statutory interpretation, and it intruded into some of his arguments at the bar.[112] In two of them he

---

[107] He had discussed the same subject in his reading (1569): below, p. 255 n. 37. He also discussed it in the Commons in 1572: *Proc. Parl. 1558–81*, p. 398.

[108] At least twelve other copies are known, one of which (at Holkham Hall) belonged to Coke.

[109] The best account is by Brooks, *Law, Politics and Society*, pp. 74–8 (where the present writer's identification of the author is accepted as likely). There are brief mentions in K. Kim, *Aliens in Medieval Law: The Origins of Modern Citizenship* (Cambridge, 2000), pp. 170–1; K. Walton, *Catholic Queen, Protestant Patriarchy: Mary, Queen of Scots, and the Politics of Gender and Religion* (2007), pp. 76–7 (where Fairfax is differently identified).

[110] This was pointed out in *Thomas Hobbes: Writings on Common Law and Hereditary Right*, ed. A. Cromartie and Q. Skinner (Oxford, 2005), p. xxviii n. 4.

[111] E.g. the discussion of 'metonomia' (metonymy), illustrated by the use of *ecclesia* to mean sometimes the men of the Church and sometimes the ordinary: Fleetwood, *Statutes*, pp. 121, 123 (*Discourse upon Statutes*, p. 126). Cf. Fleetwood, 'Notes for Arguments', fo. 309v: (tr.) 'In the law of the land you will find various forms of speech, just as in the grammar you will find a figure called synecdoche.'

[112] And in the Commons. In 1571 he made a point about Magna Carta, c. 3, which is paralleled in the treatise: *Proc. Parl. 1558–81*, p. 236; Thompson, *Magna Carta*, p. 198.

set out to give examples of equitable interpretation,[113] one of which concerned the meaning of *alga* in a charter of King Stephen, a digression which enabled him, in a typical digression, to talk about Stephen's obsession with astrology.[114] Legal philology was admittedly not a taste peculiar to Fleetwood, and it had a parallel in humanistic jurisprudence on the Continent. But his authorship of the treatise is confirmed by the existence of two different versions, or drafts, in manuscripts known to have belonged to him.[115] And it is established beyond reasonable doubt by a comparison with the Magna Carta treatise. The 'Instructions' are full of examples illustrating the principles of interpretation as they applied to particular statutes. Some thirty-three of these examples are taken from Magna Carta, and all but four of them make points of interpretation which also occur in the tract on Magna Carta.[116] Even allowing for the fact that many of them were points of common learning to be found in the readings, this is too much for coincidence.[117]

Thorne considered the date of the Ellesmere version to fall within the range 1557–71. It makes internal references to Staunford's *Plees del Coron*, printed in 1557, but no mention of Plowden, printed in 1571, which contained some pertinent passages. A possible earlier terminus *ad quem* of 1567 was suggested on the basis of an annotation, in one of Egerton's copies, referring to Christopher Wray's reading of 1567; but that rested on the assumption that the annotation was coeval with the reading.[118] The 1657 version shows signs of revision, since the opening

---

[113] *Buttell* v. *Wilford* (c. 1580) BL MS. Harley 4717, fo. 159 (citing three examples from Plowden where statutes were expounded 'epicarie'); *Norris* v. *Alsop* (1586) BL MS. Harley 1331, fo. 14; MS. Add. 35944, fo. 2 (tr. 'Serjeant Fleetwood, recorder of London, put these cases to prove what exposition the justices have made of statutes according to *epieikeia* or equity, sometimes abridging them, sometimes enlarging their text'). See also the previous note.

[114] *Norris* v. *Alsop* (1586) BL MS. Add. 35944, fo. 2v: (tr.) 'thus they expounded the grants of King Stephen astronomically, because he did everything according to astronomy; for that king gave Sagittarius for the arms of England, since that was the sign which reigned when he was elected king, and refused the two lions which were the English arms'. This report is also in YLS MS. G.R29.6, unfol. The fictional Sagittarius coat of arms was first recorded in the fifteenth century in the Kings of Britain roll (College of Arms MS. Vincent 170).

[115] Below, pp. 234–6.   [116] See Appendix 4 for a concordance.

[117] The comment in Fleetwood, *Magna Carta*, fo. 15v, that *ballivus* (in c. 8) had to be understood as meaning an escheator, or other officer who seized lands in the king's name, can also be matched in another of his tracts: CUL MS. Dd.9.17, fo. 16v (where he says it means a sheriff).

[118] *Discourse upon Statutes*, p. 94.

pages there are clearly based on Plowden's report of *Partridge* v. *Strange*,[119] but this divergent matter certainly belongs to the Elizabethan period rather than the Interregnum.[120] Plucknett, reviewing Thorne's edition, suggested a later *terminus a quo* of 1563, on the basis that a reference to Archbishop Philpot's execution for heresy in 1555 was probably taken from Foxe's *Book of Martyrs* (1563), or at the earliest 1558, since Queen Mary is referred to in one place by name rather than as 'the queen'.[121] He also suggested that Thomas Egerton wrote it himself, a suggestion which Thorne had carefully avoided making, and this attribution has since been accepted by some writers without question.[122] Fleetwood's name had not then entered into the reckoning, and no texts beyond those in the Ellesmere collection had at that time been identified.

It is now clear that Plucknett made a wrong guess. Neither Thorne nor Plucknett was aware of the printed text of 1657, or of Fleetwood's commentary on Magna Carta, or of two further versions in manuscripts which actually belonged to Fleetwood. One of these last is in a volume containing fair copies of miscellaneous drafts by Fleetwood, some of them incomplete, which came into the possession of the city of London in the 1830s.[123] The volume had belonged to John Anstis, Garter King of Arms, who wrote on the front endpaper that the book was 'in the handwriting of the learned Serjeant Fleetwood' and that he had it from his heir, then knight of the shire for Buckinghamshire, in 1719.[124] This was John Fleetwood (d. 1745) of Missenden Abbey, who gave away several of the serjeant's manuscripts. The discourse on statutes, here entitled 'Expositio Statutorum', is virtually identical with the Ellesmere version except that the first two chapters of the latter occur before the

---

[119] *Partridge* v. *Strange* (1553) 1 Pl. Com. 77v at fo. 82, *per* Saunders sjt; this was first printed in 1571.

[120] The consequence of the interpolation is that the first twenty pages or so of Fleetwood, *Statutes*, and *Discourse upon Statutes*, do not collate with each other.

[121] T. F. T. Plucknett, 'Ellesmere on Statutes' (1944) 60 LQR 242–9; *The Legislation of Edward I* (Oxford, 1949), p. 15. The thesis assumes that the author would not have had first-hand knowledge of an event in 1555. Writing before Plucknett's review was published, M. Radin, 'Early Statutory Interpretation in England' (1943–4) 38 *Illinois Law Review* 16–40, at p. 17, said Egerton was probably not the author.

[122] E.g. Youngs, p. 31; L. A. Knafla, *Law and Politics in Jacobean England: The Tracts of Lord Chancellor Ellesmere* (Cambridge, 1977), p. 46.

[123] Fleetwood, 'Miscellanea', fos. 1–9v.

[124] It was one of several given to Anstis in that year. E.g. BL MS. Harley 5154 (n. 127, opposite) is inscribed 'This is Mr Fleatwoodes boke' and 'Mr Anstis A.D. 1719'.

title, followed by some Latin maxims which are not in the other versions.[125] All is written in the same Elizabethan hand. There is an early-seventeenth-century copy of the same text among the Hargrave manuscripts.[126]

More intriguing is the second Fleetwood manuscript, which was given away by the same John Fleetwood in 1743.[127] Pasted on the last page (fo. 495v) is a paper label which reads: 'Memorandum that I William Fletewoode serjaunt at the law and recorder of the cittie of London did collect and gather into titles this booke in anno 32 Elizabethe Regine et Anno Domini 1590.' It is an alphabetical commonplace, with some idiosyncratic titles characteristic of Fleetwood, such as 'Lou un batera le bushe et auter avera le birde' (fo. 79). The hand is extremely neat and uniform, including the label, and very different from the scrawl in which the serjeant wrote his periodic reports to Lord Burghley. Whether or not it was the work of an amanuensis, it was all transcribed at the same time, gathering under titles what presumably had previously been dispersed material written before 1590. The most voluminous heading is 'Statutes', which contains over fifty pages of instructions for expounding statutes ('Instructions coment et en quel maner statutes serront expoundes'). Like the rest of the volume these instructions are in law French, but the title and the first twelve leaves are otherwise the same as the printed treatise of 1657, including the quotations from Plowden.[128] The remaining twelve leaves, however, are quite different. They are much less sophisticated, and they are based on year-book cases rather than on examples taken from the statutes themselves. The text therefore presents something of a conundrum, even if we set aside the date of 1590 as referring to the collection and transcription rather than the composition. Were it not for the quotation from Plowden, it would seem to represent a much earlier version of the treatise, written in the law French of Fleetwood's student days before he had embarked on an

---

[125] They are omitted in the 1657 edition.

[126] BL MS. Hargrave 34, fos. 32–40v. The volume also contains (fos. 55–73) some reports of *Bate's Case* (1606) and (fos. 108–127v) a copy of Coke's then unpublished reports, from 1610 to 1613, taken (with omissions) from the autograph.

[127] BL MS. Hargrave 409, fos. 376–402. Two other commonplace books of Fleetwood's in the British Library (MSS. Harley 5153 and 5154) are also written in a clear hand; they display even greater industry but contain nothing beyond the year books.

[128] The French text is more accurate: below, p. 236 n. 131.

intensive study of the statute-book.[129] There is, indeed, only one solitary reference to Magna Carta in this version,[130] suggesting prima facie that it was written before the treatise on the charter which inspired so many of the passages in the longer version. The most probable explanation is that Fleetwood (or his clerk) in 1590 brought together under the same title his very first draft of the instructions, dating from the 1550s, and his much later draft of a new introductory section, necessitated by the publication of Plowden in 1571. What is certain is that the French version of the prefatory chapter preceded the English version of the text as printed, since the latter contains some mistranslations.[131]

The treatise on justices, with which the tract on statutes was printed, was altogether unrelated. It was presumably in the same manuscript exemplar used by the printer, but its date is too problematic to assist with the chronology of its partner. In a letter to Lord Burghley on 30 July 1577, Fleetwood said he was writing a treatise on justices and that it was almost finished.[132] Several versions of the text, however, refer to a charge delivered in 'this seventh year of the queen's reign', that is, 1565.[133] It can only be supposed that Fleetwood was revising an earlier work in 1577, probably by the addition of

---

[129] Plucknett, 'Ellesmere on Statutes', pp. 243–4, expressed puzzlement that the treatise as published was not written in law French, a circumstance which he thought pointed to a young author, fresh from Oxford and 'not yet broken in to the discipline of Lincoln's Inn learning'. But Plucknett had no first-hand knowledge of student notes and commonplace books from this period, which are invariably in law French.

[130] MS. Hargrave 409, fo. 382 (corresponding with Fleetwood, *Statutes*, p. 107), referring to c. 12; this is probably based on *Hill* v. *Grange* (1556) Pl. Com. 167 at fo. 178. There is also a question on fo. 363v, under 'Roy', whether c. 27 was an affirmation of the common law or something different from the law before the statute.

[131] E.g. 'le mitter al lettre del positive ley tiel sense' is rendered nonsensically as 'the matter of the letter of the law positive such a sense', mistaking *mitter* (putting) as *matter*.

[132] BL MS. Lansdowne 74(79), printed in *Queen Elizabeth and her Times*, ed. T. Wright (1838), ii. 64.

[133] Fleetwood, *Justice*, 72; BL MS. Harley 72, fo. 74v. See *CELMC*, p. 576. Other manuscripts are BL MS. Hargrave 15, fos. 70–80 (which does not include the preface or the charge; Hargrave identified it as Marow); MS. Add. 4518, fos. 262–77; MS. Add. 26749, fos. 348–74 (late seventeenth-century copy); CUL MS. Add. 3295, fos. 178v–182v (preface only); Somerset Record Office, MS. DD/WO/52/2; HLS MS. 5080; Urbana-Champagn MS. Phillipps 10406, fos. 3–20v; HEHL MS. FBL 30, fos. 80–90 (probably late sixteenth-century). The last is the manuscript which Putnam, *Early Treatises*, p. 211 n. 6, mentioned as belonging to the duke of Westminster at Eaton Hall (MS. 9); it was in the Eaton Hall sale at Sotheby's, 19 July 1966, lot 480, and was acquired in 1981 by FBL.

precedents of precepts, warrants and indictments.[134] It was not a very original piece of work. Apart from the precedents, it was taken almost verbatim from Thomas Marow's reading of 1503, monks and all, and Bertha Putnam castigated it as a 'thoroughly discreditable appropriation of Marowe's labours'.[135] But Fleetwood excused himself by saying, 'I have presumed, as no instructor, but as a rememberer, to clothe these things in English livery that have been hidden and obscured in scattered torn pamphlets, written and noted by our elders in the French tongue ... either never, or hardly read before.'[136] These were the same scattered torn pamphlets, containing the inns of court readings of the fifteenth and sixteenth centuries, which had formed the basis of Fleetwood's legal gloss on Magna Carta.

Fleetwood's Use of Readings

Readings in the inns of court were not generally treated as authorities to be cited in legal argument in the same way as cases. At any rate, they were not in practice cited very often.[137] Fleetwood was the only legal writer to make extensive explicit use of them, often referring to 'the readers' collectively,[138] though hardly ever by name.[139] Not that he was unduly deferential to them, or unaware of their shortcomings. Some of them he criticised for 'veigne et vagarant excursions',[140] and in 1575 he denied an opinion found in the readings as that of 'some table-talkers'.[141] Half a

---

[134] In BL MS. Harley 72 the treatise is followed by a large collection of precedents (fos. 76v–142v) dated between 1568 and April 1577. Many of them are in the name of Sir William K[ingsmill], a Hampshire JP, but on fo. 88v there is one dated 1581 with the name of Serjeant Fleetwood. The date-range would fit the hypothesis of a revision in 1577.

[135] Putnam, *Early Treatises*, p. 214.   [136] Fleetwood, *Justice*, preface, sig. A5v–A6.

[137] For exceptions see Baker, *Collected Papers*, i. 353 n. 6. Another example is *Bullock's Case* (1570) BL MS. Hargrave 15, fo. 21, where Dyer CJ cited an anonymous reading on the statute *Cum duo vel tres* (Westminster II, c. 22).

[138] In *Pagett's Case* (c. 1591) CUL MS. Ii.5.12, fo. 35, he cited Spelman's reading in court.

[139] Fleetwood, *Magna Carta*, fos. 15v ('les liers sembl[ount]'), 23 ('come les lierz diont'), 30 ('les lyers diount'), 34 ('les liers pur le greinder part diount'); *Discourse upon Statutes*, pp. 105, 107, 133, 134, 141, 142, 172. Cf. Fleetwood, *Justice*, p. 90, where he refers to Sir Robert Brooke's 'travel' (i.e. reading) on Magna Carta, c. 17.

[140] Fleetwood, *Magna Carta*, 14v, *Selected Readings on Magna Carta*, p. 371. He was referring to the readings on Magna Carta, c. 7, which glossed *pro dote sua* with a full account of the common law of dower; this, as Fleetwood rightly observed, was irrelevant to an understanding of the statute.

[141] CUL MS. Dd.9.17, fo. 14. There is an explicit disagreement with 'the readers' in *Discourse upon Statutes*, pp. 133–4.

century before Coke was lamenting the decline in their clarity and authority,[142] Fleetwood made a similar complaint about the artificially abstract formalism of 'our readers at this day':[143]

> in manner their whole readings consist in shewing who shall have the remedy, against whom, in what court, and all that gear, where they please themselves much if they can plant their cases into that square difference[144] that is like a square battle:[145] as to shew where the heir shall be in ward and pay relief, where he shall pay relief and not be in ward, where he shall be in ward and not pay relief, and where he shall pay two reliefs or be twice in ward. Those cases that hereupon may be multiplied, although they be infinite whereof there is no knowledge, yet for the most part they consist of these predicaments: *Res*, as to show the nature of the thing; *Persona*, who and against whom; *Locus*,[146] where, in what court, before whom; and *Qualitas*, and such. Of which, as I have said, for the most part the readers' differences do stand and consist.

Fleetwood's Notes for Arguments

A third relevant group of texts which has not previously been associated with Fleetwood is of a completely different character. At the end of a volume of Elizabethan law reports in the Hargrave collection is a set of notes transcribed from the working papers of a senior member of the Bar, evidently in preparation for arguments in about thirty cases between 1584 and 1591.[147] They are not reports taken in court but a combination of skeleton arguments, abstracts of pleadings translated from Latin into law French, and lists of authorities or historical materials. The only personal note is a reminiscence that the author argued a

---

[142] Co. Litt. 280 ('the cases are . . . liker rather to riddles than lectures . . . and the readers are like to lapwings, who seem to be nearest their nests when they are farthest from them, and all their study is to find nice evasions out of the statute').

[143] *Discourse upon Statutes*, p. 172; Fleetwood, *Statutes*, pp. 163–4.

[144] Or 'the squared differences' (Fleetwood, *Statutes*).

[145] This apparently refers to the marshalling of troops in square formations. In CUL MS. Dd.9.17, fo. 18, he says it was the function of the marshal 'to sett the battailles'.

[146] Instead of *Locus*, Fleetwood, *Statutes* has *Tempus, Quantitas*.

[147] BL MS. Hargrave 4, fos. 289v–342 (cited here as 'Notes for Arguments'), beginning with 'Cases collected pur framer un argument pur Mr Raynold Williams en brefe de disceipt vers Brewer'. The volume came from the Yelverton collection and is annotated throughout by Sir Henry Yelverton JCP (d. 1630).

case in the King's Bench – as a 'solicitor'[148] – in 1558.[149] Since some of the cases were in the Common Pleas, they must be the notes of a serjeant at law, and the heavy concentration on historical matter points most obviously to Fleetwood. Fleetwood is known to have argued in at least fifteen of the cases,[150] and the lack of evidence about the other half is attributable chiefly to the fact that the names of counsel are often omitted from the reports – and perhaps also, in this case, to some reporters' impatience with Fleetwood's digressions.[151] Further corroboration of Fleetwood's authorship is to be found at the end of the collection, where there is a copy letter signed by him on 26 October 1583, concerning weights and measures,[152] and a brief essay on the interrelation of matter in different statutes,[153] written in the manner of Fleetwood's tract on the interpretation of statutes. There are other distinctive passages, such as a brief discussion of 'the law of the crown', and a list of different kinds of law – including the laws of Oleron,

---

[148] Whatever 'solicitor' meant here, there was nothing incongruous in a barrister acting as a solicitor, since it was not yet a distinct profession.

[149] BL MS. Hargrave 4, fo. 297v ('as touching Whetston's case, that men so much speak of, I the writer hereof, being a solicitor in that case, did argue the same in the King's Bench anno ultimo Mariae before my Lord Saunders'). The case was *Whetston v. Nethway* (1558) (ibid. 298); cited as *Whetstone's Case* in 4 Leo. 159. The reference to 'the writer hereof' confirms that these are not reports of arguments as made, but preparatory notes.

[150] (1) *Skipwith v. Sheffield* [1584] on fo. 290r–v (see *Selected Readings on Magna Carta*, p. lxxii); (2) *Case of the Tallow Chandlers* [1583] on fos. 290v–293v (see below, p. 245); (3) identifiable as *Wilford's Case* [c. 1580] on fos. 294–305 (see below, p. 240); (4) *Dolman v. Bishop of Salisbury* [1583] on fos. 305v–306 (cf. Moo. 120; above, p. 221); (5) *Knowles v. Chantour* [?1582] on fo. 301r–v (said to have been argued by Walmsley and Fleetwood); (6) *Boughton v. Bishop of Coventry* (1583) (cf. above, p. 222 n. 39); (7) *R. v. Middleton* [1584] on fos. 313v–314v (cf. BL MS. Harley 4562, fo. 30v; MS. Harley 4779, fo. 205); (8) *Scrogges v. Lady Gresham* [1585] on fos. 317–318v (cf. BL MS. Harley 4563, fo. 48); (9) *Wiseman v. Barnard* [1585] on fo. 319 (cf. BL MS. Harley 4562, fo. 63); (10) *Rudhale v. Miller* [1586] on fos. 321v–324 (cf. 1 Leo. 298); (11) *Hollinshead v. Kinge* [1587] on fo. 324v (cf. 1 Leo. 284); (12) *Bishop of Exeter v. Specott* [1588] on fos. 325, 328–330v (cf. 3 Leo. 199); (13) identifiable as *Merifeilde v. Banister* (1588) on fos. 332–3 (see above, p. 222 n. 40); (14) *Brandon v. Morist*, or *The Chamberlain of London's Case* (1590) on fos. 335–6 (cf. 3 Leo. 264; BL MS. Harley 1633, fo. 181; MS. Add. 25200, fo. 20v); (15) *Jerome v. Neale* [1587] on fos. 330v–331v (cf. 1 Leo. 106).

[151] As to which see above, p. 221. Coke's second-hand report of *The Chamberlain of London's Case* (1590), previous note, in BL MS. Harley 6686, fo. 355v (5 Co. Rep. 62), omits Fleetwood's argument completely.

[152] BL MS. Hargrave 4, fo. 338v.

[153] Ibid. 339. Note also fo. 334 (tr.) 'Where a man shall be within the express words of the statute and yet he shall not be bound'.

treaties ('Leges Trewgas'), the laws of the sea ('Hydronomiae') and forest laws – both features which have parallels in Fleetwood's *Itinerarium*.[154] The most convincing evidence of all is that some of the passages written around 1583 in preparation for an argument against the charter of the Tallow Chandlers of London recur verbatim in Fleetwood's signed opinion on the same charter amongst the Burghley papers.[155] It is thus beyond question that these notes were copied up from Fleetwood's own loose papers. And, given the authorship, it is less surprising than it would otherwise have been to find that in eight of the cases there are references to Magna Carta,[156] far more than would be found in any volume of Elizabethan law reports.

There are a few similar notes for arguments in a Harleian manuscript which was also, almost certainly, Fleetwood's.[157] The volume contains a copy of Lambarde's *Archeion* dated 1579, and other historical tracts, and a lengthy collection of notes distilled from Middle Temple readers' cases and moots between about 1546 and 1550, the period when Fleetwood was first a student there.[158] The draft arguments are in the same style as those in the Hargrave manuscript, and are written in a mixture of English and a peculiar blundered law French reminiscent of Fleetwood's Magna Carta text.[159] One is an argument in the Exchequer concerning chantries, identified as 'The argument of Mr Recorder',[160] and this is related to a long series of notes in the Hargrave manuscript.[161] Another, arising from the same dispute, contains a historical and etymological account of the office of

---

[154] Ibid. 304v, 336; Fleetwood, *Itinerarium ad Windsor*, pp. 28–9.   [155] Below, p. 243.

[156] In one case it is the only citation: *Lord Cromwell* v. *Andrewes* (1589), at fo. 334v (c. 12).

[157] BL MS. Harley 4717.

[158] Ibid. 26–112v; omitted by oversight from *Readers and Readings*. The named readers are Bradbury [1546] (fo. 63), Catlyn [1547] (fo. 91), Carus [1548] (fo. 74) and Wood [1549] (fo. 48v). A dictum of Hynde J. [1545/50] is cited on fo. 78.

[159] Above, p. 227. Much of the blundering is evidently a result of miscopying and may therefore be attributed to Fleetwood's clerk. He was perhaps the 'Walker' whose name occurs at the foot of fo. 127v. The transcript of Lambarde's *Archeion* has the initials 'W W' at the head.

[160] *Buttell* v. *Wilford* (*c.* 1580) MS. Harley 4717, fos. 158–159v. A citation from the second part of Pl. Com. dates it after 1579, and it seems to be have been heard in 1580: 4 Co. Rep. 108 (Exchequer, 1580); Dyer 368; *Dyer's Notebooks*, ii. 379. The dispute began earlier: Dal. 113 (1574); LI MS. Maynard 87, fo. 224 (1577); 4 Leo. 156 (before 1579).

[161] BL MS. Hargrave 4, fos. 294–305. This is the case in which the writer recollected his own argument in *Whetston* v. *Nethway* (1558) (opposite, n. 149). The case is anonymous here, but cf. 4 Leo. 159, where *Whetston's Case* is cited in *Wilford's Case*.

dean, which has all the appearance of being one of Fleetwood's antiquarian excursions.[162] These are in a group of cases concerning superstitious uses, gathered at the end of the volume. Earlier in the volume is a draft argument on behalf of the Joiners' Company in support of a power to imprison which they claimed under their charter.[163] This case may be dated from other reports to 1582. The company's charter was impugned by the attorney-general, John Popham, relying on chapter 29 of Magna Carta, and defended by William Daniel of Gray's Inn.[164] The draft argument follows the same course as that attributed in the reports to Daniel, but it has all the characteristics of Fleetwood's draft arguments. In particular, there is a detailed refutation of Popham's argument based on chapter 29,[165] a balanced view of the great charter which matched Fleetwood's arguments elsewhere.[166] Chapter 29, in his view, required no more than that the law of the land be observed, and the law of the land was simply 'reason'.

Opinion on the Bridewell Charter

The Bridewell prison in London, noted for its summary punishment of prostitutes, seems to have become something of a law unto itself in the sixteenth century, and the jurisdiction exercised by the city officials there became a matter of concern at the highest level after an appalling incident of 1588.[167] An Elizabethan opinion, perhaps from that time, declaring the penal clauses of the Bridewell charter to be unlawful, is almost certainly another of Fleetwood's writings which places reliance on Magna Carta. It was printed anonymously in 1643 as *Briefe Collections out of Magna Charta*,[168] and later found its way into Bacon's *Works* on the strength of one manuscript

---

[162] Bl MS. Harley 4717, fos. 162v–166. The case involved the dean of St Paul's.

[163] Ibid. 123–128v.

[164] BL Hargrave 37, fo. 57; MS. Lansdowne 1072, fos. 129v–131 (same report); CUL MS. Hh.2.9, fos. 253–254v; same report, BL MS. Hargrave 6, fo. 70r–v; MS. Hargrave 8, fos. 105v–109; MS. Hargrave 9, fos. 105v–109; below, pp. 468–72.

[165] Printed below, pp. 472–6. Some of the points were made by Daniel in the reports.

[166] Below, pp. 247–8.

[167] Above, pp. 266–70. It was also the place where suspects were sent by the Privy Council to undergo interrogation under the torture of the manacles.

[168] *Briefe Collections out of Magna Charta; or, the knowne good old Lawes of England* (1643).

attribution, though the latest editor has declared Bacon a most unlikely author.[169] In two other manuscripts it is attributed to Fleetwood,[170] and this seems far more likely on grounds of style, context and content.[171] Fleetwood had been one of those instructed in 1577 to advise on the Bridewell charter, and the city did in fact modify its orders for Bridewell while he was recorder. The core of the writer's argument was that any charter repugnant to the maxims, customs or statutes of England was void; it could not be relied on in pleading, and it could be rescinded by *quo warranto* or *scire facias*. The king could not, for example, alter the rules of law, the form of a court, or the order of pleading or make a man judge in his own cause. The relevant statutes were Magna Carta and its progeny, in particular the 1368 statute of due process. The great charter had been confirmed many times by successive kings – a typical Fleetwood point[172] – and in its final chapter it was declared that anything done by the king or his heirs which infringed or weakened the liberties granted should be void. The Bridewell charter was repugnant to chapter 29 of Magna Carta because it gave a power of imprisonment without indictment or matter of record. It was analogous to the commission in the *Liber Assisarum* case of 1368.[173] Moreover, Empson and others had been indicted for proceedings contrary to Magna Carta,[174] and in the time of the present queen a commission to Sir Ambrose Cave and others to examine felons had been abandoned when the judges advised that it was against the law. Commissions to proceed by discretion, such as bankruptcy commissions or the High Commission, were authorised by statute, and such authorising statutes would have

---

[169] *The Oxford Francis Bacon*, vol. i: *Early Writings 1584–96*, ed. A. Stewart (Oxford, 2012), pp. 52–63, at pp. 55–60. The attribution to Bacon is in BL MS. Harley 1323. The editor (at pp. 41–4) also considered Fleetwood an improbable author, in view of his professional association with Bridewell as recorder of London.

[170] LMA, CLC/539/MS. 9384, fos. 1–9 (which was Phillipps MS. 2898, not 2892 as stated in the Oxford edition); Bodl. Lib. MS. Rawlinson D. 708 (which is not noticed in the Oxford edition). None of these manuscripts seems to be contemporary. The copy in FBL MS. 30, fos. 69v–71v, is in a late-sixteenth century volume which also includes Fleetwood's *Justice* (at fos. 80–90).

[171] This was also the view of Brooks, *Law, Politics and Society*, p. 418 n. 154.

[172] Below, p. 248.

[173] *Sir John atte Lee's Case* (1368) above, p. 58. Note also the citation of a little-known 1350 case, which Fleetwood also cited in two reported cases of 1583 and 1587: above, p. 58 n. 52.

[174] The opinion cites 1 Hen. VIII, c. 8, as to which see above, p. 100. Fleetwood mentioned Sheffield rather than Empson, but this was a slip.

been unnecessary if the king could have issued them under the prerogative.[175] A very similar argument had been deployed by Fleetwood in 1583 in attacking the charter of the London Tallow Chandlers.[176] The Bridewell opinion was almost certainly his as well.

Fleetwood's Approach to Magna Carta

Fleetwood's very full commentary on Magna Carta may have reflected its perceived importance at the time it was written, although it was only one of several commentaries which he wrote (or planned to write) on all the principal *Statuta Vetera*. Magna Carta thereafter became a favourite authority of his own, as may be seen from his forensic arguments in the 1580s. He could recount the background to the events of 1215, which he said (surprisingly) were well known even to those who knew nothing of history, and moreover – although he did not know exactly where Runnymede was[177] – he had seen a copy of the 'Statute of Runnymede' and compared it with 'the Magna Carta', meaning the charter of Henry III as confirmed by Edward I.[178] He noted in passing some of the differences between the 1215 and 1225 charters, but as a guide to the law his treatise was a commentary on the latter. He observed that the wording of legal documents had changed over time, and so, although *Concessimus Deo* in the opening chapter appeared literally to be a vow to God rather than a grant, it was the form of words used in grants to churches in earlier times and words should be construed according to the usage of times. At this point he could not resist adding the wry comment that one word in an ancient charter meant more than twenty in his own day.[179] He noted elsewhere that, although the operative words of grant (*concessimus has libertates*) referred only to liberties, the grant was equally good as to the many provisions which were not liberties.[180] The 1225 charter was, in any case, not merely a charter of grant, because it had been confirmed as a

---

[175] Fleetwood was himself an ecclesiastical commissioner, but it was only in the next decade that the point was raised whether the High Commission was merely statutory or derived from prerogative powers: above, p. 142.

[176] Below, p. 245.   [177] He placed it in Oxfordshire.

[178] See the preface, printed in *Rights and Liberties*, at p. 133.

[179] Fleetwood, *Magna Carta*, printed in *Rights and Liberties*, p. 135. He was later to expatiate on metonymy and synecdoche in statutory texts: above, p. 232 n. 111.

[180] Fleetwood, *Statutes*, p. 135 (*Discourse upon Statutes*, p. 132).

statute by the parliament at Marlborough.[181] Fleetwood dealt cursorily with the statutory provision of 1368 that 'every act of Parliament made against this statute should be void' by observing, 'so much was the said statute revered'.[182] It was an indication of reverence rather than a binding entrenchment. It could hardly be disputed that many of the provisions had been altered subsequently.

The commentary has an old-fashioned flavour, reflecting that of the obscure 'scattered torn pamphlets' on which so much of it was based, but enhanced with references to *Glanvill*, *Bracton*, and some less familiar historical sources. It follows the late-medieval tradition in that, however much the charter was to be revered, its text was no more sacrosanct than that of any other statute. The author does not hesitate to point out where provisions in the charter are void,[183] repugnant,[184] incomprehensible,[185] ambiguous,[186] impliedly repealed,[187] riddled with exceptions,[188] or unenforceable. Many of its provisions were not even new, but were merely affirmations of the common law,[189] and Fleetwood argued that where

---

[181] Fleetwood, 'Notes for Arguments', fos. 335, 336v, in connection with *Brandon* v. *Morist* (1590) and *Earl of Pembroke* v. *Earl of Hertford* (1591). Likewise the Carta de Foresta: Fleetwood, *Of Forests*, fos. 13v–14 (1571).

[182] Fleetwood, *Magna Carta*, fo. 3v, *Selected Readings on Magna Carta*, p. 367; 'Notes for Arguments', fos. 335, 336v (last note); 42 Edw. III, c. 1. As to its not being legally effective see opposite.

[183] E.g. Fleetwood, *Statutes*, p. 160 (*Discourse upon Statutes*, p. 166): 'So upon Magna Carta, c. 8, the words *non seisiemus* are void, and so upon Magna Carta, c. 14.'

[184] E.g. Fleetwood, *Magna Carta*, fo. 16; Fleetwood, *Statutes*, p. 135 (*Discourse upon Statutes*, p. 133); in this case the readers held c. 8 to contain a repugnancy, but Fleetwood disagreed.

[185] In Fleetwood, *Magna Carta*, fo. 33v, it is said of c. 31 (*habebimus aliquam escaetam*) that it was so obscure that no exposition may be made which is generally true.

[186] E.g. c. 11, *in certo loco*; this did not permit the Exchequer to hear common pleas, even though it was held in a certain place and its writs were returnable at Westminster: Fleetwood, *Magna Carta*, fo. 19r–v *Selected Readings on Magna Carta*, p. 374. Cf. Fleetwood, *Statutes*, p. 126: 'So *locus certus* hath been put for *species loci certi*: Magna Carta, c. 11.'

[187] E.g. Fleetwood, *Magna Carta*, fo. 25v; *Statutes*, p. 118 (c. 19 repealed by Westminster I, c. 32).

[188] E.g. c. 11, with respect to the jurisdiction of the King's Bench: Fleetwood, *Magna Carta*, fo. 19, *Selected Readings on Magna Carta*, pp. 373–4; *Discourse upon Statutes*, p. 122; argument in *Jerome* v. *Neale* (1588), below, p. 482.

[189] E.g. the passage quoted above, p. 223. Examples are given in Fleetwood, *Magna Carta*, fos. 7v, 8, 13. Cf. Fleetwood's common-place book, BL MS. Hargrave 409, fo. 363v (under 'Roy'): (tr.) 'Query whether this statute [Magna Carta, c. 27] is a confirmation of the common law, or whether by the common law before the statute the king would have had the wardship by reason of such tenures.'

Magna Carta merely affirmed the common law it remained possible for the law to alter over time in accordance with common reason.[190] Nor was any of it entrenched. Despite the statute of 1368, 'age, which all [men] can fret and bite, hath taken it away in many things'.[191] It was evidently still not worthy to be printed in letters of gold.

Fleetwood certainly perceived some important general principles in Magna Carta. In preparing his argument against the charter of the Tallow Chandlers in 1583, he concluded, presumably from chapter 29, that 'it is directly against the law that men should be restrained from their free marts etc. or that they ought to forfeit their goods, no law set down against them, or that their goods should be seized without due inquest, or that any imposition should be set upon their goods, being the *liberi homines de regno*, as Magna Carta termeth them'.[192] By virtue of the provision at the end of the great charter, that anything done by the king or his heirs against its terms should be void, it followed that any commission or charter could be impugned if it infringed Magna Carta; and to this effect he cited *Lee's Case* (1368) from the *Liber Assisarum*.[193] This was exactly the same argument which was deployed against the Bridewell commission a few years later,[194] though almost the direct opposite of that whereby he defended the charter of the Joiners' Company a year earlier.

Despite these broad claims about chapter 29, in none of Fleetwood's works is there a discernible theme of constitutional monarchy. On many points he was inclined to exalt the royal prerogative, which was protected

---

[190] Fleetwood, *Magna Carta*, fos. 7v–8 (on c. 3): (tr.) 'when a statute is but in affirmance of the common law, if common reason alters then the statute in affirmance of the common law likewise alters, as is well proved by innumerable contrary judgments in our books'. Cf. the weaker corresponding passage in Fleetwood, *Statutes*, p. 127 (*Discourse upon Statutes*, pp. 131–2).

[191] Fleetwood, *Statutes*, p. 125 (*Discourse upon Statutes*, p. 166). He gives as examples cc. 8, 12, 14.

[192] Fleetwood, 'Notes for Arguments', fo. 293v. He also relied on cc. 14 and 30. The same passage occurs verbatim in his signed opinion against the charter, on behalf of the mayor and aldermen of London, in the Burghley papers, BL MS. Lansdowne 38, fos. 2–6, at fo. 4. Together with Robert Snagge, he had opposed a bill in Parliament in 1581 in favour of the Tallow Chandlers: G. R. Elton, *The Parliament of England 1559–81* (Cambridge, 1986), p. 237. The company complained that Fleetwood had previously supported them, producing a letter of 9 December 1576 signed by him: MS. Lansdowne 38, fo. 7.

[193] For the case see above, p. 58. This seems to be the reverse of what was argued, perhaps by him (above, p. 241), in *Att.-Gen. v. Joiners' Company* (1582) BL MS. Harley 4717, fo. 127v; below, pp. 472–6.

[194] For the case see above, p. 266.

against Magna Carta because the 'law of the crown' was part of *lex terrae*.[195] His explanation of the dispensing power was that the king was 'above his laws',[196] recalling the *Rex est supra legem* of the Ordinary Gloss,[197] though of course this did not extend to *mala in se*.[198] He also argued that by the law of the crown the king might by patent under the great seal expound a statute in favour of a 'particular part of the realm' which might suffer a special mischief by reason of the generality of its words.[199] This might be seen either as an exercise of the dispensing power or as a form of Aristotelian equity, though it was an idiosyncratic contention. In his treatise on statutes he argued, contrary to Richard Hesketh's view at the beginning of the century,[200] that where Magna Carta abridged the king's prerogative it should be construed strictly.[201] And he would argue in the Commons in 1571, long before he was a queen's serjeant, that the queen had the power to commit members of Parliament to prison.[202]

What is noticeably missing from Fleetwood's commentary on chapter 29 is any sense that it effectively protected the liberties of the subject. It is true that he identified its core principle as being that 'the pleasure of the prince should no longer have the force of law, but that justice should be used, and that from thenceforth all should be adjudged by the law of the land',[203] which was a clear enough general

---

[195] For the various laws operative in England see Fleetwood, *Itinerarium ad Windsor*, pp. 27–8; above, pp. 225, 239. He mentions the law of the crown also in one of his tracts on forest law, Fleetwood, 'Miscellanea', fo. 39v; and in *Wilford's Case* (*c.* 1580) BL MS. Hargrave 4, fo. 294v; cf. above, p. 239.

[196] Fleetwood, *Statutes*, p. 161 (*Discourse upon Statutes*, p. 168): 'And here it might aptly be shewed how the king might dispense with his statutes, for he is above his laws, and may dispense with his laws.'

[197] Above, p. 86. Cf. Morice's reading (1578), fos. 16v–17 (above, p. 87 n. 79).

[198] He continued: 'but that is true in such things as are *mala prohibita* ... but for such statutes as have the force of a law, and bind all men generally, and every man especially ... that are made, as you would say, for a common wealth, with such things he cannot dispense.' This learning was taken from *Anon.* (1495) YB Mich. 11 Hen. VII, fo. 11, pl. 35, *per* Fyneux CJ; cf. *Dyer's Notebooks*, i. lii.

[199] *Wilford's Case* (*c.* 1580) in Fleetwood, 'Notes for Arguments', at fo. 294v.

[200] Above, p. 96.

[201] Fleetwood, *Statutes*, p. 155 (*Discourse upon Statutes*, p. 161), commenting on c. 27. The point is not made explicitly in the commentary on c. 27 in Fleetwood, *Magna Carta*, fo. 29.

[202] *Strickland's Case* (1571) cited in *Itinerarium ad Windsor*, pp. 72–3.

[203] Fleetwood, *Magna Carta*, fo. 30v, *Selected Readings on Magna Carta*, p. 384.

statement of the rule of law.[204] Moreover, he held that *liber homo* was
to be taken broadly as including women, and even villeins,[205] except
in relation to trial by peers, which was extended to women only by
statute. But for Fleetwood, as for his precursors, the chapter was not
very effective. Trial by peers did not yet mean trial by jury,[206] and
Fleetwood did not explain how *judicium parium* fitted in with the rest
of the clause. The promise not to sell or delay justice was given very
limited scope, since it referred only to charging fees for writs of right.
For good measure, Fleetwood pointed out that people could in various
cases be imprisoned without any process, let alone due process, as
when they were arrested on suspicion of a felony, because such powers
of arrest were permitted *per legem terrae*. This was standard learning,
drawn from the readings. But his most significant conclusion was that
there was no remedy for deprivation of liberty other than the
common-law action of false imprisonment. The connection with
habeas corpus had not yet been made.

Fleetwood took more interest in Magna Carta than any of his contemporaries, and did all he could to promote its reputation. He approved of a
speech of 1554 in which Ralph Skinner, dean of Durham, praised Magna
Carta as a sacred text provided for the people of England by God.[207] He
adopted Roger of Wendover's saying in the early thirteenth century that
no one should write against it, and asserted that he had never read a case
which impugned it.[208] He 'stood long in proving that it was a sacred
statute' even when it 'seemed to make against him'.[209] He pointed out,
when it suited his case, the provision in the charter itself that anything

---

[204] In *Selected Readings*, introduction, p. lxxxv, there is an unfortunate misinterpretation.
The text on p. 384 was read as confining the whole clause to peers of the realm, because
it jumps from *Nullus liber homo* to *judicium parium* without a break, but 'not of every
male' must have been intended to refer only to *pares* and not *liberi homines*.

[205] The general point is made under c. 15 (*Nec villa, nec homo*, which Fleetwood read as
liber homo) in Fleetwood, *Magna Carta*, fo. 23: (tr.) 'nor indeed a villein, for as I have
suggested already, in the first chapter, *liberum* is many times understood in these statutes
as someone who is inheritable to the law, even though he is a villein de sank'.

[206] A detailed reading on trial by jury was given by Thomas Williams in the Inner Temple in
1558, praising it above all other forms of trial in the world, but it did not occur to him to
connect it with Magna Carta. He traced its origins instead through *Glanvill* and 'the
famous Bracton' (p. 6): *The Excellency and Praeheminence of the Laws of England above
all other Humane Lawes in the World asserted in a Learned Reading upon the Statute of
35 H. 8. cap. 6* (1680).

[207] Fleetwood, *Itinerarium ad Windsor*, p. 34. Skinner was speaking in the House of Lords in
1554 on the bill for the queen's regal power.

[208] *Collett* v. *Webbe* (1587) below, pp. 263, 477.   [209] *Collett* v. *Webbe* (1587) below, p. 477.

contravening it should be void.[210] Above all, he was remembered –
especially by Coke – for his saying that Magna Carta had been confirmed
by the king in Parliament over thirty times.[211] On the other hand, he was
ready to point out that it was not an elixir which could win all arguments.[212] Some of it was no longer in force, some of it had little practical
effect, and some of it was construed differently from the normal meaning
of its words. His detailed explanation of the great charter in the commentary, written early in his career, was the culmination of two hundred
years of critical exegesis in the inns of court, and a critical synopsis of the
old common learning. Yet even the most intense legal, historical and
philological analysis of the text could not by itself uncover the hidden
glories that were yet to be revealed. The Magna Carta of the Jacobean
lawyers had still not, it seems, been discovered by the start of the
Elizabethan age. Fleetwood lived long enough to observe the first strides
on the new journey, but he did not himself lead the expedition or provide
the map.

---

[210] *Brandon* v. *Morist* (1590) in Fleetwood, 'Notes for Arguments', fo. 335; BL MS.
    Add. 25200, fo. 20v.
[211] See below, p. 264.   [212] See, e.g., *Collett* v. *Webbe* (1587) below, p. 477.

7

The Resurgence of Chapter 29 after 1580

So many questions about the prerogative were stirred in the reign of Elizabeth I that Lord Buckhurst, towards the end of her reign, asked John Dodderidge of the Middle Temple to prepare a detailed treatise on the subject. As might be expected of a common lawyer with an Oxford degree and an interest in history, Dodderidge prepared a thoughtful and intricate scheme, which would have taken account of foreign authors, such as Machiavelli and Bodin,[1] Roman lawyers, and histories, as well as English legal sources.[2] The prospect of composition was daunting, not least because it was politically dangerous: as Dodderidge put it, 'He that heweth overhead shall have chips to fall in his eyes.'[3] Dodderidge was unwilling to undertake the labour himself, and there is no evidence that anyone else did, but the project demonstrates how topical and controversial the subject had become during the previous generation. It was not, however, a result of new claims founded on Magna Carta. Counsel were often warned not to dispute the prerogative,[4] and – to judge from the arguments outlined in Chapter 5 – Magna Carta was not part of their regular armoury before the 1580s.

There are occasional sightings of the charter, it is true, but they are few and fleeting. In 1554 James Dyer attributed to chapter 29 the principle

[1] Jean Bodin's *Six Livres de la Republique* (1st edn, Paris, 1576) was well known among common lawyers. Fleetwood, Coke and Egerton all had copies. A detached title-page from the second edition (Paris, 1583) with the signature 'Tho: Egerton Lincoln[iensis] 1593', taken from an old album, is in the writer's possession.

[2] The scheme survives: BL MS. Harley 5220. The dedication to Lord Buckhurst and the mention of the queen show it must have been written between 1599 and 1603. A passage on fo. 21 shows that Dodderidge intended the work to be carried out by others, who were to be provided with books, access to records, and help from the queen's counsel.

[3] Ibid. He quoted the same proverb in *Darcy v. Allen* (1602) Moo. 671 at p. 672; BL MS. Add. 25203, fo. 572. It was of medieval origin.

[4] Note the reminiscences by Serjeant Fleetwood (above, p. 191 n. 278), James Morice (above, p. 142), and Nicholas Fuller (*Proc. Parl. 1610*, pp. 156–7). Francis Bacon, as a law officer, was in the habit of trying to have his adversaries silenced: e.g. below, pp. 400, 404, 422.

that every subject had a right of access to the king's courts, 'whether bond or free, woman or infant, religious, outlawed or excommunicated'.[5] And yet, although Dyer was chief justice of the Common Pleas from 1559 to 1582, and while in office set some important precedents which inspired Coke, particularly in relation to *habeas corpus*, he did so without any reference to Magna Carta.[6] His colleague Saunders CB was another chief who had expressed concern about abuses of the prerogative,[7] but when he was asked by the Privy Council, early in Elizabeth's reign, to advise on the availability of prerogative banishment, it did not occur to him to deal with the clause 'no free man shall be exiled' in chapter 29.[8] In 1561 the Southampton charter as to malmseys was challenged by Christopher Wray as an infringement of Magna Carta, citing chapter 30 (concerning merchants) as well as chapter 29, though the outcome was unclear.[9] Wray became chief justice of England in 1574, but did not mention chapter 29 in any of his reported judgments. In 1572, upon an application for *habeas corpus* to the mayor of Exeter, Edmund Anderson of the Inner Temple explicitly made the link between that remedy and chapter 29,[10] an association which thereafter became common currency. Yet when, as chief justice of the Common Pleas, he helped prepare the memorial to the queen on *habeas corpus*,[11] he did not include any reference to it. In 1582 John Popham, as attorney-general, cited chapter 29 in challenging a power of imprisonment claimed by a London livery company;[12] it was as useful to the crown, looking downwards, as to the subject, looking upwards. In a rare 'upward' use of chapter 29, Mounson J. cited it in 1575 in denying the right of the crown to stay execution of a judgment at law until its own debts had been paid.[13] But it was only in the later 1580s that chapter 29 burst into prominence. To find an explanation for this, or at least clues which might lead to an explanation, it is necessary to return to the inns of court.

---

[5] *Anderson v. Warde* (1554) Dyer 104.   [6] Above, pp. 156–63.   [7] Above, p. 157.

[8] BL MS. Harley 6850, fo. 320. This is endorsed 'My lo[rd] chef baron' and seems to date from the first half of the reign. There is no internal clue as to authorship. Saunders was CB 1559–76.

[9] *Att.-Gen. v. Donatt* (1561) above, p. 190; the citation is in BL MS. Hargrave 37, at fo. 87.

[10] *Marshall's Case* (1572) HLS MS 1192, fo. 25.   [11] Above, p. 167.

[12] *Att.-Gen. v. Joiners' Company of London* (1582) below, pp. 468, 472. Popham had also cited Magna Carta in the Commons in 1571, in relation to monopolies: *Proc. Parl. 1558–81*, p. 211.

[13] *Manser v. Annesley* (1575) above, p. 180.

Robert Snagge's Reading

A new interest in the wider possibilities of chapter 29 was awakened in 1581, when a reading devoted to that chapter was given in the Middle Temple by Robert Snagge.[14] Only one of the lectures remains, together with some of the disputations. Although most of the reading itself is lost, we know from the notes of a student what the headings were:[15] (i) who shall be called a free man, and in what respects; (ii) what expulsions from freehold are a disseisin within this statute and what not; (iii) what denial or disturbance of liberties and customs is a disseisin of liberties and franchises; (iv) what takings, arrests or imprisonments are prohibited by this statute and what not; (v) what shall be 'destruction' within this statute; (vi) what shall be a trial by peers, and what a lawful judgment, within this statute. This lecture-syllabus suggests a traditional legal analysis, phrase by phrase, but there are indications that its content made radical departures from the older tradition discussed in chapter 3. The only part to survive is a highly polished section dealing with the Chancery, which Snagge worked up separately in 1587 for presentation to Sir Christopher Hatton on becoming lord chancellor.[16] It looks like a seventh topic, 'what shall be called the law of the land within this statute', since an exposition of 'the law of the land' (*lex terrae*) would naturally follow 'judgment of his peers'.[17] It was therefore probably the final lecture, unless he went on to deal with delaying and selling justice. He posed the question whether the law of the land included the equity of the Chancery, given that, on the face of it, the chancellor's extraordinary jurisdiction was outside or beside the law. The answer, inevitably, was in

---

[14] *Selected Readings on Magna Carta*, pp. lxxxii–lxxxiii, 256–64; *Readers and Readings*, p. 166. In *Readers and Readings*, p. 540, there is mention of a lost 'manuscript' in the Middle Temple Library; this was in fact almost certainly a copy of the printed book of 1654 (below, n. 16), though it is no longer to be found in the Library.

[15] They follow exactly the wording of c. 29 (translated above, p. 32).

[16] The only text is *The Antiquity and Original of the High Court of Chancery and Authority of the Lord Chancellor of England*, ed. T. L. (1654); *Readers and Readings*, pp. 610–11. The 1654 title-page gives the date as Lent 13 Eliz., which is a mistake for 23 Eliz., and the reader is wrongly referred to as 'Serjeant Snagg'. The serjeant was Robert Snagge's brother Thomas, who read in Gray's Inn in autumn 1574 and autumn 1580. The printed edition correctly says that the reading was in the Middle Temple, and its date is confirmed by the reader's preface, in which he says he was of twenty years standing when elected; Robert Snagge was admitted in 1560. The title-page also said the subject was c. '28', though it was c. 29 in the usual numbering.

[17] One would have expected him to continue with the last clause, deferring and delaying justice, and it is possible that he intended to do so, though no trace of this has survived.

the affirmative. Snagge had concluded, on looking into the history of English law, that the Chancery must always have been part of the law of the land and that equity was an indispensable feature of the system.[18]

Legal history was central to Snagge's thinking,[19] and its importance was pursued in the preface addressed to Hatton. Like his contemporaries, Snagge believed that English law was a form of immemorial custom, but that it had been disturbed in its operation by the Norman conquest and therefore needed to be restored to its right course in the thirteenth century.[20] This is how he put it:[21]

> That will-government in the kings, discontentment in the nobility, and continual wars within the realm, continued until King Henry III, who (being by that time by divers descents purged and purified by our English air, and by education after the order of our nation, and so become English, and of a better nature than the aliens and their offspring), of love to his subjects, was content to allow Englishmen their English laws. And thereupon, the tenth day of February in the ninth year of his reign, granted under his great seal the great charter, thereby to restore the laws of the land and the liberties of the subjects, and to limit his prerogatives so as they should be prejudicial to neither.

Forgetting his early good intentions, and presumably his innate English-ness, Henry III had subsequently been dragged into another civil war, but then in 1267 Magna Carta was given permanent statutory force in the Parliament at Marlborough. According to Snagge, the ancient laws and liberties were thereby revived and restored, and the charter (in its statutory form)[22]

> hath been by all kings and queens solemnly sworn at their coronations to be kept, and so hath been sacredly observed to this day (unless some forgetfulness in some kings, and ignorance in some officers, hath infringed the same). But now, by God's blessing plentifully poured upon it, it is in full use, to the great comfort of all good subjects, and immortal fame of her most excellent majesty.

---

[18] Snagge's treatment of the Chancery is discussed in D. R. Klinck, *Conscience, Equity and the Court of Chancery in Early Modern England* (Farnham, 2013), pp. 89–93. For the view that the Chancery was coeval with the common law see also Hake, *Epieikeia*, p. 133.

[19] He knew his ancient sources and could be found citing *Bracton* in argument: *Cordell v. Leake* (1584) BL MS. Harley 4562, fo. 11v ('Snagge de Medio Templo').

[20] Cf. Lambarde, *Archeion*, p. 62, where Magna Carta is described as 'the first letters of manumission of the people of this realm out of the Norman servitude'.

[21] Snagge, *Antiquity of the Chancery*, pp. 8–9.   [22] Ibid. 8–11.

It became an enduring belief that Magna Carta was mentioned in the coronation oath, even though it was not – at least, not by name.[23] It was enough that it should have been. And it became an equally powerful belief that it embodied law which was firmly rooted in ancient English history, long before the Norman conquest – as old as human reason itself. The myth was beginning to develop. Snagge's history embodied the very sentiments to be made familiar by Coke and others in the parliamentary debates of the 1620s. Chapter 29 was the most important piece of English legislation ever, a guarantee of liberty under the law, a source of national pride and popular reassurance. But in 1581 this seems to have been a new way of thinking. So far as we know, chapter 29 had never before been the subject of a whole reading, and had rarely been mentioned in court, whereas within a few years it would be on everyone's lips. There is no need to suppose that Snagge was individually responsible for its resurrection, but it was evidently a pivotal moment in the life of Magna Carta, now nearly four hundred years of age. Some more specific explanation for this is needed.

The principal clue is the character of the reader himself. Snagge was a truculent member of Parliament with Puritan leanings.[24] From 1571 to 1583 he was a prominent figure in the Commons,[25] and as early as 1572 he had joined with Tristram Pistor of the Middle Temple in promoting an unsuccessful toleration bill for nonconformists.[26] He spoke

---

[23] The oath as laid down by a statute of Edward II did refer to upholding the laws of St Edward (King Edward the Confessor), which some thought meant the same thing: see Sir Roger Owen's treatise on the common law (*c.* 1615), BL MS. Harley 6605, fos. 59v–60; and Francis Ashley's reading (1616), fo. 3. But this reference had disappeared by the time of Henry VII: *English Coronation Records*, ed. L. G. W. Legge (Westminster, 1901), p. 230. It was not in Henry VIII's oath as copied in BL Cotton MS. Tiberius D VIII, fo. 89. It may have been in James I's oath: *Calvin's Case* (1608) Hawarde 353, *per* Walmsley J. It was back in James II's oath, save that it now only referred to the laws and privileges granted to the *clergy* by St Edward.

[24] For the inadequacy of the term 'Puritan' see below, p. 256 n. 40. No attempt will be made here to place individual lawyers precisely on the wide religious spectrum. Snagge is referred to by historians of Parliament as a Puritan, but in the preamble to his will, made in 1599, he made a point of professing his faith in the form set down in the 1571 Articles of the Church of England, 'whereof I am a member': PCC 31 Stafford. Rather surprisingly, he also mentioned Archbishop Whitgift among his friends.

[25] He was known colloquially as Robin (*Proc. Parl. 1558–81*, p. 318), and this form of his name was used by Sir John Neale.

[26] P. Collinson, *The Elizabethan Puritan Movement* (1967), p. 119 (where they are said to have been called 'ardent irresponsibles'); *Proc. Parl. 1558–81*, pp. 362–3. Snagge and Pistor both entered the Commons in 1571: *The History of Parliament: The House of Commons 1558–1603*, ed. W. Hasler (1981), iii. 224–5, 408–9. For Pistor's membership of

fervently in the House against the duke of Norfolk and Mary, queen of Scots.[27] He attacked the notion that the queen could not be tried because of the *jus gentium*, saying 'What have we to do with *jus gentium*, having law of our own? Shall we say our law is not able to provide for this mischief?'[28] His impassioned speeches may not always have been altogether coherent, and one of them caused him difficulties in 1571 when it was misrepresented as an attack on the Lords.[29] One may guess something of his personality from the fact that he had been put out of commons by the Middle Temple in 1570 (not for the first time) for being rude to Fleetwood while arguing a case at the Guildhall,[30] and again in 1573 for contumacy, and yet again in 1578 for insolence towards another bencher; when he was readmitted in 1581 it was on condition of behaving quietly and moderately.[31] He had suggested in the House of Commons in 1571 that there should be an investigation of religion in the inns of court with a view to further reformation,[32] which was hardly the best way to court universal popularity among his fellows. So many feathers had been ruffled in his inn that it was touch and go whether he would be allowed to read at all in 1581. The benchers were minded to pass over him, but they were forced to give way on receipt of letters from the Privy Council, probably at the instance of Snagge's supporter, Lord Burghley. He was obliged to share the reading with the inn's preferred candidate, but it seems nevertheless to have been a memorable fortnight. Dyer CJ attended, with two puisne judges (Peryam and Mead), all former Middle Templars. Snagge said he had selected chapter 29 for his text because it contained, 'as it were, the sum of all the charter and Act, and the whole mark that was shot at, to revive the ancient laws and restore the ancient

---

the Middle Temple see *The Men of Court*, ii. 1283 (Pystor). In 1587 Snagge appeared as counsel for some 'recusants', probably meaning Puritan recusants: BL MS. Harley 1693, fo. 99v.

[27] J. E. Neale, *Elizabeth I and her Parliaments 1559–81* (1952), pp. 251, 265, 275, 278, 284, 286–7.

[28] *Proc. Parl. 1558–81*, p. 324.

[29] Neale, *Elizabeth I and her Parliaments 1559–81*, pp. 200, 305–7.

[30] Fleetwood referred to Snagge as 'my fellowe' in a letter of 1575, but this meant no more than that he was a fellow member of the Middle Temple: BL MS. Lansdowne 20(8), printed in *Queen Elizabeth, her Life and Times*, ed. T. Wright (1838), ii. 20.

[31] *Middle Temple Records: Minutes of Parliament*, vol. i, ed. C. H. Hopwood (1904), pp. 151, 154, 173, 193, 228. He was apparently put out of commons even while a bencher (in 1586), but complained to Burghley that the occasion was his having expelled from his chamber a younger member who, while acting as his clerk, had used the key to his study to obtain documents for his adversary: BL MS. Lansdowne 51, fo. 15.

[32] *Proc. Parl. 1558–81*, p. 207.

liberty and liberties to the subjects'.[33] But why this emphasis on legal history and restoring ancient liberties? One of Snagge's cases concerned a hypothetical duke of Norfolk, a queen of Scots, and a trial for treason, and it is possible that he chose chapter 29 for the opportunity of arguing that it did not stand in the way of the real Queen Mary's trial and execution.[34] It was indeed a matter of anxious consideration five years later how Mary should be named in the commission to try her, since describing her as a queen might prove fatal.[35] There was a similar discussion by a fellow bencher, Richard Crompton, around the same time,[36] and it may have become a recent tradition to discuss the point in the inns of court.[37] But more likely Snagge's object was something larger. Chapter 29 had recently been identified by the 'Puritan' circle of lawyers as a potent weapon of defence against the growing activity of the Court of High Commission.[38]

Puritans and the Law

The earliest public hint that chapter 29 might be deployed in the context of the High Commission had been dropped in the reading given by James Morice in 1578.[39] Morice was another Middle Templar with Puritan

---

[33] Snagge, *Antiquity of the Chancery*, pp. 11–12.

[34] *Selected Readings on Magna Carta*, pp. liv–lv, 263–4.

[35] It was decided at a conference on 30 October 1586 by Manwood CB, three puisne judges and the law officers that it should be 'Mary, daughter and heir of James V, late king of Scotland, commonly called queen of Scots and dowager of France': BL MS. Lansdowne 50, fos. 57–63, at fo. 63 (tr. from Latin).

[36] R. Crompton, in *A Declaration of the End of Traytors* (1587), sig. Div-Dii. Crompton referred to a resolution of all the judges, as to which see *Dyer's Notebooks*, ii. 256.

[37] Fleetwood, at his Middle Temple reading in 1569, put the case that an Englishman married a Scotswoman in England, they had issue in Scotland, and the king granted the son the earldom of Northumberland in tail mail with palatine authority; he concluded that the son took nothing at all by the grant: Fleetwood, 'Miscellany', fo. 159. (Cf. his treatise on children born beyond the sea, above, p. 231.) In 1566 William Thornton of Lincoln's Inn had been punished for touching on the queen of Scots in his reading: above, p. 108 n. 204.

[38] As to which see above, pp. 133–43. The role of the Puritans in 're-creating' Magna Carta was noted with her usual perceptiveness by Thompson (*Magna Carta*, pp. 144, 198), and her account has prompted the suggestion that there was an Elizabethan beginning to the English 'revolution': N. Tyacke, *The English Revolution c. 1590-1720: Politics, Religion and Communities* (Manchester, 2007), pp. 11–14. See also A. Cromartie, 'Puritans and Anglicans' in *The Constitutionalist Revolution* (Cambridge, 2006), pp. 115–47.

[39] For what follows see *Selected Readings on Magna Carta*, introduction, pp. lxxxv–lxxxviii. The name is there spelt Morice, following the principal manuscript, but Morice usually spelt his name with a single 'r'. The principal text is BL MS. Egerton 3376, a redaction

sympathies, strongly opposed to the arbitrary jurisdiction of the commissioners and the oath *ex officio*, and he would soon become one of the
foremost supporters in the Elizabethan House of Commons of individual
liberties under the common law. Like many of the strongly Protestant
lawyers, he was highly respected and by no means on the outer fringes of
the law.[40] Patronised by Lord Burghley, he became attorney-general of
the Court of Wards in 1589 and was even proposed for attorney-general
in 1593. He was to achieve fame in the 1590s as counsel in *Cawdray's
Case*,[41] and wrote a treatise against the oath *ex officio* which engendered a
pamphlet controversy with Dr Cosin.[42] The reading of 1578, an edited
version of which was dedicated to Burghley, shows that he was already
formulating his constitutional views some years before entering Parliament. Interestingly, however, it was not given on Magna Carta. The
message would be delivered less directly. Morice chose as his text chapter
50 of Westminster I. No one else had ever read on it. It was a brief saving
of the rights of the crown, inserted at the end of the statute of 1275, but it
provided an ideal vehicle for Morice's purpose. He could show his loyalty
by lecturing on the rights of the crown, beginning with a spirited defence
of constitutional monarchy as preferable to democracy ('the government
of the inconstant, rude and ignorant multitude') or aristocracy (which
tended to be torn by faction).[43] Then, as he enumerated and discussed
the many undoubted prerogatives of the crown, he could insinuate his
constitutional points from time to time as qualifications, savings to be
read into the saving clause. It was in these savings-within-savings that
Morice's underlying message was conveyed.

---

prepared at the instance of Lord Burghley. There is a partial autograph version is BL MS.
Add. 36081, fos. 229–74. Arguments on some of the reader's cases are reported in BL MS.
Add. 16169, fos. 39–57.

[40] It has been a convenient shorthand for historians to refer to 'Puritan' clergy, lawyers or
members of Parliament, even though some of them were only mild nonconformists or
reformists. There was no such thing as a Puritan party, let alone a distinct sect, by the end
of Elizabeth's reign. The epithet became a term of abuse applied to men who were not
Puritans in any definable religious sense. It has been said that, when it ceased to be
connected with specific religious tenets, it denoted rather 'the spirit of progress in every
line of human endeavour': Usher, *Reconstruction*, i. 244–6.

[41] Above, pp. 141–3.   [42] Below, p. 274.

[43] For this part of the reading see C. W. Brooks, 'The Ancient Constitution in Sixteenth-
Century Legal Thought' in *The Roots of Liberty: Magna Carta, Ancient Constitution, and
the Anglo-American Tradition of Rule of Law*, ed. E. Sandoz (Missouri, 1993), pp. 75–114,
at pp. 92–4; *Law, Politics and Society*, pp. 79–81.

It was the first principle of constitutional monarchy, according to Morice, that the king could not dissolve or change laws without the consent of the ruled. It followed that the king could not by letters patent, or charter, make new law which affected the lives or lands of his subjects. It was true that he could grant positive liberties affecting their lives and lands, for this was the reason why Henry III could 'make and establish the laws and ordinances contained in the great charter of England'. But he could not alter the law. Thus, although he could create new local or private jurisdictions by charter, they had to follow the common law. And he could not validly grant to an individual a monopoly in a common trade or traffic, or make any occupation private unto a few. Nor could he change the law by proclamation. There were certain affairs which the king could properly regulate by proclamation, such as war and coinage. But he could not, according to Morice, by the prerogative alone, command subjects to find men at arms and armour, or to go overseas, in defence of the realm. Above all, he could not levy money or take goods for the necessary affairs of the realm, save through Parliament.[44] These issues, monopolies and taxation, were to dominate the House of Commons over the next fifty years.

Morice also discussed the prerogative of judicature. He taught that, although the king could in theory sit personally in the King's Bench, it was not customary; and he could not adjudicate by himself, in private, or appoint judges who were not learned in the law. Morice conceded that the king could in some cases imprison people, since that power was recognised by another chapter of his statute,[45] but held that in doing so he was subject to the law. The king was bound to publish and declare the cause of imprisonment, and a prisoner had to be arraigned and judged according to law, 'for this is the liberty of the subject confirmed by the great charter of England'. From this remark it may be deduced that chapter 29 was already becoming part of the armoury. It contained, said Morice, 'very excellent laws touching the liberty of the subject and the righteous government of the king'.[46]

---

[44] He attributed this to Magna Carta: BL MS. Egerton 3276, fo. 22v. In fact the relevant provision was not in the charter but was a statute made in 1297 when the charter was confirmed: 25 Edw. I, stat. 1, c. 5. The next chapter provided that the king would take no aids and taxes (*prises*) except by the common consent of the whole realm; that important statute was never made the subject of a reading.

[45] Westminster I, c. 15.

[46] Morice's reading, fo. 15. Morice owned a copy of Hervy's reading (above, p. 75) in 1560; it is now HLS MS. 88.

In relation to ecclesiastical authority, the subject of his fourth division, Morice maintained that the king was supreme governor of the Church in England by the common law, that the Church could not make constitutions to bind the laity without the royal assent, and that the spiritual courts were subject to the king's governance and jurisdiction. On the other hand, although he did not directly mention the High Commission, even a dull student could have deduced from what he had been told that the queen had no power to erect ecclesiastical jurisdictions affecting liberty or property without the authority of Parliament, and that it would be against Magna Carta to imprison subjects without lawful authority. Fifteen years later, Morice was to present a bill in Parliament to reform the High Commission, based on Magna Carta, but it earned him two months' imprisonment and the bill disappeared from view.[47]

Morice's reading, and Snagge's, spoke directly to the concerns of the Puritans, and barristers sympathetic to the Puritan cause were prominent in promoting Magna Carta, but they were not single-issue politicians and their legal doctrine was not in itself sectarian. The same progressive lawyers who fulminated against the High Commission and the oath *ex officio* used similar arguments against monopolies and taxation without consent, and some of their complaints about the ecclesiastical commissions applied equally to the provincial councils and new courts of equity. The importance of Magna Carta also struck a chord with lawyers who were concerned about recent innovations in government and jurisdiction, and abuses of the royal prerogative by favourites. Chapter 29, in particular, would now become a focus for the many and varied endeavours to formulate what is now called constitutional law. This new devotion to Magna Carta fuelled the growing sense of Elizabethan national pride, for here was a uniquely English phenomenon which helped to explain why England was favoured with happiness and prosperity above those other nations which groaned under oppression by absolutist monarchs and popes.

The newfound philosophy was taken up in 1585 in a notable speech made – or intended to be made[48] – in the House of Commons, attacking Archbishop Whitgift and the activities of the High Commission.[49] By this

---

[47] Brooks, *Law, Politics and Society*, pp. 108–9; below, pp. 272–4.

[48] Sir John Neale considered the text (next note) 'much too long to have been delivered as written': J. E. Neale, *Elizabeth I and her Parliaments 1584–1601* (1957), p. 66.

[49] BL MS. Additional 48116, fos. 154–213 (called a 'treatise' but evidently a version of the speech). There is no eye-witness account, but cf. *Proc. Parl. 1584–9*, pp. 181–3, which

time challenges to the Commission were also under way in the courts, and so the legal issues were coming to be of practical importance.[50] The speech is found among the papers of Robert Beale, but the authorship is not beyond doubt; it might perhaps have been composed by Morice. Beale was serving at the time, with Morice, on a Commons committee concerning the grievances of the Puritan ministers, and also wrote papers on the same subject for presentation to Archbishop Whitgift and others.[51] Although he was clerk of the Privy Council, he was not a barrister but had educated himself in the law,[52] no doubt with mentors from the progressive legal circle, and developed a special interest in Magna Carta. The great charter, according to the speech, was one of the principal pillars of the kingdom. It was against chapter 29 for any secular or ecclesiastical power to restrain a man of his liberties unless licensed and warranted by the laws of the realm. The statute authorising the High Commission did not confer such a power, except for heresy and schism: and yet ministers were being called up from remote parts of the country to answer for such misdemeanours as wearing gowns instead of surplices, or addressing godparents at baptism in the plural rather than the singular.[53] Might not the phrase 'disseised of his liberties' extend to religious liberty? A lawyer who understood seisin in a legal sense would have been brave to suggest such a thing;[54] but reinterpretation was now in the air. In any case, as the speech pointed out, depriving ministers of

---

shows that the queen put a stop to further debate on the grounds that it challenged her supremacy.

[50] See *Thomas Carew's Case* (1584) above, p. 160 n. 94; *Cheney v. Frankwell* (1584–8) above, p. 139; *Henry Barrow's Case* (1586–7), discussed in Usher, *High Commission*, pp. 132–5.

[51] E.g. BL MS. Additional 48039, a memorandum on the same subject which Beale sent Whitgift in 1584: C. Brooks, 'A Puritan Collaboration in Defence of the Liberty of the Subject: James Morice, Robert Beale and the Elizabethan Campaign against Ecclesiastical Authority' in *Collaboration and Interdiscipliniarity in the Republic of Letters*, ed. Scott (Manchester, 2011), pp. 1–14. Further notes on the subject by Beale are in BL MS. Lansdowne 73(2), fos. 4–13. See also Brooks, *Law, Politics and Society*, pp. 101–23; E. H. Shagan, 'The English Inquisition: Constitutional Conflict and Ecclesiastical Law in the 1590s' (2004) 47 *Historical Journal* 541–65.

[52] He proved so effective that some historians assumed he was a lawyer. Professor Collinson described him and Morice as 'acute legal minds which were now [1589] to prove the most valuable of all the resources which the puritan movement still possessed': *The Elizabethan Puritan Movement* (1967), pp. 398–9. He was admitted to Gray's Inn in 1587 but not called to the bar.

[53] The orthodox position was that, since the godparents represented the child, they should be addressed as 'thou'.

[54] Note, however, that in *Waltham v. Lunde* (1501) below, Appendix 1, at p. 457, vexing a party before the Privy Council was described in the writ as a disseisin of liberty.

their livings for such lesser offences was a disseisin of their freehold,[55] contrary to another limb of chapter 29. The concept of due process was likewise an expansive one. The oath *ex officio* was illegal because it was not how things were done in this country: 'The laws of England require an exterior fact or action contrary to law, as all human laws do or ought to do. It [sic] establisheth not an interior jurisdiction of men's hearts and thoughts.'[56] Beale told Lord Burghley that the oath 'savoureth more of a Spanish inquisition than Christian charity', a comparison which Burghley liked and immediately adopted in a letter to Whitgift.[57]

The new enthusiasm for Magna Carta seems to have spread like wildfire. Serjeant Fleetwood, when speaking in the 1585 parliament but in a different context, referred to 'the great charter, confirmed with blood,[58] redeemed with 5,000 marks,[59] confirmed by general council: no parliament ever broke it.'[60] William Lambarde, barrister of Lincoln's Inn, mentioned chapter 29 in his charge to the Kent quarter sessions in 1586.[61] Richard Crompton, bencher of the Middle Temple, described

---

[55] At common law, the incumbent of a parish owned the freehold of the church, parsonage and glebe land.

[56] Speech was another matter. According to Lord Keeper Egerton, 'Thought is free, but the tongue should be governed by knowledge': *Att.-Gen.* v. *Lady Gresham* (1596) Hawarde 64, at p. 66. See D. Cress, *Dangerous Talk: Scandalous, Seditious and Treasonable Speech in Pre-Modern England* (Oxford, 2010).

[57] HPHC 1558–1603, i. 413; P. Collinson, *Richard Bancroft and Elizabethan Anti-Puritanism* (Cambridge, 2013), pp. 44–5. Burghley's letter, dated 1 July 1584, is printed in *The Life and Acts of John Whitgift*, ed. J. Strype (1718), appendix, p. 64 ('this kind of proceeding is too much savouring of the Romish inquisition, and is rather a device to seek for offenders than to reform any').

[58] Though referring to baronial conflicts with the crown, this was meant as an analogy with the manner of establishing covenants mentioned in the Old Testament. Cf. William Hakewill's speech in 1610, where he called it 'the most ancient statute-law we have, won and sealed with the blood of our ancestors . . . no less than 29 times confirmed in Parliament': *The Libertie of the Subject against the Pretended Power of Impositions* (1641), p. 99.

[59] Fleetwood seems here to have confused the fifteenth levied at the time of the 1225 charter with the sum levied on the city of London shortly afterwards, being the sum the city had earlier given to the king's enemy Prince Louis of France. Professor David Carpenter has kindly pointed out that the confusion could have arisen from the account in Wendover's chronicle.

[60] *Proc. Parl. 1584–9*, pp. 122–3 (spelling modernised). The context was the hunting bill, which some thought interfered with the liberties of the subject. The meagre report of Fleetwood's contribution ends with the cryptic remark, 'I was shent all, all hunkers in Sir John Spence's [sic] case'. This refers to *Fines* v. *Spencer* (1571–2) Dyer 306 (trespass for a hawk), though it is unclear why Fleetwood was put to shame or criticism in respect of it.

[61] C. Read, *William Lambarde and Local Government*, pp. 79–80; Brooks, 'Ancient Constitution', pp. 104–6.

chapter 29 in 1587 as 'that most honourable, most reasonable, most indifferent law that any nation in the world hath, or that can be devised'.[62] The process of beatification was under way. Magna Carta was entering everyday legal discourse.[63] In 1589 the progressive lawyers even presented a bill in the House of Commons 'for Confirmation of a Branch of Magna Carta' (that is, chapter 29), in order to strengthen the remedy of *habeas corpus*, though it did not achieve a reading.[64] The reason why it failed is not difficult to guess, given the recorded fate of a similar bill presented in 1593.[65] The High Commission was an emanation of the queen's absolute prerogative, and too high to be meddled with.

Magna Carta in Legal Argument

A brief allusion has already been made to Popham's argument in Hilary term 1582, when (as attorney-general) he made a significant submission for a law officer. He argued that 'every subject born and begotten within the realm has two privileges, one to inherit the inheritance of his father or other ancestor, and the other to inherit the laws of this realm, from which no subject ought to be barred', citing chapter 29 of Magna Carta. He went on to explain that the queen could not alter this inheritance, for 'if the queen by her letters patent could make new laws, what would be the purpose of so great an assembly of barons, bishops and commonalty at the Parliament?'[66] It is possible that this mode of thought was one of the first fruits of Snagge's reading, which Popham (as a bencher of the Middle Temple) could have attended, although the citation here was made on behalf of, rather than against, the crown. But it is the sudden increase in citations after the middle of the decade which is more

---

[62] R. Crompton, *A Short Declaration of the Ende of Traytors and False Conspirators against the State* (1587), sig. E4v. He also praised it as 'a most honorable law' in *The Mansion of Magnanimitie* (1599), sig. C2v (citing also *Sir John atte Lee's Case*, 1368). It is quoted in full, in French, in Crompton, *Courts* (1594), fo. 97v.

[63] Note also G. Whetstone, *The English Myrror* (1586), p. 225, where there is a reference to c. 29. The author, a member of Furnival's Inn, was a professed admirer of Burghley, Dyer and Fleetwood.

[64] Neale, *Elizabeth I and her Parliaments 1584–1601*, pp. 231–2. Though it was worded in general terms, Neale thought that 'it was clearly meant to arm the Common Law Courts against the Court of High Commission'.

[65] Below, pp. 273–4.

[66] *Att.-Gen.* v. *Joiners' Company of London* (1582) below, Appendix 5(a), p. 468. See also the more detailed discussion of this case below, pp. 312–13.

striking. Although lawyers with Snagge's political leanings were at the forefront of the resurrection movement, the new learning soon became absorbed by lawyers generally into their professional mentality. Counsel suddenly found it tempting to incorporate chapter 29 into their submissions whenever possible, in all kinds of cases.

After three centuries of virtual absence from the law reports, there were eight reported cases in 1587–8 in which chapter 29 was cited in the courts. It is right to point out that this high volume of citation was not maintained thereafter, but this makes it all the more remarkable. It was not a quirk of law reporting but some kind of historical event. The cases are worth examining, because they were of considerable variety and not associated with puritan or progressive causes. In 1587 Lawrence Tanfield, arguing a case in the Exchequer, gratuitously mentioned chapter 29 as showing that liberty was favoured by the law.[67] In the same year, in the King's Bench, Snagge cited chapter 29 against Coke in challenging a custom of London,[68] and the next year Coke cited it himself in attacking an alleged custom for the mayor of Salisbury to commit for battery.[69] Later in the year Coke cited it again in another case against the city, whose authorities had disfranchised a citizen, fined him and ordered him to be set on the pillory for nine days, after conviction at the Guildhall Sessions. The indictment was merely for being of bad fame and a common deceiver, and to indict someone for such unspecific offences,[70] according to Coke, was 'directly against the statute of Magna Carta'.[71]

According to Coke's argument in the Salisbury case, 'it is against the statute of Magna Carta, chapter 29, and against the law of the land, that one should be imprisoned by anyone, or brought in to answer for any

---

[67] *Ognel* v. *Paston* (1587) 2 Leo. 84 at p. 87 ('It hath been said that executions ought to be favoured; that is true, but also liberty: see the statute of Magna Carta, *Nullus liber homo*'). Cf. Cro. Eliz. 164 (dated 1589), which omits this citation.

[68] *Anon.* (Pas. 1587) CUL MS. Dd.11.34, fo. 56 (where an executor, who was not a citizen, was imprisoned in London for not delivering up the testator's goods to the mayor and aldermen for the benefit of orphans).

[69] *Jerome* v. *Neale and Pleere* (1588) KB 27/1304, m. 515; Cro. Eliz. 93; 1 Leo. 105; 4 Leo. 47, 149; BL MS. Lansdowne 1095, fo. 48; CUL MS. Hh.2.9, fo. 416; below, Appendix 5(c), pp. 481–3. According to Croke, the court declined to deal with the Magna Carta point.

[70] The important principle that indictments must specify a particular offence was settled in the fourteenth century: Baker, *Collected Papers*, ii. 975.

[71] *Samuel Starkey's Case* (Mich. 1588) YLS MS. G.R29.8, fo. 36v (which ends with Wray CJ adjourning the case for the sheriffs to make a new return). The different report in 4 Leo. 61 mentions c. 29 but not Coke, while that in BL MS. Lansdowne 1059, fo. 62, mentions Coke but not c. 29.

offence, except by due course of the law and process of the law awarded'.[72] Serjeant Fleetwood responded scathingly that if Magna Carta was to be followed to the letter, 'no felon is duly handled at Newgate'.[73] This was not meant as an admission that the Old Bailey was unduly cavalier about procedure in those days. He was, after all, recorder of London. It was rather that, as a legal historian, he was one of the last sceptics about the unassailable magic of Magna Carta.[74] The law of the land permitted various exceptions to the requirement of due process, including reasonable local customs. In the same year he cited chapter 29 himself, even though it seemed to be against him, saying that a more learned opponent would have cited it, that it had always been revered, and that according to Roger of Wendover no one should write against it.[75] Some hearers thought he was arguing on the wrong side. Perhaps he had prepared a response to an argument which was never made, and was not inclined to waste it. The point he then made was a perfectly sensible one. Although chapter 29 was a 'sacred statute', it had always been subject to judicial qualification and could not prevail against natural law or immemorial custom. One could therefore prescribe against Magna Carta to imprison or even execute people without the usual due process of the common law. But the example he gave, of Halifax gibbet law, though mentioned in the early year books,[76] was hardly well chosen, and he lost. Whatever we might think of Fleetwood's judgment as an advocate, his measured view of Magna Carta was now distinctly old fashioned. Perhaps his immunity to the current epidemic of enthusiasm had something to do with the fact that he had been a member of the High Commission himself since 1559, albeit that as a Calvinist Protestant his preoccupation was harrying papists rather than Puritans.[77] It was also a

---

[72] CUL MS. Hh.2.9, fo. 416; below, p. 483.

[73] From both reports in Leo., which are the same. Fleetwood's 'Notes for Arguments', fos. 330v–331v, do not mention Magna Carta, but only the heads of his submissions about custom; presumably, therefore, his remarks about the charter were off the cuff.

[74] He also challenged some of the assertions in Morice's reading, which he attended: BL MS. Add. 16169, fos. 40, 45v; *Selected Readings, on Magna Carta*, p. lxxxvi.

[75] *Collett v. Webbe* (1586–7) CP 40/1461, pt i, m. 2549; BL MS. Lansdowne 1087, fo. 239; BL MS. Add. 35948, fos. 99–101; CUL MS. Ff.5.4, fo. 272; MS. Lansdowne 1095, fo. 86v; selections printed below, Appendix 5(b), pp. 476–81.

[76] Temp. Edw. I in Fitz. Abr., *Prescription*, pl. 65; also cited in *Skipwith v. Sheffield* (1584) in Fleetwood, 'Notes for Arguments', fo. 290v; *The Serjeants' Case, Munck v. Philips* (1590) BL MS. Add. 36080, fo. 51, *per* Hannam sjt; *Davies v. Cornelius* (1607) CUL MS. Gg.2.23, fo. 108, *per* George Croke.

[77] Above, p. 129.

result of knowing his history.[78] It was Fleetwood who inspired Coke's favourite saying that the charter had been confirmed thirty-two times[79] – Fleetwood was said to have made it fifty-two[80] – but he had also been imbued with the cautious common learning of the late medieval inns of court.[81]

These cases arose from relatively low-level local squabbles, in which the courts showed themselves more than willing to keep uppity mayors, aldermen and liverymen in check, but in other cases in 1587 the courts ventured higher. Two important cases are to be found in Coke's manuscript notebooks for that year, though they were not included in his printed reports. The first was *Arundel's Case*, in which the King's Bench declared as a general principle that the court could not in justice ever deny a writ of *habeas corpus*, and that the return to the writ had to be sufficiently specific for the court to assess its validity, 'because it restrains a free man of his liberty'.[82] If the return was bad in form only, the court could adjourn the case for it to be amended; if it was not then made good, the court would discharge the prisoner, either absolutely or on bail. Coke does not say how the case arose, or who Arundel was. It may have been Philip Howard, earl of Arundel, who had been imprisoned without trial for two years, on suspicion of treason,[83] but it might have been the more lowly John Arundell of Quarnack, Cornwall, who had been committed by Thomas

---

[78] See the previous chapter.

[79] Below, p. 350. Thompson counted thirty-seven confirmations ('Parliamentary Confirmations of the Great Charter' (1933) 38 *American Historical Review* 659–72; *Magna Carta*, p. 10n), while Dunham made it over forty ('Magna Carta & British Constitutionalism' in *The Great Charter*, at p. 30).

[80] *The Chamberlain of London's Case* (1591) as reported in 3 Leo. 264. '52' was perhaps a mistake for 32, though cf. *Clarke* v. *Gape* (1596) as cited in *Davenant* v. *Hurdys* (1599) BL MS. Hargrave 5, fo. 74, *per* Coke Att.-Gen. (tr. 'for the great charter (as Mr Serjeant Fleetwood once said here) has been confirmed 52 times, and [Coke] said in truth so it had'); the variant report in BL MS. Add. 25203, fo. 93, says 'over thirty times'.

[81] Above, pp. 237–8. Coke was not unaware of this learning, since he owned at least two manuscript readings on Magna Carta: *A Catalogue of the Library of Sir Edward Coke*, ed. W. O. Hassall (New Haven, CT, 1950), pp. 24–5.

[82] *Arundel's Case* (Hil. 1587) Coke's notebook, BL MS. Harley 6687, fos. 726v–727.

[83] He was held in the Tower of London by order of the Star Chamber from 1585 until his trial and attainder for treason in 1589, and thereafter under sentence of death until 1595: *ODNB*. His carved signature with the date 22 June 1587 may still be seen in a cell in the Beauchamp Tower. In an undated letter to the queen around this time he complained of being imprisoned for fifteen weeks without cause, with occasional appearances before the Council, and referred to his ancestors who had likewise been detained without trial: BL Cotton MS. Julius F VI, fos. 69v–70.

Heneage, vice-chamberlain of the Household.[84] There is a case for its having been the earl. While he was in prison, he was enjoined from pursuing a Chancery suit, and is known to have complained that this was contrary to chapter 29.[85] According to Coke's report of the *habeas corpus* case, the court had once rejected the return of a committal by Lord Keeper Bacon for contempt of the Court of Chancery,[86] a possible clue that the 1587 case concerned the earl's difficulty in that court. On the other hand, the absence of any addition of his title suggests the commoner.[87] The Cornishman was still in prison in 1594, when another motion was made for his release, though apparently without citing Magna Carta.[88] Whichever case it was, Coke mentioned chapter 29 in the margin of his report, and listed several cases which he was to cite frequently in the next century, including *Kayser's Case* (1465) from his own collection of precedents and *Lee's Case* (1568) from Dyer's unprinted reports. He also noted that he had been shown precedents of *habeas corpus*, presumably from the King's Bench controlment rolls, by the secondary of the Crown Office.

The other case in Coke's notebook was that of Sir John Perrot, who brought a *praemunire* against the chancellor of Oxford University for exercising a jurisdiction according to equity and good conscience.[89] Here it was held by all the judges that, although the common law allowed the High Court of Chancery its equitable jurisdiction, it would be against

---

[84] He had been sent up to the King's Bench upon a *corpus cum causa* (i.e. *habeas corpus*) 'a long time before' the parliamentary pardon of 1593 and committed to the Marshalsea: R. v. *Arundell* (1594) Goulds. 133; reported on another point in 6 Co. Rep. 14; Moo. 594; BL MS. Harley 1697, fos. 70v–71; MS. Hargrave 50, fo. 58. The record in J. Tremaine, *Placita Coronae* (1723), 271, is dated Trin. 1588 but does not set out the indictment. He had been suspected of involvement with the earl, to whom he was not related (see 21 Catholic Record Soc. 133); but the 1594 reports show that the committal was for murder.

[85] 'Causes to be considered for the Dissolving of the Injunction awarded against the Earl of Arundel', SP 15/30, fos. 124–5; *CSPD 1580–1625*, p. 232 (dated 1587); Jones, *Elizabethan Court of Chancery*, p. 169 n. 1. The earl did then manage to pursue a suit against Lord Dacre, which was settled by arbitrators at Serjeants' Inn in Mich. 1587: 1 Leo. 91.

[86] Probably referring to *Astwick's Case* (1567) above, p. 162 n. 103.

[87] Neither case has been found in the controlment rolls (KB 29/223).

[88] BL MS. Hargrave 50, fo. 58 (tr. 'Mr Tanfield moved Mr Arundell's case again and prayed their resolutions, for the gentleman has been long in prison [and so] he prayed their resolutions one way or the other').

[89] *Perrot v. Mathew* (1588) Coke's notebook, BL MS. Harley 6687, fo. 743v; Co. Inst. iv. 87. Cf. Coke's recollection of this case from the bench in Warburton's reports, CUL MS. Ii.5.25, fo. 100 (above, p. 29). The Chancery reached a similar decision in *Dawborne v. Garbrand* (1595): see Jones, *Elizabethan Chancery*, p. 374.

chapter 29 to erect a new inferior court of equity, since it would deprive the subject of his inheritance in having his affairs determined by the law of the land. This case, though not in any printed collection of reports, was to be much relied upon in the campaign against inferior courts of equity such as the Court of Requests.

There were other cases in 1587. In *Waram's Case*,[90] in Easter term, the King's Bench rejected a new kind of prerogative protection granted to someone on the grounds of personal misfortune. Wray CJ said that 'by the law of the land', which the judges were sworn to uphold, such a protection was not allowed.[91] This seems very likely to be an allusion to *lex terrae* in chapter 29. Another important case the same term was that of Richard Cavendish, who had been granted a patent of monopoly for making writs of *supersedeas*, a grant which prejudiced the chief prothonotary of the Common Pleas.[92] The judges of the Common Pleas were sent letters under the royal sign manual, apparently procured by Robert Dudley, ordering them not to question the grant. But the court, led by Anderson CJ, held the grant void. It amounted to a disseisin of part of the profits of the prothonotary's office, contrary to chapter 29. The decision not only confirmed that the judges would disobey orders to desist from doing their duty, but also facilitated the legal attack on monopolies. This cluster of cases in 1587–8 therefore touched the royal prerogative in matters of some importance, and they must have been well known at the time even though they were not preserved in print for the information of posterity. But there was one more case, also unreported in print, which merits separate attention.

Case of the Sheriffs of London

Brief mention has already been made of the appalling incident in July 1588 involving the sheriffs of London.[93] The facts were not

---

[90] See above, p. 177.   [91] *Waram's Case* (1587) CUL MS. Ii.5.38, fo. 237.

[92] *Cavendish's Case* (1587) 1 And. 152; BL MS. Harley 4817, fos. 56–58v (slightly more accurate version); MS. Lansdowne 512, fo. 1; cited by Serjeant Richardson from Anderson's manuscript in *Brownlow v. Michell and Cox* (1615) 1 Rolle Rep. 206 at p. 208; cf. Moo. 842 at p. 843; W. Petyt, *Jus Parliamentarium* (1739), pp. 203–4. Arguments for and against the proposed patent are in BL MS. Lansdowne 35, fo. 66 (bound with papers of 1582).

[93] *Att.-Gen. v. Skynner and Catcher, sheriffs of London* (1588) above p. 212. The case was noticed briefly in Thompson, *Magna Carta*, p. 204; Brooks, *Law, Politics and Society*, pp. 402–3.

disputed.[94] The sheriffs had, without any good reason which they could offer, apprehended in the streets Jane Smith, *alias* Nevill, gentlewoman,[95] and Jane Newnham, wife of an esquire,[96] committed them to Bridewell, a prison ordained for 'persons of most vile conversation', and caused them to be stripped to the girdle and whipped as common harlots. One of the sheriffs was present, and laughing, when the whipping was carried out. Mrs Nevill was heavily pregnant at the time, and the child died soon after its premature birth a week later. The women had not been given any opportunity to defend themselves on any charge, the sheriffs having (according to the prosecution) treated their own wills as law. It is possible from extrinsic evidence to speculate that they had motives other than arbitrary viciousness. What the record does not disclose is that Mrs Nevill's husband Edmund, who was an unsuccessful claimant to the barony of Latimer and later to the earldom of Westmoreland, had been a prisoner in the Tower for several years on suspicion of complicity in popish plots. She had married him in the Tower, but her access to him had been restricted for fear she might encourage him in the matter of religion.[97] It seems, therefore, that she was considered to be a dangerous papist and perhaps the sheriffs thought they would teach her a lesson. Her husband wrote in his account of the Nevills, compiled in the Tower around 1589, that they 'had issue a son called Ralph, who through the unchristian dealing of the two unworthy sheriffs of London, Skynner and Katcher, and through their barbarous outrage most unjustly inflicted upon his mother, was untimely born and thereby murdered by them'.[98] The son was said to have been baptised, and buried in the choir of Hoxton church, Middlesex. Assuming this was true, the sheriffs were

---

[94] The following account is based on BL MS. Add. 48064, fos. 207–208v (a full transcript from the lost Star Chamber register); heavily abridged in MS. Harley 2143, fo. 44. There is also a brief notice of the case in Crompton, *Courts* (1594), fo. 31 ('13').

[95] She was the daughter of Richard Smith, son and heir apparent of Sir Walter Smith of Shelford, Warwickshire: BL MS. Hargrave 853, fo. 118v. It is not clear why the record gave her the *alias*, unless the validity of the marriage was in doubt.

[96] William Newnham, esquire, son of Sir Thomas Newnham.

[97] The Privy Council, on her petition, ordered the lieutenant of the Tower to permit her access for one week, 12 October. 1588: 16 APC 246–7, 306. For the marriage see *Complete Peerage*, xii. 564. Edmund's first wife, whom he married abroad, was buried in Tournai: BL MS. Harley 853, fo. 118v.

[98] BL MS. Hargrave 853, at fo. 118. The date 22 August 1589 occurs on fo. 73. The volume also includes a history of the baronage, some alchemical collections, and a verse account of Edmund's misfortunes. On the verso of the front endpaper is the signature: 'Edmonde Lord Latimer me possidet'.

very fortunate not to have been indicted for murder; but Edmund was in no position to prosecute them. Edmund was eventually released and died in some obscurity on the continent, but Jane Nevill lived on until 1646 and is depicted on her monument in East Ham church wearing the robes and coronet of a peeress.

Much interest was taken in the case when, the following term, the sheriffs were prosecuted by the attorney-general (Popham) in the Star Chamber.[99] The only defence offered was an alleged custom of London to imprison and castigate prostitutes. Such a usage may in fact have been widespread,[100] but the court took the view that relying on it as a defence only served to emphasise the sheriffs' malice, and imposed a severe sentence. The defendants were imprisoned for three months, fined 1,000 marks and £500 respectively, and ordered both to ask the women's forgiveness publicly in three locations and to pay them £600 compensation.[101] Popham's speech is not preserved, but in Lord Treasurer Burghley's mind the case fell squarely within chapter 29 of Magna Carta, which he took occasion to extol:[102]

> My lord treasurer in the Star Chamber ... said that this freedom no country but ours (no, not France) can challenge by the laws of their realm, and that the procuring of this statute of Magna Carta cost many a nobleman's life and was the cause of the Barons' War; and therefore, being so hardly got, we ought not so easily to suffer it to be lost.

It was agreed by the whole court, and the queen's learned counsel, that if the queen granted to commissioners the authority to punish an offence,

---

[99] The case is noted in two surviving contemporary letters: (i) from John Adams to Percival Willoughby, Nottingham University Library, Middleton C.18; calendared in Historical Manuscripts Commission: *Report on the Manuscripts of Lord Middleton* (1911), p. 158 (dated 31 'August' 1588, though it refers to the sentence in Michaelmas term); (ii) from James Digges, 25 October 1588, Lincolnshire Archives, 8 ANC 5/55.

[100] E.g. Cambridge University claimed, under its charter, the authority to arrest prostitutes and imprison them in the Spinning House, a practice kept up by the proctors until the notorious *habeas corpus* case *Ex parte Daisy Hopkins* (1891) 61 LJQB 240.

[101] The judgment does not seem to have caused them lasting harm. They were still (or again) sheriffs in 1595, when they suffered a judgment of £440 for an escape: *Westby* v. *Skinner and Catcher* (1595) 3 Co. Rep. 71; Poph. 85.

[102] BL MS. Harley 358, fo. 201v; corrected from a slightly variant text in BL Cotton MS. Cleopatra F I, fo. 73 (in a memorandum by a common lawyer on imprisonment by ecclesiastical courts); a slightly fuller version is cited in *Maunsell's Case* (1607) below, p. 520, *per* Henry Finch. The manuscript report adds, 'This was in Skinner and Katcher's case, sheriffs of London, for whipping Mrs Nevill and Mrs Newman [Newam *in* Harleian MS.].'

and a punishment was imposed such as ought not by law to be inflicted, the party punished had a good remedy against the commissioners.[103] They also agreed that imprisonment was not allowed by the course of the law as a punishment, but only as a means to secure a party's appearance at trial or to ensure the payment of a fine to the king.

It was around this time that Serjeant Fleetwood wrote his opinion on the lawfulness of the commission authorising the governors of the London Bridewell to punish prostitutes without due process.[104] He held the commission to be contrary to the 'great charter of England',[105] which had been confirmed by Marlborough and many later statutes up to Henry VI, and reinforced by the statute of 1368. It is not certain whether the opinion preceded the Star Chamber decision or followed it, but the two were clearly in unison. Chapter 29 of Magna Carta was beginning to have practical consequences.

The espousal of the new learning by Lord Burghley was of immense significance. It could hardly be criticised as subversive or disloyal if it was approved by the queen's chief minister.[106] No doubt it could not harm the queen's interests to wax lyrical about the great charter when it was applied downwards, to deal with overbearing tradesmen who became mayors or sheriffs. But Burghley was aware that the wording of chapter 29 could not be confined to inferiors; that was not why it had been 'so hardly got'. He knew and approved of its citation against the oath *ex officio* and the excesses of the High Commission. His humanist education at Cambridge, and his legal education at Gray's Inn,[107] had given him an interest in English

---

[103] Cf. Beale's letter to Whitgift in BL MS. Add. 48039, fo. 80v (1591): 'I trust your grace can remember the resolution of her majesty's learned counsel and the judges in the Star Chamber in the case of the sheriffs of London, that a commission granted upon a statute ought to go no further than the statute and [ought] to take his interpretation according to the law of the realm.'

[104] Above, pp. 241–3. The latest edition of the text makes no mention of the case, though it is obviously related to it.

[105] I.e. c. 29, which is set out on p. 55, with the comment, 'if ye do compare the said charter of Bridewell with the great Charter of England both in matter, sense and meaning you shall find them merely repugnant'. (The word 'merely' here meant 'absolutely'.)

[106] William Cecil (d. 1598), Lord Burghley, was a secretary of state by 1550 and (with the exception of Mary I's reign) held that office until he became lord high treasurer (1572–98).

[107] Cecil was admitted to Gray's Inn in 1541 and must have been called to the bar, since he became an ancient in 1547.

history,[108] and a genuine sympathy for constitutionalism. He was on friendly terms with such troublesome advocates of the rule of law as Morice and Snagge, and gave them his protection. If, looking back from the early seventeenth century, Elizabeth's reign seemed to have been the golden age of constitutional monarchy,[109] it was in some measure a result of the balance in the state which Burghley achieved. Moreover, by the end of the reign there was a perception that the happy condition of the English nation was connected with Magna Carta. As Edward Hake wrote:[110]

> And because we are thus drawn by occasion of [a] question of the great charter to speak of the nature of our English government ... I will therefore speak somewhat of it according to my own conceiving. And first, of all the nations of the world that I have read of, the English nation is a people most free ... for whereas the peoples of other nations and kingdoms, for the most part, are ruled and governed by the absolute beck, will and power of their prince, only the English nation is ruled and governed by the laws of their country – or rather by their kings and rulers, whose rule and government is according to their law and not otherwise. And therefore the kings of England are said to rule (not to reign), I say, to rule by their laws and not to reign by their wills or absolute powers.

James Morice and the High Commission

The origins of the feud between the judges and the High Commission have already been traced,[111] and now it is time to return to the arguments about Magna Carta which Morice and Snagge clearly intended for use in this connection. Surprisingly, perhaps, it was not the context in which Magna Carta made its first reappearance in Westminster Hall. Chapter 29 seems not to have been cited in court against the Commission until the very end of the century,[112] and it is not even mentioned in the reports of the Serjeants' Inn case of 1587, when the assembled judges conceded that the commissioners had the power to fine and imprison.[113] It was

---

[108] He was a collector of manuscripts, and a supporter of historians. R. V. Turner, *Magna Carta through the Ages* (Harlow, 2003), p. 139, said that Matthew Paris's *Historia Maior*, which contained the best-known account of Magna Carta, was printed in 1571 from Cecil's manuscript. This is, however, misleading. Cecil's manuscript was indeed used for the edition, but it ended in 1208, and the later part was supplied from other texts: see the preface, sig. †iij.

[109] See above, pp. 148–50.   [110] Hake, *Epieikeia* (1603), pp. 78–9.

[111] Above, pp. 133–43, 207–8.   [112] That part of the story continues below, pp. 289–98.

[113] Above, p. 141.

deployed at first extrajudicially,[114] as in the tract which Beale addressed to Whitgift in 1591 concerning the deprivation of Puritan ministers:[115]

> This manner of proceeding taketh away the benefit of the great charter, which is the franchise of the whole realm, in arresting and depriving men without sufficient cause, in depriving them of their freehold *absque et contra legem*, being not indicted and no suit of party offered against them, as the law speaketh . . .

In the more extensive treatise which he or Morice wrote around the same time, reliance was placed instead on chapter 28 of the charter – 'No bailiff shall henceforth put anyone to open law[116] or oath upon his single word, without faithful witness brought in for this purpose' – a provision which, he said, took away the previous 'Norman' custom:[117]

> And therefore it were a great pity that a law that was debated by the space of a hundred years, with the loss of the lives of more English subjects than be at this day living in the land, so solemnly made, and so often confirmed in sundry parliaments, and corroborated by the oaths of all the kings and queens and subjects, should be now overthrown and made void by reviving of that tyrannical custom which the clergy seeketh to bring in again. But seeing by this law of Magna Carta the judge was inhibited to proceed to the putting of a man to his open law or oath, so I doubt not but the accuser or informer was bound to the like, and therefore do assure myself that I may lawfully according to the said law of Magna Carta infer that in an accusation upon the bare information of any man, judge or accuser, without other lawful witnesses, none ought to be put to his oath or proceeded against without better proofs. And therefore 5 Edw. III, c. 9, it was enacted that none should be attached nor forejudged of life, limb, lands, tenements, goods or chattels against the form of the great charter

---

[114] Note also *The Triall of Maist[er] Dorrell* (1599), pp. 41–4, where it was argued that the deprivation of a minister, for contempt against an admonition by the ordinary, was against Magna Carta. The author relied not only on c. 29 but also on c. 14, as showing that even for a serious offence a free man's 'contenement' should be saved; but this rested on the equation of contenement with freehold, which was anachronistic (see *Selected Readings on Magna Carta*, p. 157 n. 1).

[115] Draft in BL MS. Add. 48039, fos. 78–86v, at fo. 84v. This was prompted by *Cartwright's Case* (1590). James Morice also relied on Magna Carta and its progeny in *A Briefe Treatise of Oathes exacted by Ordinaries* (Middleburg, c. 1590), p. 47; there is a manuscript version in BL Cotton MS. Cleopatra F I, fos. 55–72v.

[116] I.e. wager of law, whereby a party had to clear himself by oath, supported by compurgators.

[117] BL Cotton MS. Cleopatra F I, fos. 5–44v, at fos. 22v–23. This is part of a large collection of tracts on ecclesiastical jurisdiction, and the oath *ex officio*, almost all anonymous. There is a full transcript in BL MS. Add. 28843, formerly in the library of Doctors' Commons, and a similar collection in IT MS. Petyt 538.56.

and the law of the land. And in the 25th year of the said king, that none shall be taken by petition or suggestion made to the king or to his council unless it be by indictment or presentment of his good and lawful neighbours where such deeds be done, in due manner, or by process made by writ original at the common law ... and in 42nd of the same king, chapter 3, it was in Parliament assented and accorded for the government of the commons that no man be put to answer without presentment before justices, or thing of record, by due process and by writ original according to the old law of the land ... Whereby I do infer that by the statute of Magna Carta and the old laws of this realm this oath for a man to accuse himself was and is utterly inhibited.

The rhetoric was similar to Fleetwood's, Snagge's and Burghley's, and was now becoming familiar. Of course, the mere mention of Magna Carta was not enough to win the cause. As is usual with feuds, there was no instant victory for either side. The Church regarded judicial challenges to the High Commission as an interference in the spiritual sphere, and as subversive of the queen's prerogative as supreme governor of the Church of England, a point of view to which the queen and the Privy Council were easily persuaded. On the other side, there was widespread support among the laity, especially those with legal training, for the position taken by the Puritan faction.

In February 1593 Morice was emboldened to raise the matter in the House of Commons, inveighing against the 'ungodly and intolerable inquisition', whereby 'our secret deeds, words and thoughts, no way offensive to the public peace, are abused as means and instruments to deprive us of our precious liberty, countenances, callings, freeholds and freedoms':[118]

> Where is now become the great charter of England, obtained by many difficulties, confirmed by sundry Acts of Parliament, fortified by public and solemn sentence of execration,[119] wherein is contained that no free man shall be apprehended, imprisoned, distrained, impeached, disseised or put from his freehold or franchise but by the law of the land, which law utterly forbiddeth the imposing of an oath upon him that is accused of any crime or matter of disgrace? Where is now the statute made in the sixteenth year of the reign of King Edward the

---

[118] CUL MS. Mm.1.51, fos. 55–69, at fo. 56; partly printed in *Proc. Parl. 1593–1601*, pp. 30–5 (quotation at p. 32). This is a transcript by Thomas Baker of Morice's own account of the proceedings, taken from a near contemporary copy. See also Neale, *Elizabeth I and her Parliaments 1584–1601*, pp. 267–79, where details are added from other manuscripts.

[119] I.e. excommunication.

third,[120] whereby it is provided that no man be put to answer without presentment before justices, matter of record, due process or writ original after the ancient law of the land? These and many other just and profitable laws are rejected and cast aside by our ecclesiastical judges as 'antiquated' (I use their terms) and worn out of ure.

This passionate speech, according to an eminent historian of the Elizabethan Parliament, earned Morice a 'place on Liberty's long and honoured roll'.[121] At its conclusion, Morice produced two bills and presented them to the Speaker (now Edward Coke), one against unlawful oaths, inquisitions and subscriptions, which would have subjected the high commissioners personally to the penalties and pains of *praemunire*, and the second against unlawful imprisonment and restraint of liberty. The first bill recited chapter 29 of Magna Carta and the second sought a clarification of it.[122] According to Morice's account of the day, the first was well received. When James Dalton, a senior bencher of Lincoln's Inn, tried to speak against it, he was interrupted with spitting and coughing. Henry Finch, a barrister of Gray's Inn newly elected to Parliament, spoke in favour, and even Sir Francis Knowles, treasurer of the household, made some remarks on the same side. The atmosphere was evidently tense, and the Speaker found himself in a difficult position. On the motion of Sir Robert Cecil, Coke agreed to defer the reading of the bills until the next day, the pretext being their length. That was in fact the end of them. Someone reported the business to the queen, who summoned Coke to court the same afternoon and admonished him that there should be no dealing in matters of state. The parliament had not been summoned, she said, to make new laws, let alone innovations in state or government, and since she had the power of dissolution she also had the power to direct what could be discussed. Morice was summoned the next morning before the Privy Council, to be acquainted with the queen's pleasure that he be 'sharply chidden'. Lord Burghley, evidently embarrassed by the queen's intervention, spoke kindly to him and informed him that, although his bills contained good matter, his fault was 'in form'.

---

[120] Evidently a slip for 25 Edw. III, stat. 5, c. 4. The paraphrasing suggests that both provisions were recollected from memory.

[121] Neale, *Elizabeth I and her Parliaments 1584–1601*, p. 269.

[122] Morice's account does not provide a text of the second bill, but Coke recalled in 1615 that it had asked for an explanation of c. 29 with particular reference to imprisonment by the Privy Council and excommunication: HLS MS. 109, fo. 65v; *Cases Concerning Equity and the Courts of Equity 1550–1660*, ed. W. H. Bryson (118 SS, 2001), p. 461. According to Coke, the bill failed because it concerned *arcana imperii*.

He should have informed the queen privately if there was anything amiss in the ecclesiastical commissions, so that she could redress it. Although Morice was one of the queen's counsel (as attorney-general of the Court of Wards), he would hardly have been given personal access to the queen on such a matter, so the meaning presumably was that he should have submitted a memorial for her ministers to file away. At any rate, he had hewn above his head and the chips had fallen in his eyes. To teach him a lesson, he was imprisoned in the house of Sir John Fortescue for two months, though he remained on good terms with Burghley and retained his office as attorney of the Wards. No more was heard of the bills,[123] nor was any remedial action taken by the queen or her government. During the same parliament, Beale likewise earned the queen's displeasure for speaking out against the High Commission, and he too was placed under house arrest.[124]

While Morice was in confinement, the Civilian advocate Dr Richard Cosin, protégé of Archbishop Whitgift and president of Doctors' Commons, took the opportunity to publish a lengthy response, in which he maintained that chapter 29 of Magna Carta had no application to the Church courts at all.[125] Morice's even lengthier treatise in reply, though circulated, was not printed.[126] The public case against the High Commission had therefore, if anything, been set back by these proceedings.[127] The queen had no sympathy with the nonconformists and, in the interests both of her prerogative and of uniformity in religion, she supported the archbishops. Two years later, in *Cawdray's Case* (1595), discussed in a previous chapter,[128] the judges likewise sided with the archbishops, holding that the ecclesiastical commissions were warranted not solely by the Act of 1559 but also by the royal prerogative, and therefore were not limited by the wording of the Act. Although Morice

---

[123] They, or something like them, were resurrected in most successive parliaments to no avail: Thompson, *Magna Carta*, pp. 257–8.

[124] Neale, *Elizabeth I and her Parliaments 1584–1601*, p. 277. The occasion does not seem to have been Morice's speech.

[125] R. Cosin, *An Apologie for Sundrie Proceedings by Jurisdiction Ecclesiasticall* (2nd edn, 1593), p. 104. It was an amplified version of a book printed in 1591. Cf. W. Bradshaw, *A Myld and Just Defence of Certeyne Arguments* (1606), pp. 88, 89, where it is argued that, in so far as c. 29 applied to ecclesiastical courts, *lex terrae* denoted the ecclesiastical law of the land and not the common law.

[126] HLS MS. 120; Lambeth Palace Library, MS. 234.

[127] Morice complained to Burghley in 1596 that, while Cosin was able to attack his position without check, he was unable to respond publicly: BL MS. Lansdowne 82, fo. 149.

[128] Above, p. 141.

was one of Cawdray's counsel, it had been decided not to base the argument on Magna Carta but rather on close statutory interpretation. That turned out to be a miscalculation, in view of the unexpected counter-argument that the jurisdiction did not depend solely on the statute. Morice was unable to do more. He died in 1597, just before the opportunity arose again to test in court the arguments based on chapter 29.

8

Magna Carta and the Rule of Law 1592–1606

Once chapter 29 of Magna Carta had been awakened from its long sleep, the legal profession were not slow to recognise its forensic potential in tackling the other grievances which had been building up earlier in the reign. Prominent among these grievances were those generated by the English-bill courts, derived from the royal prerogative, which had expanded their reach in a high-handed manner and shared some of the perceived deficiencies of the High Commission;[1] but equally susceptible to attack under the new jurisprudence were the controversial techniques for increasing the royal revenue, such as monopolies and impositions. The challenges were made not only in the King's Bench but also in the Court of Common Pleas. This is contrary to expectations, since the Common Pleas was the most legally conservative of courts,[2] and yet it took immediately to the new learning under the chief justiceship of Sir Edmund Anderson. Anderson was no lover of the Puritans, though Robert Snagge mentioned him in his will, together with Coke, among the 'friends that I ever found kind and constant'.[3] He had inherited from his immediate predecessor, Sir James Dyer,[4] a distaste for innovations in the state and in the legal system, and together with his brethren had found new hope in Magna Carta.[5] More striking even than this, perhaps, is that the new mood was caught even by the law officers of the crown, John Popham[6] and Edward Coke, both of whom were to become chief

---

[1] For the grievances see above, pp. 135–7, 259–60, 270–5.

[2] See Baker, 'Judicial Conservatism in the Common Pleas 1500–1560' in *Collected Papers*, i. 466–80.

[3] PCC 31 Stafford (dated 1599, proved 1606).

[4] Sir Edmund Anderson was CJCP after the death of Dyer in 1582 until his own death in 1605. After a tenure of only one term by Sir Francis Gawdy (d. 1605) he was succeeded in 1606 by Coke.

[5] It will be recalled that, while a serjeant, Anderson was (so far as is known) the first lawyer to suggest a connection between *habeas corpus* and Magna Carta: above, p. 250.

[6] Attorney-general 1581–92.

justices of England. It was no mere coincidence that many of the leading precedents were set while Coke was thus in the royal service, before he became a judge, and the present chapter will concentrate on his period of office (solicitor-general 1592–4, attorney-general 1594–1606).[7] It is true that chapter 29 was not cited in every constitutional case, or at least not noticed by the law reporters in every case, and that many of the cases in which it was cited did not immediately resolve the problems addressed; but it was cited often enough to show that it had a distinct emboldening effect on the judges and a catalytic effect on legal development. The skirmishes were fought on scattered fronts simultaneously from the mid-1590s, but it will be convenient to treat each of them separately, beginning with the various jurisdictional disputes in which Magna Carta was brought into the argument.

The Court of Requests

A notable instance of recourse to Magna Carta arose from a challenge to the jurisdiction of the Court of Requests, which was rapidly expanding its case-load under the presidency of Dr Julius Caesar.[8] It was occasioned by a suit commenced in the Requests in 1590, in which the issue was the title to a lease for years of a house in London, and a decree had been made with an injunction awarding possession to the plaintiff. This raised the fundamental question whether an inferior court of equity could determine a matter of title to real property, albeit the property was a chattel real rather than an inheritance. The case occupied much of Caesar's attention when he became master of the court in 1591, and was the impetus behind his tract on the jurisdiction of the court, with an extensive collection of extracts from its records, which was first printed in 1597.[9] The defendant Parsons was advised to seek the help of the common law, and in 1595 brought an action in the Common Pleas founded on Magna Carta – the first known example of such a suit since the time of

---

[7] Coke's role is further discussed in Chapter 9, at pp. 336–51.

[8] A register of causes commenced by petition to the king survives for the period 1603–16 (BL MS. Lansdowne 266). This seems to be the council attendant, which was the itinerant branch of the Court of Requests. Of 466 private disputes in 1603–4, all but 50 were sent to arbitration: Dawson, 'Privy Council', pp. 630–5.

[9] J. Caesar, *The Ancient State, Authoritie and Proceedings of the Court of Requests* (1597; new edn by L. M. Hill, Cambridge, 1975). Dr Hill was unaware of the action founded on Magna Carta and may have assumed the suit was for a prohibition (ibid. ix).

Henry VIII.[10] The long declaration recited the statute of 1225, setting out the wording of chapter 29, all the proceedings in the Requests from bill to injunction, and the plaintiff's imprisonment for refusing to enter into a recognisance to obey the decree.[11] This imprisonment, it was contended, was not warranted by the law of the land. The year-book case of 1368,[12] and the case of 1559 mentioned by Dyer,[13] established that the king could not without Parliament create a new power of imprisonment without due process. Counsel for the now defendant, Locke, moved that his client had 'only sued in one of the ancient courts of the queen for matters in equity, and not in a new erected court'; it was not, therefore, comparable with the commissions condemned by the judges in 1368 and 1559. He also argued that he had sued for a lease and not a freehold, 'and if there was any offence it was in the masters of requests who exceeded their authority, and therefore the action should have been brought against them and not against the party'. Anderson CJ was unsympathetic, and immediately retorted, 'the Court of Requests is not an ancient court by prescription, but began in the time of Henry VII by a commission for the servants of the king's household, and for poor people also; they may not award process to expel anyone from his freehold, but if they make a decree and [the party] does not obey they may commit him to prison.' After this equivocal conclusion, he remarked that 'such writs and commissions to put a plaintiff in possession were not awarded in any court of equity until recently'. No final decision was reached by the Common Pleas, for in 1596 the suit was stayed by the Privy Council following a reference of the case to Egerton and Popham, and Parsons was ordered to obey the injunction on pain of imprisonment.[14]

---

[10] For the precedents see above, p. 97.

[11] *Parsons v. Locke* (1595) CP 40/1540, m. 401 (two membranes; entered in Hil. 1595, imparlance to Pas. 1595); Warburton's reports, CUL MS. Ii.5.25, fos. 10v–11 (Pas. 1595); anonymous report, below, Appendix 5(d), pp. 484–7. Bonds and recognisances, enforceable at law, were widely used by courts of equity to reinforce their decrees: Dawson, 'Privy Council', pp. 636–7; Jones, *Elizabethan Chancery*, p. 272.

[12] *Sir John atte Lee's Case* (1368) above, p. 58.

[13] *Scrogges's Case* (1559–60) Dyer 175; *Dyer's Notebooks*, i. 54–7; above, p. 156. Although Dyer did not mention it, Scrogges had cited c. 29: BL MS. Lansdowne 1057, fo. 3.

[14] CUL MS. Ii.5.25, fo. 11; 26 APC 92–3; below, p. 487. According to Dr Hill (above, n. 9), not citing the source, the law officers advised the Privy Council that the Requests had not exceeded its jurisdiction. This would be surprising, given that Coke was attorney-general; but it may have been a misunderstanding of the reference to Egerton in APC. The Privy

Not longer after the dust had settled in that case,[15] Caesar became embroiled in the case of *Stepneth* v. *Lloyd*.[16] Lloyd had been ordered by the Requests to pay maintenance to his wife, a matter not determinable at common law. Stepneth, as sheriff of Carmarthenshire, had then arrested Lloyd by virtue of a writ of attachment from the Requests, and released him on his giving a bond to attend the Court of Requests forthwith at Westminster. When Lloyd failed to appear, the sheriff sued him on the bond in the Common Pleas, and he pleaded successfully a statute of 1445 that bonds taken by sheriffs would be void if no day of appearance was mentioned.[17] That was doubtless enough to justify the decision, but the court went further and declared obiter that the Requests had no power by commission, statute or common law to arrest a party or take a bond for appearance;[18] it followed that the bond was void both for duress and for want of jurisdiction.[19] Coke later made much of the decision, which he interpreted as denying altogether the jurisdiction of the court,[20] though in practice it had no such effect.

In a third case, around the same time, complaint was made that the Requests had imprisoned a party for procuring a prohibition. Anderson CJ held that in such a case an action of false imprisonment would

---

Council intervened in the same year to support the Requests in another suit after judgment at law: *Dudley* v. *Knighton* (1596) 25 APC 414–15.

[15] In *Whitney* v. *Russell* (1597) complaint was made to the Privy Council that a plaintiff in the Common Pleas was pressing ahead despite an agreement in the Requests to submit to arbitration; this was referred to Walmsley J. as umpire: 27 APC 475.

[16] *Stepneth* v. *Lloyd* (1598) CP 40/1610, m. 1157 (demurrer), abstracted in A. K. R. Kiralfy, *A Source Book of English Law* (1957), pp. 308–10; *Select Cases in the Court of Requests*, ed. I. S. Leadam (1255, 1898), p. xxxix; Co. Inst. iv. 97; Cro. Eliz. 646. Coke anglicised the defendant's name as Flood, but he was Humphrey Lloyd of Glamorganshire. Coke and Croke both said judgment was given for the defendant, though the record ends with an adjournment for advisement to Michaelmas term 1598. The following year Coke prosecuted Lloyd in the Star Chamber for misdemeanours in Glamorganshire: IT MS. Petyt 511.13, fo. 119.

[17] 23 Hen. VI, c. 9.

[18] This point had already been raised in relation to the Chancery: *Taylor* v. *Beale* (1597) BL MS. Add. 25198, fo. 225; CUL MS. Ll.3.9, fos. 482, 487v; 20 *American Journal of Legal History* 223 n. 69(c).

[19] Croke's report appears to say that they had no power at all, and Coke was pleased to read the decision in that way (next note), though the court did not in other contemporary cases deny the court any jurisdiction.

[20] Co. Inst. iv. 97 ('And it was adjudged upon solemn argument, that this which was called a Court of Requests ... was no court which had power of judicature, but all the proceedings thereupon were *coram non judice*, and the arrest of Flood was false imprisonment').

lie against the judge. Walmsley J. added that even the Chancery could only 'meddle with men's persons, and it is usurpation when they meddle with possessions, or with sequestrations out of the Court of Requests; if they meddle with goods, it is unlawful'.[21] The King's Bench at this period regularly sent prohibitions to the Requests.[22] But the matter remained controversial in the Common Pleas,[23] and the question was returned to in 1599 when that court issued a prohibition against a party who had arrested a litigant and threatened to imprison the attorney who had acted in the Requests.[24] According to Glanville J., 'the masters of Requests have no authority to commit the person of any man to prison', and the court held that 'process out of the Court of Requests is not a sufficient warrant to imprison anyone, inasmuch as it is against the statute of Magna Carta, chapter 29, and therefore it seems that a writ of false imprisonment is maintainable against the sheriff who executes the process'. For from being the exclusive property of Puritan firebrands, chapter 29 was now being spontaneously invoked from the bench.[25] In the same year the Common Pleas held that a commission of sequestration from the Requests, to seize a party's goods in execution, was illegal, and that a writ of detinue would lie against the sheriff who seized the goods.[26] This was a decision about process rather than jurisdiction: the Requests should have imprisoned the recalcitrant party rather than issued a commission of sequestration. Even that concession, however, would have to be withdrawn.

---

[21] *Anon.* (*c.* 1596) BL MS. Add. 25199, fo. 2 (tr.). The passage is here translated in its garbled form, which is ambiguous. But the last allusion is to commissions of sequestration from the Requests to seize a party's goods by way of coercion: this is spelt out in *Brograve and Heveningham* v. *Watts* (1599) BL MS. Lansdowne 1110, fo. 114v; below, n. 26.

[22] *Anon.* (1594) CUL MS. Ll.3.9, fo. 422; *Anon.* (1595) BL MS. Hargrave 356, fo. 101; MS. Add. 25198, fo. 80 (same); *Luson's Case* (1596) CUL MS. Ii.5.26, fo. 153v; *Twait's Case* (1598) BL MS. Harley 4552, fo. 164v; *Anon.* (1599) BL MS. Add. 25223, fo. 56v.

[23] Relations were not wholly hostile. Dr Hill (above, n. 9), p. xix, cites a letter of 1599 from Walmsley J. to Dr Caesar asking the Requests to give relief in a case where the Common Pleas was unable to do so.

[24] *Anon.* (1599) BL MS. Add. 25223, fo. 56v (report in English); Yelverton's abridgement, BL MS. Add. 48186, fo. 419 (quotation tr.).

[25] In the same year c. 29 was relied on by the Common Pleas in *Barham* v. *Dennis* (1599) below, p. 290; and *Davenant* v. *Hurdys* (1599) below, p. 316. Cf. the *Case of the Dyers of London* (1599) Co. Inst. ii. 47; 8 Co. Rep. 125; Coke said this also rested on c. 29, though no report has been found in which the judges themselves referred to it.

[26] *Brograve and Heveningham* v. *Watts* (1599) BL MS. Lansdowne 1110, fo. 114v.

In 1600 the Common Pleas returned to the power of imprisonment.[27] The Requests had committed two executors to the Fleet prison for refusing to pay a sum awarded by decree, and they brought a *corpus cum causa*, which was a species of *habeas corpus* for parties having privilege as litigants.[28] The underlying objection was that they had been sued upon a simple contract, and the common law as understood at that date did not allow an action of debt against executors without a bond.[29] Whether they had a remedy in conscience depended on whether the executors had sufficient assets to pay the simple debts as well as those due under bonds, and that did not appear from the record. The court held the committal unlawful and said they would discharge the prisoners unless it could be shown that the cause of imprisonment was lawful. 'This Court of Requests', said the judges, 'has no such power upon the bodies of the queen's subjects, but their office is in ease of the queen to peruse the petitions of the poor and those of the queen's household, and to direct in what place they may be relieved; and it is rather an office of discretion than of correction.' They went on to say that the name of the court was not to be read of in old books, and that it had no authority derived from Parliament. If its authority was solely by commission, it would be void as being 'against the law and the liberty given by the great charter', as was established by the case of 1368.[30] Christopher Yelverton, the queen's serjeant, told the court that recently the Star Chamber had been asked whether they could punish perjury in a deposition in the Requests, and the judges who were consulted had advised that they could not. The Common Pleas referred the case to two serjeants at law, to investigate whether the executors had sufficient assets, and in the mean time

---

[27] *Jewkes v. Smith and Gardener* (Pas. 1600) BL MS. Lansdowne 1065, fo. 50v (quotations tr.); differently reported in IT MS. Barrington 6, fos. 43v ('33'v)–46. Cf. *Anon.* (Pas. 1601) YLS MS. G.R29.16, fo. 15, where the Common Pleas said a litigant sent to the Fleet by the Requests would be released on a writ of privilege, but this was not so if he was committed by the Chancery.

[28] The court conceded that it could not release parties other than those with privilege, but they had to apply to the King's Bench. This limitation was denied in *Chapman v. Boyers* (1605) BL MS. Add. 25205, fo. 33 (Walmsley J. dissenting) and was wholly abandoned under Coke's chief justiceship: below, p. 354. The reason given in that case was that the Common Pleas was derived out of the King's Bench as a result of Magna Carta, c. 11.

[29] The long-standing doctrine was overturned by the Exchequer Chamber in the time of Coke CJ: *Pynchon v. Legat* (1611) 9 Co. Rep. 86. Cf. *Herlakenden's Case* (1604) CUL MS. Gg.4.9, fo. 146v, where the King's Bench discussed the maxim *actio personalis moritur cum persona* in relation to the Requests and a judgment in ejectment against a testator.

[30] *Sir John atte Lee's Case* (1368) above, p. 58.

discharged the prisoners under surety to appear again upon warning. The sequel seems not to be reported. Another clash of jurisdictions with the Common Pleas arose in the same term.[31] A plaintiff in that court had been sued in the Requests and had obtained a prohibition to stop the suit; the defendant had nevertheless proceeded with it, and the Requests had imprisoned the plaintiff until he entered into a bond to appear in that court. The Common Pleas were asked to resolve his dilemma: should he appear, in which case the Requests would imprison him, or should he decline to appear, in which case he would forfeit the penalty in the bond? The answer given was that the bond was void, and that the defendant should be committed for his contempt in bringing the suit in the Requests. The court could not prevent the Requests from arresting the plaintiff again but, if they did, a remedy would be given. Walmsley J. said to Yelverton, the queen's serjeant who had asked the question, 'You ought to bring such causes as this judicially before us by information, or at the queen's instance, and then you shall see what we will do.' He recalled a case in which Dr Caesar, as a master of Requests, had made a party enter into a bond to appear and to perform a decree, and had sought to enforce the bond in the Queen's Bench; the defendant had pleaded duress and won a verdict at the trial before Popham CJ, 'who seemed exceedingly offended with [Caesar's] course'. Glanville J. thought more boldness was needed: 'You know that Cardinal Wolsey might do anything till the king's attorney took him in hand, but after he was as calm as a lamb. So you of the queen's counsel should inform against them of the Court of Requests.'

Later the same year, Anderson CJ reaffirmed that it was unlawful by the law of the land for the Requests to meddle with freehold,[32] and in 1603 the court (in his absence) awarded a prohibition where the Requests sought to force a party to restore the penalty recovered in an action of debt on a penal bond.[33] In the last term of the queen's reign, John Hele, queen's serjeant, told the Common Pleas that he had been summoned with the attorney-general into the King's Bench and informed by 'all the

---

[31] *Anon.* (Pas. 1600) BL MS. Add. 25223, fos. 108–9 (report in English). This is probably the same as *Smith's Case* (1600) IT MS. Barrington 6, fo. 43v, quoted in Baker, *Collected Papers*, i. 487; here it was suggested that an information on the statute of *praemunire* would lie.

[32] *Morley's Case* (Mich. 1600) BL MS. Lansdowne 1065, fo. 67v. This was another *corpus cum causa* for a litigant who had been imprisoned for disobeying an injunction from the Requests to stay execution of his suit at law.

[33] *Anon.* (Hil. 1603) YLS MS. G.R29.16, fo. 190v.

judges ... publicly that they were all resolved that the Court of Requests cannot hold plea of anything which concerneth the common law, and whereof the common law can have cognizance; and they willed all the counsellors at the bar to take notice thereof, and if any of their clients were impleaded for any such matter there, then they shall have prohibitions'.[34] This drew immediate approval from Walmsley J.: 'I am of the same mind, for truly I am informed that if a man comes into that court and informs that he is poor, and much indebted, they will grant a commission to have his debts installed,[35] and if this be lawful I marvel to what purpose the Statute of Bankrupts was made.' In another case the same term, however, Walmsley J. drew the line at directing prohibitions to the solicitors and counsel in Requests cases, even though there were said to be precedents for it in both benches, because he said it was against the law to prohibit a servant from doing his service.[36] The Common Pleas, for all its fighting language, failed to strangle the Court of Requests, which was supported by the privy councillors, but there was no mistaking their confidence in Magna Carta as their most potent available weapon.

In 1605 Coke, as attorney-general, brought in the King's Bench to join the attack. The case concerned an executor who had accounted, and then died, and a suit had been brought in the Requests to compel the executor's executors to make a fresh account. This was properly a matter for the ecclesiastical courts. Coke moved successfully for a prohibition, saying that[37]

> the court of King's Bench has power to control any court which proceeds out of course, or meddles with things which do not belong to it, as for instance if the court of Common Bench would proceed contrary to Magna Carta;[38] and likewise of the Exchequer, the Cinque Ports, or another court of equity ... and likewise if the Court of Requests meddles with things belonging to the spiritual court.

---

[34] *Anon.* (Hil. 1603) BL MS. Add. 25212, fo. 71 (report in English).

[35] I.e. deferred in order to be paid off by instalments. These commissions had caused friction with the judges in the 1590s, although the chief justices were sometimes included in them: Dawson, 'Privy Council', pp. 640–1, 648–50.

[36] *Anon.* (Hil. 1603) BL MS. Lansdowne 1058, fo. 57; MS. Add. 9844, fo. 122v; YLS MS. G.R29.16. fos. 190v–192. The prohibition had been sought by Serjeant Hele because the party could not be found.

[37] *Trott* v. *Taylor* (1605) CUL MS. Ii.5.26, fo. 227v. Coke had also moved for a prohibition to the Requests in *Snowe* v. *Beverley* (1603), reported in his autograph notebook, BL MS. Harley 6686B, fos. 537v–544, arguing (fos. 538) that a party could not have relief in equity contrary to an express rule of law.

[38] I.e. Magna Carta, c. 11.

Soon afterwards the King's Bench considered the vexed question of injunctions granted following judgments at law,[39] a jurisdiction which had been exercised occasionally by the full Council,[40] and more controversially by the Chancery.[41] Popham CJ said he thought an injunction could be granted if the court of equity was already seised of a case before the judgment was given at law, but he was immediately challenged by Coke:

> *Coke* Att.-Gen. to the contrary. And he said that, if that were law, then the statute of 4 Hen. IV, c. 23, would serve for little or nothing, which provides that after judgments given in the king's court the parties should be in peace until they were defeated by error or otherwise. For if the court of conscience might examine the equity thereof, and compel the party to release them or endure perpetual imprisonment, it would be of the same effect as if they could undo the judgment by their decree. It would also then seem that all injunctions out of these courts are idle, if they could just as well decree this after judgment. And he said it was adjudged according to this by all the judges in a case in which he was of counsel.[42]

The outcome of that case was left uncertain, but the dispute was resumed when Coke was chief justice.[43]

The Court of Chancery

A much weightier matter which also first came to a head in the 1590s was that of the jurisdiction claimed by the Court of Chancery to stay execution of a judgment at law even when the suit in equity was not commenced until after the judgment was given. This appeared to be contrary to the enactment of Henry IV cited by Coke; but the courts of law and equity had reached a stalemate on this question in the 1580s.[44] The head-on challenge came in the leading case of *Throckmorton* v. *Finch*. The litigation began in 1590 with an ejectment action in the Court of Exchequer, in which Sir Moyle Finch recovered possession of the manors

---

[39] *Cardinal* v. *De la Broche* (1605) BL MS. Lansdowne 1075, fo. 167; MS. Add. 35954, fo. 430v; IT MS. Barrington 7, fo. 209v (quotation tr.); sub nom. *De la Becoche*, CUL MS. Gg.4.9, fo. 188; differently tr. in *Cases Concerning Equity and the Courts of Equity 155–1660*, ed. W. H. Bryson, vol. i (117 SS, 2001), p. 345. These are all versions of the same report.

[40] Dawson, 'Privy Council', p. 645.   [41] Below, pp. 286–8, 302–3.

[42] Probably *Throckmorton* v. *Finch* (1597) below. See also *Anon.* (1587) Godb. 127 (concerning London).

[43] Below, pp. 376, 410–21.   [44] See above, pp. 162–3, 212–14.

of Ravenstone and Stoke Goldington in Buckinghamshire against Thomas Throckmorton; Coke had carried the day as counsel for Finch.[45] The unsuccessful defendant then brought a writ of error, and the case was argued before all the judges at Serjeants' Inn, Fleet Street. In the time of Wray CJ, who died in 1592, the judges agreed to reverse the judgment, but no judgment was entered. Then, in 1594, the case was reargued, and it was decided (by a majority of one) to uphold the judgment, notwithstanding the strongly held opinions of the dissentients. One reporter mused: '*Sic transit gloria mundi*. The law in these days altered and changed as the justices did alter and change.'[46] The dispute was entirely one of law, because the facts were not disputed.[47] Queen Mary had leased the two manors to Sir Robert Throckmorton (Thomas's father) for seventy years, with the draconian proviso that if the rent was ever in arrear for forty days the lease would be void. In 1567 Throckmorton's servant ran away with the rent money at the day of payment,[48] so that the payment in that year was not made on time, though the queen's receiver later accepted it and further payments were made and accepted for many years. The reversion of the manor was afterwards acquired by Sir Moyle Finch, as lessee of his father-in-law Sir Thomas Heneage, and he sought to recover possession against Thomas (as Sir Robert's executor) on the footing that when the day of payment was missed in 1567 the lease had become ipso facto void, and therefore the reversion had come to him free of the lease. Evidently many of the common-law judges had been willing to find a legal way of preventing Finch from taking such unfair advantage of a minor slippage, which was not Throckmorton's fault and had been waived. But their view had not in the end prevailed.[49] Finch's success was

---

[45] *Finch v. Throckmorton* (1589–90) Moo. 291; 2 Leo. 134; Cro. Eliz. 220; BL MS. Lansdowne 1068, fos. 49v–53; HLS MS. 110, fos. 35–40v; HLS MS. 1180(1), fos. 24v–25, 278v–284v. The record is printed in E. Coke, *A Booke of Entries* (1614), fos. 191–5. Coke's notebooks for this period are missing. Notes of 'mon argument' in the Exchequer on the same side as Coke, but seemingly not his, are in BL MS. Harley 1059, fos. 5–7.

[46] *Throckmorton v. Finch* (1594) BL MS. Lansdowne 1060, fo. 141v, endnote. Judgment to affirm the previous judgment was given on 12 November 1594: ibid. There are reports of the arguments in Poph. 53, sub nom. *Finch v. Riseley*; 1 And. 303; HLS MS. 5066, fos. 251v–257. Pending the writ of error, Finch had an interlocutory injunction in the Chancery to prevent waste: Bryson, *Cases concerning Equity*, i. 136, no. 63.

[47] They were confessed by a demurrer, leaving only the question of law to be decided by the court.

[48] So says the report in MS. Lansdowne 1110, though Coke (summarising the record) said only that it was unpaid by the servant's negligence.

[49] There is no need to go into the technicalities here, but the matter may be summarised. Usually the queen could not repossess land for non-payment of rent without an

without doubt unconscionable,[50] and Throckmorton was advised to prefer a bill in Chancery to prevent enforcement of the judgment. Unfortunately, he had not thought to seek relief in equity until after the judgment had been given and affirmed upon the writ of error. Finch pleaded the judgments in bar of the Chancery suit, and thereby raised for formal decision the question whether judgments at law were sacrosanct or whether they were liable to be effectively annulled by parties who had slept on their equitable rights.[51] As with the more celebrated *Shelley's Case*,[52] there were religious undercurrents in the dispute, Throckmorton being a Roman Catholic recusant.[53] The matter attracted the queen's interest, and it was also raised in the House of Commons.[54] The lord keeper, Sir Thomas Egerton, was inclined to overrule the demurrer but agreed to refer the question to all the judges of England, ostensibly 'because the case was of great consequence and likely to be a precedent for many others',[55] but in truth because the queen herself had told him to do so.[56] The case was heard before the assembled judges in Michaelmas term 1597. Throckmorton's counsel argued that his intention was not to impeach the judgment itself but to be relieved from it on equitable

inquisition of office, which there had not been in this case until after the grant of the reversion (which divested the queen of all her interest); but most leases contained a proviso for re-entry for non-payment, whereas here the proviso was held to constitute a condition, and therefore it took immediate effect without the need for an office or indeed for any decision as to whether to continue with the lease.

[50] Coke, who had been counsel for Finch, accepted that (in the view of all the judges) 'the bill comprehended much matter of equity, and there was very good cause he should have been relieved, if he had complained before the judgment': *Courtney v. Glanvill* (1614) Cro. Jac. 343 at p. 345. Cf. Co. Inst. iii. 124 ('it appeared to [the judges] that there was apparent matter in equity').

[51] For the concept of estoppel by election, in this context, see Smith, *Sir Edward Coke*, pp. 236–7.

[52] *Shelley's Case* (1581) 1 Co. Rep. 93. For the background see A. W. B. Simpson, *Leading Cases in the Common Law* (1995), pp. 13–44. See also D. C. Smith, 'Was there a Rule in Shelley's Case?' (2009) 30 *Journal of Legal History* 53–70.

[53] He had to be released from custody in Banbury Castle for a few terms in 1597 to pursue his suit against Finch: 27 APC 64; 28 APC 14–15, 102.

[54] *HPHC 1559–1603*, ii. 118–19; iv. 500–1. The dispute was nearly resolved by legislation.

[55] *Throckmorton v. Finch* (1597) Coke's notebook, BL MS. Harley 6686A, fos. 222v–227, at fo. 223 (tr.).

[56] Co. Inst. iii. 124–5: 'Sir Thomas Egerton, then lord keeper, inclined to rule over the demurrer, saying that he would not meddle with the judgment but punish the corrupt conscience of the defendant in relieving the plaintiff in equity. Upon a petition to Queen Elizabeth, who ever favoured the due proceeding of her laws, she referred the consideration of the demurrer to all the judges of England'. Cf. Co. Inst. iv. 86, where it is said that Egerton had expressed this view in court before the queen intervened.

grounds, relying on a recent decision by Lord Keeper Egerton that such suits were not brought to reopen the point which had been adjudged, but to examine the 'collateral' matter in equity and to 'conform the corrupt conscience of the party'.[57] The argument on the other side was presented by Coke, now attorney-general, among others. The delicacy of the case may explain its absence from other reports,[58] but Coke knew its importance and made a lengthy entry in his contemporary notebook. He reported the outcome as follows:[59]

> And upon great consideration it was resolved by all the judges of England[60] that the said Thomas Throckmorton was not to be admitted to examine the matter in equity after the said judgment, for that is contrary to law and statutes. Although it has been said that the court of equity will not impeach the judgment, nevertheless by this suit all the effect and fruit of the judgment would be taken away … And it would be perilous to permit men after judgments and trials in law to surmise matter in equity and thereby put the party who recovered to excessive charges. By this means suits would be infinite, and no one could be in peace for anything which the law had given him by judgment. But a contentious and able[61] person, who had an unquiet spirit, might continually surmise matter in equity and thus vex him who recovered endlessly, which would be a great inconvenience. And it is absurd that a court which, as to equity, is not a court of record should control judgments which are of record. 37 Hen. VI, fo. 14.[62] That inconvenience was intended to be taken away by Parliament in 4 Hen. IV, c. 23, so that after judgment in the king's courts, whether in plea real or plea personal, the parties and their heirs should be in peace until the judgment should be reversed by error or attaint, as had been used in the times of the king's forebears. See Magna Carta, c. 29;

---

[57] BL MS. Harley 6686A, at fos. 223v–224 (tr.), citing *Fulwood* v. *Ward*.

[58] The report in 2 Bulst. 301 was a citation by Coke CJ in 1614. The briefer note in BL MS. Lansdowne 1110, fos. 15v–17 (printed in Bryson, *Cases concerning Equity*, vol. ii (118 SS, 2001), pp. 441–2) was a citation in 1615. Coke cited the case in the Privy Council in 1616, in defending his observation that injunctions after judgment would overthrow the common law: CUL MS. Gg.2.31, fo. 202.

[59] Ibid. 224 (tr.).

[60] Coke indicated later (on fo. 226) that there was in fact one dissentient voice, that of Walmsley J. Walmsley had been one of the strong dissenters in the Exchequer Chamber, and made something of a habit of dissenting in leading cases, on occasion to Coke's irritation: see Baker, *Collected Papers*, i. 466. Coke was therefore apt to edit him out of his reports. In Co. Inst. iii. 124 he said the decision was unanimous.

[61] *Sic*, but this is possibly the ending of a longer word beginning on the previous line (which is badly worn).

[62] *Reynolde* v. *Knotte* (1459) YB Hil. 37 Hen. VI, fo. 13, pl. 3, at fo. 14, *per* Prysot CJ; *Select Cases in the Exchequer Chamber*, ed. M. Hemmant (51 SS, 1933) p. 147, at p. 152; CP 40/ 792, m. 424.

5 Edw. III, c. 9; 25 Edw III, c. 4; 28 Edw. III, c. 3; 42 Edw. III, c. 3; 15 Hen. VI, c. 4.[63] 29 Edw. III, fo. 24:[64] the king may not undo a judgment but by course of the law ...

Coke then set out further precedents, derived from his own argument at the bar, and maintained that the main point had already been decided in an unreported case of 1465.[65] He also suggested that the Chancery came within the statutes of *praemunire*, even though it was the king's court, when its proceedings were in destruction of the common law. The various precedents cited on the other side, in support of the Chancery position, some of which dated back to the time of Henry VIII, were rejected by Coke as 'not authentical, being most of them in torn papers, and the rest of no credit'.[66] They were in any case decisions by chancellors alone, without seeking judicial advice, perhaps without any contest.[67]

Three years later, in another important case involving Sir Moyle Finch, who had a decree given against him at the suit of the trustees of Ravenstone and Stoke Goldington, it was held by all the judges of England that a Chancery decree could, upon a petition to the queen, be reversed by judges delegate appointed by letters patent.[68] According to Coke's note, the judges reported that a trust could not be imposed contrary to an express use without writing,[69] and that freehold title could not be decided in Chancery, even if a party complained that he needed a

---

[63] Unlike the foregoing, this was not a direct confirmation of Magna Carta, but a statute forbidding Chancery suits for matters determinable at common law, contrary to 'the statutes thereof made'.

[64] *Earl of Hertford* v. *Earl of Oxford* (1355) YB Pas. 29 Edw. III, fo. 24 (concerning the reversal of the attainder of Lord Maltravers: as to which see above, p. 56).

[65] *Cobb* v. *Nore* (1465) KB 27/816, m. 35. He made a note of this in Michaelmas term 1597: BL MS. Hargrave 6686A, fo. 207v ('a notable precedent'). Another precedent in point was *Russel's Case* (1482) YB Mich. 22 Edw. IV, fo. 37, pl. 21, where Hussey CJ said that if the chancellor committed a party for disobeying such an injunction, he would be released upon *habeas corpus* (that is, a writ of privilege).

[66] Co. Inst. iii. 125.   [67] Co. Inst. iv. 86, abridging the report in the notebook.

[68] *Earl of Worcester* v. *Finch* (1600) 2 And. 162; cited by Coke CJ in *Vaudry* v. *Pannel* (1615) 3 Bulst. 116 at p. 118; Calth. MS. ii. 114v. Coke CJ said the decree was reversed, though Anderson CJ's report says only that the judges advised that it should not bind the defendant and that the matter was debated again in 1601. The report in Coke's notebook (below, n. 70) does not mention the patent of delegation, but says only that the case was referred to all the judges.

[69] I.e. if land was conveyed to A. to the use of A. and his heirs, it could not be alleged without a written declaration of trust that A. had in fact been enfeoffed in trust for B. Cf. *Killio* v. *Taverner* (1595) Powle's reports, Bryson, *Cases Concerning Equity*, i. 203, no. 183.

discovery of title-deeds to clarify it.[70] Popham CJ said that the jurisdiction of the Chancery was limited to three cases, namely, fraud, breach of trust, and accident without fault of the party.[71] This second 'great case'[72] was perhaps more of a blow than the previous decision. The Chancery no longer had the last word, even in matters of equity.[73] But the new review procedure was seldom if ever used again,[74] and it is unlikely that Egerton ever gave way to *Throckmorton v. Finch* in practice;[75] he was certainly ignoring it by 1615, when all this learning would be resurrected, to Coke's undoing.[76] The broad words of Magna Carta were far too unspecific to settle the matter on either occasion; but in 1615 Egerton would take pains to refute them,[77] and it is noteworthy that Coke had thought fit to cite chapter 29, with all its progeny, as early as 1597, when he was a law officer of the crown.

The High Commission

The practical value of chapter 29 having been essayed in the later 1590s in relation to the Requests and the Chancery, an opportunity was awaited for it to be deployed against the High Commission following the setback of 1595.[78] The first instance so far discovered was in 1599,[79] when Serjeant Harris relied on chapter 29 in asking the Common Pleas to grant *habeas corpus* for a party imprisoned by

---

[70] *Earl of Worcester v. Finch* (1600) BL MS. Harley 6686B, fos. 407–408v; edited version in Co. Inst. iv. 85–6. A suit for discovery was a common pretext for bringing titles into Chancery: Jones, *Elizabethan Chancery*, pp. 455–7.

[71] In Co. Inst. iv. 85, Coke diluted this to make them examples rather than restrictions. Cf. *Malcome v. Morris* (1616) Calth. MS. ii. 136, *per* Coke CJ (tr. 'Sir Thomas Smith says in his *Commonwealth* that remedy is given in Chancery for three things, covin ... accident ... or breach of trust').

[72] Coke CJ so termed it in *Vaudry v. Pannel* (1615) 3 Bulst. 116 at p. 118.

[73] The lord chancellor could presumably refuse to seal the patent appointing the delegates, but that would have been seen as an unjustifiable interference with the course of justice.

[74] Jones, *Elizabethan Chancery*, p. 290 n. 1.

[75] In *Anon.* (1605) BL MS. Lansdowne 1112, fo. 15v, an injunction from the Chancery was cast into the King's Bench after the jury were sworn, and the court said it came too late.

[76] Below, pp. 410–21.

[77] In his widely circulated tract, 'Some Notes and Observations upon the Statute of Magna Carta, c. 29, and other Statutes concerning the Proceedings in the Chancery in Causes of Equity and Conscience' (1615) below, pp. 416–17.

[78] *Cawdray's Case* (1595) above, p. 141.

[79] For other Common Pleas cases in 1599 see above, p. 280 n. 25.

the ecclesiastical commissioners in a matrimonial case.[80] The judges remanded the prisoner for further consideration of whether bail was available after excommunication, but Walmsley J. agreed with counsel that it was 'directly against Magna Carta' for the commissioners to commit anyone to prison, and Glanville J. added that 'the meaning of the statute [of 1559] was in no case to disannul Magna Carta, so sacredly established'.[81] It is noteworthy that Thomas Walmsley, of all judges, should have taken such a strong position on Magna Carta,[82] given that he was notoriously conservative and very remote from the Puritans in point of religion.[83] His remark confirms the conclusion advanced in the previous chapter, that devotion to the great charter was not monopolised by a particular brand of lawyer, even in cases concerning the Church. Chapter 29 offered protection against novelties for the conservatives as well as protection against punishment for the radicals, and in consequence Magna Carta had become 'of no less reverence with us than the Roman Tables was with them'.[84]

After this, all three courts in Westminster Hall were active in limiting the power of the High Commission, citing chapter 29 when appropriate. Doubtless in deference to the decision in *Cawdray's Case* (1595),[85] the earliest skirmishes did not involve deprived ministers but laymen. In 1599 the Court of Exchequer refused to enforce a £40 bond taken by the commissioners to enforce a sentence for working on a Sunday, on the grounds that this was not an 'enormous' offence within their jurisdiction,[86] and the King's Bench for the same reason released a prisoner who

---

[80] *Barham v. Dennis* (Pas. 1599) BL MS. Add. 48146, fo. 422; BL MS. Lansdowne 1065, fo. 12; Yelverton's reports, BL MS. Hargrave 403, fos. 198–9 (abridged in BL MS. Add. 25212, fo. 63). Cf. *Man's Case* (1591) 4 Leo. 16, where a prohibition was issued against the Commission in a case of incest, founded on 32 Hen. VIII, c. 38, and the failure to specify the Levitical degrees.

[81] BL MS. Hargrave 403, fo. 199. Magna Carta was also cited by Anderson CJ and Glanville J. in *Paramour v. Verrall* (1600) BL MS. Harley 4814, fos. 84v, 87v; below, p. 494.

[82] Cf. *Taylor v. Browne* (1598) Sterrell's reports, BL MS. Add. 25199, fo. 9v, where Walmsley J. questioned the commissioners' power of imprisonment but was stopped by Anderson CJ: '(tr.) do not speak against it, for a resolution has been given that they may make a warrant [of arrest] by the statute'.

[83] Baker, *Collected Papers*, i. 466; iii. 1151; ODNB. He has been described as 'a semi-conforming Catholic' with a recusant wife: Collinson, *Bancroft*, p. 107.

[84] *Proc. Parl. 1610*, p. 204, *per* Dodderidge MP, referring to the Twelve Tables.

[85] Above, pp. 141–3.

[86] *Atmere's Case* (1599) in Coke's notebook, BL MS. Harley 6686B, fo. 373, and Co. Inst. iv. 332; cited by Coke CJ in *Wood's Case* (1609) YLS MS. G.R29.16, fo. 292; BL MS. Add. 9844, fo. 50v; and in his tract responding to Bancroft, BL MS. Harley 7516, fo. 9;

had refused to enter into a bond in £800 for the payment of alimony.[87] In 1600 the Common Pleas held that adultery was not an enormous offence of the kind intended by the statute,[88] and a prohibition was granted by the King's Bench where a clergyman libelled the plaintiff before the High Commission for a mere assault and for calling him a goose.[89] A different point settled around the same time was that the commissioners could not arrest anyone by sending a warrant but should proceed by citation,[90] which seems a clear application of the requirement of due process. The court further held that the commissioners could not authorise their pursuivants to break into a party's house, or to arrest someone at night.[91] Coke's report of the 1600 case shows that he had now come to a different understanding of the commissioners' jurisdiction from that which he had advanced with such unfortunate success five years earlier in *Cawdray's Case*.[92] The Act of 1559 had united the ecclesiastical jurisdiction to the crown without introducing anything new. The queen could not alter the law by commission, 'for every subject has an inheritance and an interest in the laws whereby he is governed, which cannot be abrogated, altered or changed except by Act of Parliament'. And an unlimited power of imprisonment without any ordinary remedy was 'against the liberty of the subject'. It followed that the ecclesiastical commission could not confer a new power of imprisonment, and there was no power of imprisonment vested in the Church courts at common law. Coke's

---

MS. Add. 58218, fo. 20; Warburton's reports, CUL MS. Ii.5.25, fo. 94v. Coke said the offence was carrying a load of wood on the Sabbath after evensong.

[87] *Fowler's Case* (1599) CUL MS. Dd.8.48, 61.

[88] *Thicknesse's Case* (1600) cited in 12 Co. Rep. 82.

[89] *Lovegrove v. Prime* (1600) HLS MS. 2070, fo. 44v; Moo. 840. Laying hands on a clergyman was within the ecclesiastical jurisdiction, but that did not extend to an assault without battery.

[90] This explanation was given by Anderson CJ at Northampton assizes in another case the same year: *Simpson's Case* (1600) Co. Inst. iv. 333–4, which Coke was fond of citing: e.g. BL MS. Add. 58218, fo. 21; 12 Co. Rep. 49; BL MS. Add. 9844, fo. 124 (1610) and fo. 149v (1611). Simpson had killed the commissioners' pursuivant in self-defence, and this was held not to be murder, because the pursuivant could not be considered a minister of justice executing his office.

[91] *Smith's Case* (1600) in Coke's notebook, BL MS. Harley 6686B, fos. 375v–378; also reported in Owen 145; Cro. Eliz. 741; BL MS. Harley 1679, fos. 26–27v (where Serjeant Harris this time argued in support of the power of imprisonment); sub nom. *South v. Whetwit*, BL MS. Hargrave 12, fo. 393. Smith was an attorney of the Common Pleas. The notion that the 'common people' were inheritable to the common law had been expressed by Gascoigne CJ in *Windsor's Case* (1407) YB Hil. 8 Hen. IV, fo. 18, pl. 3.

[92] Above, pp. 141–3.

arguments here were the same as Morice's. His object can hardly have been to diminish the prerogative of the queen, since he was now her attorney-general, but was rather to bring the High Commission under the rule of law. Chapter 29 of Magna Carta may have been specifically mentioned in the case,[93] and it was certainly represented by the phrase 'liberty of the subject', a figure of speech not often found in earlier reports but about to become very common.[94] When the case was cited the following year by Serjeant Williams, it was undoubtedly in the context of chapter 29.[95] In an attempt to test the limits of *Cawdray's Case*, Williams sought a prohibition to the High Commission on behalf of a parson who had been deprived for simony. This time, however, the motion was unsuccessful, because the court held that simony was within the ecclesiastical jurisdiction, that there had been no ousting from a freehold, but only a declaration that the benefice was vacant, and that in any case a prohibition would not be granted after decree.

The powers of the High Commission were further considered in 1602, when all the justices were assembled and advised the Common Pleas that the ecclesiastical courts had no power to imprison or fine;[96] they were instead dependent on the 'secular power', which would assist the spiritual court in exercising its proper jurisdiction.[97] The prohibition granted in this case was expressly founded on chapter 29 of Magna Carta, and this became common form in suggestions[98] for prohibitions shortly after-wards, so that there was no longer any need to keep mentioning it in argument.[99] In 1605, however, there was a setback.[100] It had been widely

---

[93] Not in Coke's report, but it is in the recollection of the case in *Viscountess Purbeck's Case* (1629) Hetl. 132 (also in Co. Litt. 242).

[94] It was not Coke's invention: see above, pp. 155, 257.

[95] *Baker* v. *Rogers* (1601) IT MS. Barrington 6, fos. 107–10 (tr. 'by Magna Carta no one shall be put out without judgment etc.'). Magna Carta is not mentioned in the printed reports of the case: Cro. Eliz. 788; Moo. 914.

[96] Coke discovered that there was no record of any fine imposed by the Commission having been estreated in the Exchequer until James I's time: BL MS. Harley 7516, fo. 8v.

[97] *Grey* v. *Poole* (1602) BL MS. Hargrave 403, fo. 119v; MS. Add. 9844, fo. 116; MS. Add. 25212, fos. 62v–64; cited by Coke in BL MS. Add. 58218, fo. 20v, from Trin. 44 Eliz., rot. 1233. This is probably the *Grey's Case* cited below, p. 296 n. 119.

[98] The application or petition for a prohibition was called a suggestion.

[99] Gray, *Writ of Prohibition*, 378, citing the precedents in BL MS. Stowe 424, fo. 158 (the earliest being from 1608). Cf. the more general statement in Brooks, *Law, Politics and Society*, p. 111, apparently based on the same evidence. A slightly later example is *Clifton's Case* (1610) in Usher, *High Commission*, pp. 204–5, in which the prohibition recited c. 29 and the *Articuli Cleri*.

[100] This was eight months before the discovery of the Gunpowder Plot in November.

believed among Roman Catholics that James I was going to reintroduce toleration, and the king was very keen to dispel this rumour.[101] On 13 February the lord chancellor, Lord Ellesmere, made a long speech in the Star Chamber, by the king's command, ostensibly on the subject of nonconformist ministers.[102] This was at the assembly before the Lent circuits, when the judges were told of governmental concerns before going on assize. The king, said Ellesmere, had been troubled by rumours that he intended to be tolerant of papists – rumours which had led to popular petitions[103] – and he wanted his position made clear. He wanted the laws put in execution against papists and Puritans alike, declaring both to be disturbers of the state whom he proposed to suppress. The lord chancellor then addressed some legal questions to the judges, who answered unanimously that the High Commission could lawfully deprive Puritan ministers for refusing to conform with the ceremonies appointed by the Elizabethan commissioners. The monarch had the supreme ecclesiastical power and had delegated it to the commissioners, who therefore took their power from the common law and not from the statute of 1559, which explained but did not restrict it. It followed that the king could without Parliament make ordinances and institutions to govern the clergy, and deprive them for disobedience.[104] This response was consistent both with *Cawdray's Case* and with their more recent decisions, since the latter were concerned with the fining and imprisonment of laymen and not with the discipline of the clergy by means of deprivation. The judges also advised that those who framed petitions and collected multitudes of signatures to prefer to the king could be fined, because such conduct tended to sedition, rebellion and discontent and was close to

---

[101] Usher, *Reconstruction*, ii. 91–5. For other indications of such rumours, and of the perception of Elizabeth's reign by Roman Catholics as one of bloody persecution, see Hawarde 162–3, 183, 224, 255, 267, 268–70, 295.

[102] *Case of the Nonconformist Ministers* (1605) CUL MS. Gg.2.5, fos. 280–281a. There are different but closely corroborative reports in Cro. Jac. 37; Moo. 755; SP 14/12, fo. 168 (also in BL MS. Harley 3209, fos. 39v–40; MS. Add. 25223, fos. 182–3), listing those present as including the two chief justices and eight puisne justices. Cf. the shorter account in Hawarde 186–9, which does not mention the judges' opinion. There is also a brief report in Noy 100.

[103] It is salutary to remember that religious liberty was not necessarily a popular cause. In 1646 Hanserd Knollys, a graduate of St Catharine's College, Cambridge, was stoned out of the pulpit at Dallinghoo, Suffolk, for preaching tolerance: M. James, *Religious Liberty on Trial* (Franklin, TN, 1997), p. 141.

[104] Brooks, *Law, Politics and Society*, pp. 113–14, suggested that the new problems had arisen from the Canons of 1604. Cf. Usher, *High Commission*, pp. 167–8.

treason.[105] It was even finable for Puritans to stir rumours that the king would tolerate 'papistry', for the king had stated categorically that he would never do so as long as he had a drop of blood in his body.[106] To make the king's intentions clear, Parliament later in the year passed an 'Act to prevent and avoid Dangers which grow by Popish Recusants', forbidding recusants from coming to London or holding public office, forbidding the importation, printing or sale of popish books, and giving magistrates the power to search recusants' houses and deface 'popish relicts'.[107]

If these were unfavourable times for freedom of religion, it must be remembered that they were nervous times. The statute of 1605, passed only nine months after Ellesmere's speech, was a reaction to the Jesuit Plot (as Coke called it), following the country's narrow escape from a catastrophic mass murder in the name of religion.[108] And yet, although external conformity was still required by law, there was no intention to meddle with freedom of private belief. The judges, and Coke (as the principal law officer of the crown), had taken the view that bishops no longer had the power to imprison for heresy,[109] but could only proceed by the censures of the Church, and that they should observe the limitation in the Act of 1559 that nothing should be adjudged heresy unless it was so declared by scripture or by Parliament with the assent of the Convocation.[110] Convictions were

---

[105] This point was also noted by Coke, BL MS. Harley 6686B, fo. 634v. Coke and Popham CJJ both declared in 1606 that 'gathering of hands' to petitions was punishable in the Star Chamber: *Att.-Gen.* v. *Glover* (1606) Hawarde 302 at p. 305.

[106] As early as April 1603 he had made it plain that he would rather die in the field than grant toleration to papists, though he would not use extremity against them: *The Diary of John Manningham of the Middle Temple 1602–03*, ed. R. Sorlien (Hanover, NH, 1976), p. 245. Another version had it that he would 'rather fight in blood to the knees than give toleration of religion': Wilbraham, *Journal*, p. 62.

[107] 3 Jac. I, c. 5. This was the parliament nearly blown up by Guy Fawkes. Even so, it may not have been intended that the statute be strictly enforced: Usher, *Reconstruction*, ii. 110–12.

[108] Above, pp. 131–2.

[109] They had been given the power by the statute 2 Hen. IV, c. 15, which had been repealed: see above, p. 114. Nicholas Fuller said of the statute that 'the popish prelates, by the example of the man of sin at Rome, snatched the temporal sword out of the hand of the temporal magistrate by a statute gotten by themselves without the free consent of the Commons in Parliament . . . which statute since was made void': *Proc. Parl. 1610*, ii. 407.

[110] 12 Co. Rep. 56 (conference with Popham CJ and others, 1601); *Anon.* (*c.* 1607/9) Warburton's reports, CUL MS. Ii.5.25, fos. 105v–106 (rejecting a return to a *habeas corpus* that the prisoner had been committed by the archbishop of Canterbury for Arianism). It was thought unsafe to leave the jurisdiction in the hands of a single bishop: *Lady Throckmorton's Case* (1610) CUL MS. Ii.5.25, at fo. 177.

in practice almost unheard of. The last heretic executed in England was the eccentric, if not insane, Edward Wightman, who was burned at Lichfield in 1612, in the teeth of the advice which Coke CJ gave the law officers.[111] He had not only denied the divinity of Christ, in the Arianist manner, but also claimed himself to be the Messiah. Such extreme cases were rare. As far as the common law was concerned, heresy was best consigned to the history books, albeit some of its traces were difficult to eradicate.[112] Contention now raged over matters of dress and ritual, areas of fierce controversy until well into the Victorian period; but these concerned the clergy more than the laity, and affected their livings rather than their lives.

The king's concerns at the beginning of his reign, which had been broached at the Hampton Court conference in 1604,[113] aired by Ellesmere in the Star Chamber meeting of February 1605,[114] and pursued further by the bishops in a Privy Council session about prohibitions,[115] explain why Coke – in what was to be his last year as attorney-general – decided to publish an expanded report of *Cawdray's Case* (1595), declaring to a wide audience the authority of the High Commission.[116] While writing this at home during the Lent vacation of 1605, Coke wrote to Secretary Cecil that he had himself proposed the essay to James I in order to make generally available 'the very words of the ancient laws and statutes of England', and that the king had approved of his intentions. The underlying purpose was to demonstrate clearly what ecclesiastical jurisdiction belonged to the crown 'by the ancient laws of England', and that 'the laws made by King Henry VIII or since are for the most part declaratory

[111] *Anon.* (1612) 12 Co. Rep. 93 (and see ibid. 56). Another Arianist, Bartholomew Legatt, was executed earlier the same month, after James I had personally tried to convert him. He had made an appeal to Magna Carta, c. 29: Thompson, *Magna Carta*, pp. 280–1; 2 St. Tr. 727–42. No Roman Catholic was ever executed for heresy: above, p. 131.

[112] When Coke was nominated against his will to be sheriff of Buckinghamshire in 1625, he found to his surprise that the sheriff's oath (which he refused to take) still included the pursuit of Lollards, even though the legislation against them had been repealed: Yale Law School MS. G.R24.1, fos. 138, 139.

[113] Usher, *High Commission*, pp. 164–7, citing Coke's autograph notes in Holkham Hall MS. 677; Usher, *Reconstruction*, i. 327–8; above, p. 135 n. 133.

[114] Above, p. 293.

[115] 'Articuli Cleri' (1605) 2 St. Tr. 131–59 (with the judges' answers); Usher, *Reconstruction*, ii. 74–88. These complaints were about prohibitions in general, especially in tithe cases, rather than the High Commission in particular.

[116] 'Of the King's Ecclesiastical Law', 5 Co. Rep., part 1. This was published in Latin as well as English, in double columns.

of the old'.[117] It is doubtful how spontaneous this venture was, since he had already come to doubt the wisdom of the 1595 decision, and he buried the report of the case in a lengthy historical justification of the king's supremacy. Coke's main object was not to extol the High Commission, but to show 'without any inference or bombasting' that both the papists and the Puritans were wrong.

The tenor of the report might easily be misunderstood, but reports of other cases make Coke's position plain. So far was he from accepting the doctrine of *Cawdray's Case* as to the source of the Commission's authority that later in 1605 he argued in the King's Bench that the Commission was founded entirely on the Act of 1559 and had no power to fine or imprison, except in cases of enormous heresy or schism, and no power to deal with 'every little offence against the law of Holy Church, or any private controversy between man and man, for that were to take away the jurisdiction of all lesser ordinaries'. He said that this point had been decided in the time of Wray CJ (who died in 1592), omitting any mention of Cawdray. And his argument met with success. Perhaps Cawdray was distinguished on the basis that the discipline of the clergy rested primarily on the prerogative, but this does not appear in the reports. The party was a layman who had been committed to the Gatehouse by the commissioners, for insulting a minister,[118] and on Coke's motion he was released by *habeas corpus* and granted a prohibition as well.[119] It was one of a number of decisions around the same time concerning insolence to ministers ('irreverent speeches'), incidents which were symptomatic of the heated disagreements in the Church but clearly

---

[117] Autograph letter to Viscount Cranbourne, dated from Stoke [Poges], 8 March 1605: SP 14/13, fo. 116. Coke's date must have been new style. The letter was calendared with the date April 1605: *CSPD 1603–10*, p. 210.

[118] He said the minister was 'a knave priest and fitter to wear a white cloak than a black', evidently meaning that he was not Puritan enough. Puritan ministers refused to wear the white surplice.

[119] *Needham v. Price* (1605) CUL MS. Gg.4.9, fo. 174v; BL MS. Lansdowne 1075, fos. 154; MS. Lansdowne 1111, fos. 141v–142v; MS. Add. 35954, fos. 417v–418 (all the same). In *Anon.* (1606) BL MS. Add. 25205, fo. 25, Williams JKB said the same point (as to the fine) had been decided after a long debate in the Exchequer in a case in which he had been of counsel (i.e. before 1604). This seems to be *Grey's Case* (1602) YLS MS. G.R29.16, fos. 179v–180v, where a fine for laying hands on a clergyman was estreated into the Exchequer, and the party imprisoned in the Gatehouse for not paying it; all the judges of the Common Pleas held that the High Commission was to be guided by the *lex ecclesiae* and not the wording of the commission, and that its jurisdiction was grounded on the statute of 1559. Cf. above, p. 292 n. 97.

not 'enormous' offences akin to schism.[120] It was asserted in Parliament that punishment of this kind was often imposed in retaliation for bringing to light offences by the clergy.[121] A further buffet was delivered by the Common Pleas decision that the new Canons Ecclesiastical of 1604 could not override customary rights, which in theory rested on immemorial usage and were therefore triable by jury.[122]

Relief was also granted against the Commission on procedural grounds. In the case of Henry Chambers, the commissioners had thought to outwit the judges by sheltering under a vague royal authority. Chambers had been imprisoned by the High Commission, and his *habeas corpus* was returned to the effect that he was committed 'for contempt against the king'. The court held that the Commission had no general power to imprison, and said it was a great mischief when men were drawn forty miles from home for minor matters. The return 'for contempt against the king' was unacceptable, since it did not enable the court to judge whether the cause was sufficient, for it might be a temporal matter or bailable. Chambers was therefore discharged.[123] In the same term the judges rejected a general return to *habeas corpus* that the prisoner had been committed 'for certain ecclesiastical causes'. The case was adjourned for the return to be amended, and the revised return said that the prisoner had been committed for irreverent speeches and 'saucy carriage' towards a Dr Newman. This too was held bad, and the prisoner was discharged.[124] The court remarked that 'saucy carriage' was a trivial matter and might have meant no more than failing to doff his cap. Early the

---

[120] E.g. *Massye v. Taylor* (1602) Mich. 44 & 45 Eliz., rot. 1255, cited by Coke in BL MS. Add. 58218, fo. 20v (also for carrying corn on a holiday, keeping out the rogation-tide procession, and whistling and knocking on the parson's barn door 'to make music for his daughter's marriage'); *Berry v. Newman* (1605) below, n. 124; *Williams' Case* (1606) CUL MS. Gg.4.9, fo. 207; BL MS. Lansdowne 1075, fo. 185v; MS. Lansdowne 1111, fo. 210; MS. Add. 35954, fos. 443v–444 (all the same) (irreverent words spoken of the bishop of Llandaff and his wife); *Wood's Case* (1609) YLS MS. G.R29.16, fo. 292 ('scurvy priest').

[121] *Proc. Parl. 1610*, ii. 265 (complaint by the Commons that 'laymen are by the commissioners punished for speaking ... of the simony and other misdemeanours of spiritual men, though the thing spoken be true').

[122] *Nutter v. Parishioners of St Mary Somerset* (Hil. 1606) BL MS. Add. 25205, fo. 41, where a prohibition was on this ground awarded against the High Commission in a case concerning the election of churchwardens. In the parish in question the election was claimed to belong to the parishioners by immemorial custom.

[123] *Chambers' Case* (1605) BL MS. Hargrave 19, fos. 169v–170v; MS. Hargrave 29, fos. 85v–86; Christopher Yelverton's notebook, BL MS. Hargrave 430, fo. 197v.

[124] *Berry v. Newman* (1605) BL MS. Lansdowne 1062, fo. 169v; sub nom. *Birry's Case*, Godb. 147; sub nom. *Bery's Case*, BL MS. Add. 25205, fo. 22.

following year, the King's Bench frustrated an attempt by the High Commission to remove a London minister for offending against the Canons of 1604. The parson was sent to prison, and the grantee of the next avoidance sought to obtain possession by suing a writ of *vi laica removenda*, with an affidavit that only the parson's wife and children, and his reader, remained in possession. The court held that the reader could not be removed, because he was a spiritual person, and after some disagreement they held that even the wife and children could not be removed. They therefore granted a writ of restitution, and subsequently fined and imprisoned the sheriff for not obeying it.[125]

Around the same time, the assembled judges rejected the argument made by Dr Cosin and Dr Ridley that, since all ecclesiastical power was now annexed to the crown, *praemunire* was no longer available in respect of the spiritual courts.[126] It was on the same footing, said the judges, as prohibition.[127] The ecclesiastical lawyers were wrong if they supposed that the royal supremacy over the Church was a Tudor innovation. It was ancient;[128] the only change had been to remove the usurped power of the pope. If an ecclesiastical court trespassed on the common law it was still, as in the past, an encroachment upon the king's crown and dignity.[129] Only months after this, Coke was appointed chief justice, and the skirmishing over the High Commission was to turn into open warfare during the eleven stormy years of his judicial career.[130]

---

[125] *Hodkinson's Case* (1605–6) BL MS. Add. 25205, fo. 23 (motion for a writ of restitution, Mich. 1605; decision in favour of the reader, Hil. 1606, and in favour of the family, Pas. 1606; sheriff fined and imprisoned, Trin. 1606).

[126] This was also Selden's view: *Table Talk of John Selden*, ed. F. Pollock (1927), pp. 111–12.

[127] It had been argued in 1598 that prohibition also was unnecessary since the uniting of jurisdictions in the crown: BL Cotton MS. Cleopatra F I, fo. 111. This was, however, a hopeless cause.

[128] See above, p. 220.

[129] 'Praemunire' (Pas. 1606) 12 Co. Rep. 37; this may have arisen from the debate on prohibitions which began in 1605 and went into the same issues: 'Articuli Cleri', 2 St. Tr. 131–59. Cf. *Trevor's Case* (1611) BL MS. Add. 25215, fo. 78v (in prohibition to the Court of Audience before Dr Dunn), where it was said (tr.) 'that it was a gracious time, or else Dr Dunn would have incurred a *praemunire* by holding plea of a temporal matter; and the lord Coke [CJ] said that it was spoken in his hearing that no *praemunire* lies at this day, because the jurisdiction spiritual and temporal is in one sovereign; but he would advise everyone to know that the opinion of him and of all his brother justices of England is that *praemunire* lies as well today as in any time before'. See further D. C. Smith, 'Remembering Usurpation: the Common Lawyers, Reformation Narratives and the Prerogative' (2013) 86 *Historical Research* 619–37 at pp. 621–6.

[130] The story is resumed below, pp. 353–75.

The Borough of Berwick

An entirely different jurisdictional question arose in 1600 with respect to the town of Berwick-upon-Tweed on the Scottish border. Berwick had a peculiar status, being within the dominion of England but not part of the realm.[131] It was generally outside the reach of the English courts,[132] out of sight and out of mind; but this was to be the first major test of the reach of *habeas corpus*.[133] Henry Brearley, a freeman of Berwick, had been committed by the mayor and bailiffs for refusing to pay a fine, and he applied to the King's Bench at Westminster for a writ of *habeas corpus*.[134] A writ was sent, but it was ignored, as was the second and third, and so the court awarded an attachment against the mayor and bailiffs directed to the governor (Lord Willoughby d'Eresby), who had them arrested. The prisoners refused to give a bond for their appearance, saying they feared mutiny in Berwick if they did so, but they appeared of their own volition and the mayor was bailed, as was Brearley. Popham CJ observed that the court had written to Gascony when it was under English dominion, and that 'no place ought to disobey this court'. Counsel for the mayor agreed, and said they could not excuse the disobedience. The prisoners then made a return to the writ, which was immediately disallowed because it began by reciting that 'Scotland was an ancient realm by itself'. They then submitted a revised return showing that Berwick was outside the realm of England, that by their charter of 1356 they were to be governed by the old laws used in the time of King Alexander of Scotland, and since time immemorial, and that no writ from Westminster Hall could be sent there.

This bold claim attracted the notice of the queen's attorney-general. Coke argued that the old laws by which they claimed to be governed, like any other local customs, had to be consonant with the law of the land, and therefore they could not impose punishment without due process. A prescription to imprison men without an opportunity for them to answer was contrary to the provision in Magna Carta that no one should

---

[131] See M. Hale, *The Prerogatives of the King*, ed. D. E. C. Yale (92 SS, 1976), p. 42. The Isle of Man was in a similar position: *Powell* v. *Vawdrey* (1615) Calth. MS. ii. 82, *per* Coke CJ.

[132] In 1601 however, it was held to be within the jurisdiction of the Council at York: *Thomas Norton's Case* (1600–1) 30 APC 411, 718–20; 31 APC 108, 143–4; 32 APC 9–13.

[133] See Halliday, *Habeas Corpus*, pp. 259–67, based on the records of the case but not the report, which had not then been found.

[134] *Brearley's Case* (alias *Breerley*) (1601) BL MS. Lansdowne 1088, fos. 52–4 (quotations tr.).

be imprisoned until he was condemned by his peers.[135] For this he cited a case of 1596, reported in his notebooks, which will be considered later.[136] Lawrence Tanfield, for the mayor, submitted that the Scots laws were not to be treated as local custom subject to English law but as a distinct legal system:

> We do not rely only on the prescription, for it is alleged there were laws used there in the time of King Alexander. Therefore, since it pleases the king that the town should be governed by the old laws there used, they are not to be examined by the rule of our law. One law ought not to be examined by another. Some things in our law seem unreasonable to Civilians, and vice versa. There are laws in the Isle of Man and Guernsey and Jersey which would be utterly unreasonable if expounded according to the level of the common law, and yet they are good because those places are not governed by the common law of the land.

As to procedural fairness, he pointed out that Brearley had been called before the aldermen and twelve 'feering men' (affeerors), and had confessed, and so due process had been observed. There was no breach of Magna Carta, because there could be 'no greater conviction than the confession of the party himself, and so it is not against the statute'. In any case, Magna Carta 'does not extend to Scottish laws'. Coke replied that, notwithstanding the charter of 1356, Berwick ought to be governed by English law, and that had been the practice, because Berwick had always been within the commission of the justices of assize, and the assizes could not meddle with Scottish law. It was more difficult for Coke to answer the points about procedure, so he fell back on the different argument that the proceedings were entirely oral; no written record had been made.

The judges waded into deeper water in considering the effect of conquest, a topic which had been of anxious concern in the first years of the new reign.[137] Gawdy J. said that the return was good with respect to the charter and the prescription, since the two had to be taken together; the charter showed why they were allowed to use the law used before the conquest of Berwick, but the prescription was necessary to show how it became law. Fenner J., however, thought they should not have prescribed from time immemorial. When the king conquered a country, the laws of that country ceased, and if the king did not appoint other laws they would be ruled by the laws of the conqueror; therefore,

---

[135] It will be noted that Coke here did not confine 'judgment of his peers' to peers of the realm.

[136] *Clarke* v. *Gape* (1596) below, p. 314.   [137] Below, pp. 341–2.

when the king appointed that they should use the laws used in the time of Alexander, they were no longer the laws of Alexander but the laws of the king of England, and a new law given to them, the reference to Alexander being 'but an expression of what their laws should be'. Popham CJ disagreed with both of them:

> I understand, as my brother Fenner has said, that by the conquest the laws of the country cease and they are to be ruled by such laws as the conqueror will impose upon them. But that does not change the laws of the conquering country. Therefore, when the Normans conquered this realm they made a mixture of the Norman laws and of the old laws used here before,[138] but the Normans did not change their laws,[139] as is proved inasmuch as the Isles of Guernsey and Jersey use the Norman laws to this day, and they were parcel of Normandy. Also, I have seen an old charter whereby King Henry [II], after the conquest of Ireland, granted to them the English laws.[140] But if the conqueror permits the conquered country to use their old laws, they have them as their law by permission. For the Isle of Man has [sic] at this day, and therefore those laws are made the laws of the conqueror. By the conquest of Berwick the laws of Scotland ceased there, and therefore when the king granted to them to be governed by the laws used in the time of Alexander they are not governed by those laws but by the charter which established those laws.

This reasoning led Popham to reject the return as bad with respect to the prescription. He nevertheless held that an oral examination was a sufficient trial to impose punishments, for that was the usual procedure in town guilds, and if it were not allowed 'the government of all towns would be overturned, for offences there often require a speedy trial'. The court therefore granted the mayor a day to amend the return, though in the end the matter was ended by a settlement.

The King's Bench thus successfully asserted its jurisdiction to send *habeas corpus* to dominions outside the realm, and Magna Carta seems to have been treated as applying outside the realm, with respect to imprisonment, even though, on the facts, there had been no infringement of due process. The decision, though omitted from Coke's notebooks,

---

[138] Popham had made the same point in conversation with Coke in 1598: BL MS. Harley 6686A, fo. 274, quoted in Smith, *Sir Edward Coke*, p. 123. Coke later wrote against this note that, far from changing English laws, William had taken many of them to Normandy: as to which see also the next note.

[139] Cf. Sir Roger Owen's argument that the Normans took their laws from England rather than vice versa: *Common Law*, LI MS. Misc. 207, ch. 13.

[140] See above, p. 33. 'H. 3' in the manuscript must be a slip for 'H. 2'.

enabled Coke to write in 1604, in his treatise on chapter 29 of Magna Carta, that the King's Bench was the highest court in England and also the most far-reaching court, 'for it may direct a *habeas corpus* into any of the king's dominions, even though they are not parcel of England'.[141] Writs could likewise be sent to Dublin, the Channel Islands and Wales. Coke thought it worth mentioning also that there were precedents of *habeas corpus* being sent to the lieutenant of the Tower of London, the principal place of incarceration for prisoners of state.[142] Moreover, no authority beneath the king was so high that its gaolers could simply return to *habeas corpus* that they did not know the cause of committal. It was now considered to be contrary to chapter 29 to imprison someone without showing the specific cause. This principle was reaffirmed by the King's Bench in 1605 in an action of false imprisonment against two serjeants at mace in London.[143] They pleaded that the mayor, acting as a justice of the peace, had committed the plaintiff 'for good causes known to him but unknown to them'. The court held this to be no justification, because it was against Magna Carta, chapter 29, and the plaintiff recovered damages. The reporter observed that Henry Montagu, the recorder of London, defended the plea so feebly that his argument was not worth noting. Imprisonment without cause shown was becoming indefensible.

The Council in the Marches

In other jurisdictions far from Westminster, a similar reluctance to submit to central control was combined with problems of conflict similar to those touching the Requests and the Chancery. Since equitable jurisdiction depended ultimately on the power of inhibiting unconscionable proceedings at law, inferior courts of equity were asserting the same powers as the Chancery and Requests to enjoin plaintiffs at law from proceeding with their actions and even from enforcing their judgments. At first glance, the problems should have been easier to resolve than those affecting the central courts since the

---

[141] Below, p. 504 (tr.).   [142] Ibid. 505, 506. Cf. his speech below, pp. 512–13.
[143] See *Wooddy* v. *Bakers and Readhead* (1605) BL MS. Lansdowne 1075, fos. 134–5; MS. Lansdowne 1111, fos. 209–210v; MS. Add. 24846, fos. 80v–81v; MS. Add. 359454, fos. 399–400; CUL MS. Gg.4.9, fo. 135; IT MS. Barrington 7, fos. 159v–161 (all the same report).

inferior courts of equity could hardly claim parity of authority with the King's Bench and Common Pleas. In 1598 the Star Chamber decided that the warden and vice-warden of the Stannaries (in Devon and Cornwall) could not make warrants of imprisonment after a contrary judgment at common law, since it would be 'contrary to the great charter, *quod nullus liber homo imprisonetur*; and the common law is the surest and best inheritance that any subject hath: lose that, and lose everything'.[144] More difficult, however, was the authority of the grander provincial councils at Ludlow and York, which had been inconclusively challenged in the Privy Council by Anderson CJCP in 1592.[145] The Council in the North apparently accepted at this date that it could not stay proceedings at law,[146] though Anderson CJ was willing to cooperate in protecting its jurisdiction in appropriate cases.[147] Its counterpart in the Marches was not so attentive to the objections, and in 1596 another case was reported to the Common Pleas where a party who had recovered damages and obtained execution of the judgment was sued in the Marches with the object of undoing the execution and awarding restitution. The judges authorised a special writ of prohibition founded on the statute of 1402, though they agreed to send it only to the party and not to the councillors.[148] The councillors evidently regarded themselves as beyond the reach of Westminster, and in 1597 even the Privy Council had occasion to rebuke them for disobeying their order to stay a suit.[149]

The conflict came to a head after Edward, Lord Zouche, became lord president in 1602. Zouche treated Wales as his own kingdom, and was

---

[144] *Anon.* (1598) Hawarde 96 (partly tr.).

[145] *Case of the Council in the Marches* (1592) 1 And. 279; above, p. 210. The Common Pleas had granted a prohibition to stop the Council hearing an action of debt. The Councils in the Marches and the North also claimed the authority to inhibit proceedings in the Chancery: Jones, *Elizabethan Chancery*, pp. 353–5, 359–60.

[146] Jones, *Elizabethan Chancery*, pp. 359–60; R. R. Reid, *The King's Council in the North* (1921), p. 348.

[147] *Atkinson v. Readhead* (1596) 25 APC 468, 485–6, where a defendant at York procured process from the Common Pleas against his opponent, his gaoler, and a tipstaff. Here the Privy Council intervened, apparently at the queen's personal instance, and Anderson CJCP cooperated to stay the proceedings in his court. Anderson was further ordered to call for the counsel and attorneys involved and enjoin them from prosecuting the suit further.

[148] *Anon.* (Mich. 1596) CUL MS. Ii.5.25, fo. 18. There was a similar case six years later, and the prohibition went to the party and his attorney but not the lord president: *Anon.* (1602) CUL MS. Ee.3.45, fo. 8v.

[149] *Throgmorton v. Poyntz* (1597) 27 APC 225.

contemptuous of judges.[150] He made this only too clear on first taking his seat at Ludlow, when he threw down the cushion laid for the chief justice of Chester, who had customarily sat next to the president.[151] Enlarged jurisdictional claims were becoming intolerable to the judges at Westminster. When it was reported that a plaintiff in a Worcestershire case had been sued in the Marches and forced to enter into a recognisance of £100 to remove the dispute there, the Common Pleas judges reacted angrily.[152] A plaintiff was free to sue in the Marches if he wished, but if he chose the king's courts at Westminster it was 'a very bold and unlawful part for the commissioners there, having notice thereof, to draw it out from here'. Walmsley J. said the offending party should be prosecuted for a finable offence. It was also unlawful for the Council in the Marches to meddle in Worcestershire, which was in England. The judges all remembered cases where the Council had encroached on English counties, sometimes even in actions of debt. Warburton J. asked what the need was for a chancery in such cases. Walmsley exploded: 'Good lord, what doings are these? It is wonderful to see how presumptuous men are, and how they condemn the common law, being inheritance of the subject.' Anderson CJ said that the Marches did not include Worcestershire, Shropshire, Gloucestershire or Herefordshire,[153] and all their proceedings in respect of those counties were *coram non judice*, and likewise when they meddled in cities which were counties in themselves: 'they might as well take Newcastle into the Marches of Scotland'. Warburton appealed to the royal interest, saying that the king would lose 'a mass of money for fines, amercements of jurors and other things'. A prohibition was awarded, and an attachment against the offending party. Later the same term a similar case resulted in a prohibition and attachment not only against the party but also against his counsel and

---

[150] *Letters written by John Chamberlain during the Reign of Queen Elizabeth*, ed. S. Williams (Camden Soc., 1861), p. 157 ('Lord Zouche plays rex in Wales and takes upon him *comme un millord d'Angleterre* both with the Council and the justices', 15 October 1602).

[151] *The Diary of John Manningham of the Middle Temple 1602–1603*, ed. R. Sorlien (Hanover, NH, 1976), p. 95. In York there was a dispute in 1602 as to whether the assize judge (Yelverton J.) took precedence of the vice-president of the Council, but the judge lost: ibid. 76, 329; Reid, *The King's Council in the North*, ch. 6.

[152] *Heydon v. Meast* (1602) BL MS. Add. 25212, fos. 63–4 (reported in English).

[153] Manningham (above, n. 151) said in October 1602: 'The Lord Zouche . . . begins to know and use his authority so much that his jurisdiction is already brought in question in the Common Place, and the chief justice of that bench thinks that Gloucestershire, Herefordshire, etc., are not within his circuit.'

attorneys in the Marches.[154] Prohibitions were sent in the same period, and on the like grounds, to the Council at York.[155]

Lord Zouche was not inclined to accept any of this. In the summer of 1604 the territorial jurisdiction of the Council in the Marches was raised in the Privy Council and debated several times. It was argued that the king had no prerogative power to erect a court of equity, a proposition supported by the decision in *Perrot* v. *Mathew* (1588) and in a broader way by *Sir John atte Lee's Case* (1368), both of which rested on chapter 29 of Magna Carta;[156] that, as a court of equity, it could not examine cases after judgment given at common law;[157] and that the jurisdiction of the Council in the Marches could not extend to the four English counties mentioned by Anderson. Francis Bacon, as king's counsel extraordinary,[158] wrote a memorandum for the Council, suggesting that the judges had only raised the geographical objection because they had run out of arguments for attacking the jurisdiction more generally.[159] Ambitious for office, Bacon was always eager to use his legal learning to defend the new king's authority against interference by Parliament, judges and libertarian lawyers – a category which in his mind included the king's attorney-general (Coke). His memorandum therefore put the case strongly in favour of Jacobean absolutism:[160]

> The king holdeth not his prerogatives of this kind mediately from the law, but immediately from God, as he holdeth his crown; and though other prerogatives, by which he claimeth any matter of revenue or other right pleadable in his ordinary courts of justice, may be there disputed, yet his sovereign power, which no judge can censure, is not of that nature; and therefore whatsoever partaketh or dependeth thereon, being matter of government and not of law, must be left to his managing by his Council of State . . . The State, whose proper duty and eye is to the general good, and in that regard to the balancing of all degrees, will haply consider this point

[154] *Watkins* v. *Tedder* (1602) BL MS. Add. 25212, fos. 66v–67.
[155] *Savill* v. *Crooke* (1597) CUL MS. Ii.5.26, fo. 171.
[156] Above, pp. 265, 58. Around the same time it was resolved by Popham CJKB, Anderson CJCP, Gawdy and Walmsley JJ. that the king could not grant a court of equity to the queen consort because it would be in derogation of the common law: *Queen Anne's Case* (1603/5) cited in *Martin* v. *Marshall* (1615) Hob. 63; CUL MS. Mm.1.21, fo. 227v, *per* Hitcham sjt (the queen's attorney).
[157] Coke Att.-Gen. wrote to Viscount Cranbourne that 'nothing was more repugnant to law, as we have made manifest demonstration': *Hatfield House MSS*, xvi. 412, no. 883.
[158] Bacon's patent as KC (1604) was the first of its kind: Baker, *Collected Papers*, i. 125. He previously had an informal grant (1594): above, p. 197.
[159] Memorandum in *Letters and Life of Bacon*, iii. 368–92, at p. 369.   [160] Ibid. 371.

above law: that monarchies in name do often degenerate into aristocracies, or rather oligarchies, in nature by two insensible degrees. The first is when prerogatives are made envious or subject to the constructions of laws; the second when law as an oracle is affixed to place. For by the one the king is made accountable and brought under the law, and by the other the law is overruled and inspired by the judge; and by both all tenures of favour, privy counsel, nobility and personal dependences – the mysteries that keep up states, in the person of the prince – are quite abolished . . .

The prerogative of establishing courts, according to Bacon, fell into the absolute category. King Alfred introduced counties, William the Conqueror brought in the Exchequer, Henry III settled the Common Pleas, Edward III erected the Admiralty and Duchy, Edward IV the Star Chamber and the Council in the Marches, and Henry VIII the Court of Requests. If the jurisdiction were denied in the case of the Marches, it would impeach all of them and might even encourage lawyers and Parliament to assert dangerous new liberties.[161] Not one to understate his case, he suggested that it would also threaten the established religion, since the Council alone was effective in suppressing papists in the Marches, and it would dissolve the union with Wales, because Welshmen would not travel to London with their lawsuits, and Englishmen would no longer marry Welsh women if they were seen as a 'condemned people'. This prerogative, moreover, was not purely legislative but extended to the process of judgment itself:[162]

> Besides, we say that in the king's prerogative there is a double power: one which is delegate to his ordinary judges, in Chancery or common law; another which is inherent in his own person, whereby he is the supreme judge both in Parliament and all other courts and hath power to stay suits at the common law: yea, *pro bono publico* to temper, change and control the same . . . And this inherent power of his, and what participateth thereof, is therefore free from controlment by any court of law . . . [and] this free jurisdiction the king exerciseth by his Councils, which are not delegations of power but assistances thereof inherent in himself.

---

[161] Cf. ibid. 380: 'It will be the beginning of a dangerous innovation in the general government of the land. For if the king's prerogative, the ancient and main foundation upon which this jurisdiction was built, be thus questioned and shaken, then of necessity the Council at York must fall after this (which is not denied); and the Court of Requests must follow, and haply other courts of equity, which may seem to be blemished in the handling of this cause; and what further way may be opened up to Parliament or lawyers to dispute more liberties, may rather be feared than discovered at the first.'

[162] Ibid. 373.

On this footing, the Councils in the Marches and in the North had the same standing as the Privy Council. And there were positive advantages to the people in decentralisation. In another dig at the new constitutional rhetoric, Bacon asked 'whether in all Magna Carta there be any greater benefit than this – to have near and cheap justice'.[163]

The Privy Council was unpersuaded by Bacon, and held, on the advice of the justices of the King's Bench, that the four English counties were exempt from the jurisdiction of the Council in the Marches.[164] Coke reported the case slightly differently. According to his contemporary note, the judges based their opinion on Magna Carta:[165]

> It was resolved by all the justices of England in the great case of the Lord Zouche, president of Wales, that if the president prosecutes in any case which is outside his jurisdiction, either in respect of his authority or in respect of the place, both the Court of Common Bench and the King's Bench may grant a prohibition; and likewise generally of all other courts which have a limited authority and the judges thereof exceed their authority ... And the case of the four counties, namely Worcester, Gloucester, Salop and Hereford was argued before the Council at eleven separate times, and in the end it was resolved that the four counties were outside the jurisdiction of the president, for his jurisdiction extends only to Wales and the Marches of Wales, and these four counties are the Marches of England and not of Wales ... And note that that the prohibition is grounded both upon the common law and upon the statute of Magna Carta, namely *nec super eum ibimus nec super eum mittemus nisi per legale judicium parium suorum aut per legem terrae.*

Prohibition, like *habeas corpus*, was another of the remedies for the subject silently implied in chapter 29.

The display of firm judicial unanimity did not avert a major clash the following year in *Whetherly's Case* (1605),[166] probably because the king

---

[163] Ibid. 384. Cf. his further discussion of this, ibid. 381.

[164] *Farley* v. *Holder* (1604) BL MS. Add. 25244, fos. 5–33v, 74–83v; MS. Lansdowne 1113, fo. 38v; Co. Inst. iv. 242. It has been suggested that this was the first dispute with the judges: P. Williams, *The Council in the Marches of Wales under Elizabeth I* (Cardiff, 1958), pp. 224–5; but cf. ibid. 201–3, where there is mention of complaints in the 1590s.

[165] Coke's autograph notebook, BL MS. Harley 6686B, fo. 617 (tr.).

[166] *Whetherly* v. *Whetherly* (alias *Witherley*) (1605) below, Appendix 8; CUL MS. Gg.4.9, fos. 126–127v; BL MS. Lansdowne 1075, fos. 101v–103v; MS. Add. 24846, fos. 54v–56; MS. Add. 35954, fos. 370–371v (all versions of the same report; extracts tr.); record in the controlment roll, KB 29/246, mm. 22–3. Perhaps the same *Fox's Case* (undated) BL

was not himself convinced. This time the order of battle was reversed. The first suit had been brought in the Marches, where a title to land was disputed and a decree awarded. The unsuccessful party brought an action of ejectment in the King's Bench and recovered possession of the land after a jury trial. The other party then obtained an attachment and arrested the King's Bench plaintiff, who escaped and went to Bristol; a commission of sequestration was thereupon sued out from the Council in the Marches to seize his goods, and his cattle were taken. The Council did not stop there, but sent a pursuivant to Bristol, which was clearly outside their jurisdiction, and with the assistance of the sheriffs broke into the party's house and arrested him. The party again escaped, but by warrant from the Council he was rearrested and put in the dungeon called Little Ease, to remain there until he executed a bond to relinquish the benefit of his suit at law. He now sought *habeas corpus* in the King's Bench, where Coke, attorney-general, 'being present in the court when this cause was moved, asked the justices if they would give him their patience to hear him speak a little for the king's prerogative, the jurisdiction of this court [the King's Bench], and the benefit and liberty of all the king's subjects'. The justices, we are told, paid attention to him seriously, and he began:[167]

> Some men learned in the laws of this land today have privately delivered their opinion that when a subject is committed to prison by a privy councillor of the king, or by the Council of the Marches of Wales, by the Council of York, or the like, this court of King's Bench has no power to send a *habeas corpus* for the person who is thus committed; and they allege that there is no book, or law in writing, which proves such a jurisdiction to exist in this court. This is a great error. There is a written law which proves it, and that is the statute of Magna Carta, c. 29, which says, *Nullus liber homo capiatur vel imprisonetur . . . vel per legem terrae*. This is positive law in force at this day.

If this was law, he went on, there had to be a remedy, or else the law would be deficient, and that cannot have been the intention. The remedy would be provided by the King's Bench, in which the king was always by law presumed to be present. All other courts of justice were subordinate to it, and it had no geographical restraints. If the king gave authority by commission to execute justice, or even if the law gave such authority by

---

MS. Add. 25199, fo. 2. The case is discussed in Halliday, *Habeas Corpus*, pp. 11–14, citing HLS MSS. 118 and 1180, and identifying the record.

[167] For the full text see below, pp. 512–513.

Act of Parliament, the examination of what was done under such authority remained in the 'absolute and supreme power of the king, and that is in his Bench, which is the proper seat of justice'. He admitted that there were no law reports to prove this, but said he had by research found infinite precedents to prove its application through the use of *habeas corpus*. This was a reference to the precedents which he had collected from the rolls of the clerk of the crown in the King's Bench for his memorandum on chapter 29 of Magna Carta.[168]

Popham CJ told him that the court gave 'great approval to all he had said', and said his remarks were 'aptly beseeming the place in which he served, and the time in which he lived, because some subordinate courts ... have recently disobeyed these writs of *habeas corpus*', which disobedience, he said, was 'a derogation from the king's royal prerogative, and a depriving the subject of his natural freedom and of the benefit of the law'. Yelverton J. added that *habeas corpus* was important in protecting the liberty of the subject, 'if it be well maintained', because it brought the body before the court to be discharged, bailed or remanded as the court thought fit.[169] It is evident that the King's Bench had now joined the Common Pleas as firm devotees of Magna Carta, even if the magic had not yet percolated through to north Wales.

After two writs of *habeas corpus* had been sent to Hunnings (or Hemminges), the keeper of the Gatehouse prison in the Marches, which he failed to return, he deigned to respond to a third merely that the prisoner had been committed by Lord Zouche, 'Lord President of Wales', but still omitted to send the body. Hunnings was threatened with a penalty of £40, but still he failed to respond, and so the King's Bench ordered his attachment for contempt. When the Council in the Marches learned of this, they sent a *supersedeas* to the sheriff, reciting the controversies between the courts over jurisdiction, and that the king had undertaken to determine them himself, and in the mean time enjoining him to cease execution of the writ. The sheriff wisely ignored this and brought Hemmings to the King's Bench, where he was examined upon

---

[168] Below, pp. 505–7.
[169] Cf. Yelverton's remarks in *Maunsell's Case* (1607) BL MS. Add. 25206, fo. 55v: (tr.) 'Some have said that our prohibitions and *habeas corpus* are irregular. But I will have them understand that they were by the common law of great antiquity ... and it is presumed that the king sits here in his own person and is to have an account why any of his subjects are imprisoned, and for that reason the judges of this court may send for any prisoner to any prison in England without showing the cause why they send for him'. He also referred to *Kayser's Case* (above, p. 120).

interrogatories. It was proved that he had obstinately disobeyed the writs of *habeas corpus*, spoken contemptuously against the King's Bench, menaced those who brought the writs, and (after the first writ) had 'imprisoned the prisoner more harshly and inhumanely than before, in revenge thereof, putting him into a more noisome prison that before, restricting him from access to his friends, preventing food from being sent to him and giving him no sustenance, so that he was compelled to drink his own urine'. The court therefore committed Hunnings to the Marshalsea until he found bail, and fined him £100. Even this did not end the matter. When the plaintiff in the King's Bench took out a writ to execute his judgment in Gloucestershire, Lord Zouche sent another *supersedeas* as before, reciting the king's intention to arbitrate between the courts. Then, the next term, when Hemmings was ordered to obey the *habeas corpus*, he sent an elaborately evasive return framed on behalf of Lord Zouche, which he was ordered to amend on pain of £200. There the report ends, but it can by no means be assumed that the King's Bench won the victory, since the dispute continued for several more years thereafter.[170] Whetherley followed his victory by suing the porter in the King's Bench for false imprisonment, in an action founded on chapter 29 of Magna Carta. This turned out also to be inconclusive, because the porter pleaded in justification that he had acted under the authority of a known court, and the judges were equally divided as to whether this was a defence.[171]

The greatest interest of these proceedings of 1604–5 lies not in the outcome, however, but in Coke's invocation of chapter 29 of Magna Carta, its linkage with *habeas corpus* and prohibition, and his assertion of the supremacy of the King's Bench.[172] Coke's position on this subject was thus established, not when he became chief justice of the King's Bench in 1613, but eight or nine years earlier when he was the king's attorney-general. And his position was that these remedies were granted, not as a challenge to prerogative powers, but as a manifestation of the

---

[170] Below, pp. 385–9. Hunnings complained to the king of false imprisonment: *Hatfield House MSS.*, xxiv. 50–1.

[171] Sub nom. *Witherley* v. *Huninges* (1606) BL MS. Lansdowne 1062, fos. 211–12; below, pp. 514–16. This action was evidently in the same form as *Parsons* v. *Locke* (1595) above, pp. 277–8.

[172] As to the last point, which was to be warmly contested by Lord Ellesmere, see also *Warner* v. *Suckerman and Coates* (1615) 3 Bulst. 119 at p. 120, *per* Coke CJ ('We here in this court may prohibit any court whatsoever if they transgress and exceed their jurisdictions'); *Bagg's Case* (1615) below, p. 396; Smith, *Sir Edward Coke*, pp. 268–71.

'absolute and supreme' prerogative.[173] This won immediate approbation from the King's Bench judges as a perfectly proper position for an attorney-general to take, and it was designed to win over James I as well. The jurisdictions which historians sometimes characterise as 'prerogative courts', though created under the royal prerogative, were not above the law but were exercising the king's delegated authority and were therefore subject to a higher prerogative, operating in accordance with Magna Carta. An excess or abuse of jurisdiction, even by a so-called prerogative court, far from being an exercise of the king's prerogative, was properly to be viewed as an encroachment on the prerogative.[174] *Habeas corpus* and prohibition came not to destroy the prerogative but to fulfil it. It was for this reason that they (together with *mandamus* and *certiorari*) would later be termed the 'prerogative writs'. And, to Coke's way of thinking, the only royal jurisdiction which could superintend all other courts, and keep them within their bounds on the king's behalf, was the King's own Bench.[175] This approach to the prerogative powers exercised on behalf of a constitutional monarch would inspire much of Coke's judicial work.[176] But it was not embraced by the king, who found more agreeable the doctrines of Ellesmere and Bacon.[177] For the time being the Council in the Marches seems to have carried on as before.[178]

Restrictive Bye-laws and Trading Monopolies

It has already been noticed that charters and bye-laws in restraint of trade had provided the earliest target for arguments in the Elizabethan courts based on Magna Carta, and this seems to be the first context in which we regularly hear of the 'liberty of the subject'.[179] The case of the

---

[173] The point was repeated by Coke CJ, with respect to prohibition, in *Viner and Pelling's Case* (1609) YLS MS. G.R28.16, fo. 278; sub nom. *Vyner v. Polleyn*, BL MS. Add. 25209, fos. 132v–134. Prohibition was the king's action, because exceeding jurisdiction was (as the writ said) against his royal crown and dignity.

[174] Cf. the remarks of Anderson CJ, to the same effect, in *Parsons v. Locke* (1595) below, Appendix 5, at p. 485; and those of Coke Att.-Gen., below, p. 328.

[175] For the third prerogative writ, *mandamus*, which Coke also linked with Magna Carta, c. 29, see below, pp. 396–7.

[176] See also Halliday, *Habeas Corpus*, pp. 64–95; Smith, *Sir Edward Coke*, pp. 250–1.

[177] See, e.g., Caesar's minutes, fo. 414v ('the king said my lord chancellor's books to be preferred before my lord Coke's precedents', 1609).

[178] The battle continued during Coke's chief justiceship, when the Council in the North became equally troublesome: below, pp. 379–90.

[179] Above, p. 155.

Southampton charter, in 1561, was the catalyst.[180] In 1571 John Popham told the Commons that it had fixed in the minds of the learned a connection between liberty of trade and Magna Carta, doubtless referring to chapter 30 as much as to chapter 29.[181] Eleven years later, as attorney-general, Popham was the first known law officer of the crown to rely on chapter 29 in a court of law in order to curb an inferior authority.[182] It was an information against the Joiners' Company of London, at the instance of a complainant, to show by what warrant the company claimed the power to make bye-laws giving powers of search, forfeiture and imprisonment against joiners who were not members of the corporation. The company relied on a charter of Queen Elizabeth, granted in 1571 to the 'Mystery of Joiners and Ceilers'. Popham's principal argument was that the queen could not by charter confer a power of imprisonment outside the law of the land, let alone a power to make bye-laws with coercive effects on third parties. It would be against chapter 29 of Magna Carta, which guaranteed the inheritance of the subject in the laws of the realm, and this was something the queen could not alter.[183] Regulatory powers were certainly allowable when they were for the good of the community. But the bye-laws in the present case were unreasonable, because they might operate inequitably: the company might agree to admit only joiners with a stock of £100, which would be unfair on those of lesser ability; or it might agree to fix prices, which would be unfair when wares were of different values; or it might limit working hours, which would simply be 'prejudicial'. 'Such laws as these,' he argued, 'will not bind anyone, for they are absolutely repugnant to the government of a well ordered common wealth and tend to the destruction of its estate.' They were unreasonable also, according to Popham, because they were in restraint of trade. They might limit the craft to a few, which would deprive many workmen of the means of earning their living. Reference was here made to a case of 1414 where a bond not to use the trade of a dyer in a certain town was held to be invalid because it was

---

[180] *Att.-Gen* v. *Donatt* (1561) above, p. 190.

[181] Above, p. 191 n. 275. The reported text of his speech is obscure.

[182] *Att.-Gen.* v. *Joiners' Company of London* (Hil. 1582) BL MS. Hargrave 37, fo. 57; MS. Lansdowne 1072, fos. 129v-131 (same report); (Pas. 1582) BL MS. Hargrave 6, fo. 70; MS. Hargrave 8, fos. 105v-109; CUL MS. Hh.2.9, fos. 253-254v (same report); Fleetwood's draft argument, BL MS. Harley 4717, fos. 123-128v; Appendix 5(a), below, pp. 468-76; above, pp. 241, 250, 261.

[183] Cf. CUL MS. Hh.2.9, fo. 254v (tr. 'As to the imprisonment, the statute of Magna Carta, c. 29, forbids it, *Nullus liber homo etc.*').

in restraint of trade.[184] Serjeant Fleetwood defended the charter by arguing that it was reasonable to make ordinances to ensure standards of skill. Barristers had to be called to the bar, and physicians had to be approved by the College of Physicians, in the public interest. The case of 1414 was distinguishable, 'for if he offers himself to them and requests them to be admitted, and offers to do his proof-piece, and they will not admit him, he may then set up without offending the ordinance or incurring the penalty'. The reports all end without mention of any judgment, but the present interest of the case lies in the use made of Magna Carta rather than in the result. Popham's argument as to restraint of trade was not explicitly based on the charter, which was invoked only in relation to the powers of imprisonment; but the link had already been made in the *Southampton* case,[185] and it would soon be reinforced.

The case of the Joiners' Company may have been inconclusive, but the year-book case of 1414 was again cited and followed in 1587 in the case of the blacksmith of South Mimms, which was not readily distinguishable from it.[186] The blacksmith had given a bond not to exercise his trade in South Mimms or the three neighbouring vills, and this was held to be void, 'because it is against law that a man should be restrained from the exercise of his trade, whereby he gains his living and sustenance'.[187] The case had arisen upon a *habeas corpus*, because the blacksmith had been committed to prison by the Hertfordshire justices, and that was outside their jurisdiction regardless of whether the bond was good or not. Magna Carta was not cited, though when the decision of 1414 was again followed in 1601 the Common Pleas said that the restraint was against the liberty of a free man and therefore against Magna Carta:[188]

> The obligee would hereby deprive the subject of his liberty and living, and the statute of Magna Carta, c. 29, provides that men should be free [and have their] free customs, and if it were lawful to restrain him of any part

---

[184] YB Pas. 2 Hen. V, fo. 5, pl. 26. Magna Carta was not cited in this case.

[185] Above, p. 250.

[186] *The Blacksmith's Case* (1587) Moo. 242, 2 Leo. 210, 3 Leo. 217 (here dated 1588); BL MS. Lansdowne 1095, fo. 87.

[187] BL MS. Lansdowne 1095, fo. 87 (tr.).

[188] *Cleygate* v. *Batchelor* (Mich. 1601) Owen 143 (where c. '38' is obviously a slip for c. 29); sub nom. *Claggett* v. *Batchellor*, YLS MS. G.R29.16, fos. 100, 109v–110v (quotation tr. from fo. 110v); continued sub nom. *Colgate* v. *Bacheler* (Hil. 1602) Cro. Eliz. 872 (citing the record as Mich. 43 & 44 Eliz., rot. 3217); and sub nom. *Clagge* v. *Batchiler* (Hil. 1603) BL MS. Add. 35941, fo. 112 (same roll reference). The condition was not to use the trade of a haberdasher in Kent.

of his liberty, by the same reason he might bar him from the whole, whereas he cannot take from him any part of his living.

The turning point here seems to have been a Common Pleas case of 1595–6. The case was noted by Coke in 1599, doubtless in connection with *Davenant v. Hurdys*,[189] seemingly taken at second-hand from a report dated 1596, and worked up into a fuller report in 1605.[190] It is well represented in other reports, most of which date from Michaelmas term 1595.[191] The reports differ in detail but are mutually corroborative. When the law courts moved to St Albans in 1593, because of plague, the town made an ordinance imposing a rate on the inhabitants to cover the cost of setting them up. The plaintiff refused to pay (in forthright terms) and was summoned by a serjeant at mace to appear before the mayor, who imprisoned him. He now brought an action of false imprisonment against the mayor and one of the aldermen, who relied on the borough charter granting them a power to make bye-laws, and on a bye-law sanctioning imprisonment by the mayor and a majority of the burgesses for opprobrious words towards the mayor. The plaintiff argued that the words which he had used to the arresting officer were not opprobrious, and were not spoken directly against the mayor; that the mayor did not say he was acting with a majority of the burgesses; and that in any case it was against chapter 29 of Magna Carta to arrest someone merely for speaking words. The court gave judgment for the plaintiff, but on the broader ground that it was contrary to Magna Carta for the mayor to imprison anyone for breaking bye-laws or ordinances, since the only remedies available to town authorities were fines and (in the last resort) disfranchisement: 'Everyone is born a free man and is to have his liberty, and therefore without an offence against the queen, the crown, or the royal dignity, or some greater matter, no one may be imprisoned under any private act or bye-law.' Here, then, chapter 29 was at the core of a decision by the Common Pleas, very shortly after that in *Parsons v. Locke* (1595) concerning the Requests. Lord Ellesmere later criticised Coke for reporting the case, saying 'it were fitter to have lain silent than to have

---

[189] It was cited by Coke in *Davenant v. Hurdys* (opposite), laying special emphasis on Magna Carta, c. 29: BL MS. Add. 25203, fo. 93; MS. Hargrave 5, fo. 73v; CUL MS. Ee.3.45, fo. 34.

[190] *Clarke v. Gape (or Gappe)* (1595–6) BL MS. Harley 6686B, fo. 356 (dated Trin. 1596); 5 Co. Rep. 64.

[191] Below, Appendix 5(e), at pp. 487–9. The record is cited in Moo. 411 as Trin. 37 Eliz., rot. 916, and in a manuscript as Trin. 38 Eliz., rot. 124; neither reference is correct.

seen light', since Magna Carta was 'never meant to protect such obstinate persons as should refuse to set forward the erection of the court of justice'.[192] But the flaw in the report was in giving the wrong reason for the imprisonment, which according to the parallel reports was for the opprobrious words rather than for failing to pay the assessment. The decision did not in any way rest on the reason for the rate assessment. Nor did it support resistance to a reasonable tax. Coke would have done better to make clear in his report, as he did in argument in 1599,[193] that the ordinance imposing the rate was good and lawful. Although the reports do not mention it, the case really arose from a bitter internal dispute between the mayor and his predecessor.[194] Ellesmere well knew this, since the feud reached the Privy Council,[195] and at the time of writing he was himself high steward of the borough. His criticism was aimed at denigrating Coke's reports, and in no way struck at the reasoning of the court.

A better-known case arose in 1599.[196] The Merchant Taylors' Company had power by their charter to make ordinances, and they made an ordinance in 1575 that every brother of the company who sent cloths to be dressed by a clothworker who was not free of the company should thereafter send half of his cloths to another brother of the company, on pain of 10s. for each offence, the penalty to be levied by distress. The defendant Nicholas Hurdys, as beadle of the company, was ordered on 3 March 1599 to distrain all brethren who were not observing this ordinance,[197] and he duly distrained Edward Davenant by taking a broad-cloth from his house. Davenant brought an action of trespass in

---

[192] 'Observations upon Coke's Reports', p. 309. He added that, 'by casting this report abroad he hath much weakened the jurisdiction of all corporations, and disheartened them to further his majesty's service, there being no such bridle to curb forward companions as restraint of their liberty'.

[193] *Davenant* v. *Hurdys* (1599) below, p. 317: see, e.g. Moo. 580; BL MS. Hargrave 5, fo. 74.

[194] The plaintiff (John Clarke) was mayor in 1592–3, the co-defendant Francis Babbe in 1592–3, and the principal defendant Ralph Gape in 1594–5.

[195] *The Letters of Lady Anne Bacon*, ed. G. Allen (Camden Soc., 2014), p. 119.

[196] *Davenant* v. *Hurdys* (1599) Moo. 576; manuscript reports cited below. Note also *Waltham* v. *Austin* (1599) Coventry's reports, BL MS. Add. 25203, fo. 75v (sub nom. Waltam); cited in *Waggoner* v. *Fish* (1609) YLS MS. G.R29.16, fos. 339–341v; and in 8 Co. Rep. 125; Co. Inst. ii. 57. *Waltham's Case* concerned a charter granting to the Dyers' Company power search for cloth dyed with logwood, and for offending cloth to be forfeited. Coke said the charter was held to be contrary to Magna Carta, c. 29, 'for no forfeiture can grow by letters patents' (Co. Inst. ii. 57). But Coventry's report says the charter was upheld, because it was for the commonwealth.

[197] *Memorials of the Guild of Merchant Taylors*, ed. C. M. Clode (1875), p. 539.

the King's Bench to test the right to distrain. After full arguments, the judges unanimously held the ordinance void, after which it seems that the parties and the company settled the action.[198] Coke wrote a brief report at the time, noting only that 'it was adjudged that this ordinance was against law, because it was against the liberty of the subject, for every subject has a free power to send his cloths to be dressed by whatever clothworker he pleases; and this amounted to a monopoly.'[199] In his *Second Institute*, Coke glossed this with the explanation that the liberty in question was one of those protected by chapter 29 of Magna Carta.[200] If this stood alone, it might be dismissed as an *ex post facto* reinterpretation. Fortunately, however, the case was reported very fully by Francis Moore (counsel for Davenant), Thomas Coventry, James Whitelocke and others.[201] The parallel reports show that the two principal law officers of the crown, Edward Coke and Thomas Fleming, were engaged on either side. That could well be why the King's Bench was chosen as the forum,[202] rather than the amenable Common Pleas, though why they were retained in addition to the very able junior counsel, Moore and Tanfield, is far from clear. The prerogative was not directly involved; but perhaps Coke and Fleming had disagreed between themselves about restraints of trade in the city, where both had served successively as recorder.

Coke, arguing the case on behalf of the plaintiff, maintained forcefully that the Merchant Taylors' ordinance was against the liberty of the

---

[198] Francis Moore, who was counsel for the defendant, and also some of the manuscript reports, say judgment was given for the plaintiff in Trinity term 1600. But the company records say that on 15 December 1600, 'After much time spent touching the suit which hath long depended in the King's Bench ... forasmuch as the said Edward Davenant is desirous to have an end of the controversy, and to be at peace with the company and to cease upon even terms, it is agreed that his submission shall be accepted and a discontinuance entered of the [aforesaid] action': *Memorials of the Guild of Merchant Taylors* (previous note), p. 539.

[199] *Davenant v. Hurdys* (1599) Coke's notebook, BL MS. Harley 6686B, fo. 381v; record in KB 27/1356, m. 92. Coke incorporated his report into the report of *Darcy v. Allen* (1602) 11 Co. Rep. 84 at fo. 86.

[200] Co. Inst. ii. 47. There is also a brief citation in Co. Inst. iii. 182.

[201] Moo. 576–91; Coventry's reports, BL MS. Add. 25203, fos. 75v, 92–94v, 104v–108, 144–147v; MS. Hargrave 5, fos. 71–9, 81–82v (same report); Whitelocke's reports, CUL MS. Dd.8.48, 102–7; anonymous reports, BL MS. Add. 25206, fos. 109–15; MS. Add. 25223, fos. 135–140v.

[202] Coke and Fleming had no right of audience in the Common Pleas. Fleming had been created serjeant at law in 1594, but was dispensed from the coif in order to become solicitor-general.

subject as guaranteed by chapter 29 of Magna Carta. It was against liberty for work to be restricted to certain persons; it was wrong to restrict a tradesman's choice in dealing with his wares; it was wrong for one company to make laws concerning other trades; and it had been decided in 1596 that it was directly against Magna Carta for a corporation to make ordinances contrary to law.[203] Although some monopolies were allowed, when they were in the public interest, they were generally abhorred both by the common law and the Civil law. The ordinance would gradually deprive other clothworkers of work, and they would have to live on poor relief. Fleming, arguing in support of the ordinance, said that bye-laws were not *contra legem* (contrary to law) but *praeter legem* (beside the law). And it could hardly be an objection that those making them were not skilled, because 'members of Parliament often make laws concerning things in which they are not expert, and their laws are nevertheless good'.[204] Moore, arguing at greater length on the same side, accepted that monopolies properly so called were against the public interest, but denied that the ordinance in dispute did create a monopoly. It did not prohibit any clothworker from using his trade, or restrict the dressing cloth solely to the merchant tailors. Only 'a handful' of the cloth worked in London would be affected. Most towns had bye-laws restricting trades to freemen and excluding outsiders; if they were to be void as monopolies it would cause a great decay of cities and boroughs, with serious consequences for the economy. He also pointed out that the plaintiff was himself a member of the company and had taken an oath on admission, after 1575, to observe its laws and ordinances. The same principles of reasonableness should be applied as in the case of customs. And here he mentioned the supposed custom of the Cinque Ports to take goods in withernam. There was a case currently depending in the Common Pleas on that point, and Coke was able to reply that the custom had just been held by three of the judges there to be unlawful 'because of the statute of *Nullus liber homo*'.[205]

---

[203] *Clarke* v. *Gape* (1596) above, p. 314. Lawrence Tanfield, on the same side, cited the *Case of the Town of Buckingham* (1587) where the Exchequer struck down an ordinance that sheepskins brought into the town to be sold could only be sold to the Glovers of the town: BL MS. Hargrave 5, fo. 76v.

[204] BL MS. Add. 25203, fo. 146 (tr.).

[205] Whitelocke's reports, CUL MS. Dd.8.48, 105. Moore's argument is at Moo. 588. The Common Pleas case was *Paramour* v. *Verrall* (1598–1600), in which a distinction was drawn between seizing goods and arresting persons: above, pp. 26–8; below, pp. 489–94.

Davenant v. *Hurdys* thus provides another example, from the later 1590s, of Magna Carta being deployed – and again by Coke – in support of the 'liberty of the subject'. In the absence of reported judgments, however, it is impossible to know which of the many arguments advanced by counsel persuaded the court. There was nothing in the wording of chapter 29 which assisted in balancing the political and economic arguments as to what kinds of liberty it protected. The decision, even though it was not embodied in a formal judgment, nevertheless emboldened the courts to strike down more bye-laws in restraint of trade over the next few years, especially in London,[206] and to reject supposedly immemorial municipal customs which impeded freedom of trade, such as that which would have prevented outsiders from keeping shops in London.[207] Chapter 30 of Magna Carta was also invoked to justify striking down an alleged custom of Newcastle-upon-Tyne for the Merchant Adventurers there to prevent outsiders bringing in goods.[208] In 1602 an offensive custom of Canterbury was declared void by the King's Bench not only because it made a monopoly of trade but because it included a power of imprisonment, which was contrary to chapter 29 of Magna Carta.[209]

The next big step was to extend the same reasoning to the hated charters of monopoly which had burgeoned throughout the Elizabethan period.[210] In taking this step, the judges may have been emboldened by the queen's Golden Speech of 1601,[211] though they were to withhold their

---

[206] E.g. *Weavers of London* v. *Browne* (1601) BL MS. Add. 25213, fo. 1; HLS MS. 2076, fo. 90 (bye-law restricting trade to freemen of the company); *Porter's Case* (1606) CUL MS. Gg.4.9, fo. 200; BL MS. Add, 24846, fos. 124v–125v; MS. Add. 35954, fos. 438v–439v; MS. Lansdowne 1111, fos. 192–4 (bye-law restricting work as journeyman to freemen); *Franklin* v. *Green* (1610) 1 Bulst. 11 (bye-law of the Butchers' Company restricting the sale of veal by strangers).

[207] *Lowe's Case* (1605) CUL MS. Gg.4.9, fos. 190v–191; BL MS. Lansdowne 1075, fos. 134–5; MS. Add. 24846, fo. 115; MS. Lansdowne 1111, fos. 171v–172v (same report but dated Hil. 1606); MS. Lansdowne 1075, fo. 169; MS. Add. 25213, fo. 66. Lowe, a crossbow-maker in Holborn, had been gaoled by the mayor for breach of the custom.

[208] *Tonge* v. *Tempest* (1600) HLS MS. 2076, fo. 63; BL MS. Add. 48148, fo. 397; cited in MS. Add. 25203, fo. 263v. Cf. *Davies* v. *Cornelius* (1607) CUL MS. Gg.2.23, fo. 108 (custom of Southampton; no judgment).

[209] *Gobye* v. *Knight* (1602) BL MS. Add 25203, fos. 619–621v, citing the record as Trin. 44 Eliz., rot. 923; sub nom. *Gowby* v. *Knight*, cited by Fuller in Noy 183; sub nom. *Ruby* v. *Wright*, cited in Moo. 674; and see Appendix 9, p. 515. The supposed custom was that all butchers should sell their tallow to the Chandlers' Company in the same city at set prices.

[210] Above, pp. 194–8.   [211] Above, pp. 198–9.

decision from the public until the queen was dead. In fact the matter had already been debated in the Common Pleas in 1600, when the judges of that court discussed the monopoly of beer-brewing and making *aqua vitae* which had been granted to Richard Drake, an equerry of the queen's stable and a favoured courtier. The patent was one of those complained of in the Commons in 1601. The judges opined unanimously that it was a 'robbery to the subject' and void. It operated solely for the gain of the patentee, who was a gentleman with no knowledge of brewing; it would enhance prices; and it would turn qualified brewers into beggars. This was a rehearsal of the arguments which were to prevail shortly after-wards, though the Common Pleas had been unable to strike down Drake's patent because its validity did not come before them directly.[212] Walmsley J. said, 'we see the mischief of this case, and in reason and conscience we ought not to suffer it', but it would be better if the parties settled; and so, it seems, they did.

The decisive case was *Darcy* v. *Allen* (1602), or *The Case of Monopolies* (as Coke called it).[213] It has been much discussed as supposedly provid-ing evidence for the rise of a laissez-faire 'economic liberalism', and perhaps even as marking the origin of American anti-trust law.[214] Very little attention has been given to the citations of Magna Carta, which admittedly played a subordinate role, though they merit a brief digression on the case here. Edward Darcy, a groom of the privy chamber, had

---

[212] *Smith's Case* (1600) IT MS. Barrington 6, fos. 43v ('33'v)–46; also reported, but not on this point, sub nom. *Jewkes* v. *Smith and Gardener*, BL MS. Lansdowne 1065, fo. 50v; above, p. 281. It was a prohibition to the Court of Requests in a contract suit arising out of the patent.

[213] *Darcy* v. *Allen* (1602) KB 27/1373, m. 435 (record abstracted in Baker and Milsom, *Sources of English Legal History*, 2nd edn by J. Baker (Oxford, 2010), pp. 678–9); Coke's notebook, BL MS. Harley 6686B, fos. 571v–574 (printed as an appendix to Corré, '*Darcy* v. *Allen*', next note); 11 Co. Rep. 84 (a considerably altered version); Co. Inst. ii. 47; Moo. 671–5; Noy 173; Coventry's reports, BL MS. Add. 25203, fo. 678v; CUL MS. Ii.5.26, fos. 221–2. Fleming's speech on behalf of Darcy is in SP 12/286, fos. 111–23.

[214] The principal commentaries are D. S. Davies, 'Further Light on the Case of Monopolies' (1932) 48 LQR 394–414; D. O. Wagner, 'Coke and the Rise of Economic Liberalism' (1935) 6 *Economic History Review* 30–44; M. B. Donald, *Elizabethan Monopolies* (Edin-burgh, 1961), pp. 208–49; B. Malament, 'The "Economic Liberalism" of Sir Edward Coke' (1967) 76 *Yale Law Journal* 1321–58 (a convincing refutation of Wagner); D. H. Sacks, 'The Countervailing of Benefits: Monopoly, Liberty and Benevolence in Eliza-bethan England' in *Tudor Political Culture*, ed. D. Hoak (Cambridge, 1995), pp. 272–91; J. I. Corré, 'The Argument, Decision and Reports of *Darcy* v. *Allen*' (1996) 45 *Emory Law Journal* 1261–1327.

engendered much resentment by his relentless enforcement of his 1592 patent for searching and sealing leather.[215] The Council had recommended the mayor of London to bring a *scire facias* to repeal the obnoxious patent, but it was voluntarily cancelled in 1598 and Darcy was granted as compensation the sole right for twelve years to import, trade in, and manufacture, playing-cards. This monopoly had first been granted to Robert Bowes in 1588, and its stringent enforcement through the Privy Council had already caused a good deal of controversy,[216] but that did not deter Darcy from accepting a reversionary grant to commence on the expiry of Bowes's interest in 1600. It was a profitable trade, since Darcy claimed to have spent £5,000 making 4,000 gross of playing cards in 1600 alone. The patent was immediately infringed by other manufacturers, and Darcy secured the appointment of a special tribunal, chaired by Dr Julius Caesar, to enquire into these infringements.[217] This course seems not to have availed him, and so he commenced an action on the case against Thomas Allen, a London haberdasher. Allen was supported by the city of London, and at the city's instance pleaded a custom of London for haberdashers to buy and sell all manner of merchandise wherever and to whomever they wished.[218] The outcome of this dispute could greatly have affected the crown's revenue from monopolies, and on this occasion Coke was obliged to join Fleming in supporting the patent, no doubt very much against his personal instincts.[219] It seems that the custom pleaded by Allen was never seriously considered, and the only point of substance was whether the patent was valid. Coke said that there was a second question, whether the patent operated as a dispensation from a statute of 1463 prohibiting the importation of playing-cards. According to Coke's report, printed in 1615, the court ruled decisively that it could not dispense with the statute because it had been made in the public interest; but in 1616 he accepted

---

[215] Above, pp. 168, 183, 196.

[216] For Council proceedings initiated by Bowes see 18 APC 186; 24 APC 369; 25 APC 503–4; Davies, 'Further Light on the Case of Monopolies', pp. 400–03. For an earlier playing-card patent see 10 APC 431 (1578).

[217] *HPHC 1558–1603*, ii. 16; 32 APC 132–3.

[218] For the city support see Davies, 'Further Light on the Case of Monopolies', pp. 406–13. There seems also to have been a Common Pleas suit, which was stayed by the queen's letters: 32 APC 237.

[219] Besides his dislike of monopolies in general, Coke had clashed with Darcy in 1594 over an office belonging to the attorney-general: below, p. 422 n. 67.

Ellesmere's complaint that this point, though argued, had not been considered by the court at all.[220]

The law officers did not attempt to argue that granting patents of monopoly fell under the absolute prerogative, but accepted that royal grants had to be conformable to the common law. The argument in support of the playing-card patent was essentially that cards were inessential items of pleasure, potentially causing the loss of work by idle servants, and therefore it was appropriate for the queen to control their supply. This was obviously disingenuous, since the queen's interest (and Darcy's) lay in increasing the number of packs in circulation. And the tone of Coke's report of the case clearly implied that he thought the opposing argument more cogent. Monopolies such as this were against the law because they resulted in increased prices,[221] and were a restraint of trade, which led to 'idleness and beggary'[222] – presumably more idleness and beggary than was caused by cardplaying – with no corresponding public benefit, for they redounded solely to the private benefit of the patentee. The statute of 1463 showed that they were not a new invention deserving the protection accorded to entrepreneurs.[223] Not only was Darcy no inventor, but there could be no pretence that, as a groom of the chamber, he had any skill in making playing-cards, or that he was likely to suppress any abuses of cardplaying. Reliance was placed on the case of 1414, and on *Davenant* v. *Hurdys*, as showing that the law abhorred restraints of trade. Coke's report does not mention Magna Carta, though in his *Institutes* he associated the decision with chapter 29, and the charter featured, not surprisingly, in the argument by

---

[220] Ellesmere, 'Observations on Coke's Reports', 303; *Letters and Life of Bacon*, vi. 89; P. Birdsall, '"Non Obstante" – A Study of the Dispensing Power of the English Kings' in *Essays in History and Politics in Honor of C. H. McIlwain* (Cambridge, MA, 1936), pp. 37–76, at pp. 60–2. The point is not mentioned in Moo. 671 or Noy 176, though it was argued: Corré, '*Darcy v. Allen*' (above, n. 214), pp. 1307–9. The dispensing power was, however, considered in *Shaw* v. *Harries* (1606) BL MS. Add. 35954, fos. 441–442v, in which Coke Att.-Gen. persuaded the King's Bench that the grantee of a dispensation for trading contrary to a statute was not an interest which could be assigned.

[221] Nicholas Fuller, in argument, said that Darcy was selling cards at 35s. a gross, whereas the haberdashers offered to seller better cards for 20s. a gross: Noy 179.

[222] Coke's words. Fuller argued that 'if others should do the like in other trades, it would discourage men to labour to be skilful in any art, and bring in barbarism and confusion ... then will they rob and steal, and become thieves and traitors, for extremity breedeth nothing but thefts': Noy 179–80.

[223] For the favour shown to the introducers of new inventions see above, pp. 195–6.

Nicholas Fuller, the nonconformist member of Parliament and libertarian lawyer as counsel for the defendant.[224]

Fuller put to good use the learning already collected by the lawyers of his persuasion for their campaign against the High Commission, and showed that there were many cases in which commissions and patents had been held void because they interfered with the liberty of the subject:

> And how can it be said that freemen should, according to the statute of Magna Carta, use *libertatibus et liberis consuetudinibus suis* when Mr Darcy hath a patent to restrain cards, another to restrain tennis play, another hawking and hunting, and so forth? Is not this to make freemen bondmen? And if the queen cannot, to maintain her war, take from her subject 12d. but by Parliament, much less may she take moderate recreation from all subjects, which hath continued so long and is so universal in every country, city, town and household. But to punish the abuse is necessary; for common-weals are not made for kings, but kings for common-weals.

Such was the devotion to Magna Carta, and the hatred of monopolies, that even those of a Puritan bent were thus moved to defend the idle liberty of playing card-games. And they won the argument, as far as the courts were concerned.

It is impossible to know whether Magna Carta had more influence on the court than the venerable case of 1414 (in which Magna Carta was not cited), or any influence at all. According to Coke, Popham CJ and the whole court ruled Darcy's patent to be utterly void and therefore that the action did not lie.[225] The king's prerogatives were part of the law of the land, and matters touching the prerogative were to be referred to the judges. The absolute prerogatives, such as treaty-making and proclaiming war, or revaluing coin, were admittedly not examinable 'by any course of justice'. On the other hand, all prerogatives touching the lands or goods of subjects, or their callings (*artes*), or trade and traffic, were ordinary prerogatives and were 'determinable by the ordinary course of the law in any court of justice'. It was a maxim of the law that the king could not by his prerogative do wrong

---

[224] His argument is printed in Noy 173–85. This text, probably taken from his own notes, circulated in manuscript: e.g. IT MS. Petyt 516.5, fos. 347–362v; SP 12/286, fos. 124–31; Leeds Public Library, MS. SRF.942.06.c.685. For Fuller see below, pp. 356–63.

[225] What follows is from Coke's autograph note, BL MS. Harley 6686B, fo. 573. He did not print this in 11 Co. Rep.

or cause injury, for the king can do no wrong to anyone (*Rex nulli potest facere injuriam*). The reason for this maxim was that the king derived his royal power from God, and just as in his natural capacity he had a body and soul, so in his politic capacity he had a body (his royal power) and a soul (his justice).[226] That is what Coke wrote in his notebook at the time,[227] though he did not risk including it in the report published in 1615. It is just possible that Coke had ventured to improve on Popham's sentiments with his own words. If that is in fact what he did, it would be telling evidence of his own relief at losing the case. Other contemporary manuscript reports show that the judges did not deliver any opinions in public, and the record shows that judgment was not entered for Allen until after the queen's death. Darcy nevertheless regarded the patent as dead, and declined to pay the farm to the crown.[228] The common law was now clear, that no man could be prohibited from working at any lawful trade.[229] Only a few months later commissioners were appointed by the new king to consider all monopolies offensive to his subjects and report to him,[230] and later in the reign the judges struck down some proposed monopolies which would have involved administrative regulation without legislation;[231] but the financial interests of the king's favourites would keep monopolies in the catalogue of parliamentary grievances until a legislative solution was found in 1624.

---

[226] Cf. *Bracton*, ii. 305. See also Coke's commonplace, BL MS. Harley 6687A, fo. 108 (tr. 'see Bracton, 368, 369, the king by his prerogative may not do wrong'); *Bracton*, iv. 159.

[227] He had set down the same principles almost verbatim in 1594 and 1600: above, pp. 144, 145.

[228] *Att.-Gen.* v. *Darcy* (1609): see Davies, 'Further Light on the Case of Monopolies', p. 414; Corré, '*Darcy* v. *Allen*', pp. 1322–3. It was not a straightforward case of frustration by judicial decision, because there were some arrears before 1602.

[229] This was reaffirmed in three cases striking down customs and bye-laws which required seven-year apprenticeships: *Taylors of Ipswich* v. *Sheninge* (1614) 11 Co. Rep. 53; 1 Rolle Rep. 4 (sub nom. Sherring); Godb. 252; *R.* v. *Allen and Tooley* (1614) 2 Bulst. 186; sub nom. *R.* v. *Talley* (1614) CUL MS. Ii.5.26, fos. 65v–66v (upholsterers in London); *Trussell* v. *Morris* (1616–18) BL MS. Harley 5149, fos. 14v–21v; MS. Hargrave 28, fos. 176–181v, 213 (citing Magna Carta, c. 29); sub nom. *Norris* v. *Staps*, Hob. 210 (weavers in Newbury, Berks). See also *Kete* v. *Fish* (1610) BL MS. Hargrave 32, fos. 16v–17v (striking down a bye-law imposing payments for unloading wares at Puddle Dock). Cf. *Waggoner* v. *Fish* (1609–10) 2 Br. & G. 278, 284–9; YLS MS. G.R29.16, fos. 339–341v (where Coke CJ upheld a bye-law against retailing candles).

[230] 32 APC 497 (4 May 1603).

[231] In 1611 they ruled against a scheme for registering all births and deaths, and in 1614 they rejected a proposed patent for registering aliens: *Chute's Case* (1614) 12 Co. Rep. 116.

Purveyance

The perversion of purveyance for private gain was another abuse which
troubled Coke as attorney-general. In 1596 he had complained to Burghley about a purveyor in Norfolk who was not only oppressing the poor
but charging extortionate fees for his pains.[232] Some improvements were
subsequently introduced by the queen's ministers, and by the end of the
1590s Coke himself was beginning to take action in an attempt to stop
the remaining abuses.[233] The grievances nevertheless remained so
weighty than in 1604 the judges were assembled to consider 'the inso-
lences and oppressions committed by purveyors'.[234] According to Coke's
manuscript note, their unanimous resolution, and that of the law officers,
was that at common law the king could not by his prerogative take
purveyance of any part of a man's inheritance, such as glass, wainscot,
slate and lead in a house, or growing timber or fruit. If he could take part,
he might by the same reasoning take the whole. The position was clear
from chapter 21 of Magna Carta, that the king's bailiffs would not take
another's growing wood (*boscus*) without the consent of the landowner,
and that was in affirmance of the common law.[235] The king's officer who
seized anything by way of purveyance was obliged to pay instantly, unless
the owner agreed to deferment. Furthermore, they said, timber which a
man had cut in order to build or repair his houses was not liable to
purveyance, but only timber cut for sale. It was observed, no doubt by
Coke, that Magna Carta had been confirmed and commanded to be put
in execution more than thirty times by authority of Parliament, and it
could not be impugned or impaired but by equal authority, namely by
Parliament. Numerous statutes had restricted the powers of purveyors,
but none had increased them.[236]

---

[232] BL MS. Lansdowne 82, fo. 216, with supporting documents at fos. 218–22.

[233] Smith, *Sir Edward Coke*, p. 70.

[234] Coke's notebook, BL MS. Harley 6686B, fos. 606v–609 (quotations tr.); abridged in Co.
Inst. ii. 35 (in the commentary on Magna Carta, c. 21). Coke added a note at the end and
in the margin that the judges' resolutions were (tr.) 'allowed by the king and Council and
published by proclamation ... and according to this resolution divers purveyors were
punished by the Star Chamber for taking timber growing'. Also reported in BL MS.
Add. 35955, fo. 29.

[235] Chapter 21 was also cited in the House of Commons in 1606 (*JHC*, i. 282) and in the
Case of the Dean and Chapter of St Paul's (1612) BL MS. Harley 1575, fo. 103v.

[236] Even Bacon is reported as saying that 'Since Magna Carta, in Henry III's time, [it was] a part
of every king's glory to make a law against purveyors': *JHC*, i. 192 (30 April 1604).

Following this decision, the judges proceeded by the king's command to review the old form of commission issued to purveyors. This had included the taking of stone, slate, brick, tile and timber, and the judges held that these must be understood as limited to vendible chattels and not to include minerals still in the ground, or materials built into a house, because they were part of the inheritance. The clause in the commissions which authorised purveyors to imprison anyone who proved obstinate or disobedient 'until such time as the imprisonment shall be thought convenient and condign for his or their offence or offences', was resolved to be 'utterly against the common law and against the great charter of Magna Carta, chapter *Nullus liber homo* ... and against various other Acts of Parliament, which are but declarations of the common law'. Coke was active in enforcing the decision, and in February 1605 committed to Newgate a 'lewd fellow' who had taken upon himself to be a deputy purveyor and had unlawfully felled over thirty timber trees in Fulham.[237] The king affirmed the judges' decision, with respect to growing timber, by a proclamation of 1606, which resulted in several more purveyors being punished by the Star Chamber.[238]

The requirement of immediate cash payment was tested in 1605.[239] Abraham Jacob had a commission under the great seal to take purveyance of wines for the king's household in Bristol, and made a deputation to William Lamberd. When a vintner was asked to supply wine, he said he would provide it for ready money, but Lamberd said he did not have to pay ready money. The vintner therefore refused to make purveyance, and upon Lamberd's complaint to the Board of Green Cloth he was committed to prison. A group of merchant adventurers and other citizens of Bristol then went up to Westminster and prayed a *habeas corpus* on the vintner's behalf. Coke, as attorney-general, argued in support of

---

[237] Letter from Coke to Viscount Cranbourne, *Hatfield MSS*, xvii. 71, no. 145 ('All the judges of England have upon great deliberation resolved this kind of takings unlawful'). On 14 November he wrote that he was detained by purveyors' business in the Star Chamber: SP 14/16, fo. 144.

[238] Co. Inst. ii. 36 (23 April 1606); Coke's notebook, BL MS. Harley 6686B, fo. 606v, added at the foot and continued in the margin: (tr.) 'See the resolution of the justices in this case, as to the taking from subjects of trees growing, allowed by the king and Council and published by proclamation of 23 April ... and according to this resolution divers purveyors were punished by the Star Chamber for taking timber growing'); whence Co. Inst. ii. 35 (in the commentary on Magna Carta, c. 21).

[239] *Aldworth's Case* (1605) BL MS. Add. 35954, fos. 369–70. Another Bristol case, alleging extortion in buying currants, is *Anon.* (Hil. 1606) IT MS. Barrington 6, fo. 218 (where the indictment for extortion was supported by Coke Att.-Gen.).

the committal. The prerogative of purveyance was allowed by the common law, under which the purveyor did not have to pay ready money. The statute which said that purveyors should pay ready money for items worth 40s. 'or above' was misprinted, for he had seen the roll, and it said 'or under';[240] it would otherwise be unreasonable, since purveyors would have to carry the king's treasure around with them. The Board of Green Cloth was in effect the king's council for his household,[241] and had possessed authority to punish contempts against the purveyors since time immemorial:

> But because it is the king's benign will that the liberty of the subjects be precisely observed, and that his prerogative be not strained to their oppression, and inasmuch as his majesty has made known his gracious purpose unto me, I may say in this case that the patent granted to Jacob, as to the composition, and also the deputation made by Jacob to Lamberd concerning that, is void. For no composition may be made without the free assent of the subject, and when it is made the king cannot demise it over, but it ought wholly to be put in the king's coffers so that the king's provision may be made therewith; and therefore as to that (I hope) it shall be amended. Nevertheless, as to the other point, namely to make purveyance, it is good, and so is the deputation.

Coke felt unable to defend purveyors, however, without expressing once again his low opinion of them. The original name was 'cheator',[242] meaning buyer, 'and therefrom came the word caitor, a word of disgrace'. He emphasised that they could not take anything which was part of the freehold, and said that earlier in the same term a purveyor had been punished in the Star Chamber, and set on the pillory, for taking growing timber.[243]

Despite Coke's efforts, purveyors continued with their extortionate practices and were vehemently attacked in the 1606 Parliament as 'vultures, harpies, cormorants and caterpillars and vermin'.[244] An annual composition was proposed, to replace the prerogative revenue, but it

---

[240] 2 Hen. IV, c. 14. It was correctly printed in the later *Statutes at Large.*

[241] It was principal a financial body, also known as the Counting House of the King's Household: Co. Inst. iv. 131.

[242] I.e. achator. The adjustment of spelling was, of course, deliberate.

[243] Cf. *R.* v. *Ives* (1611) BL MS. Hargrave 32, fos. 43, 49v–50; 1 Bulst. 96, where the question was whether a purveyor who took felled timber without an appraisal, and without giving a tally, was guilty of felony. Magna Carta, c. 21, and the *Articuli super Cartas*, were cited. Coke included a separate chapter 'Of Felony in Purveyors' in Co. Inst. iii. 82–4.

[244] Wilbraham, *Journal*, p. 76.

found no favour in the Commons since it would have amounted to a perpetual rent-charge on the subject. It was then argued by the lawyers in the House – 'in the face of all the judges drawn to the conference by the Lords to clear all doubts, who delivered no resolute opinion, neither were much urged to, and per case doubtful in the matter' – that the king had only a prerogative right of preemption, but no prerogative in price. Reference was duly made to chapter 29 of Magna Carta.[245] The Commons complained that, if anyone gainsaid 'these ungodly people, the purveyors', they were immediately sent for and punished by the Board of Green Cloth, contrary to law and justice.[246] The Lords said the king had by long prescription a prerogative to have a reasonable price for all purchases for his household, but the lawyers pointed to statutes which said the contrary. The judges opined that a reasonable price meant a price more favourable to the king than the market price, to cover the costs of collection; but they could cite no authority for this.[247] The judges also held that the Board of Green Cloth was a court, albeit only for the purpose of punishing those who refused or resisted purveyance, and therefore if they imprisoned someone it was *lex terrae* and not against Magna Carta. They drew an analogy with the courts of equity and the Star Chamber. But they said they could send a *habeas corpus* if the Board imprisoned anyone against the law.[248] The Commons felt defeated, not least because the judges had intimated that the prerogative could not be taken away by Parliament; if it attempted to do so, the king would not be bound by the statute and could dispense with it.[249]

Later the same year, shortly after Coke became chief justice, the judges were convened again, at Serjeants' Inn, Fleet Street, to consider the legality of a commission to take saltpetre, which had been complained of in Parliament.[250] The judges upheld the prerogative as necessary for the defence of the realm, but subject to various safeguards enumerated by Coke, including the landowner's right to dig and sell saltpetre himself.

---

[245] Bowyer, *Parliamentary Diary*, p. 40 ('We are not ignorant that his majesty is sworn to Magna Carta, which saith *Nulli negabimus, nulli vendemus justiciam aut rectum ...*'); *JHC*, i. 297, *per* Coke Att.-Gen. (12 April 1606) (where the reference to Magna Carta is unintelligible); Thompson, *Magna Carta*, p. 247.

[246] Bowyer, *Parliamentary Diary*, p. 40.   [247] Wilbraham, *Journal*, p. 84.   [248] Ibid. 85.

[249] *JHC*, i. 278, *per* Nicholas Fuller MP. This had also been pointed out in 1604: ibid. 223. It may explain why one member in 1606 proposed a new great charter: ibid. 274.

[250] *Case of Saltpetre* (1606) Co. Inst. iii. 83–4; 12 Co. Rep. 12; French text in IT MS. Misc. 21, fo. 96; above, p. 194. The commission was granted by patent to John Evelyn in 1604, and was complained of in Parliament in 1606: Wilbraham, *Journal*, p. 88.

The commissioners were not allowed to sell saltpetre, or make any private profit from it. And the judges resolved, according to Coke, 'that the common law hath so admeasured the prerogatives of the king that they should neither take away nor prejudice the inheritance of any; and these monopolies, being *malum in se* and against the common laws, are consequently against the prerogative of the king, for the prerogative of the king is given to him by the common law and is part of the laws of the realm'. These resolutions were put in writing and approved of by the Privy Council. As with the prerogative writs, the royal prerogative was here being harnessed to provide a legal justification for striking down abuses under colour of the prerogative, since those could not be attributed to the king in his politic capacity. The king, as God's lieutenant, could do no wrong.[251]

Impositions

The other great debate in which Magna Carta played a part in this period was the prerogative of taxation by means of impositions.[252] In 1596 Coke, as attorney-general, brought an information in the Exchequer against the executor of Customer Smyth, late farmer of the customs, for over £1,000 due from impositions on imported alum. The lawfulness of the impost was questioned, but the court eventually decided that the queen had the right to set impositions, as parent of the common weal, and that the imposition would be presumed to have been lawful unless the contrary appeared.[253] The prevailing position before the time of James I was therefore that impositions were lawful. They belonged to the absolute prerogative, which could not be questioned.

The question was, however, raised again in 1606 after a fierce debate in the Commons. The test case was fought in the Court of Exchequer, though Coke was relieved from playing a substantial part in it, since

---

[251] Coke was fond of this principle: e.g. *The Case of Alton Woods* (1600) 1 Co. Rep. 40 at fo. 44; Co. Litt. 19. It meant, inter alia, that the king was not exempted by implication from a statute made to suppress wrong: *Case of Ecclesiastical Persons* (1601) 5 Co. Rep. 14; *Warren v. Smith* (1615) 11 Co. Rep. 66, at fo. 72; 1 Rolle Rep. 166, 167; Co. Inst. ii. 681. See also above, p. 311.

[252] See above, pp. 185–6.

[253] *Att.-Gen. v. Smyth* (Hil. 1600) cited by Hall, 'Impositions and the Courts' (below, n. 255), pp. 213–16, from Bodl. Lib. MS. Rawlinson C.756, fo. 52.

he was appointed chief justice of the Common Pleas in the summer.[254] The arguments are well known, chiefly because of the light they throw on contemporary interpretations of the royal prerogative,[255] but for present purposes the focus will be on the invocations of Magna Carta by counsel.[256] John Bate, a Levant merchant and a grocer, had imported 3,266 cwt of currants from Venice (probably ultimately from Greece), paying £244. 19s. subsidy and poundage at the port of London, but had refused to pay the further £898. 3s. demanded as an imposition. He was committed to the Marshalsea, and his case was taken up in the House of Commons by Nicholas Fuller, bencher of Gray's Inn, and Thomas Hitchcock, a bencher of Lincoln's Inn,[257] who were opposed by Francis Bacon, as king's counsel. Parliament was, however, prorogued before the matter could be resolved, and it was decided to proceed instead in the Exchequer. One of Coke's last acts as attorney-general was to lay the information against Bate, but by the time the case came to be argued in July he had been replaced by Sir Henry Hobart and the prosecution was left to John Dodderidge, the solicitor-general, and Bacon. Bate's plea, on the record, was simply that the imposition was against the law and custom of the realm. He was represented by Hitchcock and his junior Humphrey Davenport, barrister of Gray's Inn. Davenport, perhaps alluding to the decisions on restraint of trade, said that merchants had 'quasi an inheritance and birthright in their trading, so that the king may no more impose upon the merchandise of a merchant than upon the inheritance of his subject'.[258] Such impositions were therefore prohibited by Magna Carta, chapter 29. Chapter 30 was also relied on, together with the confirmatory statutes, which granted to all merchants the freedom to

[254] *Att.-Gen.* v. *Bate* (1606) BL MS. Harley 37, fo. 182; CUL MS. Dd.2.23, fos. 27–33v; MS. Gg.4.9, fos. 227–233v (same report); MS. Lansdowne 1062, fos. 188v–197; Lane 22 (reprinted in 2 St. Tr. 382); other manuscripts noted in 69 LQR 200 n. 3. The only printed report, Lane's, omits the arguments of counsel.
[255] See, e.g., G. D. G. Hall, 'Impositions and the Courts 1554–1606' (1953) 69 LQR 200–18; P. Croft, 'Fresh Light on Bate's Case' (1987) 30 *Historical Journal* 523–39; Brooks, *Law, Politics and Society*, pp. 135–42; J. S. Hart, *The Rule of Law 1603–1660: Crowns, Courts and Judges* (2003), pp. 91–8; above, pp. 146–7.
[256] The use of Magna Carta was commented upon by Hall, 'Impositions and the Courts' (previous note), at p. 201.
[257] Hitchcock was not then MP, but spoke at the bar of the House on behalf of Bate: *JHC*, i. 297 (11 April 1606). He also represented Bate in the Exchequer.
[258] CUL MS. Ee.3.45, fo. 18v (all quotations tr.).

come and go by land or sea to buy and sell, free from 'maletolts'.[259] Hitchcock here drew the distinction, made famous in the subsequent judgment of Fleming CB,[260] between limited and absolute prerogatives. The latter were *arcana regni*, not within the jurisdiction of any court. But taxes and impositions, in his submission, were of the former category and were bounded by the common law.[261] This was clearly in accordance with the judgment which Popham CJ did not deliver in *Darcy v. Allen*.[262] The decision of the Court of Exchequer, however, was that impositions on foreign imports were in the absolute category. The currants were to be treated as Venetian goods. The king could control their coming in, and so he could impose taxes for permission to bring them in, especially when (as here) the goods were not essential food but mere luxuries. The additional cost would be passed on to customers, and would only affect 'delicate persons, and those who are of most able and best estate, for their pleasure'.

The decision has been condemned, with reason, as showing a lack of judicial independence. The barons were put under pressure by the lord treasurer, the earl of Dorset, who was both responsible for collecting impositions and nominal president of the Exchequer. Fleming CB, the presiding judge, had also corresponded about the politics of the case-management with the earl of Salisbury, who shared with the earl of Suffolk a lease of the impositions on currants.[263] Fleming had cultivated the king's favour, and was promoted to be lord chief justice of England the following year. The case was not a landmark in the history of Magna Carta, save to the extent that it was relied on by Bate's counsel as their last hope. On the view that was taken, however, it was of no assistance. Impositions were seemingly part of the *lex terrae*. It was nevertheless agreed at a subsequent meeting between Coke and Popham CJJ that the right of laying impositions was limited to the advancement of trade and traffic, for it would otherwise infringe chapter 30 of Magna Carta.[264] It is

---

[259] BL MS. Hargrave 34, fo. 57v. The response to this was that the saving in c. 30 of the 'ancient and rightful customs' was enough to show that the liberty did not preclude import charges: Lane 24. Davenport also cited c. 9, confirming the liberties of London, and c. 14, concerning the amercement of merchants, without elaborating on their relevance: loc. cit.

[260] Above, p. 146.

[261] BL MS. Harley 37, fo. 175v; MS. Hargrave 34, fo. 61v; and other manuscripts.

[262] Above, pp. 322–3.   [263] Hart, *The Rule of Law* (above, n. 255), pp. 93–4.

[264] 'Customs, Subsidies and Impositions' (1607) 12 Co. Rep. 33.

not wholly clear how they would have applied this distinction in practice, but they evidently disapproved strongly of the Exchequer decision.

The judiciary being thus divided, the debate was resumed in Parliament,[265] and pursued at the same time in a learned written debate between John Davies[266] and James Whitelocke,[267] both barristers of the Middle Temple, who unearthed the whole history of taxation in England from record sources. Whitelocke identified the essence of the dispute in the fundamental constitutional maxim, 'The king cannot alter the law'. The king could not take a subject's goods without his consent, and he could not issue a commission authorising someone else to take them, because either course would be against the law.[268] Nicholas Fuller, in the 1610 parliament, spoke to much the same effect as Davenport's argument in the Exchequer. The laws were the highest inheritance of the subject, and by the laws of England subjects had property in their lands and goods which the king could not take away by impositions. The liberty of subjects in their lawful trades was protected as tenderly as lands and goods. And the king could not change this law by charter.[269] This part of the argument, like Whitelocke's, was obviously an argument drawn from the learning on Magna Carta,[270] though the only chapter which either of them discussed explicitly was chapter 30.[271]

William Hakewill of Lincoln's Inn also spoke in the Commons.[272] He said he had been present when *Bate's Case* was argued, and at the time

---

[265] *Proc. Parl. 1610*, ii. 152–65; Thompson, *Magna Carta*, pp. 250–6.

[266] 'An Argument upon the Question of Impositions', which survives in over 35 manuscripts but was not printed until 1656: *CELMC*, p. 242. Cf. 2 St. Tr. 399–408, 477–520 (attributed to Yelverton).

[267] This survives in fewer manuscripts but was printed in 1641: *CELMC*, p. 6 (listing thirteen manuscripts); *A Learned and Necessary Argument to prove that each Subject hath a Propriety in his Goods, shewing also the Extent of the King's Prerogative in Impositions* (1641); *Rights of the People concerning Impositions, stated in a learned Argument* (1658); 2 St. Tr. 479–529; *Proc. Parl. 1610*, ii. 221. His preparatory collections are in IT MS. Petyt 537.14, fos. 187–213v. The treatise was based on a speech in Parliament but may have been expanded. See D. X. Powell, *Sir James Whitelocke's Liber Famelicus 1570–1632* (Bern, 2000), pp. 73–97.

[268] *A Learned and Necessary Argument* (1641), p. 11.   [269] *Proc. Parl. 1610*, ii. 152–3.

[270] Chapter 29 is cited in the margin, ibid. 153, and *Sir John atte Lee's Case* (1368) (above, p. 58) is cited ibid. 158.

[271] Ibid. 161–2; Whitelocke, *A Learned Argument* (1641), pp. 22–4. Whitelocke (p. 16) also relied on *Sir John atte Lee's Case* (1368) and *Scrogges's Case* (1559).

[272] W. Hakewil[l], *The Libertie of the Subject against the pretended Power of Impositions maintained by an Argument in Parliament an. 7 Jacobi Regis* (1641); reprinted in 2 St. Tr. 407–76. There are copies in manuscript: e.g. BL MS. Harley 1059, fos. 24–67;

had been persuaded by the torrent of citations, but on looking into all the records (at the request of the House) he had changed his mind. He too emphasised the importance of chapter 30, in language which was now becoming familiar in speeches:[273]

> The first statute is in Magna Carta, c. 30 ... The statute of which this is a branch is the most ancient statute-law we have, won and sealed with the blood of our ancestors, so reverenced in former times that it hath been by Parliament provided that transcripts thereof should be sent to all the cathedral churches of England, there to remain; that it should be twice every year publicly read before the people; that likewise twice ever year there should be excommunication solemnly denounced to the breakers thereof; that all statutes and all judgments given against shall be held as void; that it should be received and allowed as common law by all such as have the administration of justice; and it hath been no less than twenty-nine times solemnly confirmed in Parliament. I will therefore with so much the more care endeavour to free this from all the objections that have been made against it ...

Thomas Hedley, of Gray's Inn, delivered an even more impressive and eloquent speech,[274] with Magna Carta at its core:[275]

> It is a rule or principle in the common law of England that the king without assent of Parliament cannot alter any law, no more than he can make a law ... This hath been agreed by all the king's learned counsel, and by one of them it was upon another occasion most worthily said that, as there were some principles in divinity which could not be disputed without blasphemy, so there were some principles in government that could not be disputed without sedition, whereof he held this to be one. Seeing, therefore, the king cannot alter the law, the chief subject or object whereof is property in lands and goods, ... seeing also in this kingdom of England the laws of the kingdom are the inheritance not only of the king, but also of the subjects, of which the king ought not to disseise them or disinherit them, therefore it followeth consequently and necessarily that the king cannot alter the property or goods of any of his free subjects without their consent, for that is to disseise them of the fruit and benefit of the law, which is all one as to disinherit them of the law itself. And this appeareth yet more plainly in the great charter of the liberties of England, that the law is not only to protect us

---

Columbia Law School MS. H12; Philadelphia Free Library MS. LC 14.55, fos. 21–37; Yale University, Osborne shelves MS. b.73 and fb.130.

[273] Hakewill, *Impositions* (previous note), at p. 99. Chapter 30 is discussed ibid. 6, 8, 99–112. Cf. ibid. 4, where he said impositions were 'against the great charter of our liberties'.

[274] *Proc. Parl. 1610*, ii. 170–97.   [275] Ibid. 188–9.

against the absolute power and prerogative of the king in life and member, but also in lands and goods. Therefore he that cannot alter the law, cannot alter property ... [and] he that cannot alter property, cannot impose.

Towards the end of the speech, he laid stress again on the central importance of Magna Carta, and took occasion to refute recent attempts to belittle its importance on the grounds that it was originally extorted from the king by duress of arms:[276]

> My last reason is drawn from the ancient freedom and liberty of subjects of England, which appeareth and is confirmed by the great charter of the liberties of England, but more plainly and particularly by reports and judgments printed and published in our law books. For I do not take Magna Carta to be a new grant or statute, but a restoring or confirming of the ancient laws and liberties of the kingdom which by the Conquest before had been much impeached or obscured. And therefore these cavils are easily blown away that have been of late objected for the extirpating of the honour and strength of this charter, that it was sealed in blood, gotten by force and arms taken up by subjects against their sovereign, and thereby enforced to agree to this law or charter ... I think there is little question, that if the subjects do obtain a grant of their ancient laws and liberties at the conqueror's hands, though it be first gotten by force, yet if after several times and in several ages in time of peace it be confirmed by continual consent and oath of king and people and hath so continued and been continually approved for many hundred years, then they will be as firm and strong as any human laws whatsoever ... This charter, if it was first gotten in time of war, hath been since confirmed in time of peace at the least thirty times by several parliaments in several kings' times and ages, which charter (as I said) doth notably confirm the freedom and liberty of the subjects.

Liberty and sovereignty were not incompatible, because the happiness of all kingdoms rested in the 'right mixture' of both. They were like twins, and had 'such concordance and coalescence that the one can hardly long subsist without the other'. The sovereignty of the king was principally concerned with government, the liberty of the subject with property. This matter of taxation was a matter of property, and rested on common law, which kings could not change without Parliament. The motion was for a petition of grievances, asking (inter alia) that all

---

[276] Ibid. 190. There is a further mention of Magna Carta, c. 29, ibid. 192, where an argument is made about the difference between a *liber homo* and a villein resting on property rather than liberty of the person.

impositions without the consent of Parliament should be void. They interfered with the law of property, which was 'as ancient as the kingdom itself'.

It was not to be. The petition passed the lower house but not the Lords, and it was to fail again in 1614. In 1614 the king promised, in his speech to the parliament, not to lay any impositions on home-bred commodities, and that he would accept the opinion of all the judges as to his right, but that he regarded impositions as a great flower of his prerogative and that he would die a thousand deaths rather than give them up.[277] James Whitelocke bluntly told the Commons that they were not a flower of the prerogative, that they had not been judicially recognised before *Bate's Case*, and that the decision of the Exchequer Chamber in that case had been overruled by vote of the House in 1610.[278] The other counsel who had argued in 1610 spoke to the same effect, and another speaker referred to the decision as 'evil',[279] but all to no avail.

In many of the cases surveyed in this chapter, the outcome was for the time being inconclusive. But in all these diverse issues of state, Magna Carta had become the hill on which judges, counsel and legally trained members of Parliament took their stand. This was a notable departure from previous generations. The charter was no longer a curiosity of medieval history, to be explained out of practical usefulness in the law schools. Nor was it tainted with nonconformity, as a newfound device for resisting the discipline of the established Church. Its most beneficial provisions, chiefly but not exclusively chapter 29, were becoming part of the orthodox framework of English constitutional law – if legal orthodoxy may best be discerned from the words of the judges of the two benches and the attorney-general. That is not to say that their purport and reach were as yet fully settled. Unwritten constitutions are not settled overnight. But the front line was about to be moved further forward, following the appointment of Sir Edward Coke as chief justice of the Common Pleas on 30 June 1606.

---

[277] *Proc. Parl. 1614*, pp. 138, 142 (two versions). He pointed out that his right had been confirmed by all the judges in the Exchequer Chamber, but said that if a writ of error were brought he would accept the outcome.

[278] Ibid. 95, 149.

[279] Ibid. 100, *per* Sir Maurice Berkeley MP ('evil Chequer Chamber case'). Another report of the same speech says that 'the case of the currants in the Exchequer opened the floodgate of these impositions': ibid. 93–4.

9

Sir Edward Coke and Magna Carta 1606–1615

The beatification and canonisation of Magna Carta are indelibly associated with Sir Edward Coke, partly because of his lengthy published commentary (written in the 1620s),[1] but mainly as a result of his parliamentary campaign against arbitrary taxation and imprisonment, leading to the Petition of Right in 1628. Yet his devotion to the great charter was far from being a newfound creed, opportunely adopted by the disgruntled former lord chief justice in his role as leader of the opposition faction in the House of Commons. He had taken a keen interest in its potential uses ever since his earlier days at the Bar, and this developed into an even keener interest during his career as a law officer and chief justice.

Allusion has been made in the previous chapters to the fact that Coke's own ascendancy coincided closely with the resuscitation of Magna Carta, and that most of his constitutional thinking was developed during his days at the Bar. By 1588 he was reported as speaking in about a hundred cases a year – a different one more or less every day[2] – and such was his reputation by then that one law reporter was moved to describe him as 'the famous utter-barrister of Inner Temple',[3] a note of fame bestowed on no other junior barrister in any of the law reports in any period. Those were the very years in which he immediately latched on to the newly appreciated importance of chapter 29 of Magna Carta. He was soon citing chapter 29 in his own arguments, and reporting significant cases

---

[1] Co. Inst. ii. 1–78. This was first published in 1642, having been suppressed by Charles I's government, but had been composed between 1616 and the mid-1620s.

[2] In 1587 and 1588 together, a total of 190 cases have so far been noted in which Coke was reported as speaking, chiefly in the King's Bench and Common Pleas. There must have been others, especially in other courts. The courts at Westminster were open for little more than a hundred days a year.

[3] BL MS. Add. 25196, fo. 121v (tr.), repeated (without mentioning his inn) on fos. 138, 139 (1588); and cf. Goulds. 95, 99 ('the famous Coke'). The degree of utter barrister was a step below that of reader or bencher.

in his notebooks.[4] In 1592 he entered the royal service as solicitor-
general. The queen, having summoned him to her Withdrawing Chamber at Greenwich, teasingly chided him for acting against her in some
recent cases, whereupon (in his own words):[5]

> I was so wholly appalled and dismayed (and being surprised with an
> incomparable grief that so gracious a prince should in any sort suspect my
> loyalty and inward duty and allegiance to her highness, and feeling a
> wonderful natural fear and love which God hath grafted in a subject's
> heart towards his natural sovereign) that my heart shaked within my body
> and all the parts of my body trembled, so as I neither could mark the
> conclusion of her speech nor make any answer at all, nor until mine eyes
> gushed out with tears could be reduced to perfect memory . . .

He nevertheless managed ('in sobbing manner') to express his acceptance, with suitable outpourings of gratitude.

When the queen promoted him to be attorney-general two years later,
she reminded him of his former discomfiture:[6]

> I have not seen any man so appalled and dismayed as thou wert when
> I called thee first to my service, but indeed I did then lay sore to thy charge
> such things as (I dare say) thou didst not expect for at my hands; but,
> seeing thou hast been of counsel in many great cases against me, it
> behoveth thee now in these cases to be the more wary and circumspect,
> and to carry thyself in my service as no suspicion may be had of thee of
> any respect or inclination to favour any of those matters. And now . . .
> thou shalt reap in gladness further advancement at my hands, for I have
> made choice of thee to be my attorney-general, an office of great trust and
> charge.

Although she went on to charge him with ensuring that justice be done to
her subjects,[7] it might have been supposed that in fulfilling this great
trust and charge Coke would become a subservient and prerogative-
minded law officer. It was certainly a delicate role, and his emotional
and intemperate oratory as a state prosecutor earned him a posthumous
reputation of that nature which it has been difficult to eradicate. It was
now, without question, his duty to interrogate and prosecute alleged
traitors with vigour, according to the standards of the day,[8] and to

---

[4] Above, pp. 264–6.   [5] Autograph notebook, BL MS. Harley 6686A, fos. 34–5.
[6] Ibid. 86.   [7] This part of the speech is quoted above, pp. 148–9.
[8] For his signing of torture warrants see above, p. 172. For his signing a warrant for
detention by command of the Privy Council, without cause shown, see Halliday, *Habeas
Corpus*, p. 25. For his work as a law officer generally see also Boyer, *Coke and the
Elizabethan Age*, pp. 242–96.

represent the crown's interests in court to the best of his ability.[9] He was required to settle charters and letters patent which he must have found distasteful, including patents of monopoly[10] instructions for the Council in the Marches,[11] and three ecclesiastical high commissions.[12] In 1600 he went so far as to contend that the commission under the great seal issued in 1599 to the earl of Essex on his expedition to Ireland – 'the largest and most absolute commission ever granted either for ordinary justice or for war' – could be modified by the queen's letters and oral instructions alone, since the conduct of war fell within the absolute prerogative, and that the earl could be prosecuted for breach of the supplemental instructions before a 'selected council' rather than a court of law.[13]

The typical historian's verdict has been that 'Coke the champion-of-the-common-law was a later phenomenon than Coke the Queen's-man-and-vigorous-Attorney-General'.[14] This is, however, wide of the mark. In many areas of public law, Coke as attorney-general consistently showed a judicious concern for the central importance of the common law in a constitutional monarchy. Time and again, as has been shown in the previous chapter, Coke resorted to Magna Carta in his speeches at the bar: not to undermine the royal prerogative, but rather to nurture a concept of the prerogative which supported the rule of law, and to represent the protection afforded by the machinery of the common law

---

[9] E.g. in defending the prerogative power of staying suits, which Coke argued was above the law (*ultra legem*): above, p. 183. He was obliged to argue in support of the playing-card monopoly in *Darcy* v. *Allen* (1602) above, p. 319.

[10] In 1604 he wrote to Lord Hume of Berwick justifying a monopoly of importing logwood to be used in dyeing, on the grounds that the king could prohibit their import altogether, but said he had inserted a proviso in the patent for revocation in the case of abuse: *Hatfield House MSS.*, xvi. 226, no. 411.

[11] Below, p. 380 n. 245.

[12] BL MS. Lansdowne 160, fo. 409 (so stated in the Privy Council, 1611). Coke even had to sit as a commissioner: Boyer, *Coke and the Elizabethan Age*, p. 298.

[13] Coke's autograph notebook, BL MS. Harley 6686B, fos. 408v–410 (passage quoted above, 145); Smith, *Sir Edward Coke*, pp. 258–9. The 'selected council', which met at York House, included the principal judges of the realm (Egerton LK and the three chiefs, with Gawdy and Walmsley JJ.). The report does not mention Coke's own role, but it is known that he spoke as counsel (led nominally by Serjeant Yelverton): Boyer, *Coke and the Elizabethan Age*, pp. 276–7.

[14] Youngs, p. 57. See also W. S. Holdsworth, *History of English Law*, iv (1924), p. 186 ('Coke was often inconsistent because he had the mind of an advocate, and therefore often allowed himself to be carried away by the argument which he was urging at the moment'); G. Burgess, *Absolute Monarchy and the Stuart Constitution* (New Haven, 1996), pp. 197–203.

against undesirable innovations in the state as the highest exercise of the prerogative.[15]

The year after he became attorney-general, Coke argued – with an unmistakable allusion to chapter 29 of Magna Carta[16] – that every subject had an inheritance in the law, which could only be changed by Parliament, and therefore no one could be imprisoned by virtue of the royal prerogative as expressed in a commission.[17] Two years later he persuaded the assembled judges that the Chancery could not grant an injunction to prevent a party from enforcing a judgment already obtained at law,[18] a principle which he also urged in relation to the Court of Requests.[19] In 1598 he wrote that discretion was a science of discernment, and so even when commissioners were given authority by the king to act according to their discretions, they could not act 'according to their wills and private affections' but were bound by the rule of reason and law.[20] When reinforced by the prerogative writ of *certiorari*, this principle would become a cornerstone of administrative law.[21] In 1599 Coke argued that a bye-law in restraint of trade was contrary to chapter 29,[22] and in 1601 that imprisonment by a mayor under an alleged custom, without due process, was an infringement of the same statute.[23] In this last case he persuaded the King's Bench judges that they had a jurisdiction in *habeas corpus* outside the realm. He intervened to prevent injustices arising from the undue exploitation of concealments and

---

[15] See especially his remarks in *Whetherly's Case* (1605) above, pp. 307–11; below, pp. 512–13.

[16] He was echoing the words of Popham Att.-Gen., referring to c. 29, in *Att.-Gen. v. Joiners' Company of London* (1582) above, p. 261.

[17] The context was the High Commission: *Smith's Case* (1600) above, p. 291. He made the same argument in *Needham v. Price* (1605) above, p. 296.

[18] *Throckmorton v. Finch* (1597) above, p. 287.

[19] *Cardinal v. De la Broche* (1605/6) above, p. 284.

[20] *Rooke v. Withers* (1598) 5 Co. Rep. 99; the quoted passage occurs also in his contemporary autograph report, BL MS. Harley 6686A, fo. 250v. He was to apply the principle, as chief justice, in *Hetley v. Boyer, Mildmay and others* (1614) 2 Bulst. 197; Cro. Jac. 336. For the context of these cases, and ongoing problems with the commissioners of sewers, see Smith, *Sir Edward Coke*, pp. 91–114.

[21] For the emergence of *certiorari* see above, p. 201 n. 332. The 1598 case arose from a special verdict in an action of replevin in the Common Pleas.

[22] *Davenant v. Hurdys* (1599) above, pp. 316–17.

[23] *Brearley's Case* (1601) above, pp. 299–300. Cf. *Att.-Gen. v. Milward* (1605) Hawarde 237–41, where he prosecuted a party and a serjeant at mace for arresting the dowager countess of Rutland upon a feigned action in London, in pursuance of a custom, and this was held by the judges to be a bad custom 'against the freedom of the great charter'.

purveyance,[24] and in 1604 advised the Privy Council that purveyors could not interfere with a man's freehold.[25] He praised Queen Elizabeth for assuring her judges that they should never desist from doing right by reason of any royal command, for that would be contrary to chapter 29 of Magna Carta.[26] In 1605 he again took on Lord Ellesmere's Chancery by halting proceedings in the Exchequer to enforce a fine for breach of a decree touching title to land, the lord chancellor having no jurisdiction to meddle with the common law.[27] Here chapter 14 of Magna Carta seems to have been relied on.[28] Also in 1605, in a notable speech founded on chapter 29, he advocated the supremacy of the Court of King's Bench and – in direct opposition to Bacon's earlier assertions in the same case as king's counsel, and in the teeth of the Privy Council – submitted forcefully that *habeas corpus* would lie to the Council in the Marches of Wales.[29] These were hardly the arguments of a meekly subservient law officer. It is a strong testimony to Coke's reputation, and indeed to the political wisdom of the new king, that he was continued in office at all after the queen's death.

The Accession of King James

The accession of James VI of Scotland to the English throne in 1603 could have changed everything. It was seen by many English lawyers as potentially catastrophic from the constitutional point of view. In his *Trew Law of Free Monarchies* (1598), reprinted in 1603, James had expounded the extreme monarchical position that kings were answerable to God alone; that kings were makers of laws, not laws of kings, because monarchy preceded laws; that in Parliament the subjects did no more than crave the king to legislate, which he could do just as well without Parliament; that it was for the king to interpret doubts in the law; and that the king could suspend the law at will. To an English lawyer, this was nothing other than

---

[24] Above, pp. 200, 324.   [25] Above, p. 324.   [26] Above, p. 149.

[27] *Themilthorp's Case* (1605) in Coke's autograph notebook, BL MS. Harley 6686B, fo. 645v; Co. Inst. iv. 84. Themilthorp had pleaded that the chancellor had no jurisdiction to impose the fine, and Coke as attorney-general confessed the plea to be true, to which the court agreed.

[28] Assuming it to be the case reported as *Thomlinson's Case* (1605) BL MS. Hargrave 19, fos. 79v–81v, where it is said that neither the Admiralty nor the Chancery could fine, because of Magna Carta, c. 14. This report, however, suggests that the question arose in a *habeas corpus* for a prisoner of the Admiralty.

[29] Above, pp. 308–9; below, pp. 512–13.

the Romanist doctrine that what pleases the king has the force of law.[30] It was completely contrary to constitutional monarchy as understood in England since the fourteenth century, to everything that Coke believed in. But in March 1603 James became king of England, and Coke was kept in position as the king's attorney-general. This placed him in a most uncomfortable position.

James began his reign by frightening the English legal establishment to the core. On his first journey south, at Newark-on-Trent on 21 April, he commanded the summary execution of a cut-purse caught red-handed.[31] The knight-marshal (Lord Gerard) who carried out the sentence was privately warned to procure a pardon, since he would otherwise be liable to conviction for murder.[32] The assertion of such arbitrary power brought home to lawyers that the country now had a foreign-born king apparently ignorant of, and indifferent to, English civilisation. Even a convicted criminal was *liber homo*, entitled to the protection of Magna Carta, until he was sentenced. Such arbitrary action by the king was clearly a 'going or putting' upon, and a 'destroying' of, a free man against the law of the land, as prohibited by chapter 29.[33] But the king's declared opinion was that 'immediately on our succession, divers of the ancient laws of this realm are ipso facto expired'.[34] Did this mean that the great charter of liberties was now defunct? No one seriously suggested that. But Coke would have a difficult time defending all the common-law

---

[30] See above, pp. 120, 145. Fortescue, in the fifteenth century, had denied that this principle applied in Scotland, where the king ruled constitutionally: J. Fortescue, *The Governance of England*, ed. C. Plummer (Oxford, 1885), p. 112.

[31] T. M., 'A Narration of the Progress and Entertainment of the King's Most Excellent Majesty' (1603) printed in E. Arber, *An English Garner* (1877–90), viii. 509; J. Stow, *Annales, or, a Generall Chronicle of England*, ed. E. Howes (1631), p. 821. Sir Winston Churchill thought the execution was not carried out: *A History of the English-Speaking Peoples* (1956), ii. 89. But the contemporary sources say it was. The king did, however, pardon all the other prisoners in the castle, and in several others on his journey.

[32] Francis Ashley's reading (1616) CUL MS. Ee.6.3, fo. 119. Ashley remembered the incident occurring at Belvoir Castle, which was the king's next stop (on 22 April). The sources cited in n. 31 say that the order was given to the recorder of Newark: presumably Samuel Bevercotes of Gray's Inn, who died a few months later.

[33] Ashley's reading, fo. 119. For the convict as *liber homo* see ibid. 114. Hake may have been alluding to the incident when he wrote, in the context of Magna Carta, c. 29, that the king could not put anyone to death: *Epieikeia* (1603), 81–2; the book was mostly written in the 1590s but was finished by July 1603 and a copy presented to the king.

[34] *Stuart Royal Proclamations*, ed. J. F. Larkin and L. Hughes (Oxford, 1973–83), i. 95 (20 October 1604). See further G. Garnett, '"The Ould Fields": Law and History in the Prefaces to Sir Edward Coke's Reports' (2013) 34 *Journal of Legal History* 245–84 at p. 248.

protections which had come to be associated with the charter. He would be hindered by a dangerously well-read and opinionated king, by two archbishops of Canterbury (Richard Bancroft and George Abbot), by the lord chancellor (Lord Ellesmere[35]) and by his own eventual successor as attorney-general (Francis Bacon[36]). The rhetoric of Magna Carta, so eloquently expressed by Lord Burghley in the 1580s,[37] would never be heard from their lips, or indeed from those of Burghley's son Robert, earl of Salisbury (secretary of state until 1612).

Further tremors of alarm followed a proclamation which the king issued in May 1603, announcing that he would take steps to perfect a union of England and Scotland, and directing that in the mean time his subjects were to treat the two realms as 'presently united'.[38] This occasioned a great debate in Parliament when it was summoned the following year.[39] James wanted a single kingdom, to be called Great Britain, with one Parliament and one system of law, a codified amalgam of English and Scots law. Coke and the judges did not want this at all. Nor did the House of Commons. Nor did the Scots, come to that. The English judges advised that there was no precedent at home or abroad for combining two separate kingdoms into one name except in case of conquest, and that 'the alteration of the name of the king doth inevitably draw on an erection of a new kingdom or estate and a dissolution or extinguishment of the old, and that no explanation, limitation or reservation can clear or avoid that inconvenience, but it will be full of repugnancy and ambiguity, and subject to much variety and danger of construction'. The name Great Britain would cast the names of England and Scotland into oblivion; the king would lose his precedence over other nations, since his kingdom

---

[35] Thomas Egerton, newly ennobled (with the title of lord chancellor) in 1603. Elizabeth I had refrained from granting peerages to any of her chancellors, and had only allowed Egerton the title of lord keeper of the great seal.

[36] Bacon had to wait until 1613 to achieve this position, though he became solicitor-general in 1607 after serving as the first (and at that time the only) king's counsel extraordinary.

[37] Above, p. 268.

[38] *Stuart Royal Proclamations*, ed. J. F. Larkin and L. Hughes (Oxford, 1973–83), i, no. 9. The proclamation conceded that the advice of Parliament would be sought.

[39] For what follows see B. P. Levack, 'English Law, Scots Law and the Union 1603–1707' in *Law-Making and Law-Makers in British History*, ed. A. Harding (1980), pp. 105–26; idem, *The Formation of the British State: England, Scotland the the Union 1603–1707* (Oxford, 1987), pp. 68–101; idem, 'Law, Sovereignty and the Union' in *Scots and Britons*, ed. R. A. Mason (Cambridge, 1994), pp. 213–37; B. Galloway, *The Union of England and Scotland 1603–08* (Edinburgh, 1986); Brooks, *Law, Politics and Society*, pp. 130–5; Garnett, 'Prefaces to Coke's Reports', pp. 248–50.

would become the newest; the status of treaties would be thrown into doubt; the old offices of state would all be determined; popular opinion would be against it; and so on.[40] More problematically still, Parliament would be permanently dissolved and all the laws would be changed.[41] It would be a conquest, and the accepted thinking was that a conqueror could choose the laws to be followed in the conquered country.[42] The common law might be abrogated, or mixed with Roman law, or imperfectly codified, as the king saw fit. Magna Carta and the statutes of due process might be consigned to the history books.

English lawyers interpreted the accession very differently. James was king by inheritance, not by conquest: so, indeed, was he firmly informed by Mr Serjeant Phelips, speaker of the Commons in his first parliament.[43] Even though God had chosen him as heir, and as king he was God's vicar upon earth, with no terrestrial superior,[44] it was nevertheless the law of England which made him king. *Lex facit regem*.[45] As Chief Baron Fray had memorably said in 1441, 'the law is the greatest inheritance which the king has, for by the law he himself and all his subjects are governed, and if this law did not exist there would be no

---

[40] 'Objections against the change of the name or style of England and Scotland into the name or style of Great Britain, to be moved and debated in the conference between the Lords and Commons', with notes in Coke's hand, YLS MS. G.R24.1, fos. 149–50. For other versions of this, and related papers, see BL MS. Harley 292, fos. 133–7; Garnett, 'Prefaces to Coke's Reports', p. 248 n. 26; Levack, 'English Law, Scots Law and the Union', p. 112 n. 26.

[41] *JHC*, i. 186–7, *per* Sir Edwin Sandys MP. Sandys went so far as to say it would be against the king's coronation oath.

[42] See the discussion about Berwick in 1601 (above, p. 300) and the notes there. Robert Cecil said it would mean 'an utter extinction of all the laws now in force': Garnett, 'Prefaces to Coke's Reports', p. 248.

[43] *JHC*, i. 146 (22 March 1604): 'the imperial throne of this most victorious and happy nation, where you now do . . . sit, not as a conqueror, by the sword, but as an undoubted inheritor, by the sceptre'.

[44] Coke CJ said in *Middlecote's Case* (1615) Calth. MS. i. 353v, that the king could not abdicate the crown (tr.) 'because he holds it immediately of God, and there is no power superior to him beneath God'): this was proved by the attainder for high treason of those who murdered Edward II with a featherbed after his purported abdication. He had made notes on this in the previous century, but without reference to God: BL MS. Harley 6687B, fo. 495v.

[45] *Bracton*, ii. 33. This maxim was known even to English divines, and had been expounded in R. Hooker, *Of the Lawes of Ecclesiastical Politie* (1593–7), reprinted in *The Folger Library Edition of the Works of Richard Hooker*, ed. W. S. Hill (Cambridge, MA, 1977–98), iii. 336–42. Dr Hooker was well known to Coke, not only as a writer but as master of the Temple (the incumbent of Temple Church) from 1585 to 1591.

king and no inheritance'.[46] The law embodied the rules as to the inheritance of the crown, whether they were seen as customary or statutory,[47] and defined the nature of that inheritance. The law had stood firm as a rock 'against all storms and against the change of all nations here in England, as against the Danes, the Saxons, the Romans, and Normans; and had there not been found some excellency in it, it would surely have been altered by some of them, as by the Romans who gave laws to all the world'. The laws were written in blood, especially in the thirteenth century, when Magna Carta was obtained from the king and settled by Act of Parliament.[48] The judges' argument was heartfelt and powerful, and James, while continuing to proclaim his absolutist theories,[49] and his desire to see a union, was persuaded to concede much of it in practice. In 1609 he protested that he did not wish to depart from the common law or Magna Carta, though he knew he was suspected of it,[50] and in reporting to the 1610 parliament he accepted that he was bound, if only by his oath, to observe the fundamental laws of the realm. He even admitted that 'though he did derive his title from the loins of his ancestors, the law did set the crown upon his head, and he is a king by the common law of the land'.[51] Despite the king's insistence on using the title 'king of Great Britain' on his seals and coinage, the judges were adamant that the name Great Britain could not be used for legal purposes; the union did not occur for another hundred years, and the legal systems have remained separate to this day.[52]

Early in 1604, Mr Attorney Coke drove the point home in the preface to the fourth volume of his reports, 'published' – as the title-page tactfully proclaimed – 'in the first year (the springtime of all happiness) of the

---

[46] *Rector of Edington's Case* (1441) YB Pas. 19 Hen. VI, fo. 63, pl. 1 (tr.). This had been quoted the previous year by Popham CJ in *Darcy* v. *Allen* (1602), as reported in Coke's autograph notebook, BL MS. Hargrave 6686B, fo. 572v. It was quoted by Queen Elizabeth II on opening The Queen's Building at the Royal Courts of Justice in 1968.

[47] They were certainly not derived from the *jus gentium*: see *R.* v. *Duke of Norfolk* (1571) 1 St. Tr. 1016, *per* Thomas Bromley Sol.-Gen. Note also Fleetwood's remark in Parliament on the same subject: *HPHC 1558–1603*, iii. 408.

[48] Report of the Judges on the proposed Union, printed in *Letters and the Life of Bacon*, iii. 331–2. For other citations of Magna Carta in the debate see Thompson, *Magna Carta*, pp. 248–9.

[49] E.g. in addressing Parliament in 1610 on the subject of Cowell's *Interpreter*: below, p. 392.

[50] Below, p. 370.   [51] *Parliamentary Debates in 1610*, ed. S. R. Gardiner (1862), p. 24.

[52] In 1607 it was argued in the House of Commons that extradition to Scotland, for a felony committed there, was against Magna Carta, c. 29, because a felony there was no felony in England: Bower, *Parliamentary Diary*, p. 305.

most happy rule of the most high and most illustrious King James'.[53] It was obviously intended for the eyes of the new monarch. The king, said Coke, had honoured him with a request to continue with the publication of his reports:[54]

> whose commandment, being to me *suprema lex*, hath both encouraged and imposed a necessity upon me to publish this fourth edition: which containeth nothing but his majesty's own, being sweet and fruitful flowers of his crown; for the laws of England are indeed so called *jura coronae*, or *jura regalia* ... because, as Bracton saith ... the king is under no man, but under God and the law, for the law makes the king.

It was a carefully framed passage. The law was the king's, let that be admitted; but his majesty was not to assume that he had any control over it. Only 'the reverend judges and sages of the realm' could interpret it, and only the High Court of Parliament could amend any defects.[55] The changing of laws was particularly dangerous, since it required much experience and learning both to understand why change was needed and 'to foresee that a proportional remedy be applied, so as that for curing of some defects past there be not a stirring of more dangerous effects in the future':[56]

> For any fundamental point of the ancient common laws and customs of the realm, it is a maxim of policy, and a trial by experience, that any alteration of any of them is most dangerous. For that which has been refined and perfected by all the wisest men in former succession of ages, and proved and approved by continual experience to be good and profitable for the common wealth, cannot without great hazard and danger be altered or changed.

This had been demonstrated well enough, he said, by the Statute *De Donis* (1285) and the Statute of Wills (1540), each of which had led to endless intricate questions, 'to the ruin of many, and hindrance of multitudes'. As for Bacon's scheme to codify the law, which had met with the king's prima facie approval,[57] there was (Coke admitted) a

---

[53]   E. Coke, *Le Quart Part des Reportes del Edward Coke Chivalier ... publies en le primier An (le printemps de tout heureusitè) de tresheureux regiment de trehault et tresillustre Jaques ...* (1604). The first year of the reign ended on 23 March 1604.

[54]   Ibid. sig. B5. For the *Bracton* quotation see below, p. 367.   [55]   Ibid. sig. B2.

[56]   Ibid. sig. B2v.

[57]   In his speech to Parliament in 1607, James was still complaining about the uncertainties of case-law, though he conceded that the 'grounds of the common law' were the best in the world: *King James VI and I: Political Writings*, ed. J. Sommerville (Cambridge, 1994), p. 161.

strong argument for consolidating some of the confused body of statutes, but none whatever for tinkering with the common law:[58]

> For bringing the common laws into a better method, I doubt much of the
> fruit of that labour. This I know, that abridgments in many professions
> have greatly profited the authors themselves, but as they are used have
> brought no small prejudice to others. For the advised and orderly reading
> over of the books at large, in such manner as elsewhere I have pointed at,
> I absolutely determine to be the right way to enduring and perfect
> knowledge, and to use abridgments as tables and to trust only to the
> books at large.

For an attorney-general thus to school his royal master in print was both
unprecedented and audacious, especially since the Bractonian passage
was directly contrary to what the king himself had written about
monarchy.

Coke's defence of the common law at this moment was hardly the act
of a career-minded prerogative-man. He had much to lose, since his was
the most lucrative position at the Bar, a position sorely coveted by the
more pliable Francis Bacon. It is difficult to imagine Bacon or Ellesmere
similarly risking their careers by taking on so directly the king's political
philosophy. Their public expressions inclined in the opposite direction.
In addressing the judges in 1605, Ellesmere told them that 'the king's
majesty, as it were inheritable and descended from God, hath absolute
monarchical power annexed inseparably to his crown and diadem, not by
common law nor statute law, but more anciently than either of them'.[59]
A few years later, Ellesmere attacked the 'new-risen philosophers' who
argued that the king was beneath the law; the king, he said, was the law
speaking: *Rex est lex loquens*.[60] Coke took a very different view. He was
indeed the chief law officer to this king, sworn to serve him, and obliged
to defend the royal prerogative so far as it was allowed by law.[61] But he

---

[58] Ibid. sig. B3v. Coke has been misunderstood as favouring the codification of the common
law: see P. Christianson, 'Royal and Parliamentary Voices on the Ancient Constitution *c.*
1604–1621' in *The Mental World of the Jacobean Court*, ed. L. L. Peck (Cambridge, 1991),
p. 75; repeated in *The Roots of Liberty: Magna Carta, Ancient Constitution, and the
Anglo-American Tradition of Rule of Law*, ed. E Sandoz (Missouri, 1993), at p. 119.

[59] Hawarde 188 (defending the authority of the High Commission). Cf. *Att.-Gen.* v. *Graves*
(1606) ibid. 279; below, p. 350 n. 86.

[60] *Calvin's Case* (1608) 2 St. Tr. at col. 693. Ellesmere was quoting from the king's speech to
Parliament in 1607: *Political Writings*, ed. Sommerville (above, n. 57), p. 161. Coke
countered that *Judex est lex loquens*, the judge is the law speaking (7 Co. Rep. 4).

[61] Francis Bacon, when he was attorney-general in 1614, referred to himself as the procur-
ator of the king's prerogative: *Proc. Parl. 1614*, p. 63.

had learned from the late queen that the attorney-general also had a nobler calling which transcended politics.[62] Never had that calling been under greater stress. Coke shared with the judges the duty of ensuring the survival of English law, and his commitment to that mission pervaded his thinking for the rest of his life. He was to press the case to the point of sacrificing his own judicial career, though he was politic enough to avoid direct criticism of the king. It would have been futile to fight against the king, the only permanent element in the state, irremovable even by gunpowder; but it was both practicable and necessary for someone to engage him in argument. The object was to persuade him of the merits of the common law and of the importance of the rule of law, not as a force in opposition to the prerogative but rather as the brightest jewel in his crown. The current grievances were therefore not attributed to the king himself but to his court favourites and all those who exercised authority under him in such a way as to extend their personal power, or advance their own ends, at the expense of the subject.[63] The king's subjects depended on his judges to protect them, in the king's name. This was an argument to which the king was prepared, at least, to listen. And he was shrewd enough to admire Coke's learning and integrity, the qualities which for the past decade had made him the leader of the Bar in general estimation as well as in importance.[64]

It was in this context, in Michaelmas term 1604, that Coke composed his remarkable little tract on chapter 29 of Magna Carta.[65] The immediate prompting, as shown in the previous chapter, was the overweening claim by Lord Zouche that as President of the Council in the Marches of Wales he was beyond the reach of *habeas corpus*.[66] Coke considered this outrageous. The tract was not a draft of Coke's speech in the case itself,[67] but a memorandum drawing together observations and authorities concerning chapter 29 and *habeas corpus*, many of them unearthed through research in the rolls. Coke was motivated by the current importance of the subject, and there are

---

[62] Above, p. 148.   [63] Cf. Smith, *Sir Edward Coke*, p. 277.

[64] Strictly speaking, the attorney- and solicitor-general were at this date outranked by the king's serjeants, but in reality they were far more important.

[65] BL MS. Harley 6686B, fos. 600–604v; printed in translation below, Appendix 7, pp. 500–10. It immediately follows Coke's report of the opinions of the judges given in Parliament concerning trade with infidels, but these seem to belong to the previous term or the Long Vacation.

[66] Above, pp. 303–11.

[67] For his speech of 1605, using the material he had discovered, see below, p. 512.

signs that he intended the tract to be circulated, though only one other copy has been found. It is an early example of systematic research in legal records to bolster a constitutional argument.[68] The most significant and novel part of Coke's message was that effective remedies were now available for infringements of chapter 29. These included actions of trespass founded on the statute, but foremost among them was the writ of *habeas corpus*, which would lie to any of the king's dominions, whether or not they were part of England, including Wales, Ireland and Guernsey. The linkage between Magna Carta and *habeas corpus* was obvious to Coke, and the two were soon to become inseparable in the popular mind, though the link had only been forged in the previous reign. Around the same time, Coke connected the ancient writ of prohibition with chapter 29,[69] and he would soon add *mandamus* to the list of its progeny.[70] The main interest of the tract is in showing that Coke did not suddenly produce a mythical new interpretation of Magna Carta in the troubled Parliament of 1628. He was already perfecting his Magna Carta hyperbole, as the king's attorney-general, in the critical first year of James's reign. The charter, he wrote then, protected 'everything that anyone has in this world, or that concerns the freedom and liberty of his body or his freehold, or the benefit of the law to which he is inheritable, or his native country in which he was born, or the preservation of his reputation or goods, or his life, blood and posterity'.[71]

Coke's devotion to Magna Carta, though bolstered by historical research,[72] was not primarily that of a historian. He insisted on the value

---

[68] Some of the precedents had been drawn to Coke's attention as early as 1587 by the secondary of the Crown Office: above, p. 265. Cf. *Bate's Case* (1606), in which extensive research was conducted in the public records with respect to the history of taxation: above, pp. 328–31.

[69] *Lord Zouche's Case* (1604) in Coke's autograph notebook, BL MS. Harley 6686B, fo. 617, where he says it was founded both on common law and on Magna Carta, c. 29.

[70] *Bagg's Case* (1615) below, p. 396.

[71] Elsewhere he attributed these same blessings to the common law: see *The Fift Part of the Reports* (1605), preface, sig. A6 ('The ancient and excellent laws of England are the birthright and the most ancient and best inheritance that the subjects of this realm have, for by them he enjoyeth not only his inheritance and goods in peace and quietness, but his life and his dear country in safety'); Co. Litt. 142 (a similar passage).

[72] The best introductions to Coke's use of history are I. Williams, 'The Tudor Genesis of Edward Coke's Immemorial Common Law' (2012) 43 *Sixteenth Century Journal* 103–23, and Smith, *Sir Edward Coke*, pp. 115–38; see also Boyer, *Coke and the Elizabethan Age*, pp. 135–55; W. Klein, 'The Ancient Constitution Revisited' in *Political Discourse in Early Modern Britain*, ed. N. Phillipson and Q. Skinner (1993), pp. 23–44, at pp. 23–8, 32–3.

of historical accuracy and the need to contextualise sources.[73] He continued to investigate the past avidly, and to modify his understanding of it, throughout his life.[74] But he sometimes gave too much weight to strictly legal sources,[75] and – like his contemporaries – he was too apt to presume a continuity of institutions, and their immutability, from the slightest of indications.[76] The present-day historian should beware, however, of anachronism in censuring Coke. The inns of court were arguably ahead of the universities in encouraging the study of original records, and insisting on a critical approach to historical evidence, at a time when some schoolmen seriously believed that Oxford University was founded by King Alfred and that Cambridge University was founded by King Cantaber in the time of the Trojans. Coke's historical approach was not, in fact, far removed from that of John Selden, one of the patron saints of English history.[77] But his agenda was more practical and more important than that of the antiquary. Magna Carta provided an argument against the growing misuse and abuse of the royal prerogative, a problem which had been perceived under Elizabeth but became a burning concern after the accession of James. As such, it was an argument to be deployed with care. It might well be the great charter of the liberties of England,[78] and 'the fountain of all the fundamental laws of the realm',[79] but it could not

---

[73] See, e.g., Co. Inst. iv. 52: 'Many records of Parliament can hardly be understood unless you join thereunto the history of the time.' Cf. Co. Litt. 43: 'oftentimes, for the better understanding of our books, the advised reader must take light from history and chronicles, especially for distinction of times.'

[74] See Williams, 'Coke's Immemorial Common Law' (above, n. 72), at p. 123.

[75] See Garnett, 'Prefaces to Coke's Reports', pp. 258–60. His warnings against using monkish chronicles were chiefly directed against their being used as sources of law rather than of history, on the grounds that monks knew nothing of English law. But he was too inclined to treat assertions in legal sources and records as authoritative evidence of earlier history.

[76] See, e.g., his remarks about the jury in 1579, above, p. 38 n. 216; and his remarks about the Star Chamber in 1614, below, p. 405. For two other examples see Pocock, *Ancient Constitution*, pp. 38–41.

[77] See J. P. Sommerville, *Royalists and Patriots: Politics and Ideology in England 1603–1640* (2nd edn, Harlow, 1999), pp. 85–7. Selden firmly put paid to the Brut legends, but still attributed much of English law to the Anglo-Saxons or even the Britons. Sommerville pointed out that, while Selden in 1610 considered justices of the peace to be of Anglo-Saxon origin, it was Coke who pointed out that they were introduced in 1337.

[78] Coke pointed out that this phrase was used in several writs in the Register, and that liberties were 'so called of the effects, because they make free': *La Huictieme Part des Reports* (1611), preface, sig. §§5v.

[79] Co. Inst. ii. proeme. He cannot have meant that they began then, because he was a firm believer that they existed before the Norman Conquest.

be admitted that the charter was the source of the English constitution, because the constitution could on no account be attributed to a royal grant. If it derived its force from a concession by a medieval king, that was an act of beneficence which might, perhaps, be revoked by a monarch schooled in a Romanist view of kingship. It was for the same reason that the common law could not be attributed to the Norman Conquest. It had to be something more ancient, or at least coeval with the monarchy.[80] For the same reason, it could not safely be allowed that the great charter introduced anything significant which was not already embedded in the immemorial common law. If the common law was the inheritance of the subject, it must have been inherited down the generations, time out mind.

The common law was held to be immemorial, not in the sense that it could be proved in any specific way to date from before 1189,[81] but in that it could not be shown to have begun at any particular moment in history.[82] That did not mean that every detail of it was prehistoric,[83] an absurd idea which Coke never considered.[84] Nothing, taught Coke, could be invented and brought to perfection at

---

[80] Coke's 'ancient constitution' has attracted an enormous literature since J. G. A. Pocock, *The Ancient Constitution and the Feudal Law* (Cambridge, 1957; reissued, with a retrospective essay, 1987). Much of it refers to the parliamentary debates of the 1620s. For the present purpose, it is enough to know that Coke – like all or most of his lawyer contemporaries and precursors – believed the common-law system to have originated before the Conquest.

[81] This is the notional beginning of legal memory for the purposes of prescription and custom. But the validity of a custom or prescriptive right, if accepted for a long time, does not depend on positive proof of its existence in 1189. It is merely an objection to its establishment if it can be proved to have begun at a particular time after 1189 (e.g. by statute or grant): see J. Baker, 'Prescriptive Customs in English Law 1300–1800' in *Limitation and Prescription*, ed. H. Dondorp, D. J. Ibbetson and E. J. H. Schrage (forthcoming).

[82] Snagge, *Antiquity of the Chancery* (1587), p. 17; Hake, *Epieikeia*, p. 133 (where the Chancery is said to be coeval with the common law, which dated from before the Conquest, even though no evidence of a chancellor had as yet been discovered before William I). Cf. Pocock, *Ancient Constitution*, p. 41.

[83] Cf. Pocock, *Ancient Constitution* (1987 edn), pp. 274–5, qualifying a remark in his first edition (1957); A. Cromartie, *The Constitutionalist Revolution* (Cambridge, 2006), pp. 198–9.

[84] The claim related only to the fundamental principles and basic system: above, p. 86. Cf. *La Huictieme Part des Reports* (1611), preface, sig. §§4 ('the *grounds* of our common laws were beyond the memory or register of any beginning, and the same which the Norman conqueror then found within this realm of England'). This was a widespread belief, shared by Selden.

the same instant.[85] It was enough that some of it was British, some Anglo-Saxon, some even Norman, so long as it was seen as a product of continuous perfection rather than of sudden imposition from above or outside. The special force of Magna Carta likewise derived, not from any innovative genius, but from the fact that it had been confirmed over thirty times by successive kings in Parliament – a point which Coke never tired of making[86] – and that it had been treated as unalterable in its essential parts.[87] The most essential part was chapter 29, the broad words of which guaranteed the 'liberty of the subject' as the inheritance of all the English people since time beyond the memory of man. The rights thereby assured may have been interrupted on occasion, and the remedies may have taken centuries to establish, but they were never extinguished and the repeated confirmations had rendered them sacrosanct. True it might be that kings in biblical times had wielded absolute power, that medieval popes had encouraged absolutism, and that some of the bishops in King James's time still favoured a form of absolute monarchy in order to insulate the governance of the Church from Parliament. Religious arguments carried great weight, and in supporting the king's authority it suited ambitious lawyers such as Ellesmere and Bacon to produce legal arguments in the same vein. But it was the most powerful counter-argument that the kings of England had for four hundred years, almost without exception, confirmed and upheld Magna Carta as an inviolable guarantee of the fundamental principles of the common law. And it was a counter-argument which generally prevailed. James persisted with his campaign for a united kingdom, a 'perfect union of laws and persons',[88] though he acknowledged that it could not be imposed on an unwilling

---

[85] *Nihil simul inventum est et perfectum*: 10 Co. Rep. 142; Co. Litt. 230, 377. Cf. Co. Litt. 97: 'the law of England ... by many successions of ages ... has been fined and refined by an infinite number of grave and learned men'.

[86] E.g. *Clarke v. Gape* (1596) 5 Co. Rep. 65; *Davenant v. Hurdys* (1599) BL MS. Hargrave 5, fo. 74; 'Resolutions concerning Purveyance' (1604) Coke's notebook, BL MS. Harley 6686B, at fo. 607; *Att.-Gen. v. Stokes* (1605) Hawarde 193–4 ('22' times, presumably misreported); *Att.-Gen. v. Graves* (1606) Hawarde 278 ('34 or 35 times'; this was one of his last arguments at the bar, on 16 May); *Bate's Case* (1606) 12 Co. Rep. 33; *La Huictieme Part des Reports* (1611), preface, sig. §§5v ('confirmed and commanded to be put in execution by the wisdom of thirty several parliaments and above'); *R. v. Allen and Tooley* (1614) 2 Bulst. 186; Calth. MS. i. 267; *Langdale's Case* (1608) 12 Co. Rep. 58; *Bagg's Case* (1615) Tourneur, at fo. 7v; Co. Litt. 81; Co. Inst. ii. proeme; above, p. 264.

[87] Above, pp. 21, 24.

[88] Speech to Parliament (1607) in *Political Writings*, ed. Sommerville (above, p. 344 n. 57), at p. 161.

people through his own authority. He continued to claim absolute powers by divine right, but accepted that in practice they should usually be exercised in accordance with inveterate English law. He did not order any more summary executions, or try to change the law in any significant way independently of Parliament. He even told the judges (in 1609) that he had no desire to change anything in Magna Carta.[89] And he thought well enough of Coke not only to retain his services as attorney-general for four years, but also to raise him to the bench as chief justice of the Common Pleas.[90]

Chief Justice of the Common Pleas

When the chief justiceship of the Common Pleas fell vacant by the death of Sir Francis Gawdy in December 1605, Coke as attorney-general was well placed to claim the position, and he did so in the new year,[91] though the appointment was not made until June. The Common Pleas was regarded as constitutionally inferior to the King's Bench, which could reverse its judgments, and it was thought by some to have a more limited jurisdiction in relation to the prerogative writs of prohibition, *habeas corpus* and *mandamus*. The chief justiceship, though more lucrative, was not for these reasons as prestigious a position as that of the King's Bench, which carried the traditional informal title of lord chief justice of England. Coke would be translated to that office in 1613, against his will,[92] and enjoy it for three turbulent years; but in 1606 he did not see the need to wait for such an uncertain eventuality in his striving to protect the core principles and institutions of the common law against novel encroachments. The Common Pleas had already shown a

---

[89] Below, p. 370.

[90] He also received, on 22 March 1603, the knighthood which Elizabeth had denied him, albeit he was one of a thousand created by the new king in the first year of his reign.

[91] Letter to the earl of Salisbury dated 2 February 1606: *Hatfield House MSS.* xviii. 42, no. 75. According to Bacon, Coke had applied for the position of master of the rolls in 1597: *Letters and Life of Bacon*, ii. 63.

[92] For Coke's plea to the king to be excused see Birch, *Court and Times*, i. 276. He is said to have been transferred 'by the earnest solicitation of the earl of Somerset': Calth. MS. ii. 188 (tr.). Bacon also had recommended the transfer, hoping either that Coke would become more subservient or (as must have seemed more likely) would overreach himself: cf. *Letters and Life of Bacon*, iv. 381. It was noticed that, on the day of his installation, Coke left the Common Pleas weeping: ibid. 390. Bacon had once been a contender for the post himself: ibid. 378–9. So had Montagu, Hobart and Tanfield: Birch, *Court and Times*, i. 267, 274.

predilection for arguments founded on Magna Carta,[93] and counsel must have known that, under Coke, such arguments would be at least as welcome as in the days of Sir Edmund Anderson (1582–1605). That may explain why, during his seven years in that court (1606–13), Coke seems to have been as active in awarding writs of *habeas corpus* and prohibition as the King's Bench was under Sir John Popham (1592–1607) or Sir Thomas Fleming (1607–13).

The authority of Magna Carta came to be considered by the Common Pleas only a year after Coke's appointment, in a revealing case which escaped the printed law reports.[94] An attorney of the court had been put in the stocks by a London churchwarden after representing his client in a dispute with the parish, and had been left there in his velvet jacket for three or four hours under the gaze of 'infinite spectators'. He brought an action founded on chapter 29 of the great charter granted in the ninth year of Henry III (1225), and the jury awarded him £100 damages for the aggravated injury. The recital of the 1225 charter in the writ was in accordance with the precedents,[95] though the earlier cases had all been brought in respect of process from prerogative courts. Serjeant Barker moved the court, in arrest of judgment, that Magna Carta was not a statute until it was confirmed by Parliament in 1267 at Marlborough, and also that it was not the intention of chapter 29 to give an action against common persons such as churchwardens but only against the king's officers, or where some 'new usurped authority or upstart court' imprisoned a party. These arguments fell on stony ground. According to the reporter, 'the whole court was against him in every respect (*in omnibus*)', and Coke seized the opportunity to clarify the status of Magna Carta:

> Magna Carta was an Act of Parliament in 9 Hen. III, and Coke said that he had heard it held to be so in the King's Bench.[96] He said it had been confirmed by thirty-two parliaments at least, but that was no argument to prove that it was not an Act of Parliament before the latest

---

[93] Above, p. 276.

[94] *Bulthorpe v. Ladbrook* (Trin. 1607) CUL MS. Mm.1.21, fo. 92; MS. Gg.2.23, fo. 146; MS. Gg.5.6, fo. 55 (all the same); MS. Gg.5.6, fo. 52 (another report); translation in Appendix 10, below, pp. 531–3.

[95] See Appendix 1, below, pp. 452–5; *Parsons v. Locke* (Common Pleas, 1595) above, pp. 277–8; *Witherley v. Huninges* (King's Bench, 1606) below, pp. 514–16. The precedents are not mentioned in the 1607 reports.

[96] Despite the word 'heard', this probably refers to the actions on Magna Carta found in the plea rolls: Appendix 1, below.

confirmation ... Secondly, an action lay for such imprisonment by the common law, before the statute of Magna Carta. The point of the present suit is the imprisonment, and the statute is put in only for a flourish: therefore, even if it is misrecited, the plaintiff should still have his judgment ...[97] Thirdly, everyone is within the said statute, whether he be a great man or a mean person who is not involved in the administration of justice as a minister thereof. And Coke said that it was well done to mention the statute, for when a statute gives an action which was at common law, a plaintiff who wishes to take any advantage of the statute ought to mention it. When an action is given by statute in a specified form, there is no need to mention the statute; but it is otherwise when a statute gives an action without specifying the form of the writ.[98]

The court approved the award of exemplary damages, though another reporter said they were scaled down to 100 marks, since it was not appropriate to award more damages by reason of Magna Carta than could be recovered at common law. Although the decision did not weaken the status of Magna Carta in reality, it came dangerously close to an admission that it had no legal effect at all. There was no new law in chapter 29, and the plaintiff could just as well have succeeded without mentioning it.[99] It was added 'for a flourish'. No doubt that was equally true of most citations of chapter 29 in argument, and Coke was perfectly capable of brushing aside such a citation when it was inapt.[100] And yet the flourishes were added for a reason. The statute had come to represent much more than the legal content of the mere words, and it was to play a continuing part in Coke's judicial work.

The High Commission

After becoming chief justice, Coke lost no time in asserting that the Common Pleas as well as the King's Bench could issue prohibitions to

---

[97] Coke then suggested that all the laws in Magna Carta were laws in the time of Edward the Confessor: see above, pp. 15–16.

[98] Writs on Magna Carta were authorised in general terms by Marlborough, c. 5.

[99] This probably put an end to such actions. It was around this time that Coke decided to allow *habeas corpus* to be awarded by the Common Pleas: below, p. 354 n. 105.

[100] E.g. *Sir George Reynell's Case* (1611) CUL MS. Ee.3.54, fos. 63v–65v, where c. 29 was cited by Thomas Richardson of Lincoln's Inn in arguing unsuccessfully that the king could not seize an office of trust without giving the officer an opportunity to be heard. Cf. Coke's report of the case (9 Co. Rep. 95), which does not mention Magna Carta. Another example is *Chune v. Piott* (1615) 2 Bulst. 328, where c. 29 and the thirty confirmations were cited to no avail.

the Church courts,[101] a subject on which he later wrote a treatise,[102] that the High Commission had no power of imprisonment,[103] and that the interpretation of statutes governing ecclesiastical jurisdiction belonged to the common-law judges.[104] Coke's earlier acceptance of the court's inability to award writs of *habeas corpus*, except in cases of privilege, seems to have been withdrawn soon after he took office.[105] In the year of his appointment Coke was summoned to the Privy Council together with Popham CJKB to advise as to when ecclesiastical judges might lawfully use the oath *ex officio*.[106] According to Coke's own report, they answered, firstly, that no one could be constrained to swear generally without being given the articles on which he was to swear, as in the Chancery and Star Chamber; secondly, that 'no man, ecclesiastical or temporal, shall be examined upon secret thoughts of his heart, or of his secret opinion: but something ought to be objected against him what he hath spoken or done'; and, thirdly, that laymen should not be examined *ex officio*, except in matrimonial and testamentary causes, because being mostly

---

[101] *Anon.* (c. 1607?) BL MS. Lansdowne 1062, fo. 225v; *Langdale's Case* (1608) 12 Co. Rep. 58. He later discovered precedents, beginning with *Evans* v. *Jefferies* (1575) Co. Inst. iv. 334, margin. Cf. *Bankes* v. *Wharton* (1609) BL MS. Hargrave 52, fo. 6; CUL MS. Hh.2.2, fos. 2v–3 (tr. 'Coke said he could show precedents for 100 years where this court awarded prohibitions . . . by suggestion, without a plea pending here'). The explanation that the Common Pleas was derived from the King's Bench (see *Chapman* v. *Boyers* (1605) above, p. 281 n. 28) did not fit Coke's belief that the Common Pleas antedated Magna Carta, c. 11: *La Huictieme Part des Reports* (1611), preface, sig. §§6.

[102] Mentioned in *Langdale's Case* (previous note) and *Anon.* (1605) 12 Co. Rep. 109 ('see my particular treatise of the jurisdiction of the Court of the Common Bench in this point').

[103] 'High Commissioners, if they have power to imprison' (1606) 12 Co. Rep. 19 (a post-prandial discussion at Serjeants' Inn).

[104] *Fuller's Case* (1607) 12 Co. Rep. 41; *Anon.* (c. 1607) BL MS. Lansdowne 1062, fo. 225v; *Porter* v. *Rochester* (1608) 13 Co. Rep. 4; *Huntley* v. *Clifford* (1611) BL MS. Add. 9844, fo. 149. In the 1608 case, Coke referred to *Kayser's Case* (above, p. 120) 'in my book of precedents'. Coke complained that Ellesmere had told the king the interpretation of statutes concerning ecclesiastical causes belonged to bishops and canonists: 'Dangerous and Absurd Opinions', no. 5.

[105] E.g. *Bulbrook* v. *Roper* (1607) BL MS. Lansdowne 1061, fo. 48; *Ball's Case* (1608) 12 Co. Rep. 50; Yelverton's abridgment, BL MS. Add. 48186, fo. 422v; *Hawes' Case* (1609) BL MS. Harley 1679, fo. 148. For the previous limitation see above, p. 281 n. 28; Coke's memorandum on c. 29 (1604), below, at p. 507. In the memorandum, Coke pointed out that actions on c. 29 could be brought in the Common Pleas. The reversal of opinion as to *habeas corpus* was probably the main reason for the disappearance of such actions.

[106] 'Of Oaths before an Ecclesiastical Judge ex Officio' (dated Pas. 1606, but evidently after Coke's appointment in July) 12 Co. Rep. 26. This resulted from the bill moved in the House of Commons by Nicholas Fuller in 1606 against the oath *ex officio*.

uneducated they could easily be inveigled and entrapped in matters of heresy. There was no mention of Magna Carta, but Coke cited *Lee's Case* (1568) and *Hynde's Case* (1576) from Dyer's manuscript, which he now owned.[107] These, as he said a few years later, were valuable in interpreting the 1559 statute because they were close to it in date.[108] He also relied on the statute of 1534 which declared that no person should be put in peril of his life for heresy upon a bishop's own fancy without due accusation or presentment.[109] The following year Sir Henry Hobart, the attorney-general, on behalf of the House of Commons, proposed that the commissioners' activities should be confined to London and York, where learned counsel were available; that their hearings should be held in public and not in chambers, and with the advice of men of credit; that citations to appear should contain the causes and the accusers' names; and that defendants should not be compelled to accuse themselves. John Dodderidge, the solicitor-general, also argued that excommunication should not be used for trivial causes. These reforms would have met most of the objections and reduced, if not ended, the conflict. But the Lords refused to join in the petition, since it would be 'public and scandalous', and the archbishop of Canterbury desired more time to answer.[110] The conflict was therefore prolonged.

While Parliament was approaching deadlock on these issues, heated discussions were taking place in the King's Bench.[111] The Puritan

---

[107] He cited the same cases in *Arundel's Case*, (1587) above, p. 265; *Person v. Parke* (1608) CUL MS. Ee.6.13, fo. 11; *Maunsell's Case* (1609) below, p. 358 n. 122; *Anon.* (1609) 2 Br. & G. 271; *Darrington's Case* (1609) CUL MS. Mm.1.21, fo. 159; MS. Gg.5.6, fo. 87 (the same report); BL MS. Hargrave 52, fos. 20v–22; sub nom. *William Warrington's Case*, BL MS. Add. 25209, fos. 161v–163; *Huntley v. Clifford* (1611) below, p. 372; *Boyer's Case* (1614) 2 Bulst. 182; Calth. MS. ii. 160; BL MS. Harley 4948, fo. 70; CUL MS. Ii.5.26, fo. 65; *Codd v. Turback* (1615) 3 Bulst. 109; 1 Rolle Rep. 245; *Holt and Dighton's Case* (1615) Tourneur, fo. 8; *Samuel Hodd's Case* (1615) 3 Bulst. 146 (probably the same); *Anon.* (1615) BL MS. Add. 25211, fo. 146v; and in Coke's tract on prohibitions, BL MS. Harley 7516, fo. 9v. They were also cited by Ashley, who presumably knew of them through Coke: below, p. 430.

[108] *Sir William Chauncy's Case* (1611) BL MS. Add. 9844, fo. 156v. When Coke cited the cases from Dyer in *Holt and Dighton's Case* (1615) Tourneur, fo. 8, (tr.) 'he much blamed those who did not report the case of Hinde, being adjudged and entered by Dyer in his book of reports for this year, as Coke – who has the book in his custody – observed').

[109] 25 Hen. VIII, c. 14; above, p. 124.

[110] Wilbraham, *Journal*, pp. 81–2. For Nicholas Fuller's speech on 20 June 1607, introducing a bill to regulate the High Commission, see Bowyer, *Parliamentary Journal*, pp. 344–9.

[111] *Maunsell's Case* (1607) below, Appendix 9, pp. 517–30; *The Argument of Master Nicholas Fuller in the Case of Thomas Lad and Richard Maunsell* (1607) (published by

ministers, following the setback in *Cawdray's Case*, had as yet been unable to take legal advantage of the ideas propagated by their sympathisers in the 1580s and 1590s, but the way had been prepared, and in 1607 a new test-case was begun. A *habeas corpus* was returned to the effect that three defendants before the High Commission, Richard Maunsell (a Presbyterian minister) and two Yarmouth merchants,[112] had been imprisoned for refusing to answer questions upon oath about their attendance at conventicles. Schismatical conventicles might today be called theological seminars or bible-reading classes; but they were thought to be highly subversive, because they were always associated with people of a puritanical disposition, who would meet to talk about religion and sometimes to rant against the ecclesiastical establishment. The Church had never countenanced self-education of that kind. Coke's report of the 1605 proceedings in Council was not yet in print. But Nicholas Fuller, the Puritan member of Parliament who represented the defendants,[113] knew the arguments very well.[114] He contended that the oath *ex officio* was unlawful because it required a person to incriminate himself; that, even if it was lawful, it could not be enforced with temporal punishment, since the commissioners had no such power; and that, even if they could imprison, it could not be for an indefinite period.[115]

William Jones's secret press, without Fuller's permission). There is a discussion of some of the BL texts in Gray, *Writ of Prohibition*, ii. 338–70; 'Self-Incrimination', pp. 70–7; see also Usher, *Reconstruction*, ii. 134–53; *High Commission*, pp. 171–9.

[112] The reports mention only one layman. Fuller names the lay defendant as Thomas Lad, merchant of Yarmouth; he is also called Ladd in the report in BL MS. Lansdowne 1061, fo. 47; CUL MS. Ee.5.17, fo. 106v. But the other manuscript reports give the co-defendant's name as Edward Owner, who was also a Yarmouth merchant. There were thus evidently two lay defendants.

[113] Fuller was a bencher of Gray's Inn, a common pleader in the city of London, and an MP from 1593: *Readers and Readings*, p. 46; *ODNB*; *HPHC 1604–29*, iii. 324–33; S. Wright, 'Nicholas Fuller and the Liberties of the Subject' (2006) 25 *Parliamentary History* 176–213 (where, at pp. 191–205, there is a more detailed account of his role in *Maunsell's Case* than that given here). As early as 1582 he represented a minister who was informed against for non-residence: BL MS. Lansdowne 1101, fo. 22 (the defendant pleaded he was on the queen's business). And in 1587 he represented a minister indicted for omitting to make the sign of the cross in baptism: Godb. 118. He was imprisoned in 1591 for defending Puritan ministers: 21 APC 393; Collinson, *Bancroft*, p. 115. He represented the Puritan ministers Udall and Cartwright, and in 1602 appeared for the defendant in *Darcy v. Allen* to argue against monopolies (above, p. 322).

[114] The printed report of his speech (Fuller, *Argument*) was published without his permission and may not have been delivered in exactly the same words: Usher, *Reconstruction*, ii. 151. It may be taken, nevertheless, to represent the general effect of his argument.

[115] The defendants had already been in prison for nine months.

Although most of the dispute, as in the 1590s, was about the wording and scope of the statute of 1559, Fuller relied in a general way on Magna Carta:[116]

> The laws of England are the high inheritance of the realm, by which both the king and the subject are directed, and ... such grants, charters and commissions as tend to charge the body, lands or goods of the subjects otherwise than according to the course of the laws of the realm are not lawful or of force unless the same charters and commissions do receive life and strength from some Act of Parliament ... For the laws of England did so much regard and prefer the liberty of the subject as that none should be imprisoned *nisi per legale judicium parium suorum vel per legem terrae*, as it is said in Magna Carta, c. [29], which charter by divers other statutes after is continued with such strong enforcements in some of them as to make void such statutes as should be contrary to Magna Carta.

If, he said, the statute of 1559 was not interpreted according to its general words – which could hardly be taken to repeal the great charter by implication[117] – 'there might be erected in this common wealth of England a course of an arbitrary government at the discretion of the commissioners, directly contrary to the happy long-continued government and course of the common law of the realm, and directly contrary to Magna Carta'.[118] His clients had done nothing illegal. They had simply gone, after divine service, to a place where they 'repeated the sermon', and this was something expressly commanded by the word of God.[119]

When the case was reargued the following term, Fuller became over-emotional in his language. The intention of the statute of Henry VIII which liberated the Church from Rome, he said, was 'to establish a government of the church of Christ, and this cannot be governed by the laws of anti-Christ, which these days are such as oaths, imprisonments and

---

[116] Fuller, *Argument*, pp. 3–4. Cf. his argument in Easter term, below, p. 517: (tr.) 'Every subject convented before a magistrate for any offence is to have his lawful and honourable trial by a jury of his peers by the law of England, so that all subjects are instruments of justice to each other; and a subject ought not to be imprisoned before such lawful trial, and that is by the statute of Magna Carta, *Nullus liber homo etc.* Also by the statute of 5 Edw. III, c. 5 ... and the statute of 25 Edw. III, c. 4 ... 27 Edw. III and 38 Edw. III ... and although these statutes do not extend to ecclesiastical proceedings, for at that time they could not imprison, they nevertheless show the care and respect which the law has for the liberty of the subject.'

[117] See the quotation above, p. 24 n. 128.   [118] Fuller, *Argument*, p. 29.

[119] This argument is reported in BL MS. Add. 35955, fo. 37, with a brief supporting argument by Henry Finch.

the like'. Yelverton J. interrupted him at this point and said he should not
speak in such terms of any authority established by Parliament, and if he
would not be more temperate he would be silenced. Fuller apologised, and
went on to argue that a statute could not be interpreted, by implication,
against the common law.[120] George Croke followed, to the same effect,
arguing that the oath *ex officio* was against the law of God and of nature.
There was a third argument from Henry Finch. There is no reported
argument on behalf of the commissioners. Popham CJ, who had spoken
on the first occasion, died while the case was pending and was not present
at the final hearing. The other judges delivered tentative opinions in favour
of the High Commission, but proposed to refer the matter to all the
justices of England. The reference seems not to have occurred, and in the
absence of a decision the parties remained for the time being in prison.

It has been suggested that the provisional indication given by the
King's Bench judges applied to the lay applicants as well as Maunsell,[121]
though it is clear from subsequent citations that Fuller's argument was
rejected only with respect to Maunsell, who was a preacher subject to
canonical obedience. The position of laymen may not have been explicitly considered. But the case was soon taken to have confirmed that
laymen were not subject to the same regime, presumably because the
merchants had been released. The position was clarified by Coke in
1609 when Maunsell, still in prison, sued a *habeas corpus*, returnable in
the Common Pleas. He received short shrift from the court. For a
minister to preach against the Book of Common Prayer was clearly an
'enormous' offence within the statute of 1559.[122] The court was nevertheless anxious to draw an important distinction. As had been resolved in
1605, laymen could not be interrogated upon the oath *ex officio*, save as
to matters of fact in matrimonial and testamentary causes. That conclusion was now fortified by the discovery, among the apocryphal
fourteenth-century statutes, of an order to the prelates and ecclesiastical
officials of the Norwich diocese not to require laymen to be sworn except

---

[120] Below, p. 528.

[121] Gray, *Writ of Prohibition*, ii. 338, 344, 362; 'Self-Incrimination', pp. 70–7.

[122] *Maunsell's Case* (Trin. 1609) BL MS. Add. 9844, fo. 54v (tr. below, pp. 529–30); CUL
MS. Hh.2.2, fo. 8v (sub nom. Munsfeild). Ladd was not involved in this hearing, having
presumably been released; Coke CJ emphasised that the ruling did not apply to laymen,
citing *Lee's Case* (1568) 'in Dier written reports'. The decision was confirmed later the
same term in *Gray's Case* (Trin. 1609) BL MS. Add. 9844, fo. 59v (tr. 'neither the [High]
Commission nor the ordinary has power or jurisdiction to commit any layman to
prison; contrary of a parson').

in such cases. This document was hailed by Coke as a binding statute.[123] Coke explained the distinction on the grounds that clergymen ought to be capable of rendering an account of their religious beliefs, whereas laymen were not sufficiently educated to be examined on questions of religion.[124] Three years later he held that it was illegal for the commissioners to interrogate a party about not standing for the creed, or about saying that episcopal constitutions were not by divine law.[125] Fuller's advocacy in 1607 had thus been partly successful, but he would pay the price for it. The king himself had taken an interest in the case and wanted Fuller silenced.

The High Commission decided that the best way to assert its power of imprisonment was to have Fuller himself prosecuted and imprisoned for contempt, and this they did as soon as the parliament was prorogued. On 25 June Fuller presented the King's Bench with a lengthy 'suggestion' for a prohibition, in effect claiming freedom of speech for the English Bar.[126] He recited that he had been for forty-three years a fellow of Gray's Inn, which time out of mind had been an inn of court of the common law, and for thirty-two years an utter-barrister and a counsellor learned in the law; that it was the immemorial custom of the realm that all those who sued or defended any suit or cause, excepting only treason and felony, had retained counsel learned in the law to explain their causes to the justices, and such counsel had been accustomed in arguing their causes to say

---

[123] Coke cited this not only in Maunsell's 1609 case (BL MS. Add. 9844, fo. 54v, below, p. 530) but also in his answer to Bancroft, 2 St. Tr. 131 at col. 133; in an undated dictum in Warburton's reports, CUL MS. Ii.5.25, fo. 105; in *Sir William Boyer's Case* (1614) BL MS. Harley 4948, fo. 70; and in Co. Inst. ii. 687. It was printed in *Statutes at Large* (1762 edn), i. 403, as 'Prohibitio formata de statuto Articulorum Cleri'. As Coke pointed out, Bryan CJ described it as a statute in YB Hil. 19 Edw. IV, fo. 10, pl. 18.

[124] See, e.g., Warburton's reports, CUL MS. Ii.5.25, fo. 105v: (tr.) 'if a spiritual person is convented before them for heresy or schism they may administer an oath to him, but not to a lay person, for a lay person believeth points of religion but cannot depose them'. Coke CJ explained in *Darrington's Case* (1609) BL MS. Hargrave 52, fos. 20v–21, that '(tr.) clergymen ... may well be examined upon their oath concerning heresy or any other matter of religion, because they have more knowledge to render an account of their religion than laymen have, but if they should be examined concerning anything which does not touch religion or their jurisdiction ... they need not answer, for *nemo tenetur seipsum prodere*.'

[125] *Jenour's Case* (1610) CUL MS. Gg.5.6, fo. 100 (prohibition granted).

[126] Transcript of the record in BL MS. Lansdowne 1172, fos. 97–106v, which includes a copy of the writ of consultation on fo. 106; other copies in BL MS. Hargrave 33, fos. 123v–128v; Kansas University MS. D152, pp. 443–66. Usher, *Reconstruction*, ii. 138 n. 4 (citing other versions) confused this with a law report; he was unaware of the existence of reports of the arguments.

what they could for their clients, modestly and decently, not only against the king's commissions and grants but against all private liberties, jurisdictions and privileges, as the causes required, leaving the decision to the judges; that all pleas of trespass, contempt and slander belonged to the king's courts, and by ancient custom no free man ought to be vexed or punished except by lawful judgment of his peers; that Ladd, when he was brought into the King's Bench by *habeas corpus*, had prayed that counsel might be assigned him; that the court had assigned Fuller (with others) to argue the cause on 6 May, and that is what he did; and yet, notwithstanding all this, while the case was still depending undecided, the archbishop of Canterbury and other high commissioners examined Fuller for words which he was falsely alleged to have spoken, and committed him to prison. According to Coke, this 'great case' was referred to all the judges of England, who decided that it was for them alone to determine the meaning of the 1559 statute and the jurisdiction of ecclesiastical judges. Fuller may have been punishable for contempt, but not by the High Commission.[127] On the other hand, the commissioners did have jurisdiction over schism. Where someone was charged before an ecclesiastical court with matters which were outside its jurisdiction and also some which were within, he was entitled to a general prohibition, but then a special consultation[128] could be awarded indicating the matters on which the court could proceed. The King's Bench therefore granted a special consultation, allowing the commissioners to proceed on the question of schism or heresy but leaving the prohibition in force with respect to slander, contempt and matters punishable at common law, and also with respect to the interpretation of the 1559 statute and of the commissioners' letters patent. That was enough for the commissioners' purpose. Fuller was duly convicted of schism, fined £200 and imprisoned.[129]

---

[127] With respect to jurisdiction over contempt, the authority cited by Coke was *John Hales's Case* (1564) in Dyer's manuscript reports, as to which see *Dyer's Notebooks*, i. 94–5. The decision as to imprisonment for contempt was confirmed in *Lady Throgmorton's Case* (1610) 12 Co. Rep. 69.

[128] This was the procedure for withdrawing a prohibition if the court was satisfied upon argument that the case could properly proceed.

[129] *Nicholas Fuller's Case* (1607) 12 Co. Rep. 41; BL Cotton MS. Cleopatra F I, fos. 160v–161. The special consultation in this case is discussed in Gray, *Writ of Prohibition*, i. 306–8.

Fuller applied for a writ of *habeas corpus*, and in Michaelmas term 1607 the King's Bench assigned two serjeants at law to present his case.[130] On the other side, no doubt at the king's insistence, both law officers were brought in to argue in support of the High Commission. The return to the writ stated that Fuller had 'published various false, impious and schismatical affections, namely that the proceedings of the high commissioners were popish and anti-Christian and that the administration of the oath *ex officio* tended to the damning of men's souls'. Serjeant Harris argued that this return was bad, because it did not indicate by what authority the commissioners had imprisoned him, and no power of imprisonment was mentioned in the statute of 1559. He cited chapter 29 of Magna Carta, and the statute of due process, to prove the 'precious liberty' of the person, presumably the liberty of not being imprisoned without good cause shown. Moreover, the return did not say where the words were spoken, so they might as well have been in the West Indies,[131] and in any case they did not amount to schism. Henry Hobart, the attorney-general, responded that it was unnecessary to state the place, since the return was not traversable, and made some attempt to answer the other points. Francis Bacon followed, as solicitor-general, with his usual eloquence. He said that there were two kinds of imprisonment, one custodial (*ad custodiendum*) and the other penal (*ad puniendum*). Even if the commissioners had no power to imprison as a punishment, they could imprison heretics and schismatics to prevent them dispersing their erroneous and contagious opinions. But they did have the power to punish, for whereas the ecclesiastical judges used to rely on the secular arm to impose punishment, as by means of the writ *de haeretico comburendo*, the king had now put his secular sword into ecclesiastical hands. In any case, it was not, he said, for the king's court to determine what schism was. According to a recollection two years later, the return was held to be too unspecific.[132] But that was not the actual decision.

---

[130] *Nicholas Fuller's Case* (1607) CUL MS. Gg.2.23, fos. 122v–125; BL MS. Add. 25213, fo. 81. Coke (previous note) mentioned the *habeas corpus* but not its outcome.

[131] Everyone knew (as the reporter pointed out) that they had been spoken at the King's Bench bar; but this was a formal objection to imprecision in the return.

[132] *Stamford's Case* (1609) BL MS. Harley 3209, fo. 97v: (tr.) 'therefore a return that Fuller was *schismaticus* generally was adjudged bad'. Stamford was released on *habeas corpus*, because the return that he had disturbed a preacher in Sheffield church was too general, not setting out the manner of disturbance so that the court could judge of it, and Fuller's case was evidently cited as authority; cf. a later argument in the same case in CUL MS. Ee.3.54, fos. 53v–54.

A contemporary report says the case was referred to all the justices, who held the return sufficient, and Fuller was accordingly remanded.[133] The judges said they were the king's strong arms, and had the power to grant prohibitions in proper cases, tactfully observing that they had never suspected the bishops and principal commissioners of any encroachment.[134] The king remarked in private to Sir Thomas Lake on 27 November that the judges had done well, because if they had granted the *habeas corpus* he had been minded to imprison them.[135] Roger Wilbraham noted that after this case preachers began to rail against lawyers, and that there was a division between the clergy and the temporal law, 'full of great peril to the state'.[136]

At first sight the decision looks like a capitulation by the judiciary to the king's wishes; but it was not wholly unreasonable. Even if Fuller had not used every word as alleged, he had clearly overstepped the line of modesty and decency. He was a fiery radical, and his enthusiasm had alarmed the king, irritated the lord chancellor,[137] and forfeited the sympathy of the judges. Words spoken in heat may not look much like schism; but it was not for the common-law judges to define schism. The best way of demonstrating that the words were not meant as serious theology would be simply to retract them.[138] And that was the chosen outcome, which Coke may have facilitated.[139] Fuller was remanded until he confessed his fault and submitted, which he agreed to do.[140] Early the following year Fuller was prosecuted in the Star Chamber for publishing his argument in the case, but the law officers were unable to prove that he was responsible for the printing and he

---

[133] Cf. the report in BL MS. Add. 25213, fo. 81, which says the judges all held the return sufficient.

[134] Letter from the earl of Salisbury to the king, 28 November 1607: *Hatfield House MSS.*, xix. 344–5, no. 733.

[135] *Hatfield House MSS.*, xix. 343, no. 731. The king also spoke angrily about prohibitions, and said he would proscribe them.

[136] Wilbraham, *Journal*, 96 (tr.). Salisbury (n. 134) said the judges had complained of 'men that spoke by tradition and out of their elements, some in pulpits'.

[137] As early as 1596 Egerton LK had said of him, in the Star Chamber, 'Fuller of all lawyers [is] the worst': *Att.-Gen. v. Kinge* (1596) Hawarde 44 at p. 45.

[138] See 12 Co. Rep. 44: 'if they convict Fuller of heresy, schism or erroneous opinion etc., [it was resolved] that if he recant the said heresy, schism or erroneous opinion he shall never be punished by ecclesiastical law.'

[139] Usher, *Reconstruction*, ii. 149, 210, says Coke earned the king's thanks for mediating between the High Commission and the King's Bench.

[140] CUL MS. Gg.2.23. fo. 125. See also *ODNB*, sub nom. Nicholas Fuller.

was eventually released from custody.[141] The citation of Magna Carta had here failed to secure the imposition of natural justice on the High Commission, but the courts had nevertheless managed to avoid an impasse.

In the Common Pleas, Coke and his brethren were facing similar questions. In 1607 Coke set out, albeit in conciliatory language, the uncompromising approach of the judges of that court:[142]

I am sorry there should be any kind of discord between the spiritual courts and this court. The ecclesiastical court is like a fountain of sweet water to refresh all the earth,[143] but if the fountain does not contain itself within its banks it will flood the lower lands. The policy of this state has always been that the common law should be the bounder, to reduce it within its channel when it runs over. And I am sorry that the high commissioners trouble themselves with matters of *meum et tuum*,[144] which was never the intention of the statute of 1 Eliz., for it was solely to give them power in exorbitant causes: for when the bishops of the realm who were of contrary religion were to be deprived, it was not fit to wait until they were proceeded with by the ordinaries in their ecclesiastical courts. The High Commission was therefore erected for this purpose, and for great offences, namely heresies and schisms, or such as the civil law[145] does not punish. Therefore it is fit for them to employ themselves in dealing with recusants etc. For these causes it is called the High Commission, because they deal with high and sublime causes. But for private men's causes, matter of inheritance, *meum et tuum* or such like, as in case of marriages, divorces, testaments and so forth, it is not convenient. It also takes away and subverts the power and the verity of the

---

[141] *Att.-Gen. v. Fuller, Maunsell and others* (1608) STAC 8/19/7 (depositions); *HPHC 1604–29*, p. 327, citing BL MS. Add. 11402, fos. 135, 137v; *Hatfield House MSS.*, xix. 437.

[142] *Sir Anthony Roper's Case (Bulbrook v. Roper)* (1607) BL MS. Lansdowne 1061, fo. 47v (tr.); differently reported in CUL MS. Mm.1.21, fos. 95, 106–107 (also in MS. Gg.2.23, fos. 148 and MS. Gg.5.6, fos. 57, 64v–65); Noy 149; 12 Co. Rep. 45. The decision was that the High Commission could not imprison a party for failing to pay a pension out of an impropriated rectory. The quotation is translated from the Lansdowne MS.

[143] Cf. CUL MS. Mm.1.21, fo. 106v: (tr.) 'Coke resembled the spiritual law to a sweet fountain which is comfortable and profitable to the common wealth'. He had used the same metaphor in *Bird v. Smith* (1606) Moo. 781 at p. 782.

[144] Cf. *Lane's Case* (1608) CUL MS. Mm.1.21, fo. 128 (and the other MSS cited above), *per* Coke CJ: (tr.) 'the high commissioners have no power to meddle with *meum et tuum*, as for legacies, tithes etc. The reason is because no appeal lies from their sentence; but their power is only to meddle with heresies, schisms, contempts and enormities, which upon the alteration of religion were requisite to be suppressed, not with such petty trifling matters as giving the parson a box on the ear.'

[145] Meaning here the secular common law.

spiritual courts, for an appeal lies there if someone is aggrieved, but no appeal lies from the High Commission other than a commission of review, which is of grace and not of right.[146]

Coke was keen to stress that he was not advocating tolerance of the Puritan opposition towards the ecclesiastical hierarchy or its jurisdiction: 'the episcopal authority is so respected in our law that the state cannot stand without it, and therefore the clerico-laicans who bring in their presbytery would overthrow the whole course of the laws with us; they cannot stand in this common wealth'. It was the commissioners, not the Puritans, who were challenging and usurping the authority of the bishops. Daniel J. thought perhaps Coke was being too conciliatory, since the ordinary episcopal courts were also claiming to encroach on the common law. He referred to Dr Ridley's recent book,[147] which maintained that a widow's title to dower, and statutory questions concerning tithes, belonged to the Church courts. Warburton J. said that was amazing ('marveylous'), because only those learned in the laws of the realm could expound statutes.[148] Coke dismissed Ridley's book as 'not worthy of further response – it is erroneous in all points'. Doubtless he was well aware that the king had given it his warm approval.[149]

The clarity of the Common Pleas position helps to account for the increasing numbers of applicants to that court for prohibition and *habeas corpus*.[150] Magna Carta was regularly recited in suggestions (formal

[146] Coke later claimed that the king agreed with him that the High Commission was limited to enormous and exorbitant matters and should leave common offences to the ordinaries, because there was no appeal: *Case of Modus Decimandi* (1609) 13 Co. Rep. 37.

[147] T. Ridley, *A View of the Civile and Ecclesiastical Law* (1607). Ridley, an advocate in Doctors' Commons, was a protégé of Archbishop Bancroft and was knighted in 1619.

[148] Cf. CUL MS. Mm.1.21, fo. 106v, *per* Warburton J.: (tr.) 'a statute is to be expounded according to the rules of the common law, whereof they have no knowledge, and no one may expound statutes who does not know what the common law was before the making of the statute'. This was an old doctrine: see above, p. 222.

[149] It was said that, when the king praised it, Coke 'undertook from thence to prophesy the decay of the common law': D. Lloyd, *State-Worthies* (1670), p. 923.

[150] There were at least eight further decisions in the same vein in 1607–8: *Fawne's Case* (Mich. 1607) CUL MS. Mm.1.21, fos. 101, 103v–104 (displacement of the usher of Winchester School); *Lane's Case* (Hil. 1608) ibid. 128 (calling a parson a knave and a babbler); *Vinard* v. *Pellinge* (Pas. 1608) ibid. 131v (liability of a parson to serve a parochial chapel); *Smith's Case* (Trin. 1608) BL MS. Lansdowne 1120, fo. 3 (hearing mass, a statutory offence); *Langdale's Case* (Trin.-Mich. 1608) 12 Co. Rep. 50, 58; sub nom. *Langdon's Case* (Trin. 1608) BL MS. Lansdowne 1120, fo. 24 (maintenance); *Rochester's Case* (Mich. 1608) CUL MS. Ee.6.13, fo. 12 (incontinency); *Withers* v. *Helyar* (1608) next note (dismissal of a vicar choral); *Wotton* v. *Edwardes* (Mich. 1608) below, n. 153. For slightly later cases see below, p. 379 n. 235.

applications) for prohibitions,[151] and in 1608 Coke said that if the commissioners could arrest people by warrant, without a prior citation, it would be 'against the statute of Magna Carta and all the ancient statutes'.[152] The Common Pleas were not united on the scope of the jurisdiction, however, because Walmsley J. in another case in 1608 dissented on the grounds that the statute of 1559 had annexed all ecclesiastical jurisdiction to the crown, and this included the punishment of all spiritual offences. Walmsley – himself by this time one of the commissioners – acknowledged that 'his opinion would not do any good, and yet he would discharge his conscience'. All his brethren, however, were against him, and held that the commissioners could not deal with libel.[153] In the same case Coke held that no ecclesiastical court could examine a man upon the intention or thought of his heart, as by asking his opinions on points of religion, for no one should be punished for his thought. 'According to the proverb', he said, 'thought is free.'[154] It was a rare case, in touching on religious thought, but none the less a landmark.[155] Even canonists accepted the point: 'if it be altogether secret', wrote one of them, 'then the rule is, *Nemo tenetur seipsum*

---

[151] Above, p. 292. See also *Withers v. Helyar* (1608-10) BL Cotton MS. Cleopatra F I, fos. 159-60; BL MS. Harley 1299, fos. 138v-142 (cited in the Privy Council, 1611); MS. Add. 48148, fo. 423; MS. Hargrave 278, fos. 392v-394v; Baker, 'Magna Carta and Personal Liberty' in *Magna Carta, Religion and the Rule of Law*, pp. 104-5; cf. *Helyar v. Withers* (1610) YLS MS. G.R29.16, fos. 374v-375v (concerning lay and spiritual hospitals).

[152] *Ball's Case* (1608) 12 Co. Rep. 49; Yelverton's abridgment, BL MS. Add. 48186, fos. 422v-423. Ball had been arrested for not kneeling to receive communion.

[153] *Wotton v. Edwardes* (Mich. 1608) CUL MS. Ee.6.13, fo. 12. This was, in any case, a common-law tort since the libel affected a physician in his professional capacity. Cf. *Edwardes v. Wootton* (1607) Hawarde 343; 12 Co. Rep. 35 (in the Star Chamber). 'Wootton' was John Woolton, a prominent Exeter physician. Walmsley dissented on the same ground in two other cases noted by the same reporter the same term: *Rochester's Case*, CUL MS. Ee.6.13, fo. 12; and *Nash's Case*, ibid. 45.

[154] Sub nom. *Walton v. Edwards* (Mich. 1608) 13 Co. Rep. 9; Coke's autograph notebook, CUL MS. Ii.5.21, fo. 8v. The phrase had been used by Egerton, with the qualification that it did not extend to speech: *Att.-Gen. v. Boothe* (1596) Hawarde 65 at p. 66 ('thought is free, but the tongue should be governed by knowledge'). The proverb is often attributed to Shakespeare, but it is a pithier version of Cicero's *Liberae sunt cogitationes nostrae* (from *Pro Milone*).

[155] Gray said it was the only case he knew concerning private thoughts: 'Self-Incrimination', p. 63. In 1606, however, Coke and Popham CJJ had been questioned before the Council on the same point, and advised that no one could be constrained to answer generally as to the secret thoughts of his heart: 'Of Oaths ex Officio' (Pas. 1606) 12 Co. Rep. 26. See also *Jenour's Case* [1610] Rolle Abr. ii. 305 (here dated 18 Jac., but on p. 314 dated 8 Jac.), where the King's Bench held that a man was not compellable to answer on oath

prodere.[156] The king also accepted it, as far as matters of conscience were concerned.[157]

The archbishops disagreed profoundly with Coke's delineation of the jurisdictional boundaries and sought the help of James, as king and supreme governor, in overturning him. The judges, they said, being parties in the dispute, lacked the independence to decide it themselves. James was only too ready to oblige them, since he considered that it fell within his monarchical authority to resolve jurisdictional differences between his courts,[158] and was assured by Archbishop Bancroft that his authority to do so could be proved by the word of God.[159] He felt sure his reasoning capacities were at least equal to those of the judges,[160] and he goaded Coke by saying that the judges were but his shadows and ministers and that he might himsel sit and adjudicate in any court in Westminster Hall if he wished.[161] The king added tetchily that 'if the judges will interpret the laws themselves, and suffer none else to interpret them, they may easily make of the laws shipmen's hose ... The judges are like papists. They allege scriptures and will

concerning his faith, because he was punishable by statute for publishing false doctrine and so he might be compelled by the Church to commit an offence.

[156] 'Praxis Curiae Supremae Comissariorum Regis' (*c.* 1608/14) CUL, Ely Diocesan Records, 1/5/45, 98. The Latin maxim was also quoted in *Huntley* v. *Clifford* (1611) BL MS. Add. 48148, fos. 421v–422; MS. Add. 9844, fo. 150; *Boyer's Case* (1614) 2 Bulst. 182 at p. 183.

[157] In a proclamation of 2 June 1610 ordering the expulsion of all Jesuits and seminary priests, and the disarming of Roman Catholics, James protested that he had always been 'loath to shed blood in any case that might have any relation to conscience (though but of a deceived and disguised conscience)': Usher, *Reconstruction*, ii. 252 n. 3.

[158] Cf. the king's intervention in the disputes as to the Council in the Marches (above, p. 309; below, p. 513) and the Chancery (below, p. 420). Ellesmere made the same point in relation to the High Commission: below, p. 373. He had told the king he could decide *Calvin's Case* (1608) in person: this was the first of Coke's 'Dangerous and Absurd Opinions' affirmed before the king by Ellesmere, CUL MS. Ii.5.21, fo. 47v.

[159] Coke, 'Dangerous and Absurd Opinions', no. 2. The case was expounded in a treatise 'That the King hath Power in his own Person to Hear and Determine all Kinds of Cases', BL MS. Harley 4892, fos. 10–14v (and other manuscripts), which has been attributed to Bancroft: Smith, *Sir Edward Coke*, p. 199.

[160] Below, pp. 369, 382.

[161] 'Prohibitions del Roy' (1608) 12 Co. Rep. 63; French version in BL MS. Lansdowne 601, fo. 109, printed inaccurately in R. G. Usher, 'James I and Sir Edward Coke' (1903) 18 EHR 664–75, at p. 667; also in IT MS. Misc. 21, fos. 133–4. Coke's version, as printed, is dated Sunday, 10 November 1607. That date was not a Sunday. But the manuscript versions are dated 6 Jac. (1608) and, as Usher demonstrated, it is clear from Caesar's minutes and contemporary letters that the correct date is Sunday, 13 November 1608.

interpret the same.'[162] As for Coke's saying that the law protected the king, this was (he said) 'a traitorous speech, for the king protecteth the law and not the law the king'.

According to Coke's own version of the interchange with the king, he made a valiant reply:[163]

> True it is that God has endued[164] your majesty with excellent science and great endowments of nature; but your majesty is not learned in the laws of your realm of England, and causes which concern the life, inheritance, goods or fortunes of the subject are not to be decided by natural reason, but by the artificial reason and judgment of the law, which law is an art[165] that requires long study and experience before a man can attain to the knowledge of it.[166]

This was an orthodox position. No king had sat in a regular court of law for centuries, and it was thought unconstitutional.[167] It was unconstitutional because of the principle that the king could do no wrong: if he caused injury to someone by an erroneous decision there would be no appeal.[168] Even the concept of the law's 'artificial reason' existed before Coke formulated it.[169] In defending himself against the king's accusation that it would be treason to affirm he was under the law, Coke cited chapter 29 of Magna Carta and the passage from *Bracton* which said that the king was under the law, declaiming the sacred words in Latin.[170] That was Coke's own account, anyway,

---

[162] Caesar's minutes, fo. 423 (13 November 1608). Shipmen's hose were loose enough to fit anyone: *The Poetical Works of John Skelton*, ed. A. Dyce (1843), ii. 289.

[163] From IT MS. Misc. 21, fo. 134 (tr. and converted into direct speech).

[164] The 1658 edition says 'endowed'.   [165] Misprinted in 1658 as 'act'.

[166] Cf. Co. Litt. 97: 'the common law itself is nothing else but reason, which is to be understood of an artificial perfection of reason, gotten by long study, observation and experience, and not of every man's natural reason'.

[167] See Morice's reading (1578) above, p. 257. The Star Chamber and Privy Council were exceptions. The law reports mention King Richard III (YB Mich. 2 Ric. III, fo. 9, pl. 22) and King Henry VIII (*Reports of Cases by John Caryll*, ed. J. H. Baker, vol. ii (116 SS, 1999), p. 647) sitting in the Star Chamber. James I enjoyed hearing cases in Council: Dawson, 'Privy Council', p. 635.

[168] So it was stated in the year books: above, pp. 45–6. See also Smith, *Sir Edward Coke*, pp. 265–6.

[169] It is found in 'Le Methode de Monsieur Dodderige en son Practize del Ley Dengleterre' (*c.* 1600) BL MS. Add. 32092, fos. 161–200, at fo. 185v: 'not that every man can comprehend the [law], but it is artificial reason, the reason of such as by their wisdom, learning and long experience are skilful in the affairs of men'.

[170] He had previously quoted the *Bracton* passage in 1594 (BL MS. Harley 6686, fo. 95) and 1604 (above, p. 344), having already made a note of it in the 1570s or 1580s: BL MS. Harley 6687B, fo. 495, s.v. 'Roy'. His copy of *Bracton* (1569 edn) in the Georgetown Law Center, Washington, has the passage heavily marked; the hand was identified as Coke's

though it was a conflation of several Council meetings and had been improved with retrospect.[171]

An independent observer of the incident wrote in a letter:[172]

> After which his majesty fell into that high indignation as the like was never known in him, looking and speaking fiercely with bended fist, offering to strike him etc.; which the lord Coke perceiving fell flat on all fours, humbly beseeching his majesty to take compassion on him and pardon him if he thought his zeal had gone beyond his duty and allegiance.

This flamboyant reaction was typical of James' impetuous temperament, and it has been suggested that lawyers took it too seriously.[173] If Coke's response seems uncharacteristically obsequious,[174] it was also commendably prudent; it would have been a dangerous precedent for a chief justice to be knocked over by a king. James never did press a claim to sit in the King's Bench, though he did eventually succeed in exercising his assumed judicial power in the Star Chamber, on the advice of the lord chancellor, when the King's Bench and Chancery had reached a jurisdictional stalemate.[175] A more serious outcome of his claim to possess judicial authority was the repeated summoning of judges to the Privy Council to engage in debate with him, to be humiliated by the king's counsel and to be rebuked for their decisions.[176] But Coke's security in office was not (for the time being) endangered, and he was not deterred from continuing with the

---

by the present writer. Snagge had drawn attention to the passage around the same time: *Antiquity of the Chancery* (1587), p. 15. The same passage was quoted by Nicholas Fuller in *Darcy v. Allen* (1602) Noy 174.

[171] The king's remark about the judges being his 'shadows and ministers', which Coke reported in connection with ecclesiastical jurisdiction, were in fact made a week earlier when discussing the Council in the Marches: below, p. 382. The incident when the king was provoked to anger probably did not occur until February 1609.

[172] Letter from Sir Ralph Boswell to Dr Milborne, *Hatfield House MSS*, xxi. 23, no. 64. This was in February 1609.

[173] J. Wormald, 'James I, *Basilikon Doron* and *The Trew Law of Free Monarchies*' in *The Mental World of the Jacobean Court*, ed. L. L. Peck (Cambridge, 1991), pp. 31–54, at pp. 52–3.

[174] It was, however, common for judges to kneel in the king's presence, as will be evident from episodes in the next chapter (pp. 419, 425, 426). No doubt, at Coke's time of life, the process of kneeling without a cushion might bring the hands into temporary contact with the ground.

[175] Below, p. 420 (1616).

[176] In 1604 the king had warned the judges in parliament that he would not weary in holding them to account: *Political Works of James I*, ed. McIlwain, p. 277. For further examples see below, pp. 369, 372–3, 381–3, 424–6.

campaign.[177] As he said in 1609, he felt he was 'dancing a pavane, back and forwards'.[178] In May 1609 Ellesmere convened a conference at York House to try to settle the dispute amicably, though it made no progress. Ellesmere pressed Coke to produce precedents, hinting that the king might wish to see them. 'To what end,' asked Coke, 'should his majesty see our book-cases and precedents?' The lord chancellor thought he might wish to read and consider them. 'Oh, my lord,' Coke exclaimed, 'your lordship in your wisdom knows what would follow of that.'[179]

The matter was soon taken over by the Privy Council and degenerated into a trial of the judiciary.[180] The judges were compelled to defend themselves in the first instance about the jurisdictional status of customary tithing arrangements, their position being that a claim based on immemorial custom had to be tried by jury and not by an ecclesiastical court.[181] According to Coke's report, he protested at the disrespect shown to the judges by making them dispute with their inferiors,[182] which was an innovation, and argued that the matter ought to be determined after argument in court. The king nevertheless allowed the disputation to proceed, announcing that he could perfectly well interpret statutes by guessing at the minds of the makers, that juries were unsuitable for deciding tithe questions and that judges were not competent to decide on their own jurisdiction.[183] After sitting through three days of argument, however, he reached the perceptive conclusion that it was more difficult than he had thought. He therefore declined to decide the technical question, promising (according to Coke) that he would 'maintain the law of England, and that his

---

[177] Usher, *Reconstruction*, ii. 216, says the very next day he issued a prohibition in a simony case, citing c. 29 of Magna Carta. But Usher had misread the record as being a report of proceedings in court; it was the suggestion for the prohibition which recited c. 29.

[178] *Vinor v. Pelling* (1609) YLS MS. G.R29.16, fos. 277–278v, at fo. 278; BL MS. Add. 9844, fo. 41v.

[179] From Coke's own account of the 1609 proceedings, which was discovered by Usher in Holkham MS. 677, fo. 252: *Reconstruction*, ii. 223–5.

[180] A contemporary record was kept by Sir Julius Caesar: BL MS. Lansdowne 160, fos. 405–431v (here cited as 'Caesar's minutes'). A more detailed third account has been discovered in the Leicestershire Record Office: Smith, *Sir Edward Coke*, p. 201. Usher claimed to have found Bacon's speeches in July 1609, though the texts were in fact written breviates (or briefs) of the case: *Reconstruction*, ii. 233–5.

[181] Caesar's minutes, fos. 429–30 ('Heads of the controversy', 24 May 1609), fos. 414v–415 (7 July 1609), 405–408 (8 July 1609); *Case De Modo Decimandi* (Trin. 1609) 13 Co. Rep. 37; French text in IT MS. Misc. 21, fos. 17–22.

[182] The case was argued against the judges by Hobart Att.-Gen., Bacon Sol.-Gen. and Dr Bennett (judge of the Prerogative Court).

[183] Smith, *Sir Edward Coke*, pp. 201–2.

judges should have as great respect from all his subjects as their predecessors had had'. According to Caesar, the king said he did not wish to alter any part of the common law as found in Magna Carta and the year books – 'notwithstanding any common speech to the contrary' – but took occasion to reprimand the judges for their 'unfit and unjust' prohibitions to the High Commission, and to challenge the jurisdiction of the Common Pleas to award them.[184] On the subject of the High Commission, the attorney-general (Hobart) referred to Coke's report of *Cawdray's Case*, and to chapter 29 of Magna Carta, putting Coke temporarily on the wrong foot – being 'somewhat inclinable to allow of all that'.[185] More damagingly, Hobart argued that statutes altering ecclesiastical law should be interpreted by the ecclesiastical courts, not by the common-law judges, to which Lord Treasurer Salisbury assented. Nothing much was settled. The king was confused by all the precedents but seems to have accepted that the High Commission ought not to meddle with ordinary civil cases. Coke was given until the beginning of the next term to prepare a full response in writing; in the mean time all prohibitions were to be stayed, and the judges were told to complain directly to the king if they had occasion.[186] Coke's answer was duly prepared.[187] It was a tour de force, and seems to have been enough to stay any further controversy for the time being.[188] Archbishop Bancroft gave up the Privy Council proceedings,[189] and was to die soon afterwards. The king's inhibition seems to have been ignored; at any rate, it did not extend to *habeas corpus*, and so resistance to the power of imprisonment could continue.[190]

---

[184] Caesar's minutes, fo. 405v. The Common Pleas question he referred to Ellesmere, 'to consider of the books, and make report before the next term'.

[185] Ibid. 408.   [186] Ibid. 405v.

[187] It is identifiable as the treatise 'A Declaration of the true Grounds of the Prohibitions to the High Commissioners' (BL Cotton MS. Cleopatra F I fos. 115–169), which stated that it had been prepared at the king's request. BL MS. Add. 58218 is Coke's copy, with annotations in his hand. The copy in BL MS. Harley 7516 is entitled on the cover, 'Declaratio Domini Coke Capitalis Justiciarii del authorite des haut commissioners'. It was probably not completed until 1610: Smith, *Sir Edward Coke*, p. 204 n. 154.

[188] Even Usher admitted that it was 'a noble monument of judicial learning, honesty and integrity, and displayed that admirable courage in the maintenance of his convictions for which he deserves the unqualified respect of posterity. In some ways it was the greatest of all his legal writings, for it turned probable defeat into virtual victory, and silenced the arguments of the Church': *Reconstruction*, ii. 241.

[189] See Usher, *Reconstruction*, ii. 246: 'the Archbishop accepted Coke's precedents and maxims'. He died on 2 November 1610.

[190] At the summer assizes in 1609 Warburton J. released a Roman Catholic prisoner of the commission: Usher, *Reconstruction*, ii. 231.

In 1610 the campaign against the High Commission was taken up once more in the House of Commons, deploying the arguments collected by Coke. It was complained (inter alia) that:[191]

> the said commissioners do fine and imprison, and exercise other authority not belonging to the ecclesiastical jurisdiction restored by that statute [of 1559], which we conceive to be a great wrong to the subject, and that those commissioners might as well by colour of those words (if they were so authorised by your highness's letters patent) fine without stint and imprison without limitation of time, as also according to will and discretion without any rules of law spiritual or temporal adjudge and impose utter confiscation of goods, forfeiture of lands, yea and the taking away of limb and of life itself, and this for any matter whatsoever pertaining to spiritual jurisdiction, which never was nor could be meant by the makers of that law.

As it was, petty offenders were drawn from the most remote places to London or York, and subjected to excommunication and punishment 'by that strange and exorbitant power and commission', while it was very hard to know what offences against the ancient canon law were still within the spiritual jurisdiction. Defendants were forced to incriminate themselves on oath, there was no trial by jury, and there was no appeal.[192] The commissioners were encouraging disobedient wives to leave their husbands by regularly awarding them maintenance, presumably on a more generous scale than the regular spiritual courts. Moreover, the pursuivants sent by the commissioners were breaking open men's houses and closets, 'rifling all corners and secret custodies, as in cases of high treason'.[193] The petitioners sought a legislative remedy for these grievances, but it was not forthcoming.

The burden was therefore passed back to Coke and his brethren. The power to fine and imprison, except for heresy, schism and other enormities, was consistently denied throughout Coke's time on the bench.[194]

---

[191] *Proc. Parl. 1610*, ii. 263–5.

[192] This was a point constantly stressed by Coke: e.g. *Bulbrook* v. *Roper* (1607) BL MS. Lansdowne 1061, fo. 47v; CUL MS. Mm.1.21, fo. 106; *Lane's Case* (1608), ibid. 128; *Langdon's Case* (1608) BL MS. Lansdowne 1120, fo. 24; *Person* v. *Parke* (1608) CUL MS. Ee.6.13, fo. 11; *Case of Modus Decimandi* (1609) 13 Co. Rep. 37; *Huntley* v. *Clifford* (1611) BL MS. Add. 9844, fo. 149; *Sir William Chauncy's Case* (1611) ibid., fo. 156v.

[193] Cf. Fuller's complaints against pursuivants of the High Commission in 1607: Bowyer, *Parliamentary Diary*, p. 345.

[194] *George Melton's Case* (1610) CUL MS. Mm.1.21, fo. 167; MS. Gg.5.6, fo. 94 (the same report); BL MS. Add. 25209, fo. 197; MS. Harley 1679, fo. 172v (the same report); *Edgar's (or Eager's) Case* (1610) Yelverton's abridgment, fo. 422v; YLS MS. G.R29.16, fos.

In 1611 he reasserted that the oath *ex officio* was void, in the case of laymen, because by the custom of England a layman could not be interrogated on oath.[195] *Lee's Case* and *Hynde's Case* were once more relied on, and they were cited again in *Sir William Chauncy's Case*, when it was held that the High Commission could not imprison a man for adultery,[196] or failing to pay alimony,[197] since it was against Magna Carta to imprison anyone without lawful authority and these were not the kinds of offence intended in the ecclesiastical commission.[198] Adultery by clergy was another matter.[199]

Chauncy's Case resulted in another major collision. Coke's stance had again angered the king and the archbishops, and the possibility of removing Coke from office had already been contemplated by February 1611.[200] The commissioners decided to ignore the prohibition and imprison Chauncy, who then brought *habeas corpus* and was released on bail by the Common Pleas.[201] Archbishop Abbot complained to the Privy Council, and in May all the judges were summoned to the Council

---

407v–408; BL MS. Hargrave 5, fo. 225; *Lady Throgmorton's Case* (1610) 12 Co. Rep. 69; Calth. MS. i, fos. 127v–128v (citing *Edgar's Case*); *Bradshaw's Case* (1614) Calth. MS. i. 312v; BL MS. Add. 25213, fos. 162, 168v; *Cotle's Case* (1615) Calth. MS. i. 316v, 320v. In *Chauncy's Case* (YLS MS.), *Melton's Case* and *Cotle's Case*, it was also held that the commissioners could not take bonds for the performance of their decrees.

[195] *Huntley* v. *Clifford* (Hil. 1611) CUL MS. Mm.1.21, fo. 175; MS. Gg.5.6, fos. 101v–102 (same); Yelverton's abridgment, BL MS. Add. 48486, fos. 421v–422. Cf. *Cheekitt's Case* (Hil. 1611) cited by Usher, *High Commission*, pp. 208–9, from Coke's autograph notes in Holkham Hall MS. 677, fo. 327; in this case c. 29 was cited to justify a prohibition where a layman had not been shown a copy of the articles on which he was to be sworn.

[196] Adultery was held not to be an 'enormous' offence in *Thicknesse's Case* (1600) cited in 12 Co. Rep. 82 (*habeas corpus* in the Common Pleas); *Dr Conway's Case* (1610) 2 Br. & G. 37.

[197] As to imprisonment for alimony see also *Bradstone's Case* (1614) 2 Bulst. 300 ('alemoney'), where Coke cited *Kayser's Case* (1465) but made the party find bail and told him to use his wife better; *Codd* v. *Turback* (1615) 3 Bulst. 109.

[198] *Sir William Chauncy's Case* (1611) 12 Co. Rep. 82; BL MS. Add. 9844, fo. 156; MS. Add. 48186, fo. 201; YLS MS. G.R29.16, fo. 366 (anon., Pas. 1610). Magna Carta is mentioned in the report in MS. Add. 48186 but not in Co. Rep.

[199] *Watson's Case* (1614) Calth. MS. ii. 160, *per* Coke CJ (tr. 'incontinency in priests is a greater offence than in laymen ... and therefore the High Commission has jurisdiction over it, even though it does not over incontinency in laymen'); sub nom. *Watts* (1614) 2 Bulst. 182 ('incontinency is a heinous offence in clergymen').

[200] *CSPD 1611–18*, p. 11 (letter to Lord Salisbury from Sir Thomas Lake, clerk of the signet, who acted as the king's private secretary).

[201] Usher, *High Commission*, pp. 211–12.

chamber, once again, to explain themselves.[202] Abbot excoriated the judges for offending against God, the king and the Church. Coke complained that they had had no advance notice of the objections, and asked for them to be put in writing. It was not fitting, he said, for proceedings in courts of record to be questioned in this way. But his extempore answer was that the ecclesiastical courts had no power to fine or imprison before the statute of 1559, and so any authority to do so had to be derived from the statute.[203] The statute did not confer such a power, except for high offences, and the unlimited power claimed was unreasonable; the commissioners might fine a man all his substance and imprison him for life for a minor matter, and there would be no appeal or other remedy. At an adjourned meeting in June, an attempt was made to trick Coke's brethren into inconsistencies by examining the King's Bench and Common Pleas judges separately, one by one. Coke complained that the proper way to settle such questions was judicially, after arguments on both sides at the bar, and that the matter had already been determined in that way.[204] But Ellesmere, ominously, said he preferred the king's doctrine that questions of jurisdiction were for the king himself to decide.[205] The only outcome of the clash was a revised high commission, under which – despite intense pressure from the King's Council – Coke refused to sit.[206] The new commission, though slightly more restrictive in its wording, does not seem to have reigned in the High Commission at all.[207]

Four years later, in *Dighton's Case* (1615),[208] a *habeas corpus* for four laymen was returned that the prisoners had been committed for refusing

---

[202] BL MS. Harley 37, fos. 117–23; Caesar's minutes, fos. 409 (20 May 1611), 413v (23 May 1611, Coke's speech, setting out the precedents); 12 Co. Rep. 84 (dated the Thursday before Trinity, which was 16 May, perhaps a slip for the Thursday after Trinity, i.e. 23 May); Co. Inst. iv. 328. A specific complaint was made about *Chauncy's Case*, n. 198, opposite.

[203] BL MS. Harley 37, fos. 118v, 122. Ellesmere, however, told the king that the High Commission could fine and imprison defendants in all ecclesiastical causes: Coke, 'Dangerous and Absurd Opinions', no. 7.

[204] *Re the High Commission* (Trin. 1611) 12 Co Rep. 84. Yelverton J.'s speech in support of the High Commission, which was commended by Lord Ellesmere, is in his collection of speeches, BL MS. Hargrave 17, fos. 220–1 (reversing).

[205] BL MS. Harley 37, fo. 121.

[206] 12 Co. Rep. 88 (Mich. 1611). Coke is the only authority for this session: Usher, *High Commission*, pp. 219–21.

[207] Usher, *High Commission*, pp. 236–83.

[208] *R. v. Dighton, Holte, Burrowes and Coxe* (1615–16) 1 Rolle Rep. 220, 337, 410; Moo. 840; Cro. Jac. 388; sub nom. *Burrowes, Cox, Dyton and others v. High Commission* (Trin.-Mich. 1615 and Trin. 1616) 3 Bulst. 48; Calth. MS. ii. 31, 41, 79v, 90, 119; Tourneur, fos. 8, 13; sub nom. *Cocks's Case* (1615) CUL MS. Gg.2.5, fo. 314v; Gray, 'Self-Incrimination', pp. 77–80.

to answer upon the oath *ex officio* certain articles concerning the Book of Common Prayer. Serjeant Finch argued for their release, because they were laymen and therefore protected by the decision of 1607 concerning the Yarmouth merchants. They were entitled to refuse to answer questions which might incriminate them, and they were entitled to be heard before they were committed. He prayed in aid the usual precedents of Scrogges, Lee and Hynde. Coke agreed. The prisoners were released on bail, but Coke said it was a case of great consequence, and that he would speak to the commissioners to try to find some resolution for the future. He also held that the prisoners were entitled to have copies of the articles, and said the court would inspect them. It appeared from these that the principal issue was whether they would kneel to receive communion, and Coke considered this to be an accusation of schism, since not kneeling was 'of dangerous consequence';[209] the prisoners were therefore remanded and urged to submit. While that case was depending, another *habeas corpus* was returned that a prisoner had been committed by the High Commission upon articles for words spoken in derogation of the Book of Common Prayer, for refusing to kneel at the sacrament and persuading others to do likewise, for arranging schismatical conventicles at which words were used in disgrace of the ecclesiastical government and for refusing to be examined upon oath. Serjeant Finch once more cited the dictum of Popham CJ in 1607 that the commissioners had power to administer the oath only to a minister owing canonical obedience, and that they could not administer an oath which would bring a person in danger of any penal law. This time the court had the doubtful benefit of hearing argument also from Dr Marten, the Civilian king's advocate, who said it was necessary to suppress fanatical schismatics, and that 'this matter of order and government, being a fundamental part of the king's prerogative, ought to be maintained by the judges of the common law, and *Suprema lex salus populi*'. Coke was visibly irritated. He told Dr Marten that he had acted the part of an advocate fittingly enough, but in also acting as a statesman (in expounding the dangers posed by schismatics), and as a judge (in censuring the parties), 'he had transgressed the rules of good manners, for it did not become him to instruct judges or statesmen what they should do'.[210] Coke

---

[209] Cf. *Salter* v. *Ballinger* (1615) Calth. MS. ii. 4v, where the offence was moving around the congregation collecting offerings during devotions, which was said to be an ancient custom; Coke CJ said it was unfitting to disturb people in meditation, and refused to grant a prohibition to the High Commission, though it was hardly a matter of schism.

[210] Calth. MS. ii. 90 (tr.). Cf. 3 Bulst. 52 ('to censure a serjeant at law, this doth not beseem you').

was equally unsympathetic to the party, whose conduct was unpardonable, but he agreed with Finch's argument and brought forward again the precedents from Dyer. As he told Dr Marten, many of the judges were equally opposed to schismatics, but the question for decision was whether the return to the *habeas corpus* disclosed a sufficient ground for imprisonment, and it did not. The prisoners were nevertheless bailed, with a recommendation to submit to the commissioners and conform themselves. The reporters do not mention any public conclusion of the case.[211] It seems that the King's Bench had become a little more cautious than in the past about seizing on technicalities to oppose the High Commission, although Coke could not help himself from observing that the oath *ex officio* was 'an invention of the devil, to drive men's souls down to [hell]'.[212] This position was not far removed from Nicholas Fuller's schism and the language hardly less temperate, but it was unthinkable to prosecute Coke before the High Commission. The following term, as if to emphasise further the superiority of the King's Bench over the ecclesiastical courts in its adherence to divine law, Coke pronounced that general returns to *habeas corpus* on behalf of the High Commission were against the law of God.[213] He might equally have referred to Magna Carta and the statutes of due process, but in the context an appeal to a higher authority seemed more apposite. It was to no avail. The controversies were to rumble on until the abolition of the court in 1641,[214] though even Bacon admitted that Coke had to some extent prevailed in paring down its powers.[215]

---

[211] Equally inconclusive was *Brooke* v. *Brooke* (1615–16) Calth. MS. i. 159v, 173v, 208; ii. 24, 41, 57, 79v, 321v; CUL MS. Ii.5.26, fo. 63 (arising from an action for alimony against Ralph Brooke, York Herald). Coke CJ said the king could properly grant a commission to hold a plea of alimony, but the commissioners could not fine or imprison in the absence of an Act of Parliament.

[212] 3 Bulst. 53 ('inventio diaboli ad detrudendas animas hominum ad diabolum'). Cf. *Slade* v. *Morley* (1602) 4 Co. Rep. 92 at fo. 95, where Coke said of wager of law that swearing in one's own cause was 'praecipitium diaboli ad detrudendas miserorum animas ad infernum'.

[213] *Codd* v. *Turback* (1615) 3 Bulst. 109 ('By the law of God, none ought to be imprisoned but with the cause expressed in the return of his imprisonment, as appeareth in the Acts of the Apostles').

[214] 16 Car. I, c. 11. Only the previous year, a Middle Temple reading had been stopped on Archbishop Laud's orders because the reader had questioned some aspects of its jurisdiction: E. Bagshaw, *A Just Vindication of the Questioned Part of the Reading of Edward Bagshaw* (1660); W. Prest, *The Inns of Court 1590–1640* (1972), pp. 211, 214–15; J. Rose, *Godly Kingship in Restoration England* (Cambridge, 2014), pp. 70–3. Bagshaw had been in trouble with the High Commission himself.

[215] This was, of course, a complaint: *Letters and Life of Bacon*, vi. 90.

The Court of Requests

The campaign by the judges to keep the Court of Requests within strict limits was resumed in the Common Pleas under Coke's chief justiceship, and followed a similar course to that waged against the High Commission. In 1607 Coke held that a party could not be examined on oath in the Requests as to whether he had committed a fraud, since he was not bound to incriminate himself.[216] Later in the year there was a more substantial discussion of jurisdiction in general. [217] A widow claimed dower of a house in Ipswich, but her husband had made a secret conveyance so that she did not know who was tenant and could not bring an action at law. Her first suit in the Requests was defeated when the defendant pleaded that the house had been sold to a stranger upon good consideration. The widow then sued in Chancery and obtained a reference to two arbitrators, who awarded dower and damages, even though her husband had not died seised; she was also seeking damages in the Requests. Prohibition was now sought from the Common Pleas. According to Coke:

> Prohibition lies against every court in England which meddles where it has no authority, as to the Marches of Wales, for so it was awarded in the great case concerning the Marches,[218] or to the Cinque Ports ... or to the Exchequer if they meddle with common pleas ... or to the justices of assize if they meddle with something which is not within their patent, and to the King's Bench by Magna Carta, *communia placita non sequantur curiam nostram.*[219]

He offered to show a prohibition sent 'to a court which he would not name', but which the reporter took to mean the Chancery.[220] According to another report of this remark, Coke said that 'there is no court which the king has but which, if it goes beyond its bounds of its jurisdiction, a prohibition lies', citing a precedent in 1532 where an action was brought upon the 1368 statute of due process against a

---

[216] *Bullock's Case* (Pas. 1607) BL MS. Lansdowne 1062, fo. 223; sub nom. *Bullock* v. *Hall*, BL MS. Harley 1631, fo. 365; Gray, *Writ of Prohibition*, ii. 325–6.

[217] *Sweetman* v. *Revet* (Mich. 1607) CUL MSS Mm.1.21, fo. 112v; Gg.5.6, fo. 68 (same report; quotations tr.); BL MS. Lansdowne 1062, fo. 223v.

[218] Above, p. 307.

[219] Magna Carta, c. 11. Coke thought this could be sent by the Common Pleas: Caesar's minutes, fo. 431 (1608); below, p. 384.

[220] This was indicated by the citation of 13 Edw. III, Fitz. Abr., *Prohibition*, pl. 11; and the *Diversité des Courtes*, tit. Chancery.

party who sued in equity and 'avoided a remedy at common law'.[221] Coke must have found the record of *Parnell* v. *Vaughan* (1532), in which the Common Pleas had been asked to award damages – not a prohibition – upon the statute of 1368, in respect of a suit in Chancery.[222] And the implication of the citation is that he thought such an action would lie. The court went on to say that the plaintiff in the present case could have brought an action on chapter 29 of Magna Carta for the unjust vexation, 'for the statute is that it should be *per legem terrae*, and therefore where he seeks ways of vexing the party by undue courses, against the law, an action lies upon this statute'.[223] Daniel J. remembered the case of *Parsons* v. *Locke* (1595),[224] and Walmsley J. added that 'for such plain cases he would have the counsellors punished who gave the advice to commence the suit'. In a third case in 1607, Coke said that, whereas the Chancery had existed since before the Conquest, the Requests was erected only in recent times and therefore could not hear common pleas or stay the common law, and that the Common Pleas had never allowed its jurisdiction.[225]

The following year, Coke pronounced that 'the power of the Court of Requests is solely to dispose the parties therein to the other courts, as the case requires, but they have no authority to decide cases themselves, for they may not imprison or make a decree'.[226] It was also problematic that there was no appeal from its decisions.[227] Indeed, this was a general objection against all courts of equity:[228]

---

[221] MS. Lansdowne 1062, fo. 223v (tr.). The statute was 42 Edw. III, c. 3.

[222] *Parnell* v. *Vaughan* (1532) above, p. 98; below, p. 462 (no judgment). Coke did not mention this in his 1604 tract on c. 29.

[223] CUL MSS. The report in MS. Lansdowne 1062 said the suit could be on Magna Carta or on 42 Edw. III, c. 3.

[224] Above, pp. 277–8; Appendix 5(d), below, p. 484. The CUL MSS. say that the action was there held to lie, but the Lansdowne MS. says the matter was compounded.

[225] *Ingle* v. *Busbye* (1607) CUL MS. Mm.1.21, fo. 22v.

[226] *Anon.* (1608) BL MS. Lansdowne 1120, fo. 24. In *Anon.* (1612) BL MS. Add. 25210, fo. 4, he said that the Requests did not have a general jurisdiction in equity.

[227] In 1601 the Privy Council effectively nullified a decree of the Requests, but this was not a regular practice: Dawson, 'Privy Council', p. 644.

[228] *Downing* (or *Dearing*) v. *Hadlocke* (1614) Calth. MS. i. 225. See also *Anon.* (1614) Calth. MS. i. 159 (tr. 'decrees in the Court of Requests are like the laws of the Medes and Persians, which are inviolable, and however great an injustice they import, no appeal or writ of error lies to undo them'); 2 Bulst. 197, 215; identifiable as *Wigglesworth* v. *Everard*, CUL MS. Ii.5.26, fo. 62v (where the same point is made); *Anon.* (1614), *Cases concerning Equity and the Courts of Equity 1550–1660*, ed. W. N. Bryson, vol. ii (118 SS, 2001), no. 221; *Powell* v. *Harris and Wilcox* (1615) Tourneur, fo. 11 (below, p. 388).

Coke CJ here said that it was unreasonable for men's inheritances to be thus decided in the courts of equity, the sentence whereof is like the law of the Medes and Persians,[229] which is inviolable and wherefrom no appeal lies. And they are drawn into another jurisdiction (*ad aliud examen*);[230] for men's inheritances are to be tried by the common law of the land, either by demurrer, which is a trial by the judges, or by jury, which is a trial in the country, and the party has his remedy there, if wrong is done to him either by the judge or by the jury, for the act of the judge may be called in question by a writ of error, and the verdict of the jury by an attaint; but there is no such redress in the courts of equity. Therefore the statute of 1 Hen. VI, not printed, and the preamble of the statute of 15 Hen. VI, c. 4, say that men have several times been aggrieved by writs of subpoena obtained for matters determinable at the common law, to the great damage of the person vexed and to the impediment and subversion of the common law.

This was, no doubt, a rehearsal of the arguments against the Chancery as much as against the Requests.[231] The logic of *Throckmorton* v. *Finch* applied to the Requests as well as the Chancery.[232] The two courts were, indeed, enmeshed in the same conspiracy to override the law, because assistance was available in Chancery to support decrees from the Requests.[233]

Despite all these fulminations, however, no further actions on Magna Carta are mentioned in the law reports, nor was it necessary to keep citing chapter 29 in every case, though Coke did opine in 1615 that it was 'against the liberty of the subject' to be forced to enter into a bond to obey the decree of the Court of Requests.[234] The campaign against the Requests was only partly successful, no doubt because its authority was protected by the Privy Council and the lord chancellor. The court survived the continuous barrage of prohibitions from the Common

---

[229] Above, p. 21. Coke was fond of this analogy (see below, pp. 388, 405), though the characteristic usually associated with these laws was not the absence of an appeal but their unchangeable rigidity.

[230] This alludes to the phrase used in writs founded on the statutes of *praemunire*: 12 Co. Rep. 40.

[231] For the Chancery see below, pp. 410–22.

[232] *Maye's Case* (1615) Calth. MS. ii. 49v, *per* Coke CJ (tr. 'for the common law is the elder brother and will not have any competitor with him'). For *Throckmorton* v. *Finch* (1597) see above, p. 284.

[233] Jones, *Elizabethan Chancery*, p. 383. This was complained of in *Frevill* v. *Ewbank* (1614) Calth. MS. i. 189, 283v, one of a handful of cases in which Coke CJ was disinclined to grant a prohibition to the Requests. But see *Ramsey's Case* (1616), Bryson, *Cases concerning Equity*, ii. 470, where a prohibition was granted.

[234] *Furse* v. *Milman* (1615) Calth. MS. ii. 57.

Pleas,[235] and also from the King's Bench after Coke became chief justice there,[236] and finally disappeared only in the middle of the century.

The Provincial Councils

A third campaign continued by the Common Pleas in Coke's time was directed at the two provincial councils.[237] Only months after his appointment there was a 'great complaint' by the lord president of York that the judges had issued numerous prohibitions since the beginning of term, in contempt of a command given by the king the previous term.[238] Coke had then been summoned alone to the king's presence 'in the chamber next the gallery', in the presence of Ellesmere and other councillors. He justified the decisions in detail, and cited *Perrot v. Mathew* (1588)[239] to the effect that no court of equity could be erected without an Act of Parliament. Coke reported that 'the king was well satisfied with these reasons and causes of our proceedings,

---

[235] Prohibitions were granted in *Burwall v. Baylie* (1609) YLS MS. G.R29.16, fos. 363v–364 (meaning of a lease; here the court advised the party to bring an information against 'eux de court' for meddling); *Wagginer v. Wood* (1610) 2 Br. & G. 9 (right of way); *Reade v. Fisher* (1610) ibid. 297 (debt); *Anon.* (1611) CUL MS. Ee.3.54, fo. 40 (freehold); *Evans v. Evans* (1612) Calth. MS. i. 61 (suit after verdict in ejectment); *Fuller's Case* (1612) ibid. 61v (freehold); *Hill v. Hunt* (1613) ibid. 120 (debt for rent); *Anon.* (1613) ibid. 130v (suit after verdict in trover); *Anon.* (1613) ibid. 150v (freehold); *Anon.* (1613) ibid. 151v (sale of 'un cume de mothogling', i.e. a comb of metheglin); *Anon.* (1613) ibid. 157, 159 (legacy). Calthorpe's reports show that the barrage continued under Hobart CJ. Occasionally prohibitions were refused: e.g. *Jolly's Case* (1611) BL MS. Hargrave 18, fo. 33 (*assumpsit* to convey an acre of land to a third party); *Dyer v. Fuller* (1612) BL MS. Hargrave 15, fo. 262 (rent due from a copyholder to the lord's grantee; but cf. *Fuller's Case*, above).

[236] E.g. *Anon.* (1614) Cro. Jac. 335; 2 Bulst. 197 (freehold); *Penson v. Cartwright* (1614) Cro. Jac. 345; 2 Bulst. 207 (held that prohibition lies even if the King's Bench itself has no jurisdiction in the cause). Calthorpe, who took a particular interest in the subject, noted twenty-eight cases of reversal in his reports between 1614 and 1616. There are several more in other reports: e.g. Bryson, *Cases concerning Equity*, ii. 407, 434, 447, 469, 470. There were a few instances before Coke's translation: e.g. *Crews v. Draper* (1610) 3 Bulst. 19.

[237] For the beginning of this jurisdiction see above, p. 207.

[238] 'Prohibitions' (1607) 13 Co. Rep. 30. This is dated, both in print and in the autograph notebook (CUL MS. Ii.5.21, fo. 36), as Ash Wednesday – February 1606 [i.e. 1607], but its place in the notebook is in Hil. 1609, where it was perhaps noted in consequence of later complaints. Ash Wednesday was on 18 February in 1607 but on 1 March in 1609, so 1607 seems correct. The initial complaint to the king may have been made in 1606: *Hatfield House MSS.*, xviii. 388, no. 741 (undated letter from the president at York, assigned to 1606).

[239] Above, p. 265.

who of his royal grace gave me his royal hand, and I departed from thence in his[240] favour.'

Not long after this, Mr Serjeant Phelips moved the court on behalf of 'the attorneys and subjects of the North of England', setting out a list of their grievances against the Council in the North.[241] Attorneys were being sued at York in contravention of their privilege of being sued only in the Common Pleas; they were being summoned to explain themselves for representing clients in the Common Pleas who were also litigants before the Council; the Council was releasing parties in execution at common law, entertaining real actions, granting sequestration of lands, and refusing to allow outlawries to be pleaded. Phelips claimed that the king was losing £1,200 in fines for original writs, besides the loss to the court officers, and that these matters were 'heavy to the subject, dishonourable to the king, and derogatory[242] to the common law'. Coke responded:

> This matter touches the king in point of government: for he ought to protect his subjects, in respect of which protection they give[243] obedience. The institution of the court of the President and Council at York was presently after the suppression of the abbeys, when there was some rebellion,[244] and more was feared; and it was in order to quiet possessions, prevent riots, and so forth ... Their commission refers to some instructions which they keep so sacred that no one may see them in order to demur to their jurisdiction.[245] But if what they do is not contained in their commissions it is void. He vouched the resolution in 25 Eliz. in Parrett's case:[246] the king may grant someone to hold pleas, for there the party shall be tried by the law, and if he is wronged he may bring a writ of error, but it is otherwise of a court of equity ... He said that a court not far from here (meaning the Court of Requests) has no good warrant; one may see

---

[240] The word 'good' (*bone*) followed, but is deleted in the notebook.

[241] *Anon.* (Mich. 1607) BL MS. Lansdowne 1062, fos. 224v–225v; MS. Harley 4814, fo. 172 (same report; both undated; quotations tr.); cited in 12 Co. Rep. 55 (1608) as 'in Michaelmas term last'.

[242] The Harleian MS. says 'overthrow'.   [243] The Harleian MS. says 'owe'.

[244] I.e. the Pilgrimage of Grace. Cf. 12 Co. Rep. 52, where Coke went into this in more detail.

[245] Coke himself knew what was in them, because he had drawn them himself in 1603, when attorney-general: *Hatfield House MSS.*, xv. 113, no. 265; Caesar's minutes, fo. 431.

[246] I.e. *Perrot's Case* (1588) above, p. 265. This was also cited in *Andrew v. Webb* (1607) when the Common Pleas upheld a prescriptive court of equity (the 'Mark Court') in London: CUL MSS Mm.1.21, fo. 95, 105; Gg.5.6, fos. 63v–64; BL MS. Lansdowne 1062, fos. 83v–84v (versions of the same report). In that case, Coke said that the king could not grant a court of equity, because it would take away the birthright of the subject to have the benefit of the common law, but that a court of equity could exist by prescription.

from Hall's *Chronicle*[247] how it took its commencement in 8 Hen. VIII. What is done in a court of equity is final; the party has no remedy.

Walmsley J. spoke to the same effect, and said that if anything in their commission was against the law it was void, because the king took an oath at his coronation to govern according to law. Warburton and Daniel JJ. went further and said it was against the great charter and liberty of England, and would 'abolish and cancel the common law'. Reference was made to the now familiar medieval authorities, to *Sir John atte Lee's Case* (1368), *Cobb* v. *Nore* (1465), the statute of 1402, the 1368 statute of due process and Magna Carta. The court held that the Council was instituted to quiet possessions and prevent forcible entries until title could be determined at law, but it 'could not deal with any point of judicature, or with any interest between parties, or with *meum et tuum*'.

The position taken by Coke and the judges of the Common Pleas may have been conventional common-law wisdom, but it was not accepted by the protagonists of conciliar jurisdiction. In February 1608 the battle was reopened in the Privy Council. The first issue was the jurisdiction of the Council in the Marches of Wales over the four English shires, and the scope of its instructions.[248] The judges had signed a paper arguing that the four shires were not within the Marches, an opinion which merely earned them a rebuke from the king for an 'undutiful answer', and under pressure they agreed to grant no more prohibitions in cases where the Council acted within its instructions.[249] Three weeks later the Council at York was on the agenda, and Ellesmere went into the attack. According to the lord chancellor, questioning the king's prerogative was akin to sacrilege (*ad instar sacrilegii*); it was not fit to deny the king what other princes had; and it was dangerous to question the king's power to grant judicial commissions. If anything was amiss it should be amended, 'and not the whole frame of the constitution shaken'. The Bar were to blame. He said there was a rumour that 'twelve gentlemen of Lincoln's Inn' had been appointed to search out

---

[247] *Hall's Chronicle* (1809 edn), p. 585. Coke had noted this earlier in his commonplace book, BL Ms. Harley 6687A, fo. 233v (tr.): 'See in Hall's chronicle ... who erected the Court of Requests, namely Wolsey the cardinal; when, namely in 8 Hen. VIII; and the power thereof, which is not to bind anyone to the law.'

[248] The proceedings began on 3 February 1608: Caesar's minutes, fo. 421. For the dispute as to the English shires see above, pp. 304–7; below, p. 386.

[249] Caesar's minutes, fos. 419v–420 (5 February 1608): 'Afterwards, before the king himself in his Withdrawing Chamber, all the said judges in presence of the king's Privy Council assented to grant no more prohibitions against the Marches for exercising jurisdiction in any cause warranted within the articles of their instructions.'

precedents against the king's prerogative.[250] It seems nevertheless to have been agreed that the instructions would be reformed.[251] On 15 June the judges made a further defence of their prohibitions against the provincial councils, and Coke's historical account of the origin of the Council in the North was repeated.[252] The matter was adjourned until November, when the king resumed the hostilities.[253] He was, he announced, the supreme judge, and the ordinary judges were his shadows and ministers; he could sit and judge in any court in Westminster Hall; and he, being the author of the law, was the interpreter of the law.[254] He would maintain his prerogatives 'as much as ever English king had'.[255] Four days later, when Coke sought an adjournment to prepare the case in detail, the king again fulminated against the judges, saying he was their judge and that it was his part to interpret their oath and not theirs; the clause in their oath not to delay justice did not refer to commands from the king to stay causes, and if they disobeyed such commands they deserved to be hanged.[256] He might have spent but six years studying the law of England, but he possessed reason, and reason was the soul of the law.[257] The judges should leave the judgment to him. He could not endure prohibitions thwarting his prerogative, and gave them a caution in interpreting statutes 'not to rest upon quillets of law but to consider of the whole law'. The president of Wales then charged the judges to their face that some of them had said his court was no court. The king retorted that they might as well say the king was no king. Evidently the atmosphere was explosive. But there Caesar's notes of the proceedings leave the

---

[250] Ellesmere was himself a bencher of Lincoln's Inn. It is not clear what prompted this remark.

[251] Caesar's minutes, fo. 417v (24 February 1608).

[252] Caesar's minutes, fo. 431 (15 June 1608). The remarks are not attributed to Coke, but are almost certainly his.

[253] Caesar's minutes, fos. 425, 426v (2 November 1608).   [254] Cf. above, p. 366.

[255] Chamberlain wrote on 8 November 1608 that 'the king hath had two or three conferences of late with the judges about prohibitions, as well touching the clergy and High Commission as the courts of York and Wales, which prohibitions he would fain cut off, and stretch his prerogative to the uttermost; the judges stand well yet to their tackling, but *finis coronat opus*': letter to Sir Dudley Carleton, SP 14/37, fo. 105v; Birch, *Court and Times*, i. 80.

[256] Caesar's minutes, fo. 427 (5 November 1608). There had evidently been some staying of suits *rege inconsulto* until the jurisdictional questions were resolved.

[257] Cf. Usher, 'James I and Sir Edward Coke', p. 673, where 'ratio a[n]i[m]a legis' is misread as 'ratio omnia legis'. It is very doubtful whether James I spent much time at all studying the common law.

matter of the provincial councils, and it seems that the business was still unresolved a year later.[258]

Caesar's minutes of the hearings he attended are not easy to match chronologically with Coke's account, which may have telescoped a series of events retrospectively. According to Coke, he and Fleming (chief justice of the King's Bench) prepared a written answer, on behalf of the judiciary, in Michaelmas term 1608.[259] This went over the same ground as in the previous cases, but in greater detail, and made a new point about chapter 12 of Magna Carta. Chapter 12 provided that assizes of novel disseisin should be taken only in their proper counties, and Coke cited this as proof that the king could not alter the ancient jurisdictions of courts by letters patent, without an Act of Parliament. The judges concluded by proposing some remedies. When the report was read in Privy Council, Francis Bacon (now solicitor-general) offered to reply, but was not allowed to do so. Bacon was to make a habit of challenging the judges before the king and the Council, and already in this case Coke had complained that 'the judges of this realm have been more often called before your lordships than in former times they have been, which is much observed and gives much emboldening to the vulgar'. This time the judges, according to Coke, apparently won the day. After a retirement for discussion, the Privy Council accepted their main submissions. It was decided that the councils' instructions should be publicly recorded, in so far as they concerned criminal or civil causes;[260] that both councils should be 'within the survey of Westminster Hall'; that the councils should be represented at Westminster by counsel when a prohibition was sought; and that the judges were absolutely right in saying that it was a miserable form of slavery where the law was vague or uncertain (*misera servitus ubi jus aut vagum aut incertum*).[261]

---

[258] Lord Sheffield, the president at York, was making complaints in letters to Salisbury in the second half of 1609: SP 14/47, fo. 77 (22 July); 14/49, fo. 53 (14 November). In 1609 it was 'rumoured abroad that the judges do give forth speeches that whatsoever the instructions be they will not be restrained from prohibitions': 'Note of certain Things desired by Lord Sheffield to be inserted in New Instructions', SP 14/47, fo. 79v.

[259] 12 Co. Rep. 50 (dated Mich. 1608). This refers to the Phelips motion as having been the previous Michaelmas term.

[260] They were of record by Mich. 1609: *Coken* v. *Curteys* (1609) CUL MS. Mm.1.21, fo. 160v. See also above, p. 208.

[261] Cf. BL Cotton MS. Cleopatra F I, fo. 234 ('misera servitus est ubi jus est vagum'); Caesar's minutes, fo. 431v ('miserorum servitus est ubi jus est vagum vel incognitum'). For the aphorism see above, p. 208.

Prohibitions continued after this to be granted against the Council in the North,[262] and Coke adhered to the doctrine that it only had jurisdiction if the parties consented or were too poor to sue at Westminster.[263] Although Walmsley J. persisted in denying that the Common Pleas could grant prohibitions independently of privilege,[264] Coke claimed that there were precedents going back a hundred years and refuted Walmsley's opinion 'vehemently'. The other judges, and two of the prothonotaries, agreed with Coke.[265] This had been a touchy subject since at least the 1590s,[266] and Coke was challenged in the Privy Council on the same point in 1608. A long list of precedents had been compiled from the plea rolls back to the time of Mary, and Coke asserted that in theory his court could even send a prohibition to the King's Bench if it meddled with common pleas contrary to Magna Carta.[267] The next year the Common Pleas granted both a prohibition and a *habeas corpus* in respect of an injunction from the Council in the Marches, and Coke said that parties in such cases were also entitled to bring an action (for damages) upon the statute of 1402.[268]

The jurisdiction of the Council at York was fully debated again in 1612, in a suit brought by the archbishop of York in the nature of debt on

---

[262] *Coken v. Curteys* (1609) CUL MS. Mm.1.21, fo. 160v; *Selby's Case* (1610) BL MS. Hargrave 15, fo. 232; YLS MS. G.R29.16, fo. 426v; *Dickenson v. Ploughman* (1610) CUL MS. Gg.5.6, fo. 97v; sub nom. *Baker v. Dickenson* (1611) 1 Bulst. 110; *The Archbishop of York's Case* (1611) BL MS. Hargrave 15, fo. 239; MS. Add. 9844, fo. 148v; YLS MS. G.R29.16, fo. 436v.

[263] *Anon.* (1608) BL MS. Lansdowne 1120, fo. 8; *Beethill's Case* (1609) CUL MS. Mm.1.21, fo. 151; BL MS. Harley 1575; n. 265, below.

[264] I.e. where a party was a litigant or attorney in the court. For his objection see above, p. 281.

[265] *Wharton v. Banckes* (1609) CUL MS. Mm.1.21, fo. 153; MS. Gg.5.6, fo. 83; BL MS. Add. 25215, fo. 69; sub nom. *Baines v. Wharton*, BL MS. Harley 1679, fo. 129; MS. Add. 25209, fos. 127v–129v (where there is a full discussion of the precedents). Cf. *Sir Hugh Bethell's Case* (1609) BL MS. Add. 25209, fos. 119v–120; MS. Harley 1679, fo. 123v (same report).

[266] Above, p. 280.

[267] Caesar's minutes, fo. 431 (15 June 1608). For the precedents see 'In what cases the king's court of Common Pleas may grant prohbitions by law', BL Cotton MS. Cleopatra F I, fos. 206–35 (and cf. fos. 204–5 for a brief of the arguments against them). The first, other than a tithe case, was *Nicolls v. Chaffe* (1585) CP 40/1453, m. 2574, concerning the deprival of a vicar who had been convicted of felony.

[268] *Anon.* (1609) BL MS. Add. 25209, fo. 150; MS. Harley 1679, fo. 143 (same report). For the statute of 1402 (4 Hen. IV, c. 23) see above, p. 213. No example of an action framed on the statute has been found.

a bond, which was a matter determinable at law.[269] Coke said that even the Chancery would dismiss such a case to the common law. Although the king had granted the Council power to hold pleas in all personal actions, they could not alter the form of such proceedings without an Act of Parliament, as was shown by *Perrot's Case* (1588) and a decision of 1406 disallowing a grant to Oxford University to hold pleas according to the course of the Civil law.[270] It would contravene chapter 29 of Magna Carta, because the law of the land required matters of fact to be tried by twelve men, whereas the procedure on English bill was to examine the party on oath, 'and it is a rule in law, that *Nemo tenetur seipsum prodere*'. Then there was the king's financial interest. 'We are servants to the king and his people,' said Coke, 'and we are sworn that we will procure the profit of the king and his crown inasmuch as we may, and if we allow this the king will lose his fine': that is, the fine payable for a writ of debt. Moreover, no writ of error lay from any judgment at York, and so 'the subject should by such means be deprived of his birthright'. For all these reasons, a prohibition would be granted. It was around this time that Ellesmere had sent the law officers Hobart, Bacon and Montagu to 'confute and reprove the two chief justices' before the king, persuading him once again that the judges were acting against the prerogative. Coke complained in his notebook that this was another step in subversion of the courts, of law and of justice.[271]

The King's Bench under Fleming CJ was less assertive than the Common Pleas. In 1609, in a case concerning the jurisdiction of the Council in the Marches, an unnamed but intrepid junior barrister was silenced by the chief justice when he sought to argue – against Francis

---

[269] *Sedgwick v. Archbishop of York and Ingram* (1612) Godb. 201; sub nom. *Gay* (or *Gray*) *v. Sedgwick*, CUL MS. Mm.1.21, fos. 197v–198, 201; MS. Gg. 5.6, fo. 124v; BL MS. Harley 1575, fo. 101v; briefly noted in Moo. 874; the report in BL MS. Harley 4998, fo. 266v, is printed in Bryson, *Cases concerning Equity*, ii. 406.

[270] Coke cited it from a record 'in Agarde's office' (probably from 'Liber Agarde', a copy of Arthur Agarde's collections from the plea rolls, which he owned); it is identifiable as *Peddington v. Otteworth* (1406) in *Select Cases in the Court of King's Bench*, ed. G. O. Sayles, vol. vi (88 SS, 1978), p. 166. Cf. *Martin v. Marshall* (1615) BL MS. Lansdowne 1110, ff. 20–24v ('I have heard the lord Coke cite the precedent in this court of Pemberton and Symson, where the king granted to proceed according to the Civil law to a corporation, resolved to be a void patent, yet if the Civil law had been *ab origine* no question but it had been good. 8 Hen. IV is the precedent'); Bryson, *Cases concerning Equity*, ii. 447. Coke pointed out that the universities could in his own time proceed according to the Civil law by virtue of a statute of 1571 (13 Eliz. I, c. 29) which confirmed their customs.

[271] Coke, 'Dangerous and Absurd Opinions', no. 11 (dated Hil. 1613 in the margin).

Bacon and Henry Yelverton – that the king could not by his prerogative grant a liberty against the common law, and that the four English counties were not within the Statute of Wales.[272] One judge – Sir David Williams, a Welshman – thought that actions of trespass against the king's peace were not within the Council's instructions anyway, and that a prohibition lay in such cases because of the 'inconvenience' that no error or attaint lay. But Yelverton J. (Henry's father) disagreed, and Fleming declined to decide the point. Fleming accepted that there was no equity in the case, and that error and attaint did not lie, but said he would forbear to send a prohibition because the king had granted them the jurisdiction, 'and when the king is informed of the inconvenience he did not doubt that he would resume and revoke it'. The reporter noted that 'at the rising of the court Williams J. got up very angry (*surrexit valde iratus*) and said that by the law a prohibition lay'. As late as 1613, when Fleming was on his deathbed, the other judges declined to grant a prohibition to York until they had consulted him, because 'he had heard the conference about the same matter before the king'.[273]

The attitude of the King's Bench changed once Coke was transferred to the chief justiceship after Fleming's death.[274] The King's Bench, he said, was the highest court of ordinary jurisdiction in England, superior even to the Chancery, which was not a court of record.[275] It was the supreme court of ordinary justice within the realm,[276] and no court could better

---

[272] *Hall* v. *Haward* (1609) CUL MS. Ii.5.14, fos. 10v–11, at fo. 10v (tr. 'he was interrupted by my lord Fleming, who said that more had been said of this matter than he ought to say'). Complaint was made in the House of Commons the following year that after many hearings, and much investigation of historical records, the judges had failed to reach a decision about the four counties: *Proc. Parl. 1610*, ii. 261–3. But the matter went unresolved: *Anon.* (1610) BL MS. Lansdowne 1120, fo. 23; *Botery's Case* (1616) Calth. MS. ii. 124v.

[273] *Anon.* (Trin. 1613) Calth. MS. i. 102.

[274] For this appointment, forced on Coke against his will, see above, p. 351.

[275] *Bowler* v. *Songer and Croke* (1614) Calth. MS. i. 214v, 219v, 235; perhaps the same as *Wright* v. *Fowler* (1614) 2 Bulst. 284 (left without judgment). Here Coke held that a prohibition would lie to the Duchy Chamber if it sought to interfere with a judgment at law; this had been decided in *Beaumont* v. *Wigston Hospital* (1614) 1 Rolle Rep. 42; Calth. MS. i. 163v, 198; and it was reaffirmed in *Cottes and Suckerman* v. *Warner* (1615) Calth. MS. ii. 80v–81, 84v; BL MS. Lansdowne 1110, fo. 32 (printed in 118 SS 451); 3 Bulst. 119. For the Chancery see below, pp. 411–12.

[276] *Powell* v. *Vaudry* (1615) Calth. MS. ii. 72, 82, *per* Coke CJ (tr. 'this court, being the supreme court of ordinary justice within the realm, has power to supervise the proceedings in other courts'). In this case a prohibition was awarded against the Chancery of Chester: see the report sub nom. *Vautrey* (or *Vaudrey*) v. *Pannell* (1615–16) 1 Rolle Rep. 246, 331; 3 Bulst. 116; Bryson, *Cases concerning Equity*, ii. 450.

keep other courts within their bounds than the court where the king himself sat.[277] The writ of prohibition was designed to maintain the king's jurisdiction, in accordance with the judicial oath, because it recited that the encroached jurisdiction was 'to the harm, disinheritance and derogation of the crown'.[278] There was a qualification to be made concerning the counties palatine. They were not completely beyond reach, because writs of error lay to reverse judgments by the courts of record there;[279] but their equitable jurisdictions were on a different footing from those of the provincial councils. The palatine jurisdictions were treated, like the High Court of Chancery, as coordinate with the common law and part of the immutable state of things.[280] The King's Bench would therefore only interfere with the equitable jurisdictions of the palatinates if they sought to interfere with judgments at law, or if a chancellor there gave judgment in his own cause.[281]

Such autonomy could not be accorded to courts created in recent times through the royal prerogative. Coke agreed soon after his translation to grant a prohibition to the Council at York, albeit on the specific ground that it was a suit by a solicitor for his fees, and 'a solicitor is not a person of whom

---

[277] *Cottes and Suckerman v. Warner* (1615) Calth. MS. ii. 84v. Although Coke was willing to take advantage of the king's notional presence in the court *coram rege seipso*, he did not allow that the king might take any part in its decisions: above, p. 367. Coke's language in this case was inspired ultimately by Catlyn CJ: above, p. 159; memorandum on c. 29 (1604) below, p. 504.

[278] *Cottes and Suckerman v. Warner* (1615) Calth. MS. ii. 84v, and 3 Bulst. 120, *per* Croke J.

[279] Cf. *Anon.* (1613) 2 Bulst. 158, where Coke CJ said the court would be very loath to use its power to send a *certiorari* to Durham 'to oust them of their judgment', because they used common-law due process.

[280] These questions were fully aired in *Powell v. Vaudrey* (1615–16) Calth. MS. ii. 72, 82, 113v, 114v; Tourneur, fos. 23v, 33, 34v; 3 Bulst. 119, upon a motion by Sir Lawrence Hyde that the Chester jurisdiction in relation to the possession of land was contrary to Magna Carta, c. 29. They were also discussed in *Martin v. Marshall* (1615) Hob. 63; Tourneur, fo. 13; CUL MSS Mm.1.21, fo. 227v; Gg.5.6, fo. 146v (same report); BL MS. Lansdowne 1110, fos. 20–24v (concerning a prescriptive claim to a court of equity made by the mayor of York); in this case Winch JCP said that 'private' courts of equity were contrary to Magna Carta, c. 29. Cf. the shorter discussion in *Andrew v. Webb* (1607) above, p. 380 n. 246.

[281] This was decided by Coke CJ and Dodderidge J., as assistants to the Court of Chancery, in overturning a decree made by the earl of Derby as chamberlain of Chester (equivalent to a chancellor): *Egerton v. Earl of Derby and Kelly* (1613) 12 Co. Rep. 114; cited in Calth. MS. ii. 82, 114v; Tourneur, fo. 33; 3 Bulst. 117. The plaintiff, Sir John Egerton (d. 1614), was not the lord chancellor's son of the same name but the MP, first son of Sir John Egerton of Egerton, Cheshire: *HPHC 1558–1603*, ii. 80.

the law takes notice'.[282] He also advised the Common Pleas to grant one, on the grounds that 'it was not to be permitted that English decrees should be preferred before matters of record'.[283] Numerous prohibitions were sent in his time to the Marches.[284] Repeating one of his favourite adages, Coke said that 'no favour is to be given to these English courts, for their decrees are like the decrees of the Medes and Persians, whereon no error or attaint lies, be they right or wrong'.[285] They certainly could not interfere with judgments of record in the common-law courts, which were 'so sacred that there ought to be no meddling with them save only by error of attaint, as appears by the statute of 4 Hen. IV'.[286] The award of a prohibition was by no means automatic. It would be denied, for example, after a decree had been given,[287] or where the matter in suit was not determinable at law.[288] On the other hand, the King's Bench would protect the common law against encroachments. If a party who was entitled to bring an action for breach of contract at common law was able to go to a court of equity, 'then the titles of Action on

---

[282] *Anon.* (Pas. 1614) Calth. MS. i. 184v, 188v. The plaintiff at York was solicitor to the mayor of Durham. Cf. *Solomon Leech's Case* (1614) in Baker, *Collected Papers*, i. 97 (a solicitor in the Common Pleas).

[283] *Walker v. Bateman* (1614) Calth. MS. i. 273 (Common Pleas), 282 (King's Bench), 335 (King's Bench, while Coke CJ was absent in the Star Chamber); sub nom. *Walter v. Heyford* (1614) 1 Rolle Rep. 86; BL MS. Harley 1110, fo. 17v.

[284] *Barneham v. Blake* (1614) Calth. MS. i. 188; *Foxe v. Clifford* (1614) ibid. 176; sub nom. *Foxe v. Prickwood*, 2 Bulst. 216; Cro. Jac. 347; *Dellahay's Case* (1614) Calth. MS. i. 179v; *Anon.* (1614) ibid. 220; *Jones v. Davies* (1615) ibid. ii. 45v; BL MS. Lansdowne 1110, fo. 32; *Parslow v. Dennis* (1615) 3 Bulst. 34; *Cotton v. Cooke* (1616) 1 Rolle Rep. 294; BL MS. Lansdowne 1110, fo. 29v (printed in Bryson, *Cases concerning Equity*, ii. 470); Calth. MS. ii. 93; *Brommage v. Jennings and Jennings* (1616) 1 Rolle Rep. 368; Calth. MS. ii. 120v, 141v; Tourneur, fo. 39v; BL MS. Add. 35954, fos. 514, 521v–522; *Mason v. Mason* (1616) Calth. MS. ii. 120; BL MS. Add. 25211, fo. 154v (*habeas corpus* also); *Gilman's Case* (1616) Calth. MS. ii. 141; *Mathill's Case* (1616) ibid. 145v; *Dean and Chapter of Bangor v. Beckanshawe* (1616) ibid. 170v; Tourneur, fo. 58v; *Anon.* (1616) Calth. MS. ii. 178.

[285] *Powell v. Harris and Wilcox* (1615) Tourneur, fo. 11 (tr.); also reported in 1 Rolle Rep. 263; BL MS. Lansdowne 1110, fos. 31–2; Calth. MS. ii. 38.

[286] *Cottes and Suckerman v. Warner* (1615) Calth. MS. ii. 80v–81 (tr.). The case concerned the Duchy Chamber, but the dictum referred to all 'English' courts (Latin being the hallmark of a court of record). Cf. ibid. 84v (a continuation): (tr.) 'no judgment is to be shaken in any English court after it has been given upon a lawful proceeding at common law'; 1 Rolle Rep. 252 (tr. 'no court of equity may meddle after a judgment'). For the statute of 4 Hen. IV, c. 23, see above, p. 213.

[287] *Glascock v. Rowley* (1613) 2 Bulst. 142; *Dansey v. Pasloe* (1615) Calth. MS. ii. 4v; 1 Rolle Rep. 190; sub nom. *Parslow v. Dennis* (1615) 3 Bulst. 34 (a decree for quieting possession).

[288] *Curtis v. Scarlett* (1615) Calth. MS. ii. 26; BL MS. Hargrave 47, fo. 61; Tourneur, fo. 3v.

the Case and Covenant could be put out of the books'.[289] Inferior courts could not be permitted to use stricter process than was available in superior courts, such as fines or imprisonment for non-appearance.[290] Nor could they force a party to enter into a bond to abide by the order of the court, because that might result in his goods and lands becoming liable to execution, which was 'an encroachment upon the liberty of the subject'.[291]

This war was no easier to win than that with the Requests, and Coke did not live to see the ultimate victory when the prerogative courts expired in the 1640s. But the many skirmishes in Coke's time undoubtedly prepared the way for their extinction.[292] Although Magna Carta was not cited in every case, it was a recurrent and increasingly familiar theme. The liberty of the subject under the common law had, in Coke's view, to be protected by the King's Bench against jurisdictional innovations made under cover of the prerogative. As Coke said in the *Case of the Marshalsea* (1612), the meaning of chapter 29 was that 'if anyone against the law usurp any jurisdiction, and by colour thereof arrest or imprison a man, or in any manner by colour of a usurped authority oppress any man (which is a manner of destruction) against the law, he may be punished by that statute'.[293] Usurpation was a strong word to use for a jurisdiction exercised under royal authority, but in Coke's thinking any jurisdiction not warranted by the law of the land was necessarily usurped. He explained that chapter 3 of the *Articuli super Cartas* (1300), which limited the jurisdiction of the Marshalsea, was not introductory of new law but declaratory of old:[294]

---

[289] *Brommage v. Jennings and Jennings* (1616) Calth. MS. ii. 141v.

[290] *Oliver's Case* (1615) Calth. MS. ii. 32v, 115v, 119v; Tourneur, fo. 35v; 1 Rolle Rep. 339; BL MS. Harley 1692, fo. 58v.

[291] Council in the North: *Atkinson's Case* (1616) Calth. MS. ii. 113; sub nom. *Atkinson v. Hobbs* (1616) 1 Rolle Rep. 338. Council in the Marches: *Mason v. Mason* (1616) Calth. MS. ii. 120, *per* Coke CJ.

[292] Bacon complained in 1616 that Coke had prevailed against the provincial councils 'in such sort as the presidents are continually suitors for the enlargement of the instructions ... and the jurisdictions grow into contempt, and more would if the lord chancellor did not strengthen them by injunctions where they exceed not their jurisdictions': *Letters and Life of Bacon*, vi. 91.

[293] *Hall v. Stanley* (1612) 10 Rep. 68 at fo. 74 (tr.).

[294] Calth. MS. i. 46v (tr.). This is a report in direct speech of the passage which Coke paraphrased in 10 Co. Rep. 74 ('this Act of *Articuli super Cartas* is not introductory of new law but an explanation of the great charter, which was declarative of the ancient common law of England'). The final sentence of the translation overleaf is a slight paraphrase of the French: 'et que greynder destruction ou disseisin de libertyes poet la estre que a berever eux des leyes del terre, quant le ley dicitur un liberty entant que il fait homines liberos?'

And if anyone should ask where there is any statute which speaks of [limiting] the Marshalsea before this, I answer that, even if no statute speaks expressly of it, nevertheless there is a statute called Magna Carta, chapter 29, which gives a general hint at it; for that enacts that 'no man shall be disseised of his liberties or free customs, or in any other way destroyed'. And what greater destruction or disseisin of liberties can there be but to bereave men of the laws of the land? The law itself is called a liberty, because it makes men free.[295]

Proclamations

Jurisdiction was by no means the only sphere of controversy touching the prerogative during the period of Coke's chief justiceship. Concerns also arose about the misuse of proclamations as a way of avoiding the need for parliamentary legislation. They may have been in the mind of Mr Serjeant Phelips, as speaker of the Commons in 1604, when he declared in the king's presence that the only law-making power in the kingdom was the 'commanding and imperial court' of Parliament.[296] They were fed by the rumour, at the beginning of the reign, that the king intended to relieve Roman Catholics in some way by proclamation, contrary to statute and contrary to the wishes of the House of Commons. This occasioned a long but amateurish tract, evidently written by a cleric with Roman sympathies, advocating a generous approach to the king's power of legislating by proclamation.[297] It drew upon legal as well as scriptural authorities, and is of some interest in setting out a position. The writer argued that proclamations were allowed by the common law to create criminal offences not touching the lives of the subjects, or their freedoms in blood, or the charging or changing of their lands, or exposing them to forfeiture:

> they ... have *legis vigorem* as being declaratory of the king's pleasure upon some sudden urgency or necessity of state ... especially [such] as tend to the performance of the regal office touching the defence of the liberties of holy Church, the preservation of the rights of the crown, the upholding of

---

[295] This proposition recurs in R. v. *Allen and Tooley* (1614) 2 Bulst. 186 at p. 191, *per* Coke CJ; Co. Inst. ii. 3; and cf. ibid. 4 (courts of justice are also called liberties, because in them are administered the laws of the realm which make men free).

[296] *JHC*, i. 146 (22 March 1604). He added that the king's absolute prerogative could only be exercised by refusing his assent to new law, not by initiating it. Cf. his speech on 7 July 1604 (ibid. 254), when he said that all the king's commands ought to be warranted by law.

[297] 'The force and strength of the king's proclamations or edicts', BL MS. Hargrave 29, fos. 136–139v. For the toleration rumour see above, pp. 293–4.

the common law, right and justice of the realm, the peace and concord between the kingdom and the priesthood, the establishment and reviver of good laws and the abrogation or annullation of bad and evil laws derogatory to Magna Carta, or the points aforesaid, for to this the king is solemnly sworn.

The coronation oath would be pointless, he wrote, if the king did not have the power to enforce the law himself by edict or proclamation. Magna Carta was itself 'founded on the king's grant, signed, sealed and witnessed without Parliament'.[298] The writer went on to list a number of statutes and pseudo-statutes which did not mention that they had been made in Parliament, but were nevertheless 'retained at the [present] day for good and authentical even as though the same had been made in Parliament'. This was proof that the king's legislative power was not dependent on Parliament. The writer complained that the 'malice towards the ease of poor Catholics' was such that 'if the king without a Parliament should ease them, the people will think that he takes a liberty to throw down laws at his pleasure'. This he refuted. The king 'would not touch with his little finger those immutable laws which tend to the good of all', but only 'those other which are mutable and merely of men, or of the time, which divide the natives, and serve but a few turns only, and which upon the points aforesaid are of themselves void or voidable'. The only precedent which the writer could vouch was the revocation of the New Ordinances of 1311 in 1322, which he misrepresented as a revocation of an Act of Parliament by the king. The statutes revoked were in fact those made by the Lords Ordainers, without Parliament, whereas the revocation was made in Parliament. But the writer was clearly making a claim that the king could repeal parliamentary statutes without troubling Parliament.

The same claim was made by the Regius Professor of Civil Law at Cambridge.[299] Dr Cowell wrote in 1607 that the practice of seeking the

---

[298] The solecism that the charter was signed is thus an old one. A lawyer would have known that charters and letters patent were never signed by the king, and also that Magna Carta was ratified by Parliament.

[299] The English Civilians generally aligned themselves with an absolutist view of the monarchy: see B. Levack, *The Civil Lawyers in England 1603-1641: A Political Study* (Oxford, 1973), pp. 86-121. Cowell has been condemned by posterity for supporting that cause, but a more generous view of him as a learned but naive and cloistered scholar, more concerned with abstract ideas than current political controversies, is to be found in S. B. Chrimes, 'The Constitutional Ideas of Dr Cowell' (1949) 64 EHR 461-87; this contains a full account of the proceedings. See also Thompson, *Magna Carta*, pp. 235-8.

advice of Parliament before legislating was merely an exercise of the king's benignity, or perhaps or consequence of the concession in his coronation oath, because he was 'above the law by his absolute power'. This absolute power was more than merely theoretical. Despite his oath, the king could 'alter or suspend any particular law that seemeth hurtful to the public estate'.[300] In another passage, he wrote that there was no prerogative belonging to the most absolute king which did not also belong to the king of England. Although by custom he made no laws without the consent of Parliament, 'he may quash any law concluded of by them. And whether his power of making laws be restrained *de necessitate*, or of a godly and commendable policy, not to be altered without great peril, I leave to the judgment of wiser men. But I hold it incontrollable, that the king of England is an absolute king.'[301] This was anathema to the common lawyers, and in 1610 the barristers in the House of Commons – led by John Hoskins of the Middle Temple – demanded that the book be suppressed. The bewildered Cowell was briefly imprisoned, and was questioned by the king himself in the Privy Council, but was too overcome to give sensible answers. The king, even if he liked much of what Cowell wrote, was indignant that anyone should presume to expound the mystery of his royal authority in a law dictionary, and even more troubled that it should be debated in the Commons. James petulantly informed the House that monarchy is 'the supremest thing upon earth, for kings are not only God's lieutenants upon earth and sit upon God's throne, but even by God himself they are called gods ... they have the power of raising and casting down, of life and of death, judges over all their subjects and in all causes, and yet accountable to none but God only'. His indignation having been relieved by this explosion, the king soon afterwards displayed his political prudence by ordering the book to be suppressed of his own volition. No doubt intending to tease the lawyers, he did it by proclamation. Cowell resigned from his chair in disgrace, and died the following year.[302]

This royal gesture was hardly sufficient in itself to defuse the concerns about proclamations, which were serious and fundamental,

---

[300] J. Cowell, *The Interpreter* (1607), sig. Qq1, s.v. 'King'.

[301] Ibid., sig. Ddd4, s.v. 'Praerogative of the King'. He made a similar point s.v. 'Parliament'.

[302] B. Levack, 'John Cowell (1554–1611)' in *ODNB*, and the references there. For the king's speech see J. R. Tanner, *Constitutional Documents of the Reign of James I* (Cambridge, 1930), pp. 14–16.

and were currently being voiced in the Commons.[303] Their number had increased under the new king, and they were being used, so it was said, to implement policies which Parliament had rejected,[304] to interfere with freeholds (by imposing planning regulations)[305] and with personal freedoms (by controlling trades), to authorise punishments and forfeitures without due process, to introduce new penalties without parliamentary sanction, and to enable offenders to be punished in 'courts of arbitrary discretion' such as the Star Chamber.[306] Lawyers foresaw that these gradual innovations might easily slide, in the future, into arbitrary government without Parliament. According to the petition of grievances presented by the House of Commons in 1610:[307]

> Amongst many other points of happiness and freedom which your majesty's subjects of this kingdom have enjoyed under your royal progenitors, kings and queens of this realm, there is none which they have accounted more dear and precious than this, to be guided and governed by certain rule of law ... Out of this root hath grown the indubitable right of the people of this kingdom not to be made subject to any punishment that shall extend to their lives, lands, bodies or goods other than such as are ordained by the common laws of this land or the statutes made by their common consent in Parliament. Nevertheless it is apparent, both that proclamations have been of late years much more frequent than heretofore, and that they are extended not only to the liberty but also to the goods, inheritances and livelihood of men ... By reason whereof there is a general fear conceived and spread amongst your majesty's people that proclamations will by degrees grow up and increase to the strength and nature of laws: whereby not only that ancient happiness, freedom, will be as much blemished (if not quite taken away) which their ancestors have so long enjoyed, but the

---

[303] R. W. Heinze, 'Proclamations and Parliamentary Protest 1539–1610' in *Tudor Rule and Revolution*, ed. D. J. Guth and J. W. McKenna (Cambridge, 1982), pp. 237–59, at pp. 248–59.

[304] A proclamation of 1607 even purported to revive part of a repealed statute: Heinze, 'Proclamations and Parliamentary Protest' (last note), at pp. 244–5. But it was made after consulting the judges, and the case for the repealed provision – which forbade subjects to leave the realm without licence – was that it merely restated the common law.

[305] As to these see T. G. Barnes, 'The Prerogative and Environmental Control of London Building in the Early Seventeenth Century' (1970) 58 *California Law Review* 1332–63.

[306] Petition of Grievances 1610 (next note), at pp. 327–9. Specific objections were made to proclamations prohibiting building in London and the making of wheat starch.

[307] W. Petyt, *Jus Parliamentarium* (1739), pp. 321–36, at pp. 326–7; 2 St. Tr. 519–34 at cols. 524–6; abstracted in J. R. Tanner, *Constitutional Documents of the Reign of James I* (Cambridge, 1930), pp. 148–56.

same may also (in process of time) bring a new form of arbitrary government upon the realm.

The king, in response, said he knew well that 'by the constitution of the frame and policy of the kingdom, proclamations are not of equal force and in like degree as laws', but he considered it a duty annexed to his royal authority to restrain inconveniences for which no certain law was extant. If he had extended them further than was warranted, he was glad to be informed of it, and therefore he would confer with the Privy Council and the judges.[308] This aspect of the petition was duly referred to the lord chancellor, lord treasurer, lord privy seal and the law officers. According to Coke's note, not published until 1658, he was summoned to advise them, but declined to give an opinion without consulting his brother judges.[309] Ellesmere characteristically told him that 'every precedent had first a commencement, and that he would advise the judges to maintain the power and prerogative of the king, and in cases in which there is no authority or precedent to leave it to the king to set order in it according to his wisdom and for the good of his subjects, or otherwise our king would be like the doge of Venice'.[310] Coke responded that before any novelty was established it was necessary to ensure that it was not against the common law, 'for the king cannot change any part of the [common][311] law, nor create any offence by his proclamation which was not an offence before, without Parliament'. It was thereupon referred to the chief justices and chief baron, together with Mr Baron Altham, who (according to Coke) all gave their opinion that the king could not create a new offence, 'for then he might alter the law of the land by his proclamation in a high point; for, if he may create an offence where none is, thereupon would follow fine and imprisonment'. It was also resolved that 'the king has no prerogative but that which the law of the land gives or allows to him'.

[308] SP 14/56. fo. 134.
[309] *Case of Proclamations* (1610) 12 Co Rep. 74 (reprinted in 2 St. Tr. 723); French texts in CUL MS. Ll.3.10, fos. 180–1; LI MS. Maynard 80, fos. 38–40v; MS. Misc. 162, unfol.; IT MS. Misc. 21, fos. 46v–48. The quotations are translated from the French.
[310] The wording at the end is 'come le duke de Venice'. The comparison with the doge had been made by the king: *Proc. Parl. 1610*, ii. 103. Forty years earlier, Morice had agreed that the king of England was more than a Venetian duke or Spartan king: Morice's reading (1578), fo. 5v.
[311] Word inserted in 1658.

No express mention was made of Magna Carta, but the points were precisely those which had come to be associated with chapter 29 and the explanatory statutes of due process. The opinion seems nevertheless to have had little effect at the time, and may even have been suppressed.[312] A possible explanation is provided by a previously unnoticed parallel report by a judge, which qualifies Coke's version of events.[313] According to Peter Warburton, justice of the Common Pleas, the four judges were asked by the Privy Council for their opinion on the question, 'if the king sets forth a proclamation, and any subject disobeys the proclamation, is it not a contempt, and may he not be fined and imprisoned for his contempt?' Fleming CJ, Tanfield CB and Altham B. were inclined to think that it was a contempt punishable by fine and imprisonment, whereas Coke alone 'held strongly' that the offender could not be fined or imprisoned if there was no offence at common law (*malum in se*) or by Act of Parliament (*malum prohibitum*). This may, therefore, be an example of Coke reporting – albeit not, in this instance, publishing – what he thought should have happened, and presenting his own arguments as agreed resolutions. On the other hand, it is more likely that Coke had won the others round, for a text of what appears to be an agreed opinion stated clearly that the king could not create a new offence by proclamation.[314] The compromise – which Coke did report, and which represented a partial retreat from the decision of 1556[315] – was that, although the king could not create new offences, if he issued a proclamation prohibiting something which was already an offence, the contempt of the proclamation was an aggravation which merited additional punishment.[316] In the event, the king also backed down and revoked all but one of the controversial proclamations. His politic treatment of the matter effectively

---

[312] E. S. Cope, 'Sir Edward Coke and Proclamations 1610' (1971) 15 *American Journal of Legal History* 215–21, at pp. 218, 221.

[313] Warburton's reports, CUL MS. Ii.5.25, fo. 160v (quotations tr.).

[314] 'Certain resolutions concerning proclamations, 26 Octobris 1610', BL MS. Harley 1576, fo. 18; printed in Cope (above, n. 312), at p. 221, para. 3: 'His majesty by the laws of this realm cannot by his proclamation create anything to be an offence which was not an offence before against the laws of this realm.' Cf. Ashley's reading (1616), fo. 11: (tr.) 'a proclamation may be called lawful if it adds force to the execution of a law which was already in being, or if it commands or prohibits anything which is not against any law; but if it is against any law, and prohibits what the law requires or commands what the law prohibits, it is unlawful.'; and the longer passage ibid. 22v–23.

[315] Above, pp. 151–2.

[316] 12 Co. Rep. 75. Cf. 'Certain Resolutions' (previous note), para. 2: 'the king, to prevent and prohibit any offence that is *malum prohibitum* and against the laws of this realm, may make proclamation, and the same offences being after committed may be punished in the Star Chamber ... or be determined by the ordinary course of law'.

laid the grievance to rest, but in so doing he renounced any realistic pretension to a legislative power under the absolute prerogative.

Mandamus

The history of *mandamus* began in the King's Bench before Coke's time,[317] but it was left to Coke to connect the remedy with the great charter. The opportunity arose in the case of James Bagg, who had once been a client.[318] Bagg was a wealthy merchant and former mayor of Plymouth, and had represented the borough in Parliament. He had become very unpopular locally, insulting successive mayors and refusing to contribute to the forced loan of 1615. His exasperated fellow aldermen removed him from his aldermanship in 1615, and he sued in the King's Bench for restitution.[319] Restitution was ordered, not only because the causes returned (even if sufficient for punishment) were insufficient for disfranchisement,[320] but more importantly because Bagg had not been given an opportunity to be heard and the allegations had not been tried by jury.[321] This obviously called for recourse to chapter 29.

According to Timothy Tourneur, Coke 'relied much upon the force of the statute of Magna Carta, chapter 29, which speaks forcefully for freemen; and he said that in 42 Edw. III, chapter [1], a statute was made to repeal all statutes made contrary to the statute of Magna Carta; and further said that this statute has been confirmed in Parliament thirty-two times.'[322] According to another report, by Henry Calthorpe, the removal of Bagg was against chapter 29 because there was no law allowing the corporation to do it: 'being an alderman is a "liberty", because he is a burgess of the town, one of the private council, and part of the corporation, and has an interest in the lands and goods of the town, and so he cannot be removed from it except

---

[317] Above, pp. 203–6.

[318] For Bagg see *HPHC 1604–29*, iii. 105–7; J. Barry and C. Brooks, *The Middling Sort of People: Culture, Society and Politics in England 1550–1800* (1994), pp. 130, 255.

[319] *Bagg's Case* (1615) 11 Co. Rep. 98; 1 Rolle Rep. 173, 224; Calth. MS. ii. 33v–34; Tourneur, fos. 6v–7v; discussed in Henderson, *Foundations*, pp. 46–50, 69–72. This was followed in *Taylor* v. *Mayor and Bailiffs of Gloucester* (1616) 1 Rolle Rep. 409; more fully reported in Calth. MS. ii. 129, 164, 178v, 179; Tourneur, fos. 48v–49; BL MS. Harley 1692, fo. 58v; BL MS. Add. 25211, fo. 159v; HLS 109, fos. 148v–149.

[320] The very long return is set out in full in 11 Co. Rep. 93–7. The various points are discussed in much detail in Calthorpe's report.

[321] 1 Rolle Rep. 225, *per* Coke CJ (tr. 'in this case Bagg is not disfranchised and ousted of his liberty *per pares*, that is by jury, nor *per legem terrae*'); 11 Co. Rep. at fo. 99.

[322] BL MS. Add. 35957, fo. 7v.

by the law of the land'. The law of the land would only permit his removal if the corporation had a legal power of removal, either by charter or by prescription, and no such authority had been returned to the writ.[323] The remedy in such cases sprang from the supremacy of the King's Bench:[324]

> It was resolved that the Court of King's Bench, being the king's seat, and the great court which was erected for the conservation of the peace and tranquility of the realm, had a power to reverse errors in manners just as it has a power to redress errors in judgments,[325] and therefore if anyone has a wrong offered to him, whether in taking away his liberty by imprisonment or his privilege by disfranchising him, he may well have recourse to the Court of King's Bench, and there he may have his remedy.

That may have been what was said in court, but Coke had second thoughts about the vague word 'manners'. He expressed the sentiment more expansively in his own report of the case, which was rushed out the following term while he was enmeshed in several crises to be considered in the next chapter:[326]

> It was resolved that to this court of King's Bench belongs authority not only to correct errors in judicial proceedings but other errors and misdemeanours extrajudicial tending to the breach of the peace or oppression of the subjects, or to the raising of faction, controversy or debate, or to any manner of misgovernment: so that no wrong or injury, either public or private, can be done, but that it shall be here reformed or punished by due course of law.

This passage infuriated Ellesmere, who said of it:[327]

---

[323] Calth. MS. ii. 34 (tr.). In *Taylor v. Gloucester* (1616) ibid. 178v, Trotman argued that (tr.) 'the freedom of a man being his freehold, as is said in James Bagg's case in the 11th Rep., he cannot be put out except by the law of the land, as it appears by the statute of Magna Carta, c. 29'. But Coke CJ and the court responded that an alderman could be put out for wrongdoing, if this was provided for by the charter or by prescription, because that would be *lex terrae* (a point he had made in *Bagg's Case*). The case is also reported in 3 Bulst. 189.

[324] Calth. MS. ii. 33v (tr.). For Coke's doctrine as to the supremacy of the King's Bench see also above, pp. 308–11, 386–7.

[325] Cf. 1 Rolle Rep. 225, *per* Coke CJ (tr. 'We are now in our proper element, namely in reforming abuses in manners upon a writ such as this as, well as reforming errors'). The reference to manners is difficult to understand, since Coke is clearly referring to a legal right.

[326] 11 Co. Rep. 98 (tr.).

[327] Ellesmere, 'Observations upon Coke's Reports', 307. He also mentioned it in his vitriolic speech to Coke's successor in 1616, warning him not to follow suit: BL MS. Add. 35957, fo. 63 (below, p. 439).

In giving excess of authority to the King's Bench he doth as much as insinuate that this court is all sufficient in itself to manage the state. For if the King's Bench may reform 'any manner of misgovernment' (as the words are), it seemeth that there is little or no use either of the king's royal care and authority exercised in his person and by his proclamations, ordinances and immediate directions, nor of the Council Table, which under the king is the chief watchtower for all points of misgovernment, nor of the Star Chamber, which ever hath been esteemed the highest court for extinguishment of all riots and public disorders and enormities. And besides, the words do import as if the King's Bench had a superindependency over the government itself, and to judge wherein any of them do misgovern.

It was another of the charges which led to Coke's undoing in 1616. It might have been better to limit his claims to the liberties protected by Magna Carta, which was all the decision required. Be that as it may, it was Coke's view which over time prevailed, and the remedy of *mandamus* remained firmly entrenched in the common law thereafter.

Imprisonment by the Privy Council

Arbitrary imprisonment had been one of the first infringements of liberty to be associated with chapter 29 in the Tudor period, and had been the main subject of Coke's treatise on the same chapter in 1604.[328] Magna Carta was held to protect not only against unjustified incarceration but also against unduly harsh treatment. An applicant for *habeas corpus* in 1612 complained that he had been imprisoned by the mayor of Liskeard for being rude to him, and had been thrust into a dungeon without bread or meat, or a bed, and denied bail. It also appeared that he had been imprisoned in August for an offence in June, and had then been detained for six months. The King's Bench held that this was against chapter 14 of Magna Carta, because it was disproportionate to the offence,[329] and also against chapter 29, because it was not *legale judicium*; he was therefore released.[330] No doubt he could also have recovered damages in an action of false imprisonment.

---

[328] Above, pp. 100–1, 156 n. 69, 250, 308–10, 346–7.

[329] 2 Bulst. 139, *per* Croke J. This in itself was a major piece of reinterpretation, since c. 14 referred only to amercement.

[330] *Hodges* v. *Humkin* (1612–13) 2 Bulst. 139; BL MS. Harley 1692, fo. 24v; MS. Harley 4948, fo. 48.

The great question, however, which was not finally settled until 1628, was how far Magna Carta could be taken to prevent or qualify the governmental power of imprisonment without cause shown, as claimed by the king and the Privy Council.[331] Although Coke owned a copy of Spelman's manuscript reports, he seems not to have been aware of *Serjeant Browne's Case* (1532),[332] in which the judges ruled that the king could not imprison his subjects without lawful cause, contrary to Magna Carta. The matter was therefore governed by the judges' written opinion of 1592 as reported by Anderson.[333] It had been conceded in 1592 that the courts would not examine on the merits a committal by the king himself, or the whole Privy Council, or a committal for treason. This position remained the orthodoxy and was confirmed by two cases in 1611. In the first, Thomas Caesar sought release from the Marshalsea prison, but upon the return being made that he was committed by the king's command, the court remanded him without bail.[334] Later in that year or the next, the wife of one Pinson came into the King's Bench and prayed a *habeas corpus* for her husband, who was in the custody of the marshal. He had been committed by four members of the Privy Council, but the cause was not revealed. Coke said that no one could imprison another at his pleasure without bringing him to answer within a reasonable time, for it was against the liberty of the subject; but a privy councillor could imprison for a reasonable time.[335] The wife said her husband had been in prison for fourteen days, and the court said that was not long enough to justify awarding a *habeas corpus*. But Coke 'laboured privately' to ensure that Pinson was released without the need for a writ. If correctly reported, this decision seemed to go further than the 1592 report in recognising a power of imprisonment in a small number of councillors, or perhaps even in one. But the explanation may be that the councillors, though only four in number, were deemed to be sitting in

---

[331] For the Elizabethan position see above, pp. 155–62.

[332] Above, pp. 100–1. Coke's copy of Spelman has not been found, and it may have been incomplete.

[333] Above, pp. 167–8.

[334] *Thomas Caesar's Case* (Hil. 1611) BL MS. Harley 6713, fo. 73; MS. Add. 24846, fo. 328v (same report). Williams J. pointed out that by the Statute of Westminster I, c. 15, a prisoner by the king's command was not bailable. The applicant was probably Sir Julius Caesar's nephew, the son of Sir Thomas Caesar (d. 1610), cursitor baron of the Exchequer.

[335] *Pinson's Case* (Mich. 1611) CUL MS. Mm.1.21, fo. 199; (dated Mich. 1612) BL MS. Harley 1575, fo. 100; CUL MS. Gg.5.6, fo. 123 (all variants of the same report).

Council, since in returning a committal by the whole Council there was no need to enumerate the councillors who were present.[336]

A more troubling case arose in 1613.[337] James Whitelocke, a well-established barrister of the Middle Temple, had been consulted by Sir Robert Mansell concerning the legality of a commission issued to Lord Ellesmere and others to investigate abuses in the navy and to inflict punishments according to law. He wrote a hasty opinion to the effect that the commission was unprecedented and unlawful, 'such as he hoped would never have place in this common wealth', relying on chapter 29 of Magna Carta and *Sir John atte Lee's Case* (1368)[338] as showing that the king could not authorise fines or imprisonment without due process. This must have seemed close enough to the conventional wisdom prevailing by that date. However, when Mansell produced the opinion to the authorities, Francis Bacon – who had presumably drawn the commission – prosecuted both of them in the Privy Council for some ill-defined kind of contempt. Bacon argued that the opinion was wrong, because the commission was only to punish 'according to law', and those words ruled out anything unlawful; but his main complaint was that impeaching the prerogative in such broad and general terms was beyond the scope of counsel's privilege. The reliance on Magna Carta was 'not only grossly erroneous and contrary to the rules of law, but disingenerous [*sic*] and tending to the dissolving of government'. The 'law of the land' was not confined to the ordinary courts, for 'his majesty's prerogative and his absolute power incident to his sovereignty is also *lex terrae*, and is invested and exercised by the law of the land, and is part thereof'. The commission in question was derived from the king's absolute prerogative in controlling the navy for the defence of the realm, in managing the ships (which belonged to

---

[336] *Demetrius's Case* (1614) BL MS. Add. 25213, fo. 168v. Cf. *Poynings's Case* (1454) YB Mich. 33 Hen. VI, fo. 28, pl. 1, where a sheriff returned to a writ of *capias* that the defendant had been imprisoned by two members of the Council 'for various causes touching the king himself'; the sheriff nevertheless brought the body. Coke CJ interpreted this to mean that it was a good return: *Ruswell's Case* (1615) 1 Rolle Rep. 192; Bryson, *Cases Concerning Equity*, ii. 453.

[337] *James Whitelocke's Case* (1613) PC 2/27, fo. 74; 33 APC 28, 211–19; *Letters and Life of Bacon*, iv. 348–56; 2 St. Tr. 765–8; Sir Julius Caesar's notes, BL MS. Lansdowne 160, fo. 83; *Liber Famelicus of Sir James Whitelocke*, ed. J. Bruce (70 Camden Soc., 1858), pp. 39–40, 113–18; Thompson, *Magna Carta*, pp. 281–3; G. Burgess, *The Politics of the Ancient Constitution* (1992), pp. 121–9; J. J. Epstein, 'Francis Bacon and the Challenge to the Prerogative in 1610' (1969) 2 *Journal of Historical Studies* 272–82; D. X. Powell, 'Why did James Whitelocke go to Jail in 1613?' (1995) 11 *Australian Journal of Law and Society* 169–90; idem, *Sir James Whitelocke's Liber Famelicus 1570–1632* (Bern, 2000), pp. 100–8.

[338] Above, p. 58.

him) and in correcting his own employees, and was therefore lawful. The Privy Council agreed, and gave Whitelocke a short custodial sentence for his effrontery.[339] Coke was present as chief justice, though it is not recorded what he thought of punishing a barrister for citing Magna Carta. As in the case of Nicholas Fuller,[340] it was not so much the reliance on the great charter which was punishable, but the perceived impudence of the manner in which it was done. Nevertheless, it was another ominous challenge to the independence of the Bar. Around the same time, Serjeant Harris and two fellow counsel seem to have been in trouble with the Privy Council for giving an opinion that no one ought to be imprisoned upon mere allegations made to the king before they were proved true; but they hastily qualified their opinion by explaining that this did not apply to offences against the state.[341]

Two years later Sir Samuel Saltonstall applied for a *habeas corpus* to challenge his imprisonment by the Privy Council, and it was held – citing the 1592 opinion – that 'Committed by command of the lord king's Privy Council' was a sufficient return without showing cause, for it was 'not fitting that *arcana imperii* should be disclosed'.[342] The question then arose whether he could be granted bail, but the court held that it could only be allowed in such cases upon the receipt of letters from the Privy Council, or from the attorney-general, which had to be entered of record. This had happened in the case of someone suspected of the gunpowder treason, and also in a case of 1598.[343] Coke confirmed that someone committed by the king could not be let to mainprise, and cited Staunford's interpretation that this extended to the Privy Council, 'who are the representative body of the king'.[344] He was

---

[339] Whitelocke had only just been released from prison for 'speaking too boldly against the Marshal Court' (i.e. the court of the earl marshal): Birch, *Court and Times*, i. 241 (10 June 1613); Powell, *Whitelocke's Liber Famelicus* (n. 337, above), pp. 107–8.

[340] Above, pp. 359–63.

[341] 33 APC 6–7. The others were Anthony Dyot, bencher of the Inner Temple, and Richard Godfrey, a recusant who managed to remain in active practice.

[342] *Sir Samuel Saltonstall's Case* (1615), sub. nom *Salkingstowe's Case*, 1 Rolle Rep. 219; sub nom. *Salterston's Case* (incorporated in the report of *Ruswell's Case*), Calth. MS. i. 374v (quotation tr.); Arthur Turnour's reports, HLS MS. 109, fos. 65–6 (substantially the same text as Calthorpe); Tourneur, fo. 2v. There was a decision to the same effect in *The Brewers' Company Case* (1615) 1 Rolle Rep. 134.

[343] *Harcourt's Case* (1598) KB 29/235, m. 62; above, p. 168. The record says only that the prisoner was bailed in a later term, '(tr.) as appears in the scroll of fines (*in scruetta finium*) for that term'.

[344] Calth. MS. i. 374v (tr.); W. Staunford, *Les Plees del Coron* (1574 edn), p. 72E. In 1628 Coke retracted this opinion in the Commons, saying he had been misled by Staunford, and that 1615 was 'an ill time . . . when there was clashing between the Court of Kings Bench and Chancery': 3 St. Tr. 81, 82.

perhaps already uneasy about it, because he recalled – he could hardly forget – 'a bill put in by Mr Morris [James Morice], attorney of the Court of Wards, in Parliament, in which it was desired that the statute of Magna Carta, chapter 29, might be explained, so that it could be known in what cases the Privy Council might imprison'.[345] That was unfinished business which Coke would have to resurrect when he returned to the Commons himself.

The Star Chamber

The Star Chamber was no more immune from Magna Carta than the king, whose council it was. When Coke was attorney-general, in 1602, a criminous barrister of the Inner Temple called Robert Pye, who was brought before the Star Chamber, relied on the statute of 25 Edw. III, 'that no free man should be imprisoned without judgment',[346] in support of his submission that he should not be condemned on his informal confession before bill and answer. The Star Chamber accepted this, and instructed Coke to inform against him at once.[347] The argument little assisted Pye's cause, since he was promptly convicted and sentenced to a heavy fine, pillory and loss of ears. The benchers of the Inner Temple, who had already disbarred and expelled him, were then calumniated for having admitted him to the Inn in the first place; they were told to stop calling barristers by the dozens and scores, since bad professors of the law were dangerous vermin. The Star Chamber had nevertheless acknowledged that even in cases devoid of merit they were bound to proceed in accordance with the rule of law. For the same reason, they were obliged to observe the principle against self-incrimination, by not examining defendants on oath as to alleged criminal conduct.[348]

Granted all this, it would still not have occurred to anyone that the Star Chamber might ever need correction from outside. It was invariably attended and advised by the chief justices, and on occasion a few

---

[345] Calth. MS. i. 374v (tr.). This was in 1593, when Coke was Speaker: above, p. 273.

[346] Presumably 25 Edw. III, stat. 5, c. 4; above, p. 50.

[347] *Att.-Gen.* ex rel. *Merrike* v. *Pye* (1602) Hawarde 129–33; differently reported in IT MS. Petyt 511.13, fos. 150 (omitting this aspect). Cf. Co. Inst. iv. 63 ('if his confession is too short, or otherwise than he mean, he may deny it, and then they cannot proceed against him but by bill or information, which is the fairest way').

[348] This was Coke's view, anyway: Gray, *Writ of Prohibition*, ii. 333, citing BL MS. Harley 4817, fo. 191.

puisnes as well,[349] and was responsible for overseeing its own conduct. Like the King's Bench, it sat notionally – and, unlike the King's Bench, sometimes actually – in the king's presence.[350] Coke treated it with the greatest respect throughout his career, and even in the 1620s wrote of it as 'the most honorable court (our Parliament only excepted) that is in the Christian world ... This court, the right institution and ancient orders thereof being observed, doth keep all England in quiet.'[351] But what if the right institution and ancient orders of the court were not observed? No other court could intervene directly; but the judges of the regular courts might nevertheless find themselves in the awkward situation of disagreeing with the government as to the limits of its power.

This question became the subject of a major collision between Coke and Bacon in 1614. Although Magna Carta was not mentioned in argument, the case was of considerable significance in the context of Coke's impending downfall. Richard and Thomas Brereton, and their late father's seductress Lady Townshend,[352] were convicted of forgery by the Star Chamber and ordered to pay £3,000 damages and £150 costs to the relators, Sir Richard Egerton and his children.[353] The Star Chamber had awarded damages occasionally since the 1580s, and as recently as 1612 had resolved – apparently with Coke's approval – that damages could be awarded for the malicious prosecution of a suit

---

[349] A Star Chamber reporter noted that on 2 July 1600, the last day of the legal year, there were twenty-one in attendance, only eleven of whom were members of the Privy Council and ten were judges: IT MS. Petyt 511.13, fo. 148. Similarly on 25 June 1602: ibid. 151v. But the last day was exceptional. The judges were expected to attend before going on circuit, to receive any directions from the lord keeper for communication to the country justices.

[350] Crompton, *Courts* (1594), fo. 35, said the queen was deemed always to be present. Egerton LK said in the Star Chamber a few years later that 'it is to be intended that the queen sitteth in the court, and that the lords sit there to deliver their opinions in the causes there heard, sincerely and according to their conscience, for the true informing of the prince': IT MS. Petyt 511.13, fo. 147v.

[351] Co. Inst. iv. 65. The first sentence may have been inspired by Bacon's remark, below.

[352] Dorothy Townshend, wife of Sir Henry Townshend, second justice of Chester. Barnes (p. 360) described her as 'a courtesan of no mean talent'.

[353] *Att.-Gen. ex rel. Egerton v. Brereton and Townshend* (Trin. 1614) CUL MS. Hh.2.2, fos. 142–5 (passages tr.); CUL MS. Mm.1.21, fo. 222v; MS. Gg.5.6, fo. 141v (both the same); BL MS. Add. 25223, fos. 194v–198; HLS MS. 5052, fo. 60v. Much of the background is set out in T. G. Barnes, 'A Cheshire Seductress, Precedent, and a "Sore Blow" to Star Chamber' in *On the Laws and Customs of England: Essays in Honor of Samuel E. Thorne*, ed. M. S. Arnold and others (Chapel Hill, 1981), pp. 359–82. Barnes did not know of these law reports.

there;[354] but it was uncertain how to enforce payment, since in theory
the court could only adjudicate *in personam* and could not award
execution against lands or goods. Francis Bacon now argued, as
attorney-general, that the court could levy damages and costs on the
defendants' lands and goods, that Sir Henry Townshend was liable for
the damages and costs awarded against his wife, and that the Star
Chamber could stay proceedings by the defendants in all other courts
until they paid the damages and costs which it had awarded. He began
by extolling the court, saying it was 'the great net of the realm to catch
all fish, great and small', and that no court in the Christian world was
of such consequence. There were precedents back to Henry VII's time,
and precedents were *lex terrae*.[355] Henry Finch of Gray's Inn, for the
defendants, pointed out that none of the precedents was in point
because they did not relate to awards of damages. That was the essence
of the case. But Finch was followed by William Holt, also of Gray's
Inn, a Lancastrian member of Parliament, who tried to turn it into a
major constitutional question:

> We give all power to the king, albeit such as is bound by law and reason
> (meaning in this court), and not unlimited as Mr Attorney has shown and
> endeavoured to prove. I embrace such precedents as agree with reason
> and the common law which I profess, but if any precedent passes reason
> I do not acknowledge it. Whereas Mr Attorney has said that precedents
> are *suprema lex* here, I think that *salus populi* should be *suprema lex*.

Lord Ellesmere here interrupted him and warned him to be careful how
he spoke so inadvisedly of the supreme law and the king's prerogative.
Holt nevertheless went on in the same vein, until he was ordered to
speak to the question or be silent. Bacon remarked sneeringly that he
was like a sealed dove, which flew the higher the more it was blind-
folded. No serjeant at law, he said, would speak with such audacity. Holt
persisted, saying that he expected to be shown precedents where sentences had been executed, and there were none. He also asserted that
the power of the Star Chamber had much increased since it was

---

[354] *Hersey's Case* (1612) 12 Co. Rep. 103; dated from the French text in LI MS. Maynard 80,
fo. 71v. Cf. *Anon.* (1614) Calth. MS. i. 313v, where Coke CJ said that a person who was
scandalised by a bill in Chancery, if not a party, or if the matter was outside the
jurisdiction of the court, could bring an action on the case; in other words, the privilege
of a plaintiff was lost by abusing the process.

[355] For this proposition he artfully cited *Slade's Case* (1602) 4 Co. Rep. 91, in which he had
lost to Coke when they were at the Bar.

introduced by statute in 1487. Now he had made a historical blunder, and Coke was quick to correct him by observing that it was a much older common-law jurisdiction. Sir Julius Caesar then spoke of its antiquity and of the importance of precedents, which he thought supported Bacon. But Caesar was not a common lawyer and was too ready to be taken in.

The three common-law judges present were all against Bacon. Croke J. said that it was the greatest case that had ever come under the consideration of the court. To speak of the dignity of the Star Chamber would, he said, be 'to gild gold'. It was the hammer of wrongdoers (*malleus deliquentium*), and the court had existed as long as any government had been: even so, he did not think the precedents supported Bacon, and he 'staggered' at the suggestion that lands should be bound by its decrees. Hobart CJ spoke to the same effect; the Star Chamber was not for *meum et tuum*, and damages were to be sought in other courts. Coke followed him. In a typical display of transparent historical legerdemain, he prefaced his remarks with the assertion that the Star Chamber antedated the Norman Conquest: this was evident because the King's Council was mentioned in writs, and the Register of Writs existed before the Conquest.[356] There was no harm in stressing the tribunal's antiquity, but the good point was blurred by a lapse of historical judgment worse than Holt's. Coke's main point, however, was that – although Bacon had 'done his best with eloquence' – none of the precedents came near to his submission. If Bacon was right, the plaintiff would be in a better position than the king, for no fine to the king was ever enforced in the Star Chamber,[357] and the reason (said Coke) was 'because here is like the law of the Medes and Persians: neither appeal nor error lie here'. In any case Egerton was only a relator, not a party, which meant that neither he nor the king could recover damages in the

---

[356] A comprehensive Register of Writs was itself a fiction of the legal imagination, like the 'statute-book'. The notion that it had never changed was obviously nonsense, and Coke himself acknowledged that some writs had been added, e.g. those which mentioned Magna Carta and other Acts of Parliament: see above, pp. 352–3; Garnett, 'Prefaces to Coke's Reports', 281. But even Coke's premise that it originated before the Conquest was not generally accepted. In 1597 Anderson CJ said that the Register was later than *Bracton*, because it dated from the time of Edward I, whereas *Bracton* was from Henry III's time: BL MS. Harley 1575, fo. 27v. In the same year, John Dodderidge provided a historical account of it in his argument in *Slade's Case*, BL MS. Harley 6809, fo. 46.

[357] If a party was fined by the Star Chamber, he could be imprisoned until the fine was estreated in the Exchequer: see the report in CUL MS. Mm.1.21, fo. 222v.

case: 'and so we are in a dilemma'. As to the husband's liability for his wife, Coke said the contrary position was so clear that it was not worthy to be spoken to. There was a difference between civil and criminal cases; a husband was liable for his wife in civil cases, but not in the criminal sphere. That had been decided in cases concerning recusant wives.[358] Bacon's third motion was 'fearful', since a party might be ruined by the waste and destruction of his property and have no remedy.[359] Secretary Winwood agreed with Caesar, and so did Lord Zouche, but Lord Knollys agreed with the judges.[360] The bishop of London and the archbishop of Canterbury admitted they were not lawyers, but that did not deter them from venturing the opinion that Bacon was right. Lord Ellesmere ended the discussion by saying that precedents made law; it was true that the court could not determine title to land, but the Chancery meddled with possession, and so could the Star Chamber. The husband had to be charged with the wife's fine, since the wife had nothing with which to pay; if he were not liable, he could leave his wife in prison indefinitely and she would have no means of being discharged, which would be a kind of divorce. Bacon thus won by a majority, against the unanimous opinion of the three judges, and execution was issued accordingly. It was a successful piece of extra-parliamentary legislation, and a direct affront to the judiciary, since the vote was carried by the non-professional members of the court. Probably even more significant at the time was Bacon's victory over the lord chief justice. The case was alluded to in the king's speech in the Star Chamber in 1616,[361] probably at the prompting of Bacon,[362] and was another black mark against Coke.

---

[358] See *Dr Foster's Case* (1614) 11 Co. Rep. 56 at fo. 61; cf. *R. v. Law* (1615) 3 Bulst. 87; 1 Rolle Rep. 233. Coke reported a conference on this subject with Egerton, then attorney-general, at Puckering LK's house in 1593, BL MS. Harley 6686A, fo. 54v. This may be the case referred to in 23 APC 182, 193.

[359] The three judges are said to have agreed that suits in the Star Chamber could be stayed, but not those in other courts: see the report in CUL MS. Mm.1.21, fo. 222v.

[360] The report in CUL MS. Hh.2.2 says Lord Zouche was the lay dissentient.

[361] Below, p. 420. Thompson, *Magna Carta*, p. 264, did not understand the allusion because she was unaware of the 1614 case.

[362] Bacon complained in 1616 that in this case Coke had 'bent all his strength and wits to have prevailed, and so did the other judges by long and laborious arguments; and if they had prevailed the authority of the court had been overthrown': *Letters and Life of Bacon*, vi. 91. See also below, p. 426.

Benevolences

There was another case in which Magna Carta failed to prevail. Perhaps the lowest point of Coke's judicial career was his capitulation in the case of benevolences in 1615. The king had dissolved the 'Addled Parliament' in 1614 and had no intention of calling another,[363] but this deprived him of the usual means of obtaining revenue. It was therefore decided, with considerable trepidation on the part of his advisers, including Bacon, to seek a benevolence. This was not a new idea,[364] and everyone knew that it was only a superficial pretence that the contributions would be free gifts from loving subjects. When the king's letters were received at Malmesbury, in Wiltshire, in October 1614, an obscure local gentleman called Oliver St John not only declined to pay but wrote a brave reply saying that it was against chapter 29 of Magna Carta, since it tended to the destruction of the subject, and also against the second statute of Richard III (1484),[365] and that it was unreasonable for the common people to be forced to provide what Parliament had denied. Most unwisely, he added that those who had so acted against Magna Carta had incurred the automatic excommunication imposed by the statute of Edward I, that it was against the king's coronation oath, and that the king might do well to remember the fate of Richard II.[366] The writer was not the lawyer Oliver St John who in the next reign resisted ship money on similar grounds. Indeed, he seems not to have been a member of the inns of court at all.[367] But he knew his law, and if he had framed his letter more circumspectly it is difficult to imagine that Coke would have disagreed with it. It was a sufficiently cogent argument to cause consternation in the government. Ellesmere even grumbled that it threatened the onset of democracy.[368] St John was in consequence arrested, sent to the Tower and in Easter term 1615 brought before the Star Chamber. He did not deny writing the letter but sought to justify its contents. Bacon conducted the prosecution with all the intemperance expected of him, likening the offence to treason. The essence of Bacon's case was the disingenuous assertion that the benevolence really was voluntary, and was

---

[363] The failure to pass any bills caused some legal debate whether it was truly a parliament at all. Coke CJ thought not: 2 Bulst. 235, 237.

[364] Above, pp. 185–6.   [365] 1 Ric. III, c. 2; above, p. 185.

[366] The letter is printed in 2 St. Tr. 900.

[367] The Oliver St John of Wiltshire who was admitted to Lincoln's Inn from New Inn in 1580 was the future Viscount Grandison. The writer of the letter is distinguished in one contemporary source as 'Black Oliver': Birch, *Court and Times*, i. 291.

[368] Brooks, *Law, Politics and Society*, p. 145, citing papers in the Huntington Library.

therefore not what the statute of 1484 had referred to as 'an exaction or imposition *called* a benevolence'.[369] Egerton agreed that the offence could have been treated as treason, because of the comparison with Richard II, if the king had not directed a more merciful course. It was impossible, he said, for a free man be 'destroyed' by benevolences, because supporting the king was for the safety of the realm, and therefore there was no infringement of Magna Carta. It was untrue to say that Parliament had previously denied to grant a subsidy; it had only been under consideration when it became necessary to dissolve the session because members of the Commons were speaking against the king. To the general surprise, Coke agreed.[370] He said the king's letters did not import an exaction, but rather an entreaty. There were historical examples of benevolences, some of which were admittedly illegal,[371] but (according to Coke) all the judges in 1598 had held them to be lawful provided they were truly voluntary.[372] St John, he said, had shown his ignorance by citing chapter 29 as if the law could ever destroy a man, whereas Bracton said that neither the law nor the judge destroyed a man, but only wrongdoing.[373] And he had omitted to cite a passage which worked against him. If only St John had cast his eyes on the last part of the charter, he would have found mention of a fifteenth given to the king by way of benevolence.[374] This was hardly a satisfactory judicial response to St John, but his reliance on Magna Carta had somehow to be defused. Even more remarkably, Coke dismissed the statute of Richard III as made by a usurper. It could not take away the inheritance of the crown, since the acts of a king de facto were binding only when they suppressed mischief or regulated

---

[369] His speech is in *Letters and Life of Bacon*, v. 132–51; 2 St. Tr. 902. The editors of *State. Trials*, and Spedding, thought it was the only remnant of the case. But there are full reports of the hearing, including the remarks of Coke CJ, in Calth. MS. ii. 6–8v; and in BL MS. Harley 3209, fos. 47–9. There is also a brief note in Noy 105.

[370] The surprise is evident from a letter of Bacon's, in which he remarked that it was a pity Coke had not agreed earlier: *Letters and Life of Bacon*, v. 83. In 1616 Bacon complained that Coke had at first opposed levying or even asking for contributions, 'and gave opinion that the king by his great seal could not so much as move any his subjects for benevolence. But this he retracted after in the Star Chamber; but it marred the benevolence in the mean time': ibid. vi. 92.

[371] In particular those of 1523–4 (above, p. 185): Calth. MS. ii. 8.

[372] The case is not in Coke's notebooks for 1598, but is mentioned among the precedents set out in the note 'Exaction of Benevolence' (1614) 12 Co. Rep. 119 (undated in print); the French version in IT MS. Misc. 21, fo. 76, is dated Pas. 12 Jac. [1614], which was just before St John's case.

[373] Calth. MS. ii. 7v. The aphorism ('neque lex neque judex destruunt hominem sed proprie transgressiones') has not, however, been found in *Bracton*.

[374] The charter only said 'have given' (*dederunt*). There is no mention of 'benevolence'.

matters between subjects.[375] The whole court agreed to fine St John the enormous sum of £5,000. Of course, he never paid it, but it secured an obsequious written recantation which was directed to be read at the assizes throughout the country. Even if St John had in truth given expression to respectable popular sentiments[376] – perhaps especially because he had done so – he had clearly gone too far. That may be why Coke did not choose to take a stand at that time. Coke was in difficulties enough over his support for other unworthy parties on points of principle,[377] and was engulfed in so much controversy by 1615 that he may have started to pick his quarrels more carefully. If so, it was too late.

---

[375] He was no doubt anxious to distinguish the immediately preceding statute, 1 Ric. III, c. 1, concerning uses.

[376] See the imaginary dialogue written by Sir Walter Raleigh in response to the case: J. R. Tanner, *Constitutional Documents of the Reign of James I* (Cambridge, 1930), pp. 264–5.

[377] Baker, *Collected Papers*, i. 490–2, 495–7; below, pp. 415–20.

10

A Year 'Consecrate to Justice': 1616

The year 1616 was one of the most fraught and significant in the history of the English legal system, as was only too evident to those living at the time. Bacon told the king it was 'a year consecrate to justice',[1] though many contemporaries saw it in a harsher light. It was dominated by the most serious of all the jurisdictional clashes during Coke's judicial career, that between the King's Bench and the Chancery, which was to a large extent a conflict between Coke's view of the legal system and Ellesmere's. It was long misunderstood by posterity as being a clash between law and equity, but contemporaries saw it as being a battle over the absolute prerogative, embodied in this instance by the lord chancellor. And it was paralleled in 1616 by another great case concerning the prerogative, the final straw which broke the king's patience irretrievably. As a consequence of these two thunderstorms, James was persuaded in November to accept Bacon's advice and remove Coke from the seat of justice. Many lawyers thought the common law itself was in mortal danger.

Ellesmere and the Court of Chancery[2]

The dispute between Coke and Ellesmere was not about the need for the equitable jurisdiction of the Chancery, which was both ancient and necessary. Coke never questioned that it was part of the *lex terrae* or that the relatively informal inquisitorial procedure used by the Chancery qualified as due process of law. He was occasionally a suitor there himself, he had practised at its bar, and as a judge he sometimes assisted

---

[1] *Letters and Life of Bacon*, v. 349.
[2] For the matter in this section see J. H. Baker, 'The Common Lawyers and the Chancery: 1616' (1969) reprinted in *Collected Papers*, i. 481–512; G. W. Thomas, 'James I, Equity and Lord Keeper Williams' (1976) 91 EHR 506–28; L. A. Knafla, *Law and Politics in Jacobean England: The Tracts of Lord Chancellor Ellesmere* (1977), pp. 123–81; Brooks, *Law, Politics and Society*, pp. 142–52; Smith, *Sir Edward Coke*, pp. 213–48.

its deliberations. 'The chancellor', said Coke, 'is the sole judge in matters of equity, and the Chancery is the warehouse of justice (*officina justiciae*), to which a man may have resort at any time ... and wherever the chancellor is, there is the Chancery.'[3]

The points disputed in 1616 were not new, because they had been raised and seemingly settled by the assembled judges in the previous reign.[4] The problem was that Ellesmere did not accept the judges' right to determine them. The equity of the Chancery derived from the king's absolute power.[5] The chancellor was, as Ellesmere told the king, 'keeper of the king's conscience, and therefore whatsoever the king directed in any case he would decree accordingly'.[6] This was where he and Coke differed profoundly. Although equity was not regular law, but an 'arbitrary disposition' entrusted by the king to the chancellor,[7] the lord chancellor was not free to do whatever he wished. He could not interfere with title to freehold property or other matters determinable at common law;[8] he could not lock people up without lawful cause; he could not proceed contrary to natural justice;[9] and he could not prevent the enforcement of judgments rendered by the king's courts, unless they were obtained in defiance of a prior decree. These propositions were seemingly enshrined in parliamentary legislation, the first two in chapter 29 of Magna Carta and the third in the statute of 1402.[10] Yet, whereas the first proposition was generally accepted by the Chancery, the other two were not.

The high point of contention was the means of keeping the Chancery within its bounds. Ellesmere considered himself answerable directly to the king.[11] Coke, however, adhered to the theory he had advanced while

---

[3] *Ruswell's Case* (1615) Calth. MS. i. 374v.
[4] *Throckmorton v. Finch* (1597) above, pp. 285–8.   [5] Cf. YB Trin. 9 Edw. IV, fo. 14, pl. 9.
[6] 'Dangerous and Absurd Opinions' in Coke's autograph notebook, CUL MS. Ii.5.21, fo. 47v. The notion that the chancellor was keeper of the king's conscience seems to have been no older than the Elizabethan period: T. F. T. Plucknett, *Concise History of the Common Law* (5th edn, 1956), p. 180 n. 2. Hake said that equity derived from the conscience of the chancellor as the king's representative, and that the chancellor was the king's mouth and the Chancery the king's heart: *Epieikeia* (1603), pp. 121–2, 138, 140.
[7] *Martin v. Marshall* (1615) Hob. 63, *per* Hitcham sjt.
[8] See, e.g., *Fowler v. Wright* (1614) 1 Rolle Rep. 71; *Cases concerning Equity and the Courts of Equity*, ed. W. H. Bryson, Vol. ii (118 SS, 2001), p. 437.
[9] Coke complained that Ellesmere had awarded injunctions against Magdalene College (Hospital), Colchester and Benjamin Clere, without any bill or answer: Coke, 'Dangerous and Absurd Opinions', no. 10.
[10] 4 Hen. IV, c. 23; above, p. 213.
[11] Coke, 'Dangerous and Absurd Opinions', no. 3 (tr. 'that the chancellor ought not to be judged by any judge of the law, but by the king alone').

attorney-general, that all authority under the king was subject to the survey of the King's Bench, the king's highest ordinary court of law. He found in the anonymous treatise *Diversité de Courtes*, written in the time of Henry VIII, the opinion that a prohibition would lie to the Chancery, and he announced this discovery in 1613 in open court.[12] He was never invited to award such a prohibition, and might have hesitated long before doing so, but the other prerogative writ was not in form directed against access to the court: *habeas corpus* focused on the person of the prisoner and the need for good cause to be shown for his detention.

There were precedents for issuing *habeas corpus* in respect of prisoners of the Chancery, and it was potentially a suitable remedy for dealing with both the matters in contention. Since the Chancery – like the Star Chamber – acted *in personam*, it could not impose a pecuniary penalty, but it could imprison a recalcitrant party;[13] the imprisonment could then be challenged by *habeas corpus* and the return examined. The Chancery tried to evade such challenges by returning a committal by the lord chancellor in general terms.[14] General returns had been held insufficient in Elizabethan times,[15] and the precedents were remembered, but in 1609 the Common Pleas under Coke had hesitated and the question was left undecided.[16] Their effectiveness was fully aired in 1615. A litigant called Ruswell was committed to the Fleet Prison by Ellesmere, and the return to his *habeas corpus* said he had been committed by the Court of Chancery 'for a contempt to the same court there committed', without specifying the cause.[17] George Croke, who

---

[12] *Jenour v. Alexander* (1613) Godb. 208 (printed as 'Jenoar'). Cf. *Warner v. Suckerman and Coates* (1615) 3 Bulst. 119 at p. 120 ('there is not any court in Westminster Hall but may be by us here prohibited if they do exceed their jurisdictions'). He also took the view that *praemunire* was available: below, p. 419 n. 55.

[13] See Thomas Hedley's speech in the Commons (1610) on impositions: *Proc. Parl. 1610*, ii. 193. For the Star Chamber see above, p. 404.

[14] The Chancery also claimed the power to override a *habeas corpus* by writ of *supersedeas*, but this was denied by the King's Bench: *Anon.* (1612) BL MS. Lansdowne 1110, fo. 4; Bryson, *Cases Concerning Equity*, ii. 399 (where a sheriff was fined for obeying the *supersedeas*).

[15] Above, p. 162.

[16] *Addis's Case* (1609) Cro. Eliz. 219; BL MS. Add. 25209, fo. 120; MS. Harley 1679, fo. 124; CUL MS. Hh.2.2, fo. 2v (all the same); BL MS. Hargrave 52, fos. 5v–6; CUL MS. Gg.5.6, fo. 83 (abridged).

[17] *Ruswell's Case* (1615) 1 Rolle Rep. 192, 218, 219; more fully reported in Calth. MS. i. 371v, 374v; Tourneur, fo. 2v; Arthur Turnour's reports, HLS MS. 109, fos. 65–6; BL MS. Harley 1692, fos. 55v–56; MS. Add. 25211, fo. 146; Bryson, *Cases Concerning Equity*, ii. 453–67.

complained that he was being 'watched',[18] objected on behalf of Ruswell that this was too general. Coke ruled that the King's Bench had juris-diction, for reasons reminiscent of those he had set out in his treatise on chapter 29:[19]

> The common law of England gives to every subject a remedy for his lands, his goods, and his liberty, and just as it gives an action for his lands and goods when they are taken away, so it gives in some cases a writ of false imprisonment and other actions for the restraint of his liberty if it be unjust; and the court of King's Bench has power to write for the body of a man in any place in England, and may discharge him from the imprison-ment if it finds the cause to be unlawful, though if the cause be just they are to remand him.

The lord chancellor had two powers: an ordinary power, whereby he proceeded according to the common law,[20] and an extraordinary power whereby he could commit persons to prison. In respect of the extraordin-ary power the Chancery was not a court of record, and so a writ of error did not lie. It was held on this ground that it was insufficient to return a committal by the lord chancellor, without more.[21] Here the return said it was 'by the court', and 'for a contempt', but that was not sufficiently specific to make a difference. Instead of releasing the prisoner, however, the court allowed the return to be amended so as to set out the decree. The question then raised was whether the return was bad because it did not specify the length of the sentence of imprisonment, since for all that appeared to the court it might be for twenty years. Coke said that if the cause of committal did not appear from the return to be unlawful, the court ought to remand him, since issue could not be taken between the judges and the person who made the return as to whether the cause

---

Cf. *Apsley's Case* (1615) 1 Rolle Rep. 192; Moo. 840; *Cases Concerning Equity*, ii. 468; this was very similar and was argued at the same time.

[18] BL MS. Harley 1692, fo. 55v (not MS. Harley 1691 as cited in Baker, *Collected Papers*, i. 492 n. 53): (tr.) 'Croke said before he spoke in this cause that this return was made by great advice, and it was deemed that no one would speak against it; and he said that from the beginning when he spoke in this court he had been watched, but out of his duty to the court he would speak'.

[19] Calth. MS. i. 371v (tr.). Cf. 1 Rolle Rep. 192, *per* Coke CJ: (tr.) 'there is more reason that a man should have a remedy for his person than for his goods'.

[20] I.e. on the Latin side of the Chancery. For the origin of this passage about the two powers of the chancellor, and a collection of year-book authorities suggesting the limits of his authority, see Coke's commonplace book, BL MS. 6687A, fo. 233v.

[21] He cited *Astwick's Case* (1567) and *Mychell's Case* (1577) above, p. 162 n. 103. These were evidently verified from the King's Bench controlment rolls: Moo. 839.

was good.[22] He also considered whether it was necessary for the court to see the Chancery bill and pleadings.[23] The several reports vary considerably as to the opinions expressed, and the explanation may be that Coke was exploring different ways of looking at the case as the argument progressed. The end result was inconclusive. After further argument in chambers, perhaps to avoid counsel being 'watched', Ruswell was remanded while the court took advisement. No judgment is recorded, though in a similar case in 1616 the court held insufficient a general return of a committal for contempt in not obeying an order of the Chancery.[24]

Coke had not, in *Ruswell's Case*, shown himself to be implacably opposed to the Chancery, but a seemingly much clearer situation (from the King's Bench point of view), and for that reason more hotly controverted, was that of interference with judgments. The assembled judges had decided in 1597 that the Chancery could not prevent successful plaintiffs at law by injunction from enforcing their judgments, because it would be contrary to the enactment of 1402 that judgments should be inviolate, and also (according to Coke) against Magna Carta.[25] The King's Bench had applied the same principle to lesser courts of equity,[26] and it adhered to the view that it bound the High Court of Chancery as well.[27] The Common Pleas under Coke had naturally taken the same view.[28] An attempt was even made to put the matter beyond dispute by Act of Parliament in 1614, but the bill fell with the parliament.[29] The judges did not mean to deny a remedy in

---

[22] 1 Rolle Rep. 193.

[23] BL MS. Harley 1692, fo. 55v. This was in response to Croke's argument that it did not appear from the decree whether the Chancery had any jurisdiction in the original suit.

[24] *Boulton's Case* (1616) Calth. MS. ii. 113. Here the court was informed that Boulton had been enjoined not to continue with an action of debt, but he had nevertheless continued it to judgment; the imprisonment was for disobeying the decree. But he had already served two years, which was deemed long enough for a contempt.

[25] *Throckmorton v. Finch* (1597) above, pp. 285–8. Coke CJ said in *Glanvill's Case* (1615) Calth. MS. i. 307v, that the point had also been resolved by all the judges of England in the *Earl of Southampton's Case*, for which no date was given; he followed this citation with *Throckmorton v. Finch*.

[26] Above, pp. 213, 303, 381, 384, 388.

[27] *Browne v. Heath* (Mich. 1613) BL MS. Add. 25213, fo. 159; cf. *Heath v. Ridley* (1614) opposite, n. 32.

[28] *Bride's Case* (1612) CUL MS. Mm.1.21, fo. 201; probably the same as *Anon.* (1612) CUL MS. Hh.2.2., fo. 80v; Bryson, *Cases Concerning Equity*, ii. 405.

[29] On 31 May 1614 Nicholas Fuller introduced a bill 'against the Chancery', and another was brought in the next day by Sir Jerome Horsey for subjects to be in 'common peace'

equity, but held that a party should seek it before the action at law reached the point of judgment. Equity, like law, was supposed to protect the vigilant but not the sluggish,[30] the interests of the latter being outweighed by the paramount principle of public policy – embodied in the statute of 1402 – that judgments in courts of record should be final. Lord Ellesmere however, had never accepted that limitation on his jurisdiction, and the dispute flared up in three cases in 1614 and 1615.[31] In the first case Coke gave judgment in defiance of a Chancery injunction, and expressed wonder that no one brought a criminal information against a party who exhibited a bill in Chancery after judgment.[32] The second case was that of a rogue called Richard Glanvill, who was imprisoned by the Chancery in 1613 for not performing a decree ordering him to release a judgment which had been affirmed on a writ of error. He was discharged upon *habeas corpus* in Michaelmas term 1614, on the authority of *Cobb* v. *Nore* (1465) and *Throckmorton* v. *Finch* (1597).[33] Coke remarked, 'As long as I have this coif upon my head I will not allow this.'[34] Glanvill was then imprisoned again by Lord Ellesmere on 7 May 1615, and applied for a second *habeas corpus*. This time the return was general, not mentioning any cause at all, and the court showed no hesitation in rejecting it.[35] But the lord chancellor had the trump card. He ordered Glanvill to be arrested a third time by a pursuivant, thinking that he was not a known

---

after judgment, but the parliament ended without any bills being passed: *Proc. Parl. 1614*, pp. 388, 407, 413, 418.

[30] Coke was fond of this maxim, in relation to law: *Bevil's Case* (1583) 4 Co. Rep. 8, at fo. 10; *Smith* v. *Mills* (1589) 2 Co. Rep. 25 at fo. 26; *Corbet's Case* (1599) 4 Co. Rep. 81, at fo. 82; Co. Inst. ii. 690. On the other hand, fifteenth-century chancellors had declared that the Chancery would protect the foolish: *OHLE*, vi. 42.

[31] In the time of Fleming CJ it had been decided that the Chancery could not interfere with a King's Bench judgment by *audita querela*: *Scriven* v. *Wright* (1612) 2 Bulst. 10. This remained an issue: *Mostyn* v. *Pierce* (1616) Moo. 850.

[32] *Heath* v. *Ridley* (1614) 2 Bulst. 194; Cro. Jac. 335; sub nom. *Heath* v. *Heath*, Bryson, *Cases Concerning Equity*, ii. 434, no. 220 (from HLS MS. 105, fo. 184).

[33] *Courtney* v. *Glanvill* (Pas.-Mich. 1614) Cro Jac. 343; Moo. 838; 2 Bulst. 301 (dated Hil. 1615); Calth. MS. i. 307v; BL MS. Harley 1767, fo. 37; MS. Harley 4265, fo. 75v; MS. Add. 25213, fo. 162; Bryson, *Cases Concerning Equity*, ii. 440–3; Baker, *Collected Papers*, i. 490–1.

[34] 1 Rolle Rep. 111.

[35] *Glanvill's Case* (Trin. 1615) 1 Rolle Rep. 219; BL MS. Lansdowne 1110, ff. 28v–29; MS. Stowe 296, fo. 59; MS. Add. 25213, fo. 176; MS. Add. 46410, fo. 198; CUL MS. Gg.2.31, fos. 232–3; IT MS. Barrington 29, fo. 113; HLS MS. 1034, fo 122; MS. 1035, fo. 296; MS. 2024; Bryson, *Cases Concerning Equity*, ii. 443–4.

official to whom a *habeas corpus* could be sent.[36] Coke might well have been up to that challenge,[37] but the case was overtaken by that of Dr Gooch (or Googe), master of Magdalene College, Cambridge, who had just been committed to prison by the Chancery in connection with the *Earl of Oxford's Case*.[38] The earl of Oxford and others had sued Gooch and the fellows of his college in Chancery in respect of a title which had been settled by verdict and judgment in an ejectment action (*Warren v. Smith*); the lands were different, but the title was the same. The defendants demurred to the bill, relying on the statute of 1402, but the masters certified that this was an insufficient answer – apparently because the lands were not the same – and the defendants were ordered to answer, which they refused to do. Lord Ellesmere allowed the plaintiffs to continue their suit in default of an answer, explaining that the Chancery would not meddle with the judgment at law but only with the corrupt conscience of the party.[39]

At the same time, Ellesmere set about collecting precedents and arguments in defence of his jurisdiction, with the assistance of Bacon and the other king's counsel, for the information of the king and the Privy Council. The law officers advised that there was a 'strong current of practice of proceedings in Chancery after judgment' since the time of Henry VII, and that it had been upheld on demurrer.[40] The justification for the practice was set out in the form of a 'breviate' (or brief) for the king's counsel, attributed to Ellesmere, which was widely circulated.[41] Although Magna Carta seems not to have been cited in the latest cases, it was thought vital that its spell be warded off at the outset.

---

[36] Bodl. Lib. MS. Rawlinson C.382, fo. 71; printed in Bryson, *Cases Concerning Equity*, ii. 442 at p. 443.

[37] There was a remedy by the writ *de homine replegiando*: below, Appendix 6, at p. 497.

[38] For the principal case, which has been misunderstood by posterity, see D. Ibbetson, 'The Earl of Oxford's Case (1615)' in *Landmark Cases in Equity*, ed. C. Mitchell and Mitchell (Oxford 2012), pp. 1–32. It had almost been resolved by Act of Parliament in 1614: *Proc. Parl. 1614*, p. 227 (a bill to confirm the college's title).

[39] This was the argument he had made in *Throckmorton v. Finch* (1597) above, p. 287.

[40] CUL MS. Gg.2.31, fos. 236–41 (opinions of the law officers, with the letters to them from Ellesmere); *Letters and Life of Bacon*, v. 385–95. The demurrer must have been in Chancery.

[41] 'A breviate or direction for the king's learned counsel collected by the Lord Chancellor Ellesmere' (dated September 1615) *CELMC*, p. 269 (listing 29 manuscripts); printed as *The Priviledge and Prerogatives of the High Court of Chancery* (1641) and in 1 Cha. Rep. 20–48; *Collectanea Juridica*, ed. F. Hargrave (1792), pp. 35–53; *Letters and Life of Bacon*, v. 381–95; L. A. Knafla, *Law and Politics in Tudor England* (Cambridge, 1977), pp. 319–36.

The Ellesmere brief therefore began with an essay on chapter 29, which it said had been 'urged and stood upon against the Chancery', and also on the statutes of due process.[42] Ellesmere's argument was that 'those that are sued in the Chancery are brought in to answer by due process of law for cases of equity and conscience, and that is *per legem terrae*'.[43] Justice did not rest solely in the strict application of legal rules, for *summum jus est summa injuria*,[44] and even common-law judges frequently used their discretion to prevent injustices arising from strict procedures. The common law had always allowed the Court of Chancery its proceedings in cases of equity, and many judges had themselves been litigants there. The Chancery did not 'commonly' send injunctions to the judges ordering them to desist from doing justice, but only enjoined parties not to take unconscionable advantage of the strictness of the law. This was equally true of suits brought after judgment, and the 'new concepts ... lately imagined' that parties should complain in Chancery before judgment, by reason of the statute of 1402, were 'but a cavil and sophistical distinction not worth the answering'. He drew attention to actions of ejectment, in which questions of title could be revisited after a first trial at law and judgment; this was a good point, especially in relation to Dr Gooch's case, and seems not to have been raised in the reported cases.[45] But he made no mention of the decision of all the judges of England in *Throckmorton* v. *Finch*. Perhaps it was thought too wrong to bother with.[46]

---

[42] The first part was entitled 'Some notes and observations upon the statute of Magna Carta, c. 29, and other statutes concerning the proceedings in the Chancery in causes of equity and conscience', and the second was 'Some notes and observations upon the Statutes of Provisors and *Praemunire*, especially concerning the proceedings in the Court of Chancery and other courts of equity'. Briefs on *praemunire* were also written by William Hakewill and John Davies: Brooks, *Law, Politics and Society*, p. 148.

[43] Unknown to Ellesmere, Coke had fully accepted this point in 1604 in his memorandum on c. 29: below, p. 501.

[44] Extreme right (i.e. excessive rigour in applying law) is extreme wrong. The aphorism was coined by Cicero but had become common currency in relation to equity: see, e.g., Plowd. 161v; Hake, *Epieikeia*, p. 17.

[45] Coke had himself identified it as an abuse without a legal remedy: *La Huictieme Part des Reports* (1611), preface, sig. Aii–v. It was the Chancery which eventually provided the remedy.

[46] It is not prominent in the reports of the recent cases either, though it was cited in *Glanvill's Case* in 1615 (above, p. 415). Even if the decision had not been generally publicised in 1597, it is difficult to explain why Coke himself did not make more of it in 1615.

Gooch was committed by Lord Ellesmere for contempt on 31 October 1615, and brought his *habeas corpus*.[47] The writ was returned that he had been committed for not obeying the order, and Serjeant Bawtrey submitted that this was contrary to the statute of 1402. Coke and Dodderidge J. said that it would 'tend to the downfall of the common law if judgments here given should be suffered to be called in question in courts of equity'.[48] But it did not appear from the return whether the bill in Chancery was for the same cause as the action in the King's Bench, and so the court required a copy of the bill and answer to be brought in for consideration. Examination of the pleadings showed clearly that the title was the same. Coke said, provocatively, that 'the court of King's Bench is the school of the law and ought to correct the abuses of other courts', but he acknowledged that it had become 'dangerous for any counsel to speak in this business',[49] and it seems that he himself either doubted the merits or had been troubled by the king's command to end the jurisdictional disputes.[50] The parties were bailed until the next term, and Coke said it would be best if they heard no more of it, though he let drop in passing that 'it would be well done to commit Wood, who prosecuted this bill there after judgment'.[51] The case was never moved again.[52]

There things might have been left, had not indictments been preferred in the King's Bench in 1616 by Glanvill, and a still less salubrious litigant called Allen,[53] against their opponents' counsel, together with several clerks and masters of the Chancery, for a *praemunire*, in that they had participated in procuring relief for parties in Chancery after adverse judgments at common law.[54] Glanvill had even suggested bringing a *praemunire* against Ellesmere himself, and went as far as drawing an indictment, but his most prominent target in reality was Ellesmere's favourite, Mr Serjeant Moore. It was suspected that Coke may have been behind the prosecutions, since he had in the past drawn attention to the availability of *praemunire* for impugning the judgments of the

---

[47] *Dr Gooch's Case* (1615) 1 Rolle Rep. 277; 3 Bulst. 115; Calth. MS. ii. 57v; BL MS. Lansdowne 1110, fo. 29v (printed in Bryson, *Cases Concerning Equity*, ii. 448); Baker, *Collected Papers*, i. 493–4; *CELMC*, p. 270, para. 33 (listing fifteen manuscripts).
[48] 3 Bulst. 115.   [49] Calth. MS. ii. 57v (tr.).   [50] Baker, *Collected Papers*, i. 494.
[51] 1 Rolle Rep. 277.   [52] 3 Bulst. 116.
[53] For Allen's case see Baker, *Collected Papers*, i. 492. The King's Bench had refused to deliver him upon *habeas corpus*.
[54] *Serjeant Moore's Case* (Trin. 1616) Tourneur, fos. 54v–55 (quotations tr.); Baker, *Collected Papers*, i. 495–7.

king's courts,[55] though nothing specific was ever proved against him.[56] The grand jury declined to find the bills true, but at the request of the prosecutors Coke thrice sent the jurors back to reconsider, and then – when they persisted in their decision – 'warned the sheriff to return a wiser jury the next term'. Ellesmere was incensed when he learned of these proceedings, and 'made a grievous complaint of this attempt to the king'.[57] According to Timothy Tourneur of Gray's Inn, 'the matter was much aggravated (as I heard) against Coke inasmuch as the Court of Chancery ... was the very treasury of the ancient prerogative of the crown, and the mint of new prerogatives, and ... in that the lord Coke in this matter affronted principally the prerogative'. Bacon joined in, saying it was barbarous to permit this public affront to Ellesmere when he was thought to lie a-dying, and that it was also an affront to the court of the king's absolute power. He suggested that the judges be reprimanded, on their knees, in Council.[58] It was not the time, he said, to disgrace Coke, because he was needed for an important state trial, but it might not go amiss to dismiss a puisne judge.[59] No judge was in the event dismissed on this occasion. There was no recent precedent for doing so, and it was unbecoming a law officer to propose it, though the clear implication was that Bacon would be recommending Coke's removal when the time was ripe. These interventions succeeded in working up the king's sense of indignation, and the next term Glanvill and Allen were prosecuted in the Star Chamber for bringing the prosecution, and were clogged in irons for refusing to

---

[55] E.g. as attorney-general at the time of *Throckmorton v. Finch* in 1597 (above, p. 288), and several times as chief justice: Baker, *Collected Papers*, i. 494 nn. 65–6; Smith, *Sir Edward Coke*, pp. 242–6, 271–3. This is no doubt why the statutes of *praemunire* were addressed in Ellesmere's breviate, above, p. 417 n. 42. In *Hetley's Case* (1614) 2 Bulst. 197, after fining commissioners of sewers for imprisoning a party until he released a King's Bench judgment, Coke remarked (at pp. 198–9) that they had incurred a *praemunire*, and a prosecution was actually brought against Sir Anthony Mildmay (who obtained a pardon): Cro. Jac. 336; 1 Rolle Rep. 395; Co. Inst. iii. 125. He collected a number of precedents in Co. Inst. iii. 124–5, including *Hele's Case* (1588) above, p. 214.

[56] Glanvill had obtained the assistance of King's Bench officials by pretending he had directions from Coke: BL MS. Add. 11574, fo. 44.

[57] Tourneur, fo. 54v. Cf. Birch, *Court and Times*, i. 394, as to 'great words and wars'twixt the lord chancellor and the lord Coke about the praemunire' (27 March 1616).

[58] Letter from Bacon to James I, dated 21 February 1616: *Letters and Life of Bacon*, v. 249–54. This, he said, had been done in *John Hele's Case* (1588), as to which see above, n. 55.

[59] Ibid. 252.

answer interrogatories.[60] The purpose of this harsh interrogation was, of course, to implicate Coke. More dangerous to Coke, however, was Bacon's appointment to the Privy Council the same term. It was rumoured that Bacon was to succeed Ellesmere as lord chancellor, an advancement which (according to Tourneur) was generally supposed to have been on condition of using all his power to disgrace Coke.[61] Bacon and Ellesmere decided that the king should himself sit in the Star Chamber without delay and pronounce judgment against Coke on the jurisdiction of the Chancery.

The king was pleased to do their bidding, with due ceremony, on 20 June 1616.[62] No doubt the speech owed much to Bacon's pen. The chancellor, said the king, represented his own person and was no more amenable to *praemunire* than he was himself. The judges' office was to declare but not to make law: *jus dicere, non jus dare*. They were not to meddle with the royal prerogative, or encroach on other jurisdictions, or tolerate the prosecution of great officers of state without first informing him and his Council. If his courts were at odds over the boundaries of their jurisdiction, it was for him alone to settle the dispute. The Chancery was certainly not to exceed the limits set by precedents, but only the king could correct it if it did so. And so – recalling, no doubt, that Coke had once told him that he could not decide cases in the King's Bench in person – James decided in person that Coke and the King's Bench were wrong. As Tourneur scathingly put it, 'the bias of his speech ran in favour of the Chancery and reprehension of the judges for advancing the law against his prerogative, and for raising his prerogative above the law of the realm, as if the prerogative was not to be disputed by rules of law between the king and the subject'. Chamberlain noted that the Chancery could now 'receive and call in question what judgments soever pass at the common law, whereby the jurisdiction of that court is enlarged out of measure, and so suits become (as it were) immortal'. This he blamed on

[60] Tourneur, fos. 54v–55v; Sir Julius Caesar's papers, BL MS. Add. 11574, fo. 47 (copy of the bill); Hob. 115. The prosecution brief is preserved among Ellesmere's papers: S. E. Thorne, 'Praemunire and Sir Edward Coke' (1938) 2 *Huntington Library Quarterly* 85–8.

[61] Tourneur, fo. 55 (quoted in Baker, *Collected Papers*, i. 485 n. 20). The same rumour was reported by Chamberlain: Birch, *Court and Times*, i. 411 (8 June 1616).

[62] *Letters and Life of Bacon*, v. 381–95; Baker, *Collected Papers*, i. 501–3. A formal decree in writing was promulgated on 18 July: ibid. 503–4. For the subsequent proceedings against Coke in the Privy Council on 26 June, complaining of his conduct in the matter, see below, p. 426.

Coke's mishandling of the opposition.[63] But it was not merely a jurisdictional dispute. Tourneur probably represented the prevalent view among common lawyers when he condemned the king's speech of 1616 as deeply disturbing. It was the nadir of the common law in its struggle against absolutism. The judges had endured much mortification over the previous year at the hands of Ellesmere and Bacon, and Tourneur wrote that the people had expected judges to be disgraced, presumably by some removal. It had not, in the event, happened on this occasion:[64]

> ... nor, as I hope, will it ever be, for their disgrace is a wrong to the law itself, [and] God forbid that the irregular power of chancellors, who respect nothing but their private ends, should turn the common law of the land into contempt by making decrees after judgments at common law ... For it is now usual, when the defendant at common law has tried his fortunes there, and stood out all the course of law, and in the end the matter has been adjudged against him, that he will exhibit his bill in Chancery and ground it upon points of equity for which he might have preferred his suit in Chancery before the judgment, so that there is double and infinite vexation. And this is maintained by the high power of the chancellors, who persuade the king that they alone are the instruments of his prerogative, and insinuate with the king that his prerogative is transcendent to the common law, and in a short time it will thus enthral the common law (which yields all due prerogative) and by consequence the liberty of the subjects of England will be taken away and no law practised upon them but prerogative, which will be such as no one will know the extent thereof.[65] And thus the government in a short time will lie in the hands of a small number of favourites, who will flatter the king to obtain their private ends. And if these breeding mischiefs are not redressed by Parliament, the body [politic] will in a short time die in all the parts. Some say, however, that no parliament will be held in England again.

Tourneur's fears with respect to the Chancery were exaggerated and only partly realised;[66] with respect to the state, they were prescient.

---

[63] Birch, *Court and Times*, i. 439 (14 November 1616). Chamberlain also reported that a disgruntled litigant had just shot dead a master of the Chancery in Lincoln's Inn, and Sir William Walter MP (a Puritan sympathiser) said 'the fellow mistook his mark, and should have shot hailshot at the whole court'.

[64] Tourneur, fo. 55 (tr.).

[65] Against this passage Tourneur wrote (in English), in a note dated 1658, 'This overthrew all at last and brought the whole nation under a few into that slavery under which it now labours.'

[66] The main problem was Ellesmere himself, who died in 1617: Baker, *Collected Papers*, i. 507–11; see also the entry in *ODNB*. The King's Bench in 1670 rejected James I's decision as unconstitutional: ibid. ii. 1430.

In 1616, however, this distinction was not readily apparent. The controversy with the Chancery was perceived in terms of prerogative power rather than of abstract jurisprudence.

Non Procedendo Rege Inconsulto

The Chancery, and the *praemunire* indictments, were not the only occasions for the growing rift which Bacon was levering open between Coke and the king. The royal prerogative to delay cases in the courts caused more strenuous debate in two great *causes célèbres* in 1615 and 1616. In the first one, a royal favourite had been granted a new office in the Common Pleas at the expense of Richard Brownlow, the chief prothonotary, to whose office the work (and its profits) had formerly belonged.[67] Coke thought the new office had been Ellesmere's invention.[68] When it had been first proposed in 1610, Coke wrote to the earl of Salisbury on behalf of the judges of his court, complaining that it was exactly the same proposal as that which had been condemned in 1587 as a disseisin, contrary to Magna Carta.[69] Brownlow seemed therefore to be on safe legal ground when he commenced an assize of novel disseisin in the King's Bench to recover seisin of his office.[70] When the case came on, however, Francis Bacon sought as attorney-general to stop the proceedings with a writ of *non procedendo rege inconsulto*, because of the king's interest. The case therefore raised another point arising from chapter 29, namely the delaying power, which had also been aired in the reign of Elizabeth.[71] Coke observed that such a writ was nothing new. But when Brownlow's counsel began to argue against its availability in the present case, Bacon interrupted and said he could not be heard to argue against the king. Coke could hardly tolerate that: 'Justice knows no such strange

---

[67] Interference with legal offices to benefit favourites was a mischief which Coke had experienced at first hand in the 1590s. In 1594 he fought off an attempt by the courtier Edward Darcy to obtain the office of clerk of the outlawries, which belonged to him as attorney-general. He complained to Sir Robert Cecil of the 'chaffering and merchandising' of an office of trust, which some had suspected was his own doing: *Hatfield House MSS.* iv. 511. He had to renew the fight in 1603: ibid. xv. 368.

[68] Coke, 'Dangerous and Absurd Opinions', no. 14.

[69] *Hatfield House MSS.* xxi. 194. For *Cavendish's Case* (1587) see above, p. 266.

[70] *Brownlow v. Michell and Cox* (1615–16) 1 Rolle Rep. 188, 206, 288; 3 Bulst. 32; Moo. 842; Calth. MS. i. 371v; ii. 95v–96v; Tourneur, fos. 9v–10v, 36–37; *Works of Francis Bacon*, vii. 683–725; *Letters and Life of Bacon*, v. 233–6. The assize was brought in the King's Bench since the venue was in Middlesex, a county in which there were no assizes.

[71] Above, pp. 179–84.

prerogative to shut up the mouth of the subject, so that he shall not be suffered to speak against something which seems dubious to the court'.[72] Counsel then proceeded with his argument, and brought the two Magna Carta points together: the king could not erect a new office to the detriment of an existing office-holder without an Act of Parliament, the patent was therefore illegal, and so seeking to delay the proceedings because of the patent was contrary to chapter 29. Bacon, never daunted by Magna Carta, said this was misconceived, and that Brownlow was a leveller[73] whose suit 'striketh at all the new offices erected about Westminster since 1st Elizabeth, which have hitherto stood without control'. He recalled that his own father, Sir Nicholas Bacon, had created the Subpoena Office of the Chancery out of the Six Clerks' Office.[74] The king took a personal interest in the case,[75] and the lengthy arguments by counsel were spread over three terms. In Hilary term 1616 Bacon wound them up with one of his most powerful speeches, lasting (Tourneur noted) until after the clock had struck one.[76] The delaying power was not contrary to Magna Carta, but had always been recognised by the common law. This prerogative, he said, was the mere-stone of the king's inheritance, the hedge around his vineyard. The twelve judges of the law were as the lions under Solomon's throne:[77] they ought to be lions, namely stout, but under the throne, namely with all obedience. 'This is a very great case and doth greatly concern the king in point of prerogative, and ... he were better to lose his castle of Windsor than to lose his privilege of inhibiting proceedings by this writ *de non prosequendo rege*

---

[72] Tourneur, fo. 9v (tr.). Cf. 3 Bulst. 33: 'We which are judges ought to hear the counsel of the party, and this we are to do without any colour of question.'

[73] It is not obvious what Bacon meant by this word. Brownlow was hardly a leveller in the later sense of the term. A senior member of the legal establishment, he had amassed a fortune through his clerical office, which was said to be worth £7,000 a year: Baker, *Collected Papers*, ii. 790–1.

[74] Tourneur, fo. 36. Bacon conveniently omitted to deal with *Cavendish's Case*.

[75] He wrote a private letter to Coke on 18 November 1615 earnestly requiring him to appoint a convenient time for hearing 'the great case of *rege inconsulto* ... that it may be heard *sedato animo* as a matter of such weight and consequence deserveth, lest being handled in haste some inconvenience might thereby unawares come to our prerogative': SP 14/83, fo. 69.

[76] Tourneur, fo. 37. Tourneur noted that Sir Ralph Winwood, principal secretary of state, had been sent by the king to watch the proceedings and was allowed to sit in court with his head covered.

[77] This famous aphorism was inserted by Bacon in the 1625 edition of his essay 'Of Judicature' (first published in 1612): S. Sedley, *Lions under the Throne* (Cambridge, 2015), p. 123.

inconsulto.' Even Tourneur, who had little respect for Bacon, acknowledged that 'without doubt the attorney-general argued extremely well,
and argued as much and as effectively as was possible by the ingenuity of
man to investigate in a case of this nature, consisting totally in ancient
and unusual learning'.[78] A collision with or between the judges seemed
very likely. But the case was conveniently settled before the judges had to
disgorge their opinions.

This narrow escape did not let Coke off the hook, because the matter
was concurrently under debate in a second case. The case arose from a
claim by the bishop of Coventry and Lichfield to be entitled to keep a
benefice in suspense for his own profit (*in commendam*), by royal
dispensation, at the expense of the patron.[79] This was arguably a
disseisin of the patron's freehold, but the proper action for trying this
was a *quare impedit* in the Common Pleas rather than an assize of novel
disseisin. Though brought at common law, the action raised intricate
historical questions relating to canon law and the dispensing power of
the pope. The case was therefore adjourned on account of its difficulty
into the Exchequer Chamber before all the judges of England, and was
very learnedly argued at great length over four terms, with assistance
from Civilian advocates. The judges eventually agreed that judgment
should be given for the plaintiff, but execution was stayed until further
order. Bacon then persuaded the king that to question the *commendam*
in court was to question his own supremacy as head of the Church, and
obtained the king's command to stay the proceedings *rege inconsulto.*
Coke and the other judges wrote back on 27 April 1616 that it would
be against their judicial oath to defer any case by reason of the
king's letters, which they could only suppose were not issued with
the king's personal authority. For this act of defiance, Coke and all
the judges were summoned to the Privy Council on 6 June 1616 and

---

[78] Tourneur, fo. 37.

[79] *Colt and Glover* v. *Bishop of Coventry and Lichfield* (1615–17) 1 Rolle Rep. 451; Moo. 898;
Hob. 140; Calth. MS. i. 355v–357; ii. 125–126v; CUL MS. Hh.2.2, fos. 138v–140
(Trin. 1614); Bodl. Lib. MS. Eng. hist. c. 494 (Phillipps MS. 29480); BL MS. Harley
1692, fos. 61v–62v (where Montagu CJ supported the *commendam* in 1617); MS.
Lansdowne 1062(2), fos. 313v–321v; 34 APC 595–609; *Letters and Life of Bacon*, v.
272–4, 357–70. The matter had been litigated earlier in *R.* v. *Bishop of Coventry and
Lichfield* (1602) BL MS. Lansdowne 1061, fos. 36v–39, 41v–42. On that occasion Warburton and Kingsmill JJ held the *commendam* void, with some scathing remarks about
the disingenuousness of the claim. The prerogative as to *commendam* had, however, been
judicially recognised in *Parkehurst's Case* (1564) Dyer 233; *Wentworth* v. *Wright* (1596)
Cro. Eliz. 526; Owen 144; *Armiger* v. *Holland* (1597) Cro. Eliz. 542.

rebuked by the king in person.[80] The king conceded that his ordinary prerogative, relating to his private interests, was disputable in Westminster Hall; but his 'supreme and imperial power and sovereignty' was not to be disputed 'in vulgar argument'. The court should have stopped impudent barristers who showed so little respect for his prerogative, and reported them to their inns of court so that they could be disgraced. Instead of that, 'of late the courts of the common law were grown so vast and transcendent as they did both meddle with the king's prerogative and had encroached upon all other courts of justice, as the High Commission, the Council established in Wales, and at York, and the Court of Requests'. Putting off a hearing for good cause was not denying or delaying justice but proceeding with wisdom and maturity, and the judges themselves did it all the time; it was not contrary to their oath. The judges should have consulted him before disobeying his command. There was much to be said for the king's position. Coke had allowed himself to be trapped in a corner.

Coke nevertheless proceeded to defend the judges' letter, and at Ellesmere's suggestion the attorney-general (Bacon) was invited to argue against him. Coke protested – not for the first time[81] – at having the king's counsel dispute with the judges, since (as he said) their role was to plead before the judges and not to dispute with them on equal terms. Bacon, confident of his audience, retorted that he was bound by his oath to proceed against the greatest subjects in the kingdom, if they exceeded their authority or took anything away from the king's prerogative.[82] Ellesmere gave an opinion siding with Bacon. It remained for the king to ask all the judges in turn, by now on their knees, whether they would obey a direction from him to stay a lawsuit until they had consulted him. This was the new practice, devised by Bacon and Ellesmere, for dividing and humiliating the judiciary, about which Coke had complained in the past.[83] They all submitted and said they would, except Coke, who – doubtless remembering the example set by his

---

[80] The proceedings are printed in *Collectanea Juridica*, ed. F. Hargrave (1792), i. 5–19; *Letters and Life of Francis Bacon*, v. 357–69; and see Chamberlain's account of them in Birch, *Court and Times*, i. 409.

[81] For the incident in 1609 see above, p. 369.

[82] Coke's objection to the new practice was complained of by Yelverton Sol.-Gen. in June 1616, as an instance of his 'undutiful carriage', since the law officers had acted by the king's command: CUL MS. Gg.2.31, fo. 201.

[83] Above, p. 383. It had also been a matter of complaint in *Peacham's Case* (1615): *Letters and Life of Bacon*, v. 107.

predecessor Sir William Hussey in 1486[84] – answered that, 'When that case should be, he would do that should be fit for a judge to do.' That defiant reply sealed his fate. Spedding suggested that Coke was in the wrong in refusing to answer, since he was not being asked about a specific case.[85] Judges were sworn 'lawfully to counsel the king in his business', and frequently gave opinions to the crown on questions of law submitted to them.[86] Coke's point on 6 June, however, was that the case in question was still pending before the court, and therefore the judges were not permitted to make extrajudicial promises to the king about its outcome.

Bacon decided the time had come to press home the attack, and set about drawing up a list of complaints about Coke's 'turbulent carriage', including his attempt to prevent the Star Chamber levying damages,[87] and the 'great noise and trouble' over the Chancery, which was 'a strange attempt to make the chancellor sit under a hatchet instead of the king's arms'.[88] There were further proceedings against Coke in the Privy Council on 26 June 1616, when various charges were laid against him by the solicitor-general, with Coke on his knees.[89] Chief among them were his alleged pressing of the grand jury to find the *praemunire* indictments, his conduct in the *Case of Commendams*, and his reportedly saying that the proceedings in Chancery would overthrow the common law. This further humiliation marked the end of his judicial career.[90]

---

[84] *R. v. Stafford* (1486) YB Trin. 1 Hen. VII, fo. 26, pl. 1 (tr. 'The king wished to be ascertained of their opinions beforehand ... but the next day Hussey CJ went to the king and asked his grace that he would not seek to know their opinions ... for it would come to the King's Bench judicially, and then they would do what by right they ought to do; and the king granted this').

[85] *Letters and Life of Bacon*, v. 369–70.

[86] Morice's reading (1578), fo. 36v. An example of a written opinion by the judges in response to royal letters was printed by Coke: 7 Co. Rep. 36 (1604). As recently as 25 February 1616 Coke had written a personal letter to the king setting out authorities for the opinion that felonies committed overseas could be tried by the Court of the Constable and Marshal: Lambeth Palace MS. Gibson 936, fo. 57 (ex rel. N. Saunders).

[87] *Att.-Gen.* ex rel. *Egerton v. Brereton and Townshend* (1614) above, pp. 403–6.

[88] *Letters and Life of Bacon*, vi. 90–7. Cf. Birch, *Court and Times*, i. 409: 'the lord chancellor and the attorney [Bacon] prosecute him implacably, and have won so much ground that there is a commission ... [to] examine him upon articles and points touching the *praemunire*. And withal the whole course of his life is like to be ripped up and looked into, which, if it be severely followed, many men fear it may be his utter overthrow. But he holds up his head and gives no way'.

[89] 34 APC 644–6; CUL MS. Gg.2.31, fo. 201.   [90] See below, p. 435.

Francis Ashley's Reading

As the storm clouds gathered in Westminster Hall, a remarkable reading was given in the Middle Temple, in August 1616, on chapter 29 of Magna Carta.[91] The reader was Francis Ashley, recorder of Dorchester, who had served as member for the borough in the Addled Parliament of 1614. During that troubled session he had revealed his constitutional inclinations by warning against allowing the attorney-general (Bacon) to sit in the Commons, lest he report its secrets to the king, by complaining against the management of Commons business by government 'undertakers', and by attacking impositions, though reporters noticed him only once as citing Magna Carta.[92] He had been one of those who advocated a new petition of grievances to the king, though the parliament was dissolved before the matter went further.[93] The readership of the Middle Temple fell to his turn the following year as a matter of seniority, but his choice of subject was doubtless prompted by his recent experiences in the Commons. It is difficult not to suppose also a desire to express support for Coke, on behalf of the profession, in his time of trial. He began by acknowledging the difficulties which faced him, saying 'it cannot be denied to be a perilous point indeed when a man must inevitably run the hazard of wreck, of no worse commodity than his reputation, upon the rock of censure, be it either just or unjust.' The 'trepidation of the heart' to which he admitted was not merely the modest concern traditionally expressed by readers for the good opinion of their fellows, for men had been locked up for their views on Magna Carta, including (only three years earlier) James Whitelocke of the Middle Temple.[94] Ashley foresaw that he might well earn 'an opinion of foolhardiness, that will thus expose myself to peril', but the die was cast: '*Jacta est alea*, it is now too late for me to run retrograde, and I will not doubt but the same power which first directed my perplexed cogitations to pitch and settle on this subject, without purpose of offence, will also guide me to proceed therein.'[95]

---

[91] BL MS. Harley 4841, which was probably the reader's own manuscript, though not written in his hand. Cases argued at the reading are noted in CUL MS. Ee.6.3, fos. 100–21. The importance of the reading was first noticed by Thomson, *Magna Carta*, pp. 284–93.

[92] *Proc. Parl. 1614*, p. 273. The report was misunderstood by the editor, who rendered it 'An amercement to be offered by *pares*', glossing *pares* as 'steps'. The reference is, however, to c. 14, that an amercement should be 'affeered' by peers.

[93] *HPHC 1604–29*, iii. 57–62. For its dissolution see above, p. 407.

[94] Whitelocke was three years junior to Ashley as a member of the Middle Temple and joined him as a bencher shortly afterwards.

[95] Ashley's reading, fo. 2.

Ashley's exposition of chapter 29 could fairly be described as representing the apotheosis of the new learning about Magna Carta. Barely a hint of that learning can be detected in any readings prior to Morice's in 1578, and yet little of it was Ashley's own invention, since it was largely derived from cases decided since the 1580s, from current professional thinking and from majority opinions in the House of Commons.[96] Nevertheless, in drawing the emerging notions together, Ashley managed to stretch the interpretation of the chapter to the uttermost limits. There was no longer any reticence about declaring the fundamental character of chapter 29:[97]

> If it be the common law, it is the law of laws . . . and so is this law in effect the ground, and the rest subsequent but flourishes upon it: this the base, and others the descant. But if it be a mere statute, it is the statute of statutes, for it hath begotten many of the like kind . . . And the lord Coke saith in his Fifth Report it hath been confirmed thirty times; and thirty times thirty more I suppose it would, if it lay in the power of the subject to give any strength unto it. And no marvail, if we consider either the worth or extent of it, for it is as much worth as our lives or estates are worth, and the extent is as large as anything we have which we hold precious.

Ashley was prepared to attribute almost everything positive in English law to this one chapter of the great charter:[98]

> In brief, by virtue of this statute we have property in our goods, title to our lands, liberty for our persons, and safety for our lives. But . . . in the case between *Anderson* and *Warde*,[99] it is further added another, and that justly, that by force of this statute every free subject may have remedy for every wrong done to his person, lands or goods. And not only so, for that would but give recompense for a wrong done; but this statute also *prevents* wrongs, for by virtue thereof no man shall be punished before he be condemned, and no man shall be condemned before he be heard, and none shall be heard but his just defence shall be allowed.

---

[96] He contended that decisions by the Commons were of legal authority, referring to a decision in the 1614 parliament that a clause in the patent of 1613 empowering the French Company to make orders, and to enforce them by imprisonment, was contrary to Magna Carta and void: Ashley's reading, fo. 9v ('tenus pro lege in parliamento'). He also cited a holding in 1614 that after 24 years a monopoly was an ancient trade and could no longer be restricted to a particular person: ibid. fo. 22. Cf. also above, p. 334.

[97] Ashley's reading, English preface, fo. 3. The reference is to *Clarke* v. *Gape* (1596) 5 Co. Rep. 65; above, p. 314.

[98] Ibid. 3v. Thompson, *Magna Carta*, pp. 288–9, plausibly suggested that these encomiums were derived from Coke; she was unaware of Coke's memorandum of 1604, and based the suggestion on his report of the *Case of the Marshalsea* (1612) 10 Rep. 68.

[99] *Anderson* v. *Warde* (1554) Dyer 104.

This was not reckoned to be new law, but a confirmation of the common law. An aggrieved party could therefore either bring an action founded on the statute or an action on the case generally.[100] The writ of prohibition, likewise, was attributable to chapter 29.[101] All this echoed what Coke had been saying over the previous fifteen years.

Although Ashley made his way through the clauses and words of his text in the traditional manner, in the same way as Snagge had done in 1581, he was not very precise in linking all the broad principles to the words. It would have defeated his object. He did detach *judicium parium* clearly from the peerage, holding that every free Englishman was entitled to be tried by men of the same condition.[102] But the statute, in his view, went much further; for 'by this statute are condemned and prohibited all judgments without hearing the party and without trial, and all unlawful trials and all judgments by judges not lawfully authorised, and all manner of unlawful proceedings to judgment, and all unlawful executions'.[103] This conclusion must have been based on the general spirit behind the words, taken as a whole, rather than on any literal construction. It was enough that such abuses constituted a 'going or putting upon' the subject, and were not sanctioned as *lex terrae*.

Ashley's most explicit target was the High Commission, and he was more direct than Morice had been in setting out the grievances in terms which had become familiar.[104] In taking more and more jurisdiction over all manner of ecclesiastical offences, it had undermined the jurisdiction of the regular Church courts and forced people to travel long distances to answer for relatively minor matters. In making people answer questions upon the oath *ex officio*, it obliged them to incriminate themselves, contrary to elementary principles of justice.[105] And its judgments, however irregular or oppressive, could not be reviewed in any other court.[106] The canon law was not *lex terrae* except in so far as it had been confirmed

---

[100] Ashley's reading, fo. 50v.

[101] Ashley's reading, fos. 4, 40v. Likewise *praemunire* (ibid. 40v), which was usually taken to be of statutory origin.

[102] Ashley's reading, fo. 55. Cf. fo. 59, where he treats the proceedings in Star Chamber, Chancery and Requests as *lex terrae* even though they did not involve a judgment by peers ('licet non sit per judicium parium').

[103] Ashley's reading, fo. 51.   [104] Ashley's reading, fos. 17v, 51v.

[105] Cf. CUL MS. Ee.6.3, fo. 119v, where he said that making someone incriminate himself on oath was a setting or going upon him. 'Going upon' a free man (*nec super eum ibimus*) also included arraigning him in court: ibid. 120.

[106] See also CUL MS. Ee.6.3, fo. 102v.

by Act of Parliament.[107] Ecclesiastical courts had no power to imprison except by Act of Parliament, and the Act of 1559 under which high commissions were issued – originally with the purpose of extirpating the hardline papist clergy – was concerned only with heresy, schism and 'enormous' offences. The Commission therefore had no jurisdiction over such matters as sexual offences, defamation, simony, usury, working on holidays, or even hearing mass, and if it imprisoned anyone in the course of exercising such pretended jurisdiction it was contrary to chapter 29.[108] Reference was made to *Lee's Case* and *Hynde's Case*, Coke's favourite authorities from Dyer's notebooks.[109] Quite apart from imprisonment, forcing people to accuse themselves upon the oath *ex officio* was a 'going and putting upon them' within the meaning of the same chapter, for 'no free subject may be compelled by any power to be his own accuser in judgment in causes criminal and penal'.[110] Evidence taken on oath in Chancery was distinguishable, because it was sanctioned by immemorial custom and was therefore part of the law of the land.[111]

Ashley explored further the meaning of *lex terrae*.[112] It included admiralty law, in cases arising on the high seas, the law of merchants and the equitable proceedings of the Star Chamber, Chancery and Requests. Although the Chancery subpoena had not been used before the time of Henry IV, it had been impliedly incorporated in the law of the land by parliamentary recognition.[113] On the other hand, the law of the land did not include the king's proclamations, or martial law in peace-time.[114] This learning was conventional enough, but Ashley was

---

[107] Ashley's reading, fo. 58; CUL MS. Ee.6.3, fo. 121. He also excluded Civil law, except in cases within the jurisdiction of Civilian courts (by which he presumably meant the Earl Marshal's Court).

[108] Ashley's reading, fos. 11, 17–20v; CUL MS. Ee.6.3, fo. 102. He cited authorities from the plea rolls in respect of all these propositions.

[109] CUL MS. Ee.6.3, fo. 102.

[110] Ashley's reading, fo. 51v; CUL MS. Ee.6.3, fo. 119. Ashley said it had crept in during the reign of Henry IV, who was not king *de jure* and was also anxious to please the pope.

[111] Ashley's reading, fos. 52–3.   [112] CUL MS. Ee.6.3, fo. 121.

[113] This had been Snagge's conclusion in 1587: above, p. 251. It was also part of Ellesmere's case in 1615: above, p. 417. Ellesmere's position was supported on the same ground by Anthony Benn, bencher of the Middle Temple, in his 'Discourse touching the *Praemunire* brought against Serjeant Moore' (1616) BL MS. Lansdowne 174, fos. 205–15. It was never denied by Coke.

[114] A decade later, Coke wrote that execution by martial law in time of peace was murder, being contrary to Magna Carta, c. 29: Co. Inst. iii. 52. This was in fact old law, since Parliament had ruled in the fourteenth century that it could not be used in peace-time, when the courts were sitting: above, pp. 53–5. But a precedent for its use had been set by

unusually and surprisingly restrictive about the meaning of *liber homo*.[115] It included women, because '*homo* contains both sexes', and friendly aliens, but it did not include alien enemies, outlaws, pagans and infidels, persons attainted of felony,[116] attainted jurors, or even villeins.[117] He did not deny such persons all legal rights, but their rights were less complete than those of free men. This unorthodox interpetation was seemingly arrived at by way of a logical circle: such persons did not have full rights, and therefore they could not be 'free' men within the meaning of the statute. The more orthodox position was that all were free men, but that the *lex terrae* restricted the rights of certain categories of people without placing them beyond the rule of law. The practical result was the same.

Ashley's broad interpretations meant that Magna Carta imposed limits not only on the power of the king and his ministers but also on all other forms of authority or power, including that of justices of the peace.[118] Even an innkeeper, if he detained a guest until he paid his bill, was (according to Ashley) caught by chapter 29.[119] Disseisin of liberties,

---

Mary I, who by a short-lived proclamation of 1558 threatened death under martial law for those who possessed heretical books. In 1573, when Elizabeth I was ready to sign a commission for martial law in London, it was opposed by the earls of Lincoln and Arundel because the judges were sitting in Westminster Hall: letter from the earl of Sussex to Lord Burghley, BL MS. Lansdowne 17, fo. 43. On several occasions in the 1590s the queen did nevertheless authorise its use, to put down civil unrest, and in 1605 Popham CJ said that martial law was allowed in time of insurrection and rebellion: below, p. 515. There was another instance in 1607. Some executions actually occurred after its imposition on the city of London in 1595, but they followed trials for treason upon indictment, with the advice of all the judges: Coke's autograph notebook, BL MS. Harley 6686A, fos. 114v–115v (not mentioning martial law); 2 And. 4. See further L. Boynton, 'The Tudor Provost-Marshal' (1962) 77 EHR 437–55; J. V. Capua, 'The Early History of Martial Law in England from the Fourteenth Century to the Petition of Right' (1977) 36 *Cambridge Law Journal* 152–73; J. G. Bellamy, *The Tudor Law of Treason* (1979), pp. 228–35, and the sources cited there.

[115] Ashley's reading, fos. 6–8; CUL MS. Ee.6.3, fos. 113v–114.

[116] I.e. after judgment. Persons convicted of felony, i.e. by a 'guilty' verdict, were 'free men' (though in custody) until attainted by judgment, after which they were civilly dead.

[117] As to villeins, he acknowledged that (tr.) 'there is not much use of this learning': Ashley's reading, fo. 8.

[118] CUL MS. Ee. 6. 3, fo. 115 (a discretionary sentence imposed by justices can be reviewed to ensure that it is reasonable).

[119] Ashley's reading, fo. 10; CUL MS. Ee.6.3, fo. 114v. The only authority cited was *The Six Carpenters' Case* (1610) 8 Co Rep. 146, which does not mention the imprisonment of guests, let alone Magna Carta. The decision there was that failing to pay his bill did not retrospectively convert the guest into a trespasser *ab initio*, because 'not doing is no trespass'.

which the old readers had limited to franchises granted by the crown as freeholds or in fee, was another concept given a broad reinterpretation.[120] Liberties, said Ashley, included 'every immunity and freedom to which an Englishman is inheritable; and every impeachment from enjoying the benefit thereof is a disseisin, just as much as where a freeholder is ousted'.[121] For instance, suing in a Church court for a matter justiciable at common law was a disseisin of liberty.[122] Since the offender in that case was the plaintiff, not the judge, here again a private individual was being made subject to the same limitations as those exercising authority under the crown. But the idea of liberty could be stretched still further into the economic and professional spheres. Monopolies and restrictive bye-laws contravened Magna Carta, since they were a disseisin of every free man's liberty to trade wherever and with whomever he wished.[123] A fortiori, imprisonment by a privy councillor for an offence against a patent of monopoly was unlawful.[124] Even the dispensing power was objectionable on the same principle, because dispensing with the law for one subject was a destruction of the liberty of others.[125] Therefore, if the king granted that an ecclesiastical judge could entertain a plea for tithes of wood despite a prohibition, and notwithstanding the statute of *Sylva Caedua*, this would be a disseisin of the liberty of the subject, 'for it is thraldom to all subjects that the liberty of the old common law should be taken away from them'.[126] Anxious no doubt to please his audience, Ashley put the case that electing a barrister to serve as a constable was a disseisin of his professional immunity

---

[120] Note, however, the wording of the writs founded on Magna Carta, from 1501 onwards, in which vexation by undue process was described as a disseisin of liberty: above, p. 259; below, p. 457.

[121] Ashley's reading, fo. 40.

[122] Ashley's reading, fo. 40v; CUL MS. Ee. 6. 3, fo. 116v. For this proposition he cited the very recent case of *Abbot v. Hunt* (Hil. 1616) in the King's Bench.

[123] CUL MS. Ee. 6. 3, fo. 116; cf. BL MS. Harley 4841, fos. 21–2, 40 (tr. 'trade and traffic are the life of the common wealth'). James Morice had held in 1578 that the king could not grant a monopoly of a common trade, but he did not cite Magna Carta in that connection: Morice's reading, fos. 18v–19. The connection with c. 29 was made by Coke in *Davenant v. Hurdys* (1599) above, pp. 316–17; and see *Darcy v. Allen* (1602) above, pp. 321–2.

[124] Ashley's reading, fo. 11, citing *Langley v. Heneage* (1592).

[125] Ashley's reading, fo. 41, citing 'Penal statutes' (1605) 7 Co. Rep. 36 (in which there is no reference to Magna Carta).

[126] Ibid. (tr.), referring to the statute of 45 Edw. III, c. 3. He said this was held by Coke CJ in the Council Chamber in 1612, when the Civilians argued that the king could dispense with prohibitions.

from such an office, and that he could be relieved by writ from the King's Bench.[127]

'Free customs' was an even broader expression than 'liberties'. It included not only local or particular customs, and private prescriptive rights, in accordance with the standard learning, but also 'general' customs. On this footing, the phrase seemed to encompass the whole of the common law. The law of property in goods was such a custom, and therefore a man's goods could not be taken away by a bye-law, or under a patent, even though that was nothing like a disseisin in the usual sense of the word.[128] Another ancient custom was that every man's house is his castle,[129] and therefore a house could not be broken into by a serjeant at arms executing process from a court of equity.[130] An equally open-textured word was 'destroyed'. According to Ashley, 'every oppression by virtue of a usurped authority, and by colour of law or authority, when the act done is against law, is a "destruction" within this statute'.[131] This could include not only such obvious oppressions as persecution by the High Commission, but the imposition of excessive fines, taxes and tolls, and every form of extortion.[132]

Ashley's expansive treatment of chapter 29 was possible only because there was no longer any limit to the meanings which could be read into its words by generous interpretation. Although he cited authorities for most of his propositions, they were often authorities which established the legal result as stated but without explicit reference to Magna Carta. The connection with chapter 29 was not necessary to many of the legal conclusions; it flowed inexorably from Ashley's comprehensive approach to its meaning, which reflected the professional thinking, and even the 'vulgar understanding' of the time. In his report to the bench after the reading, he claimed that it had been well received by those who attended.

---

[127] Ashley's reading, fo. 41v; CUL MS. Ee. 6. 3, fo. 116. This, he said, was the case of Mr [Thomas] Waters, an utter barrister of the Middle Temple, who was elected a constable in Sussex and discharged by virtue of Magna Carta.

[128] Ashley's reading, fo. 47. The disseisin was not of the goods, since there could be no seisin of goods, but of the 'free custom' of owning them.

[129] Trin. 14 Hen. VII, Fitz. Abr., *Trespas*, pl. 246; *OHLE*, vi. 562; *Semayne's Case* (1604) 5 Co. Rep. 91. Even Coke did not link this with Magna Carta.

[130] Ashley's reading, fo. 47v. This was not a disseisin of the house, it seems, but of the 'free custom' relating to the security of the home.

[131] Ashley's reading, fo. 49v. The authority cited here was the *Case of the Marshalsea* (1612) 10 Co. Rep. 68 at p 74.

[132] Ashley's reading, fos. 49v–50v; CUL MS. Ee. 6. 3, fo. 118v (every extortion is a 'destruction').

The general approval justified his efforts in expounding this, the worthiest statute in the statute-book:[133]

> Finding how obvious this law was upon all occasions, insomuch that no ordinary action could be brought importing violence and wrong but it had his foundation from hence, no extraordinary writ of prohibition was granted to restrain the swelling and exorbitant power of ecclesiastical or any other jurisdiction but had this law for their warrant, and finding further that no exaction, oppression, violence or grievance in the common wealth could be named but even vulgar understanding could have recourse to *Nullus liber homo*, I suppose I could not employ my labours upon a more worthy subject or more profitable, and therefore resolved farther to inform myself concerning this law so useful, so behoveful, and by that occasion found both liberty and safety, liberty to our persons, and safety to our lives and estates; and, in brief, I found that it was bought too dear in order to be sold too cheap.

Nevertheless, although Ashley was daring enough to remind his audience of the king's *faux pas* in hanging the cutpurse at Newark in 1603,[134] very little of his enthusiastic defence of English liberties was directed against the king's prerogative, and this perhaps explains how Ashley was considered fit to be made a serjeant at law two years later,[135] and knighted and then chosen as one of the king's serjeants ten years after that, in the first year of Charles I. As it turned out, Ashley was to become a strong defender of the royal prerogative in the 1620s, and to incur the wrath of the Commons led by Coke.[136] But that was in the future. The 1616 reading revealed a most notable development in English legal thinking. In under forty years, the scope of chapter 29 – which had been severely constrained for centuries by literal interpretation – had become almost limitless. It had come to be seen, even by laymen, as the basis of constitutional liberty.[137] And its new

---

[133] Ashley's reading, fo. 4.

[134] CUL MS. Ee. 6. 3, fo. 114. He said it happened at Belvoir: above, p. 340 n. 32.

[135] He was created serjeant in May 1618: J. H. Baker, *The Order of Serjeants at Law* (1984), p. 180. One of his patrons was Sir Francis Bacon LC: ibid. 437. The date 1617 in the index of serjeants, ibid. 497, was a mistake which has unfortunately been copied in *ODNB* and *HPHC*.

[136] In the interim, in 1619 one of his clients, Lord Houghton, was involved in a dispute with Coke, and Ashley was gaoled for contempt of the Privy Council in connection with the proceedings: *HPHC*.

[137] E.g. Camden: see F. S. Fussner, 'William Camden's "Discourse concerning the Prerogative of the King" [c. 1615]' (1957) 101 *Proceedings of the American Philosophical Society* 204–15, at pp. 211, 213.

importance resanctified the whole charter, other parts of which were occasionally still found to be of value. The great charter itself had in consequence completed its ascent to a more elevated position in English constitutional history than could ever have been foreseen before the time of Elizabeth I.

Coke's Dismissal

Shortly before Ashley delivered his reading, Coke had been sequestered by the Privy Council from its meetings, forbidden to go on his summer circuit, and commanded to spend the summer vacation revising the 'exorbitant and extravagant opinions' in his *Reports*.[138] But these further humiliations were only holding measures. Bacon was nearing the completion of his mission to bring down his rival, and, once he had persuaded the king, he had the final satisfaction of preparing the warrant for Coke's dismissal from office and sending it to the king on 13 November.[139] This was leaked in court circles, and Coke's downfall was common knowledge by 14 November, when John Chamberlain reported it, saying that 'Four Ps have overthrown and put him down – that is, Pride, Prohibitions, Praemunire and Prerogative'.[140] The writ of dismissal, dated 15 November, was delivered to Coke by Sir George Coppin, clerk of the crown in Chancery – accompanied by Bacon's servants to witness its safe receipt.[141] Coke received it 'with dejection and tears'.[142] It has sometimes been termed a *supersedeas*, but it took the form of a direct command (*mandamus*) that he should no longer be a justice and should desist from performing the office.[143] Coke wrote in his *vade mecum* that the writ was expressed to be

---

[138] These rulings were made on 30 June: 34 APC 649–50; CUL MS. Gg.2.31, fos. 202v–203; Birch, *Court and Times*, i. 416. Coke subsequently refused to acknowledge any but minor slips in his reports, and this was complained of to the king by Ellesmere and Bacon, who jointly conducted two or three interrogations: *Letters and Life of Bacon*, vi. 76–82; Birch, *Court and Times*, i. 432.

[139] *Letters and Life of Bacon*, vi. 97. Coke had already been suspended by writ from executing the office until the king's pleasure was known: *The Diary of Sir Richard Hutton 1614–1639*, ed. W. R. Prest (9 SS Suppl. Series, 1991), p. 13; Calth. MS. ii. 188. The writ is recited in the discharge. According to Chamberlain, the suspension was communicated to Coke by Ellesmere and Bacon in person: Birch, *Court and Times*, i. 427.

[140] Birch, *Court and Times*, i. 437.   [141] Calth. MS. ii. 188.

[142] Letter cited in Birch, *Court and Times*, i. 440, where the writer also remarked, 'A thunderbolt hath fallen on the lord Coke, which hath overthrown him from the very roots'.

[143] Calthorpe gives the Latin text: 'Cum nuper nos per breve nostrum retornabile vetaverimus vos ad serviendum nobis ut capitalis justiciarius ad placita coram nobis tenenda,

'for various causes', whereas in truth there were none.[144] There was no known precedent for discharging a lord chief justice in this way.[145] But Bacon was not much troubled by the absence of precedents. He had urged summary dismissal, because if Coke was given a hearing in the Privy Council he would have to be given time to defend himself;[146] and, of course, no good reason could be given in public. But the remedy of *mandamus*, derived by Coke from Magna Carta, and now so effective for restoring mayors and aldermen, was of no use to restore a lord chief justice.[147]

Henry Calthorpe noted what be believed to be the reasons for this shocking interference with judicial independence:[148]

> ...[Coke] having incurred the king's displeasure by not obeying a letter which was sent to him and the other judges to make a stay of the case of *commendam*, and by supporting (as it was popularly reported) the right of the subject against the prerogative of the king; and having accumulated upon him the hatred of the earl of Suffolk, and all the Howard family and their adherents, through the vehement persecution of the odious offence of the earl and countess of Somerset;[149] and having the ill will of the archbishop of Canterbury and of all the other bishops, for being so stiff against the *commendams* and in maintaining the jurisdiction of the common law against the High Commission, and against the proceedings in the spiritual courts, and also for being so prompt in granting prohibitions; and having incurred the implacable malice of Thomas Ellesmere,

---

pro diversis causis nos moventibus volumus et mandamus quod non sitis amplius justiciarius sed ab officio illo exequendo desistatis.'

[144] Coke's notebook, BL MS. Harley 6687, fo. 15v.

[145] Sir John Markham (d. 1479) ceased to be CJKB in 1468, but the circumstances of his removal are unclear. The writ appointing his successor said he had been discharged at his own request, on account of age and debility, though he is thought to have been dismissed: *The Men of Court*, ii. 1060. Sir John Fitzjames ceased to be CJKB three years before he died in 1542, but this was probably a retirement; the writ appointing his successor makes no mention of it (KB 27/1110, m. 1). Sir John Fortescue was not reappointed CJKB on the accession of Edward IV in 1461, and Sir Roger Cholmeley was not reappointed on the accession of Mary I in 1553; but all judicial offices lapsed on the demise of the crown and reappointment was not automatic.

[146] *Letters and Life of Bacon*, vi. 79.

[147] The writ appointing a CJKB did not specify any tenure at all, and so technically the office was not a freehold but occupied at the king's pleasure. For Coke's own previous decision that an office of trust could be terminated without a hearing see *Reynell's Case* (1611) above, p. 353 n. 100.

[148] Calth. MS. ii. 188 (tr.).

[149] I.e. the murder of Sir Thomas Overbury, who had conducted an affair with Frances Howard, countess of Essex, daughter of the earl of Suffolk. Frances subsequently divorced the earl on grounds of impotence and then married Robert Carr, earl of Somerset. The Somersets were convicted of the murder, but later pardoned.

lord chancellor of England, now recently created Viscount Brackley, and of all the Chancery men, for giving way to an indictment upon the statutes of *praemunire* for exhibiting bills after judgment;[150] and of the presidents of the Marches of Wales and of York, who were against him because he curbed the jurisdiction of their courts.

Timothy Tourneur, writing at the time, praised Coke as the worthiest chief justice of England since the Conquest,[151] and retrospectively wrote of his removal as the beginning of the nation's misfortunes, leading to Civil War:[152]

> This was a forerunner of the alterations that followed upon King Charles, for the Chief Justice Coke was not displaced for any crime, but for advising the king to maintain the law and not to stretch his prerogative too high – as he and his son did – and that by [Ellesmere's] advice, because the chancellor cried up the prerogative and beat down the law, [whereas] Coke's labour was to keep the balance of both even.

Calthorpe's contemporary judgment was in similar vein:[153]

> And thereupon he ceased to be chief justice, being a judge of great integrity, much sincerity, great reading, happy memory and indefatigable industry, for he had written eleven several reports besides the case *De Jure Regis Ecclesiastico*. He was the oracle and principal supporter of our law. He was aged sixty-five years, subject to some infirmities, and taxed by several or more points of indiscretion, as in being too open in the discovery of his mind and too insolent and morose against some over whom he had power, and in his too severe reprehension of counsel for every little cause.[154] But upon his being discharged from his office he was much lamented by people of all sorts, that so profitable a member of the common wealth should lie idle without making use of those excellent parts which God had bestowed upon him.

---

[150] Cf. Wilbraham, *Journal*, p. 117: 'he is taxed to have practised a *praemunire* against the lord chancellor'.
[151] Tourneur, fo. 82, reporting the trumped-up suit against him in the Star Chamber the following term.
[152] Ibid. 62v, margin. This was added in mid century.   [153] Calth. MS. ii. 188 (tr.).
[154] These defects were expanded upon in an anonymous 'letter' supposedly written to him after his downfall: SP 14/89, fos. 156–161v. Some attributed to this to Bacon, but there were several other candidates: Birch, *Court and Times*, i. 458 (22 February 1617). Cf. Wilbraham, *Journal*, p. 117: 'His arrogancy lost him many friends, to help him in need.' Even judges sometimes found him too arrogant. Williams JKB once told him he was not such a master of the law as he took upon him to be, 'to deliver what he list for law and despise all other': H. E. Huntington Library MS. EL 2184, cited by Smith, *Sir Edward Coke*, p. 212.

James Whitelocke did not think the faults worth mentioning at all:[155]

> Never man was so just, so upright, free from corruption, solicitations of
> great men or friends, as he was ... [He] was removed from his place upon
> the king's displeasure. What was the cause of the offence by the king is not
> for subjects to meddle with, but those who practised before him, or had
> causes before him, found him the most just, honest and uncorrupt judge
> that ever sat on the bench.

No time was lost appointing Coke's successor, Sir Henry Montagu,
who had bestowed thousands of pounds in acquiring the office. Bacon
had recommended the king to appoint him rather than Thomas
Coventry, who was 'a well learned and honest man, but he hath been
(as it were) schooled by my Lord Coke and seasoned in his ways'.[156]
Montagu was sworn in on 18 November and took his seat the day after.
Hutton noted the general wonder at the haste, and that 'it was not
politicly handled'.[157] Montagu had the audacity to ask Coke for his gold
collar of SS, which he refused to hand over.[158] But even less politicly
handled was Ellesmere's conduct at the swearing-in ceremony.[159] He
remarked in his speech to Montagu that his appointment was a rare
one, the position having become vacant by removal, and took the
opportunity to explain why this had happened. 'It is dangerous in a
monarchy for a man holding a high and eminent place to be ambitiously popular – take heed of it.' He bid Montagu remember his
grandfather Sir Edward Montagu, formerly chief justice of the King's
Bench (1539–45) and later of the Common Pleas (1545–53).[160] Sir
Edward did not, he supposed, arrogate to himself the title chief justice
of England.[161] He had not drawn commissioners of sewers or the

---

[155] *Liber Famelicus of Sir James Whitelocke*, ed. J. Bruce (70 Camden Soc., 1858), pp. 50, 51.

[156] *Letters and Life of Bacon*, vi. 97. Coventry, the recorder of London, became solicitor-general the following year. In 1623 Coke named his as an executor of his will, calling him a true and faithful friend: *Calendar of Inner Temple Records*, ii, ed. F. A. Inderwick (1898), p. 350.

[157] *Diary of Sir Richard Hutton* (above, n. 139), p. 16. It was observed that Montagu must have had his new robes made before Coke's dismissal.

[158] Birch, *Court and Times*, i. 442.

[159] Moo. 826; Cro. Jac. 407; *Diary of Sir Richard Hutton* (above, n. 139), pp. 14–15; *CELMC*, p. 529 (listing eighteen manuscripts).

[160] As Whitelocke hinted, Ellesmere seemed unaware that the earlier Montagu CJ was in fact imprisoned in the Tower and deprived of office after the accession of Mary I in 1553.

[161] He was in fact so described in a law report: *Reports of Cases from the Time of Henry VIII*, ed. J. H. Baker, (121 SS, 2004), p. 360. Coke's use of the informal style on his title-pages was a bugbear of the king's, but it had been used continuously since the fifteenth century

ministers of the Chancery into the dangers of *praemunire*,[162] 'an absurd
and inept construction of that old statute'. He had not cast doubt on the
right of the king to stay lawsuits *rege inconsulto*. He had not claimed the
power for his court to correct all misdemeanours, as well extrajudicial as
judicial,[163] or to adjudge Acts of Parliament to be void if he conceived
them to be against common right and reason,[164] but left it to the king in
Parliament to judge what was common right and reason. 'Remember,' he
stressed (as if Montagu needed telling), 'the removing and putting down
of your late predecessor.'

The lawyer onlookers were appalled at this public display of spleen.
According to Tourneur, 'The chorus censured my lord chancellor of
overmuch presumption, thus taking upon him to school a lord chief
justice, which (as I heard some of the graver sort say) had not been used
in former times.'[165] Whitelocke said it was 'a very bitter invective against
the late chief justice, taunting him with being ambitiously popular, and
other faults which no way touched his honest, just and upright dealing,
but rather implying faults (so esteemed to be) in a monarchical state'.[166]
But members of the profession were hardly surprised by Ellesmere's
contempt for Coke and what he stood for. According to Hutton, the
chancellor had become increasingly choleric and had in many respects
laboured to derogate from the common law and the judges.[167] Calthorpe
said that 'in recent times he had calcitrated against the common law,
which had been his raising and supporting, and therefore in his last years
had accumulated the hatred of many men'.[168] Tourneur's opinion was
that he was simply 'the bane of the law – not for any hate he bear it, but
for the love he bare to his own honour, to greaten himself by the fall of
others'.[169] Whitelocke called him 'the greatest enemy to the common law

---

and was recognised by Parliament in 1543: *OHLE*, vi. 145 n. 3; *The Men of Court*, i. 375;
ii. 1255, 1706.

[162] See above, p. 419 n. 55.

[163] A reference to *Bagg's Case* (1615) 11 Co. Rep. 98; above, p. 396.

[164] A reference to *Bonham's Case* (1610) above, p. 90.   [165] Tourneur, fo. 62v.

[166] *Liber Famelicus* (above, n. 155), p. 51.

[167] *Diary of Sir Richard Hutton* (above, n. 139), p. 17.

[168] Obituary note in Calth. MS. ii. 223v. *Calcitrare*, in Latin, means to kick or resist. Coke
complained that when Ellesmere was asked to stand up for the judges when they were
complained of to the king, 'his continual answer was that he would not lie in the gap for
any man': 'Dangerous and Absurd Opinions', no. 13.

[169] Obituary note in Tourneur, fo. 81v. John Chamberlain wrote, at the time of his death,
that he 'left an indifferent name, being accounted too sour, severe and implacable, an
enemy to parliaments and the common law, only to maintain his own greatness and the

that ever did bear office in this kingdom'.[170] Seeing Coke removed from office may have given Ellesmere his ultimate satisfaction, but it was hardly his finest hour. His own career was over, and he died on 15 March 1617. Bacon was appointed to succeed him, though he was destined to be dismissed for supposed bribery only four years later. Coke, on the other hand, far from lying idle, was destined to make much further good use of his 'excellent parts', especially in writing the *Institutes* and in his successful deployment of Magna Carta in 1628.

Even to this day Coke's defects have left him with a more negative image among historians in general than Bacon has acquired. Both were men of brilliant intellects, arrogant and covetous of wealth, and each disliked the other intensely. But Bacon was the renaissance man of letters, philosopher and scientist, whose eloquence in speech was as renowned as his elegance in writing. Coke, by way of contrast, is often caricatured as the crabbed pedant, bad historian and unreliable lawyer. *Coke upon Littleton* certainly does not compare favourably with anything which came from Bacon's pen, and posterity will draw its own conclusions from their respective writings; but this is not at all how they were seen at the time.[171] Bacon was respected for his talents rather than his deeds. Like Ellesmere, he took a pragmatic view of the royal prerogative. So long as authority was in safe hands, such as his own, and innovations in judicature were effective, there was no need to bother too much with constitutional nicety. If power fell into the wrong hands in the future, that was not today's problem. Lawyers of a more constitutional bent might fret about setting dangerous precedents, but Bacon was today's man of business, earning credit with the king by getting things done. In consequence, he could be seen as the subservient prerogative-man, ever ready to deploy his oratorical skills in advancing the king's absolutist views, more than content to see the common law disappear in a code of Anglo-Scots law if it gained him royal favour, contemptuous of the judiciary and dismissive of Magna Carta. Coke, on the other hand, was revered within the profession and without as the oracle of the English common law and the chief defender of the liberty of the subject against

---

exorbitant jurisdiction of his court of Chancery': *The Letters of John Chamberlain*, ed. N. E. McClure (1939), ii. 65.

[170] Obituary note in *Liber Famelicus* (above, n. 155), p. 53 ('It had been good for this common wealth if he had been out of the world twenty years before').

[171] The same point was made by R. Pound, *The Development of Constitutional Guarantees of Liberty* (New Haven, CT, 1957), pp. 43–4.

what was widely perceived as an absolutist regime only too ready to dispense with the rule of law and with Parliament. Though several times brought before the Privy Council to be challenged, on his knees, he had always stood his ground in defending the constitution as he saw it. In that sense he was indeed 'popular', though he had striven to elaborate plausible legal and historical arguments which might convince not only his fellow judges but the king himself. The arguments were at times defective, and Coke was wont to imperil their effectiveness by his dogged intractability,[172] but the continuity of the English constitution depended on their broad acceptance. They did not rest solely on Magna Carta, but chapter 29 was repeatedly returned to because its words resounded in the ear and their gist was widely understood even by those unfamiliar with ancient statutes and year books. Coke had not been responsible for its original resuscitation, but he had made the most of it when opportunity arose, both as attorney-general and as chief justice. It was therefore in large part his achievement that, as Ashley's reading demonstrated, the intellectual groundwork for the great debates of 1628 was all firmly in place before he was ignominiously ejected from office in 1616.

---

[172] He was, nevertheless, far more moderate in his views on the prerogative, and even in his use of prohibitions and *habeas corpus*, than some past historians have allowed: see A. Cromartie, *The Constitutionalist Revolution* (Cambridge, 2006), p. 211; Smith, *Sir Edward Coke*, pp. 179, 181, 251; Halliday, *Habeas corpus*, pp. 30, 332–3; Usher, *Reconstruction*, ii. 149, 210.

Myth and Reality

Historians have sometimes contrasted the 'reality' of Magna Carta, the true story of what happened in 1215, with the 'myth' of later centuries. It is a succinct way of contrasting two different histories, but potentially misleading. The most extreme antagonist of the supposed myth was Edward Jenks, who attempted in 1905 to overturn a century or two of 'Whig' history on the subject.[1] The great charter was great only in terms of its length. It was not a landmark in constitutional progress, or a declaration of the rights of man, but 'simply a recognition of the privileges of an aristocratic class'. Worse than that, it was 'a positive nuisance and stumbling-block to the generation which came after it'. As for its being reissued thirty-eight times, that was only necessary because it had failed to do its work. Almost everything which historians had come to believe about Magna Carta was a myth, and the author of that myth was Coke:[2]

> He was a man whose lot was cast in troublous times, amid the angry mutterings of that coming struggle which was to light the torch of civil war in England. Deeply pledged to the popular side in that struggle, he cast into it all the weight of his profound if somewhat undigested learning, and his powerful if somewhat unscrupulous intellect. It was an age in which historical discoveries were received with credulity, in which the canons of historical criticism were yet unformulated. Doubtless more than one of Coke's contemporaries (John Selden, for example) must have had a fairly shrewd idea that Coke was mingling his politics with his historical research. But, for the most part, those competent to criticise Coke's research were of his way of thinking in politics, and did not feel called upon to quarrel with their own supporter. Zeal for historical truth is apt to pale before the fiercer flame of zeal for political victory. It is a tribute to Coke's character and ability that he imposed his

[1] E. Jenks, 'The Myth of Magna Carta' (1905) 4 *Independent Review* 260–73.
[2] Ibid. 272–3. This was not new. Much the same had been written by Robert Brady in the 1680s.

ingenious but unsound historical doctrines, not only on an uncritical age, but on succeeding ages which deem themselves critical.

The essay was written with exuberant élan, in a radical political journal, and it seems possible that it was partly tongue in cheek. It nevertheless marked the start of a new historiography which cast Coke as an unscrupulous myth-maker, inventing or distorting history as it suited him,[3] and fetishising Magna Carta as the symbol of an age-old struggle against arbitrary power.[4] Yet Jenks's remarks rested on a fallacy to which legal writers are not usually prone. They assumed that the history of Magna Carta ended in 1215. Every account of Magna Carta which did not correctly capture the original intent was, on this assumption, mythical or fictional. Yet this assumption was itself profoundly unhistorical. Magna Carta was not merely an event.

It may be granted that Coke was not a good historian by modern standards, so long as it is remembered that even Lambarde and Selden – whom historians generally respect – sometimes made what seem with centuries of hindsight to have been serious errors. The more important historical fact is that Coke was not pretending to be a historian. He was not much concerned at all with what had actually happened in 1215 or 1225, or (come to that) in 1066. The scholarship was still undeveloped and, as Jenks acknowledged, even his opponents rarely challenged him on historical grounds. It has been said of Coke and his contemporaries that history was 'viewed on all sides symbolically or metaphorically' rather than factually.[5] This is a valuable insight, but it might be nearer the mark to say that lawyers used history in the same way as they used legislation and reports of cases. Statutes and law reports were all historical records of things said and done in Parliament, or in the courts, but for lawyers they were sources of legal propositions rather than of facts. They were of use to posterity not for the light they threw on what had happened in the past but for the legal rules and arguments which they contained, rules and arguments which were not frozen in time but

---

[3] See, e.g., R. V. Turner, *Magna Carta through the Ages* (2003), p. 148: 'his distortions of the English past reconfigured people's understandings of Magna Carta and medieval England … Coke interpreted or misinterpreted Magna Carta to give it relevance, misconstruing its clauses anachronistically and uncritically'.

[4] Cf. M. Radin, 'The Myth of Magna Carta' (1947) 60 *Harvard Law Review* 1060–91, at p. 1062. J. W. Gough, *Fundamental Law in English Constitutional History* (Oxford, 1955), p. 5 n. 4, described Jenks's essay as 'wittily exaggerated, but it had a substratum of truth'.

[5] H. J. Berman, 'The Origins of Historical Jurisprudence: Coke, Selden, Hale' (1994) 103 *Yale Law Journal 1651–1738*, at p. 1687.

refined over the years by constant study and debate. Magna Carta, like other statutes and charters, had certainly been an important event in English history, or rather a series of events, but it was primarily understood – chapter 29, in particular – as a codification of common-law principles. Never mind that some of those principles were unknown in 1215. The historical events had resulted in the written expression of a body of law with a life of its own, subject over time to historical arguments and consequences quite unforeseeable in the thirteenth century. This does not mean that the later law was founded on deception, or on naive Whig history. Principles of law are not facts and cannot therefore be mythical, any more than they can be fictional.[6] It is obvious that the Magna Carta of 1616 was very different from the Magna Carta of 1225, even though the words were identical; but it was just as real to those who lived in 1616 as to those who wrote it. Jenks's myth is therefore misleading, if by myth we mean something untrue, a 'noble lie' to be shunned by high-minded historians and relegated to the less scrupulous world of lawyers and politicians. The long-term story is just as factually true as the story of what happened in the early thirteenth century, and arguably much more important as a strand of world history. Coke may have got some of the early history wrong, but his consti-tutional conclusions have thrived down the centuries because they seemed right.[7]

Jenks might well have accepted much of this. He was commenting on the history of 1215, not writing law. But his argument was historically misleading at a more serious level. For the truth is that Coke did not invent anything at all of significance. He did not invent the mythical 'ancient constitution', for there never had been a time when English lawyers did not regard their system as predating the Norman Conquest.[8] A remote origin was axiomatic to Fleetwood,[9] and was still the basis of Selden's more advanced historical scholarship at the beginning of the

---

[6] J. H. Baker, *The Law's Two Bodies* (Oxford, 2001), pp. 42–7.

[7] Cf. G. Garnett and J. Hudson, introduction to Holt, *Magna Carta* (3rd edn), p. 46: 'The history of Magna Carta is the history not only of a document but also of an argument . . . If we can seek truth in Aristotle, we can seek it also in Magna Carta.'

[8] By contrast, William Camden, who was not a lawyer, had written in the 1580s that William replaced most of the ancient laws of the English with Norman customs, and established the tenurial system: *Britannia* (1586), p. 50; A. Cromartie, *The Constitutional-ist Revolution* (Cambridge, 2006), p. 197 (where it is pointed out that the passage was 'diluted' in the English edition of 1610).

[9] Above, pp. 223–4.

seventeenth century.[10] It was also Sir Roger Owen's conclusion from a thorough study of the medieval chronicles.[11] The story in some of the chronicles was that William I had adopted the old laws of Edward the Confessor's time, adding a few of his own, and this had long been the teaching in the inns of court.[12] Fleetwood believed that Edward's laws, in turn, had been merely a perfection of still earlier laws.[13] There had been many changes in the details over time, of course, and there were disagreements and misunderstandings about when some of them occurred; but the essential grounds of the common-law system, if not derived from the ancient Britons (as dubious earlier learning had it),[14] were at the latest Anglo-Saxon. This was believed to be true not only of legal institutions such as Parliament and the courts of law, sheriffs, writs and jury trial, and basic concepts such as military tenure,[15] but also of the balanced monarchical constitution. Far from being products of Coke's unhistorical imagination, the 'myths' of the 'ancient constitution' and the 'Norman yoke' were in fact medieval – so medieval, indeed, that they predated Magna Carta itself.[16]

As for Magna Carta, Coke undoubtedly revered it, and encouraged the growing general reverence for it. He sometimes exaggerated its claims.

---

[10] E.g. in his *Notes upon Sir John Fortescue*, appended to *De Laudibus Legum Angliae* (1616), at pp. 7–9. See P. Christianson, 'Young John Selden and the Ancient Constitution *c.* 1610–18' in *Discourse on History, Law and Governance in the Public Career of John Selden 1610–35* (Toronto, 1996), pp. 11–85.

[11] See, e.g., his discussion of Magna Carta: R. Owen, *Common Law* (*c.* 1615) BL MS. Harley 6605, fos. 56v–60. Like most of his contemporaries, he assumed that Magna Carta was largely a restatement of the laws of Edward the Confessor.

[12] See, e.g., Morgan Kidwelly's reading in the Inner Temple (1483), *Selected Readings on Magna Carta*, pp. 97–8; above, p. 76; anonymous reading (*c.* 1546/50) in *Rights and Liberties of the English Church*, pp. 139–40; *OHLE*, vi. 21–2. Snagge taught that the common law and the king were coeval, beginning 'before all memory of man that remaineth in the world': *Antiquity of the Chancery* (1587), p. 17. Coke set out the chronicle evidence in the preface to *La Huictieme Part des Reports* (1611), sig. §§iii and §§4v.

[13] Above, p. 226.

[14] In 1602 Coke had even hinted that the common law was pre-Roman, because the Romans boasted of their laws and would have altered the English laws had they not been better: 2 Co. Rep., preface. He repeated this in 3 Co. Rep., preface, but said of the pre-historic Brut legends that he would not 'examine these things in a *quo warranto*'. In 5 Co. Rep. (1607), preface, he tried to defend these assertions.

[15] Selden thought military tenures were Anglo-Saxon, but that William I reorganised the system with its later incidents, such as wardship in chivalry.

[16] J. C. Holt, 'The Origins of the Constitutional Tradition in England' in *Magna Carta and Medieval Government*, ed. J. C. Holt (1985), pp. 1–22, especially at pp. 17–18; Pocock, *Ancient Constitution*, pp. 42–3; Holt, *Magna Carta*, introduction, pp. 47–8.

But even he was not originally responsible for its renaissance in the mid-Elizabethan period. Moreover, as already remarked, his deductions from it were legal rather than historical. The association of *habeas corpus* with chapter 29 might well seem ludicrous to a medieval historian. But Coke never claimed that *habeas corpus* existed in 1225. He had read the records, and knew perfectly well when it began, better (in fact) than most modern historians. His argument was rather a legal one, and a good one at that: chapter 29 laid down an important principle, which was still law, but did not provide a specific remedy; it must have been intended that there should be one, or it would have been in vain, and in any case the principle was rooted in the common law; ergo, the common law had to produce the remedy.

Coke even acknowledged that Magna Carta was not absolutely essential in safeguarding the liberty of the subject, because the main principles were all inherent in the common law. Most of the charter was not new law, but an embodiment and reinforcement of more ancient maxims of law which had come under threat. This, too, was a legal rather than a historical argument, though it had some roots in fact. One of the main purposes of the original Magna Carta was to restore what were thought to be the good old laws of King Edward the Confessor, or at least the common law as it had been in 1199. It did not follow that the charter was of little independent value, as Jenks suggested, especially since many of its provisions – especially the broad principles in chapter 29 – were not to be found explicitly stated in older legal texts such as *Glanvill*, and some may never have been made explicit before. Nor was it a stumbling-block for the future.[17] The passage of time only increased its power. Magna Carta became a hereditary royal guarantee, won by blood (as the rhetoric went), reinforced by oaths and seals and threats of anathema, that no government would ever violate the fundamental principles which it was deemed to enshrine. Even James I could be persuaded to acknowledge that it placed limitations on his monarchical inheritance. And that was the main reason for Coke's devotion to it, and for his retrospective linking of various established features of the common law with the words of chapter 29. His object was not innovation but conservation. He wanted to save the common law from the combined threats of Romanism and absolutism, and laboured harder than any other chief justice, or law officer of the crown, to secure its safety. He also wanted to

---

[17] To be fair to Jenks, he said only that it was a stumbling block to the next generation (in the singular).

put a stop to the creeping abuse of power by court favourites and provincial oligarchs, not to mention lord chancellors and archbishops, men who were not fundamentally evil but preferred to rule others by discretion rather than law. Perhaps with more tact and diplomacy he would have made still more headway; but he did achieve much through his fearless confrontations with the king and his ministers. King James, for all his expedient concessions, never gave up his earlier theories of absolute monarchy, which he was prone to expound with alarming erudition and threatening language. They had somehow to be countered. Magna Carta may not have been legally indispensable to the counter-arguments, but it had a powerful emotional effect on the high as well as the low. It was ancient and peculiarly English, the inheritance of every subject, and capable of trumping the Continental learning on which the king relied.

The almost magical power which Magna Carta came to acquire over the centuries was based not on its detailed wording but on its symbolism. Its concise Latin may have seemed lengthy enough to the clerks who once had to cram the words onto a single piece of parchment, but the most significant provisions were vague and imprecise. It was, no doubt, the open texture of the broadest statements which protected them, in the longer term, from repeal. It has been said that a constitution ought to be brief and obscure,[18] and the same holds true of any declaration of principles capable of lasting for centuries. The most enduring and influential part of Magna Carta – chapter 29 – may still have the power to stir the blood,[19] but it was never of much decisive value in the courts. In that sense, the teachers of law in the inns of court were right in their negative textual criticism. Although everyone knew more or less what it was about, it was not a masterpiece of draftsmanship for practical juridical purposes. Whatever 'peers' meant, it was not at all clear how judgment by peers could be an alternative to the law of the land, something extralegal. Yet it could not be read conjunctively with the law of the land, because outlawry and imprisonment did not always require a decision by peers (however understood). Whatever 'the

---

[18] The quip is often attributed to Napoleon, but in fact it was Talleyrand. On being advised in 1802 that a constitution ought to be 'brief and ... [clear]', he interrupted with 'and obscure': *Oeuvres du Comte P. L. Roederer*, ed. A. M. Roederer (1854), iii. 428 (translated).

[19] So said Professor Holt, beginning a radio broadcast on Magna Carta in 1965. Cf. T. Bingham, *The Rule of Law* (2008), p. 56 ('power to make the blood race').

law of the land' meant, it could hardly be supposed that Magna Carta froze the common law as it was in the early thirteenth century and rendered it impervious to alteration. That would have prevented the development of parliamentary democracy. Others pointed to the gloss in the statutes of Edward III and held that it meant 'due process of law', the procedures of the common law: in other words, an indictment by grand jury to initiate a criminal prosecution, or an original writ under the great seal to initiate a civil case. But that interpretation did not stand up to legal analysis either. It would have excluded the Star Chamber, the Chancery, the Admiralty and the ecclesiastical courts, and also local jurisdictions, which would all be left without coercive powers. It would have prohibited police powers before trial. The only sensible interpretation left was that no one could be locked up, or have his property taken away, save as authorised by law. Such a formulation would suit tyrants perfectly well, since a tyrant can change the laws of the land to suit his will.[20] Even in a democracy, if and in so far as the law allows governments a power to lock people up, or to seize their property for public purposes, or to tax them, doing those things is perfectly consistent with Magna Carta. This is perhaps why little is heard of Magna Carta in the English courts of the twenty-first century.[21] Ministers nowadays usually arm themselves with statutory powers.

Magna Carta lost any practical usefulness it might have had after Coke's time as a result of the work of historians. By introducing a more scientific form of historical understanding, Sir Henry Spelman and Robert Brady put an end to the artificial conceptions of an ageless common law and a timeless Magna Carta.[22] History and law became separated, and the legal reinterpretations of the great charter became myths, quaint fallacies to be discarded by an age of reason. After the great debates of 1628, and the fight against ship-money in the later 1630s,

---

[20] It may be recalled that Hitler took the trouble to acquire legislative authority for most of what he wanted to do (apart from the very worst): J. Baker, 'Our Unwritten Constitution' (2010) 167 *Proceedings of the British Academy* 91–117, at p. 105.

[21] It is most usually cited, not by lawyers, but by litigants in person. One of the few cases in which it could have made a difference (see Baroness Hale in 129 *Graya* at p. 65) was the case of the Chagos islanders, in which the House of Lords held by a bare majority that an Order in Council was *lex terrae* and therefore a forced exile by virtue of such an order was not against the *nullus exuletur* clause of c. 29: *R. v. Secretary of State for Foreign and Commonwealth Affairs*, ex parte *Bancoult* [2009] 1 AC 453; upheld by the Supreme Court in *Bancoult* (No. 2) [2016] UKSC 35, without reference to Magna Carta.

[22] See H. Butterfield, *Magna Carta in the Historiography of the 16th and 17th Centuries* (1969).

Magna Carta was almost a spent force in England.[23] So was the guiding power of history. Lawyers no longer spend long hours poring over ancient rolls looking for solutions to the problems of the present in the records of the past. Nor, of course, do politicians and their aides. Despite all this, the words of chapter 29 have lived on until the present day in the popular consciousness, with no loss of vitality.

So powerful are the words that they exert their spell even on those who cannot read them. They are seen simply as forbidding the exercise of absolute authoritarian power. The privilege of being governed by 'certain rule of law',[24] rather than by the arbitrary discretion of rulers, is now known as the rule of law. There is, admittedly, little agreement as to what precisely this denotes.[25] And it must be acknowledged that real life rarely lives up to legal or constitutional ideals, even when they are expressed in writing. There is inevitably a gap between ideals, which are normative rather than descriptive, and what people – including governments – actually do. But that does not invalidate the principles. And the essential principle derived ultimately from Magna Carta, even if not spelt out in its words, is that every person's rights and duties should be defined by certain law, that governments should exercise no powers other than those conferred upon them by law, and that the law for these purposes is to be interpreted solely by independent and professional judges. It follows that no one should be treated arbitrarily, by unknown law or *ad hoc* law, or outside any law; that everyone should be treated equally; and that everyone should have access to justice in the form of judicial remedies.

Although those have become universal aspirations, most of Coke's particular concerns now seem very remote. English people in general have been content to give up many of their freedoms, as Coke perceived

---

[23] See H. M. Cam, *Magna Carta – Event or Document?* (Selden Soc. lecture, 1965), p. 24: 'With the granting of the Petition of Right Magna Carta ceases to be a battlecry . . . Its last appearance is in the preamble to the Act abolishing the court of Star Chamber. It is not mentioned in the 1689 Bill of Rights. It has become a legend and a symbol.' Cf. W. H. Dunham, *The Great Charter* (1965), p. 41: 'The grand debates in the 1628 Parliament that produced the Petition of Right gave to Magna Carta an additional crowded hour of glorious life. When that Parliament had ended, the Great Charter's part in forming British constitutionalism was about played out.'

[24] The phrase used in the House of Commons petition of grievances in 1610: above, p. 393.

[25] Dicey, who is supposed to have fathered the concept, did not define it, and his description has bewildered many generations: A. V. Dicey, *Lectures Introductory to the Study of the Constitution* (Oxford, 1885), pp. 167–340. Lord Bingham recently proposed a definition, but since it encompasses human rights and natural justice it is difficult to find in it any independent meaning: *The Rule of Law* (2010).

them, on the advice of their elected rulers; to allow governments to change the conventions of the constitution as it suits them; to allow legislative power, including the power to amend parliamentary statutes, to be delegated to government ministers and others; to allow ever-increasing discretionary powers to be exercised over them and their resources by quasi-autonomous bodies, or even by potentates across the seas; and (though more controversially) to submit to the jurisdiction of judges educated in Civilian legal traditions. Perhaps the only serious concerns of Coke's which would still be understood by most English people today are those associated with religious terrorism, a context in which Magna Carta is no more helpful now than it was then. Even so, the old learning continues to find new applications.

That part of chapter 29 which was explained in 1354 as a guarantee of 'due process of law' is now incorporated in the concept of Natural Justice,[26] which – as applied through the machinery of the prerogative writs developed in Coke's lifetime – still underlies English administrative law.[27] Other aspects of chapter 29 are known today in the guise of Human Rights, which were formulated in writing in the 1940s as a means of extending to all human beings the ancient liberties of the English. Already by 1616 those liberties had included, for all men and women, freedom from slavery and arbitrary arrest, detention or exile; freedom from cruel or inhuman treatment; recognition as a person before the courts, with judicial remedies for any infringement of rights; a presumption of innocence until proved guilty according to law at a public trial, after an opportunity to be heard in one's defence; freedom from arbitrary confiscation of property; protection of one's good name; freedom of thought and conscience; and freedom from restraints in one's employment. These liberties, all of which were associated by 1616 with chapter 29 of Magna Carta, were only slightly rephrased and enlarged in the

---

[26] One of the most prominent English judges of the twentieth century wrote that he understood the term in much the same way as the statute of 1354, and that it meant 'the measures authorised to keep the streams of justice pure: to see that trials and inquiries are fairly conducted; that arrests and searches are properly made; that lawful remedies are readily available; and that unnecessary delays are eliminated. It is in these matters that the common law has shown its undoubted genius': Lord Denning, *The Due Process of Law* (1980), preface, p. v.

[27] Due process has acquired an entirely different meaning in the United States, where it has in the past been deployed to deny liberty as now understood, e.g. by upholding slavery (above, p. 35) and the disabilities of married women, and preventing social reforms. Dean Griswold dismissed these older decisions as mere 'eddies in the stream which carries on the great idea': E. N. Griswold, *The Fifth Amendment Today* (Cambridge, MA, 1955), p. 36.

Universal Declaration of Human Rights (1948), and constitute more than two-thirds of that document. They were not, of course, created in 1215, when many of them would not have been recognised. They were not in any realistic sense derived from the individual words of chapter 29. They might well have developed within the common law even if there had been no Magna Carta. But they were all gathered under the wing of its protection, and thereby acquired a special sanctity. Indeed, natural justice, human rights and the rule of law may all be seen as descendants of the core provisions of the great charter of liberties, as reinvented by common lawyers in the half-century before 1616.

Appendix 1

Two Fifteenth-century Readings
on Chapter 29

Probably in Lincoln's Inn, *c.* 1455/60

'No free man shall be taken or imprisoned or disseised of his freehold etc.' This statute is a recital of the common law; for this was the common law, and it provided all that this statute sets out. Therefore we must see what the common law is, and how it shall be understood according to this statute. This statute goes on to say, 'except by the lawful judgment of his peers or by the law of the land'. If a lord, namely a duke, earl, baron or other lord, does something against the law, by this statute he shall be adjudged by his peers. And all other men, whether merchants or others, shall be adjudged according to this statute by their peers and shall be put to answer by their peers.[1] Nevertheless, in some cases the law shall pass upon them not in accordance with this statute. For twelve men may present anyone, in any court, if they so wish: and so a duke, earl, baron or other man of dignity, or any man of lesser or greater estate, may be presented or indicted by twelve men before justices of peace or assize, or other justices who have power to take presentments or offices or verdicts of twelve men. Nevertheless a lord shall not be put to answer except in accordance with this statute, to be acquitted or attainted by his peers, so that he shall be put to answer, acquitted or adjudged by the peers. Thus everyone, whether of greater estate or lesser, shall be adjudged by his peers according to this statute. According to some, if a lord, namely a duke, baron or other lord, is to be acquitted or adjudged, he shall be adjudged by the barons of the Exchequer because they are called barons. But this cannot be so, for this statute does not so provide, albeit the barons of the Exchequer together with other peers may assess a fine or amercement upon any lord, according to the custom of the court (*place*).[2]

The readings were first printed, with parallel French text, in *Selected Readings on Magna Carta*, pp. 249–54. The translations here are slightly paraphrased. For the date of these two readings and the probable connection with Lincoln's Inn, see ibid. x–xi, xliii.

[1] This was unorthodox learning at the time. Presumably the reader meant only that a common person was entitled to a jury, not to a jury of merchants or whatever.

[2] This was the gloss placed by the readers on 'peers' in Magna Carta, c. 14.

The statute further says, 'to no one shall we sell, to no one deny or delay right or justice'. According to some, this word 'right' ought to be understood as the writ of right, and 'justice' shall be understood as a *justicies*, which is in effect a commission giving power to the sheriff to hold plea in the county. But it was said [by the reader] that these two words 'right' and 'justice' shall not be understood in that way, but should be understood to mean that the king will deny to no one right or justice.

By the words 'to no one shall we sell etc.' the king shall take nothing – that is to say, no fine, whether in gold or silver – for anyone to have right, that is, to have an action. Notwithstanding this, however, the law is otherwise. For if someone sues any action for land which exceeds the value of forty shillings, or if someone sues an action for a debt which exceeds £40, or an action of trespass in which the damages exceed £40, in all these cases the king shall have a fine according to the usage of the Chancery. This usage is, nevertheless, contrary to this statute, and therefore it is wrongly done; and it is extortion to do contrary to this express law. It was said to be the law that the clerks shall have their fees for writing the writs, and the chancellor shall have somewhat for the wax and the seal, and on top of all that the king should have a fine as before, but that is contrary to this statute. In some cases one shall not make fine, as where someone sues a *justicies* directed to a sheriff to hold a plea of debt before him for £30, or £100, or £1,000 or more: in this case the plaintiff who sues this *justicies* shall not make fine, for the writ is not returnable ...

This statute provides that the king shall not deny anyone right. Suppose, then, that the king disseises someone. The disseisee cannot have an action against the king, but he shall have his remedy by petition: that is, he shall make his petition in a bill, and the king (of right) shall endorse and seal the bill, and [the petitioner] shall go to the Chancery with the bill, and there he shall plead with the king, and if they are at issue it shall be tried in King's Bench. If the king disseises someone, [and] enfeoffs someone in fee of the disseisiee's land, the disseisee may enter upon the feoffee, for no reversion is now in the king ...

The statute says, 'no free man shall be taken or imprisoned except by the law of the land'. Nevertheless in some cases a man may be imprisoned by process of law, and in some cases without process of law. By process of law, as where a *capias* issues to a sheriff to take me, and the sheriff takes me by virtue of this *capias* (as well he may), and afterwards the sheriff returns 'He is not found' (*non est inventus*): I shall now have a writ of false imprisonment against the sheriff, and the sheriff shall not justify it, but the party may show the fact of how he was wrongfully imprisoned. Thus the party may recover his damages against the sheriff, even though the defendant was taken by process of law. And in some cases a man may be taken and imprisoned without process of law, as where a man is taken and arrested on suspicion of felony; but there the felon must be arrested by a constable or known officer. Thus a known officer may arrest a man on suspicion of felony even though he is not caught red-handed ... And in this way a man may be imprisoned without process of law.

Probably in Lincoln's Inn, *c.* 1491/1508

'No free man shall be taken etc.' The common law before this statute was misused, for in old time men were taken, imprisoned and outlawed contrary to the law of the land, and the law was misordered. Therefore this statute was made, for more security, so that men should be treated according to the law of the land.

First it is to be seen what is 'the law of the land'. There are various laws used in this land. First there is the true common law of the land, which is between party and party to sue for a wrong done, and for which there are various courts and judges: for instance, the Common Bench for all common pleas, the King's Bench for the crown, and the Exchequer for accountants.[3] There are also in the law of the land special courts and special jurisdictions, which are also the law of the land, such as the Marshalsea, held within a certain precinct (namely the verge); courts of record by the king's grant, as in London and other places; courts of piepowders,[4] and such like. These are of record and are the law of the land, and yet they are to some extent outside the common law of the land and are used in accordance with custom and prescription, provided the customs are reasonable. There are also special jurisdictions and other courts of record, such as the Cinque Ports, where the king's writ does not run, and the counties palatine, such as Durham and such like; they have special courts, and are under the law of the land, and use the law of the land, but they have special jurisdiction. Likewise Ireland uses the law of the land, and the laws which are used there are the law of the land: so it appears from the statute *De Hibernia*,[5] where they wrote to the king for information about a question on which they were in doubt. But they have power in their own Parliament to make laws for their benefit. Wales is in another course, for they have a law to themselves which is different from the law of the land. There are also other courts which are not of record and yet are the law of the land, such as the court baron, hundred, sheriff's tourn, ancient demesne, and such like. All these are the law of the land.

There are other laws used in this realm which are not the law of the land, such as the Court of Admiralty, the Court Marshal[6] and the Chancery. The Court of Admiralty is for things done upon the high sea, whereof the admiral

---

[3] I.e. those who are required to account to the king.
[4] I.e. courts held in fairs to decide disputes arising in the fair.
[5] *Statutum Hiberniae de Coheredibus* 1236.   [6] I.e. the court of the earl marshal.

is judge, and the trial there is by proofs as the matter requires, and they have the procedure of the Civil law. The Court Marshal is for things done in time of war, that is, when the king's banner is displayed;[7] and it also uses trial by proofs and Civil law. The Chancery is to redress things done contrary to conscience, for which the common law gives no remedy; and the trial is also by proofs. These three are used in this land, and yet they are not the law of the land.

The statute says, 'no free man shall be taken etc.' It is to be seen (i) where one may be taken lawfully, and where not; (ii) where the sheriff to whom the process is made may arrest someone, and where not ...

The statute says, 'nor shall we go upon him or send upon him except by the lawful judgment of his peers'. By these words are meant such as are of the great estates of the realm, namely dukes, earls or barons; no one beneath that degree shall be adjudged by their peers. By the statute of 20 Hen. VI, c. 9, it is provided that ladies of estate shall be tried in the same way by their peers.[8] This statute is intended of indictments for felony or treason, or where their lives shall be in jeopardy, and this appears in the statute of the said year 20 Hen. VI. It shall never be applied to suits in which they do not put their lives in jeopardy, for in all other actions they shall be adjudged like another common person. Moreover, where they put their lives in jeopardy at the suit of a party, they shall be tried like another common person, as in appeals of murder, robbery or rape ...

The statute says, 'to no one shall we sell . . . . right or justice'. This means that in a writ of right, or in a *justicies*, one shall not make fine; and this is the usage at the present day.

---

[7] Cf. above, pp. 53–4.
[8] I.e. the same peers as would try peers of the realm: their husband's peers.

Appendix 2

Actions Founded on Chapter 29 (1501–32)

This is a calendar of the actions on Magna Carta so far discovered in the plea rolls before the reign of Elizabeth I.[1] The first known example is printed in full, translated from the Latin. Each of the others is in the same form; the calendar summarises only the details of the vexation complained of. An indictment of 1509, framed on Magna Carta, is also included.

Waltham v. Lunde (1501)[2]

Middlesex. Be it remembered that on the twenty-third of October this same term John Waltham, who [sued] both [for the lord king and for himself], came before the lord king at Westminster in his own person and proffered here in court a certain bill against Thomas Lunde, late of Pocklington in Yorkshire, in the custody of the marshal etc., concerning a plea of contempt and trespass against the form of the statute lately made and provided in the parliament of the lord king Henry the third after the conquest, held at Westminster in the ninth year of his reign, that no free man should be taken or imprisoned, or disseised of his free tenement or of his free customs, or outlawed or exiled or in any other way destroyed, and that the king should not go upon him or send upon him, except by the lawful judgment of his peers or by the law of the land. And there are pledges for prosecuting, namely William Buk and Robert Luk. The bill follows in these words:

Middlesex. John Waltham, who sues both for himself and for the lord king, complains of Thomas Lunde, late of Pocklington in Yorkshire, because, whereas in the statute of the lord Henry ...[3] as is more fully contained in the same statute, and whereas the same John is a free man, and according to the law and free custom of the realm of England every free man ought to implead and be impleaded in common pleas by original writs under the lord

---

[1] Only three later actions of the same type have been discovered: *Parsons v. Locke* (1595) below, appendix 5(d); *Wetherly v. Hunnings* (1606) below, appendix 8, at p. 514; *Bulthorpe v. Ladbrook* (1607) below, appendix 10. For actions on the fourteenth-century statutes of due process see *Spelman's Reports*, ii. 72 n. 11.

[2] KB 27/961, m. 74 (Mich. 1501).   [3] Magna Carta, c. 29, is set out again, as above.

king's great seal before the lord king's justices of his Common Bench and not elsewhere, and whereas writs and pleas of false judgment are a common plea [sic] and ought to be determined by original writ under the lord king's great seal at common law before the aforesaid justices of the aforesaid Bench and not elsewhere, nevertheless the aforesaid Thomas Lunde, little weighing the aforesaid statute, but scheming maliciously to aggrieve the said John and to vex, weary and destroy him the said John with intolerable labours and expenses, on the second day of July [1501] in the sixteenth year of the reign of King Henry the seventh, at the vill of Westminster in the county of Middlesex, exhibited to the lord king and his Council a certain bill, and by that bill accused the said John that, whereas a certain Thomas Mawdesley claimed a certain annual rent issuing from land of the aforesaid Thomas Lunde in Pocklington aforesaid, the aforesaid John Waltham and other suitors in William Willfosse's court of his manor of Pocklington, through the favour of the said William and of a certain Thomas Morley, steward of the same court, had adjudged that the said Thomas Lunde should pay the said Thomas Mawdesley the aforesaid annual rent, and forty shillings for his damages, outlay and costs, whereupon a certain writ of the said lord king's privy seal, directed to the said John, was then and there sued out, by which writ the lord king commanded the same John that, putting aside all delay, business and causes whatsoever, he be in his own person before the said lord king and his Council at the vill of Westminster in the quindene of St Michael then next following, there to answer the said Thomas, as is more fully contained in the same bill and writ; which writ the said Thomas Lunde delivered to the said John at Pocklington on the sixteenth day of July [1501] in the above-mentioned year; as a result of which the said John appeared in person at the said quindene and vill of Westminster before the most reverend father in Christ Henry,[4] archbishop of Canterbury, keeper of the lord king's great seal, and others of the said lord king's Council, and answered and was compelled by the aforesaid Thomas to answer the writ and bill aforesaid and the matter therein specified. And [thus] the said Thomas Lunde disseised the aforesaid John Waltham of his liberty and free custom, neither by the lawful judgment of his peers nor by the law of land, against the form of the aforesaid statute. And thereby the said John was vexed, worsened, wearied and destroyed with many labours and expenses, to the damage of him the said John twenty pounds etc.

And the aforesaid Thomas Lunde came in his own person and denied the force and wrong when etc., all the contempt and whatever etc. And the aforesaid John Waltham prayed that the aforesaid Thomas should answer to his aforesaid action etc. Whereupon the aforesaid Thomas had a day given

---

[4] Henry Deane (d. 1503).

him here by the court on the Tuesday next after the morrow of St Martin, to answer the said John etc. And the same Thomas, being solemnly called upon to answer at the same day, did not come or say anything in bar or exclusion of the aforesaid action of the aforesaid John, as a result of which the same John remains unanswered against the said Thomas. Therefore the same John prays his damages by reason of the foregoing to be adjudged to him etc. And because it is unknown to the court what damages the same John has sustained, both for the aforesaid cause and for his outlay and costs about his suit in that behalf, the sheriff is ordered that he diligently inquire by the oath of twelve good and lawful men from the venue of the vill of Westminster aforesaid, within his bailiwick, what damages the same [John] has sustained, both for the aforesaid cause and for his outlay and costs about his suit in that behalf, and send the inquisition so distinctly and openly taken, under his seal and the seals of those by whose oath he took the inquisition, in the octaves of St Hilary before the lord king, wheresoever [he should then be in England], together with the royal writ to him directed therein etc. The same day is given to the said John etc. At which day the said John Waltham came before the lord king at Westminster, in his own person, and the sheriff did not [send] the writ. Therefore, as often before, the sheriff is ordered . . .[5] At which day [23 June 1502] the aforesaid John Waltham came before the lord king at Westminster, in his own person, and the sheriff returned a certain inquisition taken before him, by which it appeared that the same John had sustained damages of twenty shillings by reason of the aforesaid trespass, beyond his outlay and costs laid out by him about his suit in that behalf, and for the outlay and costs three pounds. Therefore it is awarded that the aforesaid John Waltham do recover against the aforesaid Thomas Lunde his aforesaid damages as assessed by the aforesaid jury in form aforesaid. And let the same Thomas be in mercy etc. Thereupon the aforesaid John Waltham freely here in court remitted to the said Thomas Lunde thirty-three shillings and fourpence of the aforesaid damages. Therefore let the same Thomas Lunde be quit of thirty-three shillings and fourpence.

Juliane Draper v. *Robert Claver* (1502)[6]

Bill preferred on 2 July 1502 before the Council, complaining of the disseisin of a burgage in Wells, Somerset; appeared at Westminster. Nonsuit; writ of inquiry.

---

[5] Another writ of inquiry, as above, returnable on the Thursday before the Nativity of St John the Baptist.

[6] KB 27/965, m. 25 (Mich. 1502).

Nicholas Upton, gent. v. Prior of Newstead (1504)[7]

Bill preferred on 16 October 1503, claiming an annuity; appeared before Geoffrey Symeon,[8] Morgan Kidwelly, and other councillors. Imparlance.

Thomas Morley v. John Tripp (1506)[9]

Bill preferred on 2 February 1504, concerning two messuages in Brentwood, Essex; appeared before Geoffrey Symeon, John Sutton, and other councillors. Pleads that he did not sue him before the Council; jury summoned.

Florence Bartram v. John Barowe (1507)[10]

Bill preferred on 15 April 1506, concerning nine messuages in St Clement Danes; appeared before Geoffrey Symeon, Richard Sutton, Richard Hatton, clerk, and other councillors.[11] Imparlance to Pas. 1508.

Richard Belton, clerk v. William Dregge (1509)[12]

Bill preferred 1 February 1509, complaining of the taking of crops; appeared before the dean of the Chapel Royal, Thomas Hatton, clerk, and other councillors. Pleads that he did not sue him before the Council; jury summoned.

Bertram Younghusband v. Prior of Tynemouth (1510)[13]

Privy seal letters served on 20 December 1509, complaining of the asportation and detention of a boat, for which he could have had an action of detinue at common law; appeared before the dean of the Chapel Royal and the king's almoner (Thomas Wolsey). Imparlances to Hilary term 1512.

---

[7] KB 27/972, m. 92 (Trin. 1504).   [8] Dean of the Chapel Royal.
[9] KB 27/978, m. 26d (Pas. 1506).   [10] KB 27/981, m. 104d (Hil. 1507).
[11] For the suit see Select Cases in the Council of Henry VII, ed, C. G. Bayne and W. H. Dunham (75 SS 1958) p. xxvii.
[12] KB 27/992, m. 37 (Pas. 1509).   [13] CP 40/991, m. 529 (Pas. 1510).

Lawrence Streynsham v. Margaret Hoorne, widow (1510)[14]

Bill preferred on 23 February 1508, concerning tiles and timber taken from a messuage at Faversham, Kent; appeared before Geoffrey Symeon and other councillors. Imparlance to Pas. 1512.

R. v. John Phillip (1511)[15]

Indictment before commissioners at East Grinstead, Sussex, on 17 August 1509 setting out that the defendant, scheming to vex Thomas Wulgare and two others in their bodies and lands, and as far as in him lay to subvert the laws and ancient customs of the realm, on 9 November 1508 exhibited a bill of false information to Sir Robert Sheffield ('Sheffeld'), one of the King's Council, falsely accusing Wulgare and the others of homicides and other wrongdoing against the law, and also accused them in person, as a result of which letters of privy seal were (by the defendant's procurement) directed to them on 28 November 1508 enjoining them without delay to appear before Sheffield at London immediately upon sight of the same, and thus they were vexed,[16] to the wicked example of other wrongdoers in similar cases if a remedy should not be provided, and against the form of various statutes (unspecified). On 22 May 1511 Phillip pleaded not guilty, and the attorney-general, by authority of an undated warrant (in English) under the king's sign manual, confessed the plea to be true. Phillip was thereupon discharged. The indictment did not mention Magna Carta, but the warrant recited the indictment of John Phillip, one of the yeomen of the crown, for 'divers trespasses and contempts against the form of the statute of the great charter of the liberties of England', and other trespasses and articles.

Roger Vyseke v. William Frye (1511)[17]

Bill preferred on 1 November 1507, alleging false imprisonment; appeared before Richard Empson alone. Pleads Not Guilty; recovers 10s. damages, 20s. costs, and a further 30s. increment of costs.

---

[14] KB 27/997, m. 75 (Mich. 1510).

[15] KB 27/999, Rex, m. 5 (Pas. 1511). This is evidently the case cited by Coke, with an incorrect roll reference, in his memorandum of 1604: below, p. 503.

[16] It is not alleged that they actually appeared before Sheffield.

[17] KB 27/1000, m. 28 (Trin. 1511). Cf. *Nicholas Speccote* v. *William Frye* (Trin. 1511) KB 27/997, m. 37, a similar action but framed instead on the statute of 42 Edw. III; here the bill was presented to Empson on 12 June 1507 and accused Speccote of being accessory to theft, whereby he was summoned by privy seal to appear before Empson at Westminster to answer the accusation, 'without any presentation before justices or matter of record or due process or

Abbot of Bury St Edmunds v. William Adams
and others (1514)[18]

Bill preferred on 16 March 1514, alleging extortion in demanding an annuity; summoned by writ from the Chancery (seal not specified); appeared before the archbishop of Canterbury and other councillors. Justifies at length, setting out the cause of his suit; demurrer. The court took advisement until Pas. 1517, but no judgment was entered.[19]

John Mylde, clerk v. John Sympson, chaplain (1514)[20]

Bill preferred on 21 March 1515, claiming a debt as executor; appeared before the dean of the Chapel Royal and other councillors. Writ of *latitat*.

Sir Robert Brandon v. Sir Edmund Jenney, William Burgeys, yeoman, and Christopher Jenney (1515)[21]

Bill preferred on 4 March 1515, alleging a trespass by Burgeys and the abduction of Denise Burgeys, aged 19; appeared before the dean of the Chapel Royal and other councillors. Imparlance to Hil. 1516.

Thomas Butler v. Robert Fuller (1523)[22]

Bill preferred on 16 November 1521, for detinue of a long list of household chattels; summoned at the instance of John Stokysley by John Broune, 'nuncius'; appeared before John Stokysley alone, and was forced to stand to the arbitration of Stokysley and Richard Rawlens; demurrer. The court took advisement until Mich. 1525, but no judgment was entered.

original writ according to the ancient law and custom of the lord king's realm of England', and was compelled to attend from day to day until he was forced to pay Empson £20, being half the fine of £40. The defendant pleaded not guilty, but the jury (taken by default) found for the plaintiff with £30 damages and £7 costs, of which £5 was remitted by the plaintiff.

[18] KB 27/1011, m. 33d (Pas. 1514).
[19] According to a reading in Gray's Inn (*c.* 1520) on Magna Carta, c. 29, he recovered damages: *Selected Readings on Magna Carta*, p. 254 (where the reader says the abbot had been summoned before the chancellor and House of Lords).
[20] KB 27/1013, m. 40d (Mich.1514).   [21] KB 27/1016, m. 62d (Trin. 1515).
[22] KB 27/1048, m. 75 (Trin. 1523).

Matthew Saunders v. John Broke (1524)[23]

Bill alleging assault and mistreatment, in delay of law and good conscience and against the peace ('in retardatione juris et legis domini regis Anglie ac bone consciencie contra pacem domini regis'); referred by writ under the signet seal to Sir John Vere, Thomas Bonham and Thomas Audley, who summoned the plaintiff before them at Colchester, Essex, on 20 November 1521; he appeared before them and was adjourned before the Council at Westminster, where he was enjoined to attend from day to day, for a long time, under pain of £100. The entry ends with a *latitat* to the sheriff of Essex, returnable in Michaelmas term 1524.

John Parnell v. Geoffrey and Margaret Vaughan (1532)[24]

Bill preferred on 12 January 1523 before Cardinal Thomas Wolsey, legate *a latere*, archbishop of York, and chancellor of England, complaining of the breach of a commercial agreement (set out at length); summoned and enjoined by writ of subpoena under the great seal dated 16 January 1529 to appear in Chancery in the octave of Hilary, which he did; imprisoned in the Fleet by Sir Thomas More, chancellor of England, from 1 July 1531 until the date of the present suit, to his damage of 2,000 marks. Imparlance to Trin. 1532.

---

[23] CP 40/1044, m. 280 (Trin. 1524). This is an *optulit se* entry, with numerous amendments, recording the writ and mesne process only. More details of dates would have been given in the declaration, but the defendant never appeared.

[24] KB 27/1082, m. 37 (Hil. 1532).

Appendix 3

William Fleetwood on Chapter 29 (*c.* 1558)

'No free person etc.' The books say that in the ninth year of King Henry III, when the subjects asked the king to restore to them the laws of St Edward, which he had previously promised to do, he put off the perform-ance thereof because it was against his profit, and yet he did not dare deny it to them directly lest perhaps it would be a cause of sedition, but with the intention that he might safely deny it to them afterwards without fear of rebellion he raised an army and diminished the power of his adversaries. By this extortion he first took the possessions of Ranulph, earl of Chester, who was the spokesman in this case, which he had by the gift of the king's predecessors, and his ministers also took the lives of others and put some in jeopardy of their lives; and upon mere accusation, without law or judgment, some were imprisoned, some put out of their lands, all were in danger of their goods, and no one was in safety of his life: Polydore.[1] This grievance touched all the subjects alike, and at their petition it was now enacted[2] that the pleasure of the prince should not thereafter be taken as law, but that justice should be used, and that from henceforth all should be adjudged by the law of the land. The statute is confirmed by the statutes 28 Edw. III, c. 3; 5 Edw. III, c. 9; 25 Edw. III, stat. 5, c. 4; 42 Edw. III, c. 3. And the statute 37 Edw. III, c. 18, ordains that all accusers should prove their accusations before the chancellor.

'No free person'. Although in these statutes *homo* is understood both of male and female, nevertheless here the signification thereof does not extend to a countess, duchess or any female – 20 Hen. VI, c. 9 – and so it is to be understood only of males.[3] Yet not of every male, for if he is not a lord of Parliament or a peer of the realm he shall not have this privilege. Even if he is a peer, he shall still in some cases not have this trial, for bishops and abbots shall

---

First published, together with the French text, in *Selected Readings on Magna Carta*, pp. 383–5.

[1] Polydore Vergil, xvi. 11. The ultimate source of the account here seems to have been the Brut chronicle, printed by Caxton: Thompson, *Magna Carta*, p. 156.

[2] I.e. in Magna Carta.

[3] It is evident from the citation that the author was here thinking only of trial by peers.

not try each other: 10 Edw. IV, fo. 6.[4] Nor shall peers be tried by them (Stamford, 153[5]), inasmuch as they have no place in Parliament by reason of their creation, whereupon it appears that he who is to have the privilege must be a temporal lord of the Parliament.

'Shall be imprisoned'. The statute does not mean that a man shall not be imprisoned without process, for one may lawfully be sent to prison for a rescue made, for misbehaviour in forests, for felony (upon a warrant for suspicion), or for [disobeying] a command from various officers: 2 Hen. VII, fo. 6;[6] 5 Hen. VII, fo. 3.[7] For the law allows this, and the statute affirms the law inasmuch as it says 'except by the law of the land'. And if someone is imprisoned or disseised contrary to law, no one has a remedy by this statute other than what was at common law, namely the assize [of novel disseisin] or false imprisonment.

As to the word 'outlawed' in the statute, the readers say that before this statute one could have a *capias* and process of outlawry without an original writ, which is now redressed.

'Nor shall we go upon him or send upon him'. Littleton said that these words shall be understood to mean that the king shall not arraign anyone, or send process for anyone to answer, in crown cases, unless he is adjudged by his peers: 10 Edw. IV, fo. 6.[8] Thus it means that he shall have the privilege in all indictments of felony, treason, misprision or an offence against the statute of seditious rumours: Stamford;[9] 1 & 2 Phil. & Mar., c. 3. In an appeal, however, because it is the suit of a party and not the king's suit, no privilege is granted.[10] The number of the peers must be at least twelve. And for the procedure of the arraignment, and the manner how they should demean themselves therein, see our books: 13 Hen. VIII, fo. 13;[11] 1 Hen. IV, fo. 1;[12] 10 Edw. IV, fo. 6.[13]

---

[4] YB Pas. 10 Edw. IV, fo. 6, pl. 17, *per* Littleton J.   [5] Sta. P.C. 153A–B.

[6] *Rectius* YB Pas. 2 Hen. VII, fo. 15, pl. 1.

[7] YB Mich. 5 Hen. VII, fo. 6, pl. 10; perhaps identifiable as *Wynslowe* v. *Cleypole* (1489) CP 40/910, m. 340. Both cases relate to imprisonment on suspicion.

[8] YB Pas. 10 Edw. IV, fo. 6, pl. 17, *per* Littleton J. Fleetwood here treats this clause as applying only to peers of the realm.

[9] Sta. P.C. 153D–154E.

[10] YB Pas. 10 Edw. IV, fo. 6, pl. 17, *per* Littleton J., citing *Lord Grey of Codnor's Case* (1442).

[11] *R.* v. *Duke of Buckingham* (1521) YB Pas. 13 Hen. VIII, fo. 11, pl. 1: It is on fo. 13 of Powell's edition (1548).

[12] *R.* v. *Earl of Huntingdon* (1400) YB Mich. 1 Hen. IV, fo. 1, pl. 1. This report first appeared in the 1553 edition and it has been suggested that it was a Tudor forgery: L. W. Vernon Harcourt, *His Grace the Steward and Trial of Peers* (1907), pp. 416–29, 444–60; A. W. B. Simpson, *Legal Theory and Legal History* (1987), p. 56; *OHLE*, vi. 520 n. 97; D. J. Seipp, 'How to get rid of a King' (forthcoming).

[13] YB Pas. 10 Edw. IV, fo. 6, pl. 17, *per* Littleton J.

'To no one shall we sell'. This is intended of the great fees which were
payable in the Chancery at common law for writs of right, and therefore now
at this day one may have this writ freely and without fine, as a result of these
words. It could also mean that a justice shall not be bribed, for then it would be
called *justicia venalis*. As for the just execution of justice, Edward I promised
in Westminster I, c. 1,[14] that he would do it. Henry IV also promised it, and all
the lords promised it, in 1 Hen. IV, c. 1;[15] 2 Hen. IV, c. 1;[16] 5 Edw. III, c. 1.

[14] Westminster I, c. 1, para. 1 (tr. 'that common right be done to poor and rich alike,
without respect of persons').
[15] 1 Hen. IV, c. 1, *ad finem* (tr. 'that good justice and equal right be done to everyone').
[16] 2 Hen. IV, c. 1, *ad finem* (tr. 'that full justice and right be done to poor and rich alike').

Appendix 4

Fleetwood's Tracts on Magna Carta and on Statutes:
A Concordance of Parallel Passages

Chapters of Magna Carta: WORDS DISCUSSED[a]	Tract on Statutes[b]	Tract on Magna Carta
c. 1, *ecclesia*	pp. 121 (124), 123 (126)	fos. 4, 4v
c. 2, *relevium debeat*	pp. 124[c] (127), 144 (145)	fos. 5v, 6
c. 3, *heres*	p. 149 (153)	fo. 8
c. 3, *antequam homagium ejus ceperit*	pp. 125–7 (130–2)	fo. 7v
c. 3, *terra remaneat in custodia*		fo. 8
c. 4, *vastum*	p. 163[d] (171)	fo. 8
c. 5, *sustentent domos ... de exitibus*	pp. 145 (147), 156 (162)	fo. 11
c. 6, *disparagatione*	p. 121 (124)	fo. 12v
c. 7, *nec aliquid det*	pp. 132–3 (119), 157 (163)	fos. 13, 13v
c. 7, *nisi domus illa sit castrum*	p. 156 (162)	fo. 14
c. 7, *quousque dos sua ei assignetur*	p. 137 (135)	fo. 14
c. 7, *se non maritabit sine assensu nostro*	pp. 159–60 (166)	fo. 15v[e]
c. 8, *non seisiemus*	p. 160 (167)	fo. 15v
c. 8, *aut reddere nolit*	pp. 135–6 (133–4)	fo. 16
c. 11, *communia placita*	p. 134 (122)	fo. 19[f]
c. 11, *loco certo*	p. 123 (126)	fo. 19
c. 12, *si extra regnum fuerimus*	p. 137 (135)	fo. 20
c. 12, *non capiantur nisi in suis comitatibus*	p. 133 (121)	fo. 20v
c. 12, *semel in anno*	p. 160 (166)	fo. 20
c. 12, *in itinere suo*	p. 107 (omitted)	fo. 20v
c. 14, *in misericordiam nostram*	p. 155 (161)	fo. 22
c. 15, *facere*	p. 123 (126)	fo. 23
c. 18, *defunctus*	p. 123 (126)	fo. 24v
c. 18, *ad faciendum testamentum*	p. 155 (161)	omitted
c. 19, *quadraginta dies*	p. 132 (118–19)	fo. 25v

(*cont.*)

Chapters of Magna Carta: WORDS DISCUSSED[a]	Tract on Statutes[b]	Tract on Magna Carta
c. 22, *convicti*	omitted (p. 126[g])	fo. 26v
c. 27, *non habebimus custodiam*	p. 155 (161)	fo. 29v
c. 30, *rectas consuetudines*	pp. 157, 158 (163, 165)	fo. 17[h]
c. 31, *nos eodem modo eam tenebimus*	pp. 150, 155 (154, 161)	fo. 33
c. 33, *habeant earum custodiam*	p. 144[i] (145)	fo. 35
c. 34, *appellum femine de morte*	p. 137 (135)	fo. 36v[j]
c. 35, *integra*	p. 139 (138)	fo. 39v
c. 36, *terram*	p. 122 (125)	omitted[k]

[a] Corrected to correspond with the *Statutes of the Realm*.

[b] References are to Fleetwood, *Statutes* (with the corresponding page in the *Discourse on Statutes* in parentheses).

[c] Says Merton; corrected in the *Discourse*.

[d] Says c. 13; corrected in the *Discourse*.

[e] Notes that the law has changed, and criticises the explanation given by the readers, but does not give the same reason as in *Statutes*: see *Selected Readings on Magna Carta*, p. 372.

[f] Same point, but does not mention formedon in the King's Bench, which is the example in *Statutes*. This was, however, a stock case: YB 36 Hen. VI, fo. 32, pl. 34, at fo. 34, *per* Fortescue CJ; Hil. 1 Hen. VII, fo. 12, pl. 18; Hil. 14 Hen. VII, fo. 14, pl. 3, *per* Fyneux CJ; *Select Readings on Magna Carta*, pp. 144, 147, 155.

[g] 'So *convictus* hath been put for *attinctus*: Magna Carta, ca. 22.' This sentence is omitted from the corresponding passage in Fleetwood, *Statutes*, p. 123. Cf. Fleetwood, *Magna Carta*, fo. 26v: (tr.) '*Convictus* is here understood for *attinctus*.'

[h] The main point here, that a confirmation of customs does not invalidate bad customs, is made in the treatise on Magna Carta in connection with c. 9, where it is more apposite, rather than c. 30.

[i] Says c. 3, corrected in the *Discourse*.

[j] The gloss here does not make exactly the point mentioned in the tract on statutes, which is that, in saying that a widow shall not have an appeal for any death save her husband's, it is implied that she may have an appeal for her husband's death.

[k] Fleetwood, *Magna Carta*, omitted cc. 36–7 on the grounds that these chapters were not lectured upon by the readers.

Appendix 5

Six Elizabethan Cases (1582–1600)

(a) *Att.-Gen. v. Joiners' Company of London* (1582)

The attorney-general, John Popham, brought an information in the nature of a *quo warranto* in the King's Bench, at the instance of a complainant, against the Joiners' Company of London, to show by what warrant they claimed the power to make bye-laws giving powers of search, forfeiture and imprisonment against joiners who were not members of the corporation, and setting out ten or more articles of complaint. The company relied on a charter of Queen Elizabeth.

Hilary Term 1582[1]

Popham, the queen's attorney-general, argued that they could not justify their actions [as specified] in these articles by virtue of their patent and grant. He argued that every subject born and begotten in the realm has two privileges, one to inherit the inheritance of his father or other ancestor, and the other to inherit the laws of this realm, from which no subject ought be barred. In confirmation whereof is the statute of Magna Carta, c. 29. This is not changeable by the queen. And so, in the time of Edward III, where the king granted to someone who was bound to repair a bridge that he should be discharged from it, this was a bad grant, for then others would be burdened with doing it.[2] And he said that if the queen by her letters patent could make new laws, what would be the purpose of so great an assembly of barons, bishops and commonalty at the Parliament? He agreed, however, that by some particular means the queen by her patent might dispense with various things, if this is reasonable and not repugnant to the law. For instance, a grant of cognizance of pleas is good, for no new laws are made thereby, but she only ordains special judges

---

The texts in this appendix have all been translated from the original law French. Judges' names are printed in small capitals, counsel in italics.

[1] BL MS. Hargrave 37, fos. 57–59v; MS. Lansdowne 1072, fos. 129v–131.
[2] Presumably 3 Edw. III, Fitz. Abr., *Assise*, pl. 445, though this particular reason is not given.

of her laws and lays down for them their certain limits within which they may administer justice; and this grant is for the ease of the subjects and not against law, and therefore good. And the king may grant someone a protection for a year, for this is only an unquietness for a certain time. Likewise he agreed with the case of the Oxford scholars in 40 Edw. III, fo. 16,[3] for that was a pre-eminence given them for their learning, and an advantage to the town, and no damage ... That is how he argued in 23 Eliz.

And in 24 Eliz. he argued to the same purpose. He argued, firstly, that they may not make any law amongst themselves which touches government: that belongs solely to the prince, because the punishment of all offences which concern the state and government always belongs to the prince. And those who are incorporated may not make such laws. This is well proved by their charter, for their charter says that 'they may make laws lawfully and without punishment' (*quod licite et impune faciant leges*), which proves that if such words were not in their patent they would not be able to make laws without punishment. Those who take upon themselves to make laws which are to the trouble and disquiet of others are to be punished as the authors and stirrers up of sedition and strife in the common wealth. Therefore in 43 Ass., pl. 38,[4] someone was presented [before a London city court] because he had reported that there were wars overseas, and that wool could not be exported, so that the price of wool fell; and, according to Knyvet [CJKB], this was a good present-ment. But he agreed that men may make laws amongst themselves, for their private interest, which do not extend to any others than those who assent and agree to them. Thus, if certain people have a common in a certain place, they may agree amongst themselves at what time of the year they will use their common; but if there is any commoner who does not agree to this it will not bind him, for no one shall be bound other than parties and privies. Likewise in 43 Edw. III,[5] if a bridge is broken, and certain people assemble and agree amongst themselves that everyone should pay so much towards repairing the same bridge, this will bind those who are parties to the agreement but will not bind any stranger. Similarly in the principal case, they may not bind outsiders who were not party to their constitutions. Also, if the Joiners decreed amongst themselves that no one should occupy that trade unless he had a stock of £100, this constitution would not bind, for everyone's abilities are not alike. Or if they constituted that each of them should sell their wares at such and such a price, this would not bind, for it may be that their stuff is not all of the same value and therefore they may not without prejudice to others (and also to themselves) all sell at one price. Or if they ordained that they

---

[3] YB Hil. 40 Edw. III, fo. 17, pl. 8; above, p. 60.
[4] *The Lombard's Case* (1370) YB 43 Edw. III, Lib. Ass., pl. 38.
[5] *Abbot of Combe's Case* (1370) YB 43 Edw. III, Lib. Ass., pl. 37.

should only work for five hours a day, this would not bind, for it is prejudicial. Such laws as these will not bind anyone, for they are absolutely repugnant to the government of a well ordered common wealth and tend to the destruction of its estate. Even admitting that the Corporation of Joiners may make some laws, we must now see who shall be bound by such laws. And he argued that no stranger should be bound by them. If, for instance, a sanctuary is granted to someone who is in debt, this is a good grant as between the king and the grantee, and yet it will not bind a third-party creditor, who may still sue for his debt. This was agreed in the time of Edward VI in the Star Chamber, and (as Wray CJ said) has been so affirmed and adjudged in the time of this queen[6] ... Also he said that if a law is made for the benefit of the common wealth, the voice of the greater number is material, and *ubi major pars ibi totum*: as in the Parliament and other places. And so he concluded, as to this point, that the Joiners' private bye-laws tend to no commodity, and may not bind other joiners and strangers who are not parties or privies to the making of such laws. Then he argued as to their authority to imprison men. And he said that, if [joiners] engage in deceit, the order of punishment is not to imprison them without suit of the law, for no one may be his own judge, but they ought to be punished by way of indictment, which is the ordinary course of the law. In 42 Ass., pl. 5, it was presented that John Style had arrested S. with certain goods and chattels and taken him to Gloucester Castle,[7] and imprisoned him for three weeks; the defendant said that a commission came to him and others from the Chancery to take the said S., his goods and chattels, and take him to Gloucester Castle, by virtue whereof he took them; and the justices said that the commission was against the law, to take and imprison a man without indictment and due process of law. It has been objected that a constable may imprison a wrong-doer without indictment or process of law, and a town may detain a prisoner if the gaoler will not receive him;[8] and in Halifax (in the North) they proceed without process to men's deaths:[9] why, therefore, may not the Joiners proceed in the same way by virtue of their charter? He answered that a constable is like a judge, and if sees an affray he may arrest the parties and imprison them, just as judges who see an affray in their presence may command the parties to prison without process.[10] Next, as to the sixth article, he said that they may not seize wares as forfeited. It has been objected that their bad

---

[6] This probably refers to *Hampton and Whitacres' Case* (1569) in the Star Chamber: *Dyer's Notebooks*, i. 173. The reference to Edw. VI may be a mistake for the case of St Martin's-le-Grand, heard in the Star Chamber in 19 Hen. VI: ibid. 121.

[7] *Rectius* Colchester Castle, but the mistake is in the printed book: *Sir John atte Lee's Case* (1368) above, p. 58.

[8] YB Hil. 10 Hen. IV, fo. 7, pl. 3, *per* Gascoigne CJ.   [9] See above, p. 263.

[10] YB Hil. 22 Edw. IV, fo. 45, pl. 9.

wares may be seized and broken into pieces, just as corrupt victuals may be seized and thrown to dogs. But (he said) it is not the same, for corrupt victuals ought to be thrown to dogs and should not be given to men, which would beget disease (*corruption*), and so the throwing away of such things is a benefit to the common wealth. But the wares of joiners, even if they are insufficient for some particular purpose, may nevertheless be suitable for another purpose, and therefore breaking them up is a damage to the common wealth. Next he argued that it is not lawful for them to prohibit any man from occupying this trade, even though he is not allowed by them to occupy it, for it might be advantageous to them to allow only a small number, and by that means many workmen would have no means of living in the world, and on account of this mischief their patent is not to be allowed on this point. It is like a case in 2 Hen. V, fo. 5,[11] where someone was bound not to use his trade of a dyer within the vill where the obligee lived during a certain space of time, and the condition was there adjudged to be against the law, and so the bond was void ...[12] All these privileges claimed by them are great taxations and amount to infinite burdens to subjects. And all such grants from the king which tend to the overburdening of the subjects are void and of no effect in law ... And where the king's patent tends to the damage of many, the patent is void ... Thus, in the principal case, the king's patent tending to the oppression and vexation of strangers and outsiders shall be absolutely void and of no validity in law.

Daniel argued to the contrary ...[13] It has been said that no man ought to be imprisoned without due process or order of the law, and therefore their patent giving them this privilege is not to be allowed. This is not so, for in the time of Edw. I, Fitz. Abr., *Prescription*, pl. 65,[14] it is said that there is a usage in one part of the country that if someone has committed a burglary or other larceny and is pursued from vill to vill, and a hue raised, and he is taken in flight, he ought to be executed, and such a felony is a corruption of blood and loses his wife her dower, and yet there is no indictment, no arraignment, and no process of law, and still it is allowable; and the men of this vill by prescription may proceed to judgment of death without any process or ordinary course of law. A multo fortiori, the Joiners by their patent may lawfully imprison wrongdoers, for the commencement of every prescription was a grant.[15] ...

---

[11] YB Pas. 2 Hen. V, fo. 5, pl. 26.   [12] He then discusses the later articles of complaint.

[13] His first point was that those in authority may make laws if they are for the good of the common wealth.

[14] The Halifax gibbet case, n. 9, opposite.

[15] I.e. the Halifax custom must have begun by royal grant. This was an unorthodox argument, because customs were by their nature different from the common law and therefore incapable of being granted by the king: *Gateward's Case* (1607) 6 Co. Rep. 59 at fo. 60; *Rowles* v. *Mason* (1612) 2 Br. & G. 192 at p. 198, *per* Coke CJ.

And so he concluded that judgment ought to be given for the Joiners of London and against the outsiders.

It was adjourned.

Easter Term 1582[16]

Daniel of Gray's Inn ... Mr Attorney has said that the king may not alter the interest which his subjects have in the law, and may not take away the inheritance of any man. He also cited a case between the queen and those of the town of Southampton, where the queen granted that no one but themselves should import sweet wines, and the grant was adjudged void.[17] Likewise when the king granted to the Merchant Venturers that if any others used their trade to Muscovy their goods should be forfeited, the grant was adjudged void. He [*Daniel*] accepted those cases. As to what was said that it may not extend to strangers, he said that the clerk of the market may restrain corrupt victuallers. He confessed the case in 45 Edw. III, Lib. Ass. [pl. 5], where the king granted to someone that he should take the body of another, that is not good ... And he agreed that if the patent had said that no man should use his occupation, that would be void; but when it says that no one should do so 'without allowance', that is good. And he put a case where an imprisonment is lawful [without due process]: 22 Edw. IV,[18] where a constable put a man in the stocks who made an affray ...

Popham, attorney-general. No one by the common law may make laws, for that belongs to the king alone ... As to the imprisonment, the statute of Magna Carta, c. 29, forbids it: *Nullus liber homo imprisonetur etc.*

Heads of argument prepared by William Fleetwood[19]

Every prerogative granted, or custom, participates with the reason of the general law and is incorporated to some extent in the reason of the general law. And there are no contrarieties or absurdities between the general law and prerogatives granted, or customs, for there is no bastardy between them. The general law is the mother and the others are her children dependent on her. And this is proved by two reasons. First, if a prerogative granted by the king, or a custom, is pleaded, and thereupon a demurrer is joined, you who are judges of the law, and in whom the law is a speaking law, shall judge whether it is a good grant, or a good prerogative, or a good custom, and your judgment is

---

[16] CUL MS. Hh.2.9, fos. 253–254v; BL MS. Hargrave 6, fo. 70; MS. Hargrave 8, fos. 239v–241.

[17] Above, p. 190.   [18] YB Hil. 22 Edw. IV, fo. 45, pl. 9.

[19] BL MS. Harley 4717, fos. 123–128v.

grounded upon and understood through the knowledge of the law. Another reason is, *Consuetudo ex causa rationabili usitata privat communem legem*: Littleton.[20] *Privare legem* has the sense of taking away the course of the general law; but the judgment of the law – the life, soul or sense of the law – is not taken away, for whether it is a good custom or not, by the understanding of the general law, is for you to judge. If there is a custom that the youngest son should inherit, he may nevertheless bring his action for the land in the general courts, which proves that it is within the reason and ground of the general law even though the course of the inheritance is altered from the general course of the law. This I have spoken of to this purpose, to show that our case is to be determined and judged by the law, and that the king's grant is not allowable if it has no law to warrant it to be good, for *quod placuit regi legis vigorem habuit* is no rule for judges in our law to follow.[21] Nor is the saying of the King Antigonus, chancellor to the king [*sic*], that all things are honest and lawful to kings[22] ... Thus the kings of England, considering what the laws are – *Lex regis praesidium*,[23] *Lex regis solium sive statio*,[24] *Lex anima reipublicae*[25] – wish their grants and prerogatives to be directed and adjudged according to the law, and in law they have held that course, and you who are judges so adjudge them and have so adjudged and given judgment. The king has here founded a corporation, and granted government and power to make reasonable, wholesome and meet ordinances for government. Corporations are by the course of the law, and have the same favour in the law as other natural bodies have. It is right that they should be ready for all loans, and charges of soldiers, and other charges for the common weal. To make corporations – which are only a name, shadow or imagination – and not to give them order and government, and correction, is nothing but a vain thing. Therefore order, rule and government belong as a necessary incident to incorporation, and a corporation cannot exist without rule, and laws, and government, any more than the natural body without natural food. Take away government, and they are left as a dead body and shadow ... In our case nothing is granted but what belongs to a decent order and necessary government, and to avoid deceits in work which may happen to the detriment of the people if they are not providently forbidden. And such matters are for the benefit of the people, and the public weal. Therefore it is

---

[20] Co. Litt. s. 169 (tr. 'A custom used for a reasonable cause takes away the common law').
[21] See above, p. 120.   [22] See above, p. 147.
[23] 'The law is the king's protection': the motto of the new serjeants' rings in 1577.
[24] 'The law is the king's throne or standing-place.' Cf. the motto of the new serjeants' rings when Fleetwood was created in 1580 (*Lege firmatur solium reginae*): Baker, *Collected Papers*, ii. 834.
[25] 'The law is the soul of the common wealth.' Cf. the motto on the new serjeants' rings of 1589 (*Lex reipublicae vita*): ibid.

a good grant. The laws which are made are general and similar for all, private to none, not for any individual's benefit, but for the benefit of the whole corporation and the members over whom the laws extend. They are *jubens honesta et prohibens contraria*,[26] and the laws are not contrary to the laws of God or of nature but apt for the place and people, and they do not disinherit anyone of any matter. There is no sum of money, fine or imposition, imprisonment or forfeiture unless it is common to all and may be imposed on person or land for the general benefit of all ... Grants and privileges granted to those who have been the inventors of any art or science which is beneficial to the common weal, and which was not before, or which [make things more readily available] with lesser charge and more profitably for the common weal, have allowance in the law. [For instance,] Jacob Versulyne,[27] a privilege for making glass; a privilege for making copperas or alom [granted] to the Lord Mountjoy ('Monge'); a privilege granted to William Homfrey, who found out the smelting of lead with iron; Mr Hastings' privilege for making baize. These privileges are maintained in the Exchequer, and punishments inflicted on those who offend against the privileges. It has been conceded by Mr Attorney that the king may charge the people in respect of a general benefit, as in the case of murage and poundage, and contribution for causeways; and that is the law, for everyone benefits from it and has *quid pro quo*, for he has passage and defence in return for the contribution. ...

Objection. A grant was made to the town of Southampton that they (and no other) should have the bringing in of malmseys, and yet they could not enjoy it before they had a confirmation by Parliament. The Merchant Adventurers for Discovery of New Trades[28] had a grant that no one should travel in the places which they have found by their labour, upon pain of forfeiture of their goods adventured, and yet they could not enjoy it until the statute made in the eighth year of Elizabeth.

Answer ... The case of Southampton I grant, that in the case of merchants the king cannot restrain any merchant from bringing in merchandise to any place, for (this being the trade whereby he lives) he may not be restrained, inasmuch as it impugns the law of nations; for everyone who is a merchant may by the law of nations come and trade in any kingdom, not being an enemy, and if he is hindered he is wronged. And he may not be impeded or

---

[26] *Bracton*, ii. 22 ('ordering virtue and prohibiting its opposite'); J. Fortescue, *De Laudibus Legum Anglie*, ed. S. B. Chrimes (Cambridge, 1942), p. 8 ('lex est sanctio sancta, jubens honesta et prohibens contraria'). This phrase is from Azo's commentary on Justinian's *Institutes*.

[27] I.e. Jacob Verzalini, the Venetian glass-maker.

[28] *Sic*, but the correct name was The Merchant Adventurers for the Discovery of Regions, Dominions, Islands and Places Unknown.

restrained from importing such things as are wholly for the general benefit of the common weal, though things vain and unprofitable may be restrained . . .[29]

Objection. The case of 45 Ass., pl. 5, has been put, that a commission to take anyone's person or his goods is void. I agree, where no cause is given. But where there is a cause, they may be removed from his possession by commission, and his goods may be taken and removed for an offence . . .

Objection. But it is said that the king's grant does not extend so far that they may make laws to seize, imprison and impose fines upon those who are not of the corporation and society, and for this various statutes are cited which prohibit laws to be made in charge of the people. And it is alleged that no one may administer justice and execute laws unless by commission and authority. I grant this; but in our case we have authority . . . It is a good and reasonable ordinance whereby it may be known who is a skilful artificer in his art, for it is not right that anyone should set up who has no skill, for by tolerating it deceits and damage might ensue to everyone. And in all arts of learning no one may presume upon a calling and allowance. With us, no one may be an utter barrister or reader without election; nor may the physicians in London without allowance of the College [of Physicians], doctors in law in the Arches, or anyone in the universities, without calling.

Objection. But it has been likened to the case of 2 Hen. V,[30] where someone was bound that he would not occupy the art of dyeing within such a place for a certain time, and it was held that this was a void bond and against the law to restrain anyone from his occupation . . .

Answer. The ordinance [here] stands with reason, for if he offers himself to them and requests them to be admitted, and offers to do his proof-piece, and they will not admit him, he may set up without offending the ordinance or incurring the penalty. Imprisonment: as to this, it has been objected that our ordinances for imprisonment are not good. For this, Magna Carta has been vouched, *Nullus capiatur etc.*, and various statutes, such as 5 Edw. III, 25 Edw. III, 28 Edw. III, 42 Edw. III, all in the title 'Accusation' in Rastall's abridgement, all of which tend to the effect of Magna Carta. And an argument has been made that he would otherwise be in execution before lawful judgment, *legale judicium parium suorum vel per legem terrae*. But our case stands upon an imprisonment which may be inflicted without a judicial judgment. If their award is for breach of their ordinance, and the cause is reasonable, then it is *per legem terrae*. For *lex terrae* is reason, and when an imprisonment is upon a reasonable cause the imprisonment is *per legem terrae*. A constable ought to imprison in the common gaol, and yet if he is afraid that the prisoner will be

---

[29] There follows an argument as to whether bye-laws can bind strangers if they are for the public good.

[30] YB Pas. 2 Hen. V, fo. 5, pl. 26.

rescued or taken from him he may imprison him in his house, or in the stocks, at his discretion: 22 Edw. IV, fos. 36, 43.[31] If two are fighting together, the constable may take them and imprison them in his house until the affray is past: 22 Edw. IV, fo. 45.[32] If a constable takes someone to the common gaol and the gaoler will not receive him, anyone of the vill may imprison him to avoid an escape (and the fine which may happen as a result of the escape): 10 Hen. IV, fo. 7.[33] The rebels in the time of Jack Cade, to the number of one hundred, assembled in Bath and took someone in order to behead him, and the defendant came to rescue him from them, and put him in the mayor's house for one night, and false imprisonment was brought by him, and it was justified for this cause: 35 Hen. VI, fo. 45.[34] One may imprison someone who is suffering from madness, and correct him with rods to prevent him doing wrong and endangering others: 22 Lib. Ass.[35] . . .

(b)   Collett v. Webbe (1587)

In an action of false imprisonment in the Common Pleas by a mercer against the bailiffs of Shrewsbury, they pleaded a custom for the bailiffs to arrest anyone behaving contemptuously towards themselves, or towards the wardens of any mystery, either by words or by deeds, and to imprison them without mainprise for a day or more (or less) at their discretion, according to the seriousness of the offence; and they said they had imprisoned the plaintiff for four days for his contempt in not coming before them when summoned to answer for misbehaviour towards the wardens of the Weavers' Company. The plaintiff demurred, and the court took advisement from Michaelmas term 1586 to Trinity term 1587, when judgment was given for the plaintiff.[36]

Easter Term 1587[37]

Walmsley, serjeant, argued briefly (after the record was read) that this custom is against ancient statute law,[38] which appoints bail and mainprise for

---

[31] YB Mich. 22 Edw. IV, fo. 35, pl. 16; Hil. 22 Edw. IV, fo. 43, pl. 4.
[32] YB Hil. 22 Edw. IV, fo. 45, pl. 9.   [33] YB Hil. 10 Hen. IV, fo. 7, pl. 3, per Gascoigne CJ.
[34] YB Hil. 35 Hen. VI, fos. 44–45, pl. 6.   [35] YB 22 Edw. III, Lib. Ass., pl. 56.
[36] The plea roll (cited in the reports as CP 40/1461, pt i, m. 2549) is unfit for production.
[37] BL MS. Add. 35948, fos. 99–101; YLS MS. G.R29.6, unfol. (undated); abridged in BL MS. Lansdowne 1068, fo. 101; BL MS. Lansdowne 1078, fo. 51; HLS MS. 1180(1), fo. 411. Cf. the much shorter reports in 2 Leon. 34; BL MS. Lansdowne 1095, fo. 86v; LI MS. Misc. 361, fo. 106 (dated Trin. 1587); HLS MS. 1180(1), fo. 411. Walmsley's argument alone is reported in similar terms in BL MS. Harley 2036, fo. 153v (misdated Hil. 1587).
[38] Statute of Westminster I, c. 15.

everyone, except in special cases, for here they prescribe that their prisoner shall not be mainprised in any case. He also said that by prescription they could be keepers of the peace but not justices of the peace,[39] and they may not prescribe to detain in prison at their discretion. For this, the very case is in 22 Edw. IV, fo. 43,[40] that a town may not prescribe to keep suspects in their town gaol for four days before they carry to them to the common gaol, for then they would be irreplevisable for those four days, whereas by the law they ought to be replevied at once. Also, if they may prescribe for three or four days, they might by the like reason prescribe for three or four years, which would be unreasonable . . .

It was adjourned.

Fleetwood, serjeant, later argued that the action did not lie, and said that nothing had been objected against him but the book of 22 Edw. IV, fo. 43, which he said was of no great authority and was not adjudged as vouched. But he who would argue the case above learnedly ought to begin with Magna Carta c. 29, which says that *Nullus liber homo* . . ..[41] And he would not omit to show this, even though it seemed to make against him. This statute has always been in the greatest reverence, so much so that Roger Wendover ('Venerdall') in the time of Edward II wrote that no one could write against the statute, which was made and written with the blood of the subjects. And he stood long in proving that it was a sacred statute. Nevertheless, he said that no statute is of such great authority but that the justices have always, in exposition, qualified it, and have expounded it contrary to the words rather than that any absurdity should be committed through the rigour in respect of something against the law of nature. Therefore, if an Act is against the law of nature, it shall be expounded as void. And so, in 6 Edw. III,[42] it was adjudged that, whereas the Statute of Maintenance ordains that no one should maintain [a suit] or purchase the land in suit and controversy,[43] nevertheless a gift to John Style and his daughter in frankmarriage pending a suit against him was held clearly outside the statute, for by the law of nature a man may advance his daughter without committing champerty: note that. Likewise where a man brings an appeal of robbery, and his two sons aid and abet him, they shall nevertheless not render damages for this, and shall not be inquired into as abettors, for nature commands them to help their fathers. Moreover, a statute shall be construed against the letter rather than that an absurdity should be committed. For

[39] This was because justices of the peace were introduced by statute within time of legal memory: below, p. 482.
[40] YB Hil. 22 Edw. IV, fo. 43, pl. 4.
[41] According to the brief report by John Adams in BL MS. Harley 4814, fo. 275v, Serjeant Walmsley did argue that the prescription was against Magna Carta, c. 29. But Adams had probably reconstructed the arguments imperfectly from memory.
[42] YB Trin. 6 Edw. III, fo. 33, pl. 19.   [43] Statute of Westminster II, c. 49.

instance, Magna Carta appoints that no one should be in ward before homage done, and yet if a father dies, and his son is under two or three years, it has always been understood that he should be in ward immediately, for it would be absurd to compel him to do homage at that age.[44] And he said that continuance of time may cause something to be taken as a statute which in truth never was a statute, such as Merton, which is now taken to be a statute, though it is clear that it never was a statute ... see Bracton, fo. 222, to that effect[45] ... And he said there was an offence called *crimen stellionis*,[46] which is now punished only by the Star Chamber, but at common law was punished at the discretion of the justices and officers appointed to preserve the peace, and that was at first to be 'cut off'[47] by imprisonment or other present castigation. Belknap [CJCP] was exiled in Ireland for this crime. When the mayor of London was riding he was seized by various people and told to get down from his horse, and he got down to placate them; but he went at once to the Guildhall, and there without any law beheaded the offenders: and yet this was well done.[48] (But *Peryam* said that two years later he obtained a pardon.) Also there is an old book where a woman brought dower, and it was pleaded against her that her husband was attainted by Halifax law, and it was a good bar;[49] and yet this is nothing other than execution by prescription, without ordinary and lawful conviction; that was against the statute of Magna Carta previously recited, and yet it was good, for otherwise there would be great inconvenience if such punishments within corporate towns were not allowed. See 39 Edw. III, fo. 8, and 21 Edw. III.[50] And he vouched 27 Edw. III, tit. *Corone*, where someone brought a [diseased] pig into the market and was brought to the pillory[51] forthwith; and yet this was an imprisonment contrary to Magna Carta, c. 29. See 2 Ric. III, according.[52]

---

[44] Fleetwood made the same point in *Statutes*, pp. 125–7; *Discourse on Statutes*, pp. 130–2; *Magna Carta*, fo. 7v.

[45] Cited below, p. 480, as on fo. 202, but no such passage is to be found in the printed edition. Cf. *Bracton*, ii. 276 (fo. 96), where an enactment at Merton is referred as a 'new grace and provision' (*nova superveniente gracia et provisione*); and ibid. iv. 295 (fo. 416v), where the assembly at Merton is said to have been attended by most of the barons, summoned for the coronation. Cf. Fleetwood, *Statutes*, p. 105 ('As the Statute of Merton, the lords were assembled about the marriage of Eleanor and not summoned to a parliament, and yet hath the face of a statute, and yet is not called a statute but Provisiones [de] Merton').

[46] I.e. deceit, or cozening: Lambarde, *Archeion*, p. 84 ('cozenage'). Lambarde said that some supposed a connection between this metaphor and the name *camera stellata* (starred chamber). But *stellio* meant a kind of lizard and had nothing to do with stars: Co. Inst. iv. 66.

[47] These words are in English.

[48] This refers to an incident in 1339 during the mayoralty of Andrew Aubrey.

[49] Temp. Edw. I, Fitz. Abr., *Prescription*, pl. 65; above, pp. 190, 472, 473.

[50] Unidentified. The former reference is incorrect.   [51] YLS MS. Other texts say 'bailiffs'.

[52] YB Mich. 1 Ric. III, fo. 1, pl. 1, *per* Fairfax J.

Likewise in all cases where offenders are taken red-handed, such [summary] punishment was lawful: note that.[53] But he agreed the cases in 42 Ass., pl. 5, and 24 Edw. III, Bro. Abr., *Commission*, pl. [3], where a commission went to certain persons to take all those who were notoriously slandered for felonies and trespasses, even if they were not indicted; such a commission is *contra legem*, for the offence does not appear to them who have the commission. It is otherwise where the fact appears to them who have such authority, for there they may inflict punishments at their discretion. It is likewise in our case, for the defendants imprisoned the plaintiff for a misdemeanour which appeared to themselves and was committed against them. And he said it had always been allowed as a forest law that if a forester arrests any person in his forest with bow, net or any engine for killing game, he may imprison him forthwith. But by hearsay, or upon report of others, that a certain person has so misbehaved in the forest, the forester may not imprison. The mayor of London takes his oath to view all bakers and brewers, and if they offend against the assize [of bread and ale] he may commit them to prison. And he said that every corporation by their patent may equally well imprison offenders. And he made a discourse upon the commission of the peace, and said that this gives authority to the justices to examine offences upon various statutes even though there never were such statutes. And so he concluded, and prayed that the plaintiff should be barred from his action.

Afterwards, in Trinity term 29 Eliz. (1587), the justices said to *Fleetwood* that they would consider this case and look at the pleadings, because it seemed to them strange to prescribe to be a justice of the peace,[54] or to imprison anyone at their discretion . . . Therefore they intended to give judgment for the plaintiff unless Fleetwood showed other matter the next day. Afterwards judgment was given accordingly: which note.

A second report[55]

Fleetwood to the contrary. He said that his adversary who argued against him ought to have grounded his argument on the statute of Magna Carta, c. 29, *quod nullus liber homo capiatur vel imprisonetur aut disseisitur de libero tenemento suo vel libertatibus suis vel liberis consuetudinibus suis etc.* For he said that he never read any case which impugned this law. Nevertheless this law ought to have reasonable intelligence; for every law, be it by statute or common law, is void if it is

---

[53] See Baker, *Collected Papers*, ii. 973–4.

[54] This was because justices of the peace were introduced by statute within time of memory: below, p. 482.

[55] BL MS. Lansdowne 1087, fo. 239.

against the law of God, or the law or nature, or the common weal ...[56] And the king at the time of his coronation takes a solemn oath upon the gospel that he will govern and rule according to law, and do right and law to every subject, and this accords with the statute of Magna Carta. He made a long argument, but he never argued the very point, namely whether this prescription in the way it was now made was good or not.

Afterwards the opinion of the lord ANDERSON [CJ] and all the justices was ... that the prescription (even if it had been well pleaded) was not good, but unreasonable and against the law, for it is not fitting that anyone who is a bailiff or mayor of a corporation should be able to imprison anyone at his pleasure, for by this prescription he could by the same reason imprison someone for seven years, which is unreasonable.

Thereupon *Fleetwood* said there was such a prescription and custom in London, and in several other corporations, which was never before now quashed or disallowed, for if they were not allowed to do this they could not preserve such large places and cities in peace, which are so populous. But the justices answered him that it is not right that such towns or corporations should be allowed to do wrong to others against the law, at their pleasures and without cause, and then to say that they do it for preservation of their quietness and peace.

A third version of Serjeant Fleetwood's argument[57]

... *Fleetwood* to the contrary. The only objection which could be made would have to be framed upon the statute of Magna Carta, *quod nullus liber homo etc.* But it seemed to him that it would be too perilous in cities, where great mischiefs and outrages might easily be stirred up on the sudden, if the magistrates did not have sufficient power to imprison persons disobeying their orders. It is not like government in the country. And it appears in a case of 6 Edw. III that the Statute of Champerty does not restrain natural love, to give land in frankmarriage with his daughter pending a plea;[58] and there it is held that a son may aid his father in an appeal of robbery; and the common law has made the same construction in many cases to avoid an absurdity in any statute. Also time has worn out various statutes, just as time has also established others: for Bracton, fo. 202,[59] says that the law of Merton was not made by Parliament, but is now held to be a statute. ... I can show various precedents against the statute of Magna Carta. And he cited a case where the mayor of London, by the assent of the commonalty, beheaded two fishmongers who forced him to alight from his horse and misused him

---

[56] He then cited the case of champerty, and the commission of 1368.
[57] CUL MS. Ff.5.4, fo. 272.   [58] YB Trin. 6 Edw. III, fo. 33, pl. 19.
[59] See above, p. 478 n. 45.

contemptuously as he rode about the city proclaiming quietness in the time of the civil wars in the time of Edward II. (But *Peryam* said that those cases were not to be cited, for the mayor was glad to purchase his pardon.) *Fleetwood* said in conclusion that it would be greatly dangerous to wait until everyone offending against the ordinances of the city, and behaving himself contemptuously, could be indicted upon the statute ...

(c)   *Jerome v. Neale and Pleere* (1588)

Record: KB 27/1304, m. 515 (Hil. 1588). John Jerome and Avice his wife brought an action of trespass against Simon Neale and Christopher Pleere for assaulting Avice on 16 June 1587 in the parish of St Giles-in-the-Fields, Middlesex,[60] and causing such wounds that John spent £5 on her cure. On 22 January 1588 the defendants pleaded that Salisbury is an ancient city and that from time immemorial it has been the custom there that if anyone is assaulted or beaten within the city, the mayor as justice of the peace there, upon complaint, sends a serjeant at mace or constable, or other officer of the peace, to cause such person to come before him to answer for it; and they say that John Jerome assaulted and beat the defendants, being constables of the city, at Salisbury, and on 16 June 1587 they complained to Thomas Eyar, the mayor and justice of the peace, who commanded them to cause John to come before him, and when they came by virtue of this command to John's house in Salisbury, Avice assaulted and hindered them so that they could not do it, and would not desist, whereupon they gently laid their hands upon her to cause her to desist, which is the same assault, battery and wounding of which they complain. The plaintiff demurred to this plea, and the court took advisement until Easter term. No judgment is entered.

Hilary Term 1588[61]

It was adjudged no plea, for it seems unreasonable that a mayor may send for a man by such usage to any part of England, if he is in London, and he has not shown a place in which to send for him. Also, since the action is brought for wounding him, it seems he has not made answer by the above plea. And those were the reasons for the judgment given by the justices.

---

[60] The battery may have been alleged in Middlesex fictitiously to obtain a trial at Westminster, but it was to be the defendants' downfall, since they justified a trespass in Salisbury and therefore did not answer what was alleged.

[61] BL MS. Harley 1331, fos. 42v–43. The statutory references have been corrected. Cf. a much shorter report in 1 Leon. 105; 4 Leon. 149.

But GAWDY said they had not resolved whether or not a mayor or justice of peace might send for a man without warrant in writing, or whether this was a good prescription.

Coke in his argument argued that it was void, and against the statute of Magna Carta, which says that *Nullus liber homo de cetero imprisonetur etc.*, and against various other statutes; and he vouched 25 Edw. III, stat. 5, c. 4,[62] and 42 Edw. III, c. 3, etc.

But Mr Recorder [*Fleetwood*] argued against him, that prescriptions are now allowed against various statutes. For instance, 'common pleas shall not follow our court' etc.[63] Also the statute of Magna Carta says that the lord shall not take homage before the heir is in ward, and yet this is not now law.[64] And in 14 Hen. VII,[65] justices of peace may send for a man who breaks the peace [without a warrant]; and it is often so done in London when they do not know the names of those who offend.

Easter Term 1588[66]

Coke. This plea is bad. First, the custom is bad, being unreasonable. For the statute of Magna Carta, c. 29, is, *Nullus liber homo capietur aut imprisonetur nisi per legale judicium etc.* Therefore he cannot be arrested by [mere] suggestion of anyone. And for this see 25 Edw. III, stat. 5, c. 4.[67] He also says that he sent for him as justice of the peace, whereas being a justice of the peace does not lie in prescription, inasmuch as there was no justice of the peace before 1 Edw. III, [stat. 2], c. 16. Even if he was a justice of the peace, he could not determine any matter outside the sessions of the peace. Also he prescribes to send for him, and does not say 'within the city'. Also it is not shown that those of Salisbury are incorporated in such a way that he may be enabled to prescribe. Also their justification is bad, for the declaration was for an assault, battery and wounding, and they plead that they gently laid their hands on the wife, which is the same trespass, and yet this cannot in any sense be a wounding. Also they say that they laid their hands on her in New Sarum, which is the same trespass, and do not traverse the place, and therefore the plea is bad.

---

[62] The text says 24 Edw. III, c. 9, but there was no such parliament. The same wrong citation occurs in the different report below (BL MS. Lansdowne 1095, fo. 48).

[63] Magna Carta, c. 11. Cf. Fleetwood, *Statutes*, p. 134; *Discourse on Statutes*, p. 122; *Magna Carta*, fo. 19; above, p. 244.

[64] Magna Carta, c. 3. Cf. Fleetwood, *Statutes*, pp. 125–7; *Discourse on Statutes*, pp. 130–2; *Magna Carta*, fo. 7v; above, pp. 88 n. 85, 478.

[65] YB Mich. 14 Hen. VII, fo. 7, pl. 19.   [66] BL MS. Lansdowne 1095, fo. 48.

[67] The text says 24 Edw. III, c. 9, as in the previous report.

Afterwards judgment was given for the plaintiff. And WRAY said that the custom was not good, but [the reason was] chiefly because they did not answer as to the wounding. Also, according to CLENCH, by the custom here, as it is pleaded, he might call him to any part of England to answer him, which is not right.

A second report of the arguments in Easter Term 1588[68]

Coke argued for the plaintiff, and alleged that the plea was insufficient for four causes. First, this custom and prescription is void and against the law... As to the first point, regarding the custom, he thought it could not be good because it is against the statute of Magna Carta, c. 29, and against the law of the land, that anyone should be imprisoned by anyone, or brought in to answer for any offence, except by due course of the law and process of the law awarded: see 24 Edw. III, [Bro. Abr.], *Commissions*, pl. 3; and the statutes of 25 Edw. III, [stat. 5], c. 4, *De Provisoribus*, and 42 Edw. III, c. 3, that no one shall be taken or imprisoned unless by reason of an indictment or by due process of law, and not by reason of any complaint. Note also that he prescribes as a justice of peace, and this he may not do by prescription, for their authority commenced by the statute of 1 Edw. III, [stat. 2, c. 16], and before then there was no justice of peace in office ...

Fleetwood, serjeant, answered him, but spoke only as to the first point. Nevertheless, the next day judgment was commanded to be given for the plaintiffs unless an answer was shown on the morrow, principally by reason of the last two points. The [judges] did not wish to speak much to the first, because it touched the authority of mayors. On the next day, however, they commanded judgment to be stayed until the next term, and that in the mean time the plaintiffs should come to them: whereby it seemed that they intended to make a composition.

Heads of argument prepared by Serjeant Fleetwood[69]

The plaintiffs demurred in law, the causes being these: that the aforesaid custom alleged and pleaded in the plea is wholly against the law of the land, and that the defendant does not answer as to the wounding of the said Avice.

The argument to prove that the bar is good. When something is hardened by time it is to be seen when it shall be called custom and when usage. What is custom, what is prescription, what is usage. Note that this is a usage in

---

[68] CUL MS. Hh.2.9, fo. 416. There is a slightly abridged English version in Cro. Eliz. 93.
[69] BL MS. Hargrave 4, fos. 330v–331v.

Salisbury which touches only formality, namely sending a known officer without warrant in writing, as is requisite by the common law ... The laws of the land consist of natural law (*jus naturale*), statute law (*jus conditum*) and ancient customs (*mores antiquos*). Infer from the venue of Salisbury how the mayor has all the city within his view. Compare the matter with the experience here in London ...

(d)   *Parsons v. Locke* (1595)

Record: CP 40/1540, m. 401 (Hil. 1595). William Parsons brought an action against Matthew Locke on the Magna Carta of 9 Hen. III (1225), setting out the words of c. 29, and reciting (in a very long declaration) all the proceedings in a suit in the Court of Requests concerning the lease of a messuage in the parish of St Mary Colchurch, London, including the decree and injunction. The defendant imparled to Easter term 1595.

Hilary Term 1595[70]

An action was founded upon the statute of Magna Carta, c. 29, *quod nullus liber homo capiatur vel imprisonetur* ... (Check the pleading with Brownlow,[71] for *Daniel* at first moved that it was founded on several other statutes.)[72] And the present plaintiff showed that the defendant, by virtue of a decree made in the Court of Requests, had ousted him from his possession of a house and his goods in London, and also imprisoned him.

Warburton. The writ is not good, for it ought to be 'as well for the lady queen as for himself', inasmuch as the queen is to have a fine by it. Also the action does not lie on the matter, for the Court of Requests is an ancient court of record to redress matters in equity, like the Chancery, and it was not the intention of the statute to restrain any of the queen's courts from their lawful jurisdictions, but the statute says that if someone without authority will disseise another man, or imprison him, he shall be punished by the statute.

Daniel did not answer him but said he could demur if he wished.

ANDERSON [CJ] thought the action well lay for the matter, for it is clear that no court may be unless by some authority, and that ought to be by common law, custom or statute. It is not by common law, for I have not read one word about this court in our law. Also it is not by statute. And it cannot be by custom, for it is notoriously known that they first began to hold this court

---

[70] BL MS. Add. 25211, fos. 99v-100; MS. Hargrave 14, fo. 53 (same) (Hil. 1595); CUL MS. Ee.3.2, fo. 58v (same report but dated Pas. 1595).
[71] Chief prothonotary of the Common Pleas.
[72] It was in fact founded solely on the statute of 9 Hen. III.

in the time of Henry VII, and that was by a commission which has since expired. At the present day they have no commission, and even when the commission was in being it did not extend to any matters other than those between members of the Household. The true authority of these masters of Requests was that they were the king's officers appointed to receive the petitions of poor people exhibited to his majesty, and to help and advise them in their suits in the king's courts, and not to determine any matters by themselves as judges. That is their rightful authority. Everything that they use at the present day, and all that they do, they have encroached upon the queen's prerogative, and therefore their orders and decrees (not being warranted by the law) are mere wrongs to the parties, for which they may have a remedy in this court. This manner of encroachment upon the queen's prerogative in her laws is dangerous and corrigible, and before these times has been heavily punished several times.

WALMSLEY and BEAUMONT assented to everything he said. WALMSLEY moreover said that this court is not to be compared to the Court of Chancery, for that is an ancient court of the queen's, and we find it often named in our books. Even so, the Chancery has no authority to oust a man from his possession, for disobeying a Chancery decree is only a contempt, and the law of England is that for a contempt one may be imprisoned; but the chancellor may not by his decree bind the right or possession of anyone.

On account of the exception to the form, however, they doubted and did not deliver any opinion.[73] And this case was moved several times this term, and several days were given to the defendant to answer. In the end, the day next after the term was given peremptorily to answer.

Afterwards at another day, namely in Michaelmas term 37 Eliz. [1595], the case was moved again. This time they descended to the issue Not Guilty, and now the jurors were called. And *Harris*, the plaintiff's counsel, showed that the defendant had procured an injunction from the lords of the Council directed to the plaintiff and all his serjeants, counsellors, attorneys and solicitors, and besides that (by name) to Serjeants Harris, Glanvill and Daniel, commanding them that they should not proceed in the matter.[74] But we have received our fees from the plaintiff, and therefore we pray your advice and judgment in this matter. As it seems to me, the statute of 20 Edw. III, c. 1, in Rastell, *Justices*, 4, is that justice shall not be stayed by any such command but that you ought to certify the queen of it.

Whereupon the statute was looked at.

ANDERSON. The statute speaks only of commands which come to the justices, and this here is not directed to us; if it were, we would not stay, because we are sworn to administer justice and right to every subject, and if

---

[73] CUL MS. ends here.   [74] Cf. 26 APC 92, which does not give these details.

any command comes to us to the contrary the queen will be certified according to the statute. But we have nothing to do with the inhibition which comes to you. If you wish, we will (and we ought) to proceed.

WALMSLEY. As my lord has said, we have taken an oath which we ought to regard rather than all commands to the contrary. But you may do as seems to you good. Nevertheless, by way of exhortation, I tell you that you also are sworn to serve the queen and her people in law, which oath you also ought to regard rather than any command to the contrary. But be it at your peril: we will proceed according to the law.

So the defendants were called again until a full jury appeared, and then the solicitor for the defendant prayed the court that it might be referred to arbitration, to which the plaintiff assented; and so it was referred to the ordering of Sir Drew Drury, knight, and Robert Worth, esquire.

Easter Term 1595[75]

Matthew Locke exhibited a bill of complaint in the Court of Requests against Parsons for the title of a lease for years of a messuage in London, to which the defendant answered, and upon the hearing it was decreed that Matthew Locke should have the possession and that the said Parsons should vacate it, and an injunction was awarded against Parsons accordingly; and because the said Parsons did not perform the decree and disobeyed the injunction, Locke sued an attachment, whereupon Parsons was arrested and imprisoned until he would enter into a recognisance to obey the decree. Thereupon Parsons sued an action against Locke upon the statute of Magna Carta, chapter 29, *Nullus liber homo capietur vel imprisonetur aut disseisietur de libero tenemento suo*.

It was moved that this action does not lie, because Locke only sued in one of the ancient ordinary courts of the queen for a matter in equity, and not some new erected court, as was the case in 42 Ass., pl. 5,[76] where a man sued out [a commission] to take J. S., his goods and chattels, and bring him to Gloucester castle, and the justices said that this commission was against the law. Likewise the case in Dyer 175 between *Scrogges* and *Colshill*, where a matter was to be tried by an extraordinary course or commission, and not by the ordinary course of the law, and it was not allowed. But it is otherwise if someone sues in an ordinary course in an ancient court, for that is not an offence against the statute. Moreover, he sued only for a lease and not for freehold. And if there was any offence it was in the masters of requests in exceeding their authority, and therefore the action ought to have been sued against them and not against the party.

---

[75] Peter Warburton's reports, CUL MS. Ii.5.25, fos. 10v–11.
[76] *Sir John atte Lee's Case* (1368) above, p. 58.

To this it was said by ANDERSON CJ that the Court of Requests is not an ancient court by prescription, but commenced in the time of Henry VII by a commission for the servants of the king's Household, and is for poor people also. They may not award process to expel anyone from his freehold, though if they make a decree and the party will not obey they may commit him to prison. Such writs and commissions to put the plaintiff in possession were not awarded in any court of equity until recent times.

Afterwards the matter was stayed by the Privy Council.

Privy Council, 8 August 1596[77]

Their lordships having this day heard the cause between Matthew Locke and William Parsons about a decree set down in the Court of Requests touching a house in Bucklersbury in London, in which cause an injunction was served on the said Parsons commanding him to surcease the prosecution in the Common Pleas of an action of the case brought by him upon the statute of Magna Carta, whereby the proceeding of the Court of Requests was brought in question, wherein he did allege he did not disobey the said injunction; the cause having also been referred to the right honorable the lord keeper, then her majesty's attorney-general,[78] and the lord chief justice that now is,[79] to be considered, who certified their lordships of the state of the cause and the reason the Court of Requests had to make the said decree: their lordships have now ordered that the said William Parsons shall obey the said decree and injunction, and if it be proved he hath [disobeyed] or shall disobey the same, then their lordships have ordered he shall be committed to prison for his contempt.

(e) *Clarke* v. *Gape* (1595)

The facts appear in Coke's report.

Coke's report[80]

In an action of false imprisonment brought by Clarke against Gappe, the defendant justified the imprisonment because King Edward VI had

---

[77] 26 APC 92–3.

[78] Sir Thomas Egerton, who ceased to be attorney-general on appointment as master of the rolls on 10 April 1594. That was before Parsons's action was commenced, and so the clerk may have been in error.

[79] Sir John Popham.

[80] Coke's notebook, BL MS. Harley 6686, fo. 35 (under Trin. 1596); cf. his revised version in 5 Co. Rep. 64, and his citation of the case in *Davenant* v. *Hurdys* (1596) BL MS. Hargrave

incorporated the town of St Albans by the name of the mayor [and bur-
gesses], and granted them [power] to make ordinances, and he showed that
the queen proclaimed the term to be held there,[81] as a result of which they
(with the assent of the plaintiff and other burgesses) assessed a sum upon
every inhabitant for the charges in erecting courts, and ordained that if
anyone refused to pay he should be imprisoned, and because the plaintiff
(being a burgess) refused to pay, he justified [the imprisonment] as mayor.
And it was adjudged no plea, for it is against Magna Carta, *Nullus liber homo
imprisonetur*, [which Act hath been confirmed and established above thirty
times; and the plaintiff's assent cannot alter the law in such case. But it was
resolved that][82] they might inflict a reasonable penalty, but not imprisonment, [which penalty they might limit to be levied by distress, or for which
an action of debt would lie].[83] And the plaintiff had judgment to recover.

Another report[84]

... *Atkinson* argued that the justification is not good, for it is contrary to the
statute of Magna Carta, c. 29, which says that *Nullus liber homo
imprisonetur* . . .. This liberty everyone has by the law, and it cannot be altered
except by statute, and I do not know that in any case a man may be
imprisoned for words. In 16 Eliz., in Dyer,[85] there is a precedent where,
because a citizen would not stand to the award of two aldermen, they disfranchised him, and because this was not a sufficient cause he had a writ to restore
him to his franchise again. So is 8 Ric. II: the king granted to the men of Lynn
that if anyone took toll from them they could take as much back in withernam,
and this grant was held void because it was in oppression of the people.[86] . . .
But there is a plainer reason why it is not good, for the order says 'the mayor
and the greater part of the associates', and he shows that he himself
imprisoned him, which is quite outside the order, and the subsequent words
'at his or their pleasure' cannot help it, for those refer to his deliverance.

   5, fo. 73v; BL MS. Add. 35947, fo. 237v (in both of which he said Magna Carta had been
   confirmed fifty-two times). Most parallel reports are dated Mich. 1595.
[81] Michaelmas term 1593.   [82] Added in printed edition.
[83] Added in printed edition.
[84] BL MS. Harley 4552, fo. 35v; abridged in MS. Add. 25199, fo. 34v; MS. Add. 35947,
   fo. 23v. Cf. a shorter report, omitting the arguments, in BL MS. Hargrave 356, fos. 128v–
   129v; MS. Add. 25198, fos. 101v–102; CUL MS. Gg.5.3, fos. 70–71; HLS MS. 110, fo. 163v;
   and other short reports in BL MS. Harley 1697, fo. 89; CUL MSS Gg.6.29, fo. 33; Ll.3.9,
   fo. 496v. Most of these are dated Mich. 1595.
[85] *Middleton's Case* (Pas. 1574) Dyer 332 (restoration to freedom of London and to
   his shop).
[86] Hil. 8 Ric. II, Fitz. Abr., *Graunte*, pl. 105; (Ames Fdn), p. 217, pl. 18. Cf. the following case.

The whole court was of this opinion in this point. And POPHAM CJ said that it was no contempt, because he did not speak the words to the mayor himself but to the messenger. He also said that, if it could be justified, it ought to be as mayor, and not through the order. They also said that they may not make an order for imprisonment, but only for another penalty, or for disfranchisement. And so it was adjudged.

(f) *Paramour* v. *Verrall and others* (1597–1600)

In an action of false imprisonment in the Common Pleas, the defendants pleaded an immemorial custom of the Cinque Ports to imprison citizens of London, and seize their goods by way of withernam, whenever another citizen had failed to appear in court there.[87]

Michaelmas Term 1597[88]

Paramour brought trespass for imprisonment against Waferer and Verrall[89] because they had imprisoned him until he paid £47. The defendants justified because Sandwich is an ancient town, incorporated by the name of the mayor and jurats, and is one of the Cinque Ports, and they alleged a prescription in the Cinque Ports that if any baron[90] or inhabitant of the Cinque Ports loses anything which comes into the hands of any citizen or inhabitant of London, they have been used to direct their letters missive to the mayor of London complaining of this matter, requiring him to call the citizen before him and to examine him upon the premises, and to cause him to return a sufficient answer or plead a sufficient plea within fifteen days, and if no answer or remedy is returned within fifteen days an *alias* and a *pluries*, and if nothing is returned their usage is to signify to the mayor of London that they will proceed to the withernam, and, upon notice thus given, and an affidavit made of the

---

[87] A previous action was commenced in the King's Bench in 1595 but abandoned in 1597 because of defects in the pleading: Cro. Eliz. 418; Poph. 101; Moo. 350; CUL MS. Add. 8080, fo. 35v.

[88] BL MS. Harley 1693, fos. 194v–196; same text also in MS. Harley 1575, fo. 29; MS. Hargrave 51, fos. 128–129v; CUL MS. Add. 8080, fos. 34v–35v (dated Trin. 1598). Cf. a different report in 2 And. 151 (Hil. 1599), where there is a brief reference to c. 29; Moo. 603 (citing the roll as Mich. 38 & 39 Eliz., m. 2948).

[89] Probably the mayor and jurats. John Verrall was one of the jurats in 1589: Faversham Borough Records, Fa/J/W/31 (another case of withernam, with process from Sandwich to Faversham). In 1602 an appeal of murder was brought against one Verrall of Sandwich: *Crispe* v. *Verral* (1602) Cro. Eliz. 910; Yelv. 12. A Thomas Waferer was admitted to Gonville and Caius College, Cambridge, in 1569 from Sandwich School.

[90] I.e. a baron (man) of the Cinque Ports.

fact, and no restitution made within the fifteen days, then to arrest the first citizen and inhabitant in London who should come within the Cinque Ports, and to imprison him until he has paid the value of the thing lost, which shall be inquired into by writ of inquiry ... And the plaintiff demurred in law upon this justification.

Glanville, for the plaintiff. It seemed to him that the prescription is unreasonable, for it could have neither a lawful commencement nor a continuance by reason, for it is against the law of God and of the realm that one man should bear the offence of another. Even in the closest conjunction that may be, one shall not suffer corporal punishment for another, for a husband shall not be imprisoned for the wife's fault even though they are one flesh ...[91] And with respect to the confirmation pleaded, that the franchises and customs within the Cinque Ports are confirmed by the statute of Magna Carta, c. 9, this is answered by c. 29, *Nullus liber homo capiatur aut imprisonetur etc.*

Williams, serjeant, to the contrary ... As to the matter in law, it seems the prescription is good, for it is only common law, and that which is common law cannot be deemed [bad]. The Civilians term it *jus gentium*, for this withernam is only letters of reprisal, and where a man has his goods taken our law allows withernam by reprisal. Also these customs have been confirmed by precedent ever since the time of William the Conqueror until now. And in 18 Eliz. the inhabitants of Dieppe arrested a man from the Cinque Ports, and afterwards a Dieppe man coming within the Cinque Ports was taken in withernam; and the king of France wrote to our queen to have delivery of his subject, and the Cinque Ports were summoned before the Council to show their custom, and it was referred to the lord Dyer [CJCP], the lord Wray [CJQB] and two Civilians for their judgment upon the custom, and they reported it to be a good custom ...

ANDERSON CJ, BEAUMONT and OWEN at first thought this to be an unreasonable custom, but WALMSLEY forcefully (*totis viribus*) to the contrary. Note that these arguments and opinions were delivered in Easter term 39 Eliz. [1597], and now this term it was argued again. And it seemed to *Yelverton*, serjeant, that the custom was reasonable, and he insisted much on the antiquity, privileges and immunities of the Cinque Ports, granted to them by the old kings of England ... Two objections have been made, (1) that the custom is against common law, and (2) that it is against the statute of Magna Carta, c. 29. As to the first, if it is accompanied with the circumstances it will not seem unreasonable, for this withernam grows upon the default of the corporation of London upon letters missive, which are in the nature of the threefold process at common law of original, *alias* and *pluries* ... As to the second, it cannot be against the statute of Magna Carta, c. 29, since the

[91] He then made various objections to the pleadings.

customs are confirmed by c. 9 of the same statute, for then they may well prescribe against the statute. As in 8 Hen. VII,[92] a freeman and citizen of London may prescribe to devise his land in mortmain notwithstanding the Statute of Mortmain, inasmuch as their customs are confirmed by Act of Parliament. Likewise here . . .

Glanville to the contrary, and he took various exceptions to the plea in bar, but these in effect were those that he made before, and he argued the matter in law in the same way as before. And it was adjourned, ANDERSON and OWEN retaining their former opinions, but WALMSLEY to the contrary, strongly, as before. (From Nicholas Duck's book. Note: this case was discontinued because of the imperfections in the pleading.)[93]

Hilary Term 1599[94]

There were various faults in the pleading, which were moved (here omitted); but the material point was argued by all the justices in banc, and that was, in short, whether the imprisonment of the plaintiff was justifiable by this custom, or not. And it was held by them all that it was not a lawful imprisonment, for it was said that customs ought to be such as may by reason have a lawful commencement, or may by common presumption stand with reason . . . It was further said, that this custom is clearly contrary to statutes, against which no one may prescribe unless they are helped by another statute . . . And see further Magna Carta, c. 29; 28 Edw. III; and various other statutes in the *Abridgment of Statutes*, tit. 'Accusation', whereby it is ordained that no one shall be imprisoned unless in accordance with the law, whence it appears that this custom and imprisonment are prohibited by these laws and statutes . . . And so it was adjudged by assent of all the said justices that the custom would not be allowed, and that judgment would be given for the plaintiff. Hilary term, 41 Eliz.

Trinity Term 1600[95]

False imprisonment was brought by Paramour, a citizen of London, against Verrall (Verald), Waferer and Nevill, Hil. 41 Eliz., rot. 2695[96] . . . And the case was several times argued by the serjeants at the bar, and now [Pas. 1600] it was argued also by the justices only, upon the point whether the custom was good

---

[92] *Case of the Abbot of Winchcombe* (1493) YB Trin. 8 Hen. VII, fo. 1, pl. 1 (called the abbot of Tewkesbury's case: but see *Reports of Cases by John Caryll*, ed. J. H. Baker, vol. i (116 SS), at fo. 4, *per* Bryan CJ.
[93] Marginal note.   [94] 2 And. 151.   [95] CUL MS. Add. 8080, fo. 97.
[96] A new action.

or not. And at length in Trinity term [1600], 42 Eliz., after all four justices had solemnly argued, it was resolved by them all and adjudged that the custom as it was pleaded was a bad custom, and therefore void, and so the defendants were guilty and the plaintiff should recover. And the principal reasons upon which they insisted were that the prescription to take and imprison the body of one man for the debt or wrong of another was against the law of God, the common law of the land, and various statutes . . .[97] It is against various statute laws and Acts of Parliament that the body of a man should be taken and imprisoned without due course of law. As to this, Magna Carta, c. 29, provides that *Nullus liber homo* . . . . Likewise the statute of 5 Edw. III, c. 9, no man shall hereafter be attached by any accusation . . . and also by the statute of 25 Edw. III, c. 4, it is ordained that no one shall be arrested by petition or suggestion made to the king or his Council . . . and by 28 Edw. III, c. 3, no man of whatever estate or condition he be shall be ousted from land or tenement, arrested, imprisoned, disinherited or put to death without being brought to answer by due process of law. 37 Edw. III, c. 18, the words and scope of which statute is the same in effect as Magna Carta. And with these statutes is the opinion of the Court of Parliament in Westminster II, c. 25, where in making a new law against heirs and executors . . . they would not give any corporal punishment against the heir or executor because no one should be punished for another's wrong (*Nemo pro alieno delicto est puniendus*), whereby it also clearly appears what the common law was in this point. Admit, however, that the common law was otherwise, so that it was a good custom by the common law, nevertheless it is so directly crossed by so many Acts of Parliament – there being no saving of [customs] in those acts – that it is sufficiently clear that these customs are extinguished and made void. And whereas it has been objected that it has been put in practice in Normandy, Dieppe and other foreign places to take the inhabitants of those places in withernam, that only proves the case among foreigners, and it is either by the law of war (*jure belli*) or because the places are under several governments so that an ordinary course of justice cannot so easily be obtained; but London and Sandwich and the other Cinque Ports have one prince, one law, and one government, and therefore it is unfitting for such a common wealth to allow such writs of Mars and martial proceedings . . .

And it was furthermore held by ANDERSON, GLANVILLE[98] and KINGSMILL that the custom of taking the goods of a London citizen or such like in withernam for the goods of a resident of the Cinque Ports was a bad custom

---

[97] Reference was made, inter alia, to *Lee's Case* (1368) above, p. 58.

[98] Appointed JCP on 30 June 1598. His previous engagement as counsel evidently did not preclude him from giving judgment in favour of his former clients.

also because it is not reasonable that one man should answer from his goods for the wrong of another ...

WALMSLEY *contra,* that it would have been a good custom if it had been rightly and duly pleaded in this point, and he greatly insisted on the dignity of the Cinque Ports, and endeavoured much to find the reason why such great privileges have been granted to them time out of mind ... and he gathered that it was because the Cinque Ports are the ports and gates of the realm ... But he said that, as the custom is pleaded, it is not good, for they say that they have used to write letters missive to the mayor to cause the party to make sufficient answer or plea in bar, which is not a matter which lies in his power or knowledge ... To this point the other justices agreed ... And afterwards judgment was entered for the plaintiff: which note.

Note that ANDERSON in his argument said that the custom of Halifax was a good custom, namely to behead a man without judgment.[99]

Michaelmas 1599 to Trinity 1600[100]

Daniel, serjeant. The custom of the Cinque Ports is not good. Firstly, it is not agreeable with the law of God or the law of nature, or with the common law or statute law, and therefore as a bad custom it is to be abolished ... It is not agreeable with statute law, for by the statute of Magna Carta, c. 29, *Nullus liber homo capiatur aut imprisonetur etc.,* and various other statutes, it appears that no one shall be punished for the offence of another and without due process ... An oppression is not a custom but an abuse of the people. Moreover this custom [does not] agree with the statutes of England, for the statute of Magna Carta says that *Nullus liber homo capiatur aut imprisonetur,* and likewise the statute of 28 Edw. III. c. 3, and here is no due process made but only letters missive, and therefore upon such process (which is not good or agreeable with the law) no one may be imprisoned ...

Williams, contra. As I understand it, the custom is good and sufficient and agreeable with good reason ... First, it is apparent that these customs of the Cinque Ports were ancient customs, and it appears from the statute of Magna Carta, c. 9, and the statute *Articuli super Cartas,* c. 7, that the customs of the Cinque Ports were before the statute of Magna Carta, and it may be that they were before the Conquest, and if they are so ancient [it does not matter that] the cause of their first beginning does not appear, whether it was by a composition between the city of London and the Cinque Ports, or by an Act of Parliament, or otherwise ...

---

[99] Above, pp. 263 n. 76, 471, 478.
[100] Extracts from a lengthy report in BL MS. Harley 4814, fos. 78–87v. There is a similar but less detailed report of all the arguments in BL MS. Lansdowne 1065, fos. 58–63.

In Hilary term [1600], 42 Eliz., it was argued by *Warburton*, serjeant, for the plaintiff ... This is such a liberty that the king could not grant, because it is to the prejudice of others, and the king may do no wrong against his subjects by his prerogative ...

The case was argued at the bench in the beginning of Easter term [1600], 42 Eliz., by GLANVILLE and KINGSMILL, as follows ... The custom is against various statutes. First, it is against the statute of Magna Carta, that *Nullus liber homo imprisonetur etc.* And it is against the statute *Articuli super Cartas*, and against the statute 5 Edw. III, and against the statute of 28 Edw. III, and 37 Edw. III ....[101] In the beginning of Trinity term next following [1600] the case was argued by WALMSLEY ... A custom to take the goods of someone is allowable, but, as the case is, I think the imprisonment was not lawful and the plaintiff should recover.

ANDERSON CJ to same effect ... These customs ought not to be allowed by the common law if they are utterly repugnant to reason, and I think there is no case in which the body of a man may be taken and imprisoned except in respect of his own offence, [being an offence] which is allowable by the common law and by statute law. Although the customs of the Cinque Ports have been confirmed, nevertheless these here are not confirmed, for abuses are not customs ... It is against various statutes, such as the statute of Magna Carta, and when such a custom is against any statute, if it is not specifically preserved by a proviso in the statute, or revived by another statute, it is gone for ever. Therefore the custom of London [to devise in mortmain] was gone by the Statute of Mortmain until it was revived by a statute in 14 Edw. III ... Here the custom is against the statute of Magna Carta and the statute of 28 Edw. III, and by these statutes the customs are gone; a particular custom cannot be maintained against such generally worded statutes unless there is a special saving thereof in the statute, or a revival by a subsequent Act.[102]

Afterwards it was adjudged for the plaintiff.

---

[101] Reference was made, inter alia, to *Lee's Case* (1368) above, p. 58.

[102] Cf. 2 Br. & G. 191 (1610): 'Note that Coke said that it hath been adjudged by three judges against one in a case of Cinque Ports, that the Cinque Ports cannot prescribe to take the body of a free man in withernam ... for this is against the Statute of Magna Carta, *quod nullus liber homo imprisonetur nisi per legale judicium*, and also against the liberty of the subject'.

Appendix 6

The Judges' Resolutions on *Habeas Corpus* 1592

(a)   *John Agmondesham's Case* (Hilary Term 1590)[1]

The case was that one Edmund Amerson,[2] a double reader of the Middle Temple, had arrested[3] the servant of someone who was an ordinary servant attendant on the queen, and for this arrest the lord chamberlain committed Amerson to prison, there to remain until he would release his suit. Upon this matter all the justices in England were assembled to consider what should be done, for this was against the law and various statutes [which required] that the subjects of the realm ought to have the benefit of the law. And upon resolution it was agreed that certain articles should be made of these abuses, and the reasons and precedents, and the statutes made against it, and the oath of the justices, and that it should be presented to the queen, and that she should be moved about it; and it was agreed to make the lord chancellor and lord treasurer privy to this, and to have their aid and assistance, though the judges themselves were willing to attend upon the queen. First, however, it was agreed that he should be removed by *habeas corpus*, and then the keeper of the prison would make his return, and the court would examine by what warrant it was done, and if upon examination it appeared that it is false he would be fined; for to return that it was 'by the command of one of the Council' would not be good, and the court would enlarge him. But 'by command of the Council' would be good, for that is a matter of state. Likewise 'by command of the queen'. Nevertheless the chief justice said there were precedents that a prisoner who was committed by the king's command was removed from the prison where he was committed and committed again to the prison of the court until the king was moved. And it was held by them all that if the sheriff

---

[1]   BL MS. Harley 4998, fo. 26 (tr.).

[2]   So spelled in the margin, and below, but 'Amerton' in the text here. This must be John Agmondesham, double reader of the Middle Temple in Lent 1589. He was a Puritan member of Parliament, though this case is not mentioned in *HPHC 1558–1603*. The name may have been confused with that of Edmund Anderson, CJCP.

[3]   Evidently by process in an action at law.

makes a false return, as upon a *fieri facias* to return 'Nihil', or upon a *capias* 'Non est inventus' where the party was in his presence and he could arrest him, he shall be fined.

(b)   The Resolutions of 1592[4]

The resolution of all the judges for the enlargement of prisoners committed upon command by *habeas corpus*, in Easter term in the thirty-fourth year of Elizabeth.

Divers persons at several times were committed to sundry prisons upon pleasure, without good cause, and we according to law discharged [them] from their imprisonment, whereupon certain great men were offended and procured a commandment to the judges that they should not be set at liberty. And yet, notwithstanding, the judges surceased, but by advice amongst themselves drew certain articles, the tenor whereof ensues, and (subscribed by them) delivered them to the lord chancellor and treasurer.

[5][If any free subject be wrongfully imprisoned, he hath two ways to relieve himself and regain his liberty. The first is by *habeas corpus*, the second by the writ *de homine replegiando*. The *habeas corpus* lies where the party is detained by a known public minister of justice to whom the king's court may direct their writs, as the sheriff of the county, the warden of the Fleet, the marshal of the King's Bench, lieutenant of the Tower, constable of Dover, and in former times (when those parts of France were English) to the constables of the castle of Guisnes, Calais etc., as there be divers precedents.

This writ lies upon any commandment whatsoever, though by the king himself or the body of the Council, and requires to have the body with the cause of the commitment, in a return day, in the court that granted the writ, that they may judge thereupon either for or against the prisoner. The court that grants the *habeas corpus* is most properly the King's Bench, and in some places the Common Pleas. All commitments are either by verbal command or by warrant in writing. The commitments by verbal command are illegal. The commitment by warrant in writing is either general, without any cause expressed therein, or with cause. If without cause, the commitment is not legal and the prisoner ought upon the return to be freed, unless the

---

[4] BL MS. Harley 37, fos. 112–16 (English); MS. Lansdowne 1062, fos. 224v–225v (French); partial copy in SP 12/261, fos. 137–41 (*c.* 1595); abridged in 1 And. 297–8, pl. 305; Anderson's reports, BL MS. Harley 4817, fos. 99v–100. The preamble is in French in Anderson, but in English in MS. Harley 37. The French text from Anderson is printed in W. S. Holdsworth, *History of English Law*, vol. v (1924), pp. 496–7.

[5] This passage is not in Anderson or MS. Lansdowne 1062. It is evidently a later interpolation, since it refers to the king, and to Queen Elizabeth (as if no longer alive), and contains precedents of 1598 and 1609.

commitment be by the king or by the body of the Council for pretence of matter of state, which may require secrecy, in which case the court may give some convenient time for examination and calling the party to trial. But if such general commitment continue long, the party ought to be discharged. If the warrant in writing be with cause expressed, then the cause is either good (in which case the court will remand the prisoner) or insufficient, and then the court ought to remand[6] the prisoner. But if the gaoler express a sufficient cause in his return (but a false one) the party must take his remedy against the gaoler.[7]

There be in the time of Queen Elizabeth divers precedents of *habeas corpus* out of the King's Bench to the Tower and other prisons where the parties were committed, some 'by command of the lord king' (*per mandatum domini regis*), others 'by command of the lords of the queen's Privy Council' (*per mandatum dominorum de privato concilio reginae*), and in both cases have upon return of the writ been discharged. <These precedents are to be found in the King's Bench Treasury at Westminster in the several treasuries among the pleas of the crown.>[8]

But if the commitment be to no sheriff, gaoler or other known public officer to whom the court may direct their writs, in that case the *habeas corpus* will not help. Therefore the law (which leaves no man without remedy) in that case relieves the prisoner by the writ *de homine replegiando*. *De homine replegiando* issues out of the Chancery, and it is to be directed to the sheriff of the county where any man is detained prisoner by any private person, and is returnable in the King's Bench or Common Pleas at the party's pleasure. If upon such writ the party who detains the prisoner doth remove him into remote and unknown places, that the sheriff cannot deliver him, and [it] be so returned by the sheriff, the court ought then to grant a *capias in withernam* commanding the sheriff to take and imprison the party who so hath eloigned the prisoner, though he be a peer of the realm, until he deliver him. If the party so detaining the prisoner hide himself from the sheriff, and thereupon the sheriff return *Non est inventus*, then the court ought to grant a *capias in withernam* to stay such person's goods until he deliver the prisoner. The writ *de homine replegiando*, though it have some exceptions, as where the party is committed by the king himself, by the justices of the forest, and so forth,[9] yet doth it lie in case of a commitment by the body of the Council. But if a man be committed to his own house, in which case there is no force offered, but he voluntarily makes himself a prisoner, or will voluntarily submit himself to a

---

[6] *Sic*, presumably a slip.   [7] This was usually said to be an action on the case.

[8] *Margin.* The precedents here referred to are in the controlment rolls of the clerk of the crown, now class KB 29 in the PRO.

[9] These exceptions were set out in the writ itself: see below, p. 502.

confinement in another man's house, in which case no keeper (but [by] his own submission to such command) detains himself prisoner, the writ *de homine replegiando* lies not. And therefore if any free subject be offered a confinement to his own or another man's house, in which case he is deprived of the two legal ways to gain his liberty, it shall not be amiss for such person in dutiful manner to refuse the subjecting himself to such a voluntary imprisonment and to pray that either he may have his absolute liberty or be called to a legal trial, or at least have such an imprisonment as either by the half-year gaol delivery or by *habeas corpus* or the writ *de homine replegiando* he may have means to draw to a legal question the justness of his imprisonment.

Addis committed to Newgate by the lord chamberlain, no cause expressed. Hilary term 6 Jac. [1609], Addis's case in the Common Bench at the motion of Hutton.[10]

40 Eliz., Harcourt committed to the Gate House by the lords of the Council 'for certain causes then moving them and unknown' (*certis de causis ipsis moventibus et ignotis*).[11]

9 Eliz., rot. 68, Robert Constable, esquire, committed to the Tower by command of the Privy Council, and afterwards the same term delivered on bail.[12]]

[13]We, her majesty's justices of both benches and barons of the Exchequer, desire your lordships that by some good means some order may be taken that her highness's subjects may not be committed nor detained in prison by commandment of any nobleman or councillor against the laws of the realm, and to help us to have access to her majesty to the end to become suitors to her for the same, for many have been imprisoned for suing ordinary actions and suits at the common law until they have been constrained to leave the same against their wills, and put the same to order, albeit judgment and execution have been had therein, to their great loss and grief. For the aid of which persons her majesty's writs have been sundry times directed to divers persons having the custody of such persons unlawfully imprisoned, upon which writs no good and lawful cause have been returned or certified, whereupon according to the laws they have been discharged from their imprisonment, some of which persons so delivered have been [again][14] committed to prison

---

[10] Reported in Cro. Jac. 219; CUL MS. Hh.2.2, fo. 2v.

[11] *Edward Harcourt's Case* (1598) KB 29/235, m. 62; above, pp. 168 n. 134, 401.

[12] *Robert Constable's Case* (1567) cited as Pas. 9 Eliz., m. 68, in 3 St. Tr. 100, but not found in KB 29/202.

[13] From here also in Anderson and Lansdowne 1062. Holdsworth (above, n. 4), pp. 495–6, prints a shorter and earlier version of 9 June 1591 from the Burghley papers; this is addressed to Sir Christopher Hatton and Lord Burghley, and has the judges' names subscribed.

[14] MS. Lansdowne 1062.

in secret places and not to any common or ordinary prison or lawful officer or sheriff or other lawfully authorised to have and keep a gaol, so that upon complaint made for their delivery the queen's courts cannot learn to whom to direct her majesty's writs, and by this means justice cannot be done. And moreover divers officers and serjeants[15] of London have been many times committed to prison for the lawful executing her majesty's writs, [sued][16] forth of her majesty's courts at Westminster, and thereby her majesty's subjects and officers are hindered that they dare not sue or execute her majesty's laws, her writs and commandments. Divers others have been sent for by pursuivants[17] and brought to London from their dwellings and by unlawful imprisonments have been constrained not only to withdraw their lawful suits but have been also compelled to pay to the pursuivants for bringing such persons great sums of money. All which, upon complaint, the judges are bound by office and oath to relieve and help by and according to her majesty's laws. And whereas it pleased your lordships to will divers of us to set down in what causes a person sent to custody by her majesty, her Council, [or] some one or two of them, are to be detained in prison and not delivered by her majesty's courts or judges, we think if any person be committed by her majesty's commandment from her person, or by order from the Council Board, or if any one of two of her Council commit one for high treason, such person so in the case before committed may not be delivered by any of the courts without due trial by law and judgment of acquittal had. Nevertheless the judges may award the queen's writs to bring the bodies of such persons before them, and if upon return thereof the causes of their commitment be certified to the judges as it ought to be, then the judges in the cases before [mentioned][18] ought not to deliver him, but to remand the prisoner to the place from whence he came, which cannot conveniently be done unless notice of the cause in generality or else especially be given to the keeper or gaoler that shall have the custody of such prisoner.

And the judges and barons did subscribe their names to these articles in Easter term in the thirty-fourth year of Elizabeth [1592], and delivered one to the lord chancellor and another to the lord treasurer, after which time did follow more quietness [than before][19] in the cases before mentioned.

Finis.

---

[15] I.e. serjeants at mace.   [16] And.; MS. Lansdowne 1062.
[17] 'your servantes' in MS. Harley 37.   [18] MS. Lansdowne 1062.
[19] And.; MS. Lansdowne 1062.

Appendix 7

Coke's Memorandum on Chapter 29 (1604)[1]

It is provided by the statute of Magna Charta, chapter 29, that *No free man etc.* This Act is most beneficial for liberty of the subject: wherein eight words are to be observed, namely, he shall not be (1) 'taken' or (2) 'imprisoned', (3) 'disseised' or (4) 'outlawed', (5) 'exiled' or (6) 'destroyed', nor shall we (7) 'go' or (8) 'put' upon him. And inasmuch as everything that anyone has in this world, or that concerns the freedom and liberty of his body or his freehold, or the benefit of the law to which he is inheritable, or his native country in which he was born, or the preservation of his reputation or goods, or his life, blood and posterity: to all these things this Act extends. For the first two words, 'taken' or 'imprisoned', extend to the liberty of his body, which shall not be arrested or imprisoned 'except by the law of the land'. The third, 'disseised', extends to his freehold and inheritance; the fourth,[2] 'exiled', to his native country; the fifth, 'destroyed', to his blood, his goods and all that he has. 'Nor shall we go or put upon him' extends to his life. Now for all of these in order.

First, of these words 'taken or imprisoned'. By this Act no one shall be taken or imprisoned 'except by the law of the land', which words are well explained in Parliament by the statute of 28 Edw. III, c. 3: no man, whatever his estate or condition, shall be taken or imprisoned without being brought to answer by due process of law. And with this accords 37 Edw. III, c. 18, namely that the said words of Magna Carta 'except by the law of the land' signify 'without being brought to answer by due process of law'.[3] And, to oust all scruples,[4] these words 'by due process of law' are also expounded by Parliament in the year 42 Edw. III, c. 3: no man shall be put to answer without a presentment before the justices, or matter of record, or by due process or original writ according to the old law of the land. From which, therefore, it appears that in

---

[1] Coke's notebook, BL MS. Harley 6686B, fos. 600–604v (tr.) (inserted under Mich. 1604). There is a seventeenth-century copy in CUL MS. Gg.2.5, fos. 378–81. The French text is printed in *Selected Readings on Magna Carta*, pp. 394–402, and the translation is based on the emendations there.

[2] Coke here omits 'outlawed', which is reverted to below, with consequent renumbering.

[3] This passage also occurs in an extended form in Co. Inst. ii. 50.

[4] I.e. remove all doubts.

truth the statutes of Magna Carta, c. 29, of 28 Edw. III, 37 Edw. III, and 42 Edw. III, were merely declarations of the old common law of the land. And that appears from the books in 24 Edw. III,[5] and 42 Lib. Ass., pl. 5;[6] for it appears there that a commission was awarded under the great seal out of the Chancery, by the procurement of Sir John at Lee, and it was directed to J. de S. and others to take T. S. of T. and his goods and chattels and bring them to Colchester castle, and to imprison him there, by force whereof the commissioners took and imprisoned the said T. S. in the said castle for four weeks, and seized [his] goods and chattels. All this was presented before Knyvet CJ, Thorpe CJ and Lodelow CB, justices of oyer and terminer in the county of Essex, and it was resolved by them that this commission was against law (namely the common law of England), to take a man and his goods without indictment or suit of a party, or other due process. And the said judges of oyer and terminer took the commission, and brought it away with them, and said they would show it to the King's Council, inasmuch as it was in derogation of the common law and of the liberty and birthright of the subject. But a difficulty (*scruple*) remains concerning the said Acts of Parliament and year books, namely that a man may nevertheless be taken by due process of law without any indictment or suit of a party, to which the other party may make an answer before he is taken: for the words[7] are disjunctive, 'by indictment' (which is the king's suit), 'or at the suit of a party' (namely by any lawful and ordinary action between party and party), 'or by due process of law' – which of necessity must be by some means other than by indictment or by the ordinary suit of a party. As to this, it is to be known that warrants or precepts to arrest men of bad reputation, or who threaten anyone with death or destruction, or to burn his houses or pull them down, in order to find surety for their good behaviour or to keep the peace, are made 'by due process of law'. And these words 'by due process' have a greater extent, for it is to be known that the kings of this realm have governed not only by ordinary proceedings of the common law but also – since in some cases *summum jus foret summa injuria* – the common law has allowed that in some cases the rigour of the law should be mitigated and moderated according to equity and conscience, and for this purpose the law has allowed courts of equity, such as the Chancery and Exchequer Chamber.[8] Also, when the ordinary course of the law does not inflict sufficient punishment for certain exorbitant offences punishable by the law, such as heinous riots, great extortions and oppressions of the subjects, horrible and detestable deceits, frauds and other execrable misdemeanours, the

---

[5] Above, p. 58 n. 52.   [6] YB 42 Edw. III, Lib. Ass., pl. 5; above, p. 58.
[7] Presumably of the statute 42 Edw. III, c. 3.
[8] I.e. the equity side of the Exchequer rather than the court of error.

common law has allowed the High Court of Star Chamber to inflict condign punishment for such exorbitant offences. All this appears in our books.

And it should be observed, firstly, that in some cases a man may be taken and imprisoned without answer, notwithstanding the said act of Magna Carta. For instance, if a parson or some other spiritual man is disturbed in his church, or in his rectory thereto annexed, by force of any laymen, he shall have a writ *de vi laica removenda*, and by virtue of this writ if the lay people resist the sheriff he may commit them to prison without other process of law; and this is for the honour which the law gives to Holy Church, so that he need not use the ordinary process of the law, and for necessity, so that divine service be not disturbed or for any time interrupted, nor laymen interfere with matters consecrated to divine service. The wording of some of the writs is: 'We command you that without delay you remove all lay force which is held in the church of J. in disturbance of the said bishop, whereby he is less able to exercise his spiritual office in that church.' Thus it appears that it was necessary for the makers of the act of Magna Carta to add these words 'unless by the law of the land'; for the writ *de vi laica removenda* is warranted by the law of the land. Moreover, proceedings in courts of equity, in accordance with the jurisdiction thereof, are within the words 'by due process', for proceedings according to the law of equity in respect of things whereof the court of equity has cognizance may be called 'by due process' warranted and allowed by the law of the land. For the kings of this land do not govern only by the ordinary course of law, but in some cases by the law of equity; and for contempt and breach of a decree [of a court of equity] the party may be taken and imprisoned, and such imprisonment is not against the statute of Magna Carta but is justifiable 'by the law of the land'. The Star Chamber court may do the like in respect of anything within its jurisdiction; for the proceedings there (whether by bill or *ore tenus* upon confession), according to the authority of the precedents of the court, are but a branch of the law of the land. As to this purpose, the statute of 37 Edw. III, c. 18, is to be observed, which recites 'whereas it is contained in the great charter . . .': see the statute in Rastall's abridgment, under 'Accusation'.[9]

At common law if someone was falsely imprisoned he could have an original writ *de homine replegiando*, which writ in effect says: 'justly and without delay cause to be replevied B., C. and D., whom E. and F. have taken and keep captive (as it is said), unless they were taken by our special command or that of our chief justice, or for homicide, or for the forest, or else signify to us the reason'. Thus he ought to return the cause without having the body. And it is to be observed that in a case where another cause is returned, the cause must be returned specially, so that it may appear that the imprisonment was lawful and within the jurisdiction of whoever

[9] W. Rastall, *A Collection of all the Statutes* (1574 edn), fo. 6, no. 5.

imprisoned him. Also, when someone is imprisoned lawfully but is bailable, and bail is denied him, he may have a writ of mainprise: for which see Bracton, book 3;[10] Register, fo. 249;[11] and Westminster I, c. [15].

[12]Now, suppose someone is taken (by whatever person) and sent to prison without lawful warrant, or detained contrary to law, what remedy shall the aggrieved party have under the said act of Magna Carta, and the other statutes aforesaid, and in what court? As to that, it is to be known that the party may have three remedies: (1) to have an original action at the suit of the aggrieved party, founded upon the statute of Magna Carta, as was brought in Pas. 2 Hen. VIII, rot. 529,[13] against the prior of St Oswin's in Northumberland, for calling the plaintiff before the Council and imprisoning him for matter pleadable at common law; (2) he may indict him at the king's suit, as was done in Pas. 3 Hen. VIII, rot. 71,[14] where one was indicted for calling him before Robert Sheffield,[15] one of the Council; and Mich. 10 & 11 Eliz., an indictment for procuring an indictment in the Court of Requests for staying a trial in an action of debt;[16] (3) another remedy he has is to move the judges of the King's Bench and inform them of the truth of the cause, and thereupon obtain a *habeas corpus cum causa*, by which writ the body ought to be removed with the cause, and if it appears to the court upon the return of the body with the cause that he was lawfully imprisoned and detained, he will be remanded, but if he was imprisoned contrary to the statute of Magna Carta and the other statutes then the judges must discharge him from his unlawful imprisonment. And the court of King's Bench may do this even though the aggrieved party has no privilege there, by virtue of the said Acts.

Next, in which courts. (See the book of precedents, 162 [. . .] and 1 & 2 Ph. & Mar. in the Common Bench.) In 3 Edw. III, 18b,[17] John, bishop of

---

[10] *Bracton*, ii. 347.   [11] A slip for FNB 249–250G.

[12] The following question and answer, and the authorities cited, form the basis of the passage in Co. Inst. ii. 55.

[13] *Younghusband* v. *Prior of Tynemouth* (1510) CP 40/991, m. 529; above, p. 459. Cf. *Brandelyng* v. *Prior of Tynemouth*, ibid. m. 538, cited in Co. Inst. ii. 33 (but mistaking it for a King's Bench case); it is also cited in Coke's hand in the margin of his copy of *Magna Carta cum Statutis* (1556 edn), fo. 5, at Holkham Hall; *Collected Papers*, ii. 889.

[14] The same reference is given in Co. Inst. ii. 55, but it is incorrect; in the margin of *Magna Carta cum Statutis* (previous note), Coke cited it as m. 72 of the same term. (There are only mm. 1–31 in the Rex rolls for this term, and only mm. 1–10 in the controlment rolls.) The case referred to must be to *R* v. *Phillip* (1511) KB 27/999 (Pas. 3 Hen. VIII), Rex, m. 5; above, pp. 99 n. 155, 460.

[15] Robert Sheffield (d. 1518), bencher of the Inner Temple.

[16] Cf. '10 Eliz. Rot. [*blank*] Leas case', cited Co. Inst. ii. 55. This is evidently not the same as *Thomas Lee's Case* (1568), also in 10 Eliz., cited below from Dyer.

[17] YB Pas. 3 Edw. III, fo. 18, pl. 32; KB 27/276, m. 9d; Port's notebook, 102 SS 57; Co. Inst. iv. 15–17.

Winchester, was summoned to the Parliament at New Sarum and left without the king's permission; and in that case two points were resolved: (1) that this was a great offence, for when the Parliament is assembled of the peers of the land for the profit of the king and his people, if one of the peers does not come, or comes but then leaves without permission, this default is against all the people as well as the king; (2) although it was there objected that in respect of matters touching Parliament the peers should be the judges, and it lies in their record whether he left without the king's permission, and therefore this thing which was in the higher court should not be determined in any inferior court, nevertheless the bishop was indicted for this offence in the King's Bench, for although (as it is said there) they of the Parliament are judges of their peers, nevertheless, since this departure without the king's permission was against the profit of the king and his people (as has been said), it is an offence against the king, who ought to advance the common profit of the realm, and the king has no peer in his own realm, and so this offence ought not to be adjudged by them. Therefore it ought not to be adjudged elsewhere than in the King's Bench. And all this appears from the said book.

What is more to the honour of the king, and for the common profit of the king and his realm, than that his subjects should be free from all oppression? But there cannot be a greater oppression than loss of their liberty by unlawful imprisonment, so that they cannot in their callings serve the king or the public weal. And because these oppressions are against the king and his crown, for that reason these pleas are not entered in the King's Bench among the common pleas but among the pleas of the crown;[18] and for all matters of the crown the King's Bench is the natural court to have cognizance thereof. With this accord various notable precedents in the King's Bench, in which precedents three things are to be observed:[19] (1) that the King's Bench is the highest court for ordinary jurisdiction in matters of the crown throughout England, and all pleas there are *coram domino rege*; (2) just as this is the highest court, so is it the most wide-reaching court, for it may direct a *habeas corpus* into any of the king's dominions, even though they are not parcel of England; for, if they are nevertheless subject to the crown of England, their jurisdiction as to this purpose extends to them; (3) if it is returned upon any writ of *habeas corpus* that he is imprisoned 'by the king's command' (*per mandatum domini regis*), which is good without special cause shown, or imprisoned by someone else 'on suspicion of high

---

[18] I.e. (in the case of *habeas corpus*) in the controlment rolls of the clerk of the crown (now KB 29).

[19] This passage is influenced by the dictum of Catlyn CJ reported in Crompton, *Courts* (1594), fos. 78v–79, which Coke cites opposite. See the extract quoted above, p. 159.

treason concerning the king', or 'by command of the chief justice', or 'by command of the keeper of the forest of N.' (for causes touching the forest), the prisoner shall be remanded, except that in cases when a prisoner is imprisoned by the king's command etc. he is commonly removed by the king's command into his Bench to have his trial there etc. Trin. 21 Hen. VI, rot. 24, among the king's pleas; Mich. 18 Hen. VI, rot. 46, among the king's pleas: an attachment directed to the mayor of the city of Dublin and the treasurer of Ireland etc.[20] Mich. 38 Hen. VIII, rot. 26, a *certiorari* directed to the coroner of the castle of Guisnes in Picardy for an indictment of felony and homicide.[21] Mich. 7 Eliz., a *habeas corpus* to the captain, bailiffs and jurats of the vill of Guernsey for the body of Richard Bond. And infinite other precedents of *habeas corpus* which were directed to Wales etc., and many precedents of *habeas corpus* directed to the lieutenant of the Tower of London. Crompton, *Jurisdiction*, 78.[22] 19 Hen. VII.[23] 23 Hen. VIII, rot. 43.[24] See in the year 20 Hen. VIII, and 35 Hen. VI. See 38 Hen. VIII, rot. 13.[25] See 18 Hen. VIII. rot. 34;[26] 10 Hen. VIII, rot. 34;[27] 2 & 3 Phil. & Mar. rot. 58;[28] 33 Hen. VIII, rot. 38;[29] 28 Hen. VIII, rot. 43;[30] 38

---

[20] KB 27/714, Rex, m. 46; KB 27/729, m. 24: Giles Thorndon, treasurer of Ireland, and Nicholas Woder, mayor of Dublin, are ordered to attach John Cornewalsh (Cornwallis), chief baron of the Exchequer there, for not allowing Michael Gryffyn to assume that office in accordance with his patent (cf. *The Men of Court*, ii. 790); Woder returns that he arrested Cornewalsh and was ready to put him on board ship for England when he was forcibly rescued in the cathedral by William Chevir, secondary justice, Edward Somerton, king's serjeant, and others. The clerk of the crown prayed that Thorndon and Woder be heavily amerced for their insufficient return, but the court took advisement.

[21] KB 29/179, m. 26: George Pace, indicted for homicide, pleaded a pardon in self-defence and it was allowed the same term. The marginal note says 'Guisnes', but there is no mention of the coroner.

[22] R. Crompton, *L'Authoritie et Jurisdiction des Courts* (1594), fo. 78v, quoted above, p. 159.

[23] See n. 36, above.   [24] Perhaps a slip for 28 Hen. VIII, rot. 43: n. 30, below.

[25] KB 29/179, m. 13 (Pas. 1546): *habeas corpus* to Sir John Gage, constable of the Tower, for John Hogges and Thomas Heyth, committed by command of the Council. This was one of Dyer CJ's precedents, printed in 109 SS 78; above, p. 158.

[26] KB 29/158, m 34d (Mich. 1526): *habeas corpus* to the sheriff of Hertfordshire for John Dagnall and Maurice Edmond, committed by command of the Council.

[27] KB 29/150, m. 34 (Mich. 1518): *habeas corpus* to the warden of the Fleet for Thomas Apryse, committed by command of Cardinal Wolsey. This was another of Dyer CJ's precedents, printed in 109 SS 77; above, p. 158.

[28] Probably KB 29/189, m. 58d (Trin. 1556): *habeas corpus* addressed to the sheriffs of London for John Sweete, arrested by command of the Council on suspicion of counterfeiting money; but he was immediately tried, convicted and hanged.

[29] KB 29/174, m. 38: *habeas corpus* to the marshal of the household for Edward Foster, committed by command of Thomas, late Lord Cromwell. He was bailed.

[30] Perhaps KB 29/164, m. 43d: *habeas corpus* to the sheriffs of London for Lawrence and William Belyngham, committed by command of Sir Thomas Audley, lord chancellor of

Hen. VIII, rot. 13;[31] and many others where the body was brought by *habeas corpus cum causa*, namely 'he was committed by command of the councillors of the lord king', whereby he who brought him up was discharged and the prisoner committed to the Marshalsea etc. See Pas. 7 Eliz. and Mich. 7 & 8 Eliz.:[32] persons committed by the president and Council of the North removed: see Crompton, *Jurisdiction*, 78.[33] See Trin. 23 Hen. VIII, rot. 43;[34] 31 Hen. VIII, rot. 30;[35] 19 Hen. VII, rot. 21;[36] 1 Hen. VIII, rot. 9;[37] 9 Hen. VII, rot. 14;[38] Dyer, 10 Eliz., Lee's case, to the High Commissioners.[39]

[40]In Mich. 5 Edw. IV, rot. 143, there is a *habeas corpus* to the keeper of Maidstone gaol, who returned that he was taken by command of the archbishop of Canterbury on suspicion of heresy, against the form of the statute in such case.[41] Pas. 9 Hen. VIII, rot. 40:[42] a *habeas corpus* to John Royse, lieutenant of the Tower of London, who returned that he was detained by the king's command, and he was recommitted to the Tower. Likewise in the year 34 Hen. VI for Thomas Courtney, knight; and in Mich. 35 Hen. VI, rot. 54,[43] the lieutenant was amerced for not having the body.

England. They were immediately arraigned upon an outlawry for felony and murder and pleaded a pardon which was not yet (*adhuc*) allowed, whereupon they were bailed.

[31] See n. 25, above.

[32] KB 29/199, m. 31, for John Lambert (1565); see *Dyer's notebooks*, i. lxxix. The roll is cited in 12 Co. Rep. 54, which also refers to John Dawson's case, 'Mich. 7 et 8 Eliz. in libro de habeas corpus', also a prisoner of the Council in the North.

[33] See n. 22, above. Crompton does not give the name or date, but the case which he reports is evidently Lambert's and is the basis of the version in 12 Co. Rep. 54.

[34] Incorrect reference. Perhaps a slip for 28 Hen. VIII, m. 43, cited above; cf. n. 30, above.

[35] Perhaps KB 29/172, m. 30: *habeas corpus* to the marshal of the Marshalsea for James Thayne, arrested by the king's command on suspicion of high treason.

[36] There are no *habeas corpus* entries on KB 29/134, mm. 20 or 21. Cf. m. 23d: *habeas corpus* to the lieutenant of the Fleet for George Urswyk, committed by the king's command; committed to the Marshalsea.

[37] There are several *habeas corpus* entries in KB 29/140, m. 9, all in cases of imprisonment on suspicion of felony or homicide. The only unusual entry (m. 9d) is for Robert Harryson, detained by the steward and marshal of the king's household, who return that he was committed by command of King Henry VII for a homicide committed at sea.

[38] KB 29/124, m. 14: *habeas corpus* to the steward and marshal of the king's household for Humphrey Bothe of Cambridge, scholar, committed by the king's command 'et hac de causa et non alia'; eventually bailed.

[39] *Thomas Lee's Case* (1568) CP 40/1062, m. 1556; *Dyer's notebooks*, i. 143; above, p. 160.

[40] This paragraph is a marginal addition in the notebook which the copyist in CUL MS. Gg.2.5 inserted here, though perhaps it was meant to be inserted earlier.

[41] *Kayser's Case* (1465) KB 27/818, m. 143d; above, p. 120.

[42] Untraced. There is no m. 40 in the controlment roll for this year, and the lieutenant of the Tower in 9 Hen. VIII was Sir Richard Cholmeley.

[43] Or m. 94. The roll now missing.

See Trin. 20 Eliz.,[44] Pas. 12 Eliz.[45] In Hil. 13 Eliz.[46] a person committed by the president and Council of Wales was removed by *corpus cum causa*, and when the cause appeared to be insufficient the court discharged him, for although the president and Council have authority from Parliament to proceed in accordance with their jurisdiction, nevertheless whether they have pursued their authority or not belongs to the King's Bench and others of the king's courts to adjudge; and, if they do not pursue their jurisdiction (*power*), then the court of King's Bench or another [of the king's courts] shall discharge him. It was so resolved this very term by the justices in a great cause between the King's Bench and Lord Zouche, president, and the Council of Wales, who at first refused to send a prisoner whom he had imprisoned, with the cause, by force of a *habeas corpus* which issued out of the King's Bench.[47] The court of Common Pleas or the Exchequer may not award a *habeas corpus* for anyone unless he has privilege there, but the aggrieved party may without doubt purchase his original writ upon the said statute of Magna Carta in the Common Bench. See 9 Hen. VI, 44:[48] if upon a *habeas corpus* a sufficient confession is returned, even if it is false, this suffices and the party is driven to his action of false imprisonment.

As to the third word, 'disseised', the signification thereof is well known; and yet in some cases the king's writ may be awarded against someone to remove him from possession without an opportunity to answer. This appears from the notable book in 35 Hen. VI, *Suggestion*, pl. 9.[49] The case was that it was found by office that the duke of Suffolk held certain manors of the king in chief, and died, leaving his heir under age, and the king by Parliament granted the wardship of the heir and the land to the duchess of Suffolk during the nonage and until livery sued, 'without rendering anything therefor'; and the duchess

---

[44] See 12 Co. Rep. 55: 'Trin. 20 Eliz. ibid. [*in libro de habeas corpus*] the like writ for the body of John Rowland, committed by the Council and President of Wales, and finding by the return that the commitment of him was against law, he was discharged by the Court'.

[45] KB 29/205, m. 71d (Pas. 1570): *habeas corpus* to the sheriff of Herefordshire for Thomas ap Morgan Thomas and John Williams, committed 'per mandatum Consilii domine Regine Marchiarum suarum Wallie' for felony and murder, for which they were indicted; but they were recommitted to the sheriff. Cf. 12 Co. Rep. 55: 'Pasch. 12 Eliz. *in libro de habeas corpus*, Thomas ap Morgan committed by the Council and President of Wales, etc., and this Court finding the cause unjust, bailed him etc.'

[46] KB 29/206, m. 50d: *habeas corpus* to the sheriff of Shropshire for Lewis Evans, *alias* John Foster, committed 'per mandatum domini presidentis et ceterorum Consilii domini Regine Marchiarum Wallie et Principalitatis ejusdem'; committed to the marshal

[47] Above, pp. 303–11, 346; below, pp. 511–14.

[48] YB Mich. 9 Hen. VI, fo. 44, pl. 24: *corpus cum causa* to the sheriff of Oxfordshire, who returned to the Common Pleas that the cause was depending in the court of the chancellor of Oxford University.

[49] *Duchess of Suffolk's Case* (1456) Mich. 35 Hen. VI, Fitz. Abr., *Suggestion*, pl. 9.

was put into possession by the escheator, and was thus possessed until she was ousted from a certain manor by the duke of Norfolk and the escheator. Thereupon Choke, of counsel with the duchess, surmised this matter in the Chancery and prayed three things on behalf of the duchess: (1) that she might have an *amoveas manum* under a penalty of £1,000 directed to the sheriff (because the escheator was party); (2) that the duke should make fine for his entry upon the king; and (3) that he should answer for the mesne profits. Fortescue CJ, by the advice of his fellows, discharged him in respect of the two last points, for it is not reason that he should make fine and yield up the issues without answer (for that would be against the common law of the land and the aforesaid statutes); but he held, as to the first point, that the duchess should have an *amoveas manum* under a penalty. Should the duke have title, he would not be at mischief, for if he retained his possession notwithstanding this writ an attachment would issue, and thereupon he could show his title, and if it was good he should retain it; and so their opinion was that she could have the *amoveas manum* upon a mere suggestion, without presentment or inquiry. And it was held by all the justices that, if someone intrudes upon the king's possession, an *amoveas manum* may issue against him upon a mere suggestion, without inquiry or presentment. Note, reader, that no one may put the king out of possession or gain any seisin or possession against him, for the king's possessions are within the safe-keeping of the law, and that is *lex terrae*.

The fourth word is 'outlawed', which is as much as to say, deprived of the benefit and protection of the law, and to be put outside the law; for there is an ancient maxim that the benefit of the law is not to be taken away from anyone (*quod beneficium juris nemini est auferendum*),[50] unless it is for his contempt or contumacy. Every subject is inheritable to the laws of the land, which are to be esteemed worthier of respect than his goods or lands, and dearer and more precious to him than his wife or children, for the laws preserve and protect not only all of these but also his body and his life itself in peace and tranquility. *Quisquis ausus fuerit violare leges non aliquos laedet cives, sed totam rempublicam evertere conatus est.*[51] *Et non aliunde floret respublica quam si legum vigeat authoritas.*[52]

---

[50] This maxim, from the *Regulae juris* in the Sext, was quoted by Coke CJ in the case of prohibitions to the Council of the North (1609) 13 Co. Rep. 432.

[51] 'Whoever dares to break the laws not only harms other citizens but ventures to overthrow the whole common weal.' This aphorism was quoted again by Coke in Parliament on 5 June 1628: *Selected Writings and Speeches of Sir Edward Coke*, ed. S. Shepherd (Indianapolis, 2003), p. 1292.

[52] 'Nowhere does the common weal flourish but where the authority of the law thrives.' This aphorism was quoted on the title-page of 6 Co. Rep. Cf. C. Wolfhart, *Apophtegmatum Loci Communes* (1560), p. 571.

The fifth word is 'exiled', and that is as much as to say that a man shall not lose his native land 'except by the law of the land'. In what cases a man may be exiled by the law of the land is to be seen in Stanford, *Plees del Corone*, fo. 117;[53] 31 Edw. I, tit. *Cui in Vita*, pl. 31;[54] 10 Edw. III, 54b;[55] *Registrum Brevium*, fo. 312;[56] 1 Hen. IV, 1;[57] 2 Hen. IV, 7;[58] 11 Hen. IV, 7;[59] and the statute 35 Eliz., c. 1.[60] Note that the Statute of Gloucester, which ousts the writ *de odio et atia*, nevertheless gives the prisoner who cannot be bailed that he shall be imprisoned until the coming of the justices, so that he shall not lie in perpetual prison but shall be delivered at the next gaol delivery.[61] Note this well, because it is of the greatest use. Magna Carta, c. 26; Westminster I, c. 11; *Registrum Brevium*, fo. 133;[62] Westminster II, c. 29; *Bracton*, fo. 121.[63] See the resolution of the judges in 28 Eliz. in the book of precedents.[64]

The sixth word is 'destroyed', which is a general word and extends to all that a man has in the world, so that nothing which a man has shall be destroyed in any way unless 'by the law of the land'.

The seventh and eighth words[65] are, 'nor shall we go upon him or put upon him except by the lawful judgment of his peers'. These words 'go' and 'put' are to be understood of the king's suit, as by indictment; not of every indictment, but only of indictments which concern treason or felony.[66] And these words 'go etc.' extend only to the trial and not to the indictment, for he may be indicted by commoners[67] if the indictment concerns trespass, contempt, or

---

[53] Sta. P.C. 117 (abjuration).

[54] Trin. 31 Edw. I, Fitz. Abr., *Cui in vita*, pl. 31 (as to abjuration for felony).

[55] R. v. *Lady Maltravers* (1336) YB Mich. 10 Edw. III, fo. 53, pl. 37 (referring to her husband's exile for a certain cause); above, p. 56.

[56] Presumably *Registrum Brevium*, fo. 312v ('Carta pardonationis pro muliere bannita'). This was a pardon for a woman banned from Calais for six years on a false charge of adultery.

[57] R. v. *'Sybil' Belknap* (1399) YB Mich. 1 Hen. IV, fo. 1, pl. 2 (which says her husband was banished to Gascony for a crime against the king). Sir Robert Belknap, formerly chief justice of the Bench, was exiled to Ireland in 1388 following his attainder by Parliament; the exile was revoked in 1397, but the judgment of 1388 was restored in 1399. His wife was actually called Juliana: ODNB.

[58] YB Mich. 2 Hen. IV, fo. 7, pl. 26 (referring to the exile of Sir Robert Belknap).

[59] Probably a reference to *Belknap's Case* (1399) YB Mich. 1 Hen. IV, fo. 1, pl. 2; cited in (1406) YB Mich. 8 Hen. IV, fo. 7, pl. 26; above, n. 57. The only case of abjuration temp. Hen. IV cited in Sta. P.C. is YB Mich. 8 Hen. IV, fo. 3, pl. 5.

[60] This statute introduced abjuration of the realm for offenders against the law relating to public worship.

[61] Gloucester, c. 9.   [62] *Registrum Brevium*, fo. 133v ('De ponendo').

[63] *Bracton*, ii. 340, fo. 120v (abjuration of the vill).

[64] Cf. *Arundel's Case* (29 Eliz.) above, p. 264.   [65] I.e. 'go' and 'put'.

[66] Misdemeanours could be prosecuted by information.

[67] Coke here assumes that *parium suorum* in c. 29 only means peers of the realm.

any other offence which does not concern treason or felony, or misprision thereof: see Stanford, ff. 152–3.[68] And see the statute of 26 Hen. VI, c. 6.[69] This statute does not extend to it, and even though the suit concerns life or limb, nevertheless if it is a party's suit and not the king's this act does not extend to it. For instance in 10 Edw. IV, 6,[70] in an appeal of death against a peer of the realm, he shall be tried by commoners; likewise in appeals of robbery, rape, and such like. (And it is to be observed that the distinction as to peers is between the nobility and the commons beneath the nobility, so that a duke or an earl may be tried by barons, for such noblemen are all peers. Likewise knights and gentlemen are considered to be each other's peers.)[71]

---

[68] Sta. P.C. 152–3 ('Triall per les pieres').   [69] Evidently a mistake. Cf. 20 Hen. VI, c. 9.
[70] *Preston* v. *Lord Grey of Codnor* (1442) KB 27/725, m. 94, cited in YB Pas. 10 Edw. IV, fo. 6, pl. 17; 47 SS 63, *per* Littleton J.
[71] This is a free and conjectural rendering: the final part of this marginal addition is virtually illegible.

Appendix 8

Whetherly v. *Whetherly* (1605)

Phelips, the king's serjeant, came to the bar in the King's Bench and informed the court that before now a case of title of land between Whetherly and Whetherly was decreed in the Marches of Wales, in the court there. The person against whom the decree was [awarded] had brought an action at common law in this court, namely an ejectment; the defendant had appeared and joined issue, which was tried; it was found for the plaintiff, and he recovered and had the possession by execution by the sheriff. Afterwards the defendant here, who was plaintiff in the Marches of Wales, procured process out of the Marches against the plaintiff here and attached him, but he escaped; and afterwards he procured process – which they call sequestration – to take his goods which were upon the land, and thereupon the sheriff took seventeen of his beasts, and afterwards (by other process) took the beasts of another man which were on the land, and carried them off to the Marches. Then the Council of the Marches, being informed that the said plaintiff here was at Bristol, which is outside the jurisdiction of the Marches, sent a pursuivant there with a warrant directed to the sheriffs of Bristol to arrest him and send him to the Marches, by colour whereof the said sheriffs broke into his house and arrested him and sent him to the Marches by the pursuivant, and there he was committed. He afterwards broke the prison and escaped; and afterwards, by warrant of the Council of the Marches he was retaken by the sheriff and brought back to the Marches, where he was put in Little Ease, there to remain until he made a bond to relinquish the benefit of his suit at common law. And he prayed that this abuse to this court might be examined, and that a *habeas corpus* might be directed to the Marches to remove the prisoner.

This text is translated from CUL MS. Gg.4.9, fos. 126–127v; BL MS. Lansdowne 1075, fos. 101v–103v; MS. Add. 24846, fos. 54v–56; MS. Add. 35954, fos. 370–371v; IT MS. Barrington 6, fos. 112v–115. These are all versions of the same report. Although the report does not mention Magna Carta, the case is important as providing the context for Coke's memorandum on c. 29 (Appendix 7). The texts in this appendix have all been translated from the original law French. Judges' names are printed in small capitals, counsel in italics.

The court said it was a great abuse to this court that the king's subjects should be thus vexed for suing in this court for justice, and they said it would be well examined.

And *Coke*, attorney-general, being present in the court when this cause was moved, prayed the justices to give him their patience to hear him speak a little for the king's prerogative, the jurisdiction of this court, and the benefit and liberty of all the king's subjects. The justices attended to him seriously, and he began:

Some men learned in the laws of this land today have privately delivered their opinion that when a subject is committed to prison by a member of the king's Privy Council, by the Council of the Marches of Wales, the Council of York, or the like, this court of King's Bench has no power to send a *habeas corpus* for the person who is thus committed; and they allege that there is no book, or law in writing, which proves such a jurisdiction to exist in this court. And he said that this was a great error, and that there is a written law which proves it. This is the statute of Magna Charta, c. 29, which says *Nullus liber homo capiatur vel imprisonetur . . . vel per legem terrae*. This is a positive law in force at this day, so that if any free man is imprisoned at this day by any of these delegated, subordinate and circumscribed authorities, it shall be tried by the examination of some authority whether it be 'by lawful judgment' or 'by the law of the land' or not, or else the law would be defective in the means of execution, which cannot be intended. Therefore all courts of justice within the king's dominions are subordinate, this court alone excepted, in which the king is always presumed by the law to be present, and which is restrained to no place but extends to all his dominions; and therefore this court alone shall have the examination of all the other courts of justice. And even if the king gives authority by his commissions to some person to execute justice, or the law does so by Act of Parliament, nevertheless the examination thereof, as to what may be done by such authority, must remain in the absolute and supreme power of the king, and that is in his Bench, which is the proper seat of justice. And although there are no law reports to be found to prove this, yet he said that he had by search found infinite precedents to prove the continual use of this.[1] For the usage of this court is to send for someone committed by any court within the king's dominions by *corpus cum causa*[2] without mentioning any privilege or special cause in the writ; and no other courts may do that. And by such writ the body has been used to be brought in and the cause certified, so that this court may examine the cause of his imprisonment. And he said that such a writ has been used to be directed to the lieutenant of the

---

[1] See the previous appendix for the precedents collected by Coke from the controlment rolls (KB 29).

[2] I.e. *habeas corpus*.

Tower, which is the highest prison of the realm, and the prisoners brought, and the causes examined as aforesaid; and likewise out of all places within the dominions of the king of England.[3]

POPHAM CJ answered him and said that he and the whole court gave great approval to all he had said, and that he had spoken aptly beseeming the place in which he served, and the time in which he lived, because some subordinate courts – pursuing (as it seems) the erroneous opinion recited by him above – have recently disobeyed these writs of *habeas corpus*. He said that this was a derogation from the king's royal prerogative and a depriving the subject of his natural freedom and of the benefit of the law recited above. And he said he had seen a precedent in 3 Edw. IV,[4] where the archbishop of Canterbury committed someone for heresy, and the court sent a *habeas corpus* for him and his cause, and the archbishop refused to send him, and so his temporalities were seized until he sent him with his cause; and he said that, although in this case the court could not judge of the heresy, nevertheless it could examine whether the archbishop had pursued his authority in the imprisonment of the heretic. Likewise it may examine the authority of anyone within the king's dominions who by any authority or pretended authority commits any of the king's subjects.

YELVERTON J. said that when anyone is brought to this court with his cause by *habeas corpus*, this court ought to examine the cause, and may remand, bail or deliver him as his cause deserves, which is much for the liberty of the subject and for his protection against oppression if it be well maintained.

After two *habeas corpus* severally awarded for the prisoner to Hunnings ('Hemminges'),[5] porter of the gatehouse of the Marches, whereupon he returned nothing, upon the third he returned that he was committed by the Lord Zouche, lord president of Wales; and this was adjudged a bad return because he did not conclude 'I have the body ready'. Day was given upon pain of £40 to amend his return, but he did not amend it, and so an attachment was awarded against Hunnings, the porter, which was not returned this term. After the Council of the Marches heard that the sheriff had an attachment against their porter, they sent a *supersedeas* to the sheriff, reciting the whole of the writ and the controversies between the two courts for their jurisdictions, and that the king had taken it upon himself to determine the cause, and commanded him that in the mean time he surcease to execute his writ; and afterwards he made an injunction against him to the same effect. Notwithstanding this, the sheriff executed the writ and brought

---

[3] Above, pp. 504–6. *Habeas corpus* did not extend to Scotland.

[4] Presumably 5 Edw. IV, i.e. *Kayser's Case* (1465) above, p. 120, though it does not seem the temporalities were actually seized.

[5] Cf. below, p. 514 ('Huninges'). The name in the record is Francis Hunnyngs: Halliday, *Habeas Corpus*, p. 11.

the body of Hunnings into the King's Bench this term, and he was there examined upon interrogatories, to which he answered evasively (*doubteousment*); but it was directly proved against him that he had obstinately disobeyed the writs of *habeas corpus* and that he had spoken contemptuously against the court of the King's Bench and menaced those who brought the writs and the prisoner who was sued there, and that after the receipt of the first writ he had imprisoned the prisoner more harshly and inhumanely than before, in revenge thereof, putting him in a more noisome prison than before, restricting him from access to his friends, preventing food being sent to him, and giving him no sustenance, so that he was compelled to drink his own urine. And because all this appeared [to be true], the court committed Hunnings to the marshal until he had put in bail upon the information exhibited against him upon the statute – as it seems, that of 1 Edw. III, [stat. 1], c. 7 – for the harsh imprisonment, and also until the pleasure of the court should be further known. For disobeying the writs, they said that the fines would be estreated into the Exchequer. Afterwards he was fined £100, and put in bail as above, and then he was delivered. Immediately after that, various complaints were made in the King's Bench of the proceedings of the said Court of Marches.

Then complaint was made to the king, but before this was determined a writ of execution was awarded out of the King's Bench to execute a judgment in this court from Gloucestershire, and the president and the Council of the Marches made out a *supersedeas* thereof, reciting the controversies between the two courts and that the king (in whose name all their process was made) had taken upon himself to arbitrate between the two courts, and ordered the sheriff to surcease until it was determined.

Afterwards, in Trinity term next following, when the president was commanded to obey the *habeas corpus* from the King's Bench, [another] was sent to him, whereupon he sent the body and returned in this manner: 'without (*citra*) prejudice and harm to your royal laws (*jurium*) and customs, and to the right (*juris*) and jurisdiction of the president and of your Council in Wales and the Marches of Wales, inviolably used and observed from time immemorial, which I do not intend (and ought not) in any way to prejudice, I certify to your royal majesty as far as I am bound by law and not otherwise . . .'. And the porter Hunnings, in whose name this return was made, and to whom the writ was directed, was commanded to amend it upon pain of £200, which afterwards he did.

Action of false imprisonment against the porter (1606)[6]

False imprisonment by Walter Whetherly ('Witherley') against Francis Hunnings ('Huninges') upon the statute of Magna Charta, c. 29, *quod nullus liber*

---

[6] BL MS. Lansdowne 1062, fos. 211–12 (with the final decision dated Mich. 1606 in the margin).

homo capiatur, imprisonetur etc., declaring that he was a free man and ought to enjoy his liberties, and that the defendant (knowing this) imprisoned him notwithstanding for a period of twelve days at Bewdley in the county of Worcester. The defendant showed the statute of 34 Hen. VIII, c. 26, for the court of the Marches etc., and that there was a porter's lodge, and that he was the deputy porter; that the president and Council of the Marches aforesaid had been accustomed within the aforesaid court of the Marches to hear and determine matters concerning land or pleas personal, and R. W. exhibited a bill before the president and Council in the Marches aforesaid for certain land; and [because] the defendant there (namely Whetherly) did not obey the order of the aforesaid court they committed him to the defendant's custody: and thus the defendant justified the imprisonment. Thereupon the plaintiff demurred.[7]

Coventry, for the plaintiff, divided the case into the matter in law and the matter of pleading. The matter in law he divided into two points, (1) whether the president and Council of the Marches have authority to determine this cause, and (2) whether their officer (the defendant) should be punished when he had authority from the president and Council. He said that before the statute of 34 Hen. VIII the four counties adjoining the Marches were purely English ... Also, when a king conquers a country or realm, the laws which were there before are not thereby altered without a proclamation. 42 Ass., [pl. 5],[8] where a man [was arrested] without indictment or due process, and likewise 2 Eliz., Dyer 175, Scrogges' case: these prove that the king may not establish courts for [causes between] subjects without process, or designate causes to the president and Council of the Marches which are outside their jurisdiction. As to the second point, he thought that the officer should be punished. There is a distinction between when a court [has authority and jurisdiction][9] and when it has neither authority nor jurisdiction in the cause, as here, which distinction was agreed in this court 45 Eliz. between *Goby* and *Knight*.[10] As to the pleading ...

POPHAM [CJ]. In time of insurrection and rebellion the king may make a commission to a lieutenant with instructions to do things even though they concern possession of land, or life and limb, and [to proceed] without ordinary process, and if he does according to his instructions it is excusable. That is because in such times justice cannot take its course by ordinary means, but is hindered by the rebellion. Likewise, when Wales was a country in rebellion

---

[7] A demurrer confessed the facts as pleaded but raised the question whether in law they amounted to a defence.

[8] *Sir John atte Lee's Case* (1368) above, p. 58.

[9] There must be an omission here, perhaps resulting from haplography.

[10] Above, p. 318 n. 209.

against the crown of England, it was thought necessary to send forces there sometimes, and a commission to quieten the country, at times when law could not be established there. The commissioners could not, however, determine freehold, but only the possession for the duration of the war. The reason why the Marches should be well governed, and in quiet, is that they are fences for the body of counties. Whether [a place is within the] Marches or not is not triable by jury, or by book-cases, or recitals in Acts of Parliament.

TANFIELD. It was adjudged in 19 Eliz. in the Common Bench that in false imprisonment, where the defendant justified by a warrant out of the Admiral Court in a cause of land, with which they have nothing to do, the writ lay.

In Michaelmas term [1606], 4 Jac., the case being moved by *Stephens*, POPHAM CJ and FENNER thought the defendant not punishable because he did nothing without a court order, but YELVERTON and [WILLIAMS[11]] *contra*, that the court has only a special and limited jurisdiction.

---

[11] The manuscript reads 'Dan' or 'Dav', but the other puisne judge in 1606 was Sir David Williams.

Appendix 9

Maunsell's Case (1607)

King's Bench, Easter Term 1607[1]

Edward Owner,[2] a merchant, and Richard Maunsell, a minister,[3] were brought into the King's Bench by a *habeas corpus* directed to the keeper of the Clink,[4] who returned that they were committed by the High Commissioners for Causes Ecclesiastical, and the tenor of the several returns [was read].

Now *Fuller* came to the bar and prayed that they should be delivered, for he said that they were imprisoned against the law and without warrant. Every subject convented before a magistrate for any offence is to have his lawful and honourable trial by a jury of his peers by the law of England, so that all subjects are instruments of justice to each other, and a subject ought not to be imprisoned before such lawful trial. This is by the statute of Magna Carta, *Nullus liber homo etc.*[5] Also by the statute of 5 Edw. III, c. [9], which says 'no man shall from henceforth be attached by any accusation, nor forjudged of life or limb, nor his lands, tenements, goods or

---

The texts in this appendix have all been translated from the original law French. Judges' names are printed is small capitals, counsel in italic.

[1] BL MS. Lansdowne 1075, fos. 261v–267v, 286v–290; MS. Add. 24846, fos. 202v–208v; MS. Add. 35954, fos. 493v–497v. There is a different report of the same day's proceedings in BL MS. Add. 11681, fos. 45–46v; MS. Add. 25206, fos. 55–56v (same report); this largely agrees with the report translated here, though it places Finch's argument at the end; a few parallel passages (here cited as MS. B) have been appended in the footnotes. Fuller's argument was printed in full as *The Argument of Master Nicholas Fuller in the Case of Thomas Lad and Richard Maunsell* (1607). There are further reports in CUL MS. Ee.5.17, fo. 106v; MS. Gg.2.3, fos. 59–62v, 90–92, 95v–96; MS. Gg.4.9, fos. 272v–277.

[2] The name is spelt 'Omer' and 'Onon' in the manuscripts. But he is identifiable as Edward Owner (1575–1650), a Yarmouth merchant who became an MP in 1621; this aspect of his earlier life is not noticed in *HPHC 1604–29*. Fuller gives the lay defendant's name Thomas Lad, also a Yarmouth merchant, and he is also so named in BL MS. Lansdowne 1061, fo. 47 (below, p. 525 n. 36) and CUL MS. Ee.5.17, fo. 106v (below, p. 526).

[3] Maunsell was a prominent Presbyterian preacher.

[4] A gaol in Southwark, used for ecclesiastical prisoners.

[5] Cf. MS. B: 'Fuller, of Gray's Inn, moved that the prisoners might well refuse the said oath; and to prove this he insisted on the statute of Magna Charta, c. 29, and 25 Edw. III, c. 4; 28 Edw. III, c. 3; and 42 Edw. III, c. 3.'

chattels seized into the king's hands, against the form of the great charter and the law of the land'. And the statute of 25 Edw. III, [stat. 5], c. 4, that no man shall be imprisoned upon petition to the king and his Council but by lawful indictment. To the same effect is 37 Edw. III, [c. 18], and 38 Edw. III, [stat. 1, c. 9], which prove plainly that it is not lawful to imprison a subject without lawful indictment and proceeding against him. Although these statutes do not extend to ecclesiastical proceedings, for at that time they could not imprison, they nevertheless show the care and respect which the law has for the liberty of the subject. It is said in 10 Hen. VII, fo. 17,[6] that before the statute of 2 Hen. IV, c. 15, the clergy had no authority to proceed by imprisonment but only by the censures of the Church. A statute was invented against those who in those times began to profess the gospel in this land, such as Sir John Oldcastle and others, who then held the opinion of the sacrament which is now professed by the Church of England,[7] and I pray to God that power of that statute is not extended at this day against true professors of the gospel.[8] Also by this statute the ordinary ought to proceed to abjuration or purgation of the party within three months after the imprisonment, whereas these prisoners for whom I speak have been six months in prison. After the making of this statute many complaints were made by the Commons of oppression by the ordinaries, and during the time that this realm was drowned in idolatry and darkness they had no remedy. But afterwards, upon a petition exhibited in 23 Hen. VIII containing many grievances,[9] when the blessed light of the gospel began to appear in 25 Hen. VIII an Act of Parliament was made whereby the said Act of 2 Hen. IV was utterly repealed and a new course of proceeding was prescribed; and by that Act it is recited that the proceeding by captious interrogatories were distasteful to the Parliament, and that is the special cause of the imprisonment of these prisoners, namely for refusing the oath ex officio.[10] The new course prescribed by the statute of 25 Hen. VIII, [c. 14], is by presentment or accusation by two witnesses, which is reasonable, whereas this oath ex officio is unreasonable and repugnant to the law of nature, for a man shall thereby be compelled to

---

[6] *Warner v. Hudson* (1495) YB Hil. 10 Hen. VII, fo. 17, pl. 17; above, p. 123.

[7] I.e. the Lollards: see above, p. 118.

[8] A marginal note here reads: 'Note a contradiction, for afterwards he says that this statute was repealed, as it was.'

[9] The Supplication of the Ordinaries; above, p. 124 n. 70.

[10] Cf. MS. B: 'And 2 Hen. IV, c. 15, where it is ordained that the diocesan etc. should proceed against him within three months and determine the business in accordance with the canonical decrees; these prisoners, however, have been imprisoned for nine months. And 25 Hen. VIII, c. 14, which calls the articles of the ordinary captious interrogatories and deprives bishops of the power to administer similar interrogatories.'

accuse himself, which by the law of England shall never be suffered, much less compelled or urged. If a juror is charged for a misdemeanour in himself, he shall not be sworn to disclose it. And this oath *ex officio* is against the law, as appears by FNB, fo. 41, where it is said that the sheriff shall be commanded not to permit the king's subjects to take such oaths before ordinaries. It is objected that it is *pro salute animae*,[11] but it is the contrary, for it is in great peril of their souls, for perjury will of necessity ensue from it. It seems to me obvious that the high commissioners cannot compel such an oath to be taken. Every commission granted by the king to proceed in any case against the law of England is void, unless it is fortified by an Act of Parliament; this commission is to proceed against the law, and is not warranted by the statute of 1 Eliz. or by any other Act, and so it is void . . .[12] If the commission extends beyond what is warranted by the Act of Parliament it is void, as the case is in 42 Edw. III, pl. 5,[13] where a commission to arrest a man and his goods without indictment is void. Likewise if a writ is awarded to someone to take an indictment, it is void, for it ought to be a commission: ibid. pl. 12. Likewise was the commission granted to the earl of Bedford and others to examine the title of Scrogges to the exigentership, in Dyer, Eliz., fo. 175b.[14] Thus it seems to me that the commission here is void, for it extends beyond what the law warrants . . . And because there is no place to which a subject may more properly complain than this place, in which the king sits himself judicially, and which has the power to send for the body and the cause of committal of any subject, and which is most properly appointed to preserve the peace and tranquility of the subject in smaller things, so much the more so in this matter of his liberty. We are come here humbly, and in such manner as the petition was in 23 Hen. VIII, 'lamentably complaining of these grievances', and pray to be relieved and released at large.

Finch, to the same effect.[15] The sole doubt which I will make in this case is whether the high commissioners may exact this oath *ex officio* and imprison someone for not making it. The statute of 1 Eliz. is only a declaration of the common law and no new addition to the crown, for the queen already by her supremacy had domination and power over all her subjects, and was furnished with rule and power immediately from God, and it is impossible to make addition to that by Act of Parliament. I do not doubt that the king may give power to imprison, but not as this case is, because it was not within the ecclessiastical jurisdiction previously. There are three interpreters of the law

---

[11] 'For the health of the soul'.
[12] There follows a discussion of the wording of the statute of 1 Eliz.
[13] *Sir John atte Lee's Case* (1368) above, p. 58.   [14] Above, pp. 156-7
[15] In MS. B this is at the end.

of England: use, statutes and books.[16] This urging of the oath, or at least the punishment by imprisonment of the contempt in refusing it, was never used in this land before 1 Eliz., and thus it is well proved that it was unlawful. As the Civilians say, *Quod in practica non est receptum in jure est merito suspectum,*[17] and so at least it is suspicious. The statutes before recited by Fuller prove that before the statute of 2 Hen. IV they could not imprison anyone, either for this cause or any other. The books of the common law prove that it is against common reason that a man be compelled to swear to be his own accuser, for (as is said in 49 Edw. III, fo. 1)[18] if a juror is challenged for a thing which is only to his own reproach, he shall not be sworn. In the Register, under 'Prohibition et Attachment', fo. 36b, there is an attachment upon prohibition against the ordinary for exacting an oath from a subject 'against the custom of this realm of England', which is nothing other than the common law. And the Lord Treasurer Burghley (who is with God) once said in the Star Chamber that it was the liberty of the subject of England, more than of all other nations, that he should not be molested or imprisoned without indictment:[19] other nations have an accusation, but that is verbal and at the promotion of a party, whereas this is by the presentment of his neighbours and peers upon their oath, and should be of record. This liberty was purchased to the subjects of England with the blood of many people, noble and ignoble, and was the cause of the Barons' War, and it is the noblest accusation that can be. The statute of Magna Carta says that a free man shall not be imprisoned unless by the law of the land, and what is meant by the law of the land it well expounded (as it seems to me) in the statute of 25 Edw. III, [stat. 5], c. [4], to be by indictment. If justice in its course is against the law of nature it loses its name and essence and becomes injustice. *Natura est optima conservatrix sui,*[20] and so to compel a man to be his own accuser is against nature. By the law of God there should be accusers, for Christ said to the woman (8 *John* [v. 10]), 'Where be thine accusers'? And by the speech of Festus it appears that by the Civil law no one shall be condemned without accusers, for he says 'that it is not the manner of the Romans for favour to deliver any to death before he which is accused hath his accusers confront him': *Acts* 25, v. 26. Thus the law of God, the law of nature, the Civil law, and the law of England, are against this unnatural accusation by one man to be his own accuser. That this should be maintained by the statute

---

[16] I.e. law reports.

[17] Cf. MS. B: 'quod in practica non est receptum debito jure est suspectum', i.e. what has not been received in practice is rightly to be suspected in law.

[18] *Wyke* v. *Gernon* (1375) YB Hil. 49 Edw. III, fo. 1, pl. 1.

[19] *Att.-Gen.* v. *Skynner and Catcher* (1588) above, p. 270. It is not clear whether the following words are also attributable to Burghley.

[20] Nature is the best preserver of itself. This is a variant of the maxim, derived from Cicero, *De Finibus*, iv. 7, that all natural things wish to preserve themselves.

of 1 Eliz. is against the ordinary exposition of statutes, for if statutes are doubtful they should be expounded according to the law of reason, and they expound themselves and should not be wrested against the law of nature and reason ... The offence of which these men are accused is making conventicles contrary to the recent canons, the punishment of which offence (after conviction by the law) is not imprisonment, and it is against reason that a contempt in any case should be punished more severely than the offence itself ... That this oath *ex officio* is not warranted by any of our rightful provincial common laws will not be denied; but it is maintained by a foreign law which, as it seems to me, was abrogated by the statute of 25 Hen. VIII, [c. 19], which prescribes a review [of the canon law] to be had by commission of the common law (which was never made), but there is a proviso that the law should be exercised in the mean time, and that 'all such canons, constitutions, ordinances and synodals provincial, being already made, which are not contrariant [or repugnant to the laws of the realm or the king's prerogative, shall still be used until etc.]', and so if there is no provincial constitution which warrants the oath *ex officio* it is unlawful, and then the imprisonment for refusing it is unlawful, and I pray that, for this cause, these prisoners be forthwith delivered.

POPHAM CJ.[21] A *habeas corpus* was requested by the counsel at the bar for these prisoners, and, as we are obliged by course of justice to grant it to all men, so it was granted to them. The cause of their committal has been heard, and it appears to be a cause of great importance and deserves to be resolved upon great consideration. I will not dispute that this court may send for them, or for any other prisoner in whatever prison he may be, and examine the cause of the imprisonment; but I will speak to some of the things moved by the counsel at the bar. The statute of Magna Carta says that no free man shall be imprisoned except in accordance with the course of the law and by lawful judgment. But this ought to be qualified with this exposition, namely, not by ordinary officers or in ordinary causes; but in extraordinary causes concerning the state it is otherwise. For no one will deny that always after this statute, until the present day, it has been used that the king has committed persons to prison, and so likewise has the chief justice, without 'lawful judgment' (*legale judicium*), for it is many times very necessary that the cause of their commitment be concealed. The writ *de homine replegiando*, which is grounded upon the said statute, has the exception 'unless he be taken by our command or by the command of our chief justice', which plainly proves that the law ought to be so expounded. Before the statute of 2 Hen. IV, those who exercised ecclesiastical jurisdiction within this realm could not imprison, for the king has an interest in the liberty of every man, and the ecclesicastical jurisdiction was then understood to be foreign, and their highest

---

[21] Sir John Popham had been a member of the High Commission since he was attorney-general. He died on 10 June 1607.

522 *MAUNSELL'S CASE* (1607)

censure was excommunication only, which was fortified with *excommunicato capiendo* after it was found to be little respected and regarded.[22] As to what has been said that the ordinary ought by the statute of 2 Hen. IV to determine the cause within three months, that is not so; it says that they should proceed to the abjuration within three months, but if it is delayed by the peevishness of the party, or otherwise by his default, so that the ordinary cannot proceed, it shall not be intended that the ordinary should let him to at large after the three months. But this statute was utterly repealed by the statute of 25 Hen. VIII, and therefore it is vain and idle to speak of it. The inferences made out of the statute of 25 Hen. VIII are nothing to this purpose, for that was a statute solely against the Romish power, which no one now may execute within this land. All the doubt of this case rests solely upon the statute of 1 Eliz., and the exposition of this and of the commission granted by virtue of this statute ... And it has been adjudged upon consultation before all the judges of England that the high commissioners by force of the said statute and their commission may assess a fine upon offenders,[23] which by the common law they could not do; and that is all one with imprisonment, and stronger than the urging of the oath *ex officio* ... This oath *ex officio* is not such a rare thing, for without doubt ordinaries before the statute of 1 Eliz. could well have urged this oath upon their clerks, though they could not upon laymen, as appears by the Register cited before by Finch; for that writ says only 'if he be lay', and so is FNB, fo. 41. But if he was a clerk, then they could compel him to take this oath *ex officio*, for he has sworn canonical obedience to his ordinary on his taking orders. It was the usage that laymen were also drawn to take it, but that was by their consent and not by compulsion as with clergymen. Now after the statute of 1 Eliz. it is lawful, as it seems to me, to exact it also from laymen, for it is done by the commission, which is fortified and has its force and warrant by the Act of Parliament. I grant that if it was not for the Act of Parliament the commission would have been against law and void. But now authority is given to the king to make a commission by the Act of Parliament, it is now lawful to do as has been done, even though it was previously unlawful; for it is warranted by something which is good by the law, which is the Act of Parliament, and that was not made without great reason and consideration, for it was made quasi of necessity to appoint some men of great discretion and judgment to have the prime and chief jurisdiction in causes ecclesiastical in the troublesome time of suppressing popery,

---

[22] Cf. MS. B: 'The cause why the common law has so great a regard for the body of a man was so that he would be ready to serve the king. Therefore in old times ecclesiastical persons only had authority to excommunicate those who rejected religion, for that tended only to the peril and thraldom of the soul in this life, but in the end there were many who did not care about excommunication and therefore the writ *de excommunicato capiendo* was devised to punish the bodies of those who did not heed the punishment of their soul.'

[23] Presumably *Anon.* (1587) Sav. 83, 115; Clench's reports, BL MS. Harley 4556, fos. 195–6; above, p. 141.

when those who had ordinary jurisdiction either could not or would not suppress it. Also the law was uncertain, because the statute of 25 Hen. VIII, [c. 19], for reviewing ecclesiastical law, was never pursued and put in execution. Thus it seems to me that these prisoners cannot be relieved, but ought to be remanded ...[24] If there is error in the proceedings of the high commissioners, there is a course of law to reform it, by complaint to the king to recall the commission, or by suing in the Chancery to have a commission of review of the sentence. The court will not oppose any court of the king in their ordinary course, for the forms of the courts differ, and even if a form seems to us to be irregular, nevertheless because it appears to be the course of the court it will not be opposed. In this particular matter, which is of great consequence, great deliberation ought to be had before such great and weakening a blow be given to the ecclesiastical jurisdiction to exercise that for which at the present day there is such great necessity; and so etc.

YELVERTON. The prohibitions from this court which have been oppugned are by course of our law, and so are the *habeas corpus* awarded out of this court to any other court.[25] If anyone sues in court Christian for a cause which concerns the lay court, the law is a a prohibition in itself, so that the first process shall be that of attachment ... And whereas it is said that prohibitions are irregular, that is not so, for they are never granted without a surmise which contains matter to give jurisdiction to this court. As to *habeas corpus*, it cannot be doubted but that the king may send for any prisoner committed by any of his courts, and it may be returned before himself 'wheresoever he shall be in England': which is this court, or before himself in his Chancery.[26] That this is just as true where he is committed by an ecclesiastical judge for an ecclesiastical cause appears well from the case of 5 Edw. IV remaining of record in this court.[27] ... And in Dyer, fo. [*blank*], a *habeas corpus* was awarded to the warden of the Fleet, who sent the body and returned that he was committed by the cardinal.[28] Also in Dyer, fo. [*blank*], a *habeas corpus* was awarded to the lieutenant of the Tower, who sent the body and returned that he was committed by the King's Council. As to the

---

[24] Popham then expresses sorrow at the contentiousness of some clergymen.

[25] Cf. MS. B, quoted below, p. 525 n. 32, 34.

[26] MS. B adds: 'It is otherwise in the Common Bench, for there he ought to show a cause of privilege.'

[27] Cf. MS. B: 'There are various precedents which prove that the prisoners in cases like this have been dismissed. One was in 5 Edw. IV, where a *habeas corpus* was directed to the gaoler of Maidstone etc., who returned the cause of the committal of the prisoner to be that he did not care about being excommunicated or trouble about being absolved, and the prisoner was bailed here for two terms and in the third term discharged.' The case is Ex parte *Kayser* (1465) KB 27/818, m. 143d; above, p. 120.

[28] Ex parte *Apryse* (1518) KB 29/150, m. 34. This case, and the next two, were from Dyer's unpublished notebooks: above, pp. 157, 160–1.

matter in question, it depends solely on the Act of 1 Eliz., for a commission against the law is void. It is not to be denied but that, if this commission is warranted by the Act of Parliament, it is not against the law. I confess it has been the use, in appearance, that prisoners have been delivered by *habeas corpus* who were committed for refusing the oath *ex officio*, as the case is in Dyer, fo. [*blank*], where someone was convented before the high commissioners for hearing mass and refused to be examined upon his oath, and was committed and afterwards delivered by *habeas corpus* from this court.[29] To the same effect is the case of Hynde, set in the margin of Scrogges' case,[30] who was convented for usury and refused the oath *ex officio* and was committed, and delivered by *habeas corpus*. These cases appear to be in favour of the prisoners at the bar, but now upon better consideration of the commission and the statute my opinion is that they should be remanded.

POPHAM CJ. It is a great slander that the surmises in prohibitions should be accused of irregularity, for it is the only form of proceeding in all actions in this court and in all the king's courts: for what action is more than a surmise before it has been answered? If process should not be made upon a surmise, then no action could be commenced in any court. If the surmise upon which a prohibition is granted is insufficient, a consultation shall be granted; otherwise not. I deny the cases put by Yelverton, out of Dyer, to be like the case of these prisoners at the bar, for one of them was for usury and the other for hearing mass, which are both punishable by penal statute laws, and so it was unreasonable that they should be compelled to accuse themselves upon their oath. But when the offence is solely punishable by the ecclesiastical law, and not by the common law or statute law, as is the case of the prisoners at the bar, it is otherwise. Their offence is [attending] conventicles, which is purely spiritual, and so the cases are good in law but not alike.

FENNER.[31] It is justice to grant writs of *habeas corpus* and injustice to deny them. The clergy may not make laws and canons to oppose the laws of the land.

---

[29] Cf. MS. B: 'Likewise one Lee was convented before the High Commissioners for hearing mass at the Spanish ambassador's house, and because he would not answer upon his oath *ex officio* they comitted him; and the court of Common Bench (the said Lee being an attorney there) sent a *habeas corpus* for him and discharged him upon the *habeas corpus*. Nevertheless the hearing of mass in an ambassador's house is unlawful, even though the king permits [foreign ambassadors] to use their consciences in this realm.' *Thomas Lee's Case* (1568) was from Dyer's unpublished notebooks, i. 143; above, p. 160.

[30] *Ex parte Hynde* (1576–7) Dyer 175, margin; above, p. 161.

[31] Cf. MS. B, where the speech begins: 'I did not think to have spoken to the case at this time, yet I will briefly deliver my thinking. The king is sworn at his coronation that he will govern his people according to the law, and we are sworn to judge his people according to the law. *Rex non habet parem in regno suo* (The king has no equal in his kingdom), as Bracton says.'

It is a breach of the judges' oath to deny [prohibitions] upon suggestions.[32] The king has sworn to do justice, and it is a fearful thing for his justices to deny it, or for other men to act against it.

WILLIAMS.[33] It is needless for those who judge by a law in essence to make apologies for the law against the weak accusations of those who live under it, and are judged by it: for what law was ever so just that it was not accused by a condemned offender? It is against the gravity and majesty of the law, and the authority thereof, to be moved with such idle accusations, much less to make speeches giving the vain accusers satisfaction: for who will be satisfied with any defence of the law and justice who will not be content to submit themselves under the execution thereof? That is all the defence I will make for prohibitions and *habeas corpus*.[34] The case in question rests solely on the statute of 1 Eliz. ... If the said commissioners do not deal with these novelists, disturbers of the peace of the Church, and such also who have sworn canonical obedience to their ordinary, with whom may they deal, if they may not punish these disturbers of the settled estate of religion established in this realm, which is grounded upon these invincible thirty-two articles, against which no papist has written or impugned, or anyone else, but only our own schismatics, who are content to make a rupture in this our established and peaceable state of religion? ... I do not doubt that all that is done by the high commissioners is lawful, for it is warranted by the Act of Parliament, which may well give them power, just as it has given the College of Physicians in such a case, that it may imprison men offending against their ordinances. But I fully concede the distinction made by Popham, that if the cause on which the offender is examined is punishable by the temporal law he shall not be compelled to take the oath *ex officio*. The law is the same if the cause is mixed, as in the case of usury.[35] But if it is purely ecclesiastical, as it is here, then as it seems to me the oath may well be urged, and especially against a clergyman who has sworn canonical obedience; and so etc.

TANFEILD.[36] I will give no opinion directly on the matter in question, but I will speak somewhat as I now conceive upon the sudden. The whole matter

---

[32] Cf. MS. B: 'It is the law to grant prohibitions, and if we were to deny them we should infringe our oath. The ecclesiastical officers and commissioners ought also to judge according to the king's law etc.'

[33] Sir David Williams became a member of the High Commission in 1605.

[34] Cf. MS. B: 'I will not make any apology for prohibitions and *habeas corpus*. They were before the Conquest.'

[35] Cf. MS. B, which adds: 'I have read of one Doctor Cosen, who has written a treatise of this matter and is of the same opinion.'

[36] His exposition of the statute of 1559 is also in BL MS. Lansdowne 1061, fo. 47 (undated). It is here omitted, since it largely repeats what has gone before. Tanfield was translated to

rests on the statute of 1 Eliz.[37] . . . for if there were nothing contained in the Act of Parliament, and the commission, he has done well to refuse it. It ought to be expressly returned, and, because it was not, it seems to be that the return is bad.[38]

The prisoners were redelivered to the gaoler of the Clink.[39]

And in the Trinity term following TANFIELD said that the commission which is directed to the high commissioners is that if the commissioners suspect anyone for any offence contained in the statute they may convent him before them upon this sole suspicion. For this see afterwards, in Trinity term.

Trinity Term 1607[40]

The case of *habeas corpus*, above, was again moved by *Fuller*. And he said that the cause why Ladd,[41] one of the prisoners, was committed was for not taking the oath *ex officio*. But the reason which induced him to refuse it was that he had been examined on his oath on a previous occasion concerning the said conventicle, and then he accepted the oath and delivered his knowledge; notwithstanding that, they examined him again upon his oath, and they then menaced him that he was perjured, and so he refused to depose any further matter unless he might see a copy of his former deposition; and, because he was not permitted to see it, he refused, and was thereupon committed: which imprisonment, as it seems to me, was wrongful. This may be proved by the statute of 1 Eliz. Firstly by the title thereof, which is 'An Act restoring to the Crown the Ancient Jurisdiction over the State Ecclesiastical and Spiritual'. But

---

the Exchequer as chief baron in July 1607, whereupon he was added to the High Commission.

[37] Cf. MS. B: 'No one is ignorant but that a later parliament overrides (*tolle*) all former, and because it was not fit for the queen to be troubled in every particular it was ordained that the queen might appoint commissioners etc. But this statute is rather a declaration of the law than a new law. That appears by the title thereof, namely "An Act restoring to the Crown the Ancient Jurisdiction".'

[38] Cf. MS. B: 'It seems to me that the return of this *habeas corpus*, that they were committed for refusing to answer upon their oath a summary question touching a conventicle etc., is an insufficient return. I do not understand what they mean by the words "summary question". They ought to return precisely what the oath was which was tendered to the prisoners, and recite that it was for a matter within their commission.'

[39] The report in MS. B ends with Finch's argument, as above, and concludes with his prayer for bail: 'But he did not have his prayer, even though [only] one of the prisoners, namely Maunsell, was a clerk, and Onon a layman. For the justices said they wished to be better advised in a case of such great importance.'

[40] CUL MS. Ee.5.17, fos. 106v–107; BL MS. Add. 25206, fos. 59v–60.

[41] The name is omitted in the BL MS.

the ancient jurisdiction was to punish offenders by ecclesiastical censure, namely by excommunication, not by imprisonment or fine. Then, as to the matter of that statute: it was made for the government of Christ's Church etc., but that is derived from foreign authority and was admitted in the realm by 2 Hen. IV, c. 15, for the government of the Church which was then established, and in 25 Hen. VIII that authority was abolished as a thing unfit for the government of Christ's Church. Thirdly, he put various cases where a thing may be within the letter of the law and yet outside the intent.

Finch agreed. He insisted solely upon the words in the statute, 'according to the tenor and effect of the said letters patent', from which words it may be objected that what is contained in the commission is enacted by Parliament: to which I answer that the statute gives nothing to the queen, for it is only a declaration of the common law and does not give the queen anything other than what she had before. But she did not have such a power before, with respect to this point of the commission, ergo she does not now. Secondly, the words 'according to the tenor etc.' have a restrictive intention, namely that there should not be more commissioners than the queen nominates and that they should not deal in matters other than those she appoints. But they shall not be taken strangely to give whatever power should be named in the commission, for then (by the same reason) if it was contained in the commission that the commissioners might hang[42] me for any trespass, you could say that they had authority by Act of Parliament to do it. Even if the offence with which the prisoners are charged is confessed, the commissioners could still not imprison them for it, because it is not an ecclesiastical censure; ergo they cannot imprison them before the offence is confessed.

WILLIAMS thought the imprisonment was lawful, but he said he would deliver any resolute opinion. If a question is asked of them upon their oath which concerns felony or murder, they may well refuse it. But the question here proposed concerned an ecclesiastical matter, with which we have nothing to do, any more than where they deprive a minister, for there we cannot examine the cause of deprivation.

TANFIELD agreed. The reformation of religion required an expedient course, especially upon the first change thereof. If proceedings against heresies, schisms and so forth had been left to the legal course, perhaps a matter would have been two or three years in question, because of appeals; therefore it was enacted that there should be commissioners to hear and determine etc., who would take a shorter course in the matter. The statute does not, however, appoint any form of proceeding, but leaves it to the commissioners, and says that it should be in accordance with the tenor and effect of the letters patent – that is, as the king

---

[42] The CUL MS. misreads *pender* as *prender* (take), but the BL MS. is correct, and the sense is clear from Tanfield's remark below.

wishes – and it is as much as if the punishment had been expressed in the statute. Similarly, if someone makes his testament and thereby devises his land to John Style in accordance with a deed which he has himself previously made, this is a good testament in writing by reference of the will to the deed. The authority of the commissioners is to proceed by jury or witness or oath of the party, and these courses are allowed them by their commission. If, therefore, someone will not obey them, it is a contempt for which he may be committed. I wonder that Mr Finch should say that, by the same reason, if they had authority in their commission to hang a man they could do it. The case is not alike, for the statute says that they should have power to correct and amend, and will you say that hanging is correcting or amending?

FENNER. If a subpoena is sued against a man, and a bill is not put in against him, he is not bound to answer.

A second report of the argument in Trinity Term 1607[43]

More of the case of the prisoners committed by the high commissioners.

Fuller came to the bar and said:[44] it seems to me that the prisoners should be delivered. The whole doubt rests on the Act of Parliament of 1 Eliz. ... By the statute of 25 Hen. VIII the intent of the law was to establish a government of Christ's Church, and so it cannot be governed by the laws of Antichrist, but such are (in these days) oaths, imprisonments and such like, used by them under colour of this commission.

YELVERTON interrupted him and said: that was indiscreetly said, so to call any authority established by Parliament within the king's dominions. And he said that if he was not more temperate he would be silenced.

Then [Fuller] craved pardon and moved on, and said that a statute shall never be expounded by implication against the common law. And he put many cases to that effect ...

---

[43] CUL MS. Gg.2.23, fos. 73v–75v; Gg.4.9, ff. 291–296v; BL MS. Add. 35954, fos. 508–510v. The arguments of counsel are omitted here since they repeat what was said before. There was no chief justice this term, following the death of Popham.

[44] There is a much fuller version of Fuller's argument this term in CUL MS. Gg.4.9, fos. 294–296v. Towards the beginning he cited Magna Carta: 'the laws of England so much regarded and preserved the liberty of the subjects that no one shall be imprisoned "except by lawful judgment of his peers or by the law of the land", as it is said in Magna Carta, c. 29, which charter has been confirmed by various other subsequent statutes, with strong enforcements in some of them, such as making void such statutes as should be contrary to Magna Carta ... and if any free subject was wrongfully imprisoned the common law did not leave him to an action of false imprisonment only, but provided the writ *de homine replegiando* to set him free from his imprisonment ... which writ is part of the subjects' inheritance and ought not to be denied them.'

Croke[45] to the same purpose. It seems to me that the Act does not give authority to take this oath ...

Finch to the same purpose. The matter rests on the common law, the statute law, and the commission. Of the common law I will say nothing ...

WILLIAMS. If the matter contained in the return of the *habeas corpus* is a spiritual matter, it belongs to them, and is punishable by them, by the statute and their commission. The return contains that one Robert Ingler was deprived, and that the prisoners had many secret conventicles with him, which (being purely spiritual) belongs to them of the High Commission and not to us. This oath which is now so strongly opposed has been used for five hundred years together in this country, and is allowable by the common and ecclesiastical law of this land ... If anyone is examined by them upon articles which are impertinent, they may well refuse, and if they are committed they shall be delivered; but if they are pertinent, and they refuse, they may well by their commission commit them; and so etc.

TANFIELD. I will give no opinion for law, but only show how I think the statute should be construed. It is said that it is hard to examine a man upon his oath if he is a layman. It is true; but it is established by Parliament, and Parliament may do anything (*Parliamentum omnia potest*). Therefore this great authority which is given to the commissioners, being given by Parliament, is lawful until the statute is repealed, which statute having been first made upon great cause and consideration, and also for the necessity of the times, it shall be intended by the Parliament to be executed as it now is, which is well proved by the use at all times since the making thereof until the present. If, however, the cause ceases which was the origin of this law, the king if he sees reason may well reform it by a new Act of Parliament or by altering the form of his commission, which is to be left to him .... It would be good to be advised with all the justices before any resolution is given.

YELVERTON was not present when the justices argued, but had gone into the Chancery.

Common Pleas, Trinity Term 1609[46]

Maunsell was convented before the High Commission for speaking against the Book of Common Prayer and also for slandering his ordinary; and, because he would not answer to the articles objected there against him, he was sent by

---

[45] Probably George Croke. Sir John Croke, king's serjeant, became a justice of the King's Bench on 25 June 1607, in place of Sir Lawrence Tanfield.

[46] BL MS. Add. 9844, fo. 54v. Cf. a different report in CUL MS. Hh.2.2, fo. 8v, BL MS. Add. 25209, fos. 154v–155v, where Coke CJ cited *Lee's Case* (1568) from Dyer's written report. There is a brief report in CUL MS. Mm.1.21, fo. 157v.

them to prison; and he had a *habeas corpus* out of the Common Bench, and the body and cause were returned there. And the justices of the Common Bench had no cause to detain him, because the cause pertained to the decision of the spiritual court. The High Commission may examine this party, being a spiritual man, upon his oath, and if he refuses may commit him. But they may not examine a layman upon his oath, because the *Articuli Cleri* say 'no layman etc.' but do not say 'no clergyman'.[47] By the court, even if a false cause is certified upon a *habeas corpus* we ought still to remand him, for we are barred (*conclude*) by the return and the party cannot have an averment against it. And, by all the court there, a party who is convented before the High Commission ought to have a general understanding of that for which he is convented, not of the articles themselves, but the summary effect of them. It is immaterial if he is sworn there to answer as to all things which shall be objected against him but does not answer to all interrogatories which are administered to him: that is not perjury, for the oath refers only to all interrogatories which are material and rightfully objected against him. So it has been resolved in the Star Chamber, according to Coke CJ, that the oath is to answer [only] the articles which are pertinent and so far as he is bound of right to answer.

[47] This refers to the 'Prohibitio formata de statuto Articulorum Clerici': above, p. 359.

Appendix 10

Bulthorpe v. Ladbrook (1607)

Trinity Term 1607[1]

An action was brought on the statute of Magna Carta, chapter 29, *quod nullus liber homo imprisonetur*, by Bulthorpe[2] against Ladbrook, and the plaintiff declared 'against the custom of England and against the form of the statute'. The truth of the case was that the plaintiff, an attorney of this court, was put in the stocks by the defendant churchwarden of a church in London because he came to entreat for another. Upon a plea of Not Guilty it was found for the plaintiff and £100 damages given, for he sat there for three or four hours in his velvet jacket and throughout the time had infinite spectators. And the justices said that the damages were well given.

Barker moved in arrest of the judgment, (1) that he had declared and grounded his action upon the statute of Magna Carta, chapter 29, made in 9 Hen. III, whereas Magna Carta was no statute in Parliament until the statute of Marlborough was made in 52 Hen. III, whereby the said Magna Carta was confirmed; (2) inasmuch as it is here brought upon the common law and also the statute, it seems that he ought to have recited the statute truly; and (3) it seemed to him that when a common subject imprisons someone else this is outside the statute of Magna Carta, and therefore he ought not to have declared 'against the form of the statute', for the intention of the statute was only to provide for the king's officers, or where some new usurped authority or upstart court imprisoned the parties.

But the whole court was against him in everything. Magna Carta was an Act of Parliament in 9 Hen. III, and COKE CJ said he had heard it held to be so in the King's Bench. He said it had been confirmed by thirty-two parliaments at the least, but that is no argument to prove that it was not an Act of Parliament before the last confirmation. And he said that the king's nonage did not take away the force of the statute, even though it was doubtful at the time to the

---

The texts in this appendix have all been translated from the original law French. Judges' names are printed in small capitals, counsel in italic.

[1] CULMS.Mm.1.21, fo. 92, collated withMS. Gg.2.23, fo. 146, andCULMS. Gg.5.6, fo. 55.
[2] Boulthrop in Gg.2.23, Boulthorpe in Gg.5.6.

barons of the realm, for the king cannot be under age with respect to the administration of justice.

Secondly, an action lay for such imprisonment by the common law, before the statute of Magna Carta; and the point of the suit is the imprisonment, and the statute is put in only for a flourish: therefore, even if it is misrecited, the plaintiff should still have his judgment.

COKE CJ said that all the statutes[3] of Magna Carta were Edward the Confessor's laws, except one [or two][4] of them, as he had seen in a book of good authority, but they were overshadowed in the time of William the Conqueror, and afterwards restored again by Henry I and King John, and that was by Act of Parliament.

WALMSLEY J. I infer from this that our law is more ancient than some have said.[5]

Thirdly, everyone is within the said statute, not only the great man but also the mean person who has no part in the administration of justice as a minister thereof.

COKE CJ said it was well done to mention the statute, for when a statute gives an action which was at common law, and someone wishes to take any benefit of the statute, he ought to mention it. When an action is given by statute in a particular form, there is no need to mention the statute; but it is otherwise when a statute gives an action but not the form of the writ.

A second report[6]

Balthorpe against Ladbrooke. Balthorpe brought an action of false imprisonment against the law of the land and against the form of the statute ('contra legem terrae et contra formam statuti'), and it was objected that the action was badly brought because he has founded his action upon the common law and also upon the statute, and also that the statute of Magna Carta extends only to imprisonments by officials ('colore officii'), for between party and party he should have false imprisonment at common law. They also moved that Magna Carta was not a statute until it was confirmed by the statute of *Articuli super Cartas*.

To which COKE answered, and the court agreed with him, that Magna Carta is an Act of Parliament. In fact has been confirmed thirty-two times, but that does not prove that it was not a statute before; but the Commons were in

---

[3] I.e. chapters.   [4] Gg.2.23 only.

[5] This is a free translation on the assumption that Walmsley J.'s remark was ironic: 'Et sur ceo Walmsley inferre que nostre ley fuit pluis antient que ascuns ont dit.'

[6] CUL MS. Gg.5.6, fo. 52. This seems to be an independent report of the same hearing, though the same manuscript contains a version of the foregoing report as well.

doubt of it because the king was then under age, and therefore they confirmed it, even though in fact the nonage of the king is immaterial. For in 6 Edw. [III],[7] he shall not have his age; and in 21 Edw. IV a parson shall not have his age; nor shall anyone who claims in the capacity of a body politic.[8] Note also that Henry Beauclerk, who was Henry I, had the same charter made, and so did King John, and the same law was in the time of Edward the Confessor. And the common law is that no one shall be imprisoned [except by law]. Therefore he concluded that the action was well brought at common law and upon the statute together, because the statute does not give an action for damages, and because the statute extends to all imprisonments by officials and others. But he shall not here recover more damages by naming the statute than he would have if he had left out the statute.

The jury assessed the damages at £100, and he had judgment to recover 100 marks.

---

[7] *Anon.* (1332) YB Mich. 6 Edw. III, fo. 50, pl. 49, *per* Shardelow J. The manuscript says 'E. 4'.

[8] *Abbot of St Benet Hulme* v. *Mayor of Norwich* (1481) YB Mich. 21 Edw. IV, fo. 12, pl. 4, at fo. 14, *per* Choke J.

BIBLIOGRAPHY OF SECONDARY SOURCES

This includes modern editions of texts, under the names of their editors. It does not include books cited only once for specific items of information. For primary sources, including manuscripts, see the Table of Abbreviations. Original primary sources are not listed separately; they are cited either in the short forms indicated in the Table of Abbreviations or in full in the notes.

Alsop, J. D., 'William Fleetwood and English Historical Scholarship' (1994) 25 *Sixteenth-Century Journal* 155–76.

Axton, M., *The Queen's Two Bodies: Drama and the Elizabethan Succession* (1977).

Baker, J. H., *Catalogue of English Legal Manuscripts in Cambridge University Library* (Woodbridge, 1996).

Readers and Readings in the Inns of Court and Chancery (13 SS Suppl. Series, 2000).

The Law's Two Bodies (Oxford, 2001).

Oxford History of the Laws of England, vi (1483–1558) (Oxford, 2003).

The Men of Court 1440–1550: A Prosopography of the Inns of Court and Chancery and the Courts of Law (18 SS Suppl. Series, 2012), two volumes.

Collected Papers on English Legal History (Cambridge, 2013), three volumes.

'The Legal Force and Effect of Magna Carta', in *Magna Carta: Muse & Mentor*, ed. R. J. Holland (Library of Congress [Washington, DC], 2014), pp. 65–84, (notes) 258–61.

ed., *The Reports of Sir John Spelman* (93–94 SS, 1977–8), two volumes.

Reports from the Lost Notebooks of Sir James Dyer, i (109–10 SS, 1994–95), two volumes.

Selected Readings and Commentaries on Magna Carta 1400–1604 (132 SS, 2015).

Barnes, T. G., 'The Prerogative and Environmental Control of London Building in the Early Seventeenth Century' (1970) 58 *California Law Review* 1332–63.

'A Cheshire Seductress, Precedent, and a "Sore Blow" to Star Chamber' in *On the Laws and Customs of England: Essays in Honor of Samuel E. Thorne*, ed. M. S. Arnold and others (Chapel Hill, 1981), pp. 359–82.

Bémont, C., ed., *Chartes des Libertés Anglaises* (Paris, 1892).

Bindoff, S. T., ed., *The History of Parliament: The House of Commons 1509–1558* (1982), three volumes.

Birdsall, P., '"Non Obstante": A Study of the Dispensing Power of the English Kings' in *Essays in History and Politics in Honor of C. H. McIlwain* (Cambridge, MA, 1936), pp. 37–76.

Blackstone, W., *The Great Charter* (Oxford, 1759).

Boyer, A. D., *Sir Edward Coke and the Elizabethan Age* (Stanford, CA, 2003).

Brooks, C. W., *Pettifoggers and Vipers of the Commonwealth: The 'Lower Branch' of the Legal Profession in Early Modern England* (Cambridge, 1986).

'The Place of Magna Carta and the Ancient Constitution in Sixteenth-Century English Legal Thought' (1993) in *Roots of Liberty*, ed. Sandoz (q.v.), pp. 74–114.

Law, Politics and Society in Early Modern England (Cambridge, 2008).

'A Puritan Collaboration in Defence of the Liberty of the Subject: James Morice, Robert Beale and the Elizabethan Campaign against Ecclesiastical Authority' in *Collaboration and Interdiscipliniarity in the Republic of Letters*, ed. P. Scott (Manchester, 2011), pp. 1–14.

Burgess, G., 'Common Law and Political Theory in Early Stuart England' (1988) 40 *Political Science* 4–17

Politics of the Ancient Constitution 1603–42 (1992).

Absolute Monarchy and the Stuart Constitution (New Haven, CT, 1996).

Butterfield, H., *Magna Carta in the Historiography of the 16th and 17th Centuries* (1969).

Cam, H. M., *Magna Carta: Event or Document?* (SS lecture, 1965).

Carpenter, D., *Magna Carta* (2015).

Chrimes, S. B., 'The Constitutional Ideas of Dr Cowell' (1949) 64 EHR 461–87.

'Richard II's Questions to the Judges' (1956) 72 LQR 365–90.

Christianson, P., 'Young John Selden and the Ancient Constitution c. 1610–18' (1984) 128 *Proceedings of the American Philosophical Society* 271–315.

'Royal and Parliamentary Voices on the Ancient Constitution 1604–21' (1991) in *The Mental World of the Jacobean Court*, ed. Peck (q.v.), pp. 71–95.

'Ancient Constitutions in the Age of Sir Edward Coke and John Selden' (1993) in *Roots of Liberty*, ed. Sandoz (q.v.), pp. 115–84.

Cockburn, J. S., *A History of English Assizes 1558–1714* (Cambridge, 1972).

Collinson, P., *The Elizabethan Puritan Movement* (1967).

Richard Bancroft and Elizabethan Anti-Puritanism (Cambridge, 2013).

Cope, E. S., 'Sir Edward Coke and Proclamations 1610' (1971) 15 *American Journal of Legal History* 215–21.

Corré, J. I., 'The Argument, Decision and Reports of *Darcy v. Allen*' (1996) 45 *Emory Law Journal* 1261–1327.

Corwin, E. S., 'The Doctrine of Due Process before the Civil War' (1911) 24
    Harvard Law Review 366–85, 460–79.
Croft, P., 'Fresh Light on Bate's Case' (1987) 30 *Historical Journal* 523–39.
Cromartie, A., *The Constitutinalist Revolution: An Essay on the History of England
    1450–1642* (Cambridge, 2006).
Davies, D. S., 'Further Light on the Case of Monopolies' (1932) 48 LQR 394–414.
Dawson, J. P., 'Coke and Ellesmere Disinterred: The Attack on the Chancery in
    1616' (1941) 36 *Illinois Law Review* 127–52.
    'The Privy Council and Private Law in the Tudor and Stuart Period' (1950) 48
    Michigan Law Review 393–428, 627–56.
Derrett, J. D. M., 'The Trial of Sir Thomas More' (1964) 79 EHR 449–77.
Dietz, F. C., *English Government Finance 1485–1558* (2nd edn, 1964).
Donald, M. B., *Elizabethan Monopolies* (Edinburgh, 1961).
Dunham, W. H., 'Regal Power and the Rule of Law: A Tudor Paradox' (1964) 3
    Journal of British Studies 24–56.
    'Magna Carta & British Constitutionalism' in *The Great Charter: Four Essays on
    Magna Carta and the History of our Liberty* (New York, 1965), pp. 26–50.
Edie, C. A., 'Tactics and Strategies: Parliament's Attack on the Royal Dispensing
    Power 1597–1689' (1985) 29 *American Journal of Legal History* 197–234.
Elton, G. R., *Studies in Tudor and Stuart Politics and Government* (Cambridge,
    1974–92).
    The Tudor Constitution (2nd edn, 1982).
    The Parliament of England 1559–81 (Cambridge, 1986).
Epstein, J. J., 'Francis Bacon and the Challenge to the Prerogative in 1610' (1969) 2
    Journal of Historical Studies 272–82.
Forrest, I., *The Detection of Heresy in Late Medieval England* (Oxford, 2005).
Fussner, F. S., ed., 'William Camden's "Discourse concerning the Prerogative of the
    King" [*c.* 1615]' (1957) 101 *Proceedings of the American Philosophical Society*
    204–15.
Garnett, G., '"The Ould Fields": Law and History in the Prefaces to Sir Edward
    Coke's Reports' (2013) 34 *Journal of Legal History* 245–84.
Goldsworthy, J., *The Sovereignty of Parliament: History and Philosophy* (Oxford,
    1999).
Gough, J. W., *Fundamental Law in English Constitutional History* (Oxford, 1955).
Gray, C. [M.], 'Reason, Authority, and Imagination: The Jurisprudence of
    Sir Edward Coke' in *Culture and Politics from Puritanism to the Enlighten-
    ment*, ed. P. Zagorin (Berkeley, 1980), pp. 25–66.
    The Writ of Prohibition: Jurisdiction in Early Modern English Law (New York,
    1994), two volumes.
    'Self-Incrimination in Interjurisdictional Law' in *The Privilege against Self-
    Incrimination*, ed. R. H. Helmholz and others (Chicago, 1997), pp. 47–81.

Greenberg, J., *The Radical Face of the Ancient Constitution: St Edward's 'Laws' in Early Modern Political Thought* (Cambridge, 2001).

Griffith-Jones, R., and M. Hill, eds., *Magna Carta, Religion and the Rule of Law* (Cambridge, 2015).

Guy, J. A., *The Public Career of Sir Thomas More* (Brighton, 1980).

ed., *The Debellation of Salem and Bizance* (10 *Complete Works of St Thomas More*, New Haven, CT, 1987).

ed., *The Reign of Elizabeth I* (Cambridge, 1995).

Hall, G. D. G., 'Impositions and the Courts 1554–1606' (1953) 69 LQR 200–18.

Halliday, P., *Habeas Corpus: From England to Empire* (Cambridge, MA, 2010).

Harris, R., 'William Fleetwood, Recorder of the City, and Catholicism in Elizabethan London' (1963) 7 *Recusant History* 106–22.

Hart, J. S., *The Rule of Law 1603–1660: Crowns, Courts and Judges* (2003).

Hasler, P. W., ed., *The History of Parliament: The House of Commons 1558–1603* (1981), three volumes.

Heinze, R. W., 'Proclamations and Parliamentary Protest 1539–1610' in *Tudor Rule and Revolution*, ed. D. J. Guth and J. W. McKenna (Cambridge, 1982), pp. 237–59.

Helmholz, R. H., 'Bonham's Case, Judicial Review, and the Law of Nature' (2009) 1 *Journal of Legal Analysis* 324–53.

Henderson, E. G., *Foundations of English Administrative Law* (Cambridge, MA, 1963).

Holt, J. C., 'The Origins of the Constitutional Tradition in England' in *Magna Carta and Medieval Government*, ed. J. C. Holt (1985), pp. 1–22.

Magna Carta, 3rd edn by G. Garnett and J. Hudson (Cambridge, 2015).

Hulme, E. W., 'The Early History of the English Patent System' in *Select Essays in Anglo-American Legal History* (Boston, MA, 1909), iii. 117–48.

Ibbetson, D., 'The Earl of Oxford's Case (1615)' in *Landmark Cases in Equity*, ed. C. Mitchell and P. Mitchell (Oxford 2012), pp. 1–32.

Jenks, E., 'The Myth of Magna Carta' (1905) 4 *Independent Review* 260–73.

Jones, W. J., *The Elizabethan Court of Chancery* (Oxford, 1967).

Keir, D. L., 'The Case of Ship Money' (1936) 52 LQR 546–74.

Kelly, H. A., 'Inquisition and the Prosecution of Heresy: Misconceptions and Abuses' (1989) 58 *Church History* 439–51.

Inquisitions and other Trial Procedures in the Medieval West (Aldershot, 2001).

Kelly, H. A., with L. W. Karlin and G. B. Wegemer, eds., *Thomas More's Trial by Jury* (Woodbridge, 2011).

Kitching, C. J., 'The Quest for Concealed Lands in the Reign of Elizabeth I' (1974) 5 *Transactions of the Royal Historical Society* (5th series) 63–78.

Klinck, D. R., *Conscience, Equity and the Court of Chancery in Early Modern England* (Farnham, 2013).

Knafla, L. A., *Law and Politics in Jacobean England: the Tracts of Lord Chancellor Ellesmere* (Cambridge, 1977).

Langbein, J. H., *Torture and the Law of Proof* (Chicago, 1977).

Levack, B. P., *The Civil Lawyers in England 1603–1641: A Political Study* (Oxford, 1973).

'English Law, Scots Law and the Union 1603–1707' in *Law-Making and Law-Makers in British History*, ed. A. Harding (1980), 105–26.

'Law, Sovereignty and the Union' in *Scots and Britons: British Political Thought and the Union of 1603*, ed. R. A. Mason (Cambridge, 1994), pp. 213–37.

Lewis, A. H., *A Study of Elizabethan Ship Money* (Philadelphia, 1928).

Lidington, D. R., 'The Enforcement of the Penal Statutes at the Court of Exchequer *c.* 1558-c. 1571' (unpublished Cambridge PhD dissertation, 1988).

Loach, J., *Parliament and the Crown in the Reign of Mary Tudor* (1986).

Parliament under the Tudors (Oxford, 1991).

Lobban, M., *A History of the Philosophy of Law in the Common Law World, 1600–1900* (Dordrecht, 2007).

McGlynn, M., *The Royal Prerogative and the Learning of the Inns of Court* (Cambridge, 2003).

'From Charter to Common Law: the Rights and Liberties of the Pre-Reformation Church' in *Magna Carta, Religion and the Rule of Law*, ed. R. Griffith-Jones and M. Hill (Cambridge, 2015), pp. 53–69.

ed., *The Rights and Liberties of the English Church: Readings from the Pre-Reformation Inns of Court* (129 SS, 2015).

McIlwain, C. H., *The High Court of Parliament and its Supremacy* (New Haven, 1910).

'Due process of Law in Magna Carta' (1914) 14 *Columbia Law Review* 27–51; reprinted in *Constitutionalism and the Changing World: Collected Papers* (Cambridge, 1939), pp. 86–126.

'Magna Carta and Common Law' (1917), in Malden ed., *Magna Carta Commemoration Essays* (q.v.), pp. 122–79; reprinted in *Constitutionalism and the Changing World: Collected Papers* (Cambridge, 1939), pp. 127–77.

ed., *Political Works of James I* (Cambridge, MA, 1918).

McKechnie, W. S., *Magna Carta: A Commentary on the Great Charter of King John* (Glasgow, 1906; 2nd edn, 1914).

Maguire, M., 'Attack of the Common Lawyers on the Oath Ex Officio' in *Essays in History and Political Theory in Honour of C. H. McIlwain*, ed. C. Wittke (Cambridge, MA, 1936), pp. 199–229.

Malament, B., 'The "Economic Liberalism" of Sir Edward Coke' (1967) 76 *Yale Law Journal* 1321–58.

Malden, H. E., ed., *Magna Carta Commemoration Essays* (1917).

Matthew, H. C. G., and B. Harrison, eds., *Oxford Dictionary of National Biography* (Oxford, 2004), 61 volumes.

Moore, D., 'Recorder Fleetwood and the Tudor Queenship Controversy' in *Ambiguous Realities: Women in the Middle Ages and Renaissance*, ed. C. Levin and J. C. Watson (Detroit, 1987), pp. 235–51.

Moore, D., and C. Beem, eds., *The Name of a Queen: William Fleetwood's Itinerarium ad Windsor* (New York, 2013).

Musson, A., *Medieval Law in Context: The Growth of Legal Consciousness from Magna Carta to the Peasants' Revolt* (Manchester, 2001).

'Magna Carta in the Later Middle Ages' in *Magna Carta: The Foundation of Freedom*, ed. N. Vincent [2015].

Neale, J. E., *Elizabeth I and her Parliaments 1559–81* (1952).

Elizabeth I and her Parliaments 1584–1601 (1957).

Oakley, D., 'English Heresy Procedures in Thomas More's *Dialogue concerning Heresies*' (2008) 3 *Thomas More Studies* 70–80.

Oakley, F., 'Jacobean Political Theology: The Absolute and Ordinary Powers of the King' (1968) 29 *Journal of the History of Ideas* 323–46.

Peck, L. L., ed., *The Mental World of the Jacobean Court* (Cambridge, 1991).

Pila, J., 'The Common Law Monopoly in its Original Form' (2001) 3 *Intellectual Property Quarterly* 209–24.

Plucknett, T. F. T., *Statutes and their Interpretation in the First Half of the Fourteenth Century* (Cambridge, 1922).

'The Origin of Impeachment' (1942) 24 *Transactions of the Royal Historical Society* (4th series) 47–71.

'Ellesmere on Statutes' (1944) 60 LQR 242–9.

'The Impeachments of 1376' (1951) 1 *Transactions of the Royal Historical Society* (5th series) 153–64, reprinted in *Studies in English Legal History* (1983), ch. 8.

Concise History of the Common Law (5th edn, 1956).

Pocock, J. G. A., *The Ancient Constitution and the Feudal Law* (1957; reissued, with a retrospective essay, Cambridge, 1987).

Pollock, F., and F. W. Maitland, *History of English Law before the Time of Edward I* (2nd edn, Cambridge, 1898).

Pound, R., *The Development of Constitutional Guarantees of Liberty* (New Haven, 1957).

Powell, D. X., 'Why did James Whitelocke go to Jail in 1613?' (1995) 11 *Australian Journal of Law and Society* 169–90.

Sir James Whitelocke's Liber Famelicus 1570–1632 (Bern, 2000).

Powicke, F. M., 'Per Judicium Parium vel Per Legem Terrae' (1917) in Malden ed., *Magna Carta Commemoration Essays* (q.v.), pp. 96–121.

Prest, W. R., *The Rise of the Barristers* (Oxford, 1986).

Prichard, M. J. and D. E. C. Yale, *Hale and Fleetwood on Admiralty Jurisdiction* (108 SS, 1993).

Putnam, B. H., *Early Treatises on Justices of the Peace in the Fifteenth and Sixteenth Centuries* (Oxford, 1924).

Radin, M., 'The Myth of Magna Carta' (1947) 60 *Harvard Law Review* 1060–91.

Reid, R. R., *The King's Council in the North* (1921).

Rex, R., 'Thomas More and the Heretics: Statesman or Fanatic?' in G. Logan ed., *The Cambridge Companion to Thomas More* (Cambridge, 2011), pp. 93–115.

Reynolds, S., 'Magna Carta 1297 and the Uses of Literacy' (1989) 62 *Historical Research* 233–44.

Sacks, D. H., 'The Countervailing of Benefits: Monopoly, Liberty and Benevolence in Elizabethan England' in *Tudor Political Culture*, ed. D. Hoak (Cambridge, 1995), pp. 272–91.

Sandoz, E., ed., *The Roots of Liberty: Magna Carta, Ancient Constitution, and the Anglo-American Tradition of Rule of Law* (1993).

Shagan, E. H., 'The English Inquisition: Constitutional Conflict and Ecclesiastical Law in the 1590s' (2004) 47 *Historical Journal* 541–65.

Smith, D. C., 'Was there a Rule in Shelley's Case?' (2009) 30 *Journal of Legal History* 53–70.

  'Remembering Usurpation: The Common Lawyers, Reformation Narratives and the Prerogative' (2013) 86 *Historical Research* 619–37.

  Sir Edward Coke and the Reformation of the Laws: Religion, Politics and Jurisprudence 1579–1616 (Cambridge, 2014).

Sommerville, J. P., 'James I and the Divine Right of Kings' in *The Mental World of the Jacobean Court*, ed. L. L. Peck (Cambridge, 1991), pp. 55–70.

  Royalists and Patriots: Politics and Ideology in England 1603–1640 (2nd edn, Harlow, 1999).

Stenton, D. M., *After Runnymede: Magna Carta in the Middle Ages* (Charlottesville, 1965).

Tatnall, E., 'John Wyclif and *Ecclesia Anglicana*' (1969) 20 *Journal of Ecclesiastical History* 19–43.

Thomas, G. W., 'James I, Equity and Lord Keeper Williams' (1976) 91 EHR 506–28.

Thompson, F., 'Parliamentary Confirmations of the Great Charter' (1933) 38 *American Historical Review* 659–72.

  Magna Carta: Its Role in the Making of the English Constitution 1300–1629 (Minneapolis, 1948).

Thomson, J. A. F., *The Later Lollards 1414–1520* (Oxford, 1965).

Thorne, S. E., '*Praemunire* and Sir Edward Coke' (1938) 2 *Huntington Library Quarterly* 85–8.

  ed., *A Discourse upon the Exposicion & Understandinge of Statutes With Sir Thomas Egerton's Additions: Edited from Manuscripts in the Huntington Library* (San Marino, California, 1942).

ed., *Readings and Moots at the Inns of Court in the Fifteenth Century*, vol.i: *Readings* (71 SS, 1954).

Thrush, A. and J. Ferris, eds., *The History of Parliament: The House of Commons 1604-1629* (2010), four volumes.

Tittler, R., *The Reformation and the Towns in England: Politics and Political Culture c. 1540-1640* (Oxford, 1998).

Turner, R. V., *Magna Carta through the Ages* (Harlow, 2003).

Tyacke, T., *The English Revolution c. 1590-1720: Politics, Religion and Communities* (Manchester, 2007), 15-16.

Usher, R. G., 'James I and Sir Edward Coke' (1903) 18 EHR 664-75.

'Nicholas Fuller: a Forgotten Exponent of English Liberty' (1906-7) 12 *American Historical Review* 743-60.

The Reconstruction of the English Church (1910; reprinted in facsimile, Farnborough, 1969), two volumes.

The Rise and Fall of the High Commission (Oxford, 1913).

Vincent, N., *Magna Carta: A Very Short Introduction* (Oxford, 2012).

Wagner, D. O., 'Coke and the Rise of Economic Liberalism' (1935) 6 *Economic History Review* 30-44.

White, A. B., 'The Name Magna Carta' (1915) 30 EHR 472-5.

Williams, I., 'Dr Bonham's Case and "Void" Statutes' (2006) 27 *Journal of Legal History* 111-28.

'The Tudor Genesis of Edward Coke's Immemorial Common Law' (2010) 43 *Sixteenth Century Journal* 103-23.

Williams, I., review of H. A. Kelly and others, *Sir Thomas More's Trial by Jury* (2011) 33 *Journal of Legal History* 123-6.

Williams, P., *The Council in the Marches of Wales under Elizabeth I* (Cardiff, 1958).

Woodworth, A., *Purveyance for the Royal Household in the Reign of Elizabeth* (Philadelphia, 1945).

Wright, S., 'Nicholas Fuller and the Liberties of the Subject' (2006) 25 *Parliamentary History* 176-213.

Youngs, F. A., *Proclamations of the Tudor Queens* (Cambridge, 1976).

INDEX

Abbot, George, archbishop of Canterbury, 372, 406, 436

abdication of the crown, not legally possible, 342

abridgements of cases, 77, 345

absolutist monarchy: Francis Bacon and, 305–7; the Church of England and, 137, 293, 350–1; Civil lawyers and, 20, 119, 391–2; discretionary rule and Magna Carta, 357; Lord Ellesmere and, 345; James I and, 339–40; medieval popes and, 3, 9, 30, 120; *see also under* prerogative, royal (absolute prerogatives)

actions founded on Magna Carta: authorised implicitly by the charter, 429, 503; authorised by Marlborough, 49, 94–5; damages in, 353; first brought in the King's Bench (1501–32), 97–9, 456–62, 503; new formula including false imprisonment (1606–7), 310, 352–3, 514–16, 531–3; may be brought in the Common Pleas, 507; revived in the Common Pleas (1595), 277–8, 484–7; suit stopped by the Privy Council, 277–8, 487; used in respect of a Chancery suit, 377, 462

Acts of Parliament *see* statutes

Addled Parliament (1614), 407–8, 427; thought to be the last parliament ever (1616), 421

Adgore, Gregory, of Inner Temple, 77, 96

Admiralty, Court of, 166, 209–10, 430, 516; follows Civil law, 454–5; origin of, 306

adultery, punishment of, 139–41, 290, 372

advowson, usurpation of, contrary to Magna Carta, 61; *see also* commendams; *quare impedit*

Agmondesham, John, of Middle Temple, imprisonment of, 166, 495–6

aid prayer of the king, 94, 181

alderman, office of: as a liberty, 396; restoration to, by *mandamus*, 205–6, 396–8, 488

Alexander II, king of Hungary, 41

Alexander III, king of Scotland, 299–301

Alfield, Thomas, Jesuit missionary, 129

aliens, 34, 112, 191, 203, 431; when bound by English statutes, 105

alimony *see under* husband and wife (suits for maintenance or alimony)

Allen, Thomas, cardinal, 129

Allen, Thomas, haberdasher, 320

Altham, Sir James, B., 394

amercement, 88; of earls and barons, 92–3, 452

America *see* United States of America

Anabaptists, 131

'ancient constitution', 444–5

Anderson, Sir Edmund, CJCP: and Magna Carta, 250, 276; complains of abuses by conciliar jurisdictions, 210, 303; mentioned in will of Robert Snagge, 276; warns of danger of encroachments by Requests, 485, 487

Andrews, Euseby, of Lincoln's Inn, 23

Anger, Richard, of Gray's Inn, suspected of murder, 170

court used in his works, 225, 227,
232, 237–8; on readings in the inns
of court, 82; on statutes against the
word of God, 105; his treatise on
Justices of the Peace, 236–7
Fleming, Sir Thomas, of Lincoln's Inn,
later CJKB: as Sol.-Gen., 198, 316–
17; conduct in the case of
impositions, 330; less assertive than
Coke as CJ, 385–6
Flood *see* Lloyd
forced loans *see* benevolences and
forced loans
forest law, 96, 479, 505
Fortescue, Sir John, CJKB, 95, 105, 144
franchises *see* liberties and franchises
Fray, John, CB, 342
Freeman, Edward, of Gray's Inn, 23
French language *see* Law French
Frith, John, 122
Frowyk, Thomas, of Inner Temple, 77;
reading, 183
Fuller, Nicholas, of Gray's Inn: counsel
for Cawdray, 142; counsel for
Maunsell, 356–63, 517–19,
526–8; arguments against
impositions,
321–2, 329, 331; introduces bill to
restrict Chancery injunctions, 414
fundamental law, 14–24

gaol delivery system, a means to
prevent perpetual imprisonment,
509
Gascony, writs sent by the King's Bench
to, 299
Gawdy, Sir Thomas, JKB, 32
Gerard, Thomas, Baron Gerard, knight-
marshal, 340
Glanvill: cited in readings, 79, 85; cited
in the 1550s, 244; a guide to the law
before Magna Carta, 223, 227
Glanvill, Richard, 415–16, 418–20
Gloucester castle *see* Colchester
Gloucester, duke of, *see* Woodstock
God: not a legal person, 82; word of,
105; *see also* law of God; vow
gold and silver mines, 193

Golden Bull (1222), 41
Gooch (Googe), Dr Barnaby, master
of Magdalene College, Cambridge,
416
grant, royal: distinguished from statute,
12–13; construction of, 96, 243;
see also commissions; liberties and
franchises
Gray's Inn: an inn of court time out of
mind, 359; benchers elected to the
Reformation Parliament, 102;
murder of a bencher, 170; probable
visit by Elizabeth I, 225; a reading on
constitutional law in, 101–8
Great Britain, name favoured by
James I, 341, 343
Green, Bartholomew, of Middle
Temple, 129
Gregory XI, pope, attempt to suppress
unorthodox Oxford theology, 115,
120
Grevyle, Lewis, 171
Guala, papal legate, 5
Guernsey, island of, 300, 505
Guisnes, *habeas corpus* to, 496, 505
Gunpowder Plot (1605), 131–3, 294,
401
Gynes, Richard, of Inner Temple, 81,
220
Gypsies, 111–12

habeas corpus, 46, 141, 155–6, 261, 503;
availability out of term, 163;
availability outside the realm,
299–302, 338, 347, 413, 504, 512,
521, 523; fifteenth-century precedent
of, 156; general returns to, 161–2,
264, 297–8, 361, 375, 412–14; judges'
memorandum on (1592), 166–8, 399,
496–9; linked to Magna Carta, 169,
247, 250, 308, 310, 347, 446; for
prisoners of the Church, 120, 506,
513, 523; for recusants, 125, 158–60;
return not traversable, 361, 413–14,
497, 530
habere facias seisinam, writ of, and
nullus disseisiatur in chapter 29,
101

Lightning Source UK Ltd.
Milton Keynes UK
UKHW020108201119
353876UK00018B/542/P